Qaluyaarmiuni Nunamtenek Qanemciput

Our Nelson Island Stories

Qaluyaarmiuni Nunamtenek Qanemciput

Our Nelson Island Stories

Meanings of Place on the Bering Sea Coast

Transcribed and translated by Alice Rearden
Edited by Ann Fienup-Riordan

Calista Elders Council, Anchorage
in association with
University of Washington Press
Seattle and London

Printed and bound in the United States of America
Designed and typeset by Leon Unruh
Produced in cooperation with the Alaska Native Language Center
16 15 14 13 12 11 5 4 3 2 1

University of Washington Press
PO Box 50096, Seattle, WA 98145, USA
www.washington.edu/uwpress

Library of Congress Cataloging-in-Publication Data
Rearden, Alice.
Qaluyaarmiuni nunamtenek qanemciput : = our Nelson Island stories : meanings of place on the Bering Sea coast / translated by Alice Rearden ; edited by Ann Fienup-Riordan.
p. cm.
Includes bibliographical references.
ISBN 978-0-295-99135-1 (pbk. : alk. paper)
1. Yupik Eskimos—Alaska—Nelson Island—Interviews. 2. Yupik Eskimos—Alaska—Nelson Island—History. 3. Yupik Eskimos—Alaska—Nelson Island—Social life and customs. 4. Geographical perception—Alaska—Nelson Island. 5. Place attachement—Alaska—Nelson Island. 6. Yupik language—Texts. 7. Nelson Island (Alaska)—Social life and customs. 8. Nelson Island (Alaska) —History. I. Fienup-Riordan, Ann. II. Title.
E99.Y6R43 2011
916.4'51—dc22 2011005957

The paper used in this publication meets the minimum requirements of American National Standard for Information Sciences—Permanence of Paper for Printed Library Materials, ANSI Z39.48-1984.∞

Kalikam Imai

The Book's Contents

Quyavikelput

Acknowledgments

Our greatest thanks to the many Qaluyaarmiut (Nelson Islanders) who share their stories in these pages. They are the true authors of this book. It is their hope that both Yup'ik and non-Yup'ik readers will learn from their experiences and live better—and safer—lives. We are especially grateful to Simeon and Anna Agnus of Nightmute, Lizzie Chimiugak and Martina John of Toksook Bay, John Eric and Paul Tunuchuk of Chefornak, Elsie Tommy and Michael John of Newtok, and Susie Angaiak, Edward Hooper, and Tommy Hooper of Tununak. We also thank Paul John of Toksook Bay, the Nelson Island leader whom John Eric referred to as *akagarcailkutiit* (one who prevents them from rolling). He kept us on the right track throughout our discussions.

The Calista Elders Council (CEC), the primary heritage organization in southwest Alaska representing the region's elders, guided our work. CEC's executive director, Mark John, and its board of directors, including Bob Aloysius, Nick Andrew Sr., Peter Elachik, the late Peter Jacobs Sr., Paul John, the late Paul Kiunya Sr., Martin Moore Sr., Moses Paukan Sr., John Phillip Sr., and Moses White Sr., provided invaluable guidance and support.

The National Science Foundation (NSF), Office of Polar Programs, funded our work as part of the Nelson Island Natural and Cultural History Project, carried out under NSF's Bering Ecosystem Study (BEST) (Grant Number 0611978, Publication Number BEST BSIERP 13). BEST is a multiyear, multiproject study begun in 2006 and involving more than 100 researchers in efforts to understand the dynamics of change in the eastern Bering Sea. Our Nelson Island project was the one BEST project that dealt with sociocultural issues. The others all focused on the physical science and biology of the Bering Sea. We especially thank our NSF program officers, Anna Kerttula de Echave and William Wiseman, for allowing us to share with our partners a nearshore Yup'ik perspective on the Bering Sea.

In addition to direct NSF support, our work also benefitted from the support of the data management team at the National Center for Atmospheric

Research (NCAR), Earth Observing Laboratory, that NSF contracted to facilitate the larger BEST program. Although our Nelson Island project did not result in complex statistical information, we did produce abundant transcripts that NCAR enthusiastically helped us to archive and make available. Community members embraced the idea of using the Internet to provide public access. Janet Scannell worked with CEC staff to develop a place-based website, including the location of more than 400 historic sites and geographic features as well as oral accounts relating directly to more than 80 place names. It is at http://mapserver.eol.ucar.edu/best. This book is a direct outgrowth of what we learned working on the website.

Other organizations contributed to our work, especially during the three-week circumnavigation of Qaluyaat (Nelson Island) in July 2007 that was a major component of our Nelson Island project. Regional corporation Calista provided office space in Anchorage, financial support, and the expertise of its vice president of land and natural resources, June McAtee. The Association of Village Council Presidents (AVCP) also provided office space in Bethel as well as the services of archaeologist Steve Street. The U.S. Fish and Wildlife Service (USFWS) lent us newly hired biologist Tom Doolittle, who spent his first weeks on the delta learning from Qaluyaarmiut elders and sharing his experiences in turn. The Nelson Island project also received endorsement from the International Polar Year organizing committee as part of the larger Sea Ice Knowledge and Use (SIKU) initiative, providing linkages to other projects, primarily Exchange for Local Observations and Knowledge of the Arctic (ELOKA). Special thanks also to the Alaska Humanities Forum, the Calista Heritage Foundation, and the Rasmuson Foundation, whose generous assistance made this publication possible.

This book is the tenth produced by the CEC in our efforts to document Yup'ik oral traditions, not as arcane facts but as knowledge systems with continuing relevance in our rapidly changing world. The transformation of the social landscape during the last 50 years has been matched by dramatic changes in the lowland delta and coastal environments of southwest Alaska. The first CEC publications—*Wise Words of the Yup'ik People: We Talk to You because We Love You* and *Yupiit Qanruyutait/Yup'ik Words of Wisdom*—were compiled to share the foundational values of Yup'ik people embodied in the *qanruyutet* (words of wisdom) that continue to guide their relations with one another. This book, and its companion volume, *Ellavut/Our Yup'ik World and Weather,* present the values and *qanruyutet* that guide Yup'ik people in their relations with the land and sea. That these two books should follow the first pair is no accident, as how one should act on the ocean and the land and how one should treat one's fellow humans are closely bound.

Elders always shared information in the Yup'ik language, and my friend and colleague Alice Rearden did the lion's share of the transcription and translation, ably assisted by David Chanar and Marie Meade. Alice's commitment to accuracy and clarity and her knowledge of Yup'ik and English shine through these pages. Alice and I have been partners at gatherings during which elders shared these stories. As I worked with transcripts, organizing these accounts for publication, Alice was always my first and best editor—answering questions, spotting errors, making suggestions. I shaped the words she provided. Alice taught me as much as any elder and always with humor and kindness. She made collaboration a real joy.

Alice and I are both indebted to long-time collaborator Marie Meade for carefully reading and correcting the final text. Her years of experience give her a unique perspective on translation, which she generously shared. We also thank Steven Jacobson and his colleagues at the Alaska Native Language Center, University of Alaska Fairbanks, who painstakingly compiled the *Yup'ik Eskimo Dictionary*, which guided our work all the way. The clarity of the English text benefited from the sharp eyes and light touch of my longtime editor and friend, Judith Meidinger.

Many individuals and organizations provided illustrations for this book. Photographer Jim Barker, June McAtee of Calista, and Janet Klein shared fine photographs of rock outcrops and other features of the coastal environment, allowing readers to see what elders describe. The University Museums, University of Delaware, generously provided photographs taken on Qaluyaat in the early 1960s by Harley and Mabel McKeague during their years traveling for the Indian Health Service. Historical photographs were also supplied by the Jesuit Oregon Province Archives in Spokane, Washington, and the Alaska and Polar Regions Department, University of Alaska Fairbanks. Once again, my friend and colleague Patrick Jankanish produced a first-class map of the region. Finally, Michelle Pearson generously donated her time and expertise managing our ever-growing place name database and producing our beautiful maps of Qaluyaat.

Thanks are also due to the University of Washington Press and its fine staff who helped us through the publication process, including Beth Fuget, Lorri Hagman, Pat Soden, Marilyn Trueblood, and others. The Press closely collaborated with Larry Kaplan and Leon Unruh of the Alaska Native Language Center, who meticulously produced the final camera-ready copy.

Last but not least, thanks to our families, especially our children, Kyle, Kayla, Christopher, Frances, Jimmy, and Nicky. They make our work worthwhile.

Qaluyaarmiut

The People of Nelson Island

Qaluyaat (Nelson Island, from *qalu-*, "dip net") lies 90 miles west of Bethel on the Bering Sea coast, fanning out from the western edge of a lowland delta the size of Kansas. This vast, marshy plain between the mouths of the Yukon and Kuskokwim rivers was the traditional homeland of the Yupiit, or Yup'ik Eskimos. At present the region's population of more than 23,000 (the largest Native population in Alaska) is scattered among 57 villages, ranging between 200 and 1,200 persons each, with the regional center in Bethel. This huge region is cross-cut by historical and administrative differences, including three dialect groups, three major Christian denominations, six school districts, two census areas, and three Alaska Native Claims Settlement Act (ANCSA) regional corporations.

The Yukon-Kuskokwim delta mostly consists of subarctic marshland and tundra, spongy or frozen, depending on the season. Dotted with lakes and laced with innumerable rivers and sloughs, this mobile wetness drains more and more of the land's surface as it flows toward the Bering Sea. The abrupt rise of Nelson Island looms large, its west coast shoreline rising 500 feet at Cape Vancouver and another 500 feet at the center of the island. In geologic time this peak was below water. Volcanic activity pushed Nelson Island to the surface, and today its rocky ridges hold both pumice and sea shells. Structurally it is a continuation of the delta formed by the silting action of the Yukon and Kuskokwim rivers. Compared to nearby Nunivak Island, which is separated from the coast by 25 miles of rough, shallow sea, Nelson Island appears less imposing. Baird Inlet is a pond in the Nelson Islander's back yard in comparison, and except for the Qalvinraaq and Ningliq rivers draining the inlet into the sea, Nelson Island would be a high point along a continuous coastline.

Qaluyaarmiut (the people of Qaluyaat) were largely left alone into the early decades of the twentieth century. The bilateral extended family, numbering up to 30 persons, was the basic social unit. Spanning two to four generations, including parents, offspring, and parents' parents, the group might also encompass siblings of parents or their children. Extended family groups, joined by an overlapping network of family ties, lived together most of the year but normally not in family compounds. Rather, winter villages were divided residentially between a *qasgi* (communal men's house) and smaller *enet* (sod houses) occupied by women and young children. Married couples or groups of hunters often moved to outlying camps for fishing and trapping during spring and fall. Families gathered when temperatures dropped below freezing and during spring seal-hunting and summer fishing seasons. Winter villages ranged in size from a single extended family to a hundred people with men living in two separate men's houses.

Every man's place in the *qasgi* reflected his social position, and the men's house framed a number of internal distinctions, including that between young and old, married and unmarried, and host and guest. The social structure of the *qasgi* mirrored that of the natural world. Qaluyaarmiut believed that sea mammals lived in underwater *qasgit* (plural) from which they observed, and chose whether to give themselves to, human hunters. Hunters who extended the most thought and care toward the animals they sought were richly rewarded, both socially and materially. The *nukalpiaq,* or good provider, was important in village life. Not only did he contribute wood for the communal fire bath and oil to keep the lamps lit, but he also figured prominently in midwinter ceremonial distributions. Contemporary elders had as youths listened in the *qasgi* to their fathers and grandfathers discuss the hunt and talk about the rules for right living.

Although Qaluyaat is no time capsule, relatively late contact, geographic isolation, and a lack of commercially exploitable resources but an abundance of fish and game allowed Qaluyaarmiut some protection from outside influences. As a result they have retained a distinctly Yup'ik view of the world and rich subsistence lifestyle. Into the 1930s, life on Nelson Island had changed more from contact with other coastal and upriver Natives than from direct non-Native influences. A lack of suitable anchorages discouraged rapacious American whalers, and there was no gold, furs, or salmon in commercial quantities to attract American and European adventurers and entrepreneurs. It was left to missionaries to make the first direct contacts with Qaluyaarmiut.

Father Joseph Treca established a Jesuit mission at Tununak in 1889 and by the following year had a small school there for 11 students (Judge 1890:357). The island's remoteness ultimately made it unsuitable as a Catholic base of operations, and in 1892 the Jesuits moved to Kanelik, then in 1893 to Akulurak, 200 miles north on the Yukon delta. From 1895, only a mission station without a school or regular priest remained, visited annually, if at all, by a priest out of

Akulurak (Fienup-Riordan 1991).

In 1927 a new mission was opened in Tununak by Father Martin Lonneux but closed the next year, and from 1928 to 1934 Qaluyaarmiut (along with people in 32 other delta villages) were visited twice each year by a priest traveling out of Hooper Bay. Father Francis Menager spent one day in Tununak in spring 1929. He described the community as having 100 residents, a newly established government school taught by a husband-and-wife team, and a Northern Commercial (NC) Company store. The first airplane came to Nelson Island in 1930 (Bolanz 1975:5), and not until 1944 was there monthly mail delivery. The Qaluyaarmiut were equipped with little in the way of trade goods. They had rifles and supplemented their diet with flour, tea, sugar, and occasionally crackers. Leaf tobacco, cloth, tin pans, and iron pots were also available at the NC store.

In 1934, the church started in Tununak by Lonneux was finished by Father Paul Deschout, who lived and worked on Nelson Island until 1962. Father Deschout is remembered for preaching fire and damnation in perfect Yup'ik. Although sharing the paternalistic attitude of his contemporaries, he was more willing to accept the "simplicity" that he felt went along with the Qaluyaarmiut's isolation on the mission fringe and decried their gradual "corruption" (Deschout 1949:181).

Coming side by side as they have in so many parts of the world, both missionary and trader had a strong influence on the Qaluyaarmiut. The missionaries, including Deschout, propagated the work ethic to parents and children alike, encouraging them to spend their time in prayer and tending traplines, while the traders provided tea, crackers, and ammunition in exchange for the furs that traplines and prayers produced. By the early 1930s Moravian missionary John Kilbuck noted that the use of firearms was well established (Fienup-Riordan, ed. 1988:14), but the subsistence cycle remained essentially the same.

Disease, too, was well established by the 1930s. Population dropped by half from an estimated 10,000 along the Yukon-Kuskokwim delta coastline at the time of Russian contact in the early 1800s. Measles, influenza, and tuberculosis were the primary killers, along with smallpox and syphilis. Deschout's 1937 census for Nelson Island and vicinity, from Kayalivik to Cicing, gave a grand total of 573, including: Kayalivik with its four nearby villages, 132; Tununak, 159, and Yuukaq, 7; Nightmute, 60, and nine nearby villages, 149; and Caputnguaq and Cicing, 66. The initial period of direct contact, from 1889 through the early 1930s, was thus characterized by depopulation from the introduction of foreign diseases followed by the stabilization of a traditionally dispersed and seasonally mobile population. The rifle facilitated hunting without substantially altering hunting patterns or depleting animal populations. Thus fewer people remained in the area and were better equipped to pursue available and still abundant resources.

In 1929 the first federal school opened in Tununak and was quickly transferred to the Bureau of Indian Affairs (BIA) in 1931. BIA schools also were established in Chefornak in 1956 and Nightmute in 1957, replacing mission grammar classes and providing a pivot for further population concentration. The 1940s and 1950s were also characterized by steady population growth as health care improved and epidemics subsided. By 1977, forty years after Father Deschout counted just over 500 residents on and around Qaluyaat, the island was home to 1,037 (Fienup-Riordan 1983:42).

The elders who shared the stories in this book grew up in the 1930s and 1940s scattered in dozens of small villages and camps, moving between sites on a seasonal basis. Families moved to the coast for sea mammal hunting in April, followed by herring fishing in early June. There they harvested seafood of all kinds at prime coastal locations, including Merr'aq to the north; Engelullugarmiut, Tununeq, Up'nerkillermiut, and Umkumiut on Qaluyaat proper; and Aqumgallermiut and Qikertaar to the south.

Once seals had been butchered, oil rendered, and herring dried and stored, families began to move up the small rivers and sloughs that lined the coast, to harvest molting birds and a variety of freshwater fish. People south of Kangirrluar (Toksook Bay) moved to Kaviarmiut, Nangtuq, and Tapruar, fishing for flounder and tomcod. When caches were full they moved farther up the Tuqsuk River, stopping at Kass'aurluq and other smaller camping places to harvest food for people and dogs. At the same time, the tributaries of the Qalvinraaq River to the south, including Cakcaaq, Urumangnaq, Talarun, Qanrangaq, Manriq, and Arayakcaaq, were all rich in fish, including tomcod, pike, whitefish, and burbot. By late summer, tents were pitched up and down these winding rivers. Before freeze-up people again began to gather in winter camps, ranging in size from two to two dozen sod homes. Major winter villages north of Qaluyaat included Kayalivik, Qiingssaq, Cevtaq, and Yuukaq. To the south, in the vicinity of present-day Nightmute, people settled for the winter at Teggalqulegmiut, Quunermiut, Kassigluarmiut, Nevurtuli, and Kanerrlulek (off the Qalvinraaq River). Farther south, families gathered at Arayakcaarmiut, Cevv'arneq, and Cicing during freeze-up, when the entire surrounding area was rich in fish, including blackfish, needlefish, tomcod, flounder, and burbot.

Qaluyaarmiut learned their homeland by traveling its length and breadth along well-known trails up river valleys and over mountains as they harvested resources and visited friends and family at feasts and other gatherings. When sharing stories of their homeland, however, all preferred to talk about their immediate surroundings and the places they knew from personal experience. For example, Newtok elder Michael John spoke at length about Cevtaq, where he was raised, as well as land along harvesting routes. His family moved to either Engelullugarmiut or Tununeq for herring each spring, up to Nerevkartuli later in the summer to drive molting birds, finally stopping at Qiingssaq during fall before returning to Cevtaq for the winter. Simeon Agnus, on the other hand, was raised at Nightmute, where he followed the seasonal round of that community—moving to Umkumiut each spring, across to Kaviarmiut for tomcod, then up the Tuqsuk River—fishing and gathering berries. During late summer and early fall he also traveled up the Qalvinraaq River, stopping at Talarun, Urumangnaq, and Cakcaaq before returning to Nightmute for the winter. These are the places he knows from personal experience, and these are the places he shared stories about. Both men know the names, locations, and something of the history of the lands both north and south but were reluctant to describe them.

The last 60 years have seen dramatic change in the way Qaluyaarmiut inhabit their land. Perhaps the most significant is the concentration of people into five permanent, year-round villages and the abandonment of hundreds of small camps and settlements still vibrant through the 1940s. These five villages—ranging in size today from 250 (Nightmute) to 600 (Toksook Bay)—are small even compared to Bethel at close to 6,000. An audience the size of Toksook's entire population is easily present on Saturday night at the Century 21 Theater in Anchorage.

Yet as people gather closer together on and around Qaluyaat, the island's resources, though still abundant, recede away from settlements. In the past, a man could set his blackfish trap close to camp and within a day provide food for the entire community. Rich runs of tomcod and needlefish were also nearby and readily taken with *qalut* (dip nets). Now men often need to travel many miles, either by gasoline-hungry snowmobile or skiff, to set their nets and traps. People still harvest from the fishing sites they and their parents used when they were young, but at a cost. At a time when the cash economy of southwest Alaska continues to founder, hunting and fishing activities increasingly become difficult to afford.

Tununak (Tununeq, The area at the back), with a current population of 330, is the oldest major year-round settlement on the island, having been occupied for at least 3,000 years (Okada et al. 1982; Collins 1927). The village is well placed on a high isthmus at the mouth of the Tununeq River. A seasonal trading post was established there in the late 1800s, followed by a more permanent Northern Commercial company store. Traders brought merchandise from St. Michael, making goods more accessible. Men hunted muskrats in spring and trapped for fox and mink in winter, while women wove elegant grass baskets to exchange for what they needed. Tununak briefly served as the center for a reindeer operation on the island in the 1930s and 1940s until disease and wolf predation destroyed the herd. Missionary activities continued to focus on Tununak. Father Deschout, known as a strict taskmaster, often traveled from Tununak to Nightmute and Chefornak for services. When he was at home during summer, families to the south walked across the island from Up'nerkillermiut and Umkumiut to Tununak on Saturdays to visit family and friends, attend church, and go to the store before returning home.

The village of Newtok (Nuigtaq, Rustling sound) was established in 1950 when the BIA announced its plans to build a school on the low-lying tundra north of Qaluyaat. Men chose the present site because it was accessible to barges bringing in lumber for the new school (completed in 1962), and half a dozen families from Kayalivik to the north as well as Cevtaq and Qiingssaq to the east gathered on the banks of the Nuigtaq River. Despite Newtok's marshy location, it doubled in size between 1970 and 1990 to 357 today. At the same time Newtok was growing, the land was sinking and eroding at an alarming rate. Plans to relocate the village to a bedrock site across the Ningliq River on Qaluyaat have been developing for over a decade. During summer 2009 and 2010, military training missions began the process of constructing the new village, Mertarvik (Place to get *meq* (water)).

To the south of Qaluyaat, residents of the old village of Cevv'arneq (Cut through place) moved to Caputnguaq (Pretend weir) up the Urrsukvaaq River in the 1930s. Since they were from Cevv'arneq, they gave their new home that name. Like Newtok, the land is low, rising no more than 10 feet above sea level. Today the modern village of Chefornak has 470 residents. A number of our elders—including Paul John, Sophie Agimuk, Theresa Moses, and Brentina Chanar—grew up in Cevv'arneq but found marriage partners in Nightmute and moved north. To this day, strong ties exist between these communities.

A major turning point for the people living on the south side of Qaluyaat and along the Qalvinraaq River was the building of a BIA school in 1957 at the winter village of Negtemiut (People of the pressed-down place, referring to the wind blowing down on them from over the mountain). Dozens of camps and settlements emptied out over the next few years as families gathered at Nightmute from freeze-up in the fall until spring break-up in late April and early May, when they moved en masse to Umkumiut for sealing and herring fishing. Revisiting sites along the Qalvinraaq River in 2007, travelers found the remains of these once-vibrant camps—grass-covered sod homes and numerous tundra graves, some marked with wooden crosses.

Nightmute steadily grew, as homes, a church, and a school crowded along the banks of the Tuqsuk River. Paul John brought in goods from Bethel and ran a small store out of his house, replacing the old store at Pengurtalek to the south where Iiliaq (Elia) had run a one-room trading post. Along with limited land for expansion, Nightmute's inland location required residents to make the twenty-mile move to Umkumiut each April, where they settled in tents and small cabins during the spring sealing and summer herring seasons.

In 1964, a half dozen Nightmute families moved permanently to the spring camp Nunakauyaq, three miles east of Umkumiut. By settling on the banks of the bay between spring sealing and fall fishing, they obviated the need for the annual seasonal move. Hauling their small frame houses over the ice with dog teams, they settled what would become Toksook Bay—the island's largest community, with a current population of 605. In part due to its prime location midway between ocean and inland resources, Toksook has thrived.

Churches, schools, hospital care, National Guard recruitment, and seasonal employment in the commercial fisheries of Bristol Bay all came relatively late to the Qaluyaarmiut compared to others in rural Alaska. Older community members have lived through the entire sequence, from the coming of the first crucifix, cup of coffee, and primer to their place as Catholic shareholders in village and regional corporations with plastic plates on the table and kids in college. One consequence of experiencing the transformation to the modern world in but one generation is that cultural preservation comes easier. What many Alaska Natives would take out of mothballs Nelson Islanders never put away. Their language and subsistence patterns have remained vital and viable, supplemented rather than supplanted by new organizational configurations (single-family dwellings, corporations, organized religion, formal education) and new ideological patterns (land ownership, wage labor, and salvation). All have been interpreted through still vital and uniquely Yup'ik perspectives. Something new emerges, but what was there has a lot to do with its ultimate contours.

As elsewhere worldwide, men and women on Qaluyaat are creating their own version of a worldwide web. In the 1970s most lived their lives on the island, but families now are spread throughout the region, state, country, and world (Fienup-Riordan 2000:151–182). Even with this outmigration, villages continue to grow. Within the last several years Toksook Bay has acquired high-speed Internet, a new airport, subregional clinic, wind generators, a tank farm, and a community center. A road system connecting Tununak, Toksook Bay, and Nightmute is on the state's agenda (Braund and Associates 2005). Not only has community life been transformed, but residents also report dramatic environmental shifts—changes in ice and weather patterns, coastal erosion, decline in permafrost—which in turn affect village infrastructure and seasonal harvesting activities.

Yet much remains the same. The Yup'ik language is still the first language of most adults and many children. Daily life continues to revolve around harvesting activities and the seasonal cycle. Shared meals and both festive and informal distributions of food and gifts are still routine parts of life. Although significant outmigration has taken place over past decades as young people especially seek jobs and higher education, Qaluyaarmiut retain strong ties to their homeland and to subsistence practices that many feel ground their lives.

Perhaps the most striking feature of Qaluyaat today are the uses its people continue to make of the products of the rivers and the sea. Their way of life is inexorably bound up with the seasonal cycling of fish, sea and land animals, plants, and birds. Although communities have solidified in the last 50 years, to some extent obviating the need for seasonal migrations, the places people have chosen to settle are precisely those which in the past as today provide ready access to Nelson Island's abundant resources. For all the apparent immobility of newer villages—with schools, clinics, airstrips, and housing projects—they are far from permanent features of the landscape and continue to depend on the renewable bounty of the land, rivers, and sea.

Umyuallgutekluteng Calillruut
Working Together with One Mind

In 2006, the National Science Foundation's Bering Ecosystem Study (BEST) funded the Nelson Island Natural and Cultural History project. The project was initiated by Qaluyaarmiut community members and implemented through a grant to the Calista Elders Council (CEC). CEC is the primary heritage organization for southwest Alaska, representing 1,300 Yup'ik tradition bearers of the Yukon-Kuskokwim delta, actively documenting Yup'ik traditional knowledge. CEC was established in 1991 by Calista (the profit corporation for the Yukon-Kuskokwim delta). Mark John is CEC's executive director; Alice Rearden, Marie Meade, and David Chanar are the principal translators; and I am the team anthropologist. The five of us have worked together since

2000 on a variety of CEC projects, all of them initiated by CEC's board of elders. These nine Yup'ik-speaking men, representing villages throughout the Yukon-Kuskokwim region, actively support the documentation and sharing of traditional knowledge, which all view as still possessing value in today's world.

CEC's primary information-gathering tool has been the topic-specific gathering. The CEC pioneered this format while working with elders between 2000 and 2005 on a major traditional knowledge project. CEC staff found that specific topics were best addressed by meeting with small groups of elder experts, accompanied by younger community members, for two or three days. Unlike interviews, often conducted by the uninformed, our gatherings (like academic symposia) encourage elders to speak among their peers at the highest level.

CEC gatherings always take place in the Yup'ik language, as the form of information sharing is as important as the content. Translators Alice Rearden, Marie Meade, and David Chanar then create detailed transcripts of each gathering, and we work together to turn these transcripts into bilingual publications and accompanying English texts. To date CEC has produced three sets of "paired" books—an English one for general audiences and a bilingual one for community use (Andrew 2008; Fienup-Riordan 2005a, 2005b, 2007; Rearden, Meade, and Fienup-Riordan 2005; Meade and Fienup-Riordan 2005). This book is the bilingual companion to *Ellavut/Our Yup'ik World and Weather* (Fienup-Riordan and Rearden, in press), a regionwide account of Yup'ik understandings of the land and sea, which also grew from our Nelson Island project.

When elders gather to speak about their past, they carefully select subject matter. What is not said is often as significant as what is said. Long and careful listening to these conversations provides unique perspectives on Yup'ik knowledge, relationships, and language (Fienup-Riordan 2005a:1–41). Beyond facts, elders teach listeners how to learn. They share not only what they know, but also how they know it and why they believe it is important to remember. Finally, CEC staff and Yup'ik community members value topic-specific gatherings like these as contexts of cultural transmission, not mere documentation. The gatherings themselves enrich lives locally at the same time their knowledge has the potential to increase cross-cultural understanding globally.

The Nelson Island project likewise relied on topic-specific gatherings as its primary information-gathering tool. This project was unique for CEC in many ways. First, it dealt with five separate but closely related villages, rather than the region as a whole. Also, it incorporated additional scientists for a unified study of two topics often viewed separately—environmental change and cultural history. This is timely as both the natural and cultural environments of Nelson Island are changing rapidly. Third, the Nelson Island project depended on CEC and community collaboration with other regional agencies, including Calista Corporation, the Association of Village Council Presidents (AVCP), and U.S. Fish and Wildlife Service (USFWS)—each of which contributed the time and expertise of one staff scientist, without whom our project would not have been possible. Whereas a typical research scenario often involves agency scientists requesting permission to carry out non-local research agendas, in this case scientists, like elder experts, were invited to share what they knew.

Last, our involvement in NSF's BEST program was the first time CEC had participated in a large research initiative. The Bering Ecosystem Study was initiated to better understand the rapidly changing natural environment of the eastern Bering Sea. Most BEST projects were carried out by natural scientists doing observations and experiments from the deck of the Coast Guard icebreaker *Healy*. CEC's role in this large endeavor was to provide natural scientists and others with a view of coastal residents' understandings of the changes the scientists observe at sea.

Activities during 2007 included a January planning meeting in Toksook Bay, followed in March by a series of three-day topic-specific gatherings in each of the five communities. Mark John, David Chanar, and I traveled between villages by snowmobile and sled to hold these gatherings. The high point of our project was a three-week July circumnavigation of Qaluyaat, led by Nightmute elder Simeon Agnus.

Our initial January meeting set a clear agenda for summer fieldwork. In addition to planning the trip dates, camping sites, and travel routes, elders from all five villages emphasized the importance of sharing knowledge with their younger generation. One said that the trip would be "like going to college." Many showed enthusiasm for visiting historic and prehistoric sites and documenting place names as we traveled, including named sloughs, hills, points, even sandbars and underwater channels.

John Eric of Chefornak observed, "The ocean cannot be learned," and Stanley Anthony of Nightmute stated, "One must not say, 'The ocean isn't daunting.' The ocean is aware and knowing. A person should not approach the ocean with confidence." Simeon Agnus said, "We must teach our children about the land, also." These statements emphasized the tremendous knowledge required for hunting and how retaining it is critical to safe travel for contemporary young people in the future. Insofar as our project could record and share this knowledge, John Eric enthused, "These things that you mentioned that you will be doing are wonderful."

Our July circumnavigation began when 20 elders, students, and village helpers, along with CEC staff David Chanar and Alice Rearden and three additional scientists—geologist June McAtee, biologist Tom Doolittle, and archaeologist Steve Street—gathered at Umkumiut, a summer fish camp located three miles west of Toksook Bay. Our group included men and women, old and young, Yup'ik and non-Yup'ik. Many were related as cousins, sisters, in-laws, and friends, and we quickly jelled into a tight working group. Each village had been asked to select one elder, one student, and one village helper, which they did. Original selections would have given us far more men than women. Exceptional commercial halibut fishing, however, meant that some men wanted to continue fishing, and a number of women replaced them, becoming our most enthusiastic participants. Our elder women—three of whom were sisters—also added to our fun, especially in their good-natured teasing of their *uicungaq* (cross cousin), David Chanar.

Men and women alike were united in feeling that what we were doing had special significance. On our last night at Umkumiut, Father Tom Provinsal, the resident priest, sent us on our way with the Pilgrim's Blessing in a short but moving ceremony on the beach by our five heavily loaded boats. This was one of many signs of the profound meaning the trip had for Yup'ik participants, who shed tears of joy when we reached sites and visited graves they had not seen for 50 years. The emotional impact of our journey was profound for young people as well as elders.

After five days at Umkumiut we headed southwest into the Bering Sea, avoiding mud flats and entering the Qalvinraaq River, which separates Qaluyaat from the mainland. Simeon Agnus had worried about "allowing us to experience traveling in bad weather," but just as the tide came up and floated our boats, the winds died down and the water turned bright. Over the next two weeks we visited close to 30 of the island's 250 historic and prehistoric sites. Consulting with other group members, Simeon charted our course, leading us to sites where we gathered as a group and listened to what elders remembered about that particular place.

Conversations during our trip not only dealt with proper relations between humans, but also continually returned to the responsive and knowing character of the environment. For example, when Tom Doolittle left for a beach walk on our second day at Umkumiut, Simeon warned him to be careful, as the rocks might fall on people who they did not know. Commenting on the patches of mosquito blood on her tent wall, Ruth Jimmie said that when mosquitoes tell stories to one another they say, "I escaped five *nukalpiat,*" meaning a human hand, and "I got a leg" or "I got a *kass'aq*" when they bite someone.

During our July trip we saw all village types—spring and fall hunting camps, summer fish camps, reindeer stations, and permanent winter villages. Most had residents until 1957, when the first school was established at Nightmute and families moved there so that their children could attend. We also visited the island's varied natural environments, including coastal headlands, floodplain, lowland freshwater rivers, and uplands. Qaluyaat is a volcanic rise in a nonmarine sedimentary base, a delta lowland set down over millennia by the Yukon and Kuskokwim rivers. The Yukon-Kuskokwim delta has always been a land of change—lakes draining, rivers altering course, banks eroding. In the past, however, change was slow, as was the delta's ability to recover.

Our trip was not without its frustrations. Simeon Agnus' concern for group safety as well as the condition of our boats precluded stopping at several rocky beaches that geologist June McAtee had hoped to see. Once we left Umkumiut's gravel beach, she didn't see another rock. Biologist Tom Doolittle was equally frustrated in his attempt to set traps to gain an understanding of small mammal populations, as this required at least a two-night stay at the same site. Simeon planned his moves to maximize visits to historic places, so Tom's trapping plans were put on hold. None of our scientists complained or tried to push an agenda. The patience and understanding they displayed resulted in overwhelmingly positive relations between group members and, as the trip went on, elders increasingly felt comfortable freely sharing their knowledge.

The most striking feature of our conversations was elders' integrated way of conceiving and sharing information. Elders did not distinguish between human impacts on the environment, such as the effects of commercial fishing or overhunting, and the "natural" effects of climate change. Instead, elders consistently referred to the role of human action in the world when describing changes in the environment or species availability.

At every gathering at least one elder repeated the well-known Yup'ik adage, "The world is changing following its people." Simeon Agnus (July 2007:581) noted: "*Qanrutketukiit-am tua-i yun'i-gguq maligtaa nutaan ellam uum* [They say that the world is following [the behavior of] its people]. Since its people are becoming bad, *ella* is replicating their behavior." *Ella*—translated variously as world, weather, or universe—has always been viewed as intensely responsive to human thought and deed. Western separation between natural and social phenomena sharply contrasts with our Yup'ik counterparts, who eloquently focused on their connection (Cruikshank 2005:9).

The adage, "The world is changing following its people," captures the Yup'ik view that environmental change is directly related to human interaction as well as action (overfishing, burning fossil fuels). As Paul Tunuchuk (March 2007:216) of Chefornak said: "We are in this situation today because of not being dutiful to each other. It's as though we are sleepwalking." Elders maintain that the problems of global warming will require that we do more than change our destructive environmental habits. They also stress the importance of a return to traditional rules for living, believing that if human values improve, correct actions will follow.

In addition to leading by example, Qaluyaarmiut elders guide their youth mainly by speaking to them—as they did during village gatherings and our circumnavigation—sharing knowledge with kindness and compassion. As they say, "We talk to you because we love you." Stanley Anthony vehemently maintained the need to instruct the young, because, "The instructions aren't mine," implying they are not made up and should not be cast aside. Elders do not dissociate themselves from observed changes in their homeland. They accept personal responsibility. Now, they say, is the time to reverse their recent failure to instruct the younger generation. Observing uninstructed young men and women, John Eric (January 2007:26) remarked, "We must talk to them, to delay them from becoming like dogs." Qaluyaarmiut elders warmly embraced our work together, which they viewed as much more than passive documentation but as part of an active solution.

Qanemcitgun Atrit Pugtellruit
They Revealed Their Names in Stories

> There are actually many names of places in this area. And when they'd tell stories, they would constantly reveal their names.
>
> —*Paul Charles, Newtok*

Literature on place names and their meanings abounds. The richest published studies of place names in Alaska include works by Andrew Balluta (2008); Robert Drozda (1998); Karen Evanoff (2010); Susan Fair (2004); Jim Kari and Jim Fall (2003); the King Island Native Community and Deanna Kingston (2010); Katherine Koutsky (1981); Igor Krupnik, Rachel Mason, and Tonia Horton (ed., 2004); Elizabeth Marino (2005); Donald Orth (1967); Ken Pratt (ed., 2009); Dorothy Jean Ray (1971); and Tom Thornton (2008). Much valuable place name documentation also remains unpublished, such as a detailed mapping project carried out by the village of Chevak during which more than 200 historic sites were mapped (Boyscout 2005).

Interest in Yup'ik place names has increased, as has awareness of these names as repositories for such local knowledge as resource availability, travel routes, historic conflicts, distant-time events and creation stories, and ecological change. Using names specific to the Qaluyaarmiut homeland reveals a unique understanding of their world, taking the form of maps they hold in their minds (Basso 1996:46). Anthropologist Julie Cruikshank (1990:63) discusses how Eyak, Athabascan, and Tlingit place names encapsulate ecological information that "reflect changes in the landscape or in the movements of plants and animals." Yup'ik people do the same, as when they named a bend in the upper Cakcaaq River "Place where kayaks dock," referring to the fact that chum salmon spawn there at the end of their journey upriver. Recent work in both anthropology and cultural geography has supported a view of the enduring power of landscape features to act as points of reference for communicating knowledge. As Cruikshank (2005:11) notes, people "persist in transforming seemingly neutral spaces into places of significance." These "places of remembrance," in turn, "provide a kind of archive where memories can be mentally stored."

During our travels around Qaluyaat and at community gatherings after our return, elders shared close to 1,000 names, including historic sites and landscape features of all shapes and sizes, from tiny sloughs to deep ocean channels. Many of these names were shared as part of stories, and a single story often contained a wealth of names (e.g., the story of Kinguqermiut that follows). The variety of stories these places evoked was as rich as the names themselves. A number of stony outcrops, like Qilengpak, Teq'acugpak, and Qaluyaat itself, are associated with *qulirat* or distant-time stories of Raven the Creator, who made Qaluyaat when he cast soil on ice floating out to sea. Hilltops such as Qasginguaq and Qukaqliqutaat are home to *ircenrraat* (other-than-human persons), who some say appear there to this day. Several historic sites are associated with the period of bow-and-arrow warfare, ending in the early 1800s, including Engelumiut (the home of the warrior Apanuugpak) and Nunalleq. Other places recall events from more recent times, such as Kellarvik (Storage bag), commemorating the death of a child left beside the Qalvinraaq River when his mother waded across but was unable to return for him.

Elders evoke the idea of place and the act of naming in myriad ways.

Many stories could be called morality tales. Speakers share them because they believe that their lessons will guide listeners toward a better life. Bethel elder Peter Jacobs (January 2006:226) used the grassy knoll known as Narqainaq (One that is merely sniffed) as an example. The name recalls the woman buried there. She could attract husbands, but each would leave after a short time. Her behavior embarrassed her fellow villagers, and they told her, "It seems that when a man has come upon you, he leaves you upon merely sniffing you. We're naming you again the name Narqainaq." Peter recalled that when he and his companions were spoken to at home, their parents would use Narqainaq as an example of someone who lived improperly: "Her actions were a help in teaching us the *qanruyutet* [instructions]. They tried to be good, not wanting to be like Narqainaq, and when they got husbands, they hardly ever left them. They also called that small grassy knoll Narqainaq, and they used that place to try to make us fearful."

Some places were named simply to make us smile. When it was his turn to introduce himself to the group sitting on the beach at Umkumiut before we left on our trip around Qaluyaat, John Roy John from Newtok explained:

> Yesterday, when I was walking out in that direction, I passed a very large boulder, and when I reached that place, I felt like defecating. [*laughter*] Then I went up and defecated.
>
> Then again this morning, when I went up and reached that same place, I felt like defecating again. I looked and saw my feces down there, the place where I had defecated. Then I named that place Anaqsungaarrvik [Place where one suddenly wants to defecate] on my own. [*laughter*]

From mythic to historic to serious or funny, all these named places and their stories evoke a distinctly Yup'ik world. As in Keith Basso's (1996) experience among the Western Apache, as we worked with elders to document the history of their homeland, they continually used place names in narratives and conversations. Part of their evocativeness resides in the way these names create an autonomous and continuous spirit of "dwelling and being in the world" (Ingold 2000). As anthropologist David Samuels (2001:277) notes, their moving power is in part attributable to their continued independence from English place names and their ability to differentiate what non-Natives define as nameless wilderness. In a land Qaluyaarmiut have inscribed with hundreds of names, U.S. Geological Survey mapmakers note five year-round villages, two major rivers, and Baird Inlet, Etolin Strait, Cape Vancouver, Dall Lake, and Nelson Island (all named for non-Native men with minimal historic ties to the region).

Our work on Qaluyaat began as neither a mapping project nor a linguistic attempt to catalog place names. The project was conceived as an integrated natural and cultural history project committed to taking community direction. It originated as a major collaborative effort between Yup'ik community members and outside partners (including me) during which we made a serious attempt to coproduce the knowledge we hoped to share, including the format of such sharing. Our planning meetings went beyond cooperation, with one group providing ideas and understandings to another, to the coconceptualization and, more significant, cocommitments (moral and ethical) of true collaboration (Menzies 2008). From the beginning we wanted our project to be research with, rather than research about, Qaluyaarmiut. True collaboration, as many note, is the joint shaping of representations. These deep collaborations offer powerful alternatives to more conventional research approaches.

We did not set out to document place names. Rather, the places, their names, and their stories were what elders thought we needed to know. Their understanding of the world and their place within it is inscribed in the land they live on and the waterways they travel through. The way they decided we could best learn about their land and how they could best teach us was to travel through it together. They knew that what they could tell us would blend with the day-to-day experiences of camp life from which we would also learn, including the practical work of feeding ourselves from the land and finding shelter there. Qaluyaarmiut elders believed that both non-Native scientists and young Nelson Islanders could learn what they needed to know only through the combined experience of traveling and listening to their stories. One without the other was insufficient.

Elders took turns speaking at sites they knew from personal experience. Simeon Agnus, our leader, made sure their narratives were never long, contending that people cannot remember what is said during a lengthy speech. The brief narratives they shared focused on the speaker's relationship to the place—what she or he saw, did, thought, felt, and heard there. These narratives extended the personal experiences and relations they described. For example, listening to Rita Angaiak tell of her gratitude when she returned to where her mother and a sister were buried—a place she had not visited for more than 50 years—I received much more than a history of the place. In sharing her story, she enriched not only our relationship but also my companionship with her sisters, who were there listening to her story.

The relationships between places and their stories always seem to evoke shared human emotions. Qaluyaarmiut who later read these stories can also experience something of these extended personal relations and the elders' concern for their well-being. Even readers unfamiliar with particular narrators are often made aware of these relations through the sometimes gentle, sometimes humorous, sometimes scolding way in which stories are shared.

As our multicultural group prepared to leave Umkumiut, our travel preparations revealed our different expectations. Arriving at Umkumiut in mid-July, Steve Street tested the solar panels that he would use to recharge his state-of-art global positioning system (GPS). Biologist Tom Doolittle tinkered with combinations of seal oil and pilot bread in traps he would use to catch and measure small rodents. June McAtee and I took many photographs, both of camp life and Nelson Island's rocky coastline, and I made sure my tape recorder was in top condition. I also checked supplies of everything from bug repellant to stove fuel, concerned we would run short. Our food supplies were limited to basics such as coffee, tea, sugar, flour, Crisco, dried herring and herring aged in seal oil, and a variety of packaged meals. These limits reflected the elders' preference as much as our boats' carrying capacity. Simeon Agnus assured me that food would be available on the land—ducks, geese, fish, berries, and greens. Ours was no expedition into the wilderness. People did not need to carry food when visiting the sources of the island's true wealth.

While these practical preparations were under way, elders took turns explaining why they wanted to make this trip and what they hoped we would learn. Anna Agnus stated: "We've lost those ways; sometimes we feel resentful these days. We are speaking of the time in our lives when we gained awareness. We are constantly losing these [young] people who we are trying to help succeed. We are about to go on this trip for their sakes, because of these [young people]. We have been constantly talking about the Yup'ik way of life, about how to make a living."

Theresa Abraham described the centrality of time-tested *qanruyutet* (oral instructions) in what elders shared. *Qanruyutet* served as both practical and moral guideposts in the past, and elders believe they are no less valuable today:

> These people, including me, have been speaking and haven't said anything differently from what was said by my parents, those who gave constant instructions. And when I hear other people giving advice, they don't say it any differently.
>
> Up to this day, we have continued to recall the *qanruyutet* that we were given in the past about things that they wanted us to follow and obey. And at this time now, you two [young people, Jackie Lincoln and Linda Joe] are listening. We are Yup'ik people; our Yup'ik identity won't change.
>
> This is what my father said, too. He said our counterparts have their own way of life. And he said we Yup'ik people have our own *qanruyutet*

> that are the insignia of our Yup'ik ways, consisting of its teachings and admonishments. When I hear the *qanruyutet,* although we are from different villages, the oral instructions are the same.

Rita Angaiak revisited the motivation for elders to share their knowledge:

> A person only instructs a person he loves about what will come in his future. I care for you both. We all care about you. We don't have any animosity toward you, but we are fond of you. They used to tell us things that we would encounter in the future.
>
> And my grandparents, the people who instructed me, always gave me advice. And when they were done, they would tell me, "A person only gives advice to one he loves. And he doesn't advise one he doesn't care for." About my future [they said], "As you live, you will come upon the things that I told you." Evidently, what they said was indeed true.

Before leaving Umkumiut, Simeon Agnus initiated a pattern of visiting between two and four sites each day. Our group would fill three skiffs and motor to a site that Simeon and Paul John identified as important to know about. All would debark and gather on the beach or on the riverbank, where elders would take turns sharing their personal experiences there and what they had learned about the place from their own elders. Only after they had spoken were we free to walk around the site, exploring house pits and viewing graves.

As head of the AVCP lands office, Steve Street had printed out detailed maps of the area, including 142 ANCSA historic and cemetery sites he had helped document in the 1980s and the location of which he wanted to confirm using the latest mobile geographic information sites (GIS) technology. As a land manager, Steve is beset by issues of land ownership on a daily basis. It was thanks to his understanding of the complex jurisdictions surrounding land ownership on Nelson Island—ranging from federal lands managed by the U.S. Fish and Wildlife Service, corporation lands, and individual allotments—that we were able to secure the formal permission to use specific camping places the National Science Foundation required. Elders, on the other hand, were not concerned with boundaries or land ownership but with describing how these places were used by everyone in the past, underlining the gulf between Qaluyaarmiut understandings of rights to land based on generations of use and non-Native views of land as a commodity subject to individual and corporate ownership. As Paul John explained: "The white people revealed a plan that people should only hunt on corporation land. They won't be able to travel to a particular place to subsist. I told them about our ancestors' saying

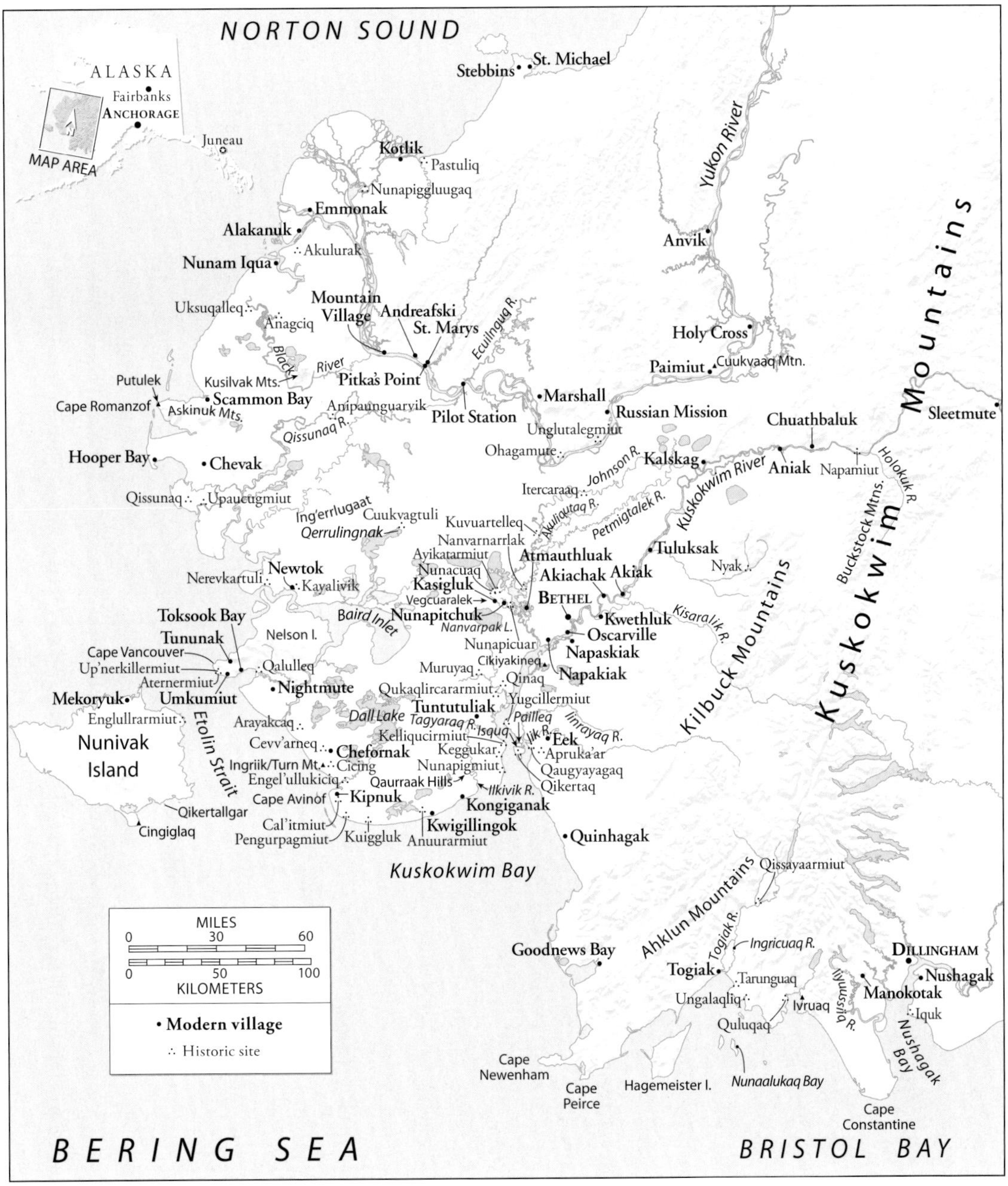

Map of the Yukon/Kuskokwim Delta region, 2010. Patrick Jankanish.

Qaluyaat (Nelson Island), looking west toward the spring camp of Up'nerkillermiut. James H. Barker

St. Mary's Mission district, including Nelson Island and vicinity, 1920s. Jesuit Oregon Province Archives, Spokane, Washington. #503.22b

Nelson Islanders gathered in front of the Tununak Church, 1940s. Jesuit Oregon Province Archives, Spokane, Washington.

Herring drying at Tununak, 1933. Otto Geist, Alaska and Polar Regions Department, University of Alaska Fairbanks.

The Hooper family at Tununak, 1942. Jesuit Oregon Province Archives, Spokane, Washington.

Graves on the tundra near Tununak, 1933, including the deceased's valued possessions. Otto Geist, Alaska and Polar Regions Department, University of Alaska Fairbanks.

Joe Post and family camped on the north side of Nelson Island, 1930s. Jesuit Oregon Province Archives, Spokane, Washington.

A half-dozen dog teams harnessed together, pulling a house over the ice from Nightmute to the newly established community of Toksook Bay, April 1964. Jesuit Oregon Province Archives, Spokane, Washington. #557.1.05

Men guiding the move over the ice from Nightmute to Toksook Bay, April 1964. Jesuit Oregon Province Archives, Spokane, Washington. #557.1.06

First communion class at Nightmute, 1968. Jesuit Oregon Province Archives, Spokane, Washington.

Toksook Bay in 1977. James H. Barker.

that in the past our people ate together from the land like [they were eating] from the contents of one bowl. We carry out the custom of camping [wherever we need to subsist]."

At an elders gathering following our trip, John Eric (December 2007:378) talked about the Qaluyaarmiut ethic of shared land and resources compared to non-Native concepts of private ownership. As an example he discussed effects of the Alaska Native Allotment Act of 1906, which gave individuals the right to apply for title to 160-acre parcels in traditional use areas. Since ANCSA would extinguish further allotments, regional organizations such as AVCP encouraged people to apply before the 1971 deadline.

> Down in the coastal area I never heard anyone say, "You cannot go and fish there." However, our [non-Native] counterparts brought about allotments on these hunting places or berry-picking places or fishing places out in the wilderness. I once had an allotment on the Cakcaaq River, but someone from Qaluyaat told me that I was trying to take land away from others. Since that person said that to me, since AVCP had workers who dealt with [allotments], when [a worker] arrived I told him, "I'm going to relinquish that allotment."
>
> I came to realize the impact of [the allotments] that our counterparts gave us. Back when our ancestors didn't have those [allotments], it was an instruction that we all must use a particular fishing spot. I must have upset that person through what was given to me by a white person.
>
> There are those [allotments] around our village, and we don't [only] go to them and pick berries from there but we go to other places [as well]. And the people of Kipnuk also go to the area behind our village since they can reach it with boats, and they pick berries there as much as they want. . . .
>
> Those things called allotments that white people brought to our people weren't around in the past. They are a source of disagreements and evidently became something that was hurtful to people.

Paul John followed by explaining the impact this change in attitude has had on the abundance of animals. He said that animals remain plentiful where people share resources but not where squabbling over exclusive rights occurs. Simeon Agnus wholeheartedly agreed with his cousin and gave the Cakcaaq River as an example: "We welcome villages beyond ours to subsist at Cakcaaq. Since it belongs to all Qaluyaarmiut, it is ours. And we open subsistence [at Cakcaaq] for the villages beyond ours." Because people today still share Cakcaaq's rich fishery, the river continues to provide abundant resources.

Reflecting on his experience traveling with elders, Steve Street observed that archaeologists tend to view sites as discrete locations possessing definable features such as springs, paths, house pits, and graves. Elders, on the other hand, immediately contextualized each site we visited, noting the season during which people camped there and how people traveled from place to place. Though as an archaeologist Steve said his original interest was each site's physical features, elders emphasized the connections between sites and the relations between families who stayed there. Elders were interested in the sites as educational opportunities and as platforms for personal narratives. For them, the present condition of the site or precise location were secondary. Their concern was not preserving sites but ensuring continuity of valued interpersonal relations between people and human and nonhuman persons inhabiting their island home.

Elders assumed the role of teachers throughout our trip. Young people, they believe, cannot understand what they do not experience, and our trip provided ample opportunities for elders to point out lessons worth remembering. Elders put each site in context, sharing a mix of very specific information—what fish were available, names of people who lived and died there—and the values that continue to animate life on and around Qaluyaat today. Throughout, they emphasized active, ongoing relations between people and the land. Even graves were viewed as connected to the present rather than remnants of the past. Instead of documenting their location and listing their features, elders wanted to say prayers and sing hymns in memory of near relatives present in the land.

Elders treated non-Native guests on the trip as they did their young people, instructing us when they deemed it appropriate. For example, on our third evening, as we traveled up the Qalvinraaq to visit Kanerrlulegmiut, a bearded seal presented itself. Our men shot it but were able to retrieve it only after the loan of a harpoon from a passing hunter. Following the hunt, when all had gathered at the site, Simeon asked David to explain to us *kass'at* (non-Natives) that we had seen genuine Yup'ik hunting—people helping one another, sharing, and never ignoring someone in need. Later in the trip Simeon used a meal of fresh whitefish to remind us why he had refrained from carrying large stores of food on our trip: "Sometimes we Yup'ik people gather together as a small group in the wilderness. And we don't have many store-bought provisions but travel with only the wilderness to provide sustenance. You know how we just set a net over there and had fresh fish to eat. The things that we cannot carry, mesh fishnets catch. And also a bird gun and a hunting gun; a man takes those for support when traveling, and we have plenty to eat."

Cat Tamarmeng Yuilqumi Atengqertut
All Places in the Wilderness Have Names

> We tried to learn the names of places in the wilderness that those before us revealed to us, and we use their names today. We didn't make up those names, but we are using the names of the sloughs, lakes, and mountains that our elders revealed to us.
>
> —*David Panruk, Chefornak*

Throughout our trip elders made clear that people traveled through and settled in places where the resources they needed to survive were located. All these places had names. CEC board member John Phillip (February 2006:169) of Kongiganak explained:

> We are speaking about the use of the land and its resources. We know the places where we will subsist. And these places all have names.
>
> My village down on the coast is called Kongiganak. My grandfather, after living in Anuurarmiut, where I was born, moved to Kongiganak. Our ancestors who formed villages apparently didn't settle just anywhere. After learning about a certain area, knowing that there were hunting areas where one could subsist, those past people established villages there. And some of the settlements also have names.

In the past, maps were rare, but knowledge was plentiful. Camilius Tulik (March 2007:474) of Nightmute recalled: "Even though they did not have maps, our ancestors knew these small villages by talking about them, and they always recognized the places." The land was also rich with names. Michael John (March 2007:1016) of Newtok exclaimed: "All these lakes have names, they do actually have names." Phillip Moses (January 2007:443) of Toksook noted: "River bends also had names in my village. Even though there was one river, their bends had names." Mark Tom (March 2007:1077) of Newtok noted that the areas around many coastal rivers were rich in names:

> When going down Kayalivik [River], the entire area is covered with names; as you're traveling along, the names change. That place has a name, and then as one is traveling, another location has a different name. And when traveling through Nerevkartuli, there are also many names.
>
> When traveling from Cevcaraq, that river has many names, with a particular place having a name. And the ones in the middle and in the lower part of the river have names to indicate location when traveling.

Joseph Patrick (March 2007:1079) of Newtok also noted that the upper, middle, and lower parts of a river were distinguished: "They call the ones farthest upriver *kiaqliit* [upper ones], the ones in the middle are called *qukaqliit* [middle ones], and the ones located downriver [near the mouth] are called *uaqliit* [lower ones]."

River bends and sections were distinguished in many ways. Paul John (September 2009:21) gave an example: "Although that river is called Tuqsuk, because that area of the river is touching the mountain, they call it Agtuqaumaneq [from *agtur-,* "to touch"]." Joseph John (June 2008:47) of Newtok added: "Areas [along the river] have names. This river that has many bends, they call this part Cingigpak [Big *cingik* (point)], this [bend] is Cingigpacuar [Small Cingigpak], and they call those [bends] Qip'acuk [from *qipneq,* "river bend"]." Elsie Tommy (February 2010:371) of Newtok declared: "Although these places are close together, they have many names; those small places all have names." Joseph John (February 2010:339) described the value of such specificity when people wanted to communicate the exact location of fish running upriver: "When we'd go and dipnet for needlefish, they knew the location of the needlefish through these places [with distinct names]. When we mention the location on the river, when the needlefish are in this river at this location, we reveal the name of the place." Paul Charles concluded: "These names were like street signs, like Fireweed Lane."

These names were important to know. In the past, they were taught to children beginning when they were very young. Phillip Moses (October 2002:228) recalled: "Back then a young boy would travel with his dad, he was expected to learn the names for all the small creeks. Each creek has its own name up to this day. Since we were small and always went with our parents we learned their names." Elsie Tommy (February 2010:326) also recalled her father instructing her while traveling: "My deceased older sister and I would slowly row, situated across from one another, when heading up Asuun River and passing by sloughs. My father would reveal their names to us, and I haven't forgotten them." Men and women also helped each other learn these names. Mark Tom (March 2007:1051) said: "I used to tell [my fellow villager] Miisaq [Peter John] about places, since I brought him with me when I traveled. When I came upon places, I'd reveal their names." Elders continue to teach these names to their descendants. John Eric (March 2005:95) said: "When I bring my grandchild Tutmalria with me, I reveal places to him since I won't always take him with me when I travel, so that if something should happen to him in the future [he will know those places], [and I tell him place names] just as my grandfather told me the names of lakes, even hills."

Emphasizing the value of knowing place names to locate critical resources, John Phillip (February 2006:170) elaborated:

> The river of the village of Kongiganak has fish. It has tomcod and smelt and needlefish in it, and it is called Kangirnaq River. And its tributaries, some sloughs also have names. We must have these [young people] know those places that can produce edible fish. And some of the rivers coming out of lakes also have an abundance of fish. We must show our children those places so they will be able to go there and harvest a particular resource.
>
> And some parts of the land have wheat grass. There was a small lake where they went to gather wheat grass in my village. That was the only place it grew. That grass would be made into containers for fish. They knew where it was and gathered it.
>
> And we had a summer fish camp downriver called Keggukar. When they cut salmon to dry there at Keggukar, when they were about to obtain grass to make containers for them, they picked *iitat* [tall cotton grass], since wheat grass wasn't the only grass made into containers. There were long [grasses] far inland in that lake they called Iitarcaraq [Place to gather tall cotton grass]. They knew that place, and when they mentioned its name, they could go there. We had to know the location of that place.
>
> They mentioned those places by name. Indeed, some sloughs have names, and some rivers are good for setting mink traps, as they say *unangviksunaqluteng* [they are good places to catch animals and fish]. It is what they refer to as *pikutak* [a good area] where there are many animals to catch. We had to know that area also if we were going to hunt for mink or muskrat to sell their fur. And we have to show our younger ones those areas if we know them.

Women, also, learned about the land and its names. John continued:

> Since our women travel out to the wilderness, some find certain places on the land where resources are plentiful. When they want to pick berries, they immediately recall the place where they are plentiful. They know that place and will go to it, mentioning it by name. And that particular hill has a name. Since there are few hills, some have names in our village.
>
> I know the places where berries are plentiful by having traveled there. When they grow, berries aren't all the same everywhere. Sometimes berries grow on a particular hill first, and they ripen and get very soft early, and other [berries] ripen later. Evidently, different areas of the land vary in their stages [of ripening]. And we must know those areas and reveal those places to our neighbors who will harvest them.

John Phillip (February 2006:172) emphasized that people travel to many places to harvest what they need each year: "They don't have just one place where they harvest things. And they name the places where they go. They know the place by its name and can go to the place with an abundance of berries." Finally, John (February 2006:173) reminded his listeners that a person only knows the names from his own area: "I don't know about the Yukon River because it's not my land."

Place names helped people find and retrieve lost property. Phillip Moses (October 2002:228) said: "If one forgets something and knows where it is, he will tell his dad or his uncle that he forgot it at a certain place so his relative will know its location. He will know the name of the river where he left it and will go to it."

Place names were also used to locate one's companions. Edward Hooper (March 2007:1433) of Tununak explained: "When two hunters were about to leave, they'd mention the place where they were going. They named the place and said that they wanted to spend the night there. That's what they constantly did. They always let them know place names." Peter Matthew (March 2008:162) of Chefornak also emphasized the safety aspect of learning place names: "That's the reason those places have names, so that a person may know where a village or river is located. Based on someone revealing that name to him, although he doesn't have a map, he can go there and know where it's located. But if he doesn't know some areas, he won't know where he is located."

Susie Angaiak (March 2007:1413) of Tununak gave a sad example of just how dangerous such lack of knowledge can be: "In the past, one of those two young men died across from the Tununak River. Since the poor things didn't know place names in the area, although the other [boy who made it home] named the place [where his traveling companion was located], he named the wrong place. They searched for him in the place that he mentioned, but he wasn't there. Finally, someone found him near that place down the coast they call Qemirpak, beyond the place that poor [young man] mentioned. Since the poor people don't know those place names, they get into tragic situations."

Place names were essential traveling tools. Mark Tom (March 2007:1016) noted: "They use these lakes that have different names to indicate location when traveling." Knowledge of place names, elders contend, helps people survive. Dangerous places were named and, therefore, known. John Walter (March 2007:1361) of Tununak named numerous *carvat* (streams with strong currents) descending from the mountains on Nelson Island—a potential hazard when traveling in winter: "*Carvat* usually do not freeze solid. Sometimes we quickly come upon them [when traveling]. A person mustn't travel along the edge of the mountains with a snowmobile, especially without a traveling partner, without knowing [where they are]."

Phillip Moses (January 2007:443) noted that knowing one's location in relation to the village ensured that travelers could find their way home: "Since there are snowstorms down [on the coast], if he gets lost he can say the river's name, and by knowing the river's location, he will know the location of his village. If he recognizes the river, he will know which way to go."

Peter John (March 2007:1004) of Newtok explained how those who travel through and use an area know its names: "Only these people who travel to this area—David Moses and Mark George—know their names. They travel through these areas, and they mention all the names of the places they traveled through. After getting wood, they mention the place where they got it from." Michael John (March 2007:1000) agreed, "I cannot talk about places where I haven't traveled." According to Tommy Hooper (March 2007:1354) of Tununak, people always knew where they were: "In the past, since we knew our land, we would ask, 'Where are you located?' After naming that particular land up there, he would say that he was located near this particular place. That's what we did since we knew our land. And although we don't want you [young people] to be [ignorant], you don't know that area. We want you to know [place names]."

Nunami Atret Tamarmeng Kangingqertut
Every Name on Land Has Meaning

Place names themselves were bestowed for many reasons. John Eric (January 2007) declared: "Our ancestors didn't give names without a good purpose. There is a meaning for everything." Some places were named after people. Michael John (March 2007:1101) gave a humorous example: "I don't think it had a name to begin with. A person named Angassaar went to get some frozen fish by just pushing his sled along. When poor Angassaar attempted to climb that hill, when he couldn't climb, he evidently cried. A person who came upon him and saw him called this hill Angassaaq. That's how the saying goes. [*laughs*]" Paul John (October 2006:73) added: "Some of the [streams] are named after a person who made a channel between [two lakes] which eventually became a small river. They named them after the person's Yup'ik name." Mark Tom (March 2007:1031) pointed out a place called Kass'aq on the map: "It was a village founded by a *kass'aq,* and that's where that person they called Kass'aq hunted." Michael John agreed, adding: "When we hunted at the place where Maklak hunted, we always called it Makliim Kuiga [Maklak's River]."

Places were also named for ways in which they were used. John Eric (March 2007) noted that fall camps were often named for what was abundant there: "Our ancestors looked at their surroundings and named the places like that. There is a place where there are many blackfish, so they named it Can'giirtupiaq [Place with many *can'giiret* (blackfish)]." Harvesting activities were not the only uses embodied in names. Places were named for events that took place there. Anna Agnus (July 2007) told the story of the Qaluyaarmiut woman who married a man in the tundra region. During a period of food shortage, she traveled back to Qaluyaat, carrying her young child and a *kellarvik* (storage bag) full of tree bark as their only provisions. Reaching the Qalvinraaq River, she left her child on the bank beside her *kellarvik* and crossed, planning to return. Unable to withstand the cold water a second time, she traveled on to a village to the south, where a childless couple took her in. The husband immediately returned to the Qalvinraaq to bring home her child:

> He finally reached [the baby], and he probably didn't travel very fast at the time. When he reached it, he saw that she had placed the baby on the tundra, and her *kellarvik* was right beside him, filled with tree bark.
>
> They say that small [baby] had been kicking, and the place where his legs had been kicking had made a deep depression. [The baby] had evidently died.
>
> That person is probably the only person [buried there] at Kellarvik. That place down there called Kellarvik, it is said that story is the reason why it was given the name.

Places could also be named for things they resembled. John Eric (March 2008:150) noted: "After observing the places that they used in the wilderness, they named them." Peter Dull (March 2007:448) of Nightmute gave an example from the Nightmute area: "They call the place on the mountainside where the bushes thin out Atkuguat [Pretend parkas]. Looking at them from far away it looks like a parka with outstretched arms, and it has a hood." During a visit to Chefornak, Paul Jenkins (March 2007:244) of Nunapitchuk noted: "Our ancestors gave names to lakes by just observing them. If it looked a certain way, they compared it to something, and that became its name. And that place called Aru [Rot] on this side of Cuukvagtuli; since there were many things including fish that tended to rot, they called it Aru after observing what it was like."

A number of places have acquired names in recent times. Paul Tunuchuk (March 2008:152) gave an example: "The area across from our village just recently got a name. Back when they lived down at Cevv'arneq, it is said two men left early in the morning day after day without saying anything. Evidently that place where they were going had formed an *aniniq* [concentration of blackfish]. Those two called that place Aassaqvik [Secret place], and it came to be called Aassaqvik. It is a tributary of the Qissivlak River."

The variety of names is as rich as the land itself. Some names are humorous, others serious, others amazing. People continue to name places. According to Paul Jenkins (March 2007:244): "Since long ago, people named lakes based on how they looked. You could actually name the places that don't have names. We can all give names to places that don't have names. You have every right to do this. If you forget the names of places, you can name them by observing what those places are like." Writing down place names on a map of the Chefornak area, Joe Maklak (March 2007:245) made a happy discovery: "The place where I set my wooden fish trap every year, evidently someone named it after me and it's written on the map."

Some places received non-Yup'ik names. Edward Hooper (March 2007:1251) said that the area above the old village of Muuguacuar was called Theresa: "After the Catholic Church came around, since Peter Post and his family used to stay there, they gave it that English name, since they placed a medal there. That medal had Theresa written on it. They gave it that English name, probably so that the place would be blessed." John Eric (March 2008:150) explained how one manmade channel got its name: "We call the channel that we made downriver from our village 'Shortcut' in English. Back when we had wooden boats, it took half an hour to travel there and back. But then we used shovels to create a channel. It has become deep today. Its name is Shortcut, and we call it Kuiliaq [Manmade river] in Yup'ik." Paul Tunuchuk (March 2008:162) gave another example from the Chefornak area: "When I hear young men talking, when asking them, 'Where are you?' [They'll say], 'Pooring.' There is now a place [at the mouth of our river] called Pooring. Its real name is Kuigeurluq [Poor river]. These days Kuigeurluq has acquired the name Pooring. These young men are giving it an English name."[1]

Places can have more than one name. Working with our map of Qaluyaat, Tommy Hooper (March 2007:1291) noted: "This place has another name, but we should give it the name Arviryaraq [Crossing place]." Tommy (June 2008:254) gave the well-known mud volcanoes north of Newtok as another example: "They say those people who were having [the fall festival] Qaariitaaq had traveled from Cakcaaq all the way to Ingrillraat and went out through there, located behind Newtok. The [people of Qissunaq] call them Ingrissaaraat. We call them different names."

Sometimes a place had no name, or at least not one contemporary elders could recall. Some wetland areas were known simply as *maraq* (marshland), and not all of the thousands of small ponds covering the delta were named. Edward Hooper (March 2007:1350) jokingly observed: "I never heard the name of the one upriver from that other river. Maybe it's called Atrilnguq [One with no name]."

Names were also given to the places on the land where people stayed in camps and villages. Simeon Agnus (March 2007:475) explained that people settled where food was available: "These are genuine villages that our parents' parents established. This village of Kanerrlulek was most populated. It was a place where our parents grew up and came to be aware of life. And that village of Qanrangaq, and Cakcaaq, Urumangnaq, and Talarun, too. [People stayed there] because food was abundant there. All these places especially were teeming with fish." Michael John (March 2007:1106) agreed: "All these small villages, people evidently formed them in places where they were fortunate [in obtaining food] back before they had schools."

In John Eric's (March 2008:150) opinion, place names, like customary sites, are passed down and should not be changed unless the place itself ceases to exist:

> They named places on land, and those names have been passed down to us. It seems to me that it won't be good if we change those place names that our ancestors revealed to us. They cannot be changed in any way, but they will probably change if water eventually erodes them.
>
> This is the only way those place names can be changed; they would say that a particular place once had that particular name. When that place turns into water [through erosion], they will mention the name it had in the past. Or even when parts of a river are eroded by water, those places that are no longer rivers are then referred to as *kuilleq* [old river]. They mention that a certain place was once a river but is no longer a river and no longer used. And when a lake empties, they say that the lake emptied when a new channel formed, and it is referred to as *cevvleq* [new channel forming and emptying into another source].

Peter Matthew (March 2008:152) agreed: "The names that we heard in the past aren't changed. They haven't been changed on purpose, but we name those places that we don't know the names of, just like we give people names that aren't their real names just for fun."

Geographic features and settlements had names. People also identified regions and local areas in relation to one another. Paul Tunuchuk (March 2008:522) explained: "They refer to the area south of these [Qaluyaat] mountains up to the mouth of the Kuskokwim River as Canineq [lower coastal area]." Lower coastal people, then, are referred to as Caninermiut, just as Nelson Islanders are known and think of themselves as Qaluyaarmiut. Paul continued: "These mountains [on Nelson Island] are referred to as Qaluyaat. And the people of the island are called Qaluyaarmiut." Space does not permit detailed discussion of these regional sociogeographic groups. Many, like Qaluyaarmiut and Caninermiut, have long histories and continue to be used today as designations of both land areas and the people living there (see Burch 1984, ed.; Fienup-Riordan 1984; Iutzi-Mitchell 1994).

Different terms are used when traveling in and between different areas. Paul Tunuchuk (March 2008:522) explained: "During spring, when they are traveling southward along the edge of the shore ice, they say *caniarluteng,* and they refer to those who travel northward as *qiiviarluteng* [possibly from *qiini-,* 'outside']. Those two have completely different terminologies." John Eric (March 2008:523) explained the terms for coastal residents relative to inland people from the tundra area:

> Those who are coming to this [Nelson Island] area from [the Kuskokwim River area] refer to it as *qagaavirrluteng* [traveling north, or outside]. They say that a snowmobile is approaching *qagaaken* [from the north, from outside], *qagken* [short for *qagaaken*].
>
> And they refer to people from the inland region as *qaugkumiut* [from *qaugna,* "the one upriver, inland, inside"], *qaugkut.* They refer to the people from the Kuskokwim River area up there as *qaugkumiut.*

And, as Paul John notes below, people living to the north of the Yukon-Kuskokwim delta refer to Yup'ik people as Avang'armiut (from *avani,* "over there").

In many cases, elders add the postbase *-miut* (lit., "inhabitants of" or "residents of") to the name of a river or hill to distinguish a camp or village site from its geographic location. Thus Kaviarmiut is the historic site where people lived along the river Kaviaq. Elders are not consistent, however, and often refer to a camp or village site using the geographic place name, leaving it to the listener to understand their reference from the context of their conversation. Elders also use terms like Cakcaarmiut to refer to the many places along the Cakcaaq River where people lived rather than to a specific site. Often people inhabited a number of sites on the same river over the years, as one place eroded and a better site was found on higher group. Thus archaeological maps note two or more places close to each other, all having the same name. Elders also use the terms Kalukarmiut and Qukaqliqutarmiut, among others, to refer to both the *ircenrraat* believed to dwell in the mountains of Kalukaat and Qukaqliqutaat and the places where these other-than-human persons live.

Many young people today are ignorant of place names. Mark John (March 2007:119), originally from Toksook Bay, gave an example: "Aparpayagaq asked him [over a VHF radio], 'Where are you?' After a second he replied, 'Next to this piece of ice.' Aparpayagaq laughed and said, 'There's probably a lot of ice around there.'" Edward Hooper (March 2007:1354) voiced the same concern: "Sometimes when we are fishing for halibut or when we're seal hunting, they say, 'Where are you located?' [They reply], 'I am down on the ocean.' It's hard to tell where those people are located." Felix Albert (March 3007:1350) of Tununak noted that many young men like himself are ignorant of the names of sloughs between major streams and sometimes refer to them as A, B, and C.

Knowing place names, Edward Hooper (March 2007:1406) declared, is part of the subsistence way of life, as important to learn as the names of one's own relatives. Susie Angaiak (March 2007:1408) explained: "Those who came before us made efforts at teaching their children about their few relatives, although they lived in other villages, because when their children grew older and were able to travel and arrived in a particular village, they might become desperate and need a place to stay."

Place names, similarly, are critical to safe travel yet, sadly, are being forgotten. John Eric (March 2008:1) spoke of the importance of documenting these many names:

> Looking at these maps, if the names of places that we used to see aren't written down [on the map], those of us who know the place names have to keep in mind that our grandchildren might not know them. Since [young people] are no longer given instruction, if these two [Ann and Alice] publish the information in the form of a book, since [young people] are able to read nowadays, the hunting and fishing sites would be documented so a person can go and obtain things that can help him live. If one of these [elders] reveals those places, the things that should have been taught will be revealed to our younger generation.

David Panruk (March 2008:163) of Chefornak noted that modern devices like GPS are not infallible and that it is one's duty to know the land:

> Recently, Puk'aq also warned my younger brother, Danny, to come the next day when the weather was good. He said [Danny] immediately started digging in his pockets and took out his GPS, and he told him that he won't get lost if we traveled using that. Puk'aq told him, "Those things aren't accurate. You have a duty to know the land."
>
> Then, like he said, recently they searched for them. Three of them got lost [while traveling]. If they had followed Puk'aq's admonishment, people wouldn't have been searching for them.

Peter Matthew agreed: "A number of people have told me that when their GPS device stopped working, they suddenly got lost. Those [devices] won't always work properly, and their batteries can be damaged, especially in the ocean."

In spite of elders' belief that technology is no substitute for knowledge, they support technology when it helps young people learn about their homeland. Our Nelson Island project also produced a map of Qaluyaat with more than 400 place names available on the web at http://mapserver.eol.ucar.edu/best. There a visitor can see photographs and read stories, in both Yup'ik and English, about 80 of these sites. Because the Nelson Island project's documentation is considered "data" by the National Science Foundation, the site was initially password protected. CEC director Mark John and I traveled to Nelson Island in April 2009 for an intervillage meeting of elders and village representations to review the results of our work together. During that meeting we asked community members about access to their website. The group voted unanimously for open and free access, arguing eloquently for the importance of making the information they had shared available to all. Sharing knowledge, Paul John explained, is like sharing food. If it is difficult to obtain in one community, those who have it must share with those who do not: "According to the traditional teachings, they were told to receive one who is trying to subsist and to help him obtain food without making the excuse that he is from another village. If this [access to information] is open [to the public], it will be like that."

Paul John then spoke about the role of our books in gaining respect for Yup'ik ways. He compared the situation today to that of African Americans before the election of President Obama:

> African Americans weren't highly respected in the past. Then when that African American desired to become president, he got an education; and after revealing his desire to the many people, he became president.
>
> We [Yup'ik people] say that we would like to take care of our own affairs. But since we haven't made documents like this, since the white

> people haven't understood us, it is as though they still don't have confidence in our abilities.
>
> If white people see these books, they will think, "These Yup'ik people evidently are knowledgeable about things and know how to take care of their affairs independently through their traditional way of life." Like the African American who has become president, our young people will be able to carry out their desire to independently practice their way of living. These [books] will prepare our younger generation for the time when they will start to take care of their own affairs.

Qaluyaarmiut are far from the only indigenous group striving for greater respect and understanding by spreading knowledge, but their methods are remarkable. While they continue to train their youth by speaking about traditional ways, their willingness to collaborate with scholars and make use of current technology distinguishes them. By sharing in these ways, Qaluyaarmiut allow insights specific to their island home to reach national audiences and contribute to all of our understanding of what makes us human.

Yugtun Igautellrit
Kass'atun-llu Mumigtellrit

Yup'ik Transcription and Translation

The Central Alaskan Yup'ik language is spoken on the Bering Sea coast from Norton Sound to the Alaska Peninsula as well as along the lower Yukon, Kuskokwim, and Nushagak rivers. Central Yup'ik is closely related to the Inuit/Iñupiaq language of the Arctic coast of Alaska, northern Canada, and Greenland, although they are not mutually intelligible. Central Yup'ik is one of four Yupik Eskimo languages. The three others are Pacific Yupik (Alutiiq or Sugpiaq), which is spoken around Prince William Sound, the tip of the Kenai Peninsula, Kodiak Island, and part of the Alaska Peninsula; Naukan, of East Cape Siberia; and Siberian Yupik, spoken on St. Lawrence Island in Alaska and across the Bering Strait in Siberia. Together, Inuit/Iñupiaq and Yupik constitute the Eskimo branch of the Eskimo-Aleut family of languages. No apostrophe is used when speaking of the Yupik family of languages, but an apostrophe is used for Central Alaskan Yup'ik and its dialects.

There are four dialects of Central Yup'ik: Norton Sound, Hooper Bay/Chevak, Nunivak, and General Central Yup'ik. All are mutually intelligible with some phonological and vocabulary differences (Jacobson 1984:28–37; Woodbury 1984:49–63). Qaluyaarmiut elders, Alice Rearden from Napakiak, and Marie Meade from Nunapitchuk are all speakers of General Central Yup'ik.

The Central Yup'ik language remained unwritten until the end of the 19th century, when Russian Orthodox, Moravian, and Jesuit Catholic missionaries, working independently of one another but in consultation with Native converts, developed a variety of orthographies. The orthography used consistently throughout this book is the standard one developed between 1967 and 1972 at the University of Alaska Fairbanks and detailed in works published by the Alaska Native Language Center and others (Reed, Miyaoka, Jacobson, Afcan, and Krauss 1977; Miyaoka and Mather 1979; Jacobson 1995).

The standard orthography for Central Yup'ik represents the language with letters and letter combinations, each corresponding to a distinct sound, as follows:

Consonants

	labials	apicals		front velars	back velars
stops	p	t	c	k	q
voiced fricatives	v	l	s/y	g (ug)	r (ur)
voiceless fricatives	vv	ll	ss	gg (w)	rr
voiced nasals	m	n		ng	
voiceless nasals	m	n		ng	

Symbols in parentheses represent the sounds made with the lips rounded.

Vowels

	front		back
high	i		u
mid		e	
low		a	

The apostrophe represents consonant gemination, or doubling (and serves several other less important functions). There are also conventions for undoubling the letters for voiceless fricatives under certain circumstances (Jacobson 1995:6–7). This standard orthography accurately represents the Yup'ik language in that a given word can be written in only one way, and a given spelling can be pronounced in only one way. Note that certain predictable features of pronunciation, specifically automatic gemination and rhythmic length, are not explicitly shown in the spelling.

Like all Eskimo languages, Central Yup'ik is a "suffixing language" in which words can be formed by adding postbases (like English suffixes but much more powerful) and an ending (indicting number, case, person, position, etc.) to word bases. For example, the word *Yupiit* is derived from the noun *yuk* "person" to which the postbase *-pik* "real" or "authentic" and the plural ending *-t* have been added, producing literally, "real people" (in the sense of "our kind").

Because suffixes in Yup'ik often serve the same function as separate words do in English, the two languages sometimes appear as mirror images of each other. For example, the English phrase "my little boat" corresponds to *angyacuarqa,* which consists of *angya-* "boat," plus *-cuar-* "little," plus *-qa* "my," so that the order of the parts within the Yup'ik word is "boat, little, my." Thus translation involves a continuous process of reordering.

Translation

"Much of great importance is lost and added in translation," linguist A. L. Becker (2000:90) reminds us. The truth of his words captures both this book's weaknesses and strengths. Each translated text is at once less than the original telling—devoid of the shapes and sounds of the speaker's voice—and more. Through the double process of translation from Yup'ik to English and from oral to written form, readers gain access to the observations and experiences of Qaluyaarmiut narrators.

Becker is not the only one to describe the deficiencies and "silences" across languages. James Clifford remarked, "The good translation gets you far enough into the other world to begin to see what you are missing. You take your translation device . . . and watch it run out of meaning" (Cruikshank 1998:98). Brian Swann (1994:xxxv) writes that one important message of his anthology of Native American literature in translation is the degree to which many Native American texts "almost successfully resist assimilation. . . . As William Bevis has written, 'We won't get Indian culture as cheaply as we got Manhattan.'" The deficiencies and exuberances of Yup'ik and English are not congruent, and recognition of the silences across languages is essential to mutual understanding.

In their roles as translators, Alice Rearden and Marie Meade offer distinctive strategies for bridging differences between Yup'ik and English without erasing them. Their goal throughout has been a "natural sounding," free translation, as opposed to either literal translation (at one extreme) or paraphrasing (at the other). Paraphrasing may communicate some of the sense of the original, but such interpretive translations modify the original to the point where the speaker's voice is alternately erased or transformed. Literal, word-for-word translation is also inadequate. At best it is awkward, and at worst it makes no sense. Alice's and Marie's translations employ a free style in which each speaker's choice of words is respected, while word order and sentence structure are modified where necessary to communicate his or her original meaning.

Several grammatical features pose potential problems in the translation of statements by Qaluyaarmiut. First, relatively free word order characterizes the

Yup'ik language. For example, the meaning of the English sentence "The man lost the dog" can be conveyed only by placing the words "man," "lost," and "dog" in this order. A Yup'ik speaker, however, can arrange the three words *angutem* (man), *tamallrua* (s/he lost it), and *qimugta* (dog) in any of six possible word orders with no significant change in meaning. Nevertheless, it is not totally irrelevant to interpreting Yup'ik sentences. Word order may be the only key to appropriate interpretation where the ending alone is insufficient. For example, the sentence *Arnam atra nallua* (literally, "woman//his/her name//s/he not knowing it") can mean either "The woman does not know his name" or "He does not know the woman's name." The same three words in a different word order, however, are less ambiguous. *Arnam nallua atra* is commonly taken to mean "The woman does not know his name." Contrasted with languages that have a freer word order, the relative position of postbases inside a Yup'ik word is very rigid. Consequently a word may comprise syntactic problems that occur only in sentences in other languages.

Translation is further complicated by the fact that the Yup'ik language does not specify gender in third-person endings. The listener is left to deduce gender from the context of the account. When a speaker describes women's tasks, we have translated the pronominal ending as "she," as that is the way an English speaker can best understand the speaker's intent. Conversely, pronominal endings are translated as "he" when the speaker is describing a hunter's activities. In general discussions we have used either "it" or "he," depending on the context. Readers should also know that Yup'ik orators sometimes mix singular and plural endings in a single oral "sentence," and we have retained these grammatical variations to reflect the complexity of the Yup'ik original.

Yup'ik verb tenses also differ from English. Although some postbases place an action clearly in the future and others place action definitely in the past, a verb without one of these time-specific postbases may refer to an action which is happening either in the past or present (Jacobson 1984:22). Accounts of events or customs that are no longer practiced in southwestern Alaska have been translated in the past tense. Readers should also note that tense may vary within a paragraph, especially in discussions of *qanruyutet* marked by the enclitic *-gguq,* which can be translated "they said," "they say," or "it is said" depending on the context. Traditional *qanruyutet* that speakers indicate still apply are translated using the present tense.

Yup'ik oral rendering values close attention to detail and consistent retellings, and Alice and Marie continue to work in that tradition. As Yup'ik scholar Elsie Mather (1995:32) notes, "The most respected conveyers of Yup'ik knowledge are those who express things that listeners already know in artful or different ways, offering new expressions of the same."

As if translation from one language to another were not challenging enough, this book involves the movement from oral to written language. Our starting point is the verbal artistry of individual elders, but critical to understanding their words is the transformation of their voices onto the page. Through the 1970s little attention was given to reflecting the dynamics and dramatic techniques of the performance, including the speakers' shifts in tone and rhythm. The oral origins of texts were all but hidden from view. Texts were routinely transcribed in paragraph form, as if the paragraph were the "natural" form of all speech.

Beginning in the 1980s, when so many tenets of anthropology were being scrutinized, the ubiquitous paragraph came under attack, especially in the work of Dell Hymes and fellow linguist Dennis Tedlock. Together Tedlock and Hymes inspired a generation of linguists and anthropologists who have since adopted and adapted their insights in a variety of ethnopoetic transcription styles, igniting a veritable "renaissance" in the translation of Native American literature (Swann 1994:xxviii). Although Alice and Marie have not chosen to employ the "short line" verse format favored by many translators, they use the prose format with a new sensitivity. In their work, paragraphs are no longer arbitrary groupings disconnected from the speaker's original oral performance, but are distinguished by prominent line-initial particles like *tua-i-llu* ("so then"), by cohesion between contiguous lines, and by pauses between units.

As we think about both the limitations and power of translation to communicate meaning across cultural and linguistic boundaries, it is useful to turn to Becker's (2000:18) recognition that translation is not the endpoint of understanding, but the beginning. Similarly the reader is invited to engage Alice and Marie's translations and use them as starting points for understanding and respecting the profound differences between literary traditions which, in turn, make it possible for us to better understand our selves.

Note

1. See David Samuels (2001) for a rich discussion of the combined use of indigenous and English place names among the Western Apache.

Qanemcillret

Those Who Told Stories

This list reflects Yup'ik protocol. Names are ordered by community, running north to south along the Bering Sea coast and upriver to Bethel. Within each community, individuals are listed by age (eldest to youngest); their Yup'ik names are in italics.

In the text the first occurrence of each speaker's name is followed by place of residence, e.g., Paul John (November 2000:81) of Toksook Bay. The gathering date and transcript page number of the statement follows the elder's name in parentheses.

Name	**Residence I Birthplace I Birth year**
Elsie Tommy / *Nanugaq*	Newtok I Kaviarmiut I 1922
Michael John / *Qukailnguq*	Newtok I Cevtaq I 1931
Mark Tom / *Nuyarralek*	Newtok
Joseph John / *Arnaucuaq*	Newtok
Peter John / *Miisaq*	Newtok I Kayalivik I 1936
Joseph Patrick / *Agiyangaq*	Newtok I Nerevkartuli I 1937
Mary George / *Nanurniralria*	Newtok I Cevtaq I 1942
Paul Charles / *Ayugan*	Newtok
John Roy John / *Aliurtuq*	Newtok I 1964
Susie Angaiak / *Uliggaq*	Tununak I Tununak I 1923
Edward Hooper / *Maklak*	Tununak I Tununak I 1925
Lucy James / *Kakgailnguq*	Tununak I 1928
Tommy Hooper / *Cuk'ayaq*	Tununak I Tununak I 1931
Rita Angaiak / *Nanurrualek*	Tununak I Chefornak I 1932
Pauline Pitka / *Ayaprun*	Tununak I Nightmute I 1934
John Walter / *Cungauyar*	Tununak I Chefornak I 1939
Helen Walter / *Nasgauq*	Tununak
Felix Albert	Tununak
Billy Lincoln / *Nuyarnerilnguq*	Toksook Bay I Tununak I 1909
Phillip Moses / *Nurataaq*	Toksook Bay I Nightmute I 1925

Name	Residence I Birthplace I Birth Year
Paul John / *Kangrilnguq*	Toksook Bay I Cevv'arneq I 1928
Sophie Agimuk / *Avegyaq*	Toksook Bay I Cevv'arneq I 1928
John Alirkar / *Allirkar*	Toksook Bay I Cevv'arneq I 1929
Lizzie Chimiugak / *Neng'uryar*	Toksook Bay I 1930
Joe Felix / *Amartuq*	Toksook Bay
Joe Asuluk / *Atrilnguq*	Toksook Bay I Kayalivik
Martina John / *Anguyaluk*	Toksook Bay I Nightmute I 1936
Ruth Jimmie / *Angalgaq*	Toksook Bay I Nightmute
Albertina Dull / *Cingyukan*	Nightmute I 1918
Dick Anthony / *Minegtuli*	Nightmute I Cevv'arneq I 1922
Simeon Agnus / *Unangik*	Nightmute I Nightmute I 1930
Anna Agnus / *Avegyaq*	Nightmute I Nightmute I 1930
Carl Mark / *Quyangun*	Nightmute I Tununak I 1931
Camilius Tulik / *Cirmirraq*	Nightmute I Umkumiut I 1935
Peter Dull / *Arcunan*	Nightmute I Qunguq I 1939
Stanley Anthony / *Inuguarpak*	Nightmute
Martina Wasili / *Cuyanguyak*	Chefornak
Maria Eric / *Qamulria*	Chefornak I Cevv'arneq
Jobe Abraham Sr. / *Kumak*	Chefornak I Nightmute I 1933
David Jimmie Sr. / *Akak'aq*	Chefornak I Kavirlirralek I 1936
Pauline Jimmie / *Kangrilnguq*	Chefornak I Cevv'arneq I 1937
Theresa Abraham / *Paniliar*	Chefornak I Cevv'arneq I 1941
John Eric/ *Cungauyar*	Chefornak I Cevv'arneq I 1942
Joe Maklak / *Acivaralria*	Chefornak I Arayakcaarmiut
Peter Matthew / *Angutekayak*	Chefornak I Cevv'arneq
John Jimmie / *Yang'aq*	Chefornak I Arayakcaarmiut
Edward Kinegak / *Sak'aq*	Chefornak I Akiachak
John Phillip Sr. / *Ayagina'ar*	Kongiganak I Anuurarmiut I 1925
Paul Jenkins / *Pugtall'er*	Nunapitchuk I Cuukvagtuli I 1925
Peter Jacobs Sr. / *Paniguaq*	Bethel I Cuukvagtuli I 1923
David Chanar / *Cingurruk*	Anchorage I Umkumiut I 1946
Mark John / *Miisaq*	Anchorage I Nightmute I 1954

Qaluyaat

Nelson Island

Qaluyaat

Kangrilnguq: Ukut waniwa Qaluyaat evunrullrunilarait, cikuuluki. Tua-i-llu cikuurraarluteng nunaurrluteng.

Tamaa-i akmalirnermi taum cikuliullri, cikum tua-i cikuliurutem tumellritun cikumi teggalqut akmalirnermi uitaut. Cikuupigtellrungatut.

Tua-i tauna-llu tuglleq, tugminek ayimciami kuiggaam kangranun, Iqallugtulim-gguq mat'um, tugmi ayimnera elliamiu, waten qanellrunilaraat: "Akwaku kinguliat iliit nalaqekuniu una tugma ayimnera camek kepqutairuciiquq." Akiuguq tayima. Tuaten taugaam tua-i wiinga qanruteksugngaaqa.

Taugaam man'a maani tua-i mer'ullrunilaryaaqaat nunaurpailgan. Wiinga qanemciuluku niitellemni qamkut qama-i Kalskag-armiut ingrit nuukait. Ukuk wani Kuigpiinkuk Kusquqviim-llu akiqliin ingrikenka akuliitni Kalskag-armiut; tua-i uatiit man' ingritailnguq.

Niitellruunga taum-gguq Ciuliaqatuum qamllerkuani ciqruskii qanerluni, "Akwaku kinguliat nunakniaraat." Tua-i-gguq nunaurtellruuq maa-i man'a taum qamllerkuaminek ciqrucillra ayagneqluku. Tuaten wii qanemciuluku nallunritetaaqa.

Qukailnguq: Ukut cali waniwa wii niitelallemni qanemciuluki tamaa-i evunrullruniluki qanrutkelallruit qanrutkestiita. Evunrullruut-gguq ukut ingrit.

Iciw' unani imarpigmi tanglalriaci evunernek. Cikunek qalliqluteng marayami naucilrianek, angturriluteng-llu. Tamakut tamaa-i evunernek pitullruit.

Tamakut-llu evunret allamiaqan nemeggni tua-i nauyarameggni nautuniaqluki.

Tua-ll' ukut waniwa, ukut cali niiteqarraalallemni avani qanemcikevkarluki, evunrullruut-gguq. Tauna-llu tulukaruk tauna nani tua-i uani nunii aperturpek'naku, nani uitallra, tuaten niitelallruaqa.

Paniak tauna, waten uksumi tua-i pinarinrakun pillermini iqalluarcurluni tamaani, cikurrami; cikumi-w' tua-i tamaani taukunun ukunun neptellermun iqalluarcurluni manallinilria. Maani-ll' maa-i pilalriaci, iqalluanek iqsagluci,

Nelson Island[1]

Paul John: They say that Nelson Island was once *evunret* [piled ice], ice. And the ice turned into land.

Along the other side, the place where [Raven] chopped with his ice pick, the rocks on the [north] side look like they've been chopped with an ice pick. I think [Nelson Island] was really once covered by ice.

And the one who was chopping the ice with his ice pick, when the tip of his ice pick broke, when he placed the broken part at the headwaters of Iqallugtuli River [Place with many chum salmon], this is what they say he said: "In the distant future, when one of the descendants finds the piece that broke from my ice pick, they won't lack anything anymore." It is probably some form of wealth. That's all I can say about it.

They say that this place was once water before it turned into land. When I heard the story, the inland village of Kalskag is located at the very end of the mountains. The village of Kalskag is located between the mountains of the Yukon and Kuskokwim rivers; as you know, there are no mountains below the village.

I heard that Ciuliaqatuk [Raven] tossed some ash from his fire and said, "In the distant future, the descendants will live on it." They say this area turned into land starting from the time he tossed some ash. I know the story to that extent.

Michael John: And when I used to hear of [Nelson Island] in stories, the person who spoke of them would say that they were once piles of ice. He said that these mountains were once ice piled up.

You've seen piles of ice down in the ocean. They are piled ice that form on sandbars [and shallow water], and they become large. They called those *evunret.*

And they'd say that those piles of ice grow in their usual places every year.

And this place here [Qaluyaat], when I first started to hear stories about them in the past, they said that they were once piles of ice. And I've heard of Raven, who lived down below, but they never mentioned where he lived.

Now, Raven's daughter, when it was time to fish for tomcod, she had gone jigging for tomcod on the ice that had stuck to this place here. Today you do that here, too, you jig for tomcod. They looked and saw that the ice she

caluci, manarluci. Piinanrani pilliniat pania augna qecuutniluku.

Tua-i-ll' taum qecuutniluku piaku, qecuutellinian, tangrramiu nunamek maaken kenirmigluni ukunun tua-i evunernun ciqrutliniluku.

Nunapigmek maaken tua-i tegulluni, qaspengqelliami, qaspemi wall'u atkumi pianun, imirluku. Imirluku tauna tua-i kenirmigluni ciqruskii, ukut waniw' nunaurtelliniluteng.

Tuaten tua-i qanemciuluku niitelallruaqa. Tua-i nunaurrluteng.

ௐ

Kangrilnguq: Tua-i nutaan aipangqataama, aipaqa kan'a kankumiunguan nutem, kassuuteqataamku uksuqan, kiagmi uksurcecarturluta tua-i Negtemun move-arluta, kiagmi Qaluyaanun tekiartaatung'erma.

Nauwa yuilqurtellrianun-llu tayim' maligutaqavtek anuqlirqan uqrucilalriit camek, nerqataarqameng-llu. Tuartang wangni Qaluyaanun kanavet nugtarcama uqrutat uqratnun uqitellrianga wangrramni.

Angayuqaagka qacigtellriatun muragkakegnek tua-i augtaqevkenaki cuukvaguanek aqvatngarcama, neqkakegnek pissu'urqama, tua-i tuarpiaq wangni uqrutat uqratnun uqiartellria man'a pingnaqelqa.

Tua-ll' kana-i kankut ilu'urma uum nunani Qaluyaat apqai; ilumun tua-i neqkaq tamaklagmi tuani tut'aqami tut'elartuq.

Taugaam tup'ailgata neqkat, waten uksuuluku ayagluku, apqait cenarayiit tamaa-i cali tamakut cenarayiit avanirpak kanautektullrulliniit, imkut Kass'atun pilaqait *mussel*-at, cat qapilaat, aliruat, terr'et, urvagnat, cat-llu imkut ussunglut.

Tamaa-i tamakunek qanruyutengqertut kankut ingrit. Avanirpak-gguq tua-i amllerqunek qilairqan man'a uitayaraat Kangirrluaraam cenii, neqet tekipailgata tamakunek-gguq tamaa-i kanaucitullruut-llu kankut Qaluyaat yuit, apeqmeggnek cenarayagnek.

was on had broken off, and she was drifting away.

When Raven was alerted that his daughter was adrift on ice, since the ice that she was on had broken off and drifted away, he filled the bottom of his garment with soil from the surrounding ground and tossed it on the piles of ice here.

He took some [soil] from the tundra around here, and since he probably had on a garment, he filled the skirt of his garment or his parka. He filled that. He filled the bottom of his garment and tossed it [on the ice], and this area here became land.

That's how I heard the story. The area turned into land.

Paul John: Finally, when I was about to marry, since my wife is originally from down there [on Nelson Island], since I was going to marry her the following winter, during summer we moved to Nightmute to spend the winter there, although I kept going to Nelson Island during summer.

When you two accompany other people traveling to the wilderness, when it's windy, you've seen people construct a windbreak out of something when they are about to eat a meal. When I moved down to Nelson Island, it felt as though I suddenly went along the side of a windbreak sheltered from the wind.

When I started to go and easily get alder wood for my parents, and when I made efforts at obtaining food for them, it felt as though I went alongside a windbreak sheltered by the wind in my efforts to subsist.

My *iluraq* [cross-cousin, Simeon Agnus] just mentioned Nelson Island where he lives; indeed when fish become available there, all different types of fish became available.

But before food became available, starting in winter, they evidently consumed what they call *cenarayiit* [seafood] to survive up to the time when food became available, the ones that they call mussels in English, including mussels, northern razor clams, sea anemones, sea cucumbers, and those *ussunglut* [possibly sea slugs].

That is what is said about the mountains down there [on Nelson Island]. They say that since time immemorial, many times when snow no longer covers the place where they live, along the shores of Toksook Bay, before fish arrive, the people living on Nelson Island consumed those they call *cenarayiit* to survive until the time when fish became available.

Tua-i kankut kana-i ilumun Qaluyaat uitanrilnguq yuk neqkailngaituq piyugngalria. Neqsungnaquralria neqkailngaituq. Uitalria taugaam tua-i neqkaicugngaluni.

Unani una-i neqkam, pisqevkenaku'urtaituq tuani. Taugaam pilegmi tuani ilaput piyugngalriit cingumaluki. Ciin-waarciiganaki-ll' "Ciin tuavet pisit?" Cingumaluki piyugngalria pisqumaluku alerquuterluta.

Naken-llu tekilluni kingunermini neqkaq nurnaan pikan ikayuusqelluku, nalluniluku taumun naken tekitellriamun, pivigkaanek apertuatesqelluku. Tua-i tuaten unani alerquuterluta, kina nallumciqkan taugaam alerqualuku pisqelluku.

Tua-ll'-am cal' tua-i nauwa niitelartukut qavani tuntuviit ikeglingniluki. Ukut avget-wa avalitkelaqait qavani Kalskag kiatmun. Makumiunek-am nunautekenritniluku qaugna wall'u-llu tamakut ellaita ungungssiqsugluki.

Tua-i quyakenritellratgun tamaa-i amlleriinarpek'nateng tua-i, wagg'uq nepliutekngatki ungungssiqestaita. Amlleriinarpek'nateng niitellrat nurnaringluteng taugaam.

Tua-llu wiinga tayima allrakuni qavcini *ten years* avatiini Yukon-amun tuntuvagculrianun ilagauquralallruunga. Tamakut cingumalua taugaam unangqaasqumayaaqlua piaqluteng. Watua-ll' maa-i kiima tayim' pinrilkiitnga, naken-llu tekilluteng pissulriit tuatnalaqait, tayim' cingumaluki.

Watua maa-i paiqsigiluteng amlleriluteng tuntuvait. Tua-i-wa Agayutem nepliutekenrilatki cingumacatki-llu naken tekilluteng pitengnaqsartunun, kiiki unangesqelluki cingumacaceteng cikiutekestiita tangrrumanrilnguum amllerivkarluki maa-i. Kuigpiim paiqvaqengraaku tuntuvaillitanrirluteng, amllekluki-ll' qanengluteng maa-i tuntuviit tamaani.

Pitarkam neqkauyugngalriim nepliutekesqenrilutii tamaa-i, neqngung'ermi. Tamaa-i tamana.

Unangik: Qaluyaani kanani inerquutaitukut wangkuta. Yaaqliput, aug'umek ava-i Cakcaamek ikirusngaaput.

Ukut-llu tua-i Qaluyaat pikngatgu ellaita, wangkuta tua-i pikluku. Yaaqliput-llu augkut ikirusngaluki.

Indeed, down on Nelson Island, a person who is capable and isn't idle will not lack food to eat. A person who continually makes an effort to obtain food will not lack food. But only one who is idle can lack food.

Concerning food down along the coast, there is no law telling people not to subsist at a particular location. But we encourage our peers who are capable to subsist at that location that has resources available. And we cannot question them, "Why did you go there?" We are instructed to encourage those who are capable to subsist.

And when someone arrives from another place because there is a lack of food in their area, they tell us to help that person, that a person who arrived from elsewhere doesn't know the area, to show him places where he can subsist. That's the instruction we are given down along the coast, to instruct a person who is inexperienced.

And also at this time we hear that moose populations are low upriver. They blame the people along the upper half [of the river], from Kalskag on up. They say to the people of this area that the land upriver doesn't belong to them or that they want to have those animals themselves.

Because they aren't grateful [that others are trying to subsist], [moose] aren't increasing in number, since those people who depend on those animals have squabbled over them. We hear that their numbers aren't increasing but that they are becoming scarce.

And about ten years ago, I went with others to the Yukon River to hunt moose many times. The people there only encouraged me and wanted me to catch one. And at the time, I wasn't the only one treated that way, but they encouraged others who came from other areas and hunted there.

At this time, their moose are starting to move down closer to the [Yukon River] mouth and their numbers have increased. Because people aren't arguing over them and are encouraging others who arrive from other places to hunt and catch them, God who gave them to us, the unseen one, has increased their numbers. They no longer lack moose, even near the mouth of the Yukon, and they are starting to say that large numbers of moose are in that area.

That's the reason why they tell people not to have disputes over animals that can be consumed, even if it's food. That's what that is.

Simeon Agnus: We don't have any admonishments [against those coming to harvest food] down at Nelson Island. We welcome villages beyond ours to subsist at Cakcaaq River.

And since it belongs to the people of Nelson Island, it is ours too. And we open subsistence [at Cakcaaq River] for the villages beyond our village.

Taugaam kiingan kuvyat tua-i inerquutaqlaryaaqaput cikucesqevkenaku civtellra kuvya. Taugaam tua-i allamineq tamalkuan kuvyaq atauciunrilnguq cikutetua.

Qilengpak

Qukailnguq: Panini-ll' tauna aglerngan pik'umi-gguq Qilengpagkun nel'i-lliniluni, nel'iluku. Ava-i qanrutkaa ukuk taman' aunrallra uitrurtellruniluku.

Tuani tua-i pikna Qilengpak kialirnerakun piyugnarquq, amingqerr-nilallruat.

Aug'um-llu Caaciquum atallran, tamaa-i-gguq tan'gurraullermini-llu amiigakun urluvminek, piteggniarqami pagaani pektaqami yaggluni-llu, tallini usgulirluku waten piqtaarqami taum neqututacia, tua-i neqututa-ssiirluku; yaggluni, urluvminek inglulirluni taum angtacia, tuaten angtallra nallunriraqluku.

Taum tayim' qanngermi, tamaa-i-gguq yuugarkaunrilnguut itqetaarluku quullra cukavkallruat. Tuaten tua-i tuaten qanrutketullruat.

Tua-i tauna Tulukaruk ciuliaqniluku-llu qanrutketullruat.

Ava-i-llu cali yaani Engelullugarmiut ketiitni teggalquq tauna ang'uq, qaill' tayim' qertutalallruuq tanglallemni. Kangrani tua-i waten ceternek tanglallruunga. Tua-i-gguq Tulukaruum tumellri, tumellri taum teggalqum qaingani. Taukut tua-i tanglallruanka tua-i tamaani nunaurcugarallemteni.

Unangik: Yaa, pikna pika-i Qilengpak alaicuituq waken, maaken. Taugaam tua-i nallunritarput pikna Qilengpak. Qilengpak tua-i uiterartellriit ullatuat.

Taugken ullangermegteggu ilait alailucuitait, alailucuitait-gguq. Tua-i tamaumaaqluki. Ilii-llu, ilait paivucuitait, paivngacuitait; tua-i manimatev-kenaki tamatum uiteram.

Ilii-gguq taugken paivngalluku tua-i, avatii man'a kavirpaugaqluni pi-llilria. Tuaten tua-i.

Pikna pikani tuaten yuunrilngermi, yuum ilii paivngalluku, ilii-ll' tamaumalluku. Tuaten tua-i ayuquq pikna.

Ilaita-gguq tua-i uiterarcaaqaqameng ullakapigtetuat tua-i camek una-ngevkenateng tua-i utertaqluteng. Tangerciqaci pikani tayima cam iliini.

Waten tua-i ayuquq pikna Qilengpak; tuaten tua-i qanrutketukiit. Ilii

But we only admonish people about fishnets, saying not to let the fishnet he set freeze in place. But every year, there is always more than one net frozen in the river.

Qilengpak[2]

Michael John: And when [Raven's] daughter had her first menstruation, he built her a house up at Qilengpak. These two just mentioned that her menstrual blood became *uiteraq* [red ocher].

At that time, they said that Qilengpak up there had a doorway, I think it was along the upper side.

And Caaciquq's deceased father said that when he was a boy, when he was roaming about up there and hunting with his bow and arrow, he extended his arm along its doorway up there and held his bow along the end of his hand to measure [the doorway]; he'd extend his arm out and adding the bow would measure its size, to see how large it was.

When he mentioned that, he said when those who weren't going to live long kept going in and out of that place, it caused [the doorway] to shrink fast. That's what they used to say about it.

And they used to say that Raven was our ancestor.

And down below Engelullugarmiut, there is a large boulder, and it used to be a certain height when I saw it. I used to see some etchings along the top like this. They would say that those are Raven's tracks, his tracks on top of the boulder. I used to see those when our village first formed.

Simeon Agnus: Yes, Qilengpak up there isn't visible from [Umkumiut]. But we know of Qilengpak up there. Qilengpak is where people go and get red ocher.

But they say that red ochre isn't visible for some people when they go. They disappear. And red ocher isn't put out for some people; the red ocher isn't displayed to some people.

But they say it's displayed to some people, and their surrounding area is probably very red. That's how it is.

Although that one up there is not human, it presents [red ochre] to some people, and it makes it absent for some people. That's how that place is up there.

It is said when some people go and get red ocher, they go there and return home without having obtained any. One of these days, you will see it up there.

That's what Qilengpak up there is like; that's what they say about it. It

paivngalluku, ilii-ll' tamaumalluku. Tua-i caulriim tuaten ayuqa pikna.

Tua-i-ll' aug'umek cali ilaqerluku, iluramnek Angutekayagmek. Tua-i-w' tayim' qanrutkekumku niiciiqan.

Kiavet Arutaam yaalirneranun arulailliniuq. Aipani-llu-qaa piuk? Yuuluni pilliniuq makut-gguq maani kavircenateng tua-i, Nanvaruum, Arutaam yaalirnerani. Maaten-gguq tang piuk uiteraullinilriit. Avurturluni cenirtelliniuq, alailnguut tegu'urluki.

Utercami cali, kingutmun caungami pilliniuq anglirikanirluteng cali tamakut alaillinilriit. Tuamtell' avurluki tua-i uterrluni. Tuamtell' kingyaami pilliniuq, anglirikanirluteng cali alairluteng. Avurluk tua-i camek pivkenani.

Yaaken cali tua-i cenirtellminek cenakun utertuq, anglirikanirluteng cali. Tua-i avurluki angyaminun ekluki, alingengaarcamek ayalliniuk.

Tua-i-llu kingunicami, nem'inun it'rucamiki taukut nek'eggluki tua-i piiyaaqellinii. Aturyuamegenki piiyaaqelliniak, uiterat tua-i tayima taukut ut'rutellri tua-i tamaumaluteng. Qaill' taukut pillruat?

Kangrilnguq: Ii-i, augna ciukarrluku, aug'um tegganrem ataataruirutma Uqamailnguum, Caucíqum Atiinek pitullrata, ikna ika-i Qilengpak qanemcikellra qanemcikqernaluku.

Ika-i-gguq ikna Qilengpak Ciuliaqatuum panian aglenrarauvikelqaa.

Tua-i-gguq taum Ciuliaqatuum panini aglenraraan ikavet ika-i Qilengpagmun pivkarluku aqumgavkallrua. Tamaa-i-llu-gguq augan mecillra uiterauluni.

Tuaten tua-i aug'um tegganrulriim qanrutkeqallrua ikna Qilengpak, Ciuliaqatuum panianun aqumgavilqeniluku. Augan tua-i mecillra tamaa-i uiteraularniluku.

Tua-i-ll' augna uum tamallernek qanellra augna; tua-i ircenertaungameng ava-i tamalriit, uyu'urma am'um avuryaaqellri.

Cali-llu maa-i augkut quugaarpiit cirunritnek ilait nalaqutlaryaaqellrullinilriit caqalriit avani. Tua-i aqvaarkauluku ilii uniciyaaqelalliniuq. Aqvayaaqnaurait-gguq tayim' tamallinilriit.

Makut maa-i avanirpak ircen'ernek kingunelget waten tamatuniluki qanrutkelarait, ircenerteggun alaitellret. Taugken ircenerteggun alaitenrilnguut tua-i uniteng'ermeng tamayuunateng. Agayutem tua-i tuanlluku yugmun

Map of Qaluyaat with place names shared by Nelson Island elders between 2006 and 2010. Michelle Pearson, Steve Street, and Alice Rearden.

Tununak at high tide, early 1960s. University of Delaware, University Museums: Mabel & Harley McKeague Alaskan Inuit Collection © Mabel McKeague.

Newtok in the early 1960s. University of Delaware, University Museums: Mabel & Harley McKeague Alaskan Inuit Collection © Mabel McKeague.

Nightmute in the early 1960s. University of Delaware, University Museums: Mabel & Harley McKeague Alaskan Inuit Collection © Mabel McKeague.

Toksook Bay in the late 1960s. Jesuit Oregon Province Archives, Spokane, Washington. #187.1.01

A group photo taken at Manriq during our circumnavigation of Nelson Island, July 2007, with Simeon Agnus holding the Bethel newspaper, the *Delta Discovery*. Seated, left to right: Michael John, Rita Angaiak, Ruth Jimmie, Ben Angaiak, Martina John, John Walter Jr., Theresa Abraham, and Anna Agnus. Standing: Simeon Sunny, June McAtee, Jackie Lincoln, Tom Doolittle, Linda Joe, Joe Felix, Steve Street, Fred Joe, Edward Kinegak, John Roy John, John Walter, Joe Charlie, Ryan Abraham, Simeon Agnus, and David Chanar. Ann Fienup-Riordan (hereafter AFR).

Simeon Agnus points out a land feature near Arayakcaaq at the mouth of the Qalvinraaq River, July 2007. Michael John sits to his right and Theresa Abraham to his left. AFR.

Men harpooning a seal on the Qalvinraaq River near Kanerrlulegmiut, during the Nelson Island circumnavigation. AFR.

Martina John smiles while using her *uluaq* (semilunar knife) to remove the blubber from the skin of an *amirkaq* (young bearded seal), while Anna Agnus works alongside, July 2007. AFR.

Elders and youth discuss place names during a CEC gathering in Chefornak community hall, March 2007. From left to right, Mark John, David Jimmie Sr., David Chanar, and John Eric. AFR.

Paul John documents the history of Kaviarmiut, on the southern shore of Toksook Bay, with a group of elders and students, July 2007. AFR.

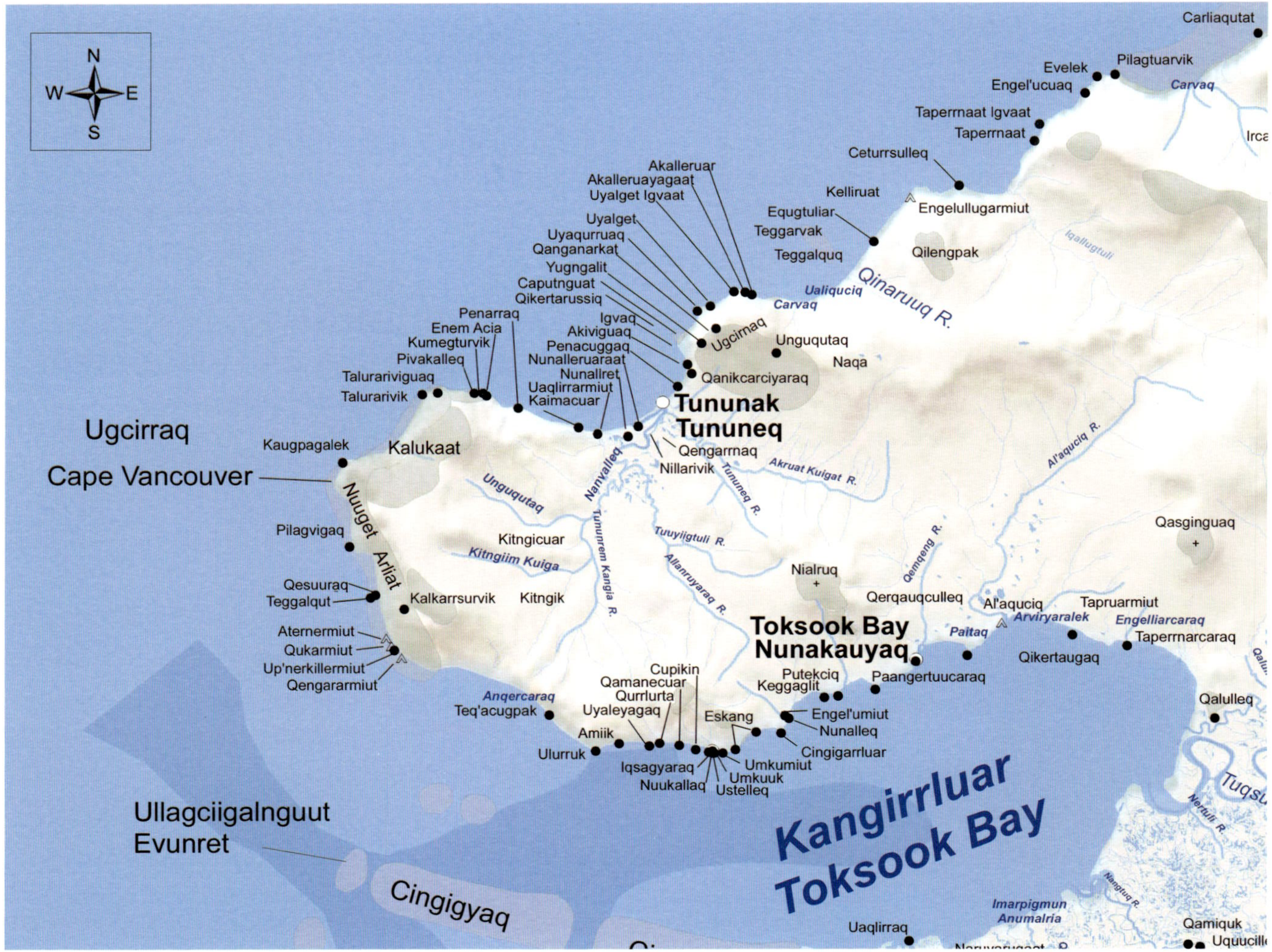

Nelson Island headlands. Michelle Pearson and Alice Rearden.

displays it for some people, and for others it makes it absent. What is that place up there that it does that.

Now I want to briefly add another thing, about my *iluraq* Angutekayak. You will hear it when I tell it.

He evidently stopped up beyond Arutaaq [from *aur-*, "to ripen or rot"]. Was it he and his wife? He got out, and he said that he saw some red things along Baird Inlet, beyond Arutaaq. They saw that they were [pieces of] red ocher. He picked them as he walked along, picking the ones that were visible.

When he returned, when he turned back, once again, larger ones appeared. Then he picked them on his way back. And again, when he looked back, he saw that they appeared even larger than before. He picked them up without thinking anything.

And when he returned from the place he went to walking along the shore, they became even larger again. He picked them and placed them inside his boat, and since they started to become afraid, they left.

And when he arrived in his village and brought them inside his home, he stored the red ocher in a good place. When they wanted to use them, they checked and saw that the [pieces of] red ocher that he had brought home were gone. What happened to those?

Paul John: Yes, starting with that story, that elder, my deceased *ataataruk* [big paternal uncle] Uqamailnguq, the one who they called Cauciqum Atii, I wanted to tell the story he told about Qilengpak across there.

He said Qilengpak across there was the place where the daughter of Ciuliaqatuk [Raven] had her first menstrual period.

When his daughter had her first menstrual period, they say Ciuliaqatuk had her go across to Qilengpak and sit there [in isolation]. And it is said the area that her blood soaked is red ocher.

That's what that elder briefly said about Qilengpak over there, that it was the place where Ciuliaqatuk's daughter sat in seclusion during her first menstrual period. He said that the area that her blood soaked is red ocher.

Now, what this person mentioned about ones that disappeared; since they belonged to the *ircenrraat* [extraordinary persons], the ones that my younger sibling had picked disappeared.

And in recent days, some people found mammoth tusks out there once in a while. Sometimes people would leave them, planning to get them at a later time. When they'd go to get them, they'd see that they had disappeared.

They mention that these things that come from *ircenrraat* disappear, the things that *ircenrraat* make visible. But things that didn't become visible to people from *ircenrraat,* they don't disappear although they leave them behind.

pikiutekumak'ngaa tamayuunani ca man' tamarmi. Tuaten tua-i ayuqluni.

Tuaten-llu ayuqngami allrakuni-ll' qavcini yuum ellillni ullaksaicimarraarluku ullagluku pikani, yuum tegunrilkani tuantarkauluni tua-i ellivillrani, ilait imumek apqiitnek tevgutenglliningermeng nunamun qap'itengluteng. Makut taugaam maa-i ircen'ernek kingunelget tuaten tua-i tamaraqluki pituniaqekait ukanirpak.

Makut ircenrraat wangkuta tangerkengamteni uitavkenateng, ellarrameg-teggun tayima, nunam-ll' acia ellauluku tayim' ellakelaryugnarqaat. Qanemciugaqameng, ciin nunamun iterluteng tamatuat tamakut ircenrraat?

Tua-ll'-am cali, tua-i wangkuta tayim' yuurpailemta pillrungatuq. Angutet iliit waten apeqmeggnek cenakun mallussurluni cenirqurallinilria. Maaten tua-i ciuneni, un'a imarpim tunglirnera tangllinia angun un'a taqukamek qamurluni tag'uralria.

Taum tua-i cumikarcamiu, cukangnaqngartelliniuq augna qamulek taqukamek. Tua-i elliin-llu yuunrilucia taringamiu tua-i angungnaqsaaqellrani waten uss'aryugmun imarpiim ceniinun tekicami, tauna imna yug' itliniuq, una-llu tua-i qamuqengaa taqukaq nunamun itqatarturtelluk pallagvikekiini tua-i uitalliniluni. Imna taugaam tayima qamurtii yuk nunamun iterluni tua-i tamarluni tua-i ircenrraungami.

Qaluyaani Cingiit

Nuyarnerilnguq: Makut-wa acirtutukait. Kiugna kia-i Qalullrem ukaqlia Engelliarcaramek pitukiit, kiugna cingik qamna.

Ingna-wa tangvakngarput Qerqaurculleq, ingna cingik, kia-i kiugna.

Una-wa, una waniw' Nunakauyaq, una nunavut pillilria, Nunakauyaq ingna yaa-i, una.

Ugna-wa ing'um Nialrum Kuigan ukatiini ingna cingik, tua-i-gguq Paangertuucaraq.

Ingna-wa Nialrum Kuigan yaaqlirraa puteggluni ingna, Putekciq-gguq tua-i.

All things that God placed there and gave to a person don't disappear. That's what it's like.

And since that's what it's like, if a person placed an item somewhere, even for a number of years, and after not having gone to get that item, when they go to it, if a person hadn't taken it, it will still be where he left it, although some things start to sink into the land. But from long ago they mention that these things that came from *ircenrraat* disappear.

These *ircenrraat* don't live in the world that we see, but they live in their own world, and I think that they view the underground as a world to live in. When they tell stories about them, why is it that *ircenrraat* go into the land and disappear?

And again, I think this occurred before we were born. One man was evidently walking along the land looking for dead, beached sea mammals. When he looked ahead toward the ocean, he saw a man towing a seal coming toward shore.

When that person noticed him, the one towing a seal started to quicken his pace. And since [the man] understood that he wasn't human, when he was trying to catch up to him, when he came upon an eroded bank along the ocean, that person went inside [the ground], and just as the seal that he was towing was going inside the land, he tripped and fell forward on top of it, and it was left behind. But the person who was towing it went into the ground and disappeared because he was an *ircenrraq*.

Nelson Island Points[3]

Billy Lincoln: They give names to these [points]. The one up the coast on this side of Qalulleq, they call it Engelliarcaraq [from *engellute-,* "to get to a destination"], the point up the coast.

Then the one over there that we see [from our village, Toksook Bay] is Qerqaurculleq [One who searched for a *qerqauq* (possibly "loon" in Norton Sound dialect)], that point over there, the one up the coast.

And this one, Nunakauyaq here, probably our village, Nunakauyaq over there, this one.

And the point down the coast on this side of Nialrum Kuiga, they call that Paangertuucaraq [Place where they raced with *paangrutet* (double-bladed paddles)].

The one right beyond Nialrum Kuiga, the one over there that bends inward, they call that Putekciq [from *puteg-,* "to bend inward"].

Yaaqlirraa-wa inga Keggaglit, Keggaglit-gguq.

Ugna-wa Nunallret yaaqliat Cingigarrluar; Cingigarrluarmek piaqluku.

Ugna-w' Umkumiut ukakaraatni, ?cingigyugyaar/cingiyaar ingna Eskang.

Umkumiut-wa quliitni penaqacuugaak imkuk Umkuuk, Umkuugnek piaqlukek.

Ugna-w' uatiit Umkumiut cali atengqerrsaaqut augkut cingicuaraat. Qugtuliaraat, Qurrlurta-wa, Uyaleyagaat-wa ugkut, augna-wa Ulurruk, ingrirpall'er ugna, Ulurruk ugna. Aterluteng tamalkurmeng makut maa-i.

Ugna-wa Up'nerkillermiut cingiat Aterneq; Aternermek piaqluku.

Aternerem-wa uatiini, ukatiini penar ingna Uyalget; Uyalegnek piaqluku penaq.

Taum-wa yaakaraani Pilagviar.

Tuani-wa yaaqlia ingna Ugcirraq. Quliini-w' pikani ingrit Kalukaat, aciatni-wa Kaugpagalek.

Kangim-wa mat'um, Ilutagmek piaqluku Kaugpagalgem yaatiini Ilutak-gguq. Piani-wa akiani cingik Talurarivik.

Taum-wa Talurariviim yaatiini Kaimarpak augna penaq cali. Penam-wa taum uatiini yaatiini cauga ingna, Kumegterviuguq-qaa? [*ngel'artuq*] Nutaan Tununermiut kia-i alaunateng.

Tununermiut-wa yaatiitni cingik Igvaq.

Yaani-wa yaakaraani cingicuar Uyaqurruaq.

Kiani-wa qamani, kangim aug'um itralriim iquani Engelullugarmiut.

Engelullugarmiut-llu yaatiitni camani Evelek, Evelek-gguq.

Tamaa-i akuliitni cat Engelucuat, Evelgem caniani Engelucuat.

The one right beyond it over there is Keggaglit, what they call Keggaglit [Those that are abrasive].

The one down the coast beyond Nunallret is Cingigarrluar [One like a *cingik* (point)]; they call it Cingigarrluar.

Then the one down the coast right along this side of Umkumiut [People of Umkuuk], the small point over there is called Eskang.

And above Umkumiut those small cliffs called Umkuuk, they call them Umkuuk.

And down the coast from Umkumiut, the small points actually have names. There is Qugtuliaraat, then there's Qurrlurta [One that cascades down a slope], and then there is Uyaleyagaat [Little *uyalget* (pelagic cormorants)] down the coast, and then there's Ulurruk, that large mountain down the coast, Ulurruk down there. These all have names.

The point of the village of Up'nerkillermiut down the coast is Aterneq; they call it Aterneq [One drifting out to sea, referring to kayaks leaving Nelson Island].

Down the coast from Aterneq, on this side of it is a cliff over there called Uyalget [Pelagic cormorants]; they call that cliff Uyalget.

A short distance beyond that is Pilagviar [Place where one butchers a seal].

The one beyond that is Ugcirraq [Small place where animals haul out, Cape Vancouver]. Above it are mountains called Kalukaat [possibly from the Cup'ig word for "bowl"], and below them is Kaugpagalek [Place with *kaugpak* (walrus)].

And along this bay, the one beyond Kaugpagalek, they call it Ilutak [One that is deep], what they call Ilutak. And up on the other side is a point called Talurarivik [Place to split sinew].

Beyond Talurarivik is Kaimarpak [Big *kaimaq* (bluff)], another cliff. Down the coast from that cliff, beyond it, what is that, is it Kumegturvik [Place where one scratched]? [*laughs*] Then finally, the village of Tununak up there is visible.

The point beyond the village of Tununak is called Igvaq [One that comes into view].

Right beyond it, the small point is called Uyaqurruaq [Pretend *uyaquq* (neck)].

Up the coast, along the end of the bay that heads up is Engelullugarmiut [People of the place resembling an *engelu* (muskrat's covered exit hole)].

Beyond Engelullugarmiut down there is Evelek [Place with *evek* (grass)], what they call Evelek.

In between are Engelucuat [Little *engeluut* (covered exit holes)], next to

Evelgem taum kiatiini nutaan augna nunaurrluni. Nulirqelriik-gguq pikani aciagni tayima Yuukarmiut, nunallret ak'allat. Tua-i tuaten atengqertut makut ingrit tamalkurmeng, nuuget.

Tamaa-i-w' tua-i aciutait tua-i quliraqluki aciutellrullikait tamakut; ateqluki qulirangqerruciinateng-llu tua-i, qulirangqerruciinateng.

Panigkaq: Ukus-mi kan'a-llu kan'a teggarvak kanani?

Nuyarnerilnguq: Qikertaugaq-qaa? Tamaani-wam camun taumun nelqenilaqiit tauna kan'a qikertacuar.

Panigkaq: Ukut-wa-qaa cingiit cam taum payugtaqamiu-qaa tutmarvillri?

Nuyarnerilnguq: Tuaten-wa qanrutketullrukiit tauna Umkumiuni imkuk qalirneragni ugna. Uini tua-i payugtaqamiu makunun cingignun tutmarluni itrarluni uiminun tua-i qantaa tun'aqluku kanani qikertami, kat'umi kana-i teggarvagmi.

Atauciullruniyaaqelaraat. Piinanermeggni tallimaurrluteng qikertat tua-i. Wiinga-ll' takumni malruullruyaaquk, aipaa tayim' catairutuq. Kana-i taugaam kan atauciurrluni.

Tuaten tua-i qanrutketullruat, tauna kanani taun angun uitaluni nulirra-ll' wani Umkuugni, Umkuuk qaingagni. Payugtaqamiu cingiit makut tutmarluki qaingitnun, amllirraarluki payugtaqluku. Tuaten-am pituniluku niitellruaqa tua-i, cauga tauna. Nalluaqa tauna, tua-i taugaam tuaten niigartelallruaqa tua-i.

Kumegturvik

Uliggaq: Taum tua-i Kumegturviim atengqerrutii.

Angun-gguq tauna tuani tua-i uani ug'um cingiim Kaimarpak, tuani cingiani, waten uksuarmi kuvyatutullruuq taqukanek, piciatun tua-i pilluni.

Taugaam-gguq tua-i tuaten tua-i kuvyani murilkelluku piaqami imna taugaam tungunquq tamakuciq-gguq taugaam napluni, imumek pug'arqan, erinani-gguq tua-i antetullrua, "Pug'artuq kan'a-aa!" Tuaten tua-i.

Tua-llu-gguq tauna kiaqlirraani uani cingigaarmi angun cali alla kuvyatuluni. Tua-i-gguq tauna tuaten tua-i erinani antaqaku taum kiaqlirraan

Evelek is Engelucuat.

Up the coast from Evelek, it finally turns into land. Underneath Nulirqelriik [Married couple, lit., "two wife-related ones"] up there is Yuukarmiut, an old village. Those are the names for all these mountains, these points.

The names they gave them, they probably told tales about them and gave them names; those are their names, and they don't seem to have tales to them.

Marie Brite: What about these ones and the large rock down there?

Billy Lincoln: Are you asking about Qikertaugaq [from *qikertaq* (island)]? They say that small island down there was the home of someone.

Marie Brite: And these points here, when something would go and give food to that one, did that one step on these points?

Billy Lincoln: That's what they used to say about that one up on top of Umkumiut. When she would go and give food to her husband, she would step on these points and head up and she would give her husband's bowl to him down on that island, down on that large rock.

They used to say that it was just one [rock]. After a while, there were five islands. And there were actually two in my presence, but the other is gone now. Only one is left down there now.

That's what they said about [Qikertaugaq], that a man was staying down there, and his wife was staying here at Umkuuk, on top of Umkuuk. When she would go and give him food, she would step on the points, taking strides along them and give him food. That's what I heard she used to do, and I'm not sure exactly what she was. I don't know what she was, but that's how I heard the story.

Kumegturvik Point[4]

Susie Angaiak: This is how that place Kumegturvik [Place where one scratched] got its name.

They say there was a man who used to use mesh nets to catch seals during fall down the coast along the point of Kaimarpak, and he would catch all sorts [of seals].

But it is said when he'd watch his net, only when an adult bearded seal would get caught in the net and surfaced, he would yell out, "That one down there has surfaced!" That's what he would do.

And it is said another man would set a net right up the coast from him in that area down the coast. When he'd yell like that, the man who was up the

angutem tua-i qamiquni kumegtelallrua. Tua-i-llu-gguq tauna pitekluku kumegcetullra, tauna tua-i taum uaqlian, cingigaar kiaqlia, Kumegturvigmek acirluku. [*ngel'artuq*]

Teq'acugpak

Angalgaq: Teq'acugpiim qanemcia nallunritan, Teq'acugpak qaillun piurtellranek, Teq'acugpak iciw' Umkumiut uatiitni. Cingyukan qanellrulria taunagguq Teq'acugpak Parum nelqaa.

Uugnaraankuk-gguq Paruq-llu eqtassiagullutek?

Nanugaq: Nunivaami Uugnar uitanillruat. Maani-llu Paruq.

Angalgaq: Naliak wani mikliritassiarluni Paruq-llu *win*-arluni mikliriluni. Nutaan tang niitellrukeka uksuq tauna.

Anguyaluk: Wiinga-llu nunakengramku niiteqaqsaitaqa.

Nanugaq: Cali-llu niigartellruluku taukuk Parunkuk Uugnar-llu ilaliurutetullrunilukek. Paruq-gguq *win*-araqluni, tua-i-wa pekcuilami pillilria. Uugnar-llu-gguq una alarqaqsugluni.

Waten niigartellrukek'a, Parum-gguq Uugnar piciqaa man'a nunavut nunamrruyugnek pitairutniluku. Uugnaraam-llu-gguq kiuluku ilani tagevkarciqniluki.

Uugnaraam-llu-gguq pikani man'a nunaseng parurtairutniluku, Parum-llu-gguq kiuluku ilani atrarceciiqniluki anuqekun.

Waten niigartellruaqa, taugaam augna iqua uunguciitaqa. Atam taun Paruq qaneryarartuniluku niitetullruaqa.

Quliraqluku niigartellruaqa, taugaam iqua augna nalluaqa.

Atam cani uitatuuq paruq.

Angalgaq: Neqni-llu. Miketkacagarluni iciw' *white*-auluteng *bunch*-augaqluteng. *You know* pekngaiciiqngalnguut tangssukuvki pektelallinilriit. Iciw' *dry fish*-ani uitatulriit tamakut parut.

Anguyaluk: Amlleraqluteng. Uitauralriani amlleriluteng. Parucuayagaat pektaqluteng taugken. Ingqitun navgurivkenateng.

coast from him would scratch his head. Because he used to scratch [his head], they called that small point up the coast Kumegturvik. [*laughs*]

Teq'acugpak[5]

Ruth Jimmie: Do you know the story of Teq'acugpak [Huge pit], the origin of Teq'acugpak? Teq'acugpak that is down the coast from Umkumiut. Cingyukan [Albertina Dull] said that Teq'acugpak was Paruq's home.

Was it Uugnar [Mouse] and Paruq [White Bug] who were trying to see who could become smaller than the other?

Elsie Tommy: They said that Uugnar lived on Nunivak Island. And Paruk [lived] here [on Nelson Island].

Ruth Jimmie: They competed to see who could become small, and Paruq won and shrunk and became small. This past winter was the first time that I heard that story.

Martina John: Although [Nelson Island] is my home, I have never heard it before.

Elsie Tommy: I also heard that Paruq and Uugnar used to tease one another. They say Paruq would win, probably because he wasn't able to move. And they say Uugnar tended to make mistakes.

This is what I heard that Paruq would say to Uugnar, that our land no longer has edible plants that grow on the tundra. Then they say Uugnar replied that he would have his relatives head up [to the mainland].

Then when Uungar would tell him that their land no longer has *parut* [small white bugs], Paruq would reply to him that he would have his relatives go down with the wind.

That's what I heard, but I don't know the end of the story. I heard that there were a lot of things said concerning Paruq.

I heard it told as a *quliraq* [legend], but I don't know the end of the story.

Paruq dwells in various things.

Ruth Jimmie: On fish also. It is extremely small and white, and a bunch of them are together. They appear as though they wouldn't move, but if you watch them, you'll see that they do actually move. You know how those *parut* dwell in dry fish.

Martina John: There are many of them. When left, they multiply. They are small *parut,* but they actually move. They don't destroy things like lice do.

Cingyukan: Ee-m. Tua-i-w' niitetukevut. Maaten ellaangua tua-i qanemcingssaarpakarluteng tua-i tuaten qanernaurtut.

Iciw' tua-i Paruq angyaaqellrulia. Ua-i Teq'acugpak-gguq assigtallra.

Tua-i-gguq imumek apqiitnek quvssaaglutek, quvnertutassiigullutek. Tua-i-ll' augna ava-i Paruq tua-i iciw' tua-i tangenrricugyaarauluni, taugken Uugnar tua-i ava-i waten angtaluni, tua-i waten angtalliniluni.

Iciw' Nunivaami Uugnar, iciw' angllermeggni-w' pillilria, qiall' pillermeggni piat, caputengqerrnilaqiit teggalqunek Uugnar.

Nauwa tua-i imumi, ak'a akaar tamaani Kass'artaitellrani, angyarpak-gguq tauna tuavet tua-i Uugnaraam caputainun picurlallrulria.

Tua-i camek nallullermeggni, makut-llu mukaat, mukaat caquit, mukaat iciw' qelekluki caquit pitekluki cailkamun kuvuurluki. Tuar-gguq tang imkut tamakut caquillrit qengarvall'er. [*ngel'artuq*]

Cauciinaki. Cauciinaki cailkamun kuvuurluki. Tuaten tua-i pikait. Cat tua-i qelkevkenaki, cat assikengermegteki cat tua-i kuvuurluki assigtait taugaam qelekluki. [*ngel'artut*] Ala-i!

Kalukaat

Cingyukan: Akaar imumi, akaar tamaani tamakussuutmun arrluyagaq, ala-i, naptell'. Iciw' imkut umyuarrluulriit.

Irniara tauna naptelliniluni tamaavet. Ala-i! Tuqulliniluni. Ala-i, tua-lli-wa-gguq tua-i akinaussaagumaaqelriit tamakut angayuqrit. Catailngaqaarluteng pugqercugluteng. Ala-i!

Pitleq tauna akinaussaagturluku cali. Aling iciw' inerquutaulalriit tamakut tamaa-i piqaasqumavkenaki. Akinrilngailnguugut-gguq. Ila-i!

Tua-i taukut pitellret, naliata picurliin taugaam tua-i tua-i-w' pinriqerrluteng. Aling tang tuaten-am.

Iciw' ua-i ugkut Kalukaat ugkut ua-i arrluunilaqait. Tamakut tamaa-i tuaten ayuqelalriit.

Albertina Dull: Yes. We hear that story. When I became aware, one of the many times they told stories, that's what they would say.

You know how Paruq was once large. They say Teq'acugpak down the coast was where he stayed.

They say they were trying to shrink, what they call *quvssaaglutek,* they were trying to see who could shrink the smallest. Then Paruq down there became small and hard to see, but Uugnar was this size, was evidently this size.

You know, Uugnar at Nunivak Island, probably when they were large, I'm not sure what they were like at the time, they say Uugnar had a stone wall.

Sometime in the past, long ago, back when there weren't any white people around, they say a large boat wrecked along Uugnar's wall.

Back when they didn't know [about Western goods], including flour, the flour sacks, they kept the flour [from the wrecked ship] because of their sacks and spilled [the flour] on the ground. They said the [flour] they spilled from the sacks looked like a very large snowbank. [*laughs*]

They didn't know what [flour] was. They didn't know what they were and spilled them on the ground. That's what they did to them. They didn't keep things, although they liked things, they spilled things but only kept their containers. [*laughter*] Oh my!

Kalukaat[6]

Albertina Dull: Long ago, a small killer whale, my goodness, got caught on one of those [nets for catching seals]. You know those [whales] that are vengeful.

Its offspring evidently got caught on one of those. My goodness! It evidently died. My, they say its parents [the killer whales] were trying to seek revenge for a long time. Although they seemed like they weren't around, they tended to suddenly surface. My goodness!

They also continually tried to seek revenge on the one who caught it. My, you know how it is an admonishment never to harm those. They said they won't fail to get revenge. My goodness!

And the people who caught [the killer whale], when one of them got into an accident, [the whales] finally stopped appearing. My, that's what happened.

You know how they say that Kalukaat down the coast are [the home of] *arrluut* [killer whales]. That's how those [killer whales] are.

Uliggaq: Tua-ll' ayagarkaurtellminek pirraarluni qanertuq, ellii-gguq tang Kalukarmiungulria.

Umyuarteqkilii, "Taugken una yuuluni waniw' ciuqamni," qaillun ircenrraullranek. Ellii-gguq Kalukarmiunguuq.

Tua-i-gguq tamakut tuani uitalriit ircenrraat tamakut tukaraaqameng-gguq-am tauna ilaseng nani uitalria taigarkaurtaqan tukaratuut; tua-i-gguq quyaluteng ilaseng tauna taiqatallinillranek. Tuaten-am tua-i qanrutellruanga.

Wiinga taugken maurluqluku. Qaillun ircenrrauga? [*ngel'artuq*] Tuaten tang qanrutellrania uunguciitellruunga. Ellii-gguq tang Kalukarmiungulria, un'gaani tamakuni ingrini.

Makut maa-i ingriput yungqerrnilarait-am tamakucinek.

Tauna taugaam marrlugaurluqa nalluvkenaku Kalukarmiungullra. Elliin apertuutellruanga. Taugken tang im' marrlugaqluku. Yuuluni tua-i cavkenani.

Tuaten-am taugaam tua-i qessayaaqellrulliami aneryaarpallaggaarluni, qanellrani tua-i-w' ayagnariqatarniluni piluni.

Cunaw' tua-i tamakut tamaa-i tuaten pilriit ilameggnek tekiteqatalriamek quyaluteng, quyatekluku pitulliniameng, iciw' kallilriatun tem'irrluteng. Quyaluteng piluteng.

Tauna tua-i elliin marrlugama call' Kalukarmiunguniluni waniw' canimni qanrutellruanga.

Nialruq

Unangik: Ii-i, kiugkut kia-i unglurpallraat yaqulpiim. . . . Tanglaqarrallemteni kiugkut nunaurpailgata avani tan'gurraullemteni atam tua-i unglurngatellruut, taugaam tua-i teggalquuluteng avatait, unglurpallraat pikani. Yaqulpak tauna angellrulliniami, angkayagluni. Atam tua-i unglui ang'ut; angkayagtut tua-i cakneq.

Tamaa-i tua-i irniari-llu angulluatun imutun atkullrani ullingalriatun ayuqekutetullruit-gguq irniari.

Ukurmiunek pikengyuunani, naken taugaam qayanek-llu iluvautaqluni tauna. Qayartuumaita tua-i qecugmigluki pikavet irniaminun nerevkatullrullinikai yaqulpiim taum.

Susie Angaiak: Then after saying that she was going to leave, [my grandmother] said that she was from Kalukarmiut.

I was thinking, "But here this one is a regular person right in front of me," wondering how she was an *ircenrraq*. She said she was from Kalukarmiut.

They say those *ircenrraat* who live there, when they kick their feet to make rumbling noises, they make rumbling noises when one of their own who is living elsewhere is about to come; it is said they are grateful that one of their own is about to come. That's what she told me.

But here she was my grandmother. How was she an *ircenrraq?* [*laughs*] I was confused when she told me that. She said she was a resident of Kalukarmiut, from the mountains down coast.

They mention that our mountains are occupied by those [*ircenrraat*].

I know that my dear grandmother is a resident of Kalukarmiut. She told me. But here she was my grandmother. Here she was a regular person and wasn't different.

But probably because she was reluctant to go, after a loud sigh, she said that it was almost time for her to go.

Evidently, those [places] that make rumbling noises like thunder do that because they are grateful that one of their own is going to arrive soon. They do that out of gratitude.

My grandmother herself told me that she was from Kalukarmiut while she was seated next to me.

Nialruq[7]

Simeon Agnus: Yes, the very large nest up the coast [that belonged to] a large bird. . . . When we first started seeing it before the village [of Toksook Bay] up the coast was established when we were boys, it looked like a nest, but there were rocks on the periphery of the very large nest up there. That large bird was enormous. Its nest is large; it is huge.

It is said they would compare the size of its fledglings to that of elderly men with their parkas turned inside out.

[That bird] would never attack or seize people from this area, but it would arrive with kayaks from other places. That large bird would use its claws to grasp people along with their kayaks and bring them up there and feed them to its fledglings.

Yaqulpak tauna, pikani Nialrum qalirnerani uitaut unglut. Taugaam maa-i mat'um nalliini unglurngairutlilriit. Avani tangerqerraalallemni unglurngatellruut atam, tan'gurraullemni.

Tua-i caqerluteng waten pikani irniallermini, arnaq tauna camek tauna erurïa tuntuugnek qasperturluni, atkugturluni. Taum tua-i alarrvikliniluku tuntuuyukluku tua-i qecugmigluku tuqulluku, makurmiu. Makurmiunekgguq piiyuitqapiarallruuq tauna yaqulpak. Tua-i tuqulluku tua-i.

Angutiin tua-i taum elpekngamiu yaqulpak tauna tua-i akngircartullinia ullagluku. Pitegcautet taugaam kiingan akngirutngutullrullilriit kapuutet-llu tamatum nalliini.

Taum tua-i yaqulpiim, cauyukluku camek erurillrani tua-i qecugmigluku, tuntuuyukluku pillrulliami tua-i alarrvikluku tua-i. Tuntuugnek atkugturluni, tunturaagnek-wa pillilria.

Pikavet tua-i mayurluni; mayuulluku tauna pillrullikii aipaa, nulirra tauna, irniaminun neresqelluku. Angutiin tua-i ullagluku pitgaryartullrullinia tuani tauna yaqulpak.

Tengeng'ami-qaa, qagaatmun tua-i tayim' ayallruuq-gguq pikaken.

Uingan-wa tua-i yaqulpak tua-i akngirrluku pitgarluku. Taugaam tua-i taum yaqulpiim qessanayugtacirmini tayima, tauna-ll' akngirtesteni ilangcillrunritlikii.

Ukurmiunek-gguq piiyuitqapiarallruuq yuitnek ukut, taugaam naken tua-i qayaq-llu qecugmikluku pikavet-gguq ellitullrua.

Taugken tang qayallernek-llu tamaa-i pikani tangerqayuitellruunga, wall'u-qaa aruluteng nevuurtellruut? Nevuurtellrungatut ak'allaurcameng. Tauna tua-i tuaten niilluku tua-i qanrutkaqatgu tua-i niitetullrukek'a tauna yaqulpak.

Qasginguaq

Kangrilnguq: Pikna-w' pika-i ircen'ernun qasgiqnilaqiit.

Tamaa-i-gguq un'a cikumaaqan qavaken-llu qamigaqsaunateng tumnek tanglallrulriit kangimek itralrianek ikamrallritnek augnek-gguq kucirturluteng pitaita tamaa-i augitnek. Pikegkut Qasginguarmiut ircenrraunilarait.

Unangik: Ava-i qanrutketullrukait kuimta kuinrakun itralriit tunguk'a-

The nest of that large bird is up on top of Nialruq. But it probably no longer resembles a nest these days. When I first saw it, it looked like a nest back when I was a boy.

One day when that bird was tending to its fledglings up there, a woman wearing a caribou parka was washing something. That bird mistook her for a caribou and snatched her with its claws and killed her, a person from here. They say that large bird never seized people from this area. It killed her [by accident].

When her husband realized what it had done, he went to that bird to injure it. Back in those days, arrows and spear points were probably the only weapons used for wounding.

That large bird, mistaking her for an animal while she was washing something, seized her with its claws, probably mistaking her for a caribou. She was wearing a caribou parka, probably a caribou parka.

It went up on top of that place; it probably brought his wife up there for its fledglings to eat. Her husband went to that large bird to shoot arrows at it at that time.

When it flew, it is said that it flew north from up there.

Her husband shot an arrow at that large bird and injured it. But that large bird, probably out of regret, didn't do anything to the person who injured it.

They say it never attacked the people from here, but it would arrive from somewhere holding a kayak with its claws and place it up there.

But I never saw old kayaks up there, or have they rotted and become soil? I think they became soil when they got old. I used to hear about that large bird when they talked about it.

Qasginguaq[8]

Paul John: They say that place up there is the *qasgi* of *ircenrraat*.

They say when the ocean down there was frozen, when they hadn't gone seal hunting, they'd see some tracks, their old sled tracks, heading from the bay along with some blood drops from the animals they had caught. They mention that people from Qasginguaq [One resembling a *qasqi* (men's house)] up there are *ircenrraat*.

Simeon Agnus: They said that the very dark killer whales that used to head

cagarluteng arrluut tua-i pikegkumiunguut-gguq. Tua-i qanrutkenaurait-am.

Atam kuimteni un'gani Kangirrluarmi arrluut kuimatullruyaaqut.

Tamakut-am agg'un akimteggun arrluut tunguk'acagarluteng amllerrluteng kiatmurrnaurtut. Cunaw' una-i ircenrraat; wavet waniw' itrarluteng.

Kangrilnguq: Cali-am uum waniw' David-am atallran qanemciskiinga; ikaken ika-i Qilengpagmek qanaatekek'ngamtenek uiterassaaggaarluni uterrnginanrani-gguq Qasginguamek tua-i kiaken atulrianek niiskengangelria.

Tuaten tua-i putrugtaqami niiskengaqsagutaqluki. Kiituan-gguq canimellian tua-i pekteng'ermi tamayuirutut erinait.

Tua-i-am caqerluni yuarucilria malrugnek ua-ua-ua-lriignek iquklicartullengqerraqlutek. Cunaw' tua-i tuani Qasginguarmiut yuarutaita aturpagallratni elitellregni malruk atullinikek tua-i. Wani tua-i iquklitellragni ua-ua-ua-rlukek iquklitnaurak', tua-i ircen'ertaungamek.

Tua-i pulengtaq call' waten qavani kangalriit, makiraaqameng-llu qanqatuut tuaten put'aqameng niitnarqaqameng, tua-i-w' kiugkut Qasginguarmiut atuagaqata put'aqata-gguq alaitaqluteng, makeskata-ll' tayim' niitnairulluteng. Tuaten tua-i ircenrraat makut qanrutkelaqait.

Cali tua-i ilait niicetqainaraqluteng, taugaam tangercetevkenateng, callermegteggun malirqellermegteggun, wall'u pillermegteggun tua-i piciatun.

Wiinga tua-i tan'gurraulua yaani Arayakcaami kal'utalrianek niitellrianun ilagautellruunga. Tuartang ilumun yuk'apiaraat. Kankiillrit-llu niitnaqluteng. Kal'utat-llu kaugturqatni, imumek tua-i cikukun elegleggluni ayallra alaitaqluni.

up our [Tuqsuk] River channel are from [Qasginguaq] up there. They would mention them.

In the past, killer whales used to swim inside our river down the coast, inside Kangirrluar [Toksook Bay].

Those very dark killer whales would go up the coast across from our village in large numbers. They were evidently *ircenrraat;* they were going upriver to this place [Qasginguaq].

Paul John: Also, David's late father [Cyril Chanar] told me a story; after going to get red ocher from Qilengpak, the place we were talking about, he said that while he was returning home he started hearing people singing from Qasginguaq up the bay.

When he'd bend forward like that and put his head down a little, he would hear them. Eventually, when he got closer [to Qilengpak], although he just walked along normally, their voices no longer disappeared.

Once he composed two songs with *ua-ua-ua* endings. Evidently, he was singing the two songs he learned that the people of Qasginguaq were singing at that time. When they ended, he'd end them with *ua-ua-ua* because they are songs of the *ircenrraat.*

Many times, people who are walking around up there, even when they are gathering greens along the land, mention that when they bend forward they can hear [*ircenrraat*] voices; when the people from Qasginguaq are singing, and [people] bend forward, their voices are audible, and when they stand up, their voices can't be heard. That's what they say about these *ircenrraat.*

Also, some [*ircenrraat*] only allow people to hear them but not see them while they are doing something, when they are pursuing seals in open water, or whatever they are doing.

When I was a young man over at Arayakcaaq, I was among a group of people who heard them playing *kal'utaq* [a game similar to hockey]. They sounded like real people. And the sound of their ice skating was audible. And the sound their sticks made when they hit what they were about to strike and it slid across the ice was audible.

Qukaqliqutaat

Kangrilnguq: Cali wii qanemciqeryugyaaqua. Niitetuukut avani ciuqvani ircenrraat alaitetullratnek. Kia-i kiugna Qasginguaq ircenrraat nunalqaat. Qamna-w' cali qamani Negtemiut ingriata, ingrim-llu qam'um kiaqlian qukaagni kiani cali ircenrraat tauna tua-i nunallrat. Ircenertangqepigtellrulliniuq.

Tamaa-i alaitaqluteng pitullratni, tauna-am kiani kia-i Qukaqliqutarni; Qukaqliqutarnek pituit kiugkut kuigek akuliigni ingrit. Tuqsucuaraam Tuqsuum-llu akuliigni Qukaqliqutarnek aterpagtetuit ingrit.

Angutet-am tauna iliit piyukacillermini, nutngenratgun, nutget alainratgun, keglunyaarnek igtem paingani tekitellinilria. Tua-i tangvaurallinii miklata. Qaillukuarpeknaki tua-i tangvaurarraarluki unitelliniluki.

Unilluki ayaagaqanrakun kegluneq mengliikun maaggun kingunranek igvaarrluni kituurcami, yaa-i ciunranun kingutmun caugarcami marualliniluni. Marualria-gguq naken akia.

Tua-i ilangcivkenaku ayaagalliniluni. Kingunrakun igvaarrluni kitu'urtaqamiu ciunranun elliirtaqami maruaraqan akistii canimellikaniraqluni.

Atam tua-i ak'anun pivkenani keglunrek malruqertellinilriik. Aren malruqercamek-gguq keglunrek imkuk uivaangartaak, iluqsigiinarlutek. Kiituangguq pamyumegnek iruakun piqercaurtaak. Tuaten tua-i keglunrek taukuk irugkengun pamyumegnek piqraqluku.

Qanruqu'uryaaqelliniak, nutni maniurluku taqesqelluni, taqsunripakaqagni mat'umek tangvaumanrilngurmek qerrulegmek akngirciiqniluku aipaak.

Tua-i taqsunrilagni, iruni-gguq pamyumegnek piqraqaku uyungleqercarpialanga'arcami aipaa nut'liniluku, tua-i nutni-ll' taman' maniurluku qanrucaaqvigminek tangvaumanrilngurmek kenermek cingestellegmek qerrulegmek.

Aipaa nutgani, tayima tua-i uacillagluni kingutmun pian igvanqigtevkenatek.

Tua-i-ll' kinguakun tayim' piinanrani tua-i-am yuilqurtelliniuq. Yuilqumi piinanrani arnaq man'a atepkussaarluni issratmek, naruumaarallinia ciunrakun.

Arnam taum tekicamiu pillinia, "Nerqerluk tang taquamnek." Tua-i

Qukaqliqutaat[9]

Paul John: I want to tell another brief story. We have heard about how *ircenrraat* were around long ago. Qasginguaq back there was where *ircenrraat* once lived. And there is another place inland, between the mountain where the village of Nightmute is located and the mountain beyond it, where *ircenrraat* once lived. *Ircenrraat* were truly around in the past.

Back when they were seen, there was once a person up at Qukaqliqutaat [Those in the middle or center]; they call the mountains between those two rivers Qukaqliqutaat. They call the mountains between Tuqsucuar River and Tuqsuk River Qukaqliqutaat.

When one of the men was hunting fur animals on foot during the time when they started to obtain guns, just as guns came around, he came upon some wolf pups along the opening of a den. He just watched them since they were little. He didn't do anything to them, and he evidently left them after watching them.

After he left them and was walking for a while, a wolf suddenly appeared alongside him from behind, and when it passed, when it turned around in front of him, it began to howl. Another wolf howled in return from somewhere.

He ignored it and continued on. When it would appear from behind him and pass alongside him, upon reaching the area in front of him, when it howled, the other wolf howling in return would get closer.

Soon two wolves were suddenly around. My, when two were suddenly there, those wolves began to circle him, getting closer and closer. Eventually they began to whip him along his legs with their tails. The wolves would strike his legs with their tails.

He repeatedly told them, holding out his gun, to stop striking him, that if they didn't stop he would injure one of them with this weapon that had a hidden bullet.

When they wouldn't stop [hitting him], when he began to almost buckle and fall on his knees when they struck him with their tails, he shot the other wolf, after continually holding out his gun and telling them about the concealed bullet triggered by a spark.

When he shot the other [wolf], when it suddenly yelped and moved back, they never appeared again.

Then after that incident, he went out to the wilderness again. While he was out in the wilderness, a woman carrying a twined grass carrying bag approached him from the area ahead of him.

nutaan-llu tangeng'ermiu angllinia.

Taquani anqaarluki, nutarinrarmek uqumek uqulgiraminek anciami pillinia, "Man'a maa-i anngarma pitaan qamigallermini uquqaa." Tua-i nernermek taqngamek pillinia, "Tua-i-w' elpet waniw' yuaqengaqellikemken. Anngarma akngircetellra elpengullilria."

Tua-ll' tua-i taum pillinia, "Callemni?"

"Tayima tua-i keglunrek malruulutek piqallrullikiigten." Neq'aqaamiu tua-i tauna qanerniarutliniluku, tua-i inerqurrsaaqvigminek pamyumegnek irugmikun piqertangellragni uyungleqercarpialangami nutellruniluk' aipaak.

Tua-ll' pillinia taum, "Kitek tua-i maligesnga. Elpengulliniuten. Qaill' pingaitaatgen; qanerniarucarturki kingunrenka maligglua." Angrani tua-i Qukaqliqutaat tungiitnun ayautenga'artellinia.

Tua-i nunanun tekitelliniuk ikgetevkenateng nunat, qasgiat-wa-gguq qukaatni. Maaten-gguq tang qasgimun itrucani piqertuq egkumi kiugna nukalpiaq taklalria, anerneni-gguq tua-i maliggluku erinani anqurluku. Qaill'-gguq piaqami puyurrluarmek anernera tapengqeqernaurtuq.

Aqumesqengatni aqumngan angullugaat iliita pillinia, "Tua-i elpet kiugna kia-i akngirtellrukuvgu, kitek' ayuqucillerpenek qanruskut."

Tua-i ayuqucilqapiaramitun qanemcitliniluki inerqurrsaaqvigminek, cali-ll' caskuni tangvaumanrilngurmek qerrungqellranek qanrucaaqvigminek, cakaniryunrilagnek pamyumegnek piqraqagni uyungleqercarpialangami nutellruniluku.

Itellriani-gguq-wa iqsulirnerem tungiini nakiqataam qukaani angulvall'er-gguq una yuukitevkenani ingelrem acianun keggatni itengqaluki, quliini-wa-gguq qugyuk. Tauna-gguq taugaam murilkelluku. Qugyuum-wa-gguq melqurrin nuugit tamarmeng takvigtarluteng, iitarluteng.

Tua-i taukut, iilliniuq, qanrumarian tauna qanresqestellra, "Iiii. Cunawa tua-i tuaten inerquayaaqellrung'erpeni, pinrilngermi pillrunilalria. Atak waten ayuqurallinili." Tua-i apervikualuki tua-i taukut ayuqucillminek piateng.

Tua-ll' tua-i taqluku. Anen'ariaku iliit pilliniuq, "Nunam-atak aalerya-rainek piqaqerlaut." Maaten-gguq tua-i iliit anrraarluni itertuq qemaggvigmek tegumiarluni. Tauna-gguq tua-i, qemaggviim imai nuutaarluteng qamaken

When the woman came upon him, she said, "Let's eat some of my provisions." Although he'd never seen her before, he agreed with her.

After taking out her provisions, when she took out some fresh seal oil that she had brought with her, she said to him, "This is the seal oil of a seal that my older brother caught when he went seal hunting." When they finished eating, she said to him, "You must be the person who I'm searching for. You must be the one who injured my older brother."

Then he evidently said to her, "What was I doing at the time?"

"Two wolves probably confronted you in the past." When he suddenly recalled that incident, he told that person that after repeatedly warning them, when they began slapping their tails on his legs until he was almost buckling, he shot one of them.

Then that [woman] said to him, "Now come with me. You are actually the person. They won't do anything to you; come with me and tell the people of my village what happened." When he agreed, she began to lead him toward Qukaqliqutaat.

They came upon a village, and there were many people in the village, and he saw that their *qasgi* was in their village center. When she brought him inside the *qasgi,* he saw a great hunter lying along the back wall, and following his breathing, he would let out his voice. Sometimes he would exhale a little smoke when breathing.

When they asked him to sit and he sat, one of the elderly men said to him, "Now if you injured that person back there, tell us what you did and your intention."

He told them exactly what happened, that after repeatedly warning them and telling them that his weapon had a concealed bullet, he shot it when they wouldn't back off and he was almost buckling when they slapped him with their tails.

When he went inside [the *qasgi*], along the left side, along the middle of the side wall, there was a very large man who wasn't small who had his chest tucked underneath the bed, and up above him was a swan. It was watching that person. And eyes were along all the tips of the swan's feathers.

The people there, after he spoke, the one who he told the story to said, "Yes. So, although you repeatedly warned him, he said that you had injured him although he had done nothing. Let him continue to be this way." That's what he said when he told them about his experience.

They were done questioning him. When it was time for him to go outside, one of them said, "Let's test him with *nunam aaleryarai* [the scurriers of the

qemaggviim iluanek, nuutaarluteng.

Maaten-gguq wavet ciuqerranun kuvai, imkut angyayagarnek pitukvut, uugnaraat aipait mikellrit, cugg'elget cingilrianek.

Arenqiapaa-gguq kuvngaceteng ciuqerranun, tua-i elliinun taugaam tua-i mayurluku, iigkenun, qengagkenun, qanranun ciutegkenun-llu itsaagluteng, iluanun tuaten iterluteng.

Aren tua-i qengagni kevirlukek pillratni epsalngunga'arcami qanmikun itsaalria aitaqanicuaqerluni qamiqurra keggutmi nalliitnun elliircan, kegqaqiini qamiqurra qiaryillakarluni. Pegcani-llu kanavet tuc'ami tukay'ayagaqerluni nalaqallinilunі.

Tua-llu-gguq taukut iliit qanertuq, "Iii-i, tuqucimayuilnguq nunam aaleryarii tuqutaa! Tuaten-atak pitaciu!" Imkut tua-i angyayagaat-am avurluki tuavet ataam ekluki tayim' anutelliniluki.

Tua-i-ll' anuqaartelluk' itran pilliniuq iliit, "Nauggun anevkaqatarceta? Qullirkun-qaa wall'u-q' atlirkun anevkaqumteni cayarta?"

Tauna-gguq atam ingelrem acianun keggatni itengqakii angulvall'er imarmiutarnek-gguq atkugturluni. Eng-aarluni tuaten piluni qanlliniuq, "Qaillukuarpek'naku itervillrakun anevkarciu. Qaillukuaquvciu wii piciqamci elpeci!" Aren imkut-gguq tuaten qanelria, "Ii-i, kitak tua-i qaillukuanritlininaurput, itervillrakun anevkallininaurput."

Tua-i itervillmikun anevkaatni anlliniuq imna uksuulleq tua-i kiakatarluni urunqilirilliniluni-ll' itrumacuarallrani. Tua-i utertellinilun'.

Kingunican, kingunrin nanlluku muluvakallrucianek apcatni, tua-i qanerniarutliniluki Qukaqliqutarmiut yungqelliniata taukut aqviitni maligutellruniluni.

Tua-i-llu tauna imna angulvall'er imarmiutarnek atkulek qanellranek qanran, taukut imkut angulluat angulluarit qanlliniut, "Tangerrluku! Ciuliamta angalkuirutkelliniat tauna." Tua-i-gguq tuavet tuqukuni Qukaqliqutarmiunun ayagciqnilallruuq.

Taum-am tua-i ikayuqallinikii kingunerminek pilriaruan tauna; qacikelliamiki ircenrraungraata tuaten qanrutlinikai. [*ngelaq'ertuq*] Augna ava-i tuaten taktaluku qanemciuluku niitellruaqa.

land].” After one of them went out, he came back inside holding a storage container. They say that the contents of his storage container were squirming around inside that container.

When he spilled them in front of him, [they were] those we call *angyayagaat* [shrews], the other type of mice that are smaller, the ones with pointed snouts.

Oh my, when they spilled them right in front of him, they only climbed on him and tried to wriggle inside his eyes, his nose, and his mouth, and they even went inside his clothing.

When they filled his nose holes, when he suddenly felt suffocated, when [a shrew] was trying to wriggle inside his mouth, he opened his mouth a little, and when its head came under his teeth, when he bit down on it, its head suddenly made a crackling noise. And when he released it and it fell on the floor, the small thing trembled and died.

Then one of the people there said, “Yes, he has killed *nunam aaleryarii* [the shrew] that has never been killed! Now let him be!” They gathered the shrews and placed them inside the container and took them outside.

After he took them out and came back inside, one of them said, “Which way are we going to let him go out? What do you think if we let him out through the top one or the bottom one?”

They say the one who had his chest tucked underneath the bed, that very large man, had a mink parka. He huffed and said, “Don’t mess with him and let him go out the way that he came in. If you mess with him, I will deal with you myself!” When he said that, the people there said, “Yes, let’s not mess with him and let him go out the way he came in.”

When they let him out the way he came in, he went outside and saw that what had once been winter was almost summer, and many patches of melted snow had appeared during the short time that he had been inside. He returned home.

When he reached his village, when the people at his hometown asked him where he had been and why he was gone for so long, he told them that since there were people at Qukaqliqutarmiut he had gone with them when people from that place came to get him.

And when he mentioned what that very large man with a mink parka said, their elderly men said, “*Tangerrluku* [Lo and behold]! That person is actually a deceased shaman of our ancestors.” They said that person had said that he would go to Qukaqliqutarmiut when he died.

That person had helped him because he came from the village where he once lived; since he could overpower them although they were *ircenrraat,* that’s what he apparently told them. [*chuckles*] That’s the extent to which I

Negtemiut Nunakauyarmiut-llu

Nightmute
and Toksook Bay

Engelumiut

Unangik: Keluqliit pingkut ciumek qanrutkerraarluki piciqut, ukut-llu kinguatgun qanrutekluki.

Pingkut pia-i keluqliit Apanuugpiim nunallri, ak'allat. Apanuugpiim pingkut pia-i anguyatullermini, tamaani yuullermini, pingkut pia-i nunakellrui.

Inglukestaita tekilluki waten qavaatni unugmi, pingkut pia-i pingkut.

Aciat qerratanilaraat pingkut pia-i, cali ilii pillilria.

Tua-i arnar'-am tauna iliit tuani nem'i, waten amillgutekngameng; atauciuluni anyaraat. Arnar'-am tauna iliit umyuarluni tua-i pillinilria. Kangcirami keluat nayugaqluku, nayugturluku. Cali uugnaraam anellra ellamun, tauna kevinrilkurqurluku.

Tua-i taukut anguyiit tekicamegteki puyilluki.

Ellii tua-i tauna kangcirami keluatnun iterluni, taum tua-i uugnaraam igtiikun ellamun anumalriakun tuaggun tua-i anertevkaarluni tua-i epevkenani.

Tua-i puyum tua-i caquateng, tua-i tauna amiingqellruami-gguq ataucimek pingna pia-i atauciuluni amiiga, taugaam tua-i enet amllellrullilriit piani.

Apanuugpiim pingkut pia-i nunalqekai tua-i ciuliaqapiaramta.

Tua-i ellani qinuirucan im' arnaq, tuaken tua-i kangcirat keluatnek anngami, anqataarluni tua-i pilliniuq, ayuqucia taman' qinungssagaunani; tua-i an'urluni pilliniuq, yugmek-llu tangyuunani.

Anngami tua-i kiarcami man'a pillinia, cenar' maa-i takelria man'a; yaaken yaa-i ayagluki yuut yagingaluteng tuqumalriit cagtellrit ingluita.

Talliit waten agtuumauraulluteng wani tua-i `gguun. Ingna yaa-i painga yaaqsilria. Yug' amlleq tua-i tuquluni tua-i.

Tua-i caarkailami uyamiit cigviit-llu taum tua-i arnam avurturallinii,

heard the story.

Engelumiut[10]

Simeon Agnus: We'll first talk about [the sites] situated farther back up there, and then we will talk about these [near the shore].

The [old site, Engelumiut (People of the *engelu* (muskrat's hole))] that is farther back up there is where Apanuugpak once lived, an old site. Back when Apanuugpak engaged in warfare during his life, the site back there was where he lived.

Their enemies came upon them while they were sleeping at night, in the place up there.

They say the ground below the site up there is elevated, and part of it is probably still that way today.

One of the women there inside that home, since they all used one doorway; they had one exit that they shared. One of the women there had an idea. She would dig out [dirt] along the area behind their wall covering to create a hole. And the mouse hole that led outdoors along that area, she would purposely not cover that.

When the warriors came upon those people, they evidently lit fires and attempted to asphyxiate them with smoke.

She crawled behind their wall covering, and she breathed through the mouse hole that led outside and didn't die of suffocation.

When smoke engulfed them, since that place up there had one doorway, it had one doorway, but there were probably many houses up there [that were connected].

That place up there is where Apanuugpak, our direct ancestor, once lived.

When it became calm and peaceful, when that woman emerged from behind that wall covering, she cautiously went out, and she felt completely calm; she cautiously went out, and she didn't see anyone around.

When she went outdoors and searched her surroundings, she looked at the shore here that extends a great distance; starting from over there, their enemies had strewn dead people with their arms stretched out along the ground.

Their arms were touching like this. You can see that the [river] mouth over there is a good distance away. Many people died.

avurturluki tua-i pillinikai taukut, tamakut taklalriit, tuqumalriit epellret.

Pingkut yuit tamarmeng tua-i epluteng. Tauna taugaam tua-i arnaq tua-i kiirrarmi tua-i maktaluni. Taum tua-i uugnaraam igtiin ellamun anumalriim, taum tua-i epevkarpek'naku.

Arnaq tauna tua-i tamakut uyamiit, makuit-llu, cait-wa tua-i uyamiit tegglit pillilriit, avulnguamiki tua-i uitangailami tua-i natmun-gguq tua-i tamaavet, pagaavet tua-i tegumiaqurngailamiki elakaulluki-gguq, elaulluki-gguq tua-i pillrui.

Akwaku kinguliat tua-i nataqekunegteki tua-i tayim', tua-i nauwa tua-i nataqumanrilnguq man'a maa-i tekilluku.

Tua-i callerkailami tauna natmun tayim' ayallrua; natmun ayauciitaqa tauna ayallra.

Apanuugpiim tua-i, ukut waniw' tua-i yugnek tua-i kaimqillri.

Tua-i tuani tua-i akinaurcillruuq. Ingluita tua-i qavaatni tekilluki muraganek amiigit kevirluki ekuavkarluki puyiilluki.

Cali waten anguyakatarqami, qapilaallernek-gguq tua-i qumikarquq. Pitegcautet pit'gaqungraatni pitegcautet agaqaquaqluteng.

Tua-i-ll'-am iliita pivakarluni aptellinia ciin tua-i pitegcautetayuitelalkegnek. Avaqutaqlikii-wa Pangalgalria. Turulua.

Pillinia Engelumiut qapilaallritnun tutmatuniluki pitegcautet. Pitegcautetarciiganatek tua-i. Engelumiut ukut qapilaallritnun tutmalarniluki pitegcautet.

Tamaa-i anguyakatarqami tuaten tua-i pilallrullinikai.

Kangrilnguq: Share-aqaqernaurtua. Tang waniw' qapilaam caqua. Tua-i-llu imutun-gguq angtatuut ciqitait waten caqukuarit.

Tua-i-llu anguyakatarqami tayim' amllenrilengraata, waten-gguq pakigluku ukuni qamavet igcecilartuq. Ava-i augna *share*-aqa'arqa qanemcia.

Tua-i `gguun igceciqerqami makucinek [qapilaanek], qainga tamarmi taum Apanuugpiim qaspengtulliniuq elliini tunukengraani-llu.

Since she had nothing to do, that woman gathered their necklaces and their nose adornments, gathering them from those people who were lying on their backs, the dead people who had suffocated.

All the people who lived up there [at the site] had suffocated to death. The only person still alive was that woman. The mouse hole that led outdoors kept her from suffocating.

That woman, when she finished gathering their necklaces, and these adornments here, probably their beaded necklaces, since she wouldn't keep them, they say that she dug a hole somewhere around here, up there, and buried them.

Our descendants may happen to find them one day in the future, but they haven't found them up to this day.

Since she had nothing to do, I'm not sure where she went; I don't know where she went.

This is the place from which Apanuugpak killed many of his enemies.

Their enemies took revenge upon him at that time. Their enemies came upon them while they were sleeping, and they filled their doorways with wood and lit them and asphyxiated them with smoke.

Also, when he was about to engage in warfare, they say [Apanuugpak] would put some mussel shells inside his clothing [along his upper body]. Although arrows were shot at him, the arrows just dangled and hung [along his upper body].

Then one day evidently someone asked him why arrows couldn't pierce [him and Pangalgalria]. Pangalgalria was probably his *avaqutaq* [lit., "son" in the Nunivak dialect]. Actually, he was his *turuluk* [a reciprocal kinship name that Apanuugpak and Pangalgalria used for each other].

He told him that the arrows hit the discarded mussel shells of the people of Engelumiut. Arrows couldn't pierce them. He said that the arrows hit the discarded mussel shells of the people of Engelumiut.

When he was about to engage in battle with his enemies, that's evidently what he did with [mussel shells].

Paul John: Let me briefly share something. Here [on this beach] is a mussel shell. They say their pile of discarded mussel shells was about this large.

And when he was about to engage in battle, he'd take a few, and he'd open [his garment's neck opening] and drop them inside. I'm just sharing this about his story.

When he'd drop these [mussel shells] through [his neck opening], Apanuugpak's entire body apparently became cloaked with [mussel shells]

Pitegcautet-llu qainganun tut'eng'ermeng aqevleqerrnaurtut-gguq, imarnitegkeni taugaam kiingan kapusngaluteng.

Nauw' makucirugarnek ellramini, qavcirrarnek igcecingermi iluminun qaspertelalliniluni tamaani yuut apqiitnek ellrinaraunritellratni, piiyuumacirluteng yuut ilait pitullrulliniameng. Augna *share*-qaqa'arqa.

Unangik: Apanuugpak tauna tua-i picurlailnguuluni yuullrullinilria.

Nani-am pivakarlukek nunani amigpitliniagket qasgimi anesqellukek.

Anlliniuk-gguq tamarmeng cavigganek akiqliqelriit tua-i tegumiarluteng.

Tua-i tekican Apanuugpak kapliniluku. Ukatmun piami, ik'um-llu akiqlian cali kapluku.

Tua-i maa-i kinguqliqu'urlutek ayalliniuk tauna-llu malini-llu.

Tua-i iqukliarcamegneki pillinia tauna aptellinia, "Naten-qaa tua-i ungilkanrituq?" Natiini-gguq tuan tallignеruakun ungilkartuq.

Wagg'uq tua-i kapullrua cavigganek tua-i kapuryaaqluku. Qaill' taukuk yuullruak? Tua-i-wa caulutek yuullrularngatuk taukuk Apanuugpiinkuk Pangalgalria-llu.

Tamaa-i nunanun piaqamek, qayanek qayinqigteqatarqamek, tamaa-i Pangalgalria aqvaqurcecetullrullinia.

Imkut paangrutet takelriit tua-i; amlliraullrini tamaa-i engelqaqutaqluteng paangrutet. Tamaa-i aqvaqullrikun Pangalgalriim elitaqaqlukek.

Yugpaullruyugnarquq tauna aipaa; Panglgalria tauna yugpaullrularngatuq.

Ukuk tua-i ava-i pikegkuk, taukut tua-i nunallerpiit pingkut, Pangalgalriim tua-i nunalqai. Tua-i anguyiit tua-i nunakluki.

Taugaam tua-i kiimek ukuk elkek tua-i anguyagaqlutek yugnek amllernek tuquciaqlutek. Taugaam tan'gurrarmek-gguq ilangqelallruuk iliini.

Avani-w' pillermegni, avani Iilgayami, tan'gurrarmek ilangqellrullinilriik tamaa-i anguyagyarturlutek pillermegni.

like a *qaspeq* [cloth parka], including his back.

And although arrows hit his body, it is said they would just dangle as they hit, and they would just pierce his seal-gut rain garment.

Although he just dropped a few [mussel shells] inside his clothing, many of these [mussel shells] would cloak his entire body like a *qaspeq* back when people weren't just human but had extraordinary abilities, *ellrinaraunritellratni* as they say, since some people evidently had certain abilities. I just wanted to share that.

Simeon Agnus: Apanuugpak evidently lived without encountering mishaps.

One day, while they were somewhere, the people there evidently lined up while they were inside the *qasgi,* making a passageway for them to walk through, and told them to go outside.

They went outside and saw that the people lined up across from one another all held knives.

When Apanuugpak reached them, they stabbed him. When he'd move this way, the person on the other side would also stab him.

He and the person who accompanied him continued on, one following the other.

When they got to the end of their passageway, he asked him, "Did any part of your body feel an itch?" He said he only felt a tickle along his arm.

They had stabbed his body with knives. I wonder how those two lived? Those two, Apanuugpak and Pangalgalria, were probably extraordinary persons.

When they'd arrive in villages, when they were about to replace their kayaks with the kayaks there, he would evidently let Pangalgalria run along the ground.

As you know, those double-bladed paddles are large; those double-bladed paddles were long enough to fit in his strides. They'd recognize them through the running strides of Pangalgalria.

His partner probably was a very tall person; I think Pangalgalria was a tall person.

These two [sites] up there, the large old village site up there was where Pangalgalria once lived. It was a place where warriors once lived.

But those two [Apanuugpak and Pangalgalria] were the only ones who engaged in war and killed many people. But it is said that a young man would accompany them sometimes.

When they were out there one time, out on Iilgayaq [Nushagak River],

Ukuk wani elkek ukuk wani Pangalgalriinkuk Apanuugpak-llu imkuuyugnarquk tua-i tuqungialnguuk, taugaam tua-i tuqunariatek tua-i tuqullrungatuk. Wangkuta taukut nalluaput ak'allaugut, ak'allauguk. Yuurcugnaunata, tamalkumta yuurcugnaunata tua-i-am anguyagturluteng pitullrulliniut augkut ciuliaput, ciuliamta ciuliarit. Anguyagturluteng eq'ukulluteng, eq'ukuqurluteng.

Qaill' tamakut yuullruat? Tua-i anguyak-am nallungermegteggu ellmeggnun tua-i pilallrullinilriit Yupiungermeng, pit'gaqulluteng. Nutgunateng, pitegcautnek taugaam caskurluteng.

Ii-I, kitak ilu'urqa.

Kangrilnguq: Augna Apanuugpak mikelnguullra apenrilaku, mikelnguullranek augna qanemcia *share*-aqernaluku umyuartequa.

Tauna tuani paningqelliniuq Apanuugpiim apaurlua. Kiingan-llu-qaa panikaa tauna Apanuugpiim apaurlurkaan tauna panini?

Tauna-am pania uingvailegmi qingalliniuq, qingarnariani-w' tua-i pillilria. Tua-i apqiitnek atailngiluni; nallunailngurmek atalguvkenani.

Tua-i-am taum apaurluan yuurcan tua-i umyuamikun cakneq cingumiimiu waten ataunani yuurtellra pitekluku, apaurluan taum tayima anguyalangneratgun pillian. . . . Imkut yaqulget qucillgarnek aptukait, erinvaulalriit, yaaqsing'ermeng-llu qalriagaqameng alaitaqluteng.

Tamakucirtaqami apaurluan taum qucillgarmek, tekitaqami nuliaminun man'a qakerlua qalriassuutii augaasqelallinia.

Tua-i-llu nuliaminun aug'arceqaarluku aug'aqaku apaurluan taum teguluku mikelnguyagaullrani tauna Apanuugpak, maavet qalriassutii qucillgam minguutelallinia, qanerluni, "Anguyagyaureskan anguyain eriniikun alikelarniaraat."

Cunawa-gguq tua-i-am nall'arulluni; anguyalangan eriniikun anguyain alikaqluku. Apaurluan-am tua-i tauna cingumatii nall'arusngaluni, erinvauluni Apanuugpak tauna pillrulliniuq.

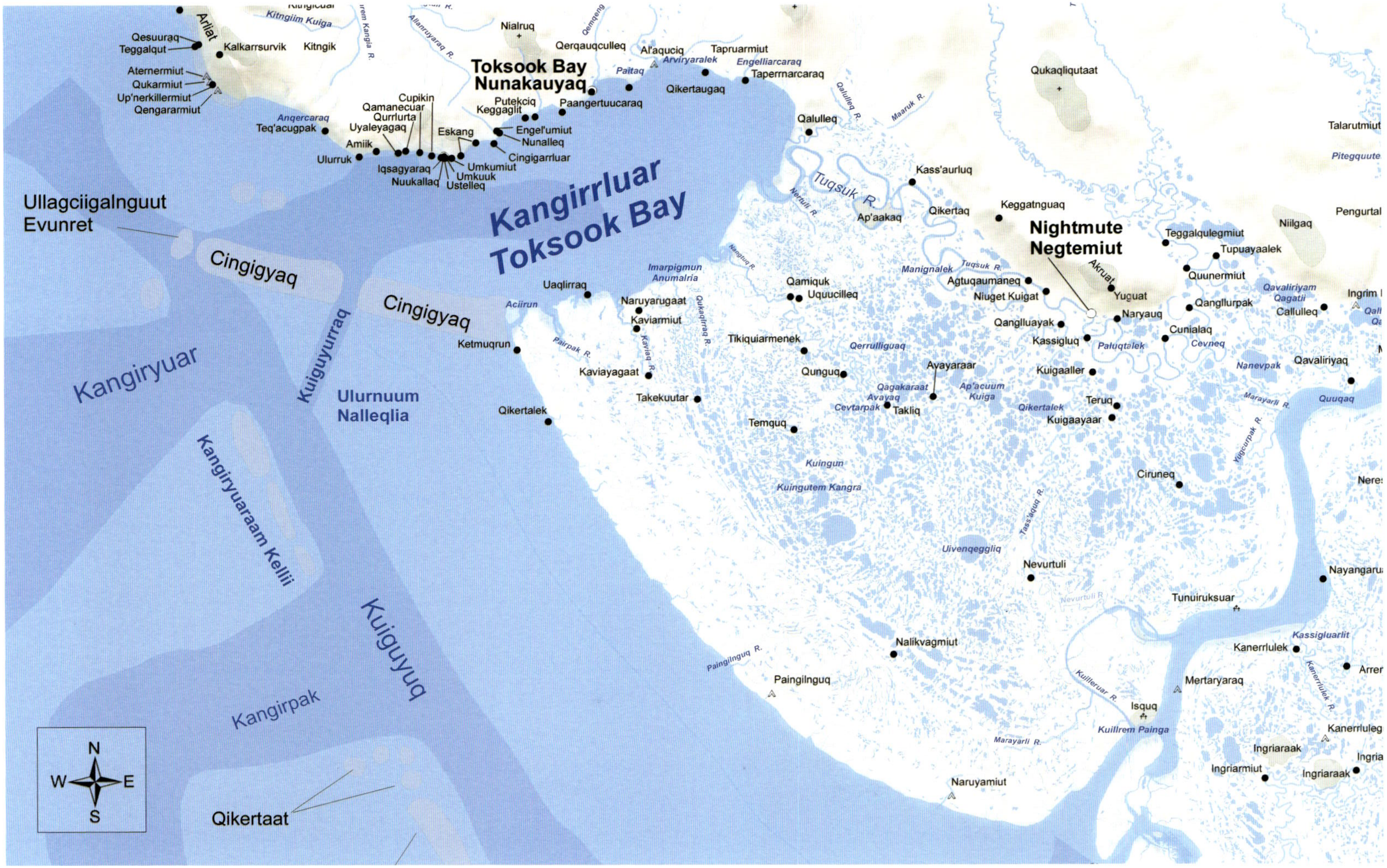

Nightmute and Toksook Bay. Michelle Pearson and Alice Rearden.

Qaluyaat/Nelson Island. AFR.

Points named by Raven on the north shore of Toksook Bay. AFR. (Pages 12–17)

Teq'acugpak. AFR. (Pages 18–19)

Snow-covered *yuguat* (lit., "pretend people") at Nialruq. Janet Klein. (Pages 22–25)

Qasginguaq. AFR. (Pages 24–27)

Engelumiut. AFR. (Pages 36–43)

Nunallret Kuigat (Nunalleq River) entering Toksook Bay at the old village site, Nunalleq. AFR.
(Pages 44–47)

Paul John, John Roy John, Simeon Agnus, and Steve Street at Nunalleq, June 2007. AFR.

Umkumiut summer fish camp. AFR. (Pages 48–61)

Umkumiut from the air, June 1962. University of Delaware, University Museums: Harley and Mabel McKeague Alaskan Inuit Collection © Mabel McKeague.

Umkuuk, the cliff on the western end of Umkumiut, from which the rock outcrop, Ustelleq, in the center of the photograph, detached. AFR. (Pages 62–71)

Tununak elder Rita Angaiak. AFR.

Amiik and Qurrlurta. AFR. (Pages 72–79.)

Up'nerkillermiut. AFR. (Pages 78–97)

Anqercaraq. AFR.

Paul John speaking at Kaviarmiut, with Qaluyaat, the mountains of Nelson Island, in the background. AFR. (Pages 98–117)

Driftwood carried to Kaviarmiut during fall flooding. AFR.

Qalulleq. AFR. (Pages 116–121)

Simeon Agnus speaking, with Qalulleq in the background. AFR.

Nightmute as seen from the village graveyard, early 1960s. University of Delaware, University Museums: Mabel and Harley McKeague Alaskan Inuit Collection © Mabel McKeague. (Pages 112–129)

Nightmute and surrounding hills. University of Delaware, University Museums: Mabel and Harley McKeague Alaskan Inuit Collection © Mabel McKeague.

Tuqsuk River from the air. University of Delaware, University Museums: Mabel and Harley McKeague Alaskan Inuit Collection © Mabel McKeague.

Tuqsuk River below Nightmute. University of Delaware, University Museums: Mabel and Harley McKeague Alaskan Inuit Collection © Mabel McKeague.

Nightmute family in the 1960s. University of Delaware, University Museums: Mabel and Harley McKeague Alaskan Inuit Collection © Mabel McKeague.

Qalvinraaq area. Michelle Pearson and Alice Rearden.

a young man was with them, when they went there to attack their enemies.

Pangalgalria and Apanuugpak seemed to be immortal, but they probably died when it was their time. We don't know what happened to them, as they lived long ago. Long before we were born, long before we were all born, our ancestors evidently frequently engaged in war, the ancestors of our forbearers. They constantly engaged in warfare out of resentment, out of constant resentment.

How did those people live? Although they didn't know about warfare, they evidently fought among one another although they were Yup'ik people, engaging in bow-and-arrow warfare with one another. They had no guns, but they used arrows as weapons.

Yes, well then, it's my *iluraq* [cross-cousin, Paul John's] turn.

Paul John: Since he didn't mention Apanuugpak's childhood, I was thinking about sharing a story about his childhood.

Apanuugpak's grandfather evidently had a daughter. And was she the only daughter of the one who would become Apanuugpak's grandfather?

Evidently, his daughter became pregnant before getting a husband, probably when she was old enough to get pregnant. [Apanuugpak] was an illegitimate child, *atailngiluni* [he was one without an *aata* (father)] as they say; he obviously had no father.

When he was born, because his grandfather really wanted him to be successful because he was born an illegitimate child, probably when they started to engage in war, his grandfather. . . . Those birds they call *qucillgat* [cranes] have very loud voices, and you can hear them when they make their call although they are a great distance away.

When his grandfather would arrive after catching a crane, he'd tell his wife to remove its windpipe, the part of its body that it uses to make noise.

After letting his wife remove it, when she took it off, his grandfather would take it, and while Apanuugpak was just a baby, he'd take the crane's windpipe and rub it [against Apanuugpak's windpipe] and say, "When he becomes a warrior and engages in battles, his enemies will fear him through his voice one day."

That evidently turned out to be true; when he started to engage in warfare, his enemies feared him through his voice. His grandfather's expectations came true, and Apanuugpak evidently had a very loud voice.

Nunalleq

Unangik: Ukut-wa call' waniw' aqumgaviput ukut wan' nunallruut call' ukut. Yungqetullruut ukut ciuliamta ciuliaritnek yungqetullrungatut ukut. Ukaqvallaugut ukut.

Tua-i anangniyarluteng tamaa-i kainiq'ngaqameng uksumi nurutaqameng pitullrullinilriit.

Kainiqurayuitellruut-gguq avani ukut wani Qaluyaat ukut, ingrit ukut, Qaluyaarmiut ukut.

Ataucimi taugaam tua-i kaillrulliniut. Ukut-wa waniw' pillrungatelalriit ukut waniw'.

Yaavet yaa-i Cev'amun anangniyarluteng tua-i piiyaaqellrullinilriit.

Tua-i-am taukut ciunrita imkurluki, tua-i-wa matarrluteng yuranrilkata akilisngaitniluki neqkaitnek tamaa-i pillrullinikait.

Tua-i-am pingaitelliniiceteng, tua-i kemgitellrit tua-i tangerrsuamegteki-am pillrullinikait tuaten tua-i.

Tua-llu cali utercameng maavet, wani tua-i up'nerkami-am, anguscii-ganateng, taukut tua-i kaigluteng tua-i tekilluteng tuavet. Wavet waniw' pillrulliniut ukurmiunun Cev'armiut.

Aren tuani imat'am ayakataameng, Qissunar augna, angalkuata pillinii, tut'ellni una, tamalkuita ellaitnun, tut'ellra una, kuigem qukaa, tut'elqurluku arviisqelluku. Tut'elqurluku tua-i arvilliniluteng qanellra una aturluku tua-i.

Cunawa-gguq wani neqet allamiku tamaavet Qissunamun iterngairulluki angalkum taum pillrullinikai. Tua-i tuaggun akinaurluki.

Tua-i kaigngata, maani maa-i, wani waniw' pillrulliniut cal' Cev'armiut ukut, akinaullrulliniit.

Nukalpiaq tauna tungunqulluni waten up'nerkami tua-i anguluni tau-mek. Aipani pillinia, una yuurqaaraam aipaa uqulirluku pisqelluku, ukut-llu ukurmiut piat carrarmek taugaam uqirluku.

Ukut tua-i wani uqip'allret allanret tamaa-i unguvang'ermeng qamiqurrit tua-i meq'ertaqluteng tua-i melqungssagairulluteng.

Atam tua-i piani tamaa-i qamuurtallrit can'gurneruuq. Unguvangraata tamaa-i tua-i qamuraqluki pilangluki, tua-i unguvaarkaunrirluki. Tua-i-gguq uquariqluteng taumek tua-i yuurqaarmek imartulriamek.

Nunalleq[11]

Simeon Agnus: This other place here where we are sitting was also an old village site. This place once seemed to be occupied by the forebearers of our ancestors. This site is a more recent site.

In the past, when they experienced a food shortage, they evidently went to other places to survive.

They say Qaluyaat here, these mountains here, these Qaluyaarmiut [people of Nelson Island] didn't constantly experience famine in the past.

They evidently only experienced famine once. I think it was the people of this village.

They evidently went to Cev'aq over there to survive [famine].

The people of that village told them that if they didn't undress and dance, they wouldn't provide them with food as payment.

Since they wouldn't provide them with any [food], since they wanted to see how thin they were, they evidently told them to do that.

Then when [the people of Nelson Island] returned to this village, during spring, since the people from that place couldn't catch enough food, they arrived here starving. The people of Cev'aq evidently came to this site [to survive famine].

I forgot to mention that before [the Nelson Islanders] left [Cev'aq to return home], their shaman told them that they should all use his footsteps as they crossed the Qissunaq River [to create one set of footprints]. They used his footsteps and crossed, following his request.

Evidently the shaman had them do that to prevent fish from entering the Qissunaq River the following year. He took revenge on those people in that way.

When they were starving, at this place here, they took revenge on the people of Cev'aq.

A great hunter caught an adult bearded seal during spring. He told his wife to put a lot of seal oil in the other broth soup that they prepared, but to only put a little seal oil in the broth served to the people of this village.

Their guests who were served an excessive amount of seal oil, although they were alive [after they ate the soup], their hair fell out, and they became completely bald.

The place up there where the people were dragged and placed is a grassy area. Although they were alive, [the Nelson Islanders] started to drag them along the ground to that place, so they would all die. They consumed too

Quyuita tua-i unguvangraata qamurluk' tua-i, unguvangairutaqata tagutaqluki.

Tuaggun-gguq tua-i akinaullruit ukurmiut waniw' anangniyallermeggni tuaten matarrluki yurallerteng tamana akilitellruat.

Tua-ll' ukut waniw' nunallret ukut waniw' aruluteng tuqullruut yuit. Tua-i-w', qaingit-wa tua-i aruluteng pillilriit. Ukut tua-i yuillruut-gguq tua-i ukut wani tua-i aruluteng.

Tua-i-w' pupigluteng pillilriit cakneq tua-i qaingit. Unguvang'ermeng tua-i kemgit makut igqaqengluteng. Arunillrularait ukut waniw' ukut nunallret ukut.

Kangrilnguq: Tamaani tamaa-i unguvaurlungraata qamurluk' ayautelallratni iliit-am qaneurlulliniluni qamullragni, "Aqsarrluugaagka nanguugarciiqelriik!" Tua-i ellani nallunriteurluryaaqngamiu.

Augna call', Chevak-armiunek nunait aprumanritellruut tamatum nalliini, Qissunamiunek taugaam ak'a tamaani.

Tamaani ciuqliput caperrnarqellruut. Ellaita taugaam unakengnaqlermeggnek akluluteng yuullermeggni, canek tua-i waten kass'allarnek aturaitqapiarluteng. Qerrullikluki, pilugukluki, atkukluki nunamiutaat unakelteng pillermeggni tamaani caperrnarqellruut.

Taumek tamaa-i tamatum nalliini tua-i-w' umyuarteqtuvkangnaqluki ayagyuateng yuullrullinilriit, cakneq ellangqertelluki tamaa-i waten elluarrluki pillerkaat pitekluku.

Unangik: Ak'allaugut ukut nunallret, pingkut taugaam kinguqliqluki. Taugaam ukut wan' nunallret ukut aruluteng tuqullruut-gguq yuit. Aruluteng tamarmeng tua-i tuquluteng.

Uitanqigtevkenateng tua-i wani.

much broth mixed with lots of seal oil.

Although they were still alive, they dragged them all there, brought them up there when they knew that they wouldn't live.

That's how the people of this village took revenge on those people [of Cev'aq] for having them undress and dance when they went to that place to survive.

And this old village site here, the people who lived here died when their flesh started rotting. Their flesh probably rotted. It is said the people of this village all died when their flesh rotted.

Severe sores probably formed all over their bodies. Although they were still alive, the skin on their bodies started to fall off. They mentioned that the flesh of the people of this old village rotted.

Paul John: During that time, even though those poor people were still alive, when they dragged their bodies along the ground, one poor person evidently said when two people were dragging his body, "You're going to chafe my belly!" That's what he said because the poor thing was aware.

Also, they weren't referred to as people of Chevak back in those days, but they were called Qissunamiut [people of Qissunaq, the ancestral home of people from Chevak] long ago.

Our ancestors in the past were remarkable. Back when they lived only having clothing and implements made of things that they tried to obtain on their own, they had no Western-made possessions at all. They were remarkable back when they made the land animals they obtained into pants, skin boots, and parkas.

That's why in the past they tried to prepare their young people to have common sense, to have a great sense of awareness so that they would lead good lives.

Simeon Agnus: This village site is old, but the ones up there are older. But this village site here, it is said the people who lived here all died from their flesh rotting. They all rotted and died.

They didn't live here again.

Umkumiut

Anguyaluk: Miktellemnek ayaglua tua-i, yuuciqluku Umkumiunun upagturluta up'nerkaraqan.

Maani tua-i April-aami anelranglalriit aklumeggnek tukuullrunrilamengllu tua-i, carrateng ilaita nekaitaqata ciumek ayaulluki piaqluteng.

Tua-i-ll' kinguakun anelrautarkairuskuneng, tua-i carra'urluteng tamalkuita anelraulluki. Tukuullrunritut, caitellruut; tua-i imairluku ena upagaqluteng maavet.

April-aam tamaani iluani anelrangaqluteng, taugaam qanikcarluni. Iliikun maani pelatekaanek-llu qiliqerluki muragat, tua-i pelatekaanek qiliqerluki qanikcaq-wa man' uruksailkii. Uitavingqerraqluta.

Ilait nengqerrluteng nepianek, nevunek nengqerrluteng.

Iliini tua-i ella natquigtaqluni-llu kiagpailgan tamaa-i anelralaamta. Unugmi nenglliraqluteng. Tua-i taugken tupagnaurtua cingquksuaralriamun kumartelliniaqata unuakumi.

Arrssaungameng tua-i aklullraarateng tamalkuita ayaulluki ayagaqluteng. Maa-irpagtun pivkenateng, nepiarrlainarnek nengqerraqluteng, nevulegnek nengqerrluteng qasgirluteng-llu.

Qasgiq tauna ak'allauluni tulugnek-llu ayapruterluni. Iteryararluni uaggun uivenqellriamek, qulmun ukinerkun itraqluteng. Wangkuta tua-i tuss'ariqerluta mayussaagluta mayuraqluta.

Tauna tua-i qasgiq angutet up'nerkami eyiumaaqluku. Qavarvikluku, calivikluku. Angullugaat uitauraraqluteng tuani.

Tua-i-ll' nernarikaki, qantanek avurtellua-ll' wii angulluarraat qantait aqvavkarluki.

Aanaka keniraqami, ciuqlirmek pitaqata, unaken unangkenganek pitaqata, angullugaat qantait imirturarraarluki, tuamtell' qasgimun aguqurtelluki.

Payugciurlua qasgimun, kiima-ll' payugciyugngallruama. Payugqurluki tua-i piaqluki.

Umkumiut[12]

Martina John: From the time I was little, it was part of our way of life that we always moved to Umkumiut during spring.

They would begin to head down the coast during April, and since they didn't have many possessions, they would bring their few belongings beforehand when they had no room to bring them along on their trip.

Then afterward, when they had nothing else to bring down, they brought all their few possessions down with them. They didn't have many possessions, they didn't have much; they took everything inside their homes and moved here [to Umkumiut from Nightmute].

They'd start heading down [to Umkumiut] during April, but there was snow around. Sometimes they'd just put a tent over a wood frame, they'd just place a tent over it, and here the snow hadn't melted in the surrounding area. Those were our dwellings.

Some people had sod homes, real sod homes.

Sometimes there would be blowing snow along the ground outdoors, since we would move down the coast before summer. It was cold at night [inside homes]. But I would wake to hear wood popping when they lit the stove in the morning.

Since they were poor, they would bring all their few possessions when they'd leave. Unlike nowadays, they all had sod homes, homes made with soil, and they had a *qasgi.*

The *qasgi* was old, and it had ivory hand supports. There was a round entryway along the front of the *qasgi,* and they'd go inside by going up through that hole. We'd just use something for a stepping stool and try to lift ourselves up and go up.

The men stayed in the *qasgi* during spring. They slept there, they worked there. The elderly men always stayed there.

And when it was time for them to eat, they also had me go and gather bowls and retrieve the bowls of the few elderly men.

When my mother cooked when they caught their first animal from the ocean, after filling the elderly men's bowls, she'd then have me bring them over to the *qasgi.*

I would constantly go and give food to people in the *qasgi,* since I was the only one who was able to go and give them food [in my family]. I would

Angutet tua-i nek'ellruat qasgiq, taugaam makut ayagyuaqsilriit-llu nemeggni uitaaqluteng. Tan'gaurluut aipailnguut atakuaqan tupigaaraat tegumiaqluki agngeciqut qasgimun pegg'aryugnaunateng-llu. Agengluteng qasgimun inarcarturaqluteng.

Tamaani qamigarnariaqan, atam ayagyaratupiallruut.

Iliini qavainanemni tupakarnaurtua unuakumi-llu agayulrianun tupagaqlua Agayunruaqan unugmi agayullerkarteng cakaarpek'naku ayagatullruameng. Unugmi agayulrianun tupagaqlua, angutet ayakatalriit quyu'urrluteng enem iluanun tamaa-i agayutullratni.

Tua-i-ll' nutaan cass'at piciqanka iliikun *two*-klaagluni-llu. Tua-i inarcecuaqerluteng makluteng ayagaaqluteng.

Iliini cal' tua-i Agayuneq nagutekaqluku. Tununermun ayallerkarteng nerilegutekluku Maqinermi, atracuaqerluteng tagluteng Tununermun ayagyarturaqluteng ikamrarnarqaqan. Ikamrarnarqellran, tamaa-i ikamrarnarqaqan arvirturaaqluteng.

Tua-i-ll' pisciigallikuneng nutaan kiangekan ikamrarciigallikuneng qanikcairuskan nutaan agayuyanrirluteng. Wangkuta taugaam pekluta piyugngalriani maaken tua-i ayagluta arvirturalallrulriakut.

Angutet agayullerkarteng cakaarpek'naku, qamigaquqatangermeng patagtung'ermeng agayuqerrlainaraqluteng Agayunermi.

Taugken tua-i ayagluteng qamigautnek inguqiqerluki qayat ayagaqluteng pekqurluteng. Tua-i tamaa-i qamigamek aprutkelallrullikiit.

Un'gaavet nengllitullrullian, ak'akik' un'gani kangia uitatullruuq Ulurruum nuniini.

Tamaa-i-llu anelraqarraarqamta Up'nerkillermiut tekilluki arnaungramta ikamratullrulriakut, taperrnarrluggluta tamaaken Up'nerkillermiunek.

Tua-i taukgen iliikun qavartaraluteng-llu angutet qamigaumaaqluteng.

Tua-i-ll' unavet pisciigalkuneng agaatmun ikamrautelluteng ayagluteng, wagg'uq uumun Kangirpagmun. Ernerni qavcini tua-i qamigaumaaqluteng tua-i agaani.

constantly go and give them food.

The *qasgi* was a home to the men, but these others, including the younger ones, stayed in their homes. In the evening, the young men who weren't married would start to head to the *qasgi* holding twined grass mats, and they wouldn't stay up late. They'd start heading to the *qasgi* to sleep.

Back then, when it was time to go seal hunting, the people used to leave very early in the morning.

Sometimes, while sleeping, I'd suddenly wake, even in the mornings, to people having religious services on a Sunday night, since they would go hunting without disregarding their duty to attend church. At night, I would wake to people attending religious services, back when men gathered inside the home for religious services.

I'd check the clock and sometimes it would be two o'clock in the morning. They'd sleep for just a short while, and then they'd wake and go hunting.

Sometimes they were held back [from hunting] on Sundays. Hindered on Saturdays because of traveling to Tununak [to attend church], they'd go down to the ocean for a short while on Saturday, then they went back to shore to leave for Tununak when the trail was good for sled travel. When the trail was good for sled travel, they always went across [to Tununak].

But when they were unable to travel, when snow started to melt during summer, when they were unable to travel with sleds when the snow was gone, they stopped going to church [at Tununak]. But those of us who were able to walk would leave from here and go across [to Tununak] all the time.

The men never disregarded their obligation to attend church services, and even when they were about to go seal hunting, although they were in a hurry, they always attended church on Sunday.

But then they'd leave, placing their kayaks on top of kayak sleds, and they'd travel by walking. That's probably the reason why [seal hunting] is called *qamigaq* [kayak sled].

They'd go down there, and since it was cold in the past, the bay [with open water] used to be far down near Ulurruk.

And when we first went down the coast [to Umkumiut], although we were women, we'd use sleds to travel and reach Up'nerkillermiut, gathering *taperrnarrluut* [wilted coarse seashore grass that had grown the previous year] from Up'nerkillermiut.

Sometimes the men would spend nights and seal hunt for a long time.

And when they were unable to go down [near Ulurruk], they'd let others take them by sled across there to the place they called Kangirpak [Big *kangiq*

Tua-i caqerluteng yug' agiirciiquq. Tamaa-i-gguq uurcalria. Agaaken imarpiim akianek. Tekiskuni tua-i qanemciluni kinkut aqvaisqelluki pitaitnek aqvalgiisqelluki.

Angutet ayaumaqulaata, wangktua-llu arnaungramta tamaa-i ikamrarluta aqvaigaqluta.

Ataucirqumek-wa wiinga Kangirpagmun aqvaillrulrianga ikamrat maliggluki, aqvalgirlua-gguq.

Un'gaaken-llu cali tuaten tua-i uurcaq agiirtaqan tekilluni qanemciaqan aqvaiquraqluta. Taugaam aarnaritullruuq, qulinret-llu angkayagluteng un'gaani nenglairutaqan.

Up'nerkami tua-i tuaten pilallruut. Ciuqlir' una pitaqerraaq qeleksuunaku nayirraungraan. Kemek yugnun tamalkuitnun nerevkaraqluku, ciuqlirmek tua-i pitaqata.

Pitetungraata, pitenraranrilengraata, unangkengaq una taqukaq ellaita kiimeng nerevkenaku, nunat tamarmeng nerqaqluki.

Tua-i-ll' kinguani nutaan, nutaan tua-i pikameggnek piluteng, pitaqluteng. Ellaita tua-i nutaan qelekluki caliaqluki.

Tuamtell' tua-i caqutekiungluki uqut; caqutekiurluki uqut tamaaken taqukat amiitnek. Qerrurarugaat ellami it'gimaluteng.

It'gait-llu makut amiiyaarturluki, tamaa-i caqutekameggnek piaqameng. Maa-irpacetun qaltanun ekurluki piiyuitellruut. Taqukarrlainarnun ekurluki pitullruut.

Tua-i egvailgata tamakut caqungnaqa'artaqluki uquuteteng. Tuamtell' kemgit kinengyaliquluki. Aulukluki arnat tua-i.

Qaqiuskuneng tuamtellu iqalluarpiit pingkata, iqalluarpiit waten tua-i nallunaitaqluteng. Qamigainanratni man'a ketvut cikurtairutaqan, unani atercequralriani cali qayat uitauraraqluteng, cikurrarni anelraqtaalriani una-i pissuraqluteng.

Nutaan tamakut pitait cugg'erit elquangareskata tua-i iqalluarpiit tekitellrit nallunriraqluki.

(bay)]. They would go seal hunting across there for a number of days.

After a while, a person would come toward the village. They referred to that person as *uurcalria* [one announcing his catch]. He'd come from across there, from across the ocean. Then he'd arrive, announcing which people needed to go and retrieve the animals they caught from there.

Since the men were gone, even though we were women, we'd take sleds and go and retrieve the animals they caught.

I went to Kangirpak once to retrieve the animals they caught, accompanying those who went by sled, *aqvalgirlua* [I went to retrieve animals they caught] as they call it.

And when a person announcing his catch approached from downcoast, when he mentioned who caught seals, we'd also go and retrieve the animals they caught. But it used to get dangerous, and the crevices in the ice were very large down the coast when it became warm out.

That's what they used to do during spring. They never kept the first animal they caught, even if it was just a ringed seal. They'd distribute all the meat and feed everyone when they caught a seal for the first time.

Although they regularly caught animals, even if they hadn't caught one for the very first time, they didn't eat the seal they caught alone, but they'd feed the entire village with it.

Then finally the next time, they caught animals for themselves. They'd keep those animals and work on them.

And again, they'd start preparing containers for the blubber; they'd prepare containers out of seal skins for the blubber. Many sealskin pokes would be inflated outside with their feet skinned.

They'd also carefully skin their small feet when they prepared sealskin pokes. They didn't place [pieces of blubber] inside buckets like they do nowadays. They always placed them inside sealskin pokes.

Before the blubber rendered, they tried to put them inside containers. They'd cut their meat into strips to dry. The women were responsible for processing and preparing them.

And when they were finished working on [seals], when the herring started to run, the herring run was obvious in the following way. While they were still seal hunting, when the ocean down below our village was free of ice, kayaks would begin to stay along floating ice down there, and they would hunt down there among the few, floating ice sheets that were heading up and down the bay.

When the animals they caught started to have herring eggs around their

Cikutairuskan-llu nutaan cikut atertenriqaki, tuamtell' kuvyirluteng iqalluarpagcuutnek.

Allanek pissuyuitellruut taugaam manignaleryagnek saginek-llu.

Natmun ayagavkenateng ukut ketiitni kanani iqsaagatullruut qayak itullukek, natmun ayagluteng pivkenateng. Taugken tua-i unangaqluteng manignaleryiit tamaa-i piullratni.

Tua-i taugken neqliateng, cali neqlinarikateng egmian-llu pivkenaki, apqemeggni qikutani, qikutanun tamaa-i pitateng piuratullruamegteki, imkunun tua-i nuna nayugluku iluturiluku. Neqkameggnek iqalluarpagnek tamana imiraqluku.

Maaken cali, waten qagaa-i taperrnat naumalriit, qanikcairtaqan taperrnarrlugnek pit'ngaqluteng piirritkameggnek. Tamakut neqet agaarkat piirritkaitnek pit'ngaqluteng arnat.

Tua-i-ll' neqlingluteng tua-i neqlingluteng, initateng imiquluki.

Imiqumarikunegteki-llu tuamtell' tamakut uqut caqullret, it'gaitgun qillerqelluki. Tuamtell' ayaulluki nunam akuliinun ellillerkameggnun, wagg'uq uquucilleryarturluteng.

Agaavet Kaviarmun, natmun tua-i uquucillervigkameggnun nunam akuliinun elliyarturluki.

Tuamtell' tua-i iqalluarpiit tamakut kinqata, nin'amayuuciluteng cali allragni uqunek imillermeggnek caqulirluki. Natmun ekularivkenateng, taqukanun taugaam tamakunun assigtaqluki caqutellret nin'amayuuciquaqluteng.

Tuamtell' kinrumalriit, yaassiillernun ekurpek'naki tut'anun, tut'anun tutmauqurluki qeculteng imiulluki tupiganun. Tupiganun nek'egtenqegcaarluk' tutmauqurluki tamakut kinerneret ekurluki.

Elagyangqetullruut taugaam cali maani. Tua-i-ll' elagyamun tamaavet, ellami piuraqarraarluki.

snouts, they knew that the herring had arrived.

And when the water was ice free, and ice was no longer floating around, they'd set herring nets.

They didn't try to obtain other types of fish, but they'd try to get *manignaleryiit* [Pacific cod] and halibut.

They didn't travel anywhere, but they'd jig for fish with hooks down there below this place by connecting two kayaks side-by-side, and they didn't travel anywhere else. But they'd obtain fish back when *manignaleryiit* were around.

But the fish they cut to dry, when it was time for them to cut and prepare [herring] for drying, they didn't immediately work on them, but they always placed the fish they caught inside pits, what they call *qikutat,* inside deep pits dug in the ground. They'd fill that pit with the herring they would harvest and consume.

And from around here, you see the *taperrnat* [coarse seashore grass] that have grown out there, when the snow melted, they would start to gather *taperrnarrluut* to use for braiding fish. The women would begin to obtain grass for braiding the fish that would hang to dry.

Then they began to cut and process fish for drying, and they'd fill their fish racks.

When they finished filling the sealskin pokes, they'd tie them along their feet. Then they'd bring them to a place where they would store them underground, *uquucilleryarturluteng* [they'd go and store seal-oil pokes in underground storage caches] as they called it.

They'd go across to Kaviarmiut and other places where they usually went to store their seal oil underground.

And again, when those herring dried, they'd prepare *nin'amayuut* [fat, partially dried herring, stored and aged in seal oil] using sealskin pokes they had filled the previous year with seal oil. They didn't place them inside other types of containers, but they'd use those old sealskin pokes to store them to prepare *nin'amayuut.*

And again, they didn't store the dried [herring] inside cardboard boxes, but they'd place them inside *tut'at* [twined grass storage containers, lit., "ones stepped on"], periodically stepping on the dried herring that they had pulled from the strands of braided herring as they placed them inside twined grass containers. They'd place the dried herring inside twined grass storage containers, constantly stepping on them to pack them down tightly.

They also had storage caches that were partially underground here [at

Ilait-am qassavleruluki pillret, apqiitnek puqelqeraqluteng tamakut tut'at imait. Puqelqerqata anlluki piaqluki, anlluki caggluki kinevsiarraarluki ataam nutaan cali elliaqluki.

Tua-i-ll' imkurluteng cali, tamakut amirkatamegnek nillaringluteng angutet. Amirkat tamakut meqciralteng nillangluki.

Nillaringluteng tua-i nunam qainganun, apeqmegnek qengat nillaucirluteng. Augkut allegturluki avatait, muraganek kapurqurluki nillautengqetullruut, ussukcaquvkenaki.

Nunam qaingani tua-i kinercirluki. Kinrumariqreskata-llu arnat imkut pilagtuarluteng naterkauluki navgurturluki.

Tua-i-llu ilait akikessaagarluki qavavet tengalrarluteng ayaulluki. Uqunek tuaten akingqessaagarluteng Mamterillermiut nuniitnun ayagalluki cipneteng.

Tua-i-ll' ut'reskuneng nutaan tua-i caarkairuskuneng, cakartairuskan nutaan cali natmun calliggnaluteng qanengluteng.

Aren tamaa-i imat'am up'nerkami-llu ilait qayat cimirnarqelriit amiit cimingetullrukait-llu.

Tua-i-llu amirkaq tauna arnat talliman mingeqluku. Amirluteng-gguq. Arnat tallimauluteng qayarkaq mingqetullruat tamaa-i qamigaqungvailegmeng.

Tua-i tamakut kinngekata nutaan caarkaireskuneng uitatairuskuneng maani, tuamtell' upaketaarluteng kuiggarnun, Kaviarmiunun, Nangtumun, Tapruar-llu. Wavet-llu Al'aqucimun. Yuut tua-i avverqelluteng upagaqluteng, quyurmeng pivkenateng.

Piviggameggnun ayagaluteng. Tamaa-i call' naternanek ciumek, iqalluarurrluteng-llu kumlangkan. Arnat qaluquluteng.

Ikani tangvalallrenka nangelriit tayim', kiugna taugaam tua-i acacungaqa kiimi kia-i qalutullerni napalria.

Umkumiut]. They'd place [the containers filled with herring] inside that partially underground cache after keeping them outside for a while.

Some of the dried herring that had been stored a little raw and not fully dried, some of the contents of the *tut'at* got soft from being warm, *puqelqerluteng* as they called it. When they became soft from getting warm, they'd take them out and scatter them and dry them for a while longer, and then they'd place them inside [grass storage containers] again.

Then the men would start to stretch out and dry the skins of the young bearded seals that they caught. They'd start to stretch out and dry the skins that they had dehaired.

They'd begin to stretch out skins to dry on top of the ground, using what they call *qengat* [wooden pegs] for stretching out the skins. They'd tear holes along the outside of the skin, and they'd insert wooden pegs in them when they stretched skins, not using metal nails to nail them down.

They'd dry them on top of the ground. And when they eventually dried, the women cut out patterns for their skin boot soles when they cut them to pieces.

Then they'd bring some of the skins up [to the Kuskokwim River] to sell, bringing them up there using boats with sails. They'd even bring their extra seal oil to Bethel to sell.

And when they returned home, when they no longer had any work to do [at Umkumiut], when there was nothing else to do, they'd begin to talk about moving somewhere else.

Oh, I forgot to mention that back in those days during spring, they'd start to replace some of the kayak skin coverings that needed to be replaced.

Then five women would sew the skin covering of the kayak. They called it *amirluteng* [sewing the skin covering]. Five women sewed the skin covering that would go over the kayak frame before they started seal hunting.

When [the fish] started to dry and they had no other work to do here [at Umkumiut], they'd begin to move to the sloughs, to Kaviarmiut, Nangtuq [from *nangte-*, "to abuse or torment"], and Tapruar [Skin rope]. And they'd also move to Al'aquciq. The people would split up and go their own ways and move, and they didn't move together as one group.

They'd travel and move to their customary places. They'd obtain flounder first, and then the fish were replaced by tomcod when it got cold. The women would periodically dipnet.

The people who I used to watch [dipnet for tomcod] over there are all gone now, except for my *acacungaq* [lit., "little father's sister," referring to Albertina

Qaluyarluteng qaluqutullruluteng, tamaa-i naternanek iqalluanek-llu pitaqluteng.

Tuamtell' tua-i kinercirluki tamakut pitait. Qimugtenun tuaten; qimugteteng tuaten nerevkarturluki.

Tuamtell' tua-i kinrumarikata tamakut, tuatmell' itraqanirluteng qavavet Tuqsuum iluanun, arulairvigluteng kiani Kass'aurlurmek pitukiitnek. Tua-i qimugtaita-w' tamaa-i nerengnaqelriit arulairturcet'lallrullikait.

Nutaan-llu tua-i man'a kumlangareskan, qakurnalangareskan nutaan uksuivigkameggnun kiavet Negtemun itrarluteng.

ଓ

Aquitulput wangkuta-w' tua-i ayagyuarluta tamaa-i maani; maani maa-i nunaniqpiatullruuq. Man'a maa-i, yaaken ing'um elavkaam keluani ilutulria; qukitiimi atam tuani qukitiitullruut. Tua-i-ll' tamana kiagpak *baseball*-arviuluni, inuguarviuluni; tua-i inuguarvikluku.

Canguarturtelluki, tua-i yuungnaqevkarluki tamakut inuguat pitullruukut yugcetun.

Pinariaqan uqiqurcetaqluki; pinariaqan kelgivkaraqluki. Tua-i yuut caciryaraitnek, caciryarait tua-i.

Tua-ll' tan'gaurluq una tan'gaurluq una taikan tauna angutnguaq ayautelluku uugnarrsurluni wall'u tekcitayaarrssurluni. [*ngel'artuq*]

Uugnaraat-llu keniraqluki. Tua-i tekiutellriit-am ciuniurluki keniraqluki.

Wiinga-ll' tamaani uugnaraat-llu qungvakevkenaki. Inuguamnun atkugkiurluki. Quyak'acagaraqlua amiirluki, nillacuarluki kinercirluki, iquarrluki-ll' atkuliluki-llu.

Tua-i yuut tangelput maligtaquluki. Tuaten pitullruukut.

Tuamtell' tua-i tamaani up'nerkaraqan waten qugtaqunariqerreskan, angutet qasperit ayaulluki ull'arrluki aliitgun qill'errluki, muragayagarnek imirluki atmagluki ut'ruqu'urluki.

Ellami-ll' tamaa-i, kaassautellruar *five gallon*-aat avgitgun kenillengqetullruluta maniarluta-ll' tuaggun uqulegmek.

Ii-i, ciumek nutarinraq uquq ukliurarraarluku, maniarrsuutmun-llu ekluku qallarvaulluku, egnera allakarluku.

Dull] up there who is the only person still living among all the people who used to dipnet [for tomcod and flounder].

They would go and dipnet from time to time, and they'd obtain flounder and tomcod.

Then they'd dry the fish they caught. They also fed the fish to their dogs; they also constantly fed their dogs.

And when those fish dried, they'd move farther up to the Tuqsuk River, and they used to stop upriver at a place they call Kass'aurluq. They probably constantly stopped along the way because of their dogs that needed to eat.

Then when this area started to get cold, when frost started to form, they'd move up to Nightmute, where they would stay during winter.

The many different games we played when we were young here [in Umkumiut]; this place was a joyous and lively place. This area here, the deep area that is back behind the wooden building; they had a Fourth of July celebration at that place. And that area was a baseball field all summer long, it was a place where they played with dolls; it was our doll-playing area.

We would pretend to have the dolls carry out work and try to make a living just like people.

When it was time, we'd have [our dolls] give seal parties; when it was time, we'd have them invite other people over to their homes to eat. We'd have them carry out the same responsibilities as people.

And when a boy came over, we'd have him take that male doll with him to go hunt mice or small birds. [*laughing*]

And we'd cook the mice. We'd be pleased with the things they brought when they arrived, and we'd cook them.

And I didn't find mice creepy back then. I'd make my dolls' parkas out of them. I'd be so grateful for them and skin them, and I'd stretch the little skins out to dry and tan them, and I'd cut patterns and make parkas out of them.

We'd imitate things that we saw people do. That's what we did.

And again, during spring, when it was time to gather wood, we'd take men's hooded garments with us and turn them inside out and tie them along their sleeves, and fill them with sticks and pack them on our back and bring them home.

And outdoors, we had stoves made out of half of a five-gallon gas container, and we'd use them to make fry bread with seal oil.

Yes, we'd first cut a fresh piece of blubber into pieces, and then we'd put

Tuaken-llu tua-i egneranek nutaramek uqirluta uqulegnek maniarluta.

Mukaaliuqutullruluta call' angutet ayagpailgata taquarkiurluki.

Tamakut pitaqerraat, ciuqlirmek nayireskan, nayireskan tua-i una amiiquniu qapiarraarluku, uquirluku.

Uqua-llu tua-i tamak'acagaan qantamun ekluku qasgimun agulluku, qaillun tua-i waten ukliaq pitaluni, angtaurluni.

Tauna tua-i qantaq imirluku; uqucuarii taum nayim qantamun ekluku qasgimun agulluku.

Tua-i-llu qanerciqut, "Aruqsaliyarci." Tengrunaqluni. Ak'a qantanek aqvat'laagluta nemtenun qasgimun tuavet, qasgimun tuavet it'ruraluta.

Tua-i-ll' itqumta aqumluta tamakut qantat imirturarraartelluki uterrluta.

Arnat tan'gaurluut-llu tamarrarmeng. Kiingan tua-i piciryaraqngameg-teggu cakneq quyaluta tuaten qanrutaqakut aruqsaliyaasqelluta.

Tuamtell' tua-i angelriamek piskan ciuqlirmek, tua-i piquratungermi allrakuaqan, ciuqliq taugaam una up'nerkami pitaqerraalleq pitullruat.

Tamaa-i tungunqumek maklagmek piskan, tuamtellu nulirra uqiquqatangaarrluni. Tua-i nalluvkenaku uqiquliyallerkarteng tuavet.

Ciuqliq tua-i tauna uqiutekluku yugnun, aruqutekluku.

Tua-i-llu keggatii una cali, angutnun qasgimelngurnun keggatiin uqua qasgimun cali agulluku, qaillun angtaurluki ukliluki. Tua-i-gguq cuanrartuq. Cuanrauluni. Tenguanek, iliikun tenguitnek ilaluki qasgimun tuavet agutaqluki.

Tua-i-ll' uqiqurluku, tuamtell' wangkuta maa-i kevgautullrulriakut tamakunun, qanercuutetgun piiyuitellruata.

Enet iquitnek ayagluta qanruqu'urluki enet, arnat tamalkuita. Un'gakenllu call' piarkangqerkuneng cali piluteng.

Tua-i kesianek ukut nunat tamarmeng tuatnatuluteng. Nunat yuit tamarmeng piuratuluteng, piuratullruluteng.

it in a frying pan and boil it, and set aside the oil that rendered.

Then we'd use the rendered oil from the fresh blubber to make bread fried with seal oil.

We'd also prepare bread before the men left to hunt, making provisions for them.

Those first animals that were caught [at Umkumiut], if they caught a ringed seal for the first time, when someone caught a ringed seal, when they removed the skin, after skinning it from the neck opening and removing the carcass through the hole, they'd remove the blubber.

Then they'd place all the blubber inside a bowl and bring it to the *qasgi*, and the pieces of blubber that were cut were about this size.

They'd fill that bowl; they'd place the small amount of blubber of that ringed seal in a bowl and bring it to the *qasgi*.

Then they'd announce, "Go and attend *aruqsaq* [a distribution of small pieces of blubber given to children]." We were eager to take part in it. Then we'd run and get some bowls from our homes, and we'd go inside the *qasgi* one by one.

Then when we went inside, we'd sit down, and after they filled our bowls with those [pieces of blubber], we'd return home.

All girls and boys participated. Since it was their only custom, we'd be so grateful when they'd tell us to go and take part in *aruqsaq*.

And again, if he caught a large [seal] for the first time, although he caught them every year previously, [they distributed] the first seal he caught during spring.

If he caught an adult bearded seal, his wife would plan to have a seal distribution party. The people around would know that they would go and attend a seal party at that person's place.

They distributed the seal meat and blubber of their first catch to people.

And the upper torso section of the seal, they'd also bring the blubber of the upper torso to the men at the *qasgi*, and they'd cut the pieces a certain size. They referred to that as *cuanrarluteng*. Sometimes, they'd include their livers and bring them to the *qasgi* there.

Then they'd distribute the seal meat and blubber at a seal party, and we were messengers for those people, back when they didn't announce events using VHF radios.

Starting from the last house, we'd inform all the houses, all the women. And if there were people to tell down on the shore, they'd also go and tell them.

Everyone in the village constantly took part in it. All the residents would

Umkuuk

Anguyaluk: Ingna-gguq yaa-i Umkuuk, una nuuk. Ugna-gguq ua-i Umkuugnek atengqertuq, qaingani-wa elanelleq nuukacagiini.

Tua-i-llu uscami, kan'a kana-i kuigaaraam akiani teggalquq waten ayuqelria, uscami, pagaaken tuavet tuc'ami Ustellermek piaqluku.

Tauna-gguq tua-i Nunivaarmiunek aciani qavalrianek qayanek tuquskengellruuq. Tauna tua-i qavallratni ustellermini, tamakut tamaa-i tuqutellruit.

Atam Nunivaarmiut-llu qayarugaat tekirqetullruut. Qayarluteng tua-i tekitaqluteng. Tuamtell' tua-i angyangameng angyakun tag'urluteng.

Cali tua-i wangkucicetun Yupiuluteng, irniateng amarluki. Tekiciiqut-llu tengalrautam natiini qurrailitat elevvlaalriit.

Qavavirtelguluteng. Tua-i-ll' ut'reskuneng maavet tekilluteng.

Wangkuta tamaa-i pikavet Umkuuk qaingagnun mayurluta kiartengtullrulriakut. Tua-i-ll' pivakarluta piciqukut akma tua-i Cingigyam amatiinek tengalrautak, malruulutek-llu. Taugken tua-i atraqumta qanemciluta angyanek.
Tua-i-ll' ciuneqluta tekicarturciqut Nunivaarmiunguluteng.

Maaken cali ayatullruut anguterrlainauluteng taugaam. Tamakut tuneniassaagarluteng up'nerkami pitullret, maaken tua-i ayagluteng, qavcini tua-i ernerugarni tayim' cataiqaarluteng tekiqurainaraqluteng.
Maani-ll' tua-i canek aquitailameng *baseball*-allermeggnek *marble*-aallermeggnek, kaukaqulluteng tuaten. Tegurpagluteng. Tua-i canek allanek aquitaunateng pilallruut.

Nunivaarmiut-llu tua-i tekiskata, angutet aataunivkenateng tamakut-llu Nunivaarmiut aataunivkenateng *baseball*-arluteng, inglukluteng taugaam makumiut-llu. Anglanaqluteng aquingaqluteng tua-i-w' caarkaitelaameng.

do that.

Umkuuk[13]

Martina John: That place over there is called Umkuuk, this point here. That place down there is called Umkuuk, and on it is an old house pit, at the very tip of the point.

And when it broke off and came down, when that rock on the other side of the stream broke off and came down from the [cliff] top and landed there, they started calling that Ustelleq [One that eroded].

It is said that [rock] killed some kayakers from Nunivak Island who were sleeping down below. While they were sleeping and that rock broke off and came down, it killed those people.

They say many kayakers from Nunivak used to arrive here in the past. They'd arrive with kayaks. And when they started to use boats, they'd continually come up with boats.

They were Yup'ik people like us, and they'd carry their children on their backs. And when they'd arrive, somewhere along the sail would be cloth diapers flapping in the wind.

They always traveled up [to the Kuskokwim River area]. And when they returned home, they'd arrive here.

We'd go up on top of Umkuuk and search the [ocean]. And then after a while, across there beyond Cingigyaq we'd see a sail, and sometimes there would be two. And when we climbed down, we'd tell them that we had seen boats.

Then they'd head our way and arrive, and we'd see that they were people from Nunivak Island.

People from here also traveled [to the Kuskokwim], but only men went. Those people who went to trade during spring would leave from this place, and after being gone for many days, they'd arrive.

Since they had no other outdoor games to play here, they only played baseball and marbles, and they also played a game of trying to have something attached to a string land inside a hole, *kaukaqulluteng*. They'd play *tegurpak* [a game similar to pick-up-sticks where they threw sticks into the air to see how many could land on the top of their hand]. They played no other games.

And when people from Nunivak Island arrived, the men, even fathers, and people from Nunivak Island without making the excuse that they were fathers, would play baseball, but they were rivals with the people of this village. They were fun to watch when they started to play, since they had nothing else to do.

Tua-i tamaani avanicetun *school*-araullrunrilameng mikelnguit qanerturayaaqtarnaurtut ellmegcecicetun anglanaqluteng.

Qangkun tua-i agayullerkarteng cali cakaarumavkenaku; pelatekam iluani Agayunraqan agayuaqluteng quyurrarmeng. Ellait ukverumallgutkenrilamceteng ellaita piciryarameggnek cali piaqluteng.

Unangik: Tua-i camek qanerkaicaaqua, taugaam pikegkunek iciw' quliriqaasqumallrukevcia watua.

Pikna pika-i, arnak pikna nunakellruak, arnarrlainaulutek. Ayugutarinwa tauna maurluan waten tua-i cayaurcan ayallra tamalkuan tua-i taquirturalliniaqekii canimelengraan-llu.

Waten tua-i kiagmi caqerluni ayallermini taitungulluku, tua-i natmun ayauciirulluni tua-i.

Anguangami anguangelliniuq kiagmi. Piinanrani tua-i anguarpakarluni ciunra ingritangelliniuq, tua-i-w' man' tungulria. Maaten-gguq tekicartuaraa ingriq, ingriullinilria.

Mecignarian pilliniuq arnak pingkuk caniqliqlutek nangerngalriik ug'um ua-i ketiini, Umkuuk.

Umkuugnek ugkuk pituagput; Umkuuguk ugkuk. Una-w' ukaqlia Ustelleq kapusngalria ingna ukaqliq teggalquq.

Taum tua-i quliigni pikani taukuk arnak eniik uitallrulliniuq tuani.

Ugircan arnak taukuk pilliniak, nalluyugnaunaku tua-i nalluvkenaku, uniurutnayukluku tegg'anernilutek tairviin. Tua-i nall'arteqapiarlukek tekillukek.

Arnak taukuk tua-i quyaqauteklinaik tua-i, malrukaqeqarak tua-i tamarkegenka taukuk arnak tua-i aipaqsagullukek.

Waten tua-i up'nerkautaqani pingnatungaqluni; imarpigmek-wa tua-i unaken angungnaquratuluni.

Paugna pava-i cenaq ngelekluku tamaa-i-gguq ultuluni, paugna pava-i cenaq ngelekluku. Tuaten-gguq ayuqellruuq.

Makut maa-i qairuat, man'a-ll' maa-i mer'ullruyaaquq, paugna-ll' qairuaruluteng makut maa-i; qairtun ayuqluteng, ilutuqtaarluteng.

Tuani tua-i uitalliniaqelria tua-i, qasgililuni-llu angyiluni-llu amimek, taqukat amiitnek angyiluni.

Uksuucani tua-i angyani tamana qer'irluku angyani palurrluku. Muragak

Back in those days, since they weren't educated in schools, their children would speak in their dialect, and they were fun to listen to.

And [Nunivak visitors] didn't disregard their duty to hold church services; on Sundays, they would have [Swedish Covenant] church services as a group inside a tent. Since we aren't of the same faith, they'd carry out their own religious services.

Simeon Agnus: I don't really have anything to say, but you asked me to tell a story about that place up there.

The place up there, two women lived up there, just women. Then there was Ayugutarin, whose grandmother would evidently always prepare provisions for him every time he traveled, even if it was close by.

One day during summer, when [Ayugutarin] traveled, it suddenly became foggy while he was out, and he completely lost his sense of direction and didn't know where he was heading.

When he started to paddle, he continued paddling during summer. After paddling for a while, a mountain appeared ahead, a dark area. As he approached closer and closer, he saw that it was a mountain.

When it became visible, he saw two women up there standing side by side, down below that place down there, down below Umkuuk.

We call the ones down the coast from us Umkuuk; those two downcoast are called Umkuuk. Then on this side of it, the rock that is sticking in the ground on this side is called Ustelleq.

The home of those two women was evidently right on top of that up there.

When he docked along the shore, those two women told him, knowing that he was there for sure, that they were afraid he might miss that place as it was very foggy. He came straight to their place.

Those women were suddenly grateful for his arrival, and so those two women became his two wives for some time.

When spring came, he would start to hunt; he continually hunted from the ocean down there.

Back in those times, when the tide would come up, they say it would reach the very edge of the land. They said that's what it was like back then.

These rocks that look like waves and this area used to be covered by water, and the [rocks along the cliffs] up there are the image of waves; the [rocks] look like waves, becoming deep intermittently.

He evidently lived there, and he built a *qasgi* and made a skin boat out of seal skins.

When winter came, he would place his boat on a rack upside down. I used

naparyallrek uitallruuk pikan' tangtullruagka, tua-i atauciq tamaqatarluni.

Tua-i-am piciuluni iqluqutnguvkenani tua-i qulirauvkenani-ll' piciuluni tua-i Ayugutarin tauna.

Tua-i uksurluni-am, uksumi piinanrani, qasgimi piinanrani, uitainanrani, taukuk aipak malrukak itqertelliniuk angyaa qagna keglunermun putuirassaagniluku, nerrsaagniluku.

Anqerrluni pilliniuq angun una nangerngalria angutnguluni. Tua-i qasgiminun itertelluku aipaquranga'artaa, aipaquranga'artellinia. Aipaqu'urluku tua-i qasgimi uitaurlutek.

Aipaa tauna tua-i uitallragni qasgimun iternanringllliniluni, nulirran aipaa. Tauna-ll' tuani qasgimi-ll' qavarnanrirluni tauna allanra, allanellra tauna. Qavayuirulluni, taugaam aipaan payugqurluku piaqluku.

Waten tua-i imarpiqunaritaqatek, up'nerkautaqatek imarpiquaqamek ner'aqamek ikna akiqlia tua-i enrungraata qangqurluk' nerrlininaurtuq taun allanra.

Tua-i Ayugutarin una elluatuunringluni. Assinringluni tua-i assiirutengluni pian, nulirran tua-i taum aipaan kellutenglliniluku. Taukuk-llu-gguq tua-i tamarmek iternanriqapiarlutek qasgimun, it'yuirullutek.

Anngami tua-i upqaarluni anngami, yaavet acianun tua-i atrallinluni.

Muragpall'ermek mimernatulriamek tekicami, tamana mimernai kepluki tamana-ll' qupurrluku, tauna-llu mimernai ayagarkiurluki, cakiurluki, ciukiurluki, pamyurkiurluni tuaken mimernamek.

Tamana-ll' qupurrluku muragaq, tua-i muragaq atauciq tua-i camek ilavkenaku muragpall'er tamana tua-i enrurrluku taqluku qayaurrluku. Up'nerkaryarturluni-gguq qakemna.

Tua-i-llu taqngamiu tua-i, taum tua-i aipaan, taum-llu tuani uniskengaan ikayullikii, amirluku.

Tauna-ll' aipaa-ll' qayiungluni cali tua-i qayaliungluni waten up'nerkaryartuucatek, tua-i-wa imarpik pinariqataan.

Ellamun ancatek qayatek tua-i qerrecqalliniluki nenglem, qatrilukek tua-i qayakek, tatkimalutek yaani Umkuuk qaingagni pillilriik.

Tua-i qerrecqaata taum aipaan qayani tauna allanran keglunruamek

to see the old wooden posts that were up there, just one, when it was about to disappear.

This is a true story and not false, and it isn't a *quliraq* [legendary tale], but the story of Ayugutarin is a true story.

Winter came, and while he was staying inside the *qasgi* during winter, his two wives suddenly came inside and said that a wolf was trying to remove the holes along the sides of the skin boat that was lashed down, that it was trying to eat it.

He ran out and saw a man standing there. He invited him inside his *qasgi* and he became his companion. He became a companion, and they stayed inside the *qasgi.*

His wife, while they were there, stopped coming into the *qasgi,* his other wife. And his guest stopped sleeping inside the *qasgi,* the person who had been his guest. He stopped sleeping there, but his other wife continually brought him food.

When it was time for them to hunt on the ocean, when spring came and they started to go down to the ocean, when they ate, the person across from him, his guest, would eat and even crunch on bones as he ate.

Ayugutarin's health started to deteriorate. When his health started to deteriorate, his other wife began to watch over him. And it is said [his guest and his other wife] no longer came inside the *qasgi* at all.

When he went outside, after preparing, when he went out, he went down below [Umkuuk].

When he came upon a very large log with its stump and roots still attached, he removed its stump and split that wood, and he prepared its stump into deck beams and prepared kayak parts with it, making the aft parts and stern part with that stump.

Then he split that log, and he made that one large log into a kayak frame, not supplementing it with any other piece of wood. It was approaching spring outdoors at that time.

And when he finished [the frame], his wife, probably with that wife who left him helping her, sewed a skin covering for it.

And his companion also began to build a kayak during the time when spring was approaching, since it was almost time to hunt down on the ocean.

When they took their kayaks outside, the cold weather bleached their kayaks, turning them white as they were on stilts over there probably on top of Umkuuk.

When they turned white, his companion, his guest painted a wolf design

paingan `gguun aciakun qaralilillinilukuu. Qaralilinermek taqngamiu, "Kitak elpet-llu qayan qaralilirru." Ayugutarin pillinia.

Imarmiutayagaruamek qaralilillinilukuu qayani.

Tua-i pinariatek qamigarlutek atrarlutek, kanavet kana-i.

Umkuuk ketiigni kangia-gguq uitallruuq uaqvaarni uani, ug'um Qurrlurtem nuniini pilliuq tauna kangia.

Atraamek tua-i kanavet ayakataqaamek taum allanran pillinia uluqaasqelluni tunulluku.

Tunulluku piani takuyallinia tunusngarraarluku, kegluneq una tuam engeliini aqumgauralria, kingulirminun-wa tua-i piluni aqumgauralria. Qayartaunani-llu-gguq ciuqerra.

Tangvakainanrani taryumek alungeqallinilunì tauna allanra.

Tua-ll' Ayugutarin im' pillinia, uluusqengani, ulurluku ulurraarluku pillinia qayami caniani nangerngaurluni tauna allanra.

Ayugutarin pillinia, "Kitak elpet."

Tua-i tunucani, tunulluku aipaan, tunucani, tunusngarraarluku takuyallinia tuam ngeliini imarmiutayagaq una qungeskiaralria meq caumaluku.

Tangvakainanrani-ll' tua-i anglluq'alliniluni tayima. Pugnerciryaaqellinia-am pugyuunani tua-i. Pugyunrilan tua-i ayalliniluni tua-i.

Ayagluni, cakemna nuuga tekitniararluku qayaq man'a uckacagarluk paircartullinia. Ayugutarin ak'a malruka'arluni utertellinilria tungunqugnek.

Tuani tua-i imarmiutayagauluni mer'em akuliikun ayallinill'. [*ngelaq'ertuq*] Tangvagarkaunriani-ll' qayaurrluni, qayamikun ayagluni.

Augna malia tua-i tekicugpek'nani. Aipaa tauna mululuni tua-i tayima tua-i.

Tua-i pivakarluni nulirra anqetaarpakarluni, uka-i-gguq agiirtuq. Tungunquyagartelliniluni temirtem mikellranek.

Tua-i nerlutek. Ner'uk-gguq-am maaten qangqurluki, enret qangqurluki nerrlinilria.

Ayugutarin pillinia tuaten pingraan ellii cakanirngairutniluni waniwa.

on his kayak underneath the [cockpit] opening here. When he finished painting an insignia on it, he said to Ayugutarin, "Now, put a design on your kayak."

He painted a small mink design on his kayak.

When it was time for them to go seal hunting, they went down there.

It is said the ice bay with open water was down the coast from Umkuuk, farther down. The ice bay with open water was probably around Qurrlurta.

When they went down and were about to leave, his guest told him to look away from him for a second by turning his back to him.

When he turned his back to him and then turned to look at him again, he saw a wolf sitting along the edge of the shore ice, sitting on its haunches. And it is said there was no kayak in front of [the wolf].

As he was watching him, his guest [the wolf] licked some salt water.

Then when he told Ayugutarin to look away from him, he looked away, and after looking away and looking back again, he saw his guest standing next to his kayak.

He told Ayugutarin, "Now it's your turn."

Then when his companion turned his back to him, after having his back to him, when he turned to look at him, he saw a small mink squatting along the edge of the shore ice, facing the water.

While he was watching him, he dove into the water and disappeared. He waited for him to appear, and he didn't appear. Since he didn't appear, he took off.

He traveled on, and just as he was about to reach the edge [of the ice], he came upon a kayak in his path that was heavily loaded. Ayugutarin had already caught two adult bearded seals and was returning home.

He had evidently swum through the water as a little mink at the time. [*chuckles*] And when he wasn't in his view any longer, he transformed into a kayak, and traveled with his kayak.

His hunting partner didn't arrive for some time. His hunting partner [the guest] was gone for a long time.

Then once when his wife entered after repeatedly going outdoors, she said that he was approaching down there. He had caught a small, adult bearded seal, one smaller than an adult.

They ate. When they ate, he saw that [his guest] crunched on the bones as he ate.

He told Ayugutarin that although he did that, that he wasn't going to change now.

Tuamtell' tua-i kayukilan ayallilriik cali, unuaquan pingatuk.

Tua-i-am Ayugutarin tua-i qayani uciviircan utertelliniluni tekilluni. Aipaa-gguq imna tekicuunani.

Anqetaarpakarluni nulirra tauna, nulirruara tauna anqetaarpakarluni pillinia uka-i-gguq-wa agiirtellria qayani qamurluku.

Tekitnerciryaaqvimeggnek anngami, anrraarluni nulirra, pillinia, itrami piuq, pika- i-gguq pikaggun Ingrirrarteggun qaklitniarartuq qayaminek qamurluni.

Anlutek pilliniak qayaminek qamurluni tua-i qulmurtellria, qayani qamurluku. Qaklicami-ll' qayani tamana ipyuqaarluku-w' pillilria, alairtelliniuq kegluneq pikna nangerngalria.

Pikegkut pika-i Ingrirrarnek pituaput pikegkut qulemteni pikegkut. Ingrirraugut pikegkut.

Pangalegluni tayim' ip'artelliniluni.

Angalkum taum qagken ullagluku. Nanurrualek pinritamken. Nanurrualgem taum angalkum ullagyaaqellinikii nulirriryarturluku Ayugutarin. [*ngel'artuq*] Elluatuuvkenani-llu-gguq tauna tua-i nulirriryarturtii taun Nanurrualek.

Angalkuum-am qaill'-tanem nallunritau-llu? Nanurrualguniluku tua-i pillrukiit. Yaa kitek tua-i tuaten pitaluku piaqa. Ilu'urma nalluyaguskengaqa call' qanrutekciqaa.

Arliat

Nanurrualek: Imkut-ll' iciw' cikaaret unani amelkacagarluteng inartetullrulriit. Nunaniqluteng cikaayagaat.

Anguyaluk: Piiyuitellruut. Maaten ellangua cikaarcuunateng. Qanemciaqluteng cikaarnek pitullruniaqluki.

Tua-i-ll' maurluugka Nunakauyami kiantetullruuk kiagaqan. Ukut-llu itratullruut iqalluarpagnek neqliyarturluteng.

Wiinga-am tamaantelqa nall'arrluku, aatamnek piuratullruaqa apaurluqa, nulirra-llu aanamnek.

Tua-i maavet tekitaqan tauna apaurluqa, nacigglainarluku, nacikum-

Then when the weather was good, they probably left to hunt again, I think it was the next day.

Ayugutarin returned home again when his kayak ran out of cargo space and arrived. Again his hunting partner didn't arrive for some time.

After going out frequently, his wife, his *nulirruaq* [pretend spouse], after going out frequently, said that he was approaching, towing his kayak.

After waiting for him to arrive for a long time, after going outdoors, his wife said upon entering that he was about to reach the summit of Ingrirraat [Small *ingriit* (mountains)] up there towing his kayak.

When they went outdoors, they saw that he was towing his kayak, going up the mountain. And when he reached the top, probably after bringing his kayak on the other side and obscuring it, he appeared again, a wolf standing up there.

We call the [mountains] up there Ingrirraat, the ones that are up above us. Those up there are called Ingrirraat.

He ran on all fours and suddenly went out of sight.

Apparently, a shaman had come to him from the north. I'm not referring to you, Nanurrualek [Rita Angaiak's Yup'ik name]. Nanurrualek, a shaman, had come to take Ayugutarin's spouses away. [*laughs*] The person, Nanurrualek, who had come to take away his spouses wasn't successful.

I wonder how that shaman knew of [Ayugutarin]? They used to say his name was Nanurrualek. Yes, that's the extent I'll tell the story. My *iluraq* will mention the part of the story that I forgot to tell.

Arliat[14]

Rita Angaiak: And there used to be many capelin that spawned and died down there along the shore. The small capelin were pleasant to watch.

Martina John: They weren't around at first. When I first became aware of my surroundings, I saw that they never obtained any capelin. The people would talk about how they used to harvest capelin.

Then my grandparents used to stay up at Nunakauyaq [Toksook Bay] during summer. And these people would also go up to process and dry herring.

One day while I happened to be there, I always called my grandfather *aataq* [father] and his wife my *aanaq* [mother].

When my grandfather would arrive here [to Umkumiut], I always cried

ni-ll' tua-i qayam iquanun camavet kingumun itertellua kitumek alrapangqerraqami. Anguarturluni itrautaqlua.

Tua-ll'-am tuani uitainanemni qanngartut cikaaret-gguq inartut. Ala-i wiinga tua-i cikaarnek paqnayuk'acagarlua cakemkunek.

Qantullruut cikaarturtenek-llu qanraqluteng. Tangrruallerkartulua, taqugvagnek tuaten piyukluki.

Tua-i cakma tua-ll' anelraryuum tekicanga, anelrarlua piunga, tamakut tamaa-i cikaarullinilriit tangrranka cimerlit makut. Cimerlinun ayuqekulluki.

Tamakut-am cikaaret ak'a tamaani ellirarnun payugutekluki pinitullruit. Iciw' tua-i cenarrarmi inangqaluteng, yugmun tegucetaalriatun ayuqluteng.

Tua-i tag'aulluki, cenami tag'aulluki. Arnaungermeng pissuquluteng. Imumek-llu waten tag'aq pikan, ataam ellureskan unegqaqelriit makut qecvaakata avulaagluki.

Qaluluki cenami qaluurluki pissuraqluki. Tamaa-i-gguq-am ellirarnek payugutkelriit.

Maa-i-llam kiagpak tayim' cikaarnek niiteqanritua. Iciw' piqtaarluteng. Maani pitullruut ketemteni tamaani tekiteqarraatullemteni maani tua-i cenami. Tua-i-ll' maavet itrarnanriameng-am un'gaani pimaqerqameng piaqluteng. Taugaam ullagluki pissulriit pitaqaqluki.

Amiik Qurrlurta-llu

Anguyaluk: Cetuat-llu cali pitullruluteng qavani. Cetuartaqluteng.

Tua-llu wani waniw' uitainanemteni arrluut agaaggun qaktaarturluteng kiatmurtengciqut. Tua-i-gguq tamaa-i cetuarculriit.

Un'gaani ugkut, amiigmek uani qanlartut Qurrlurtem uatiini, atraraqamta-ll' ua-i amiiguluni ua-i nallunaitaqluni. Tamaaken-gguq tamaa-i qayarpallaratuut.

Tua-i-llu-gguq qayarpallagallmeng kinguatni, arrluut tamakut ketmun qaktaangluteng. Tua-i-ll' itrarnaurtut qavavet tua-i tayima.

Tamakut arrluut yugmek tangssugtengqerraqameng cali tuvqatarluteng. Tamaa-i cetuanek callugaqameng tuquciaqameng ik'anek; waten ayuqelriit,

wanting to go with him when he was leaving, and when I cried when he was leaving, he'd let me get inside the aft section of the kayak if someone was sitting back-to-back with him in his kayak. He'd paddle and bring me up [to Nunakauyaq].

Then while I was there, they started to say that the *cikaaret* [capelin] were lying down. I was very curious about the *cikaaret* down there.

They also mentioned *cikaarturtet* [type of whale or porpoise]. I was imagining all sorts of things when they mentioned them, and I even thought they were talking about very large seals.

Then when I wanted to go down, I went down, and when I saw the *cikaaret,* I saw that they were just smelt. They looked like smelt to me.

They mentioned in the past that capelin were gifts to orphans. They just lie along the shore, like they are asking for people to take them.

The surf would bring them ashore. People, including women, would gather them. And when the surf came, and when it went back down, when it left fish on the shore jumping around, we'd quickly pick them up.

They'd dipnet for them along the shore when they harvested them. They would say that they were giving themselves to orphans once again.

I didn't hear about capelin this summer. They are available periodically. They used to be available here [at Umkumiut] when we first arrived along the shore. Then when they stopped coming up here, they were available down the coast [at Arliat (Mew gulls, Black-legged kittiwakes)]. People go to where they are available and obtain them.

Amiik and Qurrlurta[15]

Martina John: And there were beluga whales around up the coast. They would catch beluga whales.

Then while we were staying here [at Umkumiut], killer whales would start swimming and breaching across there, heading up the coast. They mentioned that they were hunting beluga whales.

Down the coast, they mention that there is an *amiik* [door] down below Qurrlurta, and when we'd go down, we'd see a place that is obviously a door. They mention that they hear kayak noises from that place.

Then after hearing kayak noises, killer whales would start breaching and swimming down toward the ocean. Then they'd head up the coast.

If humans witness those killer whales [hunt], they are also generous [with their catch]. When they attack beluga whales and kill them, [they give people]

aug'aumalriit ik'anek pituit.

Tua-i-gguq tauna pugleqerrvikciqaa camaken, tua-i cikirluku tauna yuk tangvagtelteng.

Maa-i-rpak-llu ukaqvaggun kina un'gaani piiyaaqellrulliniat, taugaam-gguq alikluku teguvkenaku. Ila-i!

Ii-i, tuaten-gguq ak'a pitullruut. Quyatuluteng tamakut arrluut.

Uatiini amiigtangqellruuq. Maa-i-wa uunguciirutlilria. Maaken atam alaiterpatullruuq, ua-i amiiguniluku. Nallunaunani ua-i tan'gercenani amiiguluni. Uum penarpallraam aciani kanani. Taun ircenrrarnun piknilallrukiit.

Uunguciirutlilria-w' tua-i. Tua-i tangellra yaatmun amiignganani.

Yaa qanemciqtaartukut.

Unangik: Alingnaqvaa! Yaa qanemcikaicaaqeng'erma-w, tua-i augkunek ava-i arrlugnek.

Arrlluut imkut maani kuimalgullruut atam unani ketemteni. Tamakut tamaa-i tunguk'acagarluteng pilriit Qasginguarmiunguniluki pitullruit, Qasginguarmiut-gguq.

Imkut-llu maaggun qaralilget aamarrlugutellget Kalukarmiunguluteng cakmani. Ii-i, Kalukarmiunguluteng.

Cali waten qayarpallagaluteng pinga'artaqameng, tamaa-i-gguq alaitetuut-gguq atam, alaitetullruut. Tua-i-llu-gguq piuraqerluteng arrluut tua-i cenamek maaken qakluteng, qaktaarluteng ayagluteng ircenrraungameng.

Waten tua-i inerquutauluni malirqeqaasqevkenak unani. Pisteteng-gguq nalluyuitait, nalluyuitelarait. Ilangciarayunaitut-gguq. Yugmek-gguq pikngengaicaaqut, taugaam-gguq yugmek pikengyukuneng picetaarutlermek piyugngaut. Nalluyagusngaunaku-llu.

Uani-llu Up'nerkillermiuni imna Apangssaar kuvyaa cetuarcuutii tamakucirtellruuq arrluyagarmek. Tua-i uani Up'nerkillermiuni uitallratni, tamaa-i imna-llu, arnassagaq imna Naparyarrarmiu, imna Cukiq.

Tamaa-i-gguq Apangssaar uantauratullruami waten kiagmi, up'nerkiviungameng ugkut; Up'nerkillermiut ugkut caviunritut, taugaam up'ner-

ik'at; they call [square] ones like this *ik'at* [pieces of skin and blubber removed from beluga whales].

They say a piece like that will suddenly pop out of the water near that person; they are giving a person who is watching them [hunt belugas] a share.

They evidently [gave a share of their catch] recently to a person who was down the coast, but he was afraid and didn't take it. My!

Yes, they mentioned that they did that long ago. Those killer whales are capable of expressing gratitude.

There was a door down the coast from [Qurrlurta]. It's probably not clearly visible any longer these days. It used to be very visible from here, and they said that it was a door. It was obvious down there, and was dark and was a door. It was beneath a large cliff down there. They mentioned that [the doorway] belonged to *ircenrraat.*

It's probably not visible any longer. When looking at it from a distance, it looked like a door.

Yes, we're taking turns telling stories.

Simeon Agnus: My goodness! Yes, although I don't have any stories to tell, that person over there [Martina] was just talking about killer whales.

Killer whales were always swimming around here, right down below us. People said that the ones that were very dark were from Qasginguaq. They said they were Qasginguarmiut [inhabitants of Qasginguaq].

And the ones that had designs here, the ones with breast designs, were from Kalukarmiut down there. Yes, they were from Kalukarmiut.

Also, when they started to make noises similar to kayaks preparing, they mentioned that you could hear their noise. Then after a while, killer whales would come out of the water along the shore, and they'd come out of the water and resubmerge as they left because they are *ircenrraat.*

People were admonished not to pursue them down there. They said they are aware of people who are pursuing them. They said they mustn't bother them. It is said they won't attack a person, but if they want to attack a person who is provoking them, they could attack them. And they won't forget the person, either.

And down at Up'nerkillermiut, Apangssaar's beluga net caught one of those, a small killer whale. When they were living down at Up'nerkillermiut, including that person, that elderly woman from Napakiak, that person named Cukiq.

Since Apangssaar used to stay down there [at Up'nerkillermiut] during summer, since that place down there is a spring camping site; Up'nerkillermiut

kami pissullerkarteng ullatullruat, canimenaku tua-i piarkaurrluteng uani waten taqukassuagaqameng.

Arrluyagarmek pitlinilria Apangssaar kuvyaa tamana cetuarcuutii.

Tua-i waten qacaqnillrani qairvaallrani, waten itlermini amiigem ciuqerranun aqumqalliniuq. Mikelnguq-wa-gguq una natermi aqvaqualria. Pim Nusail-am natelqau kinguqlilqellikii-llu; Can'irraam anngaqellrullikii tauna.

Ukut-llu-gguq tua-i camek pivkenateng tua-i piinanratni, arnaq ugna itliniuq mecungkacagarluni-gguq, arillugturluni ivrucirturluni-llu.

Mikelnguq-wa-gguq una natermi aqvaquall' tan'gurraq. Malkaani teguqerluku kenimkaruarluku tua-i tayim' anlliniluni.

Taukut-llu-gguq elpekevkenaku, elliin taugaam tua-i Cukim tangvagluku. Tan'gurraq tauna imna unugpailgan tuquq'alliniuq. Tua-i taum arrluum irniani tauna kuvyakngaullruan, taumek tua-i nunulirluku teguluku.

Apangssaar imna anguarluni cenak'acagarkun, tua-i-llu ketvaryarpiaqaqan naken piciinateng arrlluut makut kuimangareskata tua-i tagluni. Tua-i callra tamalkuan nalluvkenaku.

Uani ua-i Up'nerkillermiuni kuvyak'ngellruuq im' Apangssaaralleq, Nusail-am atallra.

Alingnarqut. Waten taugaam yuk picetaarutenrilnguq pingaitaat. Alingnaqsaaqut.

Angtuarpallraat-llu imkut cetuat angyaaqelriit, qanritni-gguq atam iquit tua-i caningqaluki keggmiaqaqaceteng pugumarpayuitut angelriit arrluut.

Cali-am Tuyuryami-qaa arrluut taukut callullinilriit arvermek cenami?

Tua-i-am cat makut carrateng tua-i kicetaqluki pillratni, waten uqurtallerkarteng pitekluku. Cat tua-i uyamiggateng carraat kicetaqluki.

Tua-i-ll' tauna arveq pugtaqalliniluni kana-i tuquluni. Piuraqerluni-gguq yun'erraq kan'a pug'uq amalirnerakun cungavseq tauna kic'etellrat iliita tegumiaqluku. Taum tua-i tegumiaqluku iliita kic'etellra.

Apangkuggaam-gguq arvertani cungavsermun uumun tunaa.

Tua-i arveq tauna unitqapiggluk' arrluut ayalliniut. Tua-i payugkengluteng

isn't used for any other purpose, but they would go there when it was time for them to hunt, so that they could hunt seals nearby.

Apangssaar's beluga net evidently caught a small killer whale.

While the wind was blowing against shore and large swells formed, when [Cukiq] went inside the home, she sat in front of the doorway. A child was running around on the floor, and the child was Nusail's older or younger sibling, probably his younger sibling. That child was probably Can'irraq's older brother.

While the people were just sitting there, a woman entered, completely wet, wearing fish-skin mittens and waterproof skin boots.

There was a child, a boy, running around on the floor. When [the child] got close to her, she embraced him and then went out.

And the people there didn't notice it, but Cukiq was watching her. That boy evidently suddenly died before evening. That killer whale, because her child was caught in a net, took that child to replace it.

Apangssaar would paddle right along the shore, and when he moved farther down toward the water, out of nowhere killer whales would start to swim, and then he'd go back up toward shore. They were aware of everything he did.

Down at Up'nerkillermiut, the person who was named Apangssaar, Nusail's late father, caught a killer whale in a net.

They are dangerous. But they will leave a person alone who hasn't provoked them. They are actually dangerous.

And the very large ones, you know how large beluga whales actually are, it is said when [killer whales] are biting on the lower part of the side of their bodies, the large killer whales aren't fully visible.

Also, was it in Togiak that killer whales were attacking a bowhead whale along the shore?

The people there dropped the few things they possessed in the water so that they would be given a piece of blubber. They dropped their necklaces and other small belongings in the water.

Then that bowhead whale died and surfaced in the water. Then after a while, a young man appeared along the other side [of the whale] holding a *cungavseq* [bead] that someone had dropped in the water. That person was holding the item that one man had dropped in the water.

He said that Apangkuggaq is trading the bowhead whale that he caught for the *cungavseq* he was holding.

The killer whales just left that bowhead whale behind and went. They

tua-i taukunek nunanek. Taumek tua-i nunulirluku, arverpall'ermek tua-i taumek cikillrulliniit.

Imna-llu Qilangaq imna unguvallermini maantellrani, ikani ika-i akimteni arrluut callulliniut arvermek, tua-i tuqulluku.

Tua-i nerluteng, tua-i piinanratni kingunratnek, ayagluteng ava-i kingunratni pugtertelliniuq.

Tuar tagutellratni tamaani caviggarkun un' aug'allruciqelria. Ervigissuun imarluni; tua-i tauna tua-i uqiutii.

Ii-i, tangellruaqa tua-i iigemkun maani, amiq. Tuar-llu tang caviggarkun aug'alleq. Qaill' tayim' aug'allruatgu. Arrluut-wa makut yuungameng, ircenrraungameng.

Up'nerkillermiut

Unangik: Ugkut tua-i uaqliput ugkut Up'nerkillermiut, augkut ciuliamta, angayuqallemta ciuliarita, ugkut ua-i up'nerkiviugut ugkut. Neqsurluteng iqalluarpagnek tamaa-i-llu kuvyatutullruluteng *beluga*-nek. Apangssaar iciw' qanrutkeqallrukek'a tauna Apangssaar. Apangssaar tauna kuvyatutullrulliniuq, Ermianguaq-llu tauna pillilria.

Ugkut uani nunallret caperrnarqut. Wangkutaulriani maa-i asqilingraata qessanayugaqelriakut.

Tua-lli-w' augkut ua-i ullatullrukait pavaggun ukut Ingrirrat keluatgun, yaaggun-llu atrarluteng quliitgun, Anqercaraq ugna tuaritaqan.

Ilaurluit-llu picurlagaqluteng ikamrait, qertuami waten Qengararmiut augna tua-i quliit, waten uvervagpek'nani cakneq piyaaquq. Tauna call' elluryarallrat.

Ullagaqluku up'nerkaneq tamaq'apiaraan; naken iluvarvikluku avaken Cevv'arnermek tuaten augkut ciuliamta.

Qimugteurlungqerraqluteng ilait pingayurrarnek. Wangkuta tamaa-i qaill' piqaqumta aarrarrarraaraqelriakut aarrarrarraarnariksailengraakut, mernurluta.

Angayuqalput imkut caperrnaqkacagartut yuucillrat, pingnatullrat, anrutarteng kass'allarmek-llu waten teguqerrartevkenateng yuullruameng.

gave that gift to the people of that village. They traded [that bead] with that, and gave them that very large bowhead whale.

And when Qilangaq was alive and was here [at Umkumiut], killer whales evidently attacked a bowhead whale across from us and killed it.

They ate, and after they left, [a piece of blubber] floated to the surface.

When they brought it to shore at that time, it looked like the piece had been cut off with a knife. A washtub was filled with the blubber that he was given.

Yes, I saw it with my own eyes, a piece of skin. And it looked like it had been removed with a knife. I wonder how they removed that piece. It's because these killer whales are people, because they are *ircenrraat.*

Up'nerkillermiut[16]

Simeon Agnus: The village down the coast from us, Up'nerkillermiut [People of Up'nerkilleq (old spring camping site)], that place downcoast was a spring camp for our ancestors, the forebearers of our parents. They fished for herring, and they would set nets to catch beluga. Remember I told you about Apangssaar earlier. Apangssaar evidently used to set a net, and probably Ermianguaq also.

The village down the coast is a difficult place to get to. Although our living conditions are much easier these days, even those of us here are reluctant to go there.

Here those people went to that place down the coast through the inland route behind these Ingrirraat, and then they descended over there from above the village when there was no shorefast ice down along Anqercaraq [Where one suddenly comes out, from *ane-,* "to go out"].

And some people's sleds would break, since the area above Qengararmiut is steep, but it isn't actually a very steep incline. That was where they slid down [the mountain].

Our ancestors from all over would go there every spring, even those from out in Cevv'arneq.

Some poor people had only three dogs. These days, when we experience a little strain, we say "*Aarrarrarraa*" [an expression of exhaustion] although it isn't time yet for us to say "*Aarrarrarraa,*" when feeling sore and tired.

Our parents' way of life was extremely daunting, their subsistence way of life, since store-bought goods weren't readily available to them.

Kass'arteqataquneng-llu akmavet yaaqvanun Tacimun tuavet ayatullrullinilriit. Quuniutaqateng cavluteng, tengalrarnarquskateng tengalrarluteng. Tamaa-i uaken ua-i Up'nerkillermiunek tuatnatullrullinilriit kass'artaqameng, cuyarraq pitekluku caayuaraat.

Augkut-llu angutait, augkut qaill' uquutellegnek pitullrit; qanrutketukaitwa puulingqerrniluki tekcitagaat qamiqurricetun angtalrianek.

Nutegpallraat makutun tengmiarcuutetun tua-i neqututalallrulliut, wall'u-qaa nequkilqelallruit tamakut nutgit. Cayarauluteng, puyurkamek kuvqerluki yaaggun cupluakun, puyurkirluku, piinkirluku, puulia-ll' nutaan kingumek iterrluku. Ataucirqumek nutegluni kinguani-ll' nutenqigcesciiganani calirraarpek'nani.

Tamakut tamaa-i caskullrit-llu tamakut aarnarqetuyaaqellrullinilriit, taugaam picurlauteksuunaki, kenengyuunateng-wa tua-i una wani pakigcuuteseng putkaumavkenaku kenengyuunateng.

Angayuqamta ciuqliit, una waniw' uani Up'nerkillermiuni Aciqsauq un' qanrutketukiit tua-i pulengtaq wii niitetuaqa, tua-i nukalpiaq. Elluatuuvkenani, piirrallektarnek-llu-gguq cingingqerraqluni, tua-i ikiungnaqem ugaan. Tua-i nukalpiakayak, camek kepqenrilnguq tauna angun.

Tua-i-am caqerluni qakmavet Tacimun kass'artellratni cakaminek aklukaminek, imarpigcuutekaminek kiputellrani angutet iliita pillinia, "Caka'urlurpenek usuuq pisit?" Tua-i aturallrai tangerrluki.

Waten waniw' inerquutaulria angun aklulliqengraan tua-i-w' cangakesqevkenaku. Iiput-gguq alartelartut. Nukalpiakayagmek tukurlimek pikengciqukut-gguq, aturarrliqengraan temcikesqevkenaku.

Augkut avani ciuqliput ciuliaput nukalpiat tua-i pitsaqutmek tua-i ikiukacagarluteng pitullrullinilriit.

Tauna tua-i Aciqsauq nukalpiakayak, augkut tangvagtaita calistekayuamek-qaa tua-i tuani pillrularaat, tua-i calistenguyukluku.

Tua-i ugkut uani nunallret pingayuugut. Up'nerkillermiut, Qukarmiut, Qengararmiut-wa. Taukut tua-i Qengararmiut kiaqlit, ullagaqamegteki tua-i tuaggun atraryarangqellruut, pavaggun ingrit keluatgun, paugkut qullimta. Yaaqsigluteng ugkut nunallret.

Ukut-llu yugyagpakayuunateng-gguq ukut Umkumiut. Waten up'ner-

And when they went to get store-bought goods, they'd evidently travel far away to St. Michael. They'd paddle when the weather was calm, and they'd use sails when conditions were good for sailing. Traveling from Up'nerkillermiut down there, they'd evidently go and purchase goods from there, just to get a little bit of tobacco and tea.

And their men talked about the [guns] they called *uquutellget* and mentioned that their bullets were the size of the heads of *tekcitagaat* [small birds].

Those very large guns were probably the same width as bird guns or possibly narrower. It took work to prepare them, spilling a little powder along the opening of the barrel, putting powder in it, then placing something in between [the powder and the shell], then placing its bullet in last. They shot only once, and they couldn't shoot again until after reloading it.

And their guns were dangerous, but they never got into accidents with them, as they didn't ignite and go off until they were cocked.

Our parents' forebearers repeatedly mentioned Aciqsauq who was from Up'nerkillermiut down the coast, a great hunter who I've constantly heard about. He didn't look distinguished, and it is said that his laces were from old braided grass ropes because he purposely wanted to look unsightly. He was an exceptionally great hunter, a man who didn't lack anything.

One day, when they went to St. Michael to purchase goods, when he bought items for himself, some gear for himself, some ocean hunting gear, one of the men looked at his raggedy clothes and said to him, "What are you purchasing these goods for?"

It is an admonishment not to criticize a man although he is wearing shabby clothing. They say our eyes are deceptive. They said not to laugh at him although he wore shabby clothes or we would end up criticizing an exceptionally great hunter.

Those who came before us, our ancestors who were great hunters, evidently looked extremely unattractive on purpose.

That person named Aciqsauq, an exceptionally great hunter, I think at the time they thought that he was a laborer.

There are three old settlements down the coast. There's Up'nerkillermiut, Qukarmiut [People of the *qukaq* (center)], and Qengarармiut [possibly from *qengaraq* (tibia, shinbone)]. When they went to Qengararmiut, that is, up the coast from the others, they went down through that place, from behind the mountains that are right above us. The old village sites are far away.

And they said hardly any people stayed here at Umkumiut. During spring

kami ek'artaarturallerkarteng pitekluku, unaken imarpigmek-wa tua-i taqukanek pingnaqurallerteng yaaqsigpek'naku pingnaquratullrullinilriit. Wangkuta taugaam tua-i nunakeksaitaput wangkuta maa-i kinguvritni.

Tuamtell' tua-i angutait pivakarluku atertaulliniluteng; ugkut tua-i angutairluki Up'nerkillermiut.

Anguarluteng pitullermeggni cikullaam tagviirluki pillrungatait taukut. Tamaa-i tua-i imarpigmi kiagpak uitallinilriit, up'nerkarpak. Angutait tua-i tamarmeng ayaulluki cikum.

Tua-i waten tua-i man'a cikullaq, tamaa-i tua-i imarpigmi unani pillermegni, negcik tegumiarteng waten tua-i tallim uqamiinek ukiarrluni, augna-ll' muragartaa itenrilkan, tua-i pekcugngariluteng tua-i qaingani tua-i qamigarluteng.

Naugg'un taukut tut'ellrulartat. Avaggun-wa tua-i tut'ellrularngalnguut, tut'ellrunilarait taukut. Angutairyaaqellruut, taugaam tua-i picurlagpek'nateng.

Iliit-llu, naterkairucaaqelriim. Augkut avani uquutengqetullruut ayagastait taqukat it'gaitnek. Taukugnek-am ellminek natrarluni, ellminek waten arulaingqallermini natraq'allinilria tamakucignek tamaa-i, uquutmi caquanek, caqutiinek imailan-wa tua-i pillikii.

Tamakut tamaa-i tuaten tua-i taukut qanrutkeqallruit cali; qanrutketullrukait-wa tua-i atertauyaaqellret.

Apacungaq imat'am nat'rallrunilaqiit, Mancuam aatallra, aanama anngallra tauna Apacungaq. Tan'gurrarmek taugaam kitumek Ayaprutmekqaa ukut ilangqellrulartut?

Qayarugaat cali waten tangvaurtelluteng. Unegna atam anuqlirqan anuqlinertuuq waken *north*-amek. Qayat imkut anguarumalalriit-gguq tuc'uunateng; tangerkengaqluki tua-i ellaita anuqlirqan anguarluteng. Wangkuk-llu waniw' atuqallrallrukep'uk allakuni pingayuni maani.

Anguatullruukuk-llu wangkuk. Angualrianun tua-i kingunrirtuutetullruukuk, maligcuaqetulunuk-llu ilu'urqa-llu.

Cali waten qayat makut maligcuaqetaarturluteng pituluteng anguatullermeggni. Malrutaarturluteng tua-i ikayuqu'urlutek, cacetuquteklutek. Tuaten tua-i maani tua-i cenarmiut pitulriit avavet tua-i ungalaqlimtenun qagaavet-llu.

Man'a pingnaqsaraat makut cenarmiut ayuqerrlugtuq, taugaam

like this, [they stayed at Up'nerkillermiut] so they could easily go down [to the ocean], as they always made an effort to stay close to the ocean where they would be hunting. But we, their descendants, didn't stay at that place.

And once their men evidently drifted out into the ocean; all the men from Up'nerkillermiut drifted out.

Back when they paddled with kayaks, I think the *cikullaq* [newly frozen ice accumulated by the incoming tide] prevented them from going back up to shore. They evidently stayed down on the ocean all summer, all spring long. The ice drifted all their men out to the ocean.

While they were down on the ocean, when they struck the gaffs they held with the weight of their arms and [the gaffs] pierced the ice, if the wooden [shaft] didn't go through, they were able to walk on top of [the *cikullaq*] with their kayak sleds.

I'm not sure exactly where those people reached shore. I think they said those people reached shore through the area out there. All their men drifted away, but they didn't die.

And one of them, his boot soles wore out. Back in those days, their men who traveled and hunted had sealskin containers made of seal flippers. He sewed boot soles for himself out of those, quickly sewing that material on his own when they were resting somewhere, [making boot soles] out of his seal-oil container, probably because it was empty.

They also mentioned those people; they used to mention those who drifted away.

Oh yes, they said Apacungaq sewed boot soles, Mancuaq's late father, my mother's late older brother Apacungaq. But they had a young man; was it Ayaprun who was with that group?

The people [at Up'nerkillermiut] could see the many kayaks. When it's windy down on the coast, the north wind blows for a long time. It is said the kayaks would paddle for a long time and wouldn't reach shore; they'd see them as they paddled when it was windy. [Paul John and I] experienced [paddling with kayaks] for three years around here.

We two also used to paddle kayaks. We paddled kayaks behind the others, and my *iluraq* and I paddled together.

Also, kayakers used to paddle together in pairs back then. There were always two who helped one another, who supported one another. That's what coastal people do, even those to the south of us and those to the north of us.

The subsistence way of life of the coastal people is similar, but their

alerquutait ayuqenritut.

Waten una waniw' ketgulleqluku pituat ukurmiut, Negtemiut, Tuqsugmiut-llu una. Qamigaqungartaqameng ketgullermek atengqertuq; atraryarateng ketgullruluni atraryaraat.

Ii-i, Up'nerkillermiut; ilu'urma augna Aciqsauq iquklitevsiaqerliu. Niicugniqernaurput atam.

Kangrilnguq: Augna Aciqsauq ayagneranek qanemcikcuaqeryugaqa.

Tauna-am Aciqsaum atakaa yuilqurtellermini ikamrarugarnek tangllinilria. Nulirtuqsaunani-llu tauna Aciqsaum atakaa. Ikamrarugarnek tangrrami, ciunrirluki, ciunratnun arulairluni utaqallinikai.

Tua-i tekicaaqekseng, taukut imkut ikamrarugaat elpekevkenaku. Elpekcetaaryaaqelliniuq, quspagaaqluni, irugni-llu camkuk elliuryaaqlukek, tua-i menglaingermegteggu maa-i elpekumavkenaku.

Ukna-gguq-wa ikamraq uyatu'urluki ilani. Maaten-gguq tang unicatni taukut pia, ukna tua-i nallunaunani ayagyualriaruvkenani, akiqlirrii-wa-gguq tan'gaurlurraq tua-i angliluaqaqsailnguuluni; akiqliqu'urlutek ikamratek kasmurluku uka-i.

Tekicagni-am tua-i, piiyaaqelliniuq murilkevkenaku taukuk cali. Tua-i-ll' kituqerluku, tauna angulluaq kingyalriim, tangerqalliniluku.

Waqaalliniuq, "Waqaa. Yuuguq-qaa?" Tua-i-ll' taum pillinia, "Tua-i-w' yuulrianga. Augkut ciuqlirpetek elpekenrilkiitnga elpekcetaangerma."

Taum atam tua-i angulluam ciuqlitek augkuullinii, "Augkuut." Erinii tua-i niicamegteggu kingyaarrluteng arulairrluteng piata, "Tang yuk."

Maligtesqellutek tua-i ullagluki. Nutaan tua-i maliklukek tekiucan'gu, taukut-llu imkut nutaan tangerrluku.

Tua-i pillinii ellaitnun elpekellrunritniluni, uumun taugaam kingyallrani tua-i elpekniluni. Narugniluteng qanrucateng, narullruyaaqniluki, pilliniat, "Waqaa ca pitekluku ciunemteni tua-i pingnaqsaaqsit?"

Tua-ll' qanrutlinii, "Tua-i-w' yuunritlerci taringamku narullrukemci."

teachings aren't the same.

People from [Umkumiut], Nightmute, and Tokook Bay all use the ocean down there. When they begin to go seal hunting, it is called *ketgulleq(luteng)* [those who use the same coastal area / ocean to hunt in]; the place where they go down [to the ocean], they all hunt in the same area when they go down.

Yes, the people of Up'nerkillermiut; let my *iluraq* finish the story of Aciqsauq. Let's listen to him.

Paul John: I want to briefly tell the story of Aciqsauq from the beginning.

When the one who would eventually become the father of Aciqsauq went out to the wilderness, he evidently saw many sleds. At the time the one who would become Aciqsauq's father hadn't married yet. When he saw many sleds, he went to meet them, he got in front of them, he stopped in front of them and waited for them.

When they came upon him, the many people in sleds didn't sense that he was there. Although he tried to get them to realize that he was there, coughing loudly and stomping his feet, they didn't notice that he was there although they passed alongside him.

There was another person approaching in a sled who was trailing behind a good distance away from the group. When they left him, he looked at the person approaching and saw that he was obviously not a young person, and the person alongside him was a young man who hadn't grown into an adult; they were approaching, pushing their sleds alongside one another.

When they came upon him, he tried to alert them once again, but those two didn't pay attention to him either. Then just as they passed him, the elderly man looked back and saw him instantly.

He said hello, "Hello. Is it a person?" Then that person said to him, "Yes, I'm a human person. Although I tried to get the group ahead of you to notice me, they didn't."

Then that elderly man called the people up ahead and said, "Hey, you up ahead." When they heard his voice and stopped and looked back, he said, "Look, there is a person here."

They asked him to go with them, and they went to those people. He followed the two, and when they got to the group, they finally saw him.

He told [the group] that they hadn't noticed him at all, but that [the man coming behind them] had seen him only when he looked back after passing. When he said that he had come out to meet them, they asked, "Why did you decide to go out and meet us?"

He said to them, "When I realized that you aren't human, I decided to come out and stay in your path to meet you."

Taukut atam pillinikiit curukaugut-gguq ellait, kelegtemeggnun-gguq, tamaani curukatullratni, curukaugut.

Tua-i tuaten pirraarluteng pilliniat, "Maligcugarpekut-qaa?" Tua-i-ll' taum yuum pillinii cangakenrilkatni maligciiqniluki. Tua-i maligtesqengata maligtelliniluki.

Tua-i-ll' nunarrlugnun tua-i, apqiitnek nunarrlugnun tekitelliniluteng. Tua-i nunat taukut yugyagluteng. Qukaatni-wa-gguq nunat qasgiat. Tua-i tuavet qasgimun ciunillililuteng, iterluteng.

Itrameng ciuneteng taukut pilliniit taukut yup'igmek malingqerrniluteng, qaillun taum yup'igtarteng piqatallranek.

Taukut-am ciunrita pilliniat, "Nerrlerpeceni ilaganrilengraaci, qavavet qaug'um ingelrem iquanun nugtelluku piciu." Maaten-gguq tang tuaten qavavet-aarata piuq, imna tua-i qasgim egkua inglerluni tus'arrluni.

Kiavet-gguq tua-i iqsulirnermun iquanun pisqengatni tuavet aqumuq. Maaten-gguq tang imkut neqkalgirait neqkait pii tuntut ircaqurrit, uluit-wa, camek avuunateng tua-i.

Tua-i neqkicatni nerrliniluni. Nerurarraarluteng taqngameng pilliniut ukut, "Una-mi waniwa yugtarci qaill' piqatarta? Maantellerci-qaa iquklilluku maanciiquq?"

Iliit pilliniuq, "Iquklilluku-w' maantellerput maanelkan ellaita allrakuatni cataiciiqelria, allrakuatni taugaam kinguniciiqelria." Tua-i ukut utercecungartelliniat, uterqurqan canriciiqniluku.

Tua-llu-gguq tua-i utercetqatangarcatgu, iliit qanertuq, "Aling waniwa-qaa carrarmek piqaqatanritarci? Camek-tang tua-i piqaqatanritsiyaagarci, wii carrarmek piqaqerlaku." Angratni, anlliniluni tauna.

Anrraarluni-gguq itertuq, waten maklak tegumiaqluku. Takuyartaarluni-gguq tauna maklak tegumiara. Ulliimiu pillinia, "Elpenun una piqatanritaqa. Qetunrarkarpenun piqatarqa." Tua-i-ll' tuaten qanruqaarluku acianun ingelrem kasmekiini tayim' tegumiara tamalliniluni tua-i camavet itercani tayima.

Tuamtell' tua-i anelraan iliit pinga'artelliniuq, "Atag-atak wii call' piqaqerlaku." Anrraarluni-am it'liniuq tuaten-am tua-i tegumiaqluku tuntuq cirunelek; takuyartaarluni taun tuntuq.

Then the group told him that they were on their way to a village Messenger Feast, back when they had Messenger Feasts, that they were *curukat* [invited guests].

After telling him that, they said, "Would you like to come with us?" Then that person told them that he would accompany them if they didn't mind. Since they asked him to come along, he accompanied them.

They continued on and arrived at a land or dwelling place of souls, a village we call *nunarrluk.* That village was large with many residents. At the center of the village was a *qasgi.* [The guests] went straight to the *qasgi* and entered.

When they entered, they told their hosts that they had brought a human with them, and they asked how the human should be treated.

Their hosts said to them, "He shouldn't join you when you eat, but let him go up on one end of the bench against the back wall and sit." When [the human] heard them say that, he looked at the back of the *qasgi* and saw a large bench extending from one end to the other.

When they asked him to go to the left side [of the bench], he [went back and] sat there. When food was delivered to the guests, he saw only caribou hearts and tongues and nothing else.

When food was offered, he ate. After they all finished eating, the people there said, "What is this human here with you going to do? Will he be here during your entire stay?"

Then one of the people said, "If he is here the whole time we're here, he'll be gone for a year in [human] time, and he'll only get home after a year has passed." The people there suddenly decided to allow him to go home, [saying] that it would be good if he went home.

When they decided to let him go home, one of them said, "My, are you not going to give him something little? Since you aren't going to give him something little, let me give him a little gift." When they said he could do that, he got up and went out.

After leaving, he came inside, holding a bearded seal. The seal was turning its head from side to side. He went [to the man] and said, "I'm not going to give this to you. I'm giving it to your future son." After telling him that, when he pushed the seal under the bench, it disappeared.

When [the one who gave him the seal] went back to his place, one of the people there said, "Let me also give him a little gift." After going outside, he came back in holding a caribou with antlers; that caribou was turning its head from side to side.

Ulliimiu tekicamiu pillinia, "Elpenun una wii piqatarqa." Tuaten-am tua-i ingelrem acianun kayimngani tayima.

Tua-i nutaan pilliniat, "Kitaki tua-i uterquryartua. Taugaam ankuvet ellamun kiartevkenak tallimarqunek elatmun ulpiareskina. Nangreskuvet kingyaqina yuuyuksuarpekut."

Anngami-am tua-i tuaten alerquuciacetun kiartevkenani tallimarqunek elatmun ulpiarqaarluni, kingyaryaaqelliniuq nunatangssagaunani tua-i, yuilqurruluni tamana imna.

Maaten kiartelliniuq, imna-ll' urunqiitelleq ak'a urunqinglliniluni nerqanruarmek [uitainanrani].

Tang ukut ircenrraat allrakurput erneqlinikiit. Tamaa-i tuaten tua-i pillinilriit.

Tua-ll' tua-i uterrluni, kingunilluni.

Tua-i piluni piinanermini tua-i nulirtulliniluni, nulirtuami-llu qetunranglliniluni taumek Aciqsaumek. Tua-i-gguq tauna qetunraa pissuryaurtuq, tua-i maklagculiqluku ukurmiut Qaluyaarmiut maklagculiqluku tua-i.

Taum-gguq tang taugaam iluriin, naken pikiumaluni qanrutkumanrilngermi, uum-gguq Qirnam, tua-i-gguq maligtaquluku pillgucirluku piaqamiu tua-i elliitun piculuni piaqluni tauna Qirnaq, Qirnaq-gguq una.

Tua-i-am up'nerkarpak up'nerkillermeggni maklagglainarnek tua-i uani Up'nerkillermiuni pitaqluni.

Tua-i-gguq qalliryagtellriit pequsngaluteng makliit qerturiata, nulirran pillinia, "Makus-mi-tam maa-i caqunarikuni-llu camek caqusqelluki caqutekauyugnamek-llu tekiucuitaqsit?"

Taum-gguq Aciqsaam nuliani pia, "Aa-a, tua-i-w' tang nayiit nutektangramki uniurcukenka qamiqucngaussiyaagyuata." [*ngel'artut*] Tua-i tuaten kiullinia-am.

Unuaquan-am tua-i ercan quunian, ayagaluteng, ellii-ll' tauna maligulluni Aciqsauq. Atakuyartuaraqerluku-gguq-am agiirtuq, tua-i-gguq-am uckacagarluni.

Tekicartuaraan-gguq murilkaat qayaan kinguani qamigautegken qaingani nayiik malruk tevingalriik, ciuqerrani-wa-gguq ceturyaani alla. Umyuarteqliniut, "Aling tua-i-wam pitaqetukminek maklagmek uciallilria.

Qayani-am uciillinia, nayirrlainarnek kemgirturluki tua-i ucilillinikii. Imna-am qanlleq nayiit nutektang'ermiki uniurcugniluki caqutekarrlainarnek qayani-gguq ucilillia. Tuaten-am tua-i tauna qanrutkelaqiit.

When he went to [the man], he said, "I'm going to give this to you." When he pushed it underneath the bench, it disappeared like before.

Then they said to him, "Now go out and go on home. But when you go outside, don't look around but somersault five times. When you stand, look back, for you may think that we are human."

When he went outside, just as they had instructed him, he didn't look around, but only looked back after flipping forward five times, but there was no village, only wilderness.

When he looked around, he saw that the snow had melted and the ground was visible all around in just the short time he was inside.

You see that a year for us equals a day for these *ircenrraat.* That's what happened there.

Then he went home and reached his village.

After some time, he eventually married and a son was born named Aciqsauq. When his son started hunting, he became the greatest hunter on Nelson Island.

But they say his *iluraq,* although it wasn't known he had been gifted to begin with, they say when a person named Qirnaq hunted with [Aciqsauq], he would also catch many animals like him.

All spring, when they went spring camping down at Up'nerkillermiut, he caught only bearded seals.

When a pile of bearded seals [that he caught] became high, his wife told him, "When it is time to place these in containers, what do you expect me to store them in when you haven't brought anything home to make into storage containers?"

Aciqsauq told his wife, "Aaa, although I shoot at ringed seals, I tend to miss them since they have such small heads." [*laughter*] That's what he said to her.

The next day, when the sun came up and the weather was calm, men went out hunting including Aciqsauq. In the early evening, he approached with a big load as usual.

As he slowly approached, they saw that two ringed seals were draped over the back of his kayak on top of his kayak sled, and another was draped over the front deck of his kayak. They thought, "My, he is probably carrying a load of bearded seals that he usually catches."

He unloaded his kayak, and he had loaded it with only ringed seals with their meat removed. The one who had previously said that he tends to miss although he shoots at them had loaded his kayak only with seals to be made into storage containers. That's what they say about that person.

Tua-i tauna Aciqsauq qavcinek tayima tua-i qetunrangqelliniami tamaa-i Tacirtaaraqluteng. Qetunrai tua-i taukut piyaqlegurtellerteng tekitengluku. Tamaa-i-gguq tua-i una qetunraa aprutii Enemqerralriarullinian, Enemqerralriinkunek-gguq piaqluki taukut.

Tua-i taukut qetunrani piyaqlegurtenratgun waten paqnakengllinia qagna, qaillun tayima qag'um nunakellran ayuqucia.

Paqnak'ngengamiu-am tua-i negetmurteqataami pillinii tungayani, ellii waniwa qagna paqnakengvakaamiu uksiqernaluni qagaani umyuami paqnak'ngengaku, tua-i waniw' utertevkenani negetmurteqatarniluni, piyugteqelriamun maligcesqelluni tungayaminun. Tua-i-am qavciuluteng tungayain maligculliniluku tuaten tua-i utertarkauvkenateng uksiarkauluteng.

Tua-i uksilliniluteng nunat tayim' qagaani, wall'u-q' Tacirmiuni pillrulartut. Tacimi uksilliniluteng tua-i.

Tauna-gguq tua-i taukut apqiit umialgat, waten up'nerkaryartuan waten qamigaqtaangelliniuq; nukalpiateng qagkut umialegmeggnek pitulliniamegteki.

Tua-i-gguq tallimatellrurteqerluni maklagnek qanertuq, "Aling tavaringna Avang'armiut umialekekiit. Umialekekatni-llu ak'a pitqetaangellemni agamyangyalria imarpigmun; agamyanrilnguq umialeknilangraatni Avang'armiut."

Wangkuta-am maani ungalaqlimeggni qagkut Avang'armiunek pitulliniamegtekut. Tua-i iliita-ggur-am, umciatelaata-ggur-am yuut ilait, iliita qanqautellinia taumek, tauna tua-i Aciqsauq. Ing'umun yaani umialemeggnun tuaten qanrutekniluku, Avang'armiunun nukalpiaqnilangraatgu imarpigmun paqnayuyuitellranek, ellii-llu-gguq waniw' tallimatellrurrluni maklagnek.

Tauna-am qanrucesteni qanen'ermek taqngan pillinia, "War-atak tallimarraan umyugaan piyagutkai, erenrem ataucim pitarnaari. Ak'aurtuqggem qamigaqungellra." Tuaten-am kiullinia.

Tua-i nutaan taum Aciqsaum qayani uplukụ. Tayima tua-i atralliniluni. Maaten-ggur-am tekituq maklagnek tallimatlinilria. Ataucikun anguluku.

Up'nerkarpak-ggur-am ayagaqami tallimaterrlainarluni tekitaqluni.

Tauna tuani, tua-i taum atiin cikirtellran waten qanellran, "Una elpenun piqatanritaqa; qetunrarkarpenun piqatarqa." Tauna-am tua-i nall'arusngaluni, ircenrrarnek pikiumacia.

Since Aciqsauq had a number of sons, at that time they would travel back and forth to St. Michael. His sons had become capable at the time. Since his son's name was Enemqerralria, they would refer to that family as Enemqerralriinkut [Enemqerralria and his family].

Just as his sons became capable, he started to become curious about the north, what it was like to live in the north.

When he became curious about what it was like in the north, when he was about to head north, he said to his relatives that he was thinking of spending the winter up north since he was getting curious about it. He said that he was going to head north and not return home and that his relatives who wanted to should accompany him. Some of his relatives were willing to accompany him, and they planned to spend the winter there and not return home.

They then spent the winter in some village in the north, or was it at St. Michael. They evidently spent the winter at St. Michael.

It is said the *umialek* [wealthy boat owner] of the people there began to go seal hunting periodically toward spring; the people of the north evidently call their *nukalpiat* [great hunters] *umialek.*

When he had caught five bearded seals, he said, "My, I don't think that person over there is the *umialek* of Avang'armiut. If he is their *umialek,* he would have already become restless to go down to the ocean during the time that I've been catching animals; he hasn't become restless to go down to the ocean although they say he is the *umialek* of Avang'armiut."

The people of the north evidently call us people from the south Avang'armiut [from *avani,* "over there"]. Since some people love to talk, one of the people there told Aciqsauq what he had said. He told him what their *umialek* over there had said about him, that although they had mentioned that he was the *nukalpiaq* of Avang'armiut, why hadn't he been curious about the ocean, and that [the *umialek*] had already caught five bearded seals.

When he was done talking, [Aciqsauq] said to the person who informed him about what [the *umialek*] had said, "So he is impressed by just five [animals], [animals] caught only in one day. I thought he started going seal hunting a while back." That's how he replied to that person.

Then Aciqsauq prepared his kayak. He went down. When he arrived, they saw that he had caught five bearded seals. He caught up with him all at once.

All spring long, when he left to go hunting, he always arrived having caught five.

That person there, what was said by the person who gave his father a gift, "I'm not going to give this to you. I'm giving it to your future son." That turned out to be exactly true, the ability that he was given by *ircenrraat.*

Tua-i tamaa-i uksillermeggni iqukvaryarturniarallrani, nutegcuutekaanek, aug'um ilu'urma qanrutkellra ava-i aturluku, nutegcuutekaanek, ilani-gguq tamakut tungayani umyuaqluki piami, atu'urkanen'i cipluki tua-i kiputellrani, iliita tua-i aug'utun qanellratun uum pillinia, "Cakarpenek usuurluuq amrunaurpakarcit tamakunek, qailleraan-wa tamana aturarkarpenek pinaqsaaqelria."

Kiugaa-ggur-am, "Nutegyuumirarkat-wa tua-i umyuaqluki waten amrunaulrianga."

Ataucimek kiturillrulliniunga; kituralqa utervikqaqerlaku.

Tamaa-i tua-i negetmurrnginanermeggni, tumemeggni qavartaqataameng, qetunrani pillinii, "Pelatekaq kitek naparteqerciu wani qavartarniartukut."

Qanruqaarluki kelutmun ayaumaqanrakun angun man'a atralliniuq, tua-i-gguq cumiggluni, cumiggluni pektellra. Paircamiu-gguq pia, "Enemqerralriinkut-ggem tekitniit. Unkus-kiq una-i atiit naliqatgu." Ellii tua-i atiit apluku. "Naliqatgu-kiq tayima?"

Tua-i-gguq taum Enemqerralriim Atiin qetunrani kingyaarrluni kiugaa, "Tua-i-w' tayim' unkut naliqatgu." [*ngel'artuq*] Aturaqegcinrilan elliinguyuksugnaunaku.

Tua-i pissurnarian tua-i up'nerkaan tamaani pissulliniut. Taum tua-i tamakut tungayani waten tua-i-w' inglukerrluucirteng taringumiimiu, pillinii, tuami qavarpakanrilngermeng up'nerkarpak pissuryugluteng.

Tua-i-gguq taguquriut taqukanek. Taukurmiuni tua-i unangenruluteng. Unani-gguq anuqengengaitaqan pugtalriami unugpak uitaaqluteng.

Tua-i-gguq pissullerteng taq'ercan qaugkumiut qanernaurtut, arenqiatuqgguq ukut Avang'armiut ciku ilagarluku unani-ll' unugpak uitatulliniameng cikum akuliini. Tua-i capeqluki.

Tua-i tamaa-i qetunrani pissuangengata pissunringluni. Uitaqallratni-am iliita qayaakun ayalliniuq tayima. Ayaggaarluni-am agiirtelliniuq uciarluni tamaa-i qamigarnanringnermikun.

Nulirran elpekngamiu tekicartuarallrani erinami niicugngariaku qanlliniuq, "Man'a-mta pilliuq!" Tua-i maklagcukluku piamiu.

When they spent the winter there, near the end of winter, just as my *iluraq* stated earlier, when he purchased bullets for his relatives, when he bought more items than he needed, like this person said, one of the people there said to him, "What are you purchasing those many things for? Here you dearly need clothing for your poor self."

They say he replied to him, "I'm buying a surplus of things like this, keeping in mind the ones who will want to shoot [animals]."

I forgot to mention one part of the story; let me return to the section that I passed.

While they were heading north, when they were about to spend the night along their path, he said to his sons, "Pitch the tent so that we can spend a night here."

After telling them that, as he was heading inland, a man was coming down, walking excitedly. When he came upon him, he evidently said to him, "I thought they said Enemqerralria and his family had arrived. I wonder which one of the people down there is their father." He asked their father, "I wonder which one he is?"

Looking back at his sons, Enemqerralria's father said to him, "I'm not sure which one he is down there." [*laughs*] Because he wasn't wearing nice clothing, he never guessed it was him.

When it was time to hunt when spring came, they hunted there. Since he understood that the people there opposed them a little, he told his family that they should hunt all spring without spending too many nights on the shore ice.

They say that they brought many seals up to shore. They caught more than the people of that village. It is said when it wasn't going to get windy, they'd stay down on the ocean all night on floating ice.

When they were finished hunting, the northern people would express their reverence for the people of Avang'armiut who slept all night among the [pieces of] ice. They were astonished by them.

When his sons began hunting, he stopped hunting. One day while they were just sitting, he left with someone's kayak. After leaving, he returned carrying a load, during the time that he had stopped seal hunting.

When his wife realized that he was gone, while he was approaching, when he was able to hear her voice, she scoldingly said, "Has this person once again caught one!" She thought he had caught a bearded seal.

Ciunran-gguq kiugaa, "Pilliunga-mta!" Tua-i nukalpiarulliniami tauna Aciqsauq-gguq una. [*ngel'artut*] Tua-i augna qanemciullra aug'utun ava-i qanemcikqerqa Aciqsaum.

Tamaani elluatun tamakut ayagyuat ilait, wagg'uq qanruyutmeggnun maligtaqutellriit ca man'a ukvekesteminun piciucia aturluku, tamakut-am tamaa-i qanruyun aturluku ayagmek tan'gurraat pilriit, waten apqiitnek nuqlipakarpek'nateng ilameggnek unangqayuluteng pitullrullinilriit, qavar aturpakarpek'naku, cali-ll' qanruyun maligtaquluku pilriit.

Ii-i tua-i qanerkairuteksaileng'erma waten pitaqaquma.

☙

Cingyukan: Up'nerkillermiuni ak'a ak'aqucuk, pagaavet tang tua-i qauqamun, pagna kuvyaq, pagaani ingrim kangeqngalkiini muragagnek iquulquterluni uitaluni.

Taugken tua-i maavet qacarnermun mirqekata aqesgirugaat tua-i imumek tengcetaarluki ullakaceteng tengluteng pagaagguiquneng naperqelluteng. Tuaten Up'nerkillermiut pitullruut. Pagaani tua-i kangkacagaqngalkiinun kuvyaq civvluku.

Tuaten tua-i pitaqluk' taugaam amiiyuitait eritarrlainarluki. Allguryaureskait-wa maa-i.

☙

Neng'uryar: Ugkut-llu Up'nerkillermiut ak'a ciuliaput tayim' qanrutkelaqait upagaqameng, ingriq uneg' caperrnarquq.

Tamaaken nuugetgun pilallermeggni uvertuq. Qaillun iluvalartat pagken pilallret?

Tamakut-gguq ikamrateng muragpall'ernek qaillun ellegtaluteng avatetmun qillerrluki ellutullruut. Tua-i uvercan. Atratullruut.

Tamakuirtellriamek tauna call' ataataka qanrutkellrat, kenqutii aug'arrluni aaniit qecngelliniluni. Tua-w' tuqullrullilria tauna.

Tuaten tua-i ellutullrulliniut, iluvarqameng, ikamrateng, avateteng-gguq maragak qillrullukek, muragpaulutek qaillun ellegtalutek ellurcuutekluki

The one she addressed said to her, "I probably did [catch one]!" because the one they call Aciqsauq was evidently a *nukalpiaq*. [*laughs*] I'm just briefly telling the story of Aciqsauq.

In the past, some young people who did the right thing and obeyed their *qanruyutet,* as they say, by following the principle that whatever a person believes in will ultimately become true, young men who followed the *qanruyun* from the beginning evidently hardly ever lacked things among their peers and easily obtained things, those who didn't overindulge in sleep, and also those who followed and obeyed the *qanruyun* [never lacked things].

Although I haven't run out of things to say, this is all I'll say.

Albertina Dull: At Up'nerkillermiut long ago, up along the top of the mountain, there was a mesh net with wooden stakes on both ends along what seemed to be the top of the mountain.

When many ptarmigan landed along the bottom, when they approached them and tried to make them fly, they'd get caught when they flew up along the top. That's what the people of Up'nerkillermiut used to do. They'd set a mesh net at what seemed to be the very top of the mountain up there.

They'd catch [ptarmigan] like that, but they didn't skin them but always plucked them. These days they are starting to tear their skins off.

Lizzie Chimiugak: And as to that Up'nerkillermiut down the coast, when they moved there our elders used to say that those mountains down the coast posed formidable obstacles.

Back when they traveled along the points, they were extremely steep. I wonder how they managed to arrive when they went by those steep mountains?

They say they tied large logs this thick [as brakes] around their sleds and slide down. It was because it was extremely steep. That was how they went down.

They have told of my paternal uncle, when his [log] dragging device came off and their mother flew off. She probably died then.

They evidently slid down like that when they'd arrive there, they'd tie two logs alongside their sleds, two large logs that were a certain thickness

uvercan unegna. Qaillun igvalallrat caperrnaquq.

Taulan im' qanemciqa'arqami, nanvacuartangqertuq pagna uvertellria.

Makut taugaam nervikeurluamegteggu un'a imarpik, nunam qaingani kiingan nervikngamegteggu, tamakut taugaam tamaa-i alerquutekluki enrraat pegcugnaunaki nayiungraata cat enrrait tuavet tua-i mayuuqulallrullinikait ingrim qacarneranun navacuarmun quyurtaateng quyurqurarraarluki. Peksagtevkenaki angungnaqutait tamaa-i alerquutekellrulliniamegteki.

Tamakut taugaam taqukinraaraat cagcaaqevknaki, neqekngamegteki pikavet mayuutetullrulliniit. Taulam apertullrua tauna nanvacuar. Waten-llu issran imirluku pikavet mayuulluku kuvtullrat tua-i nanvacuarmun tuavet.

Up'nerkillermiut ugkut ak'a yungqerturatullrulliniameng.

Nurataaq: Augna qanemcika iquklicugnaunaku, wiinga iigemkun tangssullrenka Up'nerkillermi-ll' uani.

Makut wani nasaurluut, kiimeng-llu pillrunritlilriit, makut inuguateng, Up'nerkillermiuni waten nallunaitut inuguarviit ingrim uvenrani. Cali tamaqsaitut.

Elagluku waten inuguarvigluteng; yaaqliqu'urluteng tua-i yaaqliqu'urluteng inuguatullruut. Cenirrnguarcetaqluki-llu tamakut ilait inuguateng tamakut.

Tegungaunaki uksumi inuguateng watqapik: Tegungaunaki inuguarngaunateng uksumi. Uumek taugaam utaqakngarluteng qaqamek. Tua-i-llu qaqamek imna qalrialriamek niiskuni tuani tua-i inuguateng teguluki. Qaqat tua-i cuqyutekluki.

Neng'uryar: Quyaqatullruukut qaqanek niitaqamta.

Nurataaq: Tua-i qaqamek niiskuneng tuani inuguateng teguarkauluki. Tuaten tua-i piuraurlutullruut. Kiagpak-llu tua-i umyugiurluteng.

were used to slide down because that place down the coast is steep. How they came up on top of the village is daunting.

And whenever Taulan [Paul Agimuk] talked a bit about it he said that there was a small lake there on the steep side.

And because their food came from the ocean and also the land, and since they were instructed to do so, instead of haphazardly discarding the bones of any animal including those of seals, they took those bones up to that small lake on the side of the mountain after they gathered those they had been saving.

They were told not to scatter them because they were their means of survival.

They did not scatter and make a mess of those seal bones because they were their food, but they carried them up there. So Taulan pointed out that small lake. He'd mention how they filled up their grass baskets with the bones they collected and dumped them into that small lake.

That Up'nerkillermiut down the coast always had inhabitants in the old days.

Phillip Moses: Long before I completed what I was talking about, [I wanted to mention] what I saw with my own eyes down at Up'nerkillermiut.

And these young girls were probably not the only ones who did that with their dolls at Up'nerkillermiut, the places where the girls played with their dolls on the side of the mountain are easy to find. They still have not disappeared.

By digging and hollowing out the ground, they had places to play with their dolls; situated beyond one another, they played with dolls. And some of them pretended to have their dolls there visit other houses.

They could not take out their dolls in winter whatsoever: They will not touch their dolls in winter and play with them. But they wait for this common loon. Only when someone hears the loon's call, then they take out their dolls. Common loons are their guides.

Lizzie Chimiugak: We [girls] used to be so glad to hear the call of the common loons.

Phillip Moses: They were thankful. So when they heard the call of the common loon, they would take their dolls then. The poor [girls] always did that. So then, the entire summer they played with their dolls as much as they wanted.

Kaviarmiut

Unangik: Tua-ll' waniw' wavet waniw' taigukut ak'allanun nunanun, nunallernun ak'allaq'apiarnun ukunun, caitellernun, nutgunateng-llu talliteng taugaam kiingita caskukluki.

Waten tua-i waten uksuaryartuutaqateng wani kaugpiit cakmaken neplirqata qayat-gguq ayagaqelriit, nutgunateng-llu. Kapurluki kaugpiit tamaa-i tuqutaqluki ugingalriit.

Uani-gguq Umkumiut uani akiatni tua-i uksuarutaqateng waten kaugpiit pitullruut.

Ukut waniw' ak'allaqapiaraugut nunallret ukut, ciuliamta-ll' ciuliarit pillilriit. Tua-i talliteng taugaam kiingita caskukluki.

Makut maa-i kaugpiit alingnarqetuyaaqelriit; wangkuta-w' tua-i nutgunata alikekput. Tamaa-i kapurluki tuqutaqluki. Aling qecigtulriit-wa tuaten.

Qaill' tamakut yullret caperrnarqeqapiarluteng yuullruvagtat. Ak'a-ll' qaill' caqaqumta-ll', aarrarrarraarluta-ll' aqumluta ayagyuarungramta.

Tan'gurraat-am ilaita mernurniaqata pilaranka, wiinga tang aqumaqama mernuciirut'lallrulrianga mernurngaqaarlua. Aqumekuma-ll' mernulqa tamarluni.

Ukut waniw' nunallret ukut ak'allaupiartut, tua-i ak'alqapiarauluteng. Uksiviuluteng tuaten. Tuaten tua-i ayuqellruut ukut nunallret; tuaten ayuqellrunilarait.

Taugaam tayim' uksuutaqateng pavavet Qukaqlirrarmun; canimetuq tua-i maan Qukaqlirraq can'giingqetuluni-llu. Can'giircurviktullrullikiit tamakut yullret ikamracuarrarluteng tamaa-i. Tuaten tua-i qanrutketullrukait.

Ugkut-wa call' ua-i ugkut ua-i Naruyaruganek pitukait, taukut nanvat, naruyat irniviketuitki ugkut imkut ilanelilriit ugkut.

Cali tua-i maaten tua-i pianka ukut nunallret, puyuunguat pikaken ika-i Umkumiunek alaitetullruut ul'aqan; tungurpauluteng tua-i alaiterpagluteng tengaurqameng, maani maa-i misngaqutullruameng.

Tua-i-am pit'gaquyugngariama-ll' wiinga Kaviarmi wani uitaqallemteni, imkut tua-i pitegcautet cingigturaularyaaqellriit, tengkata, akuliitnun pik-

Kaviarmiut[17]

Simeon Agnus: We've come here to this old village site, this ancient site here, a place where people had no modern tools and amenities, and they had no guns, but their arms were their only means of hunting.

When it was near fall, when the noise of walrus started to be heard from down there, it is said that kayaks would leave, and they had no guns. They'd kill the walrus perched along the beach by spearing and piercing them.

It is said down there, across from Umkumiut, when fall came, there were walrus around.

This old village site is ancient, and our ancestors' forebearers probably lived here. Their arms were their only means of hunting.

These walrus are actually dangerous; we ourselves are afraid to hunt them without guns. They'd pierce them and kill them. My, and their skin is actually very thick.

My, our ancestors were incomparable. And when we do a little work, we say tiredly "*Aarraarrarraa*" and sit down although we're young.

When some young men say that they are sore and tired, I tell them that when I sat down after feeling sore and tired in the past, I didn't feel exhausted any longer. When I sat down, I no longer felt exhausted.

This old village site is ancient, it is very old. It was also a fall camp. This is how this village site was. That's what they say this place was like.

But when winter came, they'd go inland to Qukaqlirraq [Small one in the center]; Qukaqlirraq River is nearby, and there are blackfish there. People probably used that site for harvesting blackfish, using just small sleds for travel. That's what they said about them.

And the ones down there [along the coast], the ones they call Naruyarugaat [Many *naruyat* (gulls)], the lakes there, since the place down there is where gulls lay their eggs, there are many small islands.

Also, when I came to observe this old village site here, a large flock of little, long-billed birds, including dunlins, appearing like puffs of smoke when they flew were visible from up there at Umkumiut when the tide was high; they were very dark and very visible when they were flying, since they used to land in this area here.

And back when I was able to use a bow and arrow when we were living for a short time here in Kaviaq, although those arrows had just one point, when

uniki pitegcautni igetqapiggluteng, qavcinek pingayunek-llu nuvumalriartangqerraqluteng, augkunek ceremrarnek pitukengamtenek.

Puyuunguat amllerraqluteng. Atam amlletullruut, tua-i-llu tamarluteng tuatnayuirulluteng.

Kangrilnguq: Augkut ava-i puyuunguanek apellri imkut yaqulecuaraat cugg'erpiit ceremraat-llu; tamaa-i waten amllerem ugaan' teng'aqameng tunguriaqluni nalliit, tua-i-wa amllerem ugaani.

Maa-i watua nauwa tamakut? Tua-i caarrluk man'a amlleriami, ellam iluani nunam-llu qaingani, tamakut tua-i tamatum ikeglivkarai nallunailngurmek.

Cali-llu, ava-i ilu'urma-am qanrutkekai ukut nunallret ak'allapiaruniluki. Tua-i ilumun qanemcimegteggun ak'allapiaruut.

Waten tua-i ava-i qanellratun uani nervingqelalliniameng, taavtaangqelallinian ugna, Aciirutem una nunii, nervikluku tua-i pilalliniameng, kaugpiit tamaa-i enucetaqata nepaitgun niilluki ullagluki, ava-i qanellratun, kapurluki caskuilameng nutegnek tuqutaqluki.

Tua-i-am una call' qanemciat wani Kaviarmiuni ukuni. Tuaten tua-i kaugpagugarnek nalacirraarluteng navgurpailegmegteki iliit-am qanlliniuq, "Camiut-kiq waniw' nerniartatki?"

Ak'akika-gguq iliit avaken nunanek Caninermiunek ap'riuq, "Pimiut-wa nerkilitki."

Tua-i-am tuaten tauna tua-i kiustellran pimiunun neresqelluki, uksuan taukunun apellrinun kevgillinilriit ukurmiut waniw' Kaviarmiullret. Kelegluki tua-i apeqmeggnek tua-i kevgirluki.

Tuani-gguq tua-i cauyait amllellruut anrutaitnek amllernek unangameng kaugpiit.

Tua-i-am cali picirkiulliniut cauyailnguarucugluki allaneteng. Yuut tamaa-i cauyiquluteng tua-i cauyarugarnek amllernek pirraarluteng, cauyailnguarucugluki piameng, allaneteng tekiteqataata qasgim-qasgit kenillrit muragnek, wagg'uq nacicirluki pitullruit-patuluki. Camavet-am cauyarugateng atrartelliit kenillermun. Cauyalqurrarmek-gguq taugaam ataucirrarmek tua-i paivngailuteng.

Taukut-gguq tua-i allaneteng nerevkarraarluki apeqmeggnek nernerr-

they flew, when one shot his arrow among them, they'd fall, and sometimes the arrow would pierce a number of them, even three of those [birds] that we call dunlins.

There were many *puyuunguat* [large flocks of birds appearing like puffs of smoke]. There were many in the past, but they soon disappeared and are no longer seen like that anymore.

Paul John: The ones that he just called *puyuunguat,* those small birds with long bills and dunlins; because there were so many in the past, when they'd fly, the area where they were got dark, since there were so many of them.

These days, where are they? Since lots of pollution is in the air and on the land now, that is obviously causing the decline of those species.

Also, my *iluraq* just mentioned that this village site is very old. Indeed, from stories they tell about this place, this place is ancient.

As he stated, since their feeding grounds are down there along the coast, since there are heart cockle clams down along the coast there, the area around Aciirun [from *aci,* "area below, area under"], since they eat in that area, when the walrus were on shore during low tide, [hunters] would go to them after hearing their sounds, and like he said, they'd pierce them and kill them since they had no guns at that time.

The story they tell about Kaviarmiut here. After killing many walrus, before butchering them, someone among them evidently said, "I wonder which village residents will eat them?"

One of them mentioned a distant village from Canineq [the lower Kuskokwim coast], "The people of this particular village should eat them."

Honoring what that person said about a particular village eating [the walrus], during winter, the people of this village, the people who once lived in Kaviarmiut, invited the village that he named to attend a Messenger Feast. They invited them, *kevgirluki* [they sent messengers to invite them to a Messenger Feast] as they called it.

It is said that they had many drums at the time, since they had obtained many walrus stomachs [to make into drumskins].

They planned to lie to their guests that they had no drums. The people made drums, and after constructing many drums, since they had planned to lie to them that they had no drums, when their guests were about to arrive—they used to place floor boards over the fire pit of *qasgit*—they covered them. They lowered their many drums down into the firepit. They only left out one small, mangy drum.

After feeding their guests, when they were about to sing songs and dance

lugcetaariqataameng iliit qanlliniuq, "Arenqialngukut-wa tua-i cauyailngalriakut."

Tauna-ll'-am ilu'urqelliamiu ilaseng avalitkani kina tua-i yuk tauna aperluku, "Pim qenqertellermini cauyaput navgullrukai. Una taugaam waniw' tua-i cauyalqurraq taugaam kiingan cauyaqkevvut."

Tua-i-gguq imkut allanret umyugait qac'uqerrluteng; tua-i-gguq cauyaunateng kevgilriit yurallerkaatnek picirniyugpek'nateng.

Mumigarutarkauluteng apqiitnek pilliniameng, ilait-gguq umyuartequt, "Wiinga-w' cauyaunaki amllermek yurautekama ilait pivkenaki piciqelrianga."

Tua-i-am tuaten tua-i yuarutmek aturraarluteng, yuarun ciuqliq-qaa iquklican piut, "Nacitet pakigluki!"

Aren cauyarugarnek-gguq nugcingameng nugcingut. Tua-i-gguq kassugluku qasgi cauyanek tegumialegtarluni. Aren cauyaitni-llu-gguq kaugtullratni cakneq qaskeggngaqu'urpaa-gguq miikeggngapaa.

Imkut-gguq tuaten cauyaitellratnek ukatairciluteng yurautekateng ilait uitatnaluki umyuarteqsaaqellret, tua-i-gguq yurauciryugyaaqluteng umyuarteqequyaaqluteng [*ngel'artuq*], cauyateng anlluki cauyarugateng kaugtuallratni.

Tua-i-am taukut picingssaaraqallrulliniut tuaten taum nalliini allanerugangqellermeng. Camiunguyaaqut-am avani. Ii-i Cal'itmiunek tua-i kelgillrungatut taum nalliini, ingkut Qipnermiut nunapiallritnek ciuqlirmek.

Tua-i tamaani nunat ayuqluteng kevgirtaaruquratullruameng waten yaaqsingraata piyukteng apeqmeggnek kevgirluki pitullrulliniameng.

Ukurmiut-am tua-i yaaqsingraata Qipnermiut taukut nunaqerraallrit Cal'itmiut kelellrullinikait kaugpagugartameggnek tamakunek, iliita taukunun neresqellruaki. Tua-i neresqellri aturluki tua-i taukurmiunun kelegluki tua-i taukut pillrullinikait.

Unangik: Man'a maa-i kuik Kaviarauguq. Cali tua-i waten uksuarutaqateng iqalluanek tamaa-i qaluquluteng tamaa-i neqkameggnek pitullrulliniut. Man'a maa-i kautuat ceturrnat; kautuat man'a maa-i kuig-man'a.

Tak'uq atam; maaggun ingigutem engeliikun kiatmurtuq maa-i man'a.

to try to purposely interfere with their eating, *nernerrlugcetaariqataameng* [singing songs of indigestion] as they called it, one of the people there said, "Unfortunately, we have no drums."

Since that particular man who he was to blame for the situation was probably his *iluraq* [teasing cousin], he named that person and said, "When this person got angry, he broke our drums. This mangy drum here is our only drum."

The guests suddenly felt disappointed; they weren't too thrilled to watch the Messenger Feast presenters dance without any drums.

Since they had planned to have the guests dance and present gifts right after the host village danced and presented gifts, *mumigarulluteng* as they say, some people thought, "Since they don't have any drums, I won't present some of the gifts that I was going to present while dancing."

After singing a song, was it when the first song was over that they said, "Pull up the floor boards!"

My, when they started to take out drums, they began to take many out. It is said people held drums around the entire *qasgi*. My, it is said when they beat their drums, the sound was rich and deep.

It is said the people who were previously disappointed because they had no drums and thought that they wouldn't present some of their gifts, they wished that they had many gifts to present [*laughs*] when they took out their many drums and began beating them.

Those people carried out a hoax in that way when they had many guests. Those [guests] were from some village. Yes, I think it was people from Cal'itmiut who they invited during that time, the original village of the people of Kipnuk.

Back when all the villages would host and take part in Messenger Feasts in their villages, although the villages were far away, they would invite the villages they wanted to Messenger Feasts.

Although this village was far, they invited the original village of the people of Kipnuk, the people of Cal'itmiut, since one of the people there had wanted them to eat the many walrus that they had caught. Fulfilling their hopes that the people from that village would come to eat them, they evidently invited the people of that village.

Simeon Agnus: This river here is called Kaviaq. Also, when fall came, they would dipnet for tomcod that they ate. Tomcod enter this river; they come into this river.

This is a long river; this river goes inland along the edge of where the

Taugaam kiani Kaviayagaat nuniitni quuqerrluni tua-i amelkelliluni.

Ii-i taukut Kaviarmiungutkaat tua-i Kaviayagaat kiugkut.

Kangrilnguq: Kiugkut kia-i apellrit Kaviayagaat, ukurmiut waniwa Kaviarmiunek atengqerrutekait. Man'a-ll' maa-i kuik Kaviarautekluku qamkut ingigutem engeliini igterugaat.

Kaviaret irniluteng taukuni igterugarni kaviayagaat tua-i amlleraqluteng taukut igtet nuniitni. Taumek tua-i waniw' Kaviarmiungutekluku qamkut irniviit kaviaret igterugait, Kaviayaarnek taugaam apruterluteng.

Unangik: Waten qakurnaqungluku tamaa-i ilumun tua-i tamakut caperrnarqepigtellrulriit arnat. Waten-llu aklunek-llu teguqerrartengssaarpek'nateng, imarnitnek taugaam tua-i aturluteng pitullrullilriit imarnitpianek aturluteng tamaa-i ungumrarluteng. Qakurnaqungluku, meq-llu kumlangellran nalliini. Qaillun tamakut yugeurluut yuullruat. Pinirpagtat tamakut yuut.

Piniqapiarluteng, arnaungermeng pinillrulliniut yullret imkut. Tayima-ll' waten apquciarpakarpek'nateng pillruyugnarqut tua-i kencikulluteng yuullruameng, kencikutqapiarluteng. Aturait tua-i arnamun ngigcessngaunaki waten tua-i ayagyuarullratni. Ellaita tua-i pikluki.

Kangrilnguq: Wiinga waniwa aanamnek tangvatullruunga maurlumnek-llu uksuarmi cikut, imumek-llu cikulluarqengraan ivratullregnek.

Imkunek tua-i imarnitnek as'arrlutek naqugarrluki ivrarlutek tua-i apeqmeggnek cikulluarqengraan ivrarlutek qalu civvnaukek.

Tuamtell' tua-i qayakun ungumralriit, tuaten tua-i cikulluarqem nalliini cikulluarkun ungumratullruut angutet.

Tekiskata ungumrallrit, ukuk cali tua-i iverluteng tuaten tua-i cikulluarqengraan qalut nugtaqluki.

Tamaa-i caperrnaqvaa, kumlaqalriamek-llu tangerrnaqsuunani apqiitnek kumlam itqerreskiinek.

Caqerluni taugaam tua-i ataucirqumek aanaka ivrumavallagluni aglugugni-ll' aitartesciiganakek nugellruuq ugaan kumlatem. Puqlamek taugaam tua-i igqaqu'urluni urugluku.

marshland becomes tundra. But it suddenly gets small and becomes narrow up near Kaviayagaat [Little *kaviat* (red foxes), where fox dens are located].

Yes, Kaviayagaat upriver is the reason why [this place] is called Kaviarmiut.

Paul John: The ones he mentioned upriver, Kaviayagaat is the reason why this place is called Kaviarmiut. And the many dens up along the edge of where the marshland rises and becomes tundra are the reason why this river is called Kaviaq [Red fox].

Red foxes give birth there in those many dens, and many fox pups are there along those dens. The numerous red fox birthing dens are the reason this place is called Kaviarmiut, but the place where the dens are is called Kaviayagaat.

Simeon Agnus: When frost started to form, indeed those women were beyond compare. And they didn't have an abundance of gear, but they probably wore seal-gut rain garments, the real seal-gut rain garments to strike the water to drive the fish. When frost started to form, the water also started to get cold. I wonder how those poor people lived. How strong those people were.

Although they were women, those people of the past were evidently strong. And I think they hardly became ill because they had great respect for one another's clothing. They wouldn't allow a woman to lean or sit on men's clothes when they were young. [Those clothes] belonged only to them.

Paul John: During fall I used to watch my mother and my grandmother who used to wade in the water although it was a little icy.

They'd put on seal-gut garments and secure a belt over it, and then they'd wade in the water although it was a little icy, *cikulluarqengraan* as they call it, and set the dip net.

And again, those who were striking the water's surface and driving fish [into the nets] with kayaks, when there was a thin film of ice along the water, the men would strike the water to drive the fish during a time when it was icy.

When the driven fish came, they'd continue to wade in the water although it was a little icy and pull the dip nets out of the water.

How very difficult that was, and no one succumbed to hypothermia, one whose body succumbed to hypothermia because the cold entered the core of his body.

But once my mother waded in the water for too long, and she was unable to open her jaws when she came out of the water because she was so cold. But when she periodically drank some warm water, her body warmed up.

Cakneq-lli augkuni yugni caperrnarqellrullinivaa. Mat'um nalliini yuk pingairutuq maa-i. Tangvalallruamki tua-i qalulriit wiinga ava-i tangvalalqa augna cikulluarqengraan arnat ivralallrat qanrutkeqa'arqa.

Anguyaluk: Wiinga tangvalallruunga maani qalulrianek, qaluyalrianek. Maligutlallruunga; uavet ua-i iterluni painga augna ukatmurrluni, tua-i-ll' ukatmurtellrani, tuavet qalumeggnek civciluteng, qalunek pingayunek, kapulluki marayamun caniqliqu'urluki.

Tua-i-ll' tuaten civterraarluki arnak, malruk ayaglutek ungumraryarturlutek itrarlutek maavet. Wangkuta-ll' tua-i kingunratni aqumgaluta utaqalukek.

Tamakut qaluqatalriit uayatullruut arnat. Akluirluteng tua-i imarnitnek kiingan aturluteng, makut-llu taqmateng maavet mayurrluki taukut tangvak'ngallrenka pilallruut, naqugarrluteng-llu.

Tua-i-ll' ungumrak ayaglutek qava-i igvaryarturlutek pikagnek, nutaan yulkiasqevkenata-ll' pinauraakut.

Uani ua-i tayim' kitullrukvut; iterluni kuik ukatmurrluni, painga-ll' ua-i alaitaqluni. Tuavet civcitullruut eningarmi taugaam entaqan.

Tua-i-ll' nutaan igvaqata keluatgun wangktua; wangkuk-wa Theresa-q-llu piyartuusqelallrukiikuk. Nutaan una-i keluatnek atrarlunuk keluatgun ungumraruarturlunuk taukut ungumralriit keluatgun piurlunuk.

Tua-i-ll' tuavet qalunun tekiskuneng paingani tuani kaugtuarturluteng tua-i qalut-llu makut pugluteng. Qalut qalirnerit pugluteng neqet itraqata tuavet qalunun.

Tua-i-ll' nutaan kaugtuarturaqerraarluteng cukangnaqluteng kapusngalriit amuluki, tua-i-llu painga waten tua-i qipqerluku.

Yaaqliqu'urluteng qaluteng cenamun tagqurluki. Cenamek-llu tuaken nutaan imait issratkun cali pagaavet mayuuqurluki, imairturluki.

Imairraarluki tua-i nutaan qaluteng taggluki iniluki uani ua-i inimaluteng.

Tua-i nunaniqluteng. Tamakut avaciqerluki neqtateng unilluki tuavet.

My, how extremely daunting those people were. These days, a person won't do that again. Since I used to watch people dipnetting, I've briefly mentioned witnessing women wading in water although it was a little icy.

Martina John: I used to watch people dipnetting here at this place, people who went to dipnet. I used to accompany them; when entering the river mouth, it bends in this direction, and when it bends in this direction, that's where they set their dip nets, three dip nets, staking them in the mud side-by-side.

And after setting them like that, two women would leave to go and strike the water to drive the fish into the nets, coming upriver to this area. And after they left, we sat and waited for them.

The women who were about to dipnet would remove their clothing. They'd remove their clothing, and they'd only wear seal-gut rain garments, and the women who I watched would lift their skirts up to [their waists], and then they'd put on a belt.

Then the two who struck the water to drive the fish into the net would leave, and when they were coming into view upriver, they'd tell us to stay out of sight and not make noise.

Downriver, along the area we passed; when you enter the mouth, the river bends this way, and the mouth was visible down there. They would set nets there but only during low tide.

Then when they came into view, we would go along the shore above them; they'd ask Theresa and I to do it. We'd go down from the shore above them and pretend to strike the water to drive the fish from along the shore above the ones who were actually striking the water to drive the fish.

And when they got to the dip nets, they'd continue to strike the water along the opening of the dip net, and the dip nets would surface in the water. The tops of the dip nets would appear when the fish went inside them.

Then after striking the water for some time, they'd quickly pull out the stakes that were thrust into the mud, and then they'd just twist the opening of the net.

They'd bring their dip nets up to shore situated right beyond one another. And then from shore, they brought the contents up to shore using twined grass carrying bags, and they emptied them one by one.

After emptying them, they'd bring their dip nets up to shore and then hang them, and they'd stay hung downriver.

It was very joyful to watch them. They'd place something around the fish they caught and leave them there.

Nutaan-llu ut'reskata ulkan angutet aqvailuteng taukunek qalukengaitnek.

Wangkuta tua-i maani mikelnguuluta tamaa-i pillruamta unuakuarmi tupagaqamta, uavet qalut tua-i tekcitagnek pitqutuata, aqvaqulalriakut uatmun. Nunaniqluteng. Pitaitnek paqnayugluta.

Pilu'ugtuyuitellruukut maantellemteni. Kamilangqaurluta. Kamilarramta. Tut'eqarraami, kelugkarnun-llu piqarraami, tua-i aknirnaqluteng kapukcuallagaluteng alut piiyaaqerraarluteng elpegiuskuneng cangatenrirluteng.

Nangluteng tayim' qalutullret, acacungaqa taugaam kiugna Cingyukan kiimi kia-i qalutullerni tamakuni ilakelallritni kiimi tua-i tangrruulria.

Tua-i caqerluteng-am tua-i qaluyallermeggni, makut-wa cikuvguaraat mamkunateng aterqurqai. Tua-i qerrutkacagarluteng tagluteng qunglluteng urugcirluteng qalunermek taqngameng.

Qaluuratullruut maani arnat, angutait-llu pissurngacuunateng, arnat taugaam tua-i qalukenganek piuraraqluteng. Inialiriluteng. Inialiriluteng iqalluanek. Kinrata-llu qecugluki.

Nutaan waken cali, waken cali, maaken cali maa-i itrarvingqellruukut; mat'um ingigutem engeliikun qamavet Kaviayaarnun. Makiraquluta. Makirarluta tamaavet Kaviayagaat tekilluki.

Pelatekat imkut, takuyarnaurtukut qerratauksuarluteng ua-i pelatekat uitalriit. Tuavet tekiskumta iqvarluta, amrayaagnek aptullrit issratet iluqliit anrutat imirturluki.

Yuukitengnaqluki iqvaput amlleriaqata qagerqelluki imiraqluki, tuavet naivaqluki.

Tua-i-ll' nutaan uqamaitelaata, qertuuralriim qainganun unilluki issrateteng, unilluki nutaan uterrluteng. Tuamtell' tua-i qayakun tamakut pitait aqvaluki. Ul'aqan aqvaaqluki, unuaquani-llu iliikun aqvaaqluki ununrakun utertaqamta.

Uitavikelalput tang allayuungalnguq una. Nanvatangqertuq pavani tamaani-llu qungunek-llu pitarluni. Qavcin qungut uitallruut tamaani.

After they returned, when the tide came up, the men would go and retrieve the fish they dipnetted.

Since we were children during the time we were here, when we'd wake up in the early morning, since the [hanging] dip nets would catch *tekcitat* [small birds], we'd run down toward the mouth. It was very joyful to watch them. We were curious about what the nets had caught.

We never wore shoes when we were living here. We always went barefoot. We had no shoes. When we walked around and stepped on coarse grass for the first time, it was painful, and after the bottom of our feet felt like they were pricked, when our feet became numb to the pain, they felt okay after that.

The people who used to dipnet are all gone now, but my *acacungaq* [little paternal aunt] Cingyukan [Albertina Dull] is the only one still around of those who used to participate with the dipnetters.

One time when they went dipnetting, thin sheets of ice were dispersed floating along the river. They were very cold when they went up and placed their bodies in a fetal position and warmed up when they were done dipnetting.

Women always dipnetted here, and their men didn't seem to go hunting and fishing, but the women always worked on fish that they dipnetted. They'd obtain many fish that were hung to dry. They'd obtain many tomcod hanging to dry. And when they dried, they'd pull them [off the braided grass where they hung].

Then from this place, we had a place we went up to; we'd travel along the edge of the marshland where the land rises and becomes tundra up to Kaviayaat. We'd gather greens. We'd gather greens reaching Kaviayagaat.

We'd look back and see tents that were a little above the ground. When we'd reach that place, we'd pick berries, filling the twined grass carrying bags' inside liners that they called *amrayiit,* the [dried] stomach containers.

We tried to make them as compact as possible when we picked a lot of berries, and we'd pop them when we filled them, spilling them into those [containers].

And since they were heavy, they'd leave their twined grass carrying bags on top of a steep place and return home. And then they'd go with kayaks and retrieve the berries they obtained. They'd go and get them when the tide came up, and sometimes they'd get them the next day, if we'd returned home in the evening.

This place where we used to stay seems different. There is a lake up there, and there are some graves there. There were a number of graves there in that area.

Tua-i tangnerrarlua mat'umek. Wani uitatullrungramta tuani tua-i can'gurneret engeliitni, allaunganani taugken.

Kangrilnguq: Kic'ami-wa man'a nuna atraami.

Anguyaluk: Keluatni-wa maani uquucillret. Quagelvall'ernek tua-i pingqerraqluteng.

Tamaavet nanvanun kic'eciaqluteng naunrarnek itrarpailegmeng.

Tua-i-ll' upakataquneng nuggluki nutaan itraulluki. Atraulluki upakataquneng ayaulluki.

Maaken cali upangramta ciunitevkenata natmun avavet cali arulairluteng pelatekaqerluteng cali uitaaqluteng. Tamaa-i naternassurluteng, naternassuraqluteng.

Tuqsuum-llu iluanun pikumta, kiugna kia-i Kass'aurluq arulairviktullrukiit. Tamatum nalliini narulkaquluteng-llu malirqetullruameng, tua-i nepengnaurtut ama-i nalluvkenaki-ll' taukut malirqeniluki piaqluteng.

Nutaan tamaaken uitallemtenek nutaan tua-i nenglingengaaraqan itrarluteng nutaan uksillerkameggnun qamavet itrarluteng.

Tamakunek tamaa-i tangvalallemnek qanemciunga wantelallemteni. Qavcirqunek tua-i wantelallruukut una uitavikurluku. Ikgetevkenata, tua-i pelatekat yaaqliqluteng uitalallruut wani.

Tua-i nangluteng, nangluteng. Wani waniwa Tuquyuilnguq-llu tuqullruuq wani nunani.

Ikaken Umkumiunek iqalluarpiit kinraqata Umkumiunek tua-i ikaken caarkairutaqameng *move*-araqluteng maavet. Tamaa-i qalullerkameggnun, neqsullerkameggnek allanek. Iqalluarpauteteng tua-i elagyangqerrameng unitetullruit ikavet ava-i uitavimtenun.

Tamatum nalliini yuut assillruameng kelucamek-llu piilengraata itrarciuyuunateng tamakut elagyat elliviit. Imateng imaquraaqluki qaillukuarumavkenateng.

Tua-i unilluki. Tua-i-ll' itraquneng, nutaan uksuureskan, uksuumainanrani iqalluarpautmeggnek, neqmeggnek nangutengkuneng nutaan ikamrakun cali neqsaagaqluteng tamakunek unitallermeggnek kinernernek.

This place doesn't look the same to me. Although we stayed here, along the edge of the grassy place, it looks different.

Paul John: It's because the land has sunk, because it's gone down.

Martina John: There were underground seal-oil storage pits behind them. There were very large sourdock plants there.

Inside the lakes there, they'd sink some salmonberries underwater before they went up.

And when they were going to move, they'd pull them out of the water and bring them up. They'd bring them down when they were about to move and take them along.

And although we moved from this place, we didn't go straight to our destination but stopped someplace out there, set up the tents, and stayed there. They'd fish for flounder.

And when we went inside the Tuqsuk River, they'd stop up there at Kass'aurluq. Back in those days, since they always hunted seals by pursuing them in open water with spears, they'd get noisy up there, and they knew what they were doing out there and said that they were pursuing seals in open water.

Then from that place where we were staying, when it started to get cold, they'd go up to their winter camps up there.

I'm just telling you about things that I observed when we lived at this place. We stayed at this place a number of times, always at this place here. There weren't just a few people, but tents were next to one another at this place here.

[The people who stayed here] are all gone now. Tuquyuilnguq also died here at this place.

From across there at Umkumiut, when the herring dried, they'd move here from Umkumiut when they had nothing else to do. They'd move here to dipnet and fish for other fish species. Their dried herring, since they had partially underground storage caches, they'd leave them over there in the place where we are staying [at Umkumiut].

Since people were honest back in those days, although they had no locks, those partially underground storage caches were never broken into. Things stored inside were always there, and they weren't bothered.

They'd leave them behind. And when they went up, when winter came, during winter, when they ran out of fish, they'd go during winter with sleds and retrieve the herring they harvested, the dried fish that they had left behind.

Cali Al'aquciq yungqerrluni Tapruar-llu yungqerrluni. Tamaa-i kiagiqtaarviit. Uaken itraraqameng taugaam, ayagaqameng uaken neqsuqtaarturluteng tamaa-i, qimugtengqerrameng-llu qimugteteng nerqallerkaitni uitataqluki.

School-amek-llu piiyuitellruameng *school*-amun nerilegcugnaunateng, uksuakacagarmi taugaam itraraqluteng.

Unangik: Aren imat'anem qanrutkenritliniaqa. Ingna atam yaani nanvallrem ilua kaugpinrarnek enernek imangqertuq tua-i, enrugarnek. Ukut wani kiaqliita ketiini nanvalleq taksuryiurluni. Tamaa-i ciqicivillrat. Enrugaat kaugpiit enrit amlleret yaani.

ᴥ

Cingyukan: Qalutuluta, ivraraluta qaluaqluta maatekiirluta. Qalut-wa tegumiaput, kuig'atrarluku.

Tua-i kuinra-ll' cam' nalluvkenaku camna terr'a. Manialkan tua-i nateqvaqaniqerluta call' qalut tua-i civvluki.

It'gamtenek acia camna qemia tutmaulluku marayamun qap'iqu'urcelluku. Apqiitnek-llu initarak cali makuk tuaten cali. Qemia camna atlirnera marayamun qap'iqu'urcelluku qaluaqluta.

Qaluka tua-i taumun manillruyugnarqaqa. Taugaam yualukauguq, pelacinayagauguq.

Ang'uq. Qalurpallraat. Tak'ut.

Iqalluat naternat-llu pitaqluki ungumrarluta. Ungumrarluta tua-i imarnitnek all'uta qillerrluta.

Tua-i muragaq man'a wagg'uq ungumrautaput unrapigayagaq assirluni.

Tua-i-ll' ungumraqumta natkaarturluta ayagturluta qalum qavaken iquanek qavaken kuigmek. Ungumrarluta tua-i ungumrautaq terr'anun tus'arqurcelluku.

Qainganun pivkenaku. Camavet tua-i terr'anun. Kaugtuarluku, terr'anun agtuqaulluku.

Anguyaluk: Neqet tua-i ayagcelluki.

Cingyukan: Tuaten tua-i. Imumi tua-i canimi qaluyaryaaqellemni, aren tua-i

There were also people living in Al'aquciq, and there were people at Tapruar. Those were the summer camps. Only when they went up from down the coast, when they left that place down the coast, they'd fish periodically as they traveled, and since they had dogs, they'd stay in places where they could feed their dogs.

And since they had no schools in the past, schools didn't hold them back, but they'd go up during late fall.

Simeon Agnus: Oh, I didn't mention it. The inside of that old lake over there is filled with walrus bones, many bones. It's an old lake that is down below the place up above here, a longish lake. That was their dumping place. There are many walrus bones over there.

Albertina Dull: We used to dipnet, we used to wade with the water reaching part of our bodies and dipnet. We held dip nets, going down into the river.

And we knew where the river's deep channel was, the bottom of the river down there. When it was rough, we'd move over in either direction and set the dip nets also.

We used our feet to step on the line that was tied onto the bottom of the dip net to sink it under the mud. And we also did that to the fish fence. We had the line tied to the bottom of the net sink into the mud and we'd dipnet.

I think I showed that person [Ann] my dip net. But it is made of store-bought twine, it's made of small twine.

It's large. Dip nets were very large. They are long.

We'd catch tomcod and flounder by striking the water with sticks to drive the fish. We'd strike the water with sticks to drive the fish by putting on seal-gut rain garments and tying [belts around our waists].

The wooden stick that we used to strike the water to drive the fish was a small, good *unrapigaq* [straight-grained piece of wood with few knots].

And then when we struck the water to drive the fish, we walked along with the water up to [the middle] of our bodies, from the end of the river. We'd strike the water with the stick, having the stick constantly touch the river bottom.

We didn't just [strike] the surface. We'd touch the river bottom. We'd continuously strike [the water], lightly touching the river bottom.

Martina John: Having the fish swim.

Albertina Dull: That's what they did. In the past when I went to dipnet

tang imurtualrianga wiinga. Tuar pinritsaangerma tua-i imurtuakacagarlua. Kumlaqillua, imurtualua-gguq tua-i.

Anguyaluk: Waten [neplirluni]. [*ngel'artut*] Kumlam piluku.

Cingyukan: Yaa, ii-i tua-i-ll' tekiskumteggu kaugtuarturluta ciuqerrani. Tua-i-ll' piqerluta, qalu nuculerluku paikek ataucimurrluku. Neqet assirpak anglanaqluteng.

Anguyaluk: Imkut, qalut iquit pug'aqluteng neqet itraqata. Itqata tua-i qalu-ll' una pugyarturluni imangluni neqnek.

Cingyukan: Imangluni. Anglanaqsaaqluni. Taguqurluki-ll' tua-i.

Anguyaluk: Qamurluku cenamun tagulluku. Tua-i-llu issratnek assigcirturluta imainek mayuuqiurluta.

Cingyukan: Anglanarpak cillartellriani kuimarluteng tua-i anglanaqluteng.

Arnani, aka'ar taugaam yaqulegcutullruut. Waten wiinga ellangua imna Akagualriim aanallra kanani Kaviarmiuni, kuvyakuinrayagaq, kuvyakuinrayagaq ikgetkacagarluni issratmun ek'arrluku. Pilu'ugturyugnaunata kamilamta. Maligtelalqa.

Tua-i-ll' agaani iciw' Kaviaq arvirluku, marami agaani kangarlunuk.

Tua-i-ll' piyagarnek tangerqumegnuk, aipaqa, tua-i tauna kuvyaq teguluku, iciw' nanvam imum quuyarpiaqallra, amilkelliirtellranun civvluku iverluni.

Tua-ll' tamakut yaqulget ungukateng, tuagguiquneng naperqelluteng. Tua-i-ll' issratii imangekan uterrluni.

Cali imna iciw' Cungiim aanallra piani imkuni tunutellelilriani tuaten cali pitullruuq. Waten apqaitni akulnguuyaarni, amelkilngurni, cali kuvyarraq civvluku.

Tua-i cali tua-i ungunrilngermiu unitaqluku tua-i tunutelleliqaqluni.

Kemgit iniurluki, qetunrani-ll' imna tua-i tunutellegnek atkungevkaraqluku. Tuaten atam pitullruuq-llu, imkunek allegngiatkacagalrianek.

Tuaten-am tauna-ll' Akagualriim aanii. Waten taugaam piyagaullermeggni

close by, I was crying out from the cold. Although I tried not to, I was crying out loudly from the cold. I was reacting to the cold, and I cried out from the cold, what they call *imurtualua*.

Martina John: She was [making noise] like this. [*laughter*] The cold was causing her to do that.

Albertina Dull: Yes, and when we got to [the nets], we'd continuously strike the water in front [of the net]. Then after a while, we'd suddenly pull up the net and gather the opening together. The fish were fun to watch.

Martina John: The end of the dip nets would surface when the fish would enter. When [fish] entered, the net would become visible [along the water's surface], filling with fish.

Albertina Dull: It would fill up. It was actually fun. Then we'd bring them up to shore.

Martina John: They'd drag it and bring it to shore. Then we'd use woven grass carrying bags to bring up the [net's] contents.

Albertina Dull: It was a lot of fun watching it when it opened as [fish] were swimming. . . .

Women [also] hunted birds long ago. When I became aware of my surroundings, the deceased mother of Akagualria down at Kaviarmiut would place a very small mesh net inside a grass carrying bag. We didn't wear shoes at all but went barefoot. I used to accompany her.

Then across there, we'd cross Kaviaq River and walk along the marshland across there.

Then when we saw young birds, my companion, she'd take that net, and she set the net by wading in the water along a place where the lake almost closed in, where it became narrow.

Then when she would drive those birds, when they swam through there, they would get caught [in the net]. Then when her grass carrying bag was filled [with birds], she'd return home.

Cungiiq's deceased mother also did that up in the place where there are many Pacific loons. She'd also set a small net in places they call *akulnguuyaaret* [narrow parts of lakes] in places that were narrow.

Although she didn't drive the birds toward the net, she'd leave it there and catch many Pacific loons.

She'd constantly hang their meat to dry, and she'd make her son a Pacific loonskin parka. She also did that, [making parkas] out of [skins] that don't tear easily.

That's what the deceased mother of Akagualria used to do. When the

augkut yaqulget iciw' imumek tua-i pistemeggnek-llu anglaninritlallermeggni nalliini tuaten pitullrulriit. Tuaten tua-i kuvyiqerluteng.

Tamakut piyagaat tengqatalriit-llu makut yaqulget piyagaat, qeciit-llu tamakut qaugraraat, qecikekacaarluteng. Tuaten tamaa-i atkugkateng-llu umyuaqluki tuaten kuvyiqulallrullilriit. Tauna tua-i Cimiralria Akagualriim aanallra maligtelallemni pilallruuq.

Makut cali yaqulget iciw' uquitkacagalriit iqutellrat assiilngatlallrulria. Ciilercugpagluki. Metraat imkut uquicunqekacagallruut. Iqucunaunateng assiinateng. Kelluteng'ermi ciilercugpagluni.

Qalulleq

Unangik: Augkut Arnapagaq ilu'urqa Niugtarmi nallunrilkeci; tamaa-i wantellruut-gguq cali Qalullermiuni ukuni.

Ingkut yaa-i, augkut uqvigaat pia-i tangrraci; iquata nalliitni pia-i uitaut pingkut nunallret.

Tuaten tua-i ayuqut pingkut. Tua-i angussaagviilngalngermeng, taugaam waten amaqsut, irunat-llu tamaa-i maavet itetungatut.

Taugaam tua-i neq'rugarnek una qanernaqsuituq Qalulleq, tua-i qaneryarauluni tua-i tumyarami uitiimi una. Ikamrat iciw' tua-i kituqetaaqiit ketiitgun ukut wani.

Tua-i angutait wavet waniw' tevluteng Qalullermek uskuarmi amirkanek nayuraqluteng malirquurarkameggnek taqukanek. Amirkat tamaani paivngakacaaralallruyugnarqut, maliqniyaumaaqluteng.

Kangrilnguq: Una-ll' waniwa uitavigput, entaqan imairutetuyaaquq.

Waten ulutaqateng imarpinraat itetuata, augna-am ava-i kiavet, natmun tua-i tamaavet kuvyiryarturluni imarpinrarcurtuq, Negtemek kiaken kingunirluni ava-i. Tua-i man'a maa-i ul'aqan naptaat itetuluku.

Taugaam maa-i mermek imangqessuirutarkaurtellni ullagluku; entaqan

birds were younglings, during times when they didn't have anyone to carry out work for them, that's what they did. They'd set nets like that [to catch birds].

The younglings, and those young birds about to fly, and those small spectacled eiders had very good skins. They also probably set nets like that [to catch birds] for the parkas they would make out of them. That's what Cimiralria, the deceased mother of Akagualria, used to do when I'd accompany her.

Tanning these birds that didn't have a lot of fat on them also seemed to be ineffective. They tended to be too dry. Those common eiders tended to have no fat. They weren't good to tan. Although we watched over [the skin] while tanning it, it tended to dry up fast.

Qalulleq River[18]

Simeon Agnus: You all know Arnapagaq, my *iluraq* from Newtok; it is said they also lived here at Qalulleq [Place where one dipnets].

The ones over there, you see the small trees up there; the old village site is along the edge of those [trees].

That's how that place is up there. Although it seems as though there is no place to subsist in their surrounding area, I think pink salmon and Dolly Varden trout go into that river.

Qalulleq isn't mentioned as having an abundance of fish, since this place is along the trail. You know how snowmobiles are constantly passing down below this place.

Their men would portage overland to [the Toksook River] from Qalulleq, and they would watch for young bearded seals that they would pursue in open water. I think young bearded seals were abundant back in those days, and so they would come here to pursue seals in open water.

Paul John: And the place where we are now [Qalulleq] usually empties completely when the tide goes out.

When the tide comes in, since *imarpinraat* [whitefish] come in the river, that person who we just saw had just gone up there to fish for *imarpinraat,* coming from Nightmute upriver just now. When the tide goes in, *naptaat* [Bering cisco] enter this river.

But today, it's nearing the time when water will no longer enter this river;

kinturiluku meriulluni mat'um maa-i ilua. Kinturiluku tua-i, nallunailngurmek nunaurtarkauluni.

Kiugna kia-i kiaqlia qamna cingigpapialleq; wiinga-ll' cevpailgatgu tanglallrukeka. Maa-i nunaqapiurrluni waten kuilleq cingiulleq. Mer'em-wa tua-i carvanenmikun carrirnanriani nunaurrluni.

Una-ll' waniw' tuatnaciquq, neqsurviunrirluni. Maa-i imarpinrarcurvikluku imarpinrarnek neqkangviklaqiit.

Tua-llu ava-i qanertukuk ukut qanemcikarpakarkaitniluki. Tua-i taugaam uumek iquliqeryugyaaqaqa angalkullratnek pingkut Qalullermiut.

Una waniwa uum atqaa Qalulleq. Ping'um tua-i cingiim tua-i ateqluku. Qalullrutkaa pingna; ateqluku.

Tua-ll' tamaani ukut waniw' Qalullermiut angalkungqellrullinilriit, taumek tua-i angalkumek.

Tua-i-ll'-am piqerluni, taum arnat iliita tuquqatalriim, apqiitnek tua-i imumek-wa tua-i naulluullran mat'um avalitekluku, kapiatekluku. Piuraurlurluni tauna arnaq tuqulliniluni.

Tuquan atam tua-i uinga tauna tua-i qivruyaaqeng'ermi tauna tuqutenrilkurrluku, ikamrak taugaam navgullinikek; ikamrak tua-i navgurlukek, umyuami assiicaaqetacia tayima niilluku.

Ikamrak navgurraarlukek qasgimun iterluni, pakemna qasgim egalrakun nulirra taum angalkum qanlliniuq, "Ellmini cupuirtuq ikamrak navguamikek."

Nutaan tua-i tauna angun qenqerpallaarluni angalkuq tauna ullagluku tuququallinikii.

Tuqucamiu-llu pikavet pika-i Qalullrem qalirneranun mayuucamiu navgurluku tua-i, iik-ll' ikugglukek piaqlukek. Iik-gguq ikugngamikek, ellimalriim kenurrallran palungqalriim acianun palurullukek. Tua-i tayima.

Tua-i taumeg-am nulirran qanellran, tuqutetngurtellruniluku. Umyugaa assiileng'ermi tua-i tauna tuqutenrilngermiu, ikamrak taugaam navguryaaqellininqraakek, taum nulirran tua-i anirtaqulluk ikamrak navguamikek cupuirtuq-aalriim tuqutetnguqercetliniluku.

Ukut tua-i yuirutengluteng natmun tua-i un'gavet up'nerkillerkameggnun anelrangluteng pillrata kinguani aqvailliniuk taukuk malruulutek. Aqvai-

when the tide goes out, it has gotten drier, and there isn't any water inside this river. It has gotten drier now, and it is obvious that it will turn into land one day.

The one upriver from it that was once a very large point; I used to see it before they cut through the land to create a shortcut. Today what was once a river with a bend has turned into tundra. Since the current no longer washes out the sediment, it has turned into land.

That will also happen to this river, and it will no longer be a fishing place one day. These days, they come here to fish for *imarpinraat* and to obtain *imarpinraat* for food.

Now, we just said that there aren't many stories to tell about this place. But I want to end with a story of an old *angalkuq* [shaman] from Qalullermiut up there.

This [river] is called Qalulleq. It's the name of that point up there. The reason why it's called Qalulleq is that place up there; that's its name.

And in the past, there was evidently an *angalkuq* at Qalullermiut, a shaman.

Then one day, a woman who was about to die blamed [the shaman] for her illness, she felt anguished about dying. One day, that poor woman died.

When she died, although her husband was extremely sad over losing her, he decided not to kill that [shaman] but instead destroyed his sled; he broke his sled to pieces, reacting because he was so upset.

After breaking his sled to pieces, he went inside the *qasgi,* and from up along the *qasgi* window, the wife of that *angalkuq* said, "He's satisfied now that he has broken his sled."

That man finally became enraged, and he went to that *angalkuq* and murdered him.

And when he murdered him, when he brought him up on top of Qalulleq, he butchered his body and even scooped his eyes out. When he scooped his eyes out, he placed them underneath an old, upside-down lamp of a deceased person in a grave. Then time passed.

They mention that he decided to kill [the *angalkuq*] because of what his wife said. Although he was upset, he initially didn't kill him but just broke his sled, but he suddenly decided to kill him when his wife said that he was satisfied after breaking his sled.

When this village became empty when they started to go across to their spring camping sites on the coast, two people went to get some supplies.

llermeggni taum imum, tauna-w' imna tuqutellra tanglliniak, akuliramikun tua-i `gguun akulirami qukak'acagaakun ataucimek iiluni, iicillrek-wa imailnguuk.

Tua-ll' tua-i taukuk ullakengagni pilliniak, pilliniak taukuk, utercugngaqapiaryaaqniluni waniw' uterrluni ilagaryugngaqapiaryaaqniluki, iigni taugaam nalaqesciigalamikek tua-i waniw' utertenrit'luugutekniluku.

Waten iiluni ataucimek pikuni mikelngurnun tatamurratek'larnayuklunillu, cung'umikun iiluni pikuni. Taugaam avaggun nauggun ungalalirnerkun yuurcarturciqniluni qanrutlinilukek taukuk.

Tauna-gguq tua-i atuatuliuguq angalkuq yuarullulirluni.

Tua-i piinanermeggni makumiu tauna avatmurtelliniuq angyakun, natmun tua-i avavet Caninermiut nunat naliat, Kuigilngurmiunun-llu tayima pilliuq wall'u-q' natmun.

Tekican iliit, taum-wa tua-i ciuniumavian pillikii, ing'umek tan'gaurlurmek tua-i yuarulluitunrilngurmek alairyualriartangqerrniluku angalkuullerkaanek alairyualriartangqerrniluku.

Tua-i-gguq yuarutai ayuqevkenateng; atu'urqami tua-i uumek yuarullugmek, nalluvkenaki tua-i yuarulluni atu'uqluni. Tua-i tayima. Tua-i atam ataku atuangniartuq-allinia taum.

Tua-i qasgiamek tan'gaurlurraq tauna atuallrani taum makumium niicugnillinia, taum tua-i angalkum tuqutaullrem yuarulluinek atualria.

Tua-i-gguq tauna avaggun yuurcarturciqnillruan tuana tua-i piciukluku. Yuarulluinek atualallinian taunguyukluku tua-i yuurtenqigcukluku avaggun.

Unangik: Apaqaciitaq. Apaqaciitaulria imat'anem. Apaqaciitaq una tuaten tua-i tuquqaarluku unitelliniak. Unicaaqekiigni kingyalliniuk, maktellria. Cukariinarluni. Tuquqaarluku piaqagni kingyarciqaak-gguq makluni evculria.

Tua-i nutaan iigni ikuitkek nutaan tua-i maktenritliniluni.

Kangrilnguq: Ii-i. Tua-i-w' augna ava-i umyuamnun kanaan, qaneryararkartailata callmeggnek ukut, aug'umek tua-i ava-i ukurmiunguan qanemcika'artaqa.

Unangik: Ii-i, quyana-wam. Wii neq'aksugnaicaaqekek'a wii. Ilumun tua-i una Apaqaciitaq angarvaqapiarauguq. Ava-i Amitatugaam ateqngamiu angalkuuguq, Amitatugaq. Ilu'urpet nulirra, Ian-am.

When they went to get supplies, they saw the one he had killed. He had one eye in the middle of his forehead, and his eye sockets were empty.

Then he evidently said to the people who he approached, he told those two that he could certainly return now and join them, but that not finding his eyes was preventing him from returning.

He said that if he had only one eye like that, he was afraid that he would startle children if he returned with one eye on his forehead. But he told those two that he would be reborn somewhere to the south.

It is said that *angalkuq* was one who sang many *yuarulluut* [shaman songs].

One day, a person from here went out in that direction with a boat, to one of the villages in the lower Kuskokwim coastal area, probably somewhere near Kwigillingok.

When he arrived, I think it was his host who told him that there was a boy there who knew many *yuarulluut* who was starting to come out as a shaman.

It is said he had many different songs; when he sang this particular *yuarulluk* [shaman song], he knew his *yuarulluut* and sang them. Then some time passed. Then that person told him that he would start singing that evening.

When they went to the *qasgi,* when that boy sang, that person from [Qalulleq] listened to him, and he sang the *yuarulluut* of that murdered *angalkuq*.

Since [the murdered *angalkuq*] had said that he would be reborn somewhere in a distant village, he believed that. Since he probably sang the *yuarulluut* of that person, he suspected that it was him, that he had been reborn out there.

Simeon Agnus: Apaqaciitaq. Oh yes, his name was Apaqaciitaq. After killing Apaqaciitaq in that way, those two left him. When they left him, they looked back and saw that he got up. He got faster [coming to life again]. After killing him, they'd look back and see that he was getting up and dusting off his clothes.

When they finally scooped his eyes out, he didn't get up.

Paul John: Yes. Since that story came to mind, since there's nothing to say about what they did at this place, I'm just telling this story because it originated here.

Simeon Agnus: Yes, thanks for mentioning it. I didn't recall that story at all. Indeed, Apaqaciitaq was a very powerful *angalkuq*. Since Amitatugaq is his namesake, Amitatugaq is an *angalkuq*. Your *iluraq*'s wife, Ian's wife.

Negtemiut

Anguyaluk: Tua-i-llu nutaan qakemna nenglengareskan, iciw' tua-i kumlat'langareskan nutaan tua-i tuaken itraquneng nunakameggnun, wangkuta-w' tua-i nunaketukemtenun Negtemun tekilluta. Nunaniqluni upalleq tamatum nalliini.

Tagciqukut imkut tua-i *yellow*-rrarnek kangelget, qimugtengqetullruameng nuna tua-i man'a tamakuuluni. Pektellriani maani kavcaggluteng piaqluteng.

Tua-i-ll' tekiskumta cali tua-i uksillerkamtenun tuavet pelatekamek naparciluteng pelatekami uitaluteng enet kitugteqatarluki.

Nevuirluki. Wangkuta-llu canegnek pitquluta, aanavut-wa makut tupilriit canegnek enem *insulation*-aarkainek. Eviutekiurluteng. Tua-i-ll' angutet imkut ena tauna kituggluku, tua-i-gguq makluku.

Waten tua-i nel'inaurtut: Avatait ekitaanek piurarraarluki pagaaggun muraganek cali ellivikurarraarluki tua-i-ll' tamakut muragat qaqiskata can'get tamakut piirrallret waten tua-i ena tauna tamalkuan patuluku canegnek piirrarnek.

Nutaan nevunek elliviku'urluki ekitaanek. Ekitaanek pituluki tamakut nevut, qaill' mamtutaluki. Tua-i elliurluki, qaqiskunegteki-llu akulait makut callauralriit kevirturluki; umcigiluki tua-i kevirturluki.

Tuamtellu qilunek egalerkiurluteng. Ilait-am tua-i qimugtet-llu igteurlutuata casguliluku-llu una egalrem avatii piaqluku, qimugtet tamaa-i qimugkauyaraat may'uqerrluteng egalerkun-llu pika-i aluit alaunateng pituata. Igpakalngulaameng-wa tamatum nalliini.

Tua-ll' egalerkiurluteng, mingqurluki egalret tamakut waten piurpek'naki, mingqepiarturluki egalerkiurluteng.

Taqkunegteki-llu tua-i egaleq tauna taqkunegteggu lumarramek avacirluku elliluku-llu nanercirluku; nanercirluku tua-i elliluku egaleq.

Muragnek ilaita nanercirluki ilaita-llu nanqapigarluki canek uqamailngurnek.

Tua-i enet imkut nunaniqkacagarluteng, wangkutni tua-i nunaniqluteng itqerraaqumta.

Tuamtell' tua-i itqumta, acililaameng tua-i muraganek, inglerkiurluteng.

Nightmute[19]

Martina John: And when it started to get cold outdoors, when it started to get cold, when they headed upriver from [fall camps] to their [winter] village, we would arrive in the village of Nightmute, where we usually stayed. It was joyous to move during that time.

We'd head up to land, and since they had dogs, the land would be covered with those [chamomile] plants that have yellow tops. When walking along, the [plants] would make noise.

And when we arrived at our winter village, they'd erect a tent and stay in tents when they were about to fix their homes.

They'd remove the sod from them. And we'd obtain grass, and our mothers would weave grass for insulation for the home. They'd prepare *eviutet* [grass insulation for homes]. And then the men would repair the home, what they call *makluku* [erecting it].

They'd build homes like this: After placing *ekitaat* [pried rectangular pieces of sod] around the homes with wood placed on top of them, when they finished with the wood, they covered the entire home with those grasses that had been braided [woven].

Then they'd place sod over them, *ekitaat.* They called those [sod pieces pried from the ground] *ekitaat,* and they were a certain thickness. They'd place them [on the home], and when they were done, they'd fill gaps in between; they'd fill the gaps in tightly.

Then they'd prepare window coverings out of seal gut. Since poor dogs would fall through, some built fences around the window, since dogs, puppies would run up and their paws were visible up through the window. They constantly fell through during that time.

Then they'd prepare window coverings, and when they made window coverings they sewed them with regular [overcast] stitches and not [waterproof stitches].

And when they were done making that window, they'd place cloth around it and put it in place with weights around it; they'd put the window in place with weights around it.

Some used wood to weigh it down, and some would just use heavy things on top to hold it in place.

Those homes were very joyous inside, to us they were very joyous inside when we'd first go in.

And when I went inside, since they'd make beds out of wood, they'd

Tuamtell' tamakut canegtarugaput acinun caggluki qaill' tua-i mamturingraata caggluki. Tua-i-ll' tupiganek qallilirluki.

Tuamtell' keluteng cali canegnek cali naparqelluki iqutmun. Tuaten piurarraarluki tuamtellu piirraqegtaarnek cali taperrnanek piirraqegtaarnek, kangciranek makut qacarnermi waten napalriit kangciranek piaqluki. Aipait-wa curut. Makut-am kangcirat kenugngaluteng pagkut pinaurtut-llu.

Enem qacarneranun *straight*-arluteng. Waten pimangermi camani *straight*-anglaameng keluteng tuaten canegnek piurarraarluki capluki-llu tamakunek tupigaqegtaarnek capluki. Kangcirat-gguq tamaa-i kangciranek aperluki.

Pagna taugaam murauluni. Muragluni kiimi canegnek *insulation*-aarluni; pagaa-i tua-i can'get alaiterpagluteng.

Murak, *inside,* tua-i-llu maani wani evget, elatiini-wa *mud*. Tuaten ayuqluni pagna.

Itqerraaqumta nunaniqluni tua-i cakneq nunaniqluni. Kaminiarit-wa tua-i *tank*-allret; *tank*-allernek kaminiangqerraqluteng. Kumaurayuunateng. Waniw' taugaam nerqataquneng kumarrluku unuakutaqataquneng kumarrluku atakutaqataquneng kumarrluku; cailkami-ll' maani kumaurpek'nateng. Pingraan taugken maqarcenani, iciw' puqlanirturluni.

Tamatum nalliini wiinga tamakunek taugaam atliruarrarnek pilegnek tangtullrulrianga. Lumarraq una cayukaniqaqluku qamngaqan uqunek piluki. Ala-i tan'gercelngermeng nunaniqluteng.

Unangik: Atam makut wani qikertam yui peksagtellruyaaqut tua-i. Waten tua-i nunat makut maa-i ullaketaaqengaput yungqetullruut tamarmeng.

Tua-i-ll' 1957-aami BIA-q naparrluni. Tua-i tuaken Negtemun tua-i iluvallruut makut avaqliput, Negtemiungurrluteng.

Wangkuta kiani Negtemiuni atam enen'i qavcirraullruyaaqukut. Uum waniw' angayuqaak, wiinga-w' angayuqaagka unguvallragni, kiugum-llu Phillip Moses-aam atii, Mancuam-wa atii, Poline-aq-wa. Qavciuluteng tua-i kiani Negtemi atam uitallruut.

prepare their beds. And then we'd scatter the large amounts of grass that we had obtained along the beds, scatter them although they were thick. Then we'd cover them with woven grass.

And they also erected grass along the area behind [their beds] to the very end. After doing that, they'd also [place] wonderfully woven coarse seashore grass. They call the [woven mats] situated upright along the wall *kangcirat.* The other [type of woven grass] were *curut* [grass mats]. Those *kangcirat* up there were also nicely decorated with designs on them.

They were straight along the wall of the home. Although [the home was curved], since they became straight, after placing grass behind [their beds] like that, they'd cover them with those nicely woven [grass mats]. Those are called *kangcirat;* they call them *kangcirat.*

But the ceiling was wood. That was the only [exposed] wood, with grass insulation; the grass up there was clearly visible.

The wood was on the inside, and then there was grass, and outside it was mud. That's how the ceiling was.

When we fist went inside [the home], it was very joyous, very joyous inside. Their stoves were old tanks; they had old tanks as stoves. They weren't always on. They'd only light it when they were about to eat, they'd light it when they were going to have a morning meal, and they'd light it when they were about to have an evening meal; they weren't always on during other times. Although that was the case, it was warm, it was constantly warm.

During that time, I only saw those [lamps] that had *atliruarraat* [small saucers]. They'd periodically pull the cloth [wick] when it would start to go out, and they'd put seal oil in them. My, although it was dark, it was joyful inside.

Simeon Agnus: The people of this island were dispersed in the past. All the village sites that we will go to were all occupied once.

Then in 1957, the BIA [Bureau of Indian Affairs] was established [in the region]. From that time on, people started moving to Nightmute from the surrounding areas, and they became residents of Nightmute.

Originally, there were only a few of us with homes in Nightmute. [Martina John's] parents, my parents when they were alive, and Phillip Moses' father, and Mancuaq's father, and Polina. Originally, a number of families were living up at Nightmute.

1957-aami tua-i nutaan *school*-arvingvaalullruut ukut Negtemiut. Kinguqlikacagaungatellruut tua-i *school*-arvingqellrat. Taumek maa-i wangkuta maani waten ellilriani ilaitni tua-i [*school*-arauksaitukut].

Kiugkut kiani nayuqengaput anuqlirturangaqameng atam uksumi anuqlirturatuut. *North*-aq tua-i una anuqlirnakaat. Ukut-wa uaqliput ukut quunirturalriit.

Piiyaaqnauqa-am ilu'urqa ugna George Nevak-aq, "Tua-i-tang makut maani allurulluta pitukumta, nunavceni amllernek tamariyalriaci quunirturallerpecenek." [*ngel'artuq*] Anuqlirqan, anuqlingaqamta.

☙

Augkut ava-i neqnek ilu'urqa qanerturalria. Ukut wani Negtemiut neqet qukaatni uitaut kiugkut. Tua-i man'a neqnguuq, un'a-ll' can'giilitullruyaaqluni, qaugkut-llu carvat tamarmeng neqerluteng.

Tua-i umyuarteqaqama wii qessamkaungamta wangkuta ilaitni kainiqtuukut. Qessamkaunrilnguq taugken kaigyugnaunani.

Tua-i ukut ilumun Negtemiut ukut anuqetungermeng muragmek cali nuuqitevkenateng. Cuukvaguanek uquryaraitellermeggni cuukvaguanek teguqerrartellruut, kiatmeggni maani cuukvaguat amllerata. Cuukvaguanek tua-i murangqerrlainarluteng enet.

Tua-i maa-i ilait qugtaqayuitqapiaralriit; wiinga qugtanermek wii taqeksaitua waniw' qugtaaratuunga cali, kaminiat makut uqurkait akiturissiyaagata. [*ngel'artuq*]

Atam tua-i nunat tekisngait cuukvaguat kiugkut. Kanavet pikumta augna Nangtuq asguqumteggu piavet tangvakuvki tangerrsaraten.

Kangrilnguq: Augna neqerqelria caperrsaguciluni elagyami qavartallra. Ilumun tua-i tuaten anurvanertulliata angutet-am taukut[iliit] ikamriagni uitertellinikek tua-i tangningnaqlukek cakneq, muriit uiteraq tangnirquteknatgu.

Tua-i-ll' qer'anun mayurrlukek, ugaan tua-i kenketacim. Unukuan tua-i pirretpangllinilun. Maaten-gguq ertuq imkuk ikmaraurluuk uiterangssagaunatek, pirtuum tamaa-i uiterakek aug'alliniluk'. [*ngel'artuq*] Augna usguqerluku.

Ava-i tua-i ilumun ukut Negtemiut, uum uitalria taugaam piitullerkaanek

In 1957, they finally established a school for the first time in Nightmute. I think they were the very last village to have a school. That's why those of us who are this age now [didn't attend school].

The village where we live upriver, when it starts to get windy there during winter, it's always windy there. The north wind blows for a long time. But here the places that are downriver from us are constantly calm.

I tell my *iluraq* George Nevak, "My, if we could snatch weather away from one another, you would lose a lot of calm weather from your village." [*laughs*] When it's windy, when it starts to get windy in our village.

❧

My *iluraq* was just talking about fish. The village of Nightmute upriver is located in the middle of an area where fish is available. This area is full of fish, and this river once had many blackfish, and all the streams to the north once had fish.

When I think about it, indeed some of us go hungry because of our inclination to be lazy. But those who aren't lazy are far from going hungry.

Indeed, although the village of Nightmute is a windy place, they also don't lack wood. Back when they didn't have stoves that took stove oil, alder was readily available to them, since there is a lot of alder upriver from that place. The houses always had alder firewood.

These days, some people don't go and collect wood at all; I haven't stopped collecting wood and continue to get wood, since stove oil is getting too expensive. [*chuckles*]

The alder reach the village up there. When we go down there and up the Nangtuq River, when you look at [Nightmute] up there, you see [the trees].

Paul John: [They tell] that story about a person who went to get some fish who decided to spend a night at a partially underground storage cache because he found the conditions too bad for traveling. Probably because that place gets extremely windy like that, one of the men once painted his sled with red ocher, trying to make it look nice, since red ocher is used to make wood look attractive.

Then he placed it on top of a fish rack, since he really valued [his sled]. That night, it started to get extremely blizzardy. When the sun came up, he saw that his poor sled had no red ocher on it whatsoever, as the blizzard had removed the red ocher. [*laughs*] I just wanted to add to what he said.

Indeed, concerning the village of Nightmute, this person said that only a

qanertuq. Wiinga yaani Cevv'arnermiuni yuurtellruama, una taugaam aipaqa uksuqan teguarkaurcamku kiavet *move*-allruukut.

Tua-i-tang kiavet *move*-aamta wangrramni ayuqekutellrulrianga wangnek; tuartang wiinga uqrutat iluatnun uqiartellrianga, muragmek neqmek-llu.

Tua-i tuaten qacignarqerpallagnganani neqtengnaqleq murangengnaqleq-llu. Tua-i tuaten wangnek ayuqekutelallruunga; tuar ilumun uqrutat uqratnun uqiartellrianga.

Unangik: Tayima tua-i wiinga-llu ugkumiungurtellruyartua, upagallratni upakataryaaqlua, ilu'urqa nakmiin upiin Mancuaq.

Tua-ll' aanama inerquraanga. Pingnatugturalqa-gguq una uyaturiqercessiyaakatartuq, Negtemiut ukut nunakanka nayurlaki. Tua-i maligartaqa.

Waten tua-i arrsiqurangramta kiani Negtemi ukut avteqarraallranikut, ilumun arrsiqurallruukut. Kipusviinata tuaten. Kipusvigmek pingnaqluta *Native Store*-angluta. Aklungssuarangaqluni tua-i aklulirpek'nani-llu.

Tua-i aanama inerqunrilkanga ugkumiuni tua-i maqinertutassiigutlaryartukuk ilu'urqa-llu nayuuskumegnuk. [*ngel'artuq*]

Upagnarikakut-llu, kiugkut Negtemiut ukut-llu ilakellemteni, yuirutetullruut uavet Umkumiunun anelrarluteng. Qimugtetgun upagluta.

Taugaam nunamiunguyulriit kiani tua-i nunamiunguaqluteng. Qavcirrauluteng-llu, iliini-ll' malruingarauluteng uitaaqluteng enet yungqerraqluteng.

Quyumakumta yugyagyartukut tua-i yugyak'apiaryartukut tua-i. Hooper Bay-rmiuni ikegkuni cangallruyanrilngatukut; amllenruyalliukut-llu avvulluta pillrunrilkumta.

Ukut waniw' ilakaput. Upagyukumta ugkunun ua-i upakainauluta. Ikirusngaakut ellaita-ll' kiavet itraryukata cali ikirusngaluki tua-i. Ikirusngalluteng tua-i-w' ilakngamta qaill' inglukutevkenata. Tuaten tua-i nepaillrullrakun tuaten tua-i taqluku pillruarput.

person who sits and doesn't work will lack things. Since I was born over at the village of Cevv'arneq, we only moved up [to Nightmute] during the winter [1953] that I was to marry my wife.

When we moved up [to Nightmute], I compared my feelings at the time; it felt as though I went inside a grass windbreak to seek shelter from the wind, in terms of the availability of wood and food. Trying to get fish and wood seemed much easier.

That's the comparison that I made about how I felt; indeed it seemed as though I suddenly found shelter from the wind along the calm side of a grass windbreak.

Simeon Agnus: I would have moved down [from Nightmute to Toksook] when they moved [in 1964], and I was about to move, since my real *iluraq* Mancuaq moved.

Then my mother admonished me. She said that it was going to become too far for me to hunt, that I should stay in my hometown of Nightmute. I suddenly followed her advice.

Although we were poor up in Nightmute when they first split from our village, indeed we were poor. We didn't have a store either. We made an effort at obtaining a store, and got a Native Store. At first it obtained a little bit of merchandise and not lots of goods.

If my mother hadn't admonished me, my *iluraq* and I would try to outdo each other on who could take the longest steam bath, if we were living in the same place. [*laughs*]

And back when the village of Nightmute upriver and the people [of Toksook Bay] were together, when it was time for us to move [each spring] the village used to empty, as people would move down to Umkumiut. We'd move with dog teams.

But those who wanted to stay in the village would stay in the village upriver. And there were just a few, and sometimes there would be just two homes occupied with people who stayed behind.

If we all stayed in the same village, there would be lots of us; there would be many, many people. I think our population would be about the same as Hooper Bay now; we'd probably have more people if our village hadn't split in two.

These people here [from Toksook Bay] are our relatives. If we want to move down to that village, we can easily move. Their community is open to us, and if they want to move up there, our community is open to them. The two villages are open to one another since we are related, and we have no rivalry. We made a pact that was the most peaceful way.

ೋ *Nunakauyaq* ೋ

Kangrilnguq: Tua-ll' ava-i ilu'urma *move*-allerput uavet qanrutkaa. *School*-alangarrluteng tamatum nalliini *move*-allemteni.

Tua-i-llu ukut ellinguaracesteput qanengluteng, "Aling *school*-arat tang tua-i allurtelaqeput. *School*-allerkaat iquklipailgan upautaqluki." Tua-i tamana tamaa-i *school*-allratnek allurulluki upalallerteng uavet qanaatekluku.

Tuamtellu pinaurtut, "Aling kiagmi-llu maani qimugteput-llu nerumaurcetengnaqluki pillerkamteni Kangirrluaraam ceniini, *school*-aqatarqata nerilegutekluku *school*-allerkaat nerangnaqurallerkarput tua-i unitaqluku uneg-ken Kangirrluaraam iluanek."

Cali-llu tayima maa-i caliangqelangelriit. Kina caliyarturyung'ermi ilani taugaam yuirautellerkaat-llu un'gani uitainanratni nagutek'lallrat calissaagaqeryung'ermeng.

Tua-i makut yuungnaquucit apaaluki piurluteng, tua-i uavet umyuallgutekluteng pingameng anelrallret anelrallruut uavet Tuqsugmun, makut-wa tua-i arenqiallugtaaruteteng aprarraarluki.

ೋ

Nurataaq: Una-llu nunauvkenani uitavigput una nunaungssaarpek'nani.

Waten taugaam iqalluarpagnek, imkut pistailnguut, pistailnguut enucetaarraarluteng kuvyateng piurluki.

Angayuqaagken-llu maantauraqlutek waten itraraqamek. Tuaten tua-i murilkellruanka angayuqaagken tua-i waten wangmiurulutek, tamakut ilaten. Wani neqliuratullruut. Nunakluku tua-i.

Tangkaq-llu nel'iluni. Tom Sunny-q-llu cali.

Tauna tua-i kiimi nunauluni kiagmi; waten ullaketaatuluku kiagmi taigaqluni. Taugaam neqkarrsurvikluku uksuarmi.

Tuaten tua-i. Muralillruami unkuk avatek muragugaat. Tayima-ll' tamangluteng tamakut tamaa-i nunat muralitulit.

Nunaulutek tua-i.

Tua-i-llu una wani skularviliqatartut misvililuteng-llu. Tamaa-i ayagnirluteng. Nutaan quyurtaangartut. Wavet upagyugluteng ilait.

Toksook Bay[20]

Paul John: My *iluraq* just talked about how we moved down [to Nunakauyaq, Place that could have been a *nuna* (village)]. They started to attend school during the time we moved [1964].

And when the leaders of our village started to say, "My, we prevent the students from attending school [when we move to Umkumiut each spring]. We move with them before their school year is over." They started talking about moving down the bay because they prevented them from attending school.

And they said, "My, and our responsibility to keep our dogs fed during summer along the shores of Kangirrluar, when they are about to start school, we put our duty to hunt and fish down inside Kangirrluar over their responsibility to attend school."

And you know how people have jobs nowadays. Although someone wanted to go and work, they were hindered by their family members who would be left alone down the bay although they wanted to go and work.

Those who moved repeadedly mentioned [how it would benefit] their efforts in making a living, and when they started to come to an agreement, they moved down to Toksook Bay, after mentioning all their hardships.

Phillip Moses: And this [Toksook Bay] where we live now was not a village, it was not a place of residence at all.

But when those without providers were fishing for herring, they would let the tide go out and then [pick the fish off] their nets.

And your [David Chanar's] parents always stayed here whenever they went up. So that was the way I observed your parents and your kin; they stayed here. They always harvested fish here. So this was their place.

And Tangkaq built a house. And also Tom Sunny.

And it was the only place in the summer; he constantly came to this place during summer. But it was a place where they went to obtain food in fall.

So it was like that. Because each side of it had a lot of driftwood, there was so much wood. And those places where they had a lot of wood are no more.

So it was a place of residence.

Then they were going to build a school and an airport. They were starting then. Then they started to meet together. Some of them wanted to move here.

Taukuk skularviinkuk *airport*-aq-llu pisqumalukek wavet; imairuciiq-niluku kiugna.

Tegganret-am iqluvknateng tangrruallermegteggun kiani. tua-i-ll' kiani upanrilkuneng nunairucarluteng. Nunairucarluteng. Piviirulluni kia-i. Nu-nairulluni.

Taugaam alartevknateng ak'allaraat wavet upakata taukut napartar-kauluku, skularviinkuk, *airport*-llu.

Tua-i ilait-am waten ukanirpak-gguq umyuallguteksuitelliniut callig-teqatarqameng nunamun allamun. Ilait-am tua-i qessalriit uitaluteng.

Tua-i-ll' yugyangameng irniameggnek, allakarmeng yuurcata nunairu-lluteng kia-i. Pileryagciiganateng. Nangluni; tag'urluni. Tua-i kia-i piviirutek-saitelliniameng Negtemiungunriqsaitut.

Uksivigteng unicuirulluku maa-i kiagungraan. Tuaten tua-i ayuqluteng. Cagtenrirluteng yuut. Taugaam tua-i angyakun nerangnaqaqluteng tamaku-nun uitaviketullritnun.

Tua-i tekilluni unuaquan. Tekicami Negtemun angayuqaagminun iterluni qanrutak Tuqsugmek-gguq anluni Qikertaugaq tekiteqataqerluku nuna una wani tanqigiluni unugmi. Kenurrat-gguq amelkacagarluteng!

Tua-i pingraan, qayaa-ll' nutaraungami amia, qayaan-ll' ilua tanqigiluni taum akiqallranek. Tua-i tekitniaranrakun tamalliniluni tamana tanqik.

Tua-llu iterluni tua-i angayuqaagni qanrullukek. Nunaurcugnaunaki.

Aatama qanrutaa ircenrraat-gguq aturkaitnek avani maniitullruut. Manii-tullruut. Cunaw' waten waniwa nunaurciiqelliniata. Aglumanariksaunani-ll' tamatum nalliini.

Tuamtell'-am irniagka angqaliyarluteng Tununermun ikamrarlutek, tau-gaam, ellmegnek ikamramegnek, wii ikamrarcillrulukek; tamalkuita, panim-nun pikniluki qanrutekluki. Tua-i angqaliyarlutek nutaan ukut yung'enrat-gun.

Uyangtelliniuk piaken Nialrumek kenurrarugaat tua-i amllerrluteng! Amllerrluteng. Atrarlutek tua-i.

They wanted the school and the airport to be built here; they said that [Nightmute] would be depleted of people.

The elders up there [at Nightmute] did not lie when they foresaw the future. If they did not move, they would no longer have land to expand up there. They would run out of land. There is no longer any room up there. There is no longer any land there.

But the elders did not make a mistake [thinking] that if they moved they would build those two, the school and the airport.

Some of them, from time immemorial, do not reach consensus when they are going to move to another place. Some of them who were reluctant stayed [at Nightmute].

And since their village population has risen through their children, now that they're living on their own, they have run out of room up there. They are limited in doing what they want to do. The land is running out; it is eroding. Since they have not run out of too much land they continue to be Negtemiut.

[Toksook Bay residents] do not abandon their winter place now, even in summer. So they are like that now. People do not scatter anymore. But using boats they try to subsist at those places that they used to live at.

He arrived the next day. When he arrived he went inside his parents' house and told them that when he went out of Tuqsuk River and just before reaching Qikertaugaq [Small island], this place [Toksook Bay] was all lit up in the night. He said there were many lights there!

And since his kayak skin was new, the inside of this kayak became bright from the reflections of those lights. So just before he got there, those lights disappeared.

So entering [the house] he told his parents. This was long before [Toksook Bay] became a village.

My father told him that the *ircenrraat* used to show people about the future. They revealed future life. So it was because they were going to become a village today. And people had not even thought about making it a village at that time.

And then one time my two daughters went to Tununak for a ball game, but they were using their own snowmobiles that I had provided for them, indicating that they belonged to all of them. So they went to a ball game after [Toksook Bay] became inhabited.

When they came over Nialruq, there were a lot of lights! There were lots. So they came down.

Ip'arrnarquq pikna tekiteqatalriani. Maaten-gguq ip'arqaarlutek igvartuk ayuqucimegcetun ayuqluteng. [*ngelaq'erluni*] Tua-i tuaten tangellrulliniak.

Kass'aurluq

Anguyaluk: Yaa, kiani taugaam Kass'aurlurmek pitukiitni uitaqalallruukut, ak'anun-llu uitavkenata ataam qamaavet itrarluta.

Ak'anun tuani uitayuitellruukut. Un'gaken tua-i itraraqamta tuavet arulairluta uitalallruukut. Maurlurput-wa imna taugaam iqvaryalallrulria, paugkut-llu ingrit tekilluki pekqurluni.

Camek tua-i pivakarngatevkenata kiantetullrulriakut. Taugaam tamaa-i anguarluteng pitullermeggni malirqelriit alaitaqluteng. Neplirluteng. Nepliagaqata tua-i malirqelriaruniaqluki.

Camek pivakarpek'nata kiantetullruukut, taugaam tua-i iliikun iniangqecuaqaqluta. Tuaken-llu tua-i ayakumta, qamavet ngell'itlemtenun kiavet kia-i Negtemun ngell'itlemtenun ayagluta.

Wangkuta-ll' tua-i camek ayagallemtenek qanemcikaunata, taugaam tua-i tan'gerpagnek iqvaksuararaqluta. Taugaam ngell'itaqamta qamavet nutaan iqvapialallruukut.

Tuani-am ayagavakarlunuk, tuani tua-i Kass'aurlurmiut taukut kuicuarangqertut kelutmun. Akilirneranun-am yuulunuk kiartellmegni nanvak malruk kelutmun. Keluani pamani quagcirugarnek tekillunuk. Tua-i tuakenirnek taukut quagcirugaat ullatuyaaqellruapuk.

Paniliar: Apyutkangqertua. Ciin-gguq tamaani Kass'artaitellrungraan tauna Kass'aurlurmek acillruatgu?

Anguyaluk: Aug'um-wa Billy Dull-am aatallran uitavikeqallrularaa-qaa? Yaa, tauna tua-i Kass'aurlurmek atengqerrutekluku. Yaa, Kassartaitellrungraan tauna Kass'aurlurmek pitullruamegteggu tauna. Maanteqallermini-w' tua-i acacungamnek aipangellrullilria kiug-qetunraa.

Yaa, tua-i-w' tauna-am pitekluku uitaqallra Kass'aurlurmek pilallinikiit,

One goes into a depression where one cannot see the village as one gets near it. After they went into that depression and when they came into view of the village, they were like they normally are. [*chuckles*] So they saw them like that.

Kass'aurluq[21]

Martina John: Yes, we stayed for a short while up at the place they call Kass'aurluq, and we didn't stay there for long but continued upriver again [to Nightmute].

We never stayed at that place for long. When we went up from the coast, we'd stop there and stay there. Only our grandmother would go and pick berries, and she would walk to the mountains up there.

It seemed that we didn't obtain a lot of things when we stayed up there. But back when they used to paddle with kayaks, the noise of ones who were pursuing seals in open water was apparent. They were noisy. When they'd make noise, they'd say that they were pursuing seals in open water.

We didn't seem to obtain things when we stayed up there, but sometimes we'd have a few hanging fish. And when we moved from that place, we would travel up to Nightmute where we would stop.

And we don't have any stories to tell about traveling [while we were there], but we would pick a small amount of blackberries. But when we'd reach our destination up [at Nightmute], we'd really pick blackberries and obtain a substantial amount.

During one of our many trips, there is a small stream at Kass'aurlurmiut that heads inland. When we got out on the other side and searched, there were two lakes heading inland. Up beyond them we came upon many sourdock plants. From then on, we used to go to that large patch of sourdock.

Theresa Abraham: I have a question. Why is it that although no white people were around during that time they called that place Kass'aurluq [Poor, dear *kass'aq* (white person)]?

Martina John: Was it a place where Billy Dull's [Caucasian] father once stayed? Yes, that's the reason why it came to be called Kass'aurluq. Although there were no white people around, since they called that person Kass'aurluq [they named it after him]. His son probably married my *acacungaq* when he lived here for a short while.

Yes, they evidently call that place Kass'aurluq because he stayed there for

uitaqallrullra, aug'um Billy Dull-am aatallra. [*ngel'artuq*]

Kangrilnguq: Tamaani-wa aug'um Martina-m qanemcillran kinguakun, qetunraa taum Kass'aurluum Billy Dull-aq atami akluinek tailluni tuneniaksuararaqluni wavet Negtemun nulirturpailegmi. Tamaa-i tuatnallermi nalliini nuliani augna Cingyukan nulirqerkaurrluku tua-i pinglliniamiu nuliqsagutellrukii.

Tamaani caperqelallruaqa Billy Dull-aq. Wangkuta paltuukcikaaryugnaitellemta nalliini nengelmi uksumi ikamrarluni kitu'urqami paltuugturluni akurtunrilngurmek pilallra pitekluku caperqelallruaqa nenglliurturnikluku.

Tua-i tamaa-i aipangami makurmiungurcami avavet ayanrirluni.

Qungurmiut

Unangik: Qungurmiut ikegkut ika-i nunallerpagnek anguyiit nunallritnek kiaqlingqertut, waten qerturpalrianek.

Ikegkut atam ika-i nunallerpiit ang'ut, angkayagtut. Kiugkuni taugaam Engelumiuni mikellruut.

Ukut-wa nunallret, yullrit-llu tayim' nangluteng, kiugna taugaam kia-i acacungaq, una-ll' waniwa aipaqa nunakestellrit ikegkut Qungurmiut.

Qungurmiut ikegkut avaken ayagluteng tua-i pinricaaqut ukut uaqliit, taugaam ukut wani Qaillukayak, Caingilnguunkuk-llu Yuguayak-llu, Nickam Atii call' tua-i kiugna; cali uitatullruluni tuani avani ellangyugallemni, aug'umek ciuqlirmek aipangqellermini.

Aipaqeqerrallra ciuqliq tuqullruuq. Kituulria imat'anem? Qulvarkaq. Tauna tua-i aipaqlermini tuani tua-i uitatullruuq.

Taryuralria-ll' augna nengauga tamaa-i unguvaluni, taugaam Negtemi uitalutek aanani-llu. Qulvarkaq-llu tauna; tuani tua-i, Qungurmiuni uitatullruut, Unguiralriinkut-llu pillilriit.

Uum-wa tua-i atiin, atallran tua-i taluyirviktullrukii tauna painga aug'um Avayam. Can'giirnek tua-i uksurpak nerumavikluku, tua-i pelluyuunateng.

Kankut kana-i Qungurmiut tua-i nunakegtaarauyaaqut taugaam tua-i yungqerrnanrirluteng. Tua-i waten cikuqami avatiit tamarmi neqnguluni; tua-i can'giirnek, quarruugnek, quarruuget cukilget, cat tamakut, iqalluat,

a short while, because Billy Dull's father briefly stayed there. [*laughs*]

Paul John: In those days, after the time that Martina talked about, Kass'aurluq's son, Billy Dull, would bring his father's merchandise here to Nightmute and sell a few items before he married. During a time when he did that, since he probably decided to marry his wife Cingyukan [Albertina], he married her.

During that time, I considered Billy Dull to do things beyond my capability. Back when we never wore coats, in the cold winter when he'd pass by with a sled and dog team, because he wore a coat that wasn't very long, I used to think that he did things beyond my capability, thinking he could withstand cold weather very well.

When he married and moved to this place, he stopped traveling out there.

Qungurmiut[22]

Simeon Agnus: There is an old village that was once occupied by warriors upriver from Qungurmiut [Residents of *qunguq* (grave)], a very steep place.

The old village site across there is large, it's very large. But they are smaller than Engelumiut up the bay.

The people who once lived in that old village are all gone now, too, except for *acacungaq* up there and my wife here, among those who lived at Qungurmiut across there.

Qungurmiut across there, since long ago, not the ones downriver from them, but these people including Qaillukayak, Caingilnguq, and Yuguayak, and Nick's father up there [Albert Therchik]; he also lived there back when I first started to become aware of life, when he was with his first wife.

His first wife died. What was her name again? Qulvarkaq. When he was married to her, he lived there.

And his in-law, Taryuralria, was alive at that time, but he and his mother lived at Nightmute. And Qulvarkaq, too; they lived there at Qungurmiut, and probably Unguiralria and his family, too.

This person's father, his late father, would set his wooden fish trap along the mouth of Avayaq [Branch of a river, tributary]. That's where he got blackfish to eat all winter, and they were always available.

Qungurmiut down there is actually a wonderful place, but today people no longer live there. During freeze-up, the entire surrounding area has fish; there are blackfish, needlefish, those types of fish, tomcod, flounder. They

naternat. Maaken tua-i naternassuquluteng.

Ikani ika-i Kaviarmiunek ullallemteni, taukut tua-i Qungurmiut uitatulit ika'antetullruut Kaviarmiuni. Iqalluarcurluteng, inialiriluteng inialiriaqluteng itrarpailegmeng.

Atauciq-wa angyaat tengalratuli, aug'um Peter Dull-am atiin angyaa. Massiinirpailgani tengalratullruluni taman' angyaa.

Billy-m-llu tua-i tamak'acagaita ilani ekluki nunarraat itraulluki tua-i ikanelnguut Kaviarmiuni, ilani angyakun. Taugaam qimugteteng nunakuartelluki pitullrungatait, tamaani aug'umi Nangtuum ceniini.

Avani upatullemteni wangkuta qimugtet nunakuartelluki atam upatullruukut. Tua-i nunakuangermeng uirucuunateng petuileng'ermeng. Nalugaqluku; tua-i kuik arviqtaarluk qimugtet nalugaluki. Nutaan ciuniskuneng petugluki.

Anguyiit ikegkut nunalqait.

Anguyiit makut nunallrit tamarmeng maani qertuut. Nani-llu-w' tayim' pillilriit nunani tayima avani-llu, pavani-llu. Waten waniw' ayuqelallilriit anguyiit nunallrit. Qaill' makut anguyiit nunallrit pilriameng waten kit'ekegtauvkenateng-llu qertutuameng, qertulaameng.

Taugken makut nunapiallret, yuut nayullrit tua-i kit'etuluteng. Tayim' tua-i yaani Kanerrlulegmi tangerqumteki tayima ilait kisngaciqut, ilait usserqusngaluteng.

Tua-i yaani-ll' cali Nevurtulimi tuaten ayuqut. Uaqliqut, uaqliqelriaruut nunallret, kiaqliit-wa kiugkut. Cali tua-i waten ustem tua-i nang'arkaurrluki tua-i ika-i.

Taugaam taukut Qungurmiut kuiteng carevpanrilan qaugna ayuqucirmegcetun ayuqsaaqelriameng, taugaam nunallrit tayim' uitavillrit kit'engeng'atut aipaagni.

Man'a yuilquq avanitun ilu'urqa-ll' ayagatullermegtun ayuqenrirtuq. Cat tekitetulpuk tangnerranarqaqluteng allamiaqan. Kiq'urluteng. Nuna man'a tua-i ilii amlleq kit'uq. Tamartut nunallret ilait, tamaumaut tua-i avani ullakataqekngamteni. Kisngaut, kill'uteng.

Tua-i nuna man'a avani ellangyugallemni ayuqucimitun tua-i pingatetullruyaaquq ayagayaurtua maaten. Tua-i ayuqucirmegcetun ayuqaqluteng. Taugken maa-i mat'um nalliini tuartang kit'ellra cukarilria. Cukaringanan tua-i; cat tekitelallma ilait tangnerranarqaqluteng. Tua-i tangnerranariluni tua-i yuilquq, ayuqucirmitun mat'um nalliini ayuqenrirluni.

would fish for flounder from the area nearby.

When we went to Kaviarmiut, the people who stayed at Qungurmiut used to stay at Kaviarmiut. They'd fish for tomcod, they'd obtain many dry fish for hanging before they went up [to Nightmute].

They had one boat with a sail, Peter Dull's father's [Billy Dull's] boat. Before he put an outboard motor on it, his boat had a sail on it.

And Billy would bring all his relatives in his boat, the few residents who stayed at Kaviarmiut, and he would bring them upriver, taking his relatives with a boat. But I think they let their dogs travel the land route, along the shores of Nangtuq River.

Back when we used to move from place to place, we would have the dogs travel along the land when we moved. Although they traveled along the land untethered, they didn't fight with one another. They'd swim and take shortcuts; the dogs would swim across rivers. And when they got to their destination, we'd tie them down.

That place across there is where warriors once lived.

All the places that warriors once occupied are high. They are probably like that in other places, including out there, and inland. That's probably what places where warriors once lived are like. Why is it that places where warriors once lived don't sink too much; it's because they are steep, they are steep.

But these real villages, the places where people once lived, sink. When we see some of the places over at Kanerrlulek River [Small amount of *kaneq* (hoarfrost)], they will be sunken completely, and some will be eroded away.

That's how they are in Nevurtuli River, also. The old village sites are up and down the river from one another, and there are ones upriver, too. Erosion will cause them to disappear.

But since the river where Qungurmiut is located doesn't have a strong current, it's actually in its original state, but the village site where they stayed is probably sinking.

The wilderness no longer looks like it did compared to back when my *iluraq* and I used to travel. The places where we used to go don't look the same and seem to change every year. They are continually sinking. A lot of the land is sinking. Some village sites are gone now; they are gone in places that we will travel to. They have sunk.

When I first became aware of life, the land seemed to stay in the same state when I first started to travel. [Places] were always in their original state. But these days, [the land] seems to be sinking at a faster rate. It seems to be getting faster; some of the places where I used to go don't look at all like they did in the past. The wilderness is starting to become unrecognizable, and

Kangrilnguq: Tua-i ukut Qungurmiut tua-i avani nerumaurvimeggni uitatullruameng yuut caggluteng. Nerumaurvikegciameng Qungurmiut nayurturallrukait augkut nayurtektullrita.

Ava-i qanellratun tua-i neqkameggnek maaken yaaqsigpek'naki avakarameggnek neruurviklerteng pitekluku tua-i nunaksugcaliluku nunakestain nunakellruat.

Kiugum-llu kia-i *elder*-aaqsaguskemta mat'um nalliini Nick Thercick-aam atiin tua-i qanrutkeqaquaqamiki, cat-llu anyugyaratulit kuiggaat avatiitni waten kiagungraan ilait, kiaksingraan anyugyaratulit tamaa-i can'giirnekwa tua-i cukilegnek-llu neryara'arvik'lalteng qanrutkaqluki.

Aipaagni tayima kuikegcikata unicallrunrilngatait. Kuiget makut maa-i cat angyarpaagaat asgurciigalkait unirqengellrukait *school*-at makut pingata, ullagciigalateki angyarpaagauluteng.

Tamana tamaa-i pitekluku makut avanirpak nunallret ilait angyam ullagciigatarkaullra pitekluku angelriim unirqellrukait, *school*-arvilegnun nugtarqelluteng, irniateng *school*-allerkait pitekluki.

☙

Arcunan: Kanai-w' tua-i Qungurmiuni ellangengatellrulrianga. Qungurmiunguaqluta tua-i qavciulallruukut. Yugyaggalallruut imumi.

Umyuaqellemni-w' tua-i tamaa-i tangtullemni Kicarraankut uitatullruut, Nick-am atii-llu. Uitaqtaaraqluteng; wangkuta-wa. Yuguayiinkut-wa, imnallu Caingilnguq.

Qaillukayiinkut-wa. Ukut-wa Miisaam angayuqai. Taukullruut yugyaggallerluteng uitatullrulriit.

Tua-lli-w' tua-i uksumi tua-i up'nerkami nurutelalriit kanani Qungurmiuni, nurutelalriit. Allanret tumkelallruat kan'a Qungurmiut.

Tununertellriit avaken makut maa-i yungqetullermeggni malkuirqameng Qungurmiutguirturatullruut. Tununerrluteng kass'arrluteng maaggun ayallrutulriit. Qungurmiut tua-i allanertuluteng avaken yaaqlimtenek.

these days it's not like it was originally.

Paul John: Concerning Qungurmiut, since people lived where they could sustain themselves, they were dispersed. Since that was an ideal place to sustain them with food, the people who usually went and stayed there always occupied that place.

Like he stated, because they sustained themselves with food from the surrounding area, people who lived there were content to stay there.

And the one who has become our eldest elder up [in Toksook Bay] these days, when Nick Therchik's father [Albert Therchik] talked about them from time to time, he would talk about some of the sloughs in the surrounding area where fish became abundant, even early in summer, the places where they got blackfish and needlefish early on.

They probably wouldn't have abandoned that place if it had a good river. They started to abandon these settlements on rivers that boats could no longer go up when schools started to be established, since they couldn't get to them with large boats.

They abandoned these old village sites that existed for a long time because large boats wouldn't be able to reach them, and so the people moved to places with schools so their children could attend.

Peter Dull: I seem to have gained awareness of life down at Qungurmiut. So several of us families used to live at Qungurmiut.

When I think of it from what I saw, Kicarraq and family used to live there, and so did Nick Therchik's father's family. They would stay periodically and also our family. And Yuguayak [Micky Abraham and family] and that Caingilnguq.

Then there was Qaillukayak [Nicolas Kailukaiak] and family. And the parents of Miisaq. So those were the families, and it was sort of populated when they lived there.

But then people who lived down there at Qungurmiut would run out [of dried fish] in winter and spring, they'd run out of dried fish. People from other villages used to go through Qungurmiut [on their way somewhere)].

Those going to Tununak from these small places that were populated always went through Qungurmiut. They went by here going to Tununak to buy Western goods from the store. Qungurmiut had a lot of guests from people living to the east of us.

Tamakut tamaa-i neqvut cukanrarcet'laryukluki tamakunun kinguakun maa-i umyuarteq'lallruunga, ciin neq'rugarnek pirraartelluta nani tua-i maani April-am nuniini nurutnaurtut; neqairutnaurtukut. Taugaam unitangqelaameng Umkumiuni neqsaagturainarqami tua-i aataka iqalluarpautengnaurtukut tua-i Umkumiunek neqsaallrinek.

Nin'amayuut-wa kiingita neqput. Tua-i imkut uriluteng-llu nin'amayuut. Wiinga-llu imkut ak'allat-wa tua-i imkut qercuqat ciin neresciigat'lallrusia?

Tamakunek cikiyuitellma piurallaarcecugnarqaakut. Tauna tua-i nuruterpallrat umyuaqelaraqa tamaani tan'gurraullemni.

Maani tua-i April-ami upatullruukut cali Qungurmiunek ikamratgun Umkumiunun. Tua-i uksukacagangraan upagnaurtut pinarilliaqateng tua-i uksumi upagnaurtut.

Tua-i neqnek taugaam can'giirnek, cukilegnek-llu paivngallran makunek-llu akikarcuagurallrita melqulegnek cali avatiit pitangqerrngami, tauna pitekluku nunauluugcet'laryukluki pillruanka.

Neqtuuralriani makut yullret uitalallruata, naspaalaruarluki nunat. Nunaliaqluteng-ll' iliini tua-i uksumi tekicimaaqan allrakuan atunqigtevkenaku allamun nunamun piluteng tua-i naspaagaqluki. Naspaagurluki. Neqmek taugaam qacignanqurrarmun cali melqulegmek mat'umek akiullruami melqulek kiimi, melqulegnek tua-i paivngauralriani uitangnaqu'urluteng cagtellermeggni.

Yugnek-llu tangyuunata yugugarnek tangyuunata tamaani. Tua-i cayaqlirluta Negtemun agayuya'arqamta, aling yugyalarpaa-ll' Negtemi tallurnaqluteng tua-i cakneq! Takarnaqluteng yuut takaryutullinillemteni tamaani yugnek.

Tuamtell' cenircesqekakut cenircaqliqumta, tua-i amiigkun itqumta, tuavet-llu tua-i amiigem canianun nangerrluta, aqumleryugnaunata qavavet itraqercugnaunata. Taugaam tua-i pikestiin taum aqumesqumakunikut tua-i itrarluta aqumvigkamtenek apertuulluta pikakut, nutaan aqumluta.

Angulluarrarmek ak'allarrarmek wall' arnassagarmek pitsaqa'artevkenani qanerturalriartangqerkan, neplirngaitqapiarluta yugni tamaani. Nepliqalria nunuraqluku.

Tua-i tang caluni-ll' alerquaginrilngalengraan, alerquaginrilngalngermeng imkut kangirciluteng yuut pilallrulliniut. Ellmeggnek qanemcikluteng taringcetaarutekngganaku.

More recently I started to think that those people were the reason why our supply of dry fish went so fast, and that was why they'd run out during April after obtaining so much food; we'd run out of dry fish. But since they had some dry fish that they left behind in caches at Umkumiut, when my father finally went to get fish, we would come to have dried herring that he had gone to get from Umkumiut.

And our only food was *nin'amayuut* [herring aged in seal oil]. And those *nin'amayuut* become mushy. And I wonder why I could not eat those old frozen fish?

Maybe especially because they never offered those to me. I think of that time when we really ran short of food when I was a boy.

During April we moved from Qungurmiut by dog team to Umkumiut. So while it was still covered in deep winter, I guess they moved when it was time.

Because of the abundance of blackfish and needlefish and also because they hunted for fur animals for money because there were some in the surrounding area, I suspect that village existed there for that purpose.

Those people lived in places where there was an abundance of fish, by checking to see if places [had fish in abundance]. And some of them established places for the winter, and then they would move to another place the following winter and try it out. They kept trying new places. Because fish and also fur were the only means of obtaining money, they tried to stay in places where they were readily available when they lived scattered.

And we never saw very many people at that time. When we finally went to Nightmute to attend church, Nightmute was so crowded it caused one to cringe with respect! People caused one to be shy [out of respect for them] when we were shy of people at that time.

And when they finally told us to visit, when we finally visited, when we came through the door, we stood by the door, instead of sitting down right away and going right into the inner section of the house. We only sat when the owner of the house pointed out where we could do so.

If we happened upon an old man or old woman who was speaking, we people there could make no noise at that time. If one made a small noise, they scolded that person.

Those people did not seem to teach all the time, but they also told why things were the way they were. They told of themselves using it as if it was an example.

Taumek makut aanamta *disturb*-aasqevkenaki pilallrukait, yugmun cavkenani qanerturalria man'a nall'aruskumta cenireskumta nepliqaasqevkenata watqapik tua-i nepaitqapiaraasqelluta. Arcaqerluni qasgimi, qasgi takarnarqeqapiarluteng canek angukarnek imangqelaameng angulluanek qanrucistenek. Qanrucistenguluteng.

Uunguciitaqameng, augkut puqigngalngermeng, makut aataput, makut aatait-llu, tamakunun uunguciilkayagaqameng angulluallernun apnaurtut. Taugken nallunrilngacaaqluteng. Kangircitaqluki tua-i angulluat ayuqucianek tamakut aptellrata ayuquciqapiariinek, ilakuivkenaku.

Unangik: Uksuarmi tua-i waten melqulegculrianun-wa tua-i maligutaqamegnuk waken waniw' ayatuunga tua-i maaggun Qungurmiut tumekluki.

Qungurmiut tekiskumki maaken mat'um maa-i nuniinek ukatmurrlua, ukatmun. Naruyam kangranun; kangranek maaken kelutmun tua-i caulua. Kelutmun tua-i.

Ataam tua-i uterrlua tumelqenrilkemkun. Maani nutaan caqialua tua-i piciatun tua-i. Piciatun maani tamaani-llu, piciatun.

Tuamtell' Qalvinraam akianun pikuma Qanrangarmiut tekilluki ketmun, Ingriaraak-llu ingkuk ketairlukek cali; ukatiigni cali maani pitulua, pitullrulua. Maa-i tuaten piiyuirutellrianga.

Ilu'urma-ll' call', wani wangni ayagatunrulria yaaqvanun Etgalngurnunllu ayagatulriit avavet Etgalngurnun.

Kangrilnguq: November-aami-w' tua-i asvaingaqan, aarnairutngartaqan.

Unangik: Maani kiagmi ayagasciigatukut waten piciatun. Waten taugaam uksuarmi imarmiutartengnaquralriani tua-i ayaganarqetullrulria. Ernerpak unugluni-llu, unuakumek ayagluni.

Kapkaananek ucingqessuitut, taluyaruarugarnek taugaam. Taluyanekllu. *Hundred*-aaq naaluku civcitullruukut. Civcilangellruunga *hundred*-aaq naaluku. Nanilnguaraat.

Melqulek tua-i kiingan akikengnaqu'urluku.

Kangrilnguq: Angun piyugngauralria melqulegcuryugngauralria *welfare-*

That's why our mothers told us not to disturb them, to be extremely quiet if we visited and happened to come across someone talking. Especially in the *qasgi* because it was filled with old men who taught. They were the ones giving instructions to people.

When those who seemed to be smart got confused like our fathers and their fathers, they asked those old men. But here they appeared as though they would know things. But then those old men whom they asked told them exactly how it was. They did not leave anything out.

Simeon Agnus: During fall when we'd accompany people who went fur animal hunting, I used to travel from here through Qungurmiut on my route.

When I'd reach Qungurmiut, around this location here, I would head this way. I would head to the upper part of Naruyaq River [Gull River] and inland from its headwaters. I would travel inland.

I'd return not taking the route that I had taken. Around this area, I would start to turn here and there and go all over. I would go anywhere in this area, all over the place.

And again when I traveled to the other side of Qalvinraaq River, I would reach Qangrangarmiut and head down toward the ocean, and I would travel down below Ingriaraak [Two hills, Two small *ingrik* (mountains)] over there; I would also [go fur animal hunting] on this side of them. I no longer do that today.

And my *iluraq* [Paul John] here, he traveled more extensively than I did to areas a great distance away, and they'd also travel out to Etgalnguut Lakes [Ones that are shallow], to Etgalnguut Lakes out there.

Paul John: During November when the [ice] became thick, when it was no longer dangerous.

Simeon Agnus: We cannot travel all over during summer. But fall was the time to travel when trying to catch mink. [We'd travel] all day, and night would come, starting in the morning.

They didn't carry metal traps, but many *taluyaruat* [conical wooden mink traps]. And *taluyat* [conical wooden blackfish traps]. We used to set up to a hundred. I started setting up to a hundred. [I would set] those short ones.

They constantly tried to obtain only fur animals for an income.

Paul John: A man who was capable, one who was able to hunt for fur

aq piitellrani, ikayuun tamarmi piitellrani, *food stamp*-artaitellrani, piyugngauralria tua-i pingnaquratullruuq melqulegnek, tamarmi piyugngauralria.

Wangkuta maa-i tua-i ayagmek piiyuumariurallemtenek ayagluta tua-i pinariaqan uitasciiganata melqulegtengnaquraraqluta.

Qimugtetgun *Ski-doo*-tangvailgan tamaa-i. Cikuqami-w' kankiitullruyaaqelriakut.

Unangik: Man'a atam tua-i, Qungurmiut man' ketiit caneggluk pingqerraqami tua-i piirciigat'lallruuq atam, caneggluk amllerraqan. Kuigaaraat tua-i amelkacagartut kuicuayagaat amelkacagartut. Tamaani avani Qungurmiut nuniitni nutaan tua-i amllerpallaarluteng.

Tumekluki nallunrirnaqluteng. Ilait nutaan tekilluki, alangaanarqaqluteng.

Qimugteggun pitullemni qimugtema tua-i pillialriit asguqerrvikluki atam qimugtema. Qimugtet atam makut, kiima-ll' pinrilngua, makut-llu maa-i qimugtait pitullrulriit. Waten tua-i imarmiutalkiakan kuigaar tua-i asguqerrvikluk' asgulirnemeggni uitakan.

Tamaa-i nallunrirnaqluteng; qimugtet apertuiluteng tuaten kuigaarnek atam pitullruut pillialrianek. Ilu'urma-ll' waniw' nallunrilkai.

Man'a maa-i pivikellruaqa, man'a-llu nalluluku ukalirnera man'a, man'a taugaam tua-i maa-i Qungurmiut-llu man' ketiit tamana. Ilakluta qankutagayuunata.

Inuguarpak: Piciatun tua-i piyugngauralriit nallunricetait; piyugngauralriim yuilquq tamalkuan kangatullrua, piyugngauralriim.

Unangik: Ikingqalluku tua-i, pikniluku-ll' qanyunaunani tua-i, ikingqaluni taugaam tua-i.

Pitarkaq man' piyullminun itetuuq. Tua-i pitarkat makut waten piciqniluki qanyunaituq, "Uumek piciqua." Tamana tua-i qanruteksunaunani. Tua-i piyullminun tua-i taluyaruanun itetuut.

animals back when there was no welfare, back when there was no government assistance of any kind, back when there were no foodstamps, one who was capable always made efforts to catch fur animals, everyone who was capable.

From the time we were capable, we would leave when it was time and couldn't stay put, but constantly made efforts to catch fur animals.

We'd travel with dogs before there were Ski-doos [snowmobiles] around. We used to ice skate at freeze-up.

Simeon Agnus: This area here, when this grassy area down below Qungurmiut had an availability of [fur animals], they never became scarce when there was lots of grass. There are many sloughs, there are a great number of small rivers. There are a great many near Qungurmiut.

As you travel through them, you learn where they are. We'd come upon some for the first time, and we'd be surprised by their existence.

Back when I used to travel with dogs, my dogs would suddenly go up [sloughs] that had traces of animal activity. These dogs, and I'm not the only one who experienced this, but the dogs of these people here did that as well. If there was a trace of mink there, they'd suddenly go up a slough if it was along the place they were heading up.

You found them that way; dogs would find sloughs where there were traces of animals. And my *iluraq* here knows how they are also.

I used to [hunt for fur animals] here, and I don't know the area along this side of it, but only this area and the area down below Qungurmiut. We would all [hunt there] and didn't squabble.

Stanley Anthony: They had anyone who was capable know those places; a person who was capable would walk on foot all over the wilderness, one who was capable.

Simeon Agnus: [The wilderness] was open to them, and it was unacceptable for a person to say that he owned it, but it was open [to all people].

An animal enters [a trap] that it chooses. A person must not say that he will catch animals in the following way, "I will catch this." A person musn't say that. They enter *taluyaruat* that they choose to enter.

Tuqsuk

Unangik: Tuqsugmek maa-i man'a atengqertuq. Tuqsuuluni, ugna-w' uani avvneruara ketmun Nertuli.

Cali-w' kiani, tuani tua-i canimetuq tuani, Kass'aurluq. Ketmun-wa cali ayalria Manignalek. Uaqlirput-wa ugna Tass'aquq.

Uatmurqut-llu tua-i ilakluteng, ataucimek taugaam anllerlutek. Tua-ll' qavani kiatiini kuigmek tua-i at'legtairulluni, Tass'aqucuar taugaam qavani kiaqvani.

Tamaa-i manignassurviktaatukait. Manayuitellruyaaqut, manarluteng manigniqsaurrluteng maa-i, manarluki. Maninpallraat atam angluteng.

Tua-i imkunek taluyarpangqellriatun maa-i mat'um nalliini ayuqliriut makut tan'gurraat.

Unugmi taugaam mikunruaqluteng tamaa-i manaqungaqameng waten cikuaqan. Usuarmi tua-i aarnairtaqan-wa tua-i pitullrulriit, piiyaurtellriit maa-i.

Kangrilnguq: Wiinga tua-i maani anglillrunricaaqngama, qanemciullritgun taugaam tua-i niitelallruanka.

Maani maa-i ipukaqutuluteng iqalluanek, ceturrnanek, mat'um maa-i iluani. Camkut-wa kelliit Nangturmiut; cali tua-i tuaten ipukaqutulliniluteng ceturrnanek.

Tua-i-gguq imumek carvanrirararulluki qaluteng naparrluki piciqut, camkut-llu-gguq kelliit tua-i cali tuaten qaluteng naparrmillinikait Nangturmiut.

Tua-i uum pinritqallra augna ipukaqulallrat, maani qanemciuluteng Tuqsuum iluani cikuqami ceturrnanek.

Tua-i cali man'a maani Tuqsuk ceverqellruuq.

Cevnertangssagaunaku-ll' wii murilkellruaqa. Qamani taugaam Negtemiut uatiitni nutaan cevteqarraartengluni. Tuamtell' tua-i kinguakun kiugna Negtemiut tungliat cevteqarraartengluni.

Tuamtell' uum waniwa, maa-i man'a kuilqessaaqaa; kiugna kangia cali cevvluku.

Tuqsuk River[23]

Simeon Agnus: This river is called Tuqsuk River. It's called Tuqsuk, and its small tributary downriver that heads toward the shore is called Nertuli [One who eats lots, from *nere-,* "to eat"].

Also, upriver, it's right up close there, is Kass'aurluq River. And another that heads toward the shore is called Manignalek River [Place with *manignaq* (burbot)]. Then the one downstream from us is called Tass'aquq River.

They all head downstream, but they have one outlet. Then upriver, there is no other named river but Tass'aqucuar River, which is pretty far upriver.

Those are the places where they go and fish for burbot. They never used to jig for fish with hooks, but they have started to jig for fish and catch a lot of burbot by fishing with hooks. Those very large burbot are huge.

These days, it's as though these young men have large wooden fish traps [when they fish with hooks].

But [burbot] are more abundant at night when they start to jig with hooks when the river freezes. They have started [to fish with hooks] during fall when conditions are no longer dangerous these days.

Paul John: Although I didn't grow up in this region, I used to hear about this place through stories they told.

In this [river] here, they would fish with dip nets under the ice for tomcod, inside this river. And the ones down below them, Nangturmiut; the people there evidently also dipnetted under the ice for tomcod.

It is said when the current slacked and they posted their dip nets [in the water], they'd see that the people down below them, people of Nangtuq, had also posted their dip nets like that.

What this person here didn't mention about how they would dipnet under the ice for tomcod, they told stories about how they would dipnet for tomcod here in the Tuqsuk River after freeze-up.

They also made new channels here in the Tuqsuk River by cutting through the land.

I started to see [the Tuqsuk River in the 1950s] back when there were no man-made channels. But upriver, downriver from Nightmute, someone had made a new channel there at the time. Then after that, someone made a new channel along the [bend] toward Nightmute.

Then this here, this was its original river; they also made a new channel [shortcut] by cutting through the land along the upper part.

Tuamtell' upallemta kinguani qamani Negtemiut uaqliat uaqlingluni waten cali kangia cingiim cevengluni.

Man'a maa-i qamavet Negtemun itrallra *four*-aanek cevnengqertuq, waten cingiit takelriit cevtaqluki. *Four*-aaruluteng cevenret.

Ak'allaq taugaam qamna qama-i Negtemiut kiatiitni Cevnermek pitukiit, ak'allaq tayima ak'a tamaani cevellrulallrilria, Cevnermek pilaqiit.

Unangik: Ilaita-am narulkaquyulit, qayat amlleng'ermeng malirqaqameng, piculit tua-i-w' waten nagiiquyat elluarrluki ayagatulim pilek, tua-i qayarugaat amlleret allurtaqluki.

Tua-i taqukam qainganun kapuckaquneng nagiiquyat napaurluteng, cegg'ulluteng ayagaqluteng. Ayagluteng tuaten tua-i.

Ilait anglluutetuyaqait, taugaam tua-i quyigikan mermi alairluteng-llu taukut. Tuaten tua-i pitullruut.

Tua-i nutaan aarpagaluteng aaqata'arpek'nateng malirqelriit tuaten. Ilateng qamcara'arluki. Narulkaqataqatgu tua-i yaaqsigpek'naku pugkani, tua-i qungvagyulriit ilait narulkacurlagaqluki-gguq tua-i ilaita.

Arulaquyaq-ll'am uani, taukugnek nukalpiagnek maligluni, nukalpiakayiignek. Tuqsugmi, aug'umi asgullemteni, Qalullermun ayallemteni asgullemteni, tamaani tua-i amirkam pugglinikek, pugglinikai ua-i uatiitgun.

Arulaquyaq-gguq tauna keniqatarluni. Taukuk tua-i nukalpiakayiik maligtellrullinikek tuavet tua-i anssiilragni pillilria. Tua-i kenirteknaluku wall'u-q' taukuk tua-i unayaqellruak.

Kiatmegteggun pugngan, ilagni taukuk up'ngarcagnek, piak ilagken, "Caqatacit? Malirqellmegni tangssuarkuk, kenirturaa. Pitaqekumegnegu taikumta nerniartukut."

Aren Arulaquyaralkuk pingraagni taukuk nukalpiakayiik, ilu'urqelliamegnegu-w' tua-i pilria, piqtangraagni uptellralliniuq.

Tua-i tamaa-i pug'aqluni tua-i pillrani, tua-i elkek tua-i nukalpiak piculiungamek, nagiiquyatek tua-i waten cassingalluki piinanrani, Arulaquyaq

Then after we moved [to Toksook Bay], another new channel formed downriver from the channel right downriver from Nightmute, as a new channel started to form along the base of that large river bend.

This river that goes up to Nightmute has four man-made channels. They'd cut across the land and form channels along large points of land on the river. There were four channels that were made by cutting across the land.

But an old channel right upriver from Nightmute, the one they call Cevneq [from *ceve-*, "to cut through land"], is old, and it probably cut through the land and formed a channel long ago, the one they call Cevneq.

Simeon Agnus: Some who were good at spearing, although there were many kayaks that were pursuing seals in open water, those who were good at catching, those who were accurate at throwing spears took away animals from many kayaks.

When their points struck a seal, the *nagiiquyat* [seal-hunting spears] would stay upright and move in the water making a wake. They'd move [in the water] like that.

Some [seals] went underwater with them, but when they got close to the surface, those [spears] appeared. That's what they used to do.

At that time, people who were pursuing seals would shout without any inhibitions. They tried to get their fellow hunters to become frantic and lose focus. When they were about to spear [the seal], if it appeared not far from a person, they say those who were frantic didn't spear them correctly.

And once Arulaquyaq accompanied two great hunters, exceptionally great hunters. In the Tuqsuk River, the river that we went up when we headed upriver to Qalulleq, a young bearded seal evidently surfaced while they were there, downriver from where they were.

They say Arulaquyaq was about to cook at the time. He had accompanied those two great hunters to that place, probably when they were hunting for seals in open water at that place. Or did those two ask him to come along so that he could cook for them.

When it appeared downriver from them, when the two who he was with started to get ready, his two companions said to him, "What are you going to do? Just watch us while we're pursuing the seal and continue to cook. When we catch it and come back, we can all eat."

Although the two great hunters told that wily Arulaquyaq to stay, probably because he was their *iluraq*, although they asked him to stay, he got ready.

When the seal repeatedly surfaced, since those two great hunters were good at catching animals, while they held their two seal-hunting spears ready

akuliigni anguarluni kitulliniak. [*ngel'artuq*]

Tua-ll' taukuk, "Arulaquyaraaq amci kakiten!" Arulaquyiim takuyarluni pilliniak, "Uitaurlutek malirqitek!" [*ngel'artuq*]

Arulaquyaralleraam pugkan pugellrani canik'acagami narulkaqallerallia. Tua-i taukuk ilagken unitekugtaaryaaqerraarluku ikayullrukiik.

Aren tuani imat'am ekqataamek qanelriik nukalpiaruamek, "Nalimegnukkiq pitaqniartau." [*ngel'artuq*]

to throw like this, Arulaquyaq paddled past between them. [*laughs*]

Then those two [said], "Arulaquyaraaq, hurry up and get ready to spear and shoot!" Arulaquyaq looked back at them and said to them, "Just stay where you are and pursue the seal!" [*laughs*]

When it appeared, that wily Arulaquyaq speared it from close by. After his companions considered leaving him, they helped him.

Oh, I forgot to mention that when they were about to go down to the [Tuqsuk River], they said because they were great hunters, "I wonder which one of us two will catch it." [*laughs*]

Imarpik

The Ocean

Akuluraq

Nurataaq: Cikuyuinaku, cikuyuicaaqluku taugaam cikuq utqetaarluni, tumaunani. Pissurviuvkenani cikuq amllerraqan, pektelangermi.

Tua-i tuaten cali-am qanemcirluni ak'a tayima, ak'a tayima tamarmi cikullra.

Allirkar: Cumikellemni nengla tukniarutellria. Ugna ua-i Ulurruk up'nerkami maavet taigaqamta ngel'ekvallulallrua, tua-i qamigat tauna ngel'ekvallurluku. Tuavet tuani qayatgun pitullratni tauna tua-i ngel'ekvallulallrua. Tuam tua-i arulairvikluku.

Nurataaq: Ak'anun taugaam tua-i uitaurvikqerluku kepulartuq cali. Cali-am navgurturallermini piciatun-am cali kevkarcuunani. Allamikuaqan ayuqluni kepurturluni nang'uratullruuq.

Allirkar: Carvaneq man'a pinikayalliniuq imarpigmi carvaneq.

Tuani cali tua-i angenqiullermini qagkumiutaq angenqaaq tekitellria Akulurami kanani. Qavartallruunga qavcirqunek; qavautellruatnga-w' tua-i qaingani.

Nurataaq: Cikurpall'er cikuq. Mamtukayagluni.

Allirkar: Tua-i cungaguakayagluni waten acitmun tayima.

Tua-i-llu makumiutaq-llu puukautellriik waten carvanrem pillrani. Waten tua-lli-wa mayulria aling aren ustaqlutek. Makumiutaq tua-i elnguillruami taum puukaqungraani uitauraqeryaaquq. Mamkillruami taugaam tua-i qainganun ugirqaqluni ustaqluni.

Nurataaq: Ii-i. Tangellruaqa-ll' call' tamana qagkumiutaq taugaam angevkenani. Tanqigcetkacagaluni cikua. Menuunani.

Allirkar: Maavet-llu Kangirrluarmun iterciiganani. Etgallekluku. Etgalqitaqluni ugaan mamtum. Qagkumiutaunilallrikiit-wa.

Iqangssagaunani tua-i cungagpak. Mat'um taugken pillra iqangtagnganani amtall' cali iqaicaaqluni.

Etolin Strait[24]

Phillip Moses: [Akuluraq (Etolin Strait between Nunivak and Nelson islands, from *akula,* "area between")] doesn't freeze; it does not freeze, but the ice goes back and forth and there's no way through it. It is not a place to go hunting when there is a lot of ice, though [the ice] moves.

And there is a story that [Etolin Strait] all froze up long ago.

John Alirkar: As I've observed it, the cold is getting weaker. That Ulurruk down there, when we come here in spring, that was as far as the ice froze, so that's as far as the seal hunters always went. When they used to go by kayaks, that was the usual place that the ice froze to. So that was where the shore ice stopped.

Phillip Moses: But after it has been there a while, the ice breaks up again. But while [the ice] kept breaking up, it did not break randomly. Every year, it breaks to pieces the same way.

John Alirkar: The current is evidently extremely strong in the ocean.

Then one time one big ice flow came from the north to the Akulurat down there. I spent a night on it a number of times; they had me sleep with them there on top of it.

Phillip Moses: A floeberg [massive piece of sea ice]. It was really thick.

John Alirkar: So it was greenish all the way to the bottom.

Then the [floeberg] from here collided with that [massive piece of sea ice] when the current moved it. And it went up like this and, oh my, parts of the floebergs would fall off. Since the floeberg from around here wasn't as sturdy, even though that one was rammining it, it stood its ground for a bit. But since it was thinner, it got on top of it and kept crumbling.

Phillip Moses: Yes. I also saw [that floeberg] from the north, but it was not big. Its ice was very bright and transparent. It was clean.

John Alirkar: And it couldn't come into this Kangirrluar. [The bay] was too shallow for it. It would hit bottom because it was so thick. They said it was from the north.

It was absolutely clean. It was deep green. But the ice from around here seemed to be real dirty compared to it, but here it was really clean.

Unangik: Augna-ll' ava-i imarpik-llu qanrukeqaqii tua-i. Imarpik una kia elitniluku qaneryaqunani, tan'gurraam-gguq elitaa imarpik. Elitestaituq imarpik up'nerkami, ciku amllerrluni. Tamakut pellaassuutet atungermiki, taitugmi cikum tuskani, cikumek tumaireskuni arulairciquq.

Waten tua-i taitugmi makut tan'gurraat tua-i umyuama alingilkeqa'arqekai waten ayagaaqata, waten taitugmi, kingunrat tua-i waten tagviirutlerkaat.

Kan'a kanaan Akuluraq kan'a avatmitun ayuqenrituq; nequkilami kan' carvanra tuknituuq negetmurneq. Tuknituuq ernerpak negetmun carvanituami. Unuakumi-ll' ancarnirluni yaatmun, unuakuarmi.

Tuani tua-i pitarkaq paivngaqatuuq ancarnerem taugaam nalliini. Paivngaqatullra tua-i tamana tua-i nallunrivguarallrukek'a imum' pilallemni. Pitarkaq man'a paivngaqatullruuq erenrem iliini [ancarnirluku].

Negetmurnengkan-llu pitarkat imkut tua-i tamalriatun ayuqluteng. Unuakuq taugaam una tua-i pitarkam tua-i ancarneq una elluarrluku kuimaryaraqaa.

Waten avani ayakata'arqama unuakumi aanaka an'aqelria, kiarciiquq ella kiarciiqaa. Piciqaanga, "Ernerpak quunirciquq."

Waten-llu ellassuralua piiyuilama iluramtun, nallunruaqa ellam pagna qaill' ayuqellra. Ingrit taugaam ingkut tua-i ingriput, nuuget tua-i taituum uyangtaqaki tua-i nallunrit'larqa.

Cali una tungunquq pilakuni puy'illakuni tua-i anuqengarkaurtuq tua-i, puyiquni. Ullireskuni, puyiquni tua-i anuqengarkaurrluni tua-i qakma qaill' pivkenani. Tamana call' tua-i piciuluni cali.

Tuaten tua-i ayuquq imarpik. Tua-i una wani imarpik waten qanrutkeqa'arqamku una alerquutaqtukek'a tua-i iliini waten: "Imarpik elitnarqenrituq. Kia elitniluku qanquni iqluciquq." Elipailemku-ll' waniw' ayagayuirullua up'nerkami.

Ilumun man'a imarpik caperrnarquq. Taugaam maa-i angyarluteng pilangameng caperqenriqiit.

Anguatullemteni caperrnarqellruuq, caperrnarqellruuq anguarluta.

Simeon Agnus: He also briefly talked about the ocean earlier. Let no one say that they've learned the ocean, or a young man say that he has learned the ocean. There is no one who has learned the ocean during spring when lots of ice is around. Although he is using a GPS device, when ice comes upon him in the fog, when the ice obstructs his path, he will stop [and not continue traveling].

When these young men travel in fog, I consider them to be fearless when they travel in fog, concerned that they may not be able to get to shore.

Akuluraq down there isn't like other places around here; since it is narrow, its northern current is strong. It is strong, since the current flows north all day. And in the morning, the current flows out [away from shore] toward that direction, in the early morning.

Seals are readily available only during the outgoing tide. I learned that animals are available during that time back when I used to hunt. Animals used to be readily available some days during the outgoing tide.

And when the current started to flow north, it was like animals were no longer around. The morning outgoing tide is the time when animals tend to swim more.

In the past, when I was about to leave [to go hunting], my mother would go outside and search the sky. She'd tell me, "It will be calm all day."

Since I don't observe the weather to predict coming conditions like my *iluraq* here, I am less knowledgeable than he is about the weather. But when fog is visible over the mountains over there, over our mountains, the points, I know what the weather conditions will be like.

And when butchering an adult bearded seal, if it suddenly sprays [blood], it means that it is going to get windy, if it sprays [blood]. When it is split down the belly, and it sprays [blood], it means that it will get windy outside for sure. That is also true.

That's what the ocean is like. When I briefly talk about the ocean, this is the instruction that I constantly give: "The ocean cannot be learned. If someone says that they have learned [the ocean], they will be lying." Before I've learned it, I have stopped traveling [and hunting] during spring.

Indeed the ocean is daunting. But since they are starting to [hunt and travel] with boats nowadays, they no longer fear it.

Back when we used to paddle [with kayaks] it used to be daunting, it was daunting back when we paddled.

Waten-llu anuqenga'arrluni ingrit caumallrat caperrnarquq; atam cakviurnarquq anuqengluku anguarluni pilleq.

Tamana tua-i anguarluni pilallrat angullruarpuk ilu'urqa-ll' una-llu.

Caqerluku-am Nick-am Atiin pillinia una ilu'urqa, alingiltaarpiiqnanuk pilaasqellunuk. Tua-i alingyuitellruukuk camek. Quuniutaqakuk taqukassurpek'nanuk ituklunuk anguangaqamegnuk. [*ngel'artuq*]

Tua-i caqerluni yaani tungunqumek nutkengluni, quunirluni-llu. Ullagluku tua-i teguteqaqiin pekervagluni.

Aling, qayarluni; qayaa atam canircartuqalria. Ingna-w' qayami paingani akesvaumaluni usaam iqukluku.

Qayaa tua-i canirmi ayagturaqerluni, tua-i-ll' qayaa man' tungiinun uvercartungaarrluni; tua-i-am qayapagaqa pegcesqelluku. Peg'areskii, uvaaluni tua-i. [*ngel'artuq*] Qalutevkenani.

Kangrilnguq: Amirkamek-wa uciilkuma paluarcaqiinga. Amirkamek uqamalkutangqerran qayaqa paluartevkenii.

Unangik: Tua-i kiarrluni tua-i pugciqngan tua-i cirliqengkuni. Pugngan tua-i anguyugngangalamku tua-i nutgesqelluku. Nutgaku tua-i curukarluku teguteqerluku.

Anguarqamegnuk waten cumigtaqamegnuk nuqlicetetullruaqa cumigglunuk ayagaqamegnuk. Piciqaanga, "Iluq, qayan tamana iqkillruan cukanraryugtuten." [*ngel'artuq*]

Tua-i ilumun Nick-am Atiin piyunailengraan pitullruamegnuk inerquryaaqellrullinikii alingiltaarpiiqnanuk pilaasqellunuk. Tua-i picuktalaamegnuk tua-i pitarkamek tua-i kiartaqamegnuk tua-i alingiltaatullrulriakuk.

Ii-i, ircaqurpaulunuk tua-i. Anglanitullruukuk waten ayagatullemteni.

It is also difficult when facing the mountains when it starts to get windy; it is difficult when paddling when it starts to get windy.

My *iluraq* [Paul John] and I happened to catch the time when they paddled [with kayaks].

One time Nick's father [Albert Therchik] evidently told my *iluraq* that he and I should stop being so fearless. We were never afraid of anything. When the weather became calm, we wouldn't hunt seals but would put our kayaks side by side and paddle. [*laughs*]

One time, he shot an adult bearded seal, and it was calm. When he approached it and harpooned it, it suddently thrashed violently.

Gosh, he was using a kayak; his kayak started to go on its side. And that person over there positioned himself and held on to prevent himself from tipping over along the cockpit of the kayak, holding the end of the harpoon line.

His kayak moved while on its side, then his kayak started to tip toward [the animal]; I yelled to him to let [the line] go. When he let go [of the line], his kayak started tipping from side to side. [*laughs*] It didn't take in water.

Paul John: If I wasn't carrying a young bearded seal [in my kayak], it would have capsized me. Since my kayak was carrying a young bearded seal, I didn't suddenly capsize.

Simeon Agnus: He searched his surroundings since [the wounded seal] would appear when it got weak. When it appeared, since I felt I could reach it, I told him to shoot it. When he shot it, I went up to it and harpooned it.

When we'd paddle fast, I would leave him behind when we'd paddle fast. He'd tell me, "Iluq, since your kayak is narrower, you tend to paddle fast." [*laughs*]

Indeed, since we used to travel although conditions were dangerous, Nick's father evidently told him that we shouldn't be so fearless. Since we wanted to catch an animal when we'd search for animals, we were fearless.

Yes, we had big hearts [as we were unafraid]. We used to have fun when we traveled [with kayaks].

Kangirpak Kuiguyuq-llu

Unangik: Augna-w' man'a maa-i, Kangiryuarmek kanaken amavet Taqukatulimun, igyarairutuq; igyarairucukluku wii pila'arqa taqukangqerrnanrian augna Kangirpak.

Imumi atam avani tua-i pissuryugaralallemegni-llu ill'aqa-llu, angyat imkut uaqliqu'urluteng yaani yaa-i Taqukatulim ukatiini, Kangirpagmi. Angyat uaqliqu'urluteng tua-i taqukaliutullruut tua-i. Tamana taqukat kuimarvikellruat.

Amaken tua-i Akiliinek taingami Kuiguyuq, unaggun yaavet Taqukatulimun, tua-i-ll' igyaraqluku, Kangirpiim tua-i ciuneqluku. Tua-i-ll' nutaan marayaq ketmurrluni tuaken.

Tua-i taqukangqetullret. Kessiganaitetullruuq augna tua-i tuaten piqarralallemegni ill'aqa-llu.

Taugaam watua-im' qanrutekqallruyaaqaqa, marayaq un'a, unkut kuiguyuut, marayingami-llu kan'a Kangirpagmek pitukengarput, tauna iqua, Taqukatuli; aug'um tua-i Cevv'arnermiut ketiitni kuiguyuum aug'um *west*-atmun ayalriim, kan'a, tauna Taqukatuli iqukekii.

Kangirpak tua-i imkuqluku, cali anumaluni, qikertarluni-ll' taun ketii. Tamana tamaa-i kuiguyuullruuq.

Tua-i-ll' maa-i qamna igyarani marayangan, carevpatulleq-llu Kangirpak aug' carevpayuirulluni, taqukangqerrnanrirluni-llu.

Atam avani pissuryugarallemnuk Kangrilnguq-llu ilu'urqa-llu, tua-i uaqliqu'urluteng tungunqunek pitullruyaaqluteng angyat qayat-llu pitullruluteng tuaten.

Qayalrianun angutellruunga tua-i; allrakuni pingayuni tua-i anguarlua pitullruunga. Ilu'urqa-ll' call' cangallruvkenani wangni call'; pingayuni tua-i aipaagni pillrunganani.

Marayat unkut qerturiut. Kat'um Kangiryuaraam ketiinelnguq qaill' pilarta. Et'galilartuq-qaa?

Nallustaitnun, una wani Cingigyaq tua-i, imairrluku waten anuqmi tua-i-w' tevengnaqaqatgu ilaita tegg'anernarqelartuq.

Atam avaken tailriani, ugna ava-i Ulurruk tangvagluku tua-i ciuneqluku ullagnarquq, imairulluni pikani.

Kangirpak and Kuiguyuq Channels[25]

Simeon Agnus: The following area, from [the ice bay] Kangiryuar [from *kangiq* (bay)] over to Taqukatuli Channel [Place with many *taqukat* (seals)], there is no longer an outlet; I suspect that it no longer has an outlet, since there are no longer any seals at [the ice bay] Kangirpak [Big *kangiq* (bay)].

Back when my *Ill'aq* [Paul John] and I first started to hunt, there were boats situated up and down [the channel] on this side of Taqukatuli, at Kangirpak. Boats were lined up and down hunting for seals there. That's where seals used to swim in the past.

As Kuiguyuq [Channel] headed [south] from [ice beached in shallow water called] Akiliit over there, extending down below Taqukatuli, that was where its outlet was, and Kangirpak flowed into Taqukatuli. Then from there, there was a sandbar extending down toward the ocean.

Those were waters where seals swam. One didn't have to go out far from land back when my *Ill'aq* and I first started [to hunt].

But I mentioned the sandbar down there, the channels down there, since the [ice bay] we call Kangirpak has many sandbars now, the lower end of [Kangirpak] they call Taqukatuli; the channel that is right below the village of Chefornak that heads west, that channel connects to Taqukatuli.

[Taqukatuli] flowed out to [the ice bay] Kangirpak, and there is an island down below. That was where the channel was at one time.

But nowadays, since [the river] outlet has many sandbars now, Kangirpak that once had a strong current no longer has a strong current, and it no longer has seals.

Back when my *iluraq* Kangrilnguq [Paul John] and I first started to hunt, boaters and kayakers used to hunt for adult bearded seals right up and down there [at Kangirpak] in the past.

I happened to catch the time when they used kayaks during my life; I paddled [and hunted with a kayak] for three years. And I think my *iluraq* was no different; he seemed to [hunt with a kayak] for a period of three years.

The sandbars are getting higher down there, but I don't know about the one located down below Kangiryuar. Is it getting shallow?

For those who are unfamiliar with it, when some people attempt to travel over [the sandbar] Cingigyaq when the water is low when it's windy, it's distressing.

When heading this way from out there, one has to face and head toward Ulurruk [point] when the waters get shallow.

Qagret, qagngermi tua-i qagerpang'ermi, tua-i-ll' kuiguyuq tauna nall'arciiqaa tua-i, qaingssagaunani tua-i. Ikna taugaam anellra qailirluni Ulurruum nallii.

Ulurruum tua-i nalliini tua-i Kuiguyuq. Ukatii taugaam et'gallruami qailinruuq.

Tauna kuiguyurraq ikna Kangiryuarmun tua-i anumiimi qailiyuitelartuq.

Tauna cali tua-i elissautekluku qanruyutekluku makunun tan'gurranun pikuni atawaunruciquq. Amllerem nallua; nallularaa.

Unkut tua-i marayat-llu kankut, tua-i nallunrilkenganka kankuk, pingayuulriit tua-i.

Qikertaq-llu kan'a kanan Kangirpiim kellia, ketmun kuiguyungqertuq. Kangiryuar tua-i ketmun kuiguyurluni. Un'umun iginianun anumalutek tamarmek.

Cali-ll' ingna Taqukatulim iqra, kellirneq cali marayaq cali ketmun cali takluni, ilua man'a kuiguyuuluni.

Ingna-ll' cali Qalvinraam ciunrani cali marayaq kan'a, Qalvinraallrem ukaqlia. Tauna cali tua-i imairtemi cali tua-i amllerem etgalqitaq uitaqatuuq.

Nallunaunani tua-i marayaq qertulria, ing'um Qalvinraallrem igyaraan tua-i ukalirnera. Tauna tua-i qertutulria cali. Arcaqerlukek tua-i ukut tua-i nallunrit'laqenka.

Augna tua-i yaatii Cevv'arnermiut maani nuniit augna ketiit, wii nalluaqa, kuiga-ll' wii nalluluku, kuinra. Un'a taugaam Qalvinraaq tua-i ullaketaatuamku nallunritevguarqeka-w' tua-i.

Augkut imkut angayuqamta augkut, imarrliqutullret qayarluteng tamaa-i qanruyutektukiit una. Kangirpak-gguq una nullra kessigaqami, Kangirrluraam ciuqerranun tekitetuuq, kat'um tuavet tua-i.

Tua-i-llu tamarmi cikuliqan angyaq-gguq tua-i qayaq-llu qes'aruskan, negetmuruceskili-gguq anangnaqevkenani.

Tamaani-gguq Kangirrluaraam ciuqerrani ciku qaciglituuq, taum Kangirrluaraam ciuqerrani. Qaciglilini tua-i, ayayunarituuq. Nallunrilken tua-i qavcirqunek malik'lallrulriakut.

Pirrlainatuuq, unuakuq un' enta ancarnituuq, unuakuqliq. Tua-i-ll' ulkuni

Although there are many breaking waves, when one reaches that ocean channel, there won't be any waves inside it whatsoever. The only place that has large and rough waves is where it goes out, directly across from Ulurruk [point].

Kuiguyuq is situated in line with Ulurruk. But since this side of it is shallower, it has more waves.

Since that small channel down there flows out into Kangiryuar, large waves don't develop there.

It would be better if we teach these young men about it. Many people don't know that; they aren't aware of it.

And the sandbars down there, there are three [sandbars] that I know of down there.

And the island that is down below Kangirpak has an ocean channel that heads down toward the ocean. Kangiryuar has a channel that heads down toward the ocean. They both flow out to the deeper channel of the one down there.

Also the edge of Taqukatuli, the sandbar down below also extends and is long out toward the ocean with a channel inside it.

And there is another sandbar in front of Qalvinraaq River, on this side of Qalvinraalleq. During low tide when the waters are shallow, many people that get stuck in shallow water are stuck there for a while.

The steep sandbar is visible, alongside the outlet of the Qalvinraaq River. That is also steep. Those are the main ones that I know about.

The area beyond that, the shore around Chefornak, I don't know that area, and I don't know its river, its deep navigable channel. But since I frequently travel to the Qalvinraaq River, I know that area a little.

Our parents who encountered dangerous conditions down on the ocean using kayaks mention the following. They said when ice that is pulled in by the current at Kangirpak is farther out, it reaches the area in front of Kangirrluar [Toksook Bay] down there.

And they said if a lot of ice is throughout the whole area, and a boat and kayak are stuck within the packed ice, they should allow the current to drift them north and not try to get out [of the ice jam].

They said there in front of Kangirrluar, the ice disperses, right in front of Kangirrluar. When it disperses, one can leave. You know of this occurence as we all traveled together a number of times.

The morning tide is always an outgoing tide, the morning tide. Then when

negetmurnirluni, enteng'ermi-ll' cakanirpek'nani negetmun, taugaam tua-i ketmurninruluni. Tuaten tua-i ayuquq.

Tua-i-ll' augna. Ava-i Cungauyam qanrutekqallrukii. Augkut ava-i marayat ukut pingayun nallunrilkenganka tua-i nallunritanka. Una Kangiryuaraam ketii, Kangirpiim ketii, ingna-llu Taqukatulim kellirnera ketmun marayaq nengelria.

Taugaam tauna imairteng'ermi etgaliyuituq. Etgalqitarnarqessuituq tauna.

Una taugaam Cingigyaq arcaqerluni tua-i anuqmi alingnarqelartuq, *west*-amek. Tauna qailituami, ketiikun pingnaqlerkaq tua-i tegg'anernarquq.

Cingigyaq una arcaqerluni kiagmi tua-i tegg'anernanqurrauguq.

Inuguarpak: Avaken tailriani, anuqliulriani, anuqlilriani, uum nalliini ketiini, qikertaq wani tayim' uitiimi, Kuiguyuq-wa keluani maani, qikertaq wani nallunaitetuuq anuqlirqan. Kiimi tua-i qaterluni qagraluni.

Keluirnaqluni ketaingnaqevkenaku, kuiguyukun maaggun keluakun pinarqelaami, nani tayima maani qikertaq takngami.

Tauna tua-i qatetuuq anuqlirqan, qairem patussiyaagpailgani, etgataqan. Kiimi tua-i qaterrluni kana-i nallunaunani, Kuiguyum kelua.

Tauna tua-i nallunritlemtun wiinga atulaamku iliini, qagralriit keluatgun maaggun ayagaqama, tauna tua-i nallunritaqa. Et'urivailgan tauna tua-i Kuiguyuum keluani, kellirnerani, tauna tua-i qagratuuq qaterluni kiimi.

Kangirrluar

Unangik: Uani Tuqsugmi aqvailunuk uksuarmi aanaput-llu, angyarlunuk itrarlunuk, angyat unkut amllerrluteng.

Itraamegnuk-llu tua-i Tuqsugmun kipussaagaqerlunuk-am calqurrarnek aptanka, "Cat unkut unani tuaten pilriit?" Cetuanek-gguq piut.

the tide comes in, [the current] flows north, and even when the tide goes out, it doesn't change and continues to flow north, but it flows out toward the ocean a little more. That's what it's like.

And the other thing. Cungayuaq [John Eric] briefly mentioned it. The three sandbars that I know of, I know those. There is one down below Kangiryuar, one down below Kangirpak, and one in front of Taqukatuli over there, a sandbar that stretches out toward the ocean.

But in that particular [channel], although the water goes out and gets low, it doesn't get shallow. One doesn't encounter shallow areas when traveling there.

But Cingigyaq is especially dangerous when it's windy, when the wind is blowing from the west. Since there are large waves, it's distressing to try to travel down below that area.

Cingigyaq is the most difficult area to navigate through during summer.

Stanley Anthony: When coming from [Chefornak] out there when it's windy, right around this area here, right below it, since there is an island here, and Kuiguyuq is behind it here, the island that is located here is visible when it's windy. It's the only thing that is white as there are breaking waves around it.

You have to go through the channel nearest to land and not down below it, since you have to travel through the channel here behind it, since somewhere here is an island that is long.

That [island] is white when it's windy before waves cover it, when the water is shallow. The area behind Kuiguyuq is the only thing that's white down there and is obvious.

Based on experience, since I've traveled through there sometimes when traveling behind breaking waves, I know that area. I'm aware that before the water gets deep, the area down below Kuiguyuq is the only place where waves are breaking and the only area that is white.

Toksook Bay[26]

Simeon Agnus: Down at Toksook, when our mother [my wife] and I went to fetch some things [at Umkumiut] by boat during falltime, there were lots of boats down there [in Kangirrluar (One like a *kangiq* (bay)].

When we headed up to Tokook Bay to buy knickknacks at the store, I asked them, "What are [those boats] doing down there [in Kangirrluar]?"

Tua-i-ll' piaqa aanavut, "Aling cetuanek cikiqeryuaraitkuk ilagauskumegnuk taugaam unkunun cetuanek ungulrianun."

Angyarugaat tua-i Kangirrluar man'a tut'enritaraumaluku kuinra tua-i waten tua-i piluteng.

Tua-i-ll' atrarlunuk maaggun ualirneratgun. Avani tangvallemni maaten tua-i pianka ava-i qak'artaqameng pingayuungatnaurtut tua-i augkut cetuat.

Ungulriit Taulan-wa atanrat, angageurluqa. Cavutet kaugtuaraqluki.

Tua-i-ll' pivakarluni qayagpagtuq, "Amci tua-i taggnariyaaqai!" Tuqsuunkuk akuliignun Nangtuq-llu.

Aling, tua-i qaviruskaiteng cetuat imkut tua-i tagluteng tua-i kelutmun. Pingayurraungatnaurtut augkut.

Tua-i-ll' keluqsigiata qavlunangarcata—wiinga tua-i pingayuuyukluki umyuarteqlua—qavlunangluteng qavelvangqerluteng, maani waniw' Nangtunkuk akuliigni Tuqsuk-llu, wavet maavet tua-i taggluki; ulumaluni-llu.

Pinariniaki tua-i angyat curukaulluteng. Wiinga-ll'-am tua-i uitangailama curukaullua tua-i. Tua-i angyat makut pingaartut tua-i.

Piuraqerluni cetuaq man'a qatqillagtuq ciunemegni qavelvalria! Narugarrluku ullagluku menglairluku tegutet kapusvikluki maavet, nutegpek'naku.

Aanavut alingkacagarluni tua-i! Palucetnayukluni. Qelluqicami tua-i qiperrlugpek'nani qaktaarturlun' taugaam tua-i waten; ter'ani piqtaarturluku.

Tegutmek tua-i ucingqerrama tuani tua-i cetuamek teguteqaqengellruunga tua-i unguvalriamek puulitaumanrilngurmek. [*ngelaq'erluni*]

Cetuat makut ungusciryakacaartut. Tuaten tua-i pulengtaq augkut-llu ciuliamta teguteqerturluki pitullrukait. Tua-i ungukaceteng tua-i etgatkacagalria.

Tua-i tuani Taulan pinari[niaki], tuani maaten piaput qulngunritaraullinilriit cetuat; qulngunrita'arnek tuquciluteng tua-i.

Tamakut ciulaput-ll' augkut qayatgun taugaam ungutullrukait; marayamun tua-i taggluki tua-i.

Up'nerkami-llu wani Ulurruum ketiini, uum ketiini, cetuamek nutegyaaqellruunga taugaam nall'artevkenaku ukatmun cauqapiaraumaluni pin-

They said they were hunting for belugas.

And then I said to our mother, "I declare, in hopes that they may give us some beluga, we should join those herding beluga down there."

There were a lot of boats practically all across the channel of Kangirrluar.

So going down we went down the bay from them. When I observed, whenever the beluga breached, there seemed to be three of them.

They were herding them, and Taulan [Paul Agimuk] was their boss, my poor maternal uncle. They would beat [the boat] with oars.

Then eventually he yelled, "It's about time to take them toward land!" [He meant to take them toward land] between Tuqsuk River and Nangtuq River.

My, when they turned them, those belugas went up toward land. There seemed to be only three of them.

And when they were way up toward the edge of land and beginning to make wakes—I thought there were three—so they were beginning to make large wakes, and this was between Nangtuq River and Tuqsuk River where they brought them up to shore; and the tide was in.

When they said that it was time go get them, the boats attacked them. Since I wasn't going to just stay there, I also pursued one. So all these boats were all [in the frenzy of a kill].

Pretty soon, the beluga flashed in white and created a large wake just in front of us! We moved toward it, and as it was positioned on the side of the boat, I speared it instead of shooting it.

Our mother was beside herself with fright! She thought we might capsize. When the rope became taut, it didn't thrash around but kept breaching like this; it kept moving its tail flipper.

Since I had a spear in my boat, that was the first time that I speared a live beluga that had not been previously shot. [*chuckles*]

Belugas are easy to herd. So spearing them like that, our ancestors used to get them like that. So they herded them to a shallow area.

At that time when Taulan told us that it was time, we found out that there were nine belugas; so they killed nine.

Our ancestors used to herd them using kayaks; they'd push them all the way to the mudflats.

And in spring, in front of Ulurruk [point], in front of this place here, I shot at a beluga, but I didn't hit it since it wasn't facing this way completely. I shot

rilan. Wiinga-am nutegyararaqerluku pillrukek'a tuani. Cikut akuliitni. Pitaqevkenaku tua-i tayima natmun ayagartellrua.

Man'a maani levaat piurayuitellratni man'a maa-i kuig asgutullruyaqaat; atam ilaita nunat-llu ilaita.

Ilangciyuunaki-llu. Ilait tua-i piqatuyaaqellrullikait. Iliini cetuarugaat kautetullruut atam maavet. Tua-i kangivarluteng tua-i.

Imna-ll' Aluskaq nallunrilken, Peter Aluskaq, kiugumek agayuvilillrani malrugnek qavaken qava-i cetuartellruuq cetuarpallraagnek malrugnek qatellriignek. Ava-i kiatemtenek.

Qagaani negemteni maani Niugtarmiut ketiitni pinriyuitut; maa-i pituut piuratuut. Hooper Bay-irmiut ikegkut call' cetuarquratulriit, Cev'armiut-llu ikegkut.

Cirmirraq: Tamana-wa Kangirrluaraam ilua avani ak'a amaqsuut amlletullratni cetualirrlainatullruuq-gguq una Kangirrluaraam ilua. Kanavet Al'aqucimun tamaa-i cat makut neqrugaat amaqsuli ? tamakut maliggluki. Tuaten tua-i ayuqellrullilria tauna. Levaarturayuitellratni.

Tua-i-gguq pinricuunateng-gguq tua-i tuaten cetuanek. Cetuarculriit tua-i tuaten ungulliniaqluteng.

Unangik: Tua-i-wa tamaani ellangyugallemni cetuaricuitkacagallruuq tua-i man'a waten kiagmi.

Akiliit

Unangik: Avani qamigaqarraatullemni unani taugaam Akiliini kiingan tamakunek tangtullruunga, etgalqitanek. Akiliit unani, Akiliinek tamakut piaqluki etgalqitat.

Akiliit ingkut caqerluku up'nerkami tekitellruanka, Cevv'arnermiut ketiit kan'a, Qussauyarmek maliglua.

Ingna-w' angyaq ciunemteni, Nuqarrluunkuk ilurapaka-ll' Nurauq. Kinallu pillruat. Kayirayuaq-llu malikellrukiit.

Ilurapaka aptaqa arulaiqaamegnuk, arulairvikngamegneki, "Ukut wan' evunpallraat caugat?" Akiliiruut-gguq.

Iluatni waten mayuumaurluni. Pianga, "Ilurapak, yuurqernaurtukut, mayurluten."

at it too soon at that time. In the middle of the ice floes. So it wasn't caught, and I don't know where it fled to.

[Beluga] used to go up this [Tuqsuk River] before many outboard motors were around; some of them even went past [Nightmute].

And they ignored them. They probably hunted some of them though. Sometimes many beluga came into this [Tuqsuk River]. So they come all the way up [river].

And you know Aluska, Peter Aluska, when he was building that church up there, he got two, big white belugas upriver. Upriver from our village.

[Beluga] never stop coming up north of us, like in front of the village of Newtok; they are always there. And the village of Hooper Bay across there always gets belugas; that village of Chevak, too.

Camilius Tulik: They say that in those bygone days when there were a lot of humpies inside Kangirrluar, there were a lot of belugas inside Kangirrluar. When there used to be a lot of humpies at Al'aquciq, they followed those. It was probably like that. When they didn't constantly travel with outboard motors.

They say that belugas never failed to come. So those who hunted for beluga herded them like that.

Simeon Agnus: When I came to be aware, this area never lacked belugas in summer.

Akiliit[27]

Simeon Agnus: Back when I first started to go seal hunting, I only saw *etgalqitat* [ice beached along shallow water] down at Akiliit. The Akiliit down in the ocean, they called those *etgalqitat* Akiliit.

I arrived at Akiliit one day during spring, along the area down below the village of Chefornak, traveling with Qussauyaq.

There was a boat ahead of us, occupied by Nuqarrluk and my *ilurapak* Nurauq. I don't know who else was with them. Kayirayuaq was with them, too.

I asked my *ilurapak,* when we stopped next to them, "What are these very large *evunret* [ice piles] called?" He said they were called Akiliit.

He had climbed up and was inside them. He told me, "*Ilurapak,* climb up and let's have some tea."

"Aren yuurqeryuumiitua. Tua-i tang alingelrianga, quuqerrutnayuklua."

Pianga atam-gguq Ugcirraq un'a tangerqerlaku. Anuqetaituq ugna cakemna. "Tua-i taituk atrarqami tua-i uani Ugcirraq, pagken atrarqami, qalirnera taitungareskuni tua-i anuqengenrilngaituq." Tauna tua-i Ugcirraq tangvatulliniamegteggu avaken.

Yuurqerraarlunuk taqngamegnuk taqukassullma kiinguan tamalkisngaluk utertukuk. Qavani taugaam Kangirrluaraam ketiini angyanek tekitengamegnuk nutaan massiinaqa cukairrluku. Tua-i alingelqa.

Cingigyaq

Cuyanguyak: Wangkuta-ll' cali kiagmi waten Umkumiunun neqliyarluta ayagyaaqluta. Ayagluta pingayuuluta. Amaqigcim nangcarluta, wangkutallu David-am angyaani uitaluta. Nangcaqluta elliin Amaqigcim. Ukut-wa Qiurtarralgenkut cali kinguqlikacaaqluki. Maaken arvilriakut uaken Aqumgallermiunek. Ernerpak quunirluni ayaagalriakut.

Tua-i qaill' pivkenata ayagluta. Tua-i-llu tauna Cingigyaq ikani qaitunilallrat mallegpallalliniluku.

Ciunerput augna qatriluni. Qairet qagerturallrat. Ullagluku, natetmunllu ayayuunata.

Tua-i-llu tamana tekitarput qairet. Amaqigcim angyaa ayagaqluni waten mayurluni qairmi, tuamtell' tayima atrarluni.

Wangkuta tuamtellu kiimta, ilanka-wa, Tuguyak-wa. Cali tuaten atrarluta tuavet Amaqigcim atrallranun.

Amkut-wa amatmun cali qairem amatiinun ipluteng. Wangkuta tua-i tuaten cali ayagluta elliitun.

Ukut-llu kinguqlikacaarput, Qiurtarralegenkut; tuavet-llu tekicameng qairmun, ukatmun pirraarluni mayuqan, nangcautarput augna ilavkuk qalriayaarluni kinguqliuluni. Taukut kinguqlimta nangcautaat qalrialuni imumek qelluqiarrluni. Wangkuta akunleqliuluta, arvilriakut ernerpak.

Tua-i-llu David-aam waten qanrutaa, qayagpagluku Amaqigciq yaa-i nangcartevut, keluqvaqaniqaqumta-gguq qairet utumaqanirciqut. Kessigiqertelliniluta.

[I said], "My, I don't want to have tea. I'm afraid that the ice may close in on me."

He told me to look at Ugcirraq [Cape Vancouver] down there. There was no wind down there at the time. He said, "When the fog goes down from up there, the top of Ugcirraq suddenly forms fog, it gets windy for sure." He knew that because they've apparently always observed Ugcirraq since long ago.

After we finished drinking tea, after hunting for seals, we returned home with our motor running at full speed. I only decreased the speed of my motor up below Kangirrluar when we started to come across boats there. I was afraid at that time.

Cingigyaq[28]

Maria Eric: We also went to Umkumiut to harvest fish during summer one time. There were three boats that went. Amaqigciq towed us, and we were in David's boat. Amaqigciq was towing us. Then Qiurtarralek and his family were at the very back. We went across from Aqumgallermiut [Residents of Aqumgalleq (One who sat there)]. It was calm and windless all day as we traveled slowly.

We traveled and were okay. Then we evidently got too close to Cingigyaq [One similar to a *cingik* (point)] that they say forms large waves.

The area ahead started to turn white. They were breaking waves. We went toward it, and we never turned in any direction.

When we got to that area, there were waves. Amaqigciq's boat would go like this, would go up on top of a wave, and then it would go down.

Then there was just us, and others with me, and Tuguyak. We'd go down like that also, to the place where Amaqigciq's boat had gone down.

Then those in front of us would disappear on the other side of the wave. We also went through the path that he had taken.

Then the people who were at the very back, Qiurtarralek and his family; when they reached a wave, after going down, when it went up, the rope that we were towing would make a faint noise, as it was in the very back. The rope that towed the people behind us would make noises from getting taut. Our boat was in the middle as we went across all day.

Then David told him, shouted to Amaqigciq who was towing us, that if we moved a little toward shore, the waves would be much calmer. We had gone a little too far away from shore.

Tua-i tamakut qairet aturluki ayagluta. Angyam uciini wangkuta tua-i cakneq qailiukacagarluta. Angyaq-llu mayurraarluni atrarqan malikluku-ll' wangkuta.

Tua-i tuaten ayagluta. Tua-i-llu ika-i Umkumiut alairluteng. Qailillra utumaqerluni keluqvaqanillemteni.

Arvirluta, tua-i-ll' painganun yaa-i Tuqsuum tekiteqatarluta, ketmun caqirtellemteni, tuartang wangni quunermun tekitellriakut. Quunillruuq tuani cakmaken uaken ayallemteni.

Tuartang wangni angayaput tuavet painganun tua-i atraqertellemteni tuartang wangni ellu'urtellriakut, nauw' tayim' qairpallraat avani kingunemteni. Cunaw' cakma Umkumiut uatiitni cali tuani tangvallinikaitkut taillemteni, tua-i tangerrluta.

Tua-i-llu Umkumiunun tekilluta. Tua-i tua-i qairtaiteqerluni. Umkumiut yugyagluteng pelatekarugaat qavavet itraumaluteng. Neqliyaryaaqluta iqalluarpagnek.

Taukut-gguq tua-i pikani, cakmani nayuryaaqelliniluta, ilavut waten angyaq qelluqiskan ilavut katagnayukluki kellutelliniluta. Nayulliniluta.

Tua-i tekicamta cakmaken taukut nayurteksaaqelput itraraluteng. Quyaluteng ilavut picurlanritellranek, angyaq-llu kevkautenritellranek.

Amkut-llu pamani kinguqlikaacaurlulput qialriit aanatuumarmeng. Kayungiaraam qanemcikluki yuungamta. Qialriit-gguq alingluteng atatuumarmeng. Tacuuq-llu alingkacagalliniluni qailiuyuilami, qailiuyuitelliniami.

Tagglemteni, wiinga aayalngualua, ?James-aankugnek ukuurluq-llu maliglua. Angayiim atrarluni piakut natmun ciuniusqevkenata, nem'inun agucugluta.

Iterluta. Aren, irniagka ukuk nepenglutek elliinek Angayiimek alinglutek. Aiggacungarcecugnaunatek. Tua-i tayim' ilaput natmun tayima ciunirluteng.

Tua-i-llu nerluta tekicamta, itramta elliinun. Arenqialagnek irniagka taukuk alingagnek, qiagurlutek anyuglutek, alinglutek taumek arnarpall'ermek. Tua-i-ll' anullukek.

Anucamkek tuamtellu waniwa ? cungaka; tuamtellu nem'inun itrucugluta. Itertukut aanaurlullra imna kiani aqumgauralria. Nepiamek nel'uteng ellait. Iterluta. Tuartang imkut irniagka tuavet itramta nepaiteqerlutek, alingellrek, alingellruyaaqellrek.

We continued on through those waves. Those of us who were inside the boat were going through really large and rough waves. After going up, when the boat went down, we'd follow it.

That's how we traveled. Then Umkumiut came into view over there. The waves got much calmer when we moved in toward shore.

We went across, and when we were about to get to the mouth of the Toksook River, when we turned toward shore, it seemed to me that we arrived in calm waters. It was calm when we traveled on from down there.

To me it seemed that when our boat suddenly went down into the mouth that we slid down, and all the waves behind us were gone. Evidently, down below Umkumiut, they watched us as we came, and they saw us.

Then we arrived in Umkumiut. There were no waves the rest of the way. There were many people at Umkumiut, many tents that extended up the coast. We went to harvest herring at the time.

Some people were evidently watching out for us from up [on the bluff] down the coast, evidently watching us just in case one of us fell out when the tow line became taut. They were evidently watching over us.

When we arrived, those people who had been watching us went back up from downriver. They were happy that no one in our group had experienced a mishap and that the tow line hadn't broken.

The people who were in the very last [boat] cried along with their mothers. Kayungiaraaq told us what they did when we got out [of the boats]. He said they cried out of fear, including their father. And Tacuuq was really terrified since he evidently hadn't gone through large waves before.

When we went up, I was dizzy, and James and this poor person were with me. Angayiik came down and told us not to go anywhere else but wanted to take us to her home.

We went inside. My children started to whine, afraid of Angayiik. They wouldn't let her shake their hands. The others went to other places when they arrived.

Then we ate when we arrived, when we went inside her home. Since my children were so afraid, they kept crying, wanting to go outside, afraid of that very large woman. Then I brought them outside.

When I brought them outside, I saw [another woman]; she again wanted to take us inside her home. We went inside and saw her late mother sitting back there. They had a sod home. We went inside. It seemed as though my children quieted down when we went inside there, the ones who had been previously afraid.

Taum tua-i pikiitek, irniagka kinguqliqlutek arviqerrlutek, aiggacungarluku. Tamarkenka aiggacungarlukek.

Aiggacungarraarlukek pianga, kituusia-gguq. Tua-i-ll' atqa aperturluku.

Tua-i-ll' waten pianga, elliin taum aaniita arnassak'acagaam. Pianga irniagka-gguq ukut unatekek tegullrit waten, arivnekek makut arivnerit unatekenka, "Aivkangqanritliniut." Waniwa-gguq assirlutek yuuguraqatalliniuk. Quyaluku anelrarluta.

When [their mother] acknowledged them, they quickly walked across one after the other and shook her hand. She shook both their hands.

After shaking their hands, she asked me who I was. Then I told her my name.

Then their mother said to me, that very old woman. She told me that my children, taking their hands like this, referring to the joints along their hands, she said, "They are solid." She said they would lead good lives. I thanked her and went across.

Qalvinraaq Avayai-llu

Qalvinraaq River and Its Tributaries

Qalvinraaq

Unangik: Man'a maa-i Qalvinraaq makunun nunacuarnun pivailegmeng uitavigkameggnun, uksivigkameggnun, man'a maa-i Qalvinraaq uksuarpak tua-i atutullruat, nayutullruat. Neqsurvikluku, makunek-llu taqukanek tamaa-i malirqu'urvikluku tuaten. Tuaten tua-i ayuqellruut.

Tayima-llu nayurterugallri anguterugaat, pelatekat atam maani kiaqliqluteng pitullruut. Uani-ll' ua-i kitullruavut Mertaryararmiunek pitukait. Taukut cali tua-i pelatekarugaat amlletullruut tuani.

Angungnaqvikluku tua-i man'a yullret imkut nayutullruat. Waten peksagpailegmeng makunun nunalqurrarnun uksivigkameggnun, tamaa-i tua-i angungnaqvikluku pitullruut.

Ukut-llu waniw' qavciuluta waniw' angumakput, ukuuluta waniw', augkutciulqiputangayuqaput. Wangkutakass'allamekanglaninritqapiarallruukut mat'umek maa-i nertukevcenek. Neqa taugaam tua-i pikluku.

Cali piciatun neqmek tegulluta pisciigatkacagarluta, aanaput apterraarpek'naki. Kass'at iciw' makut erneq quka'arqan nertulriit atakumi-ll' *five o'clock.* Tuaten tua-i nertullruut quyurmeng kina imna ilaseng irniarteng katagpek'naku. Nernarikan irniarit quyu'urrluteng nalluvkenateng angayuqateng ilagarluki nerluteng, piciatun neryugnaunateng.

Cali maniartangqerqan kaigayaaqekumta qunuskakut qepirtevkenata-ll' uitaluta. Mukaaq taugaam tua-i man'a wangkuta tua-i pikangqeqa'arqamta nertullrukvut. Camek-llu *pop*-ataunani, cataunani, *candy bar*-artaunani.

Ikna ikan' *Native Store*-aq Tununermi kiimi kipusviullermini makut maa-i Caninermiut ullagluku uksumi ikamrarluteng ikavet kass'artequtullruut, augkut yaaqliput ungalaqliput.

Tua-i catangssagaunani, angret taugaam tua-i kiimeng piuluteng. Taugken *North Star*-aq tekiskuni, imna kituulria-ima, Moe-q, kantinek tagulluni tua-i aruqeciquq imkunek kantirugarnek imkunek urugcitulinek qanermi. Quyak'acagarnaurtukut tua-i tangrraqamteggu tekitaqan, waten pirrlainatuan. Nunat imkut tuaten pitullruyugnarqai tamalkuita uciirviktukni *North Star*-am.

Qalvinraaq River[29]

Simeon Agnus: The Qalvinraaq River here, before they moved to the villages where they would stay for the winter, they stayed at the Qalvinraaq River all fall. They fished here, and they also pursued seals in open water here. That's how people were.

And the many men who stayed here, tents were situated up and down the river along [the banks]. We also passed the place they call Mertaryararmiut [Residents of Mertaryaraq (One along the way to get water, from *mertar-*, "to fetch water"] downriver. Many tents were also there in the past.

People stayed at this place to subsist in the past. Before they dispersed to villages where they would spend winter, it was a place where they hunted and fished.

Including these people here, a number of us here happened to catch the way of life of those who came before us, our parents. We didn't have an abundance of store-bought goods that you all eat now. We only had traditional foods.

And we couldn't just take whatever type of food there was before asking our mothers. You know how white people eat at noon and in the evening at five o'clock. They ate together as a group like that, not leaving any of their children out. When it was time to eat, their children gathered and knew when mealtimes were, and they ate with their parents at set times.

And if there was fry bread and we asked for some and they declined to give it to us, we didn't demand to eat any and just stayed. We'd eat bread only when we had some available. There were no soda pops, nothing of that sort, no candy bars.

When the Native Store over at Tununak was the only store around, the people of the lower Kuskokwim coastal area, the people to the south of us, would go there during winter with sleds to buy store-bought goods.

There weren't a great variety of things, but only chewing gum was available. But when the *North Star* arrived, that person whose name I've forgotten, Moe, would bring some candy to shore and distribute them, many candies that melted in the mouth. We'd be extremely happy when we'd see him when he arrived, since he always [distributed candy]. I think the *North Star* did that to all the villages where it stopped to unload merchandise.

Augna tekiteqarraatulleq tangelqa muragaullruuq atam, muragauluni tua-i angyarpall'er augna. Tua-ll' kinguqlingluni aug'umek tegglimek. Tauna tua-i ak'anivkenani tayima tangrruunrillruuq, makutgun tengssuutekun *freight*-aquluki piyaurcatki makut kipusviit akluit. Tayima tua-i tangrruunanrirluteng tua-i tayima. Tuaten tua-i ayuqellrulriit.

Makut-llu mat'um maa-i yullri tayima catairulluteng tamaq'apiarmeng, mat'um maa-i yugugaat nayurtellrit. Anirtima imkut angayuqaput waten qanlallruut, "Nauw' imkut yuut?" Waten waniw' wangkuta waniw' yuaryugngaaput.

Man'a yugyatullruuq Qalvinraaq qamavet Cakcaaq tekilluku. Nunalqurraat amllertut.

Augkut angayuqaput imkut ciuqliit neqelget taugaam nayurluki uksiviketullruit. Neqairucuilnguq uksurpak can'giirnek, tua-i tamakut arcaqerluki.

Can'giiq maa-i kiingan makut maani qimugtetgun pitullermeggni; can'giiret, uqtaqngat iqalluat, naternat. Camek tua-i avungqerpakallrunritut maani.

Taugken ukut ingrit, tua-i waten uksuutaqateng picimegcetun tua-i nertuluteng uksuarmi; manignanek, qassayaarnek, qaurtunek, cuukvagnek.

Tua-i waten ilaitni man'a qanruyun imutun caunricukeng'erpeceni ciunerpeceni caningqauq. Tekitniarci atam. Tuaten ayuqurngaituci. Wangkucicetun ak'allingekuvci umyuarteqciquci erenrem iliini, augna-ll' im' qanerturallerput umyuaqluku; umyuaqeciqluku ilavci avaunrilkuniu.

Man'a ciulirneq qantuuq cingumailuni taugaam makunek kinguqlirminek, eq'ukevkenaki. Tuaten tua-i qantuut Yupiit.

Arayakcaaq

Kangrilnguq: Arayakcaaq kan'a una kiagiurviksunarquq, tamaa-i kass'inrarmek nerucingvailemta.

Neq'linricaaquq ayuqenrilngurnek, imkunek tua-i naternanek, ceturrnanek, imarpinrarnek; kiagmi tua-i tamakunek taugaam neqerluni. Taugaam maavet carvanun pissurluteng-llu carvarmiutartutullruluteng.

Cali yaqulget up'nerkamek ayagluteng kayanguitnek yaqulget-llu tua-i nerumatkeurluki, tamaa-i kiagmi.

Tua-i neqkartuyarrnarqenricaaqeng'ermi taugaam neryuuminarqevke-

The [ship] that first arrived that I saw was wooden, a large wooden ship. Then after that, it was a metal [ship]. That boat wasn't around for long when they started shipping merchandise as freight for stores with airplanes. [The ships] were no longer around after that. That's how they were.

And all the people who once lived here are gone now, the many people who once lived in these settlements are all gone now. No wonder our parents used to say, "Where are those people?" We, too, can ask where those people are.

Many people once lived along the Qalvinraaq River, reaching the Cakcaaq River up there. There are many small settlements.

Our parents, the first ones only lived in places where there was an availability of fish during fall and winter. They especially lived in places that had an availability of blackfish all winter.

Back when they traveled with dogs, blackfish was the only thing they obtained; blackfish, tomcod caught with hookless lures, flounder. They didn't obtain much else besides those around here.

But along these mountains, when winter came, they ate various things during fall; burbot, frozen raw whitefish, broad whitefish, pike.

Although some of you think that the *qanruyun* [instruction] is useless, it is in your future. You will come upon it one day. You won't always be like this. When you get older like us, one day you will think about it and remember the things that we talked to you about; if some of you haven't forgotten it, you will recall it.

An elder gives instructions only to encourage young people toward success, without any hatred toward them. That's what Yup'ik people say.

Arayakcaaq River[30]

Paul John: Arayakcaaq River down there was a good place to spend summer, back before we started eating Western foods.

There isn't actually a variety of fish there, but there are flounder, tomcod, *imarpinraat* [whitefish]; those types of fish are there during summer. But they also fished here in streams and had freshwater fish from streams.

And starting in spring, they also gathered bird eggs, and they had birds to eat during summer, too.

Although there isn't a large amount of food to obtain there, it was a place

nani kaignaunani; neqsurturluni nerumaurnaqluni.

Wangkuk waniw' Cevv'arnermiuni yuurtellrungramegnuk una-llu anglivsiarvilqerpuk una Arayakcaaq.

Tua-i angliurlunuk tamaani ellangellruyaaqengramegnuk Cevv'arnermiuni. Tamaa-i mik'nanuk angayuqamegnuk nugtarullunuk wavet Arayakcaamun anglivsiarturallruukuk.

Uksumi-llu can'giirnek quarruugnek, tua-i neqkarturyarrnarqenrilngermi, neru'urnaqluni.

Kiagmi-llu ceturrnat naternat-llu kinercirturluki, uksumi kinerneqluki tua-i piurnaqluni.

Naptat-llu amllenrilngermeng cali imarpinraat, cali tua-i kiagmi nerqaqu'urnaqluteng.

Kaignarqenrilnguq ayuqenrilngurnek neqaileng'ermi Arayakcaam anaakurallra.

Allirkar: Waken painganek, Araykcaam paingani kiagaqan uitatullruukut. Tuani kiituan kayangut an'ut, irniarit-llu tukerluteng tengluteng.

Maavet tua-i imna ellangellemni aanaka issratmek atmagluni ayalalria, piyagaat pingaqata. Iralum anngairutma urluvranek aturluni tayima ayagaqluni. Tekiciiquq issratni muirumaluki; aananek pitgaqutuluni aanaka.

Tuamtell' atkugkarcuqunikut kuvyamek civciluni nanvamun tunutellegnek, qaqanek, tamakunek allyuilngurnek; kelugartaqameng taugaam tunutellget qaqat-llu altullrulriit. Qucillgaat-llu call' allyuunateng kelugartaqameng taugaam. Qugyuut-llu.

Kangrilnguq: Tua-i kaiyuunata wani Arayakcaam tayim' paingani.

Allirkar: Arayakcaam paingani. Up'nerkiyarauluteng tuaten. Up'nerkami kiagcecarauluteng; tamaaken tamaa-i Arayakcaamek atrarluta tuantaqluta.

Iliini-ll' Naruyamiuni uitaaqluta up'nerkami, urugcelluteng, maaken imkut anangnaqestelput uqurrangengnaqlallruameng imarpigmek.

Tuani tua-i, tuamtell' maavet mat'um Qalvinraam avayaanun, avayainun upagaqluteng neq'legnun cali. Cali tamaani iqalluanek ceturrnanek neqsuraqluteng naternanek-llu.

where one didn't go hungry; it was a place where one could continually fish and stay fed.

Although [John Alirkar] and I were born at Cevv'arneq, Arayakcaaq River was where we spent the rest of our childhood.

We grew up there although we became aware of our surroundings at Cevv'arnermiut. When we were small our parents moved us here to Arayakcaaq River, where we spent the rest of our childhood.

And although there wasn't an abundance of food there in winter, enough blackfish and needlefish were there to eat.

And in summer, they constantly dried tomcod and flounder, and those were the types of dried foods they had during winter.

And although there weren't many *naptat* [Bering cisco] and *imarpinraat,* one could also eat them from time to time in summer.

Arayakcaaq River isn't a place to go hungry, although it doesn't have a variety of fish.

John Alirkar: We stayed at the mouth of the Arayakcaaq River during summer. While we were there, birds laid their eggs, and their fledglings hatched and flew.

When I became aware of life, my mother would carry a grass bag on her back and travel to this area when there were fledglings around. She would leave using my deceased older brother Iraluq's bow. She'd arrive with her grass carrying bags full; my mother would shoot arrows [and catch] mother birds.

And when she went to obtain birds for parkas for us, she'd set a fishnet inside a lake and catch Pacific loons, red-throated loons, those birds whose skins don't tear; the only time Pacific and red-throated loonskins would tear was when their stitches came out. And cranes didn't tear either, only when their stitches came out. And also swans.

Paul John: We never went hungry along the mouth of the Arayakcaaq River.

John Alirkar: Along the mouth of the Arayakcaaq River. It was also a spring camping site. It was a site where we went during spring and spent the summer; we'd go down from Arayakcaaq and stay there.

And sometimes we'd stay at Naruyamiut [Residents of *naruyaq* (gull)] during spring, until the snow and ice melted, since the people who provided for us tried to obtain seal oil from the ocean here.

At that place, again they would move to the tributaries of the Qalvinraaq River to places where there were fish also. They would fish for tomcod and flounder there.

Tuamtell' itraqanirluteng qavavet carvallarnek cali qassayaarnek, qaurtunek. Wall' aqvataqluteng angyakun ayagluteng.

Naunrat-wa tua-i tekitaqata ullagluki pilallrulriit iqvalriit, naugaqata.

Waniw' taugaam paingani piciatun nerangnaquralallruut.

Kangrilnguq: Apqiitnek piyagarcuquaqamta pekluta ayagaqluta, tua-i unangvimtenun ayagaqamta. Kingunerput-llu yaaqsigirrarluku ayagaqluta piyagat nalliitni tamaa-i. Nut'gayugnaunaki pitgaquluki taugaam. Anglanaqluni pissuraqamta.

Qaugret, piciatun. Irnitulriit tamarmeng yaqulget; tamaa-i piyagaitnek tua-i pissuraqluta.

Amlletullruameng-llu nacaullget, unguluteng piaqameng piliqaqluteng.

Ilagautetullruukuk. Apeqmeggnek aqvaquryugngauralrianek iivkaristerluteng pitullruut. Tua-i aqvaqurturluteng ayagluteng yaqulget maani evesrarni uitalriit ketmun qimagtelluki, unavet marayamun.

Tua-i taugken cuqkiuraat, cali alerqurrluta pilaitkut ca imna tekiskumteggu ketmurcesqelluta.

Ketmureskumta cali tua-i ellait upingaluteng kuvyat waten kuvyat usgulluki, iteryarirluki, qasgililuki apeqmeggnek.

Cali amani ellait ciunerkamteni cagingaluteng utaqaluteng. Waken tua-i qasgimek ayagluteng ketmun cagingaluteng mer'em engeliinun.

Tamaa-i unguaqaceteng mermun atrarpek'nateng marayakun taugaam qimatuameng.

Tua-i waten iluvalriani, amkut-llu amani tekitniarallinikaceteng nangerrluteng yaqulegnun call' tangertelluteng.

Yaqulget tua-i tamakut nangerngalriit akitmigutekluki, wangkuta-ll' tua-i ungusteni tekiskumta tuavet kuvyamun tua-i iterrluki nutaan kaugtuarluki nalarqelluki.

Iliini piliqaqluteng. Amllenritaqameng-wa tua-i amllessiyaagmek pitnaunateng.

Anen'iluki tang wii tangvakallrunrilkenka, tua-i nalluvkenaku ketmun waten cagingalaameng meq tekilluku. Tua-i akitmigutnguluteng.

Allirkar: Waken atam waniw' ayalallruut maaggun. Naugg'un-llu tayim'

Then they would move farther upriver and fish from streams for freshwater fish, including round whitefish and humpback whitefish. Or they'd travel by boat and get that type of fish.

When salmonberries grew, berry pickers would go to the berries when they grew.

They subsisted for many things only along the mouth [of the river].

Paul John: When we were hunting for young birds, we'd travel by walking, when we'd travel to places where we could catch. And we'd travel a great distance from our place during the time when young birds were around. We wouldn't shoot them [with a gun] but just shoot arrows at them to catch them. It was fun when we hunted.

[We hunted] spectacled eiders, all different types. As you know, all birds give birth; we'd hunt their young.

Since there were many emperor geese in the past, when they'd drive the birds to catch them, they'd catch lots.

We used to participate. They recruited those who could run and drive the birds, *iivkaristet* as they called them. They'd leave by running, having the birds situated along the small grass run down toward the shore, down to the mud.

But they would tell us to start heading down toward shore when we got to a certain place.

When we started heading toward shore, [the people along the shore] were prepared, connecting fishnets like this, making an entrance, what they call *qasgililuki* [lit., "making them into a *qasgi*"].

And up ahead where we were heading, those people would be dispersed waiting. From the *qasgi,* they were dispersed down toward shore, to the water's edge.

When they drive [birds], [the birds] don't usually go down to the water but run along the mud.

When coming into view, when [the birds] were about to reach those people over there, [the people] would stand and let the birds see them.

The people who were standing acted as a barrier to the birds, and those of us who were driving them, when we reached that area, we'd drive them inside the fishnet and strike them and kill them.

Sometimes they caught lots. When there aren't many [birds], you couldn't catch too many.

I never saw them come out [of the net], since [people] knew what to do and were dispersed like this, reaching the water. They acted as a barrier.

John Alirkar: They used to leave from here and head this way. And then

maaggun kanarluteng ketmurrluteng. Wani-ll' call' tayim' pilallruut, nuugani wani.

Wiinga ciuqliuvkatullruatnga wani. Tua-i ciumek ayagglainarlua, aqvaqurturlua ayagyuallemni. Ilanka utaqaaqluki tangenrriqertaqamki. Alairaqata ayagaqlua.

Waken ciuqlikacaar ayalalria, kessigiinarluteng kinguqliit ketvaqanirluteng ayagaqluteng.

Yaaggun-llu maaken qayatgun ayaulluki cali, maaggun mer'em engeliikun cali. Unaggun cali aqvaqurluteng, yaaggun, tua-i-ll' kacgulluteng.

Kangrilnguq: Elisngallruut augkut ciuliaput cam pingnaqsaraan tungiinun.

Allirkar: Nacaullegpallurnek. Makut-am tuutangayiit anssaagyunqeggata, ikgetaqata aug'arluki anevkarluki qaritngulaameng.

Makut taugaam nacaullget ungusciryarluteng pissurciryarluteng, narugaqameng caqirtaqluteng. Tamakut taugken tuutangayiit piqtang'ermeng anssaagturluteng. Anevkaraqluki.

Cucuaq: Caameng-kiq tuaten ayuqat, tuutangayiit.

Kangrilnguq: Umyuallgutkenritliiceteng-wa. [*ngel'artuq*]

Cucuaq: Atkukluki-ll' piiyuitellruamegteki.

Kangrilnguq: Yaa, atkuuyuitut tuutangayiit nacaullget taugaam.

Cucuaq: Augkunek-mi ceturrnanek pissulallermeggni?

Allirkar: Qaluluki pilallruit, augkunek waten iverluni piyaranek, qalurpall'ernek.

Kangrilnguq: Tamakucimi ilagauskuvet qaluq iverluten civteqataquvgu atrarluten, qaillun-llu tayim' pugumataluten nakrit kapulluki. Arnat ivrarluteng qaluaqluteng.

Cucauq: Wani-q' Arayakcaami pitullruut?

Kangrilnguq: Ii-i, pitullruut.

Allirkar: Maani-ll' Qalvinraam avayaini pilallruut, maani marami. Isquq, tamaa-i Kassigluaralek; piciatun uaqsilriit qaluviuluteng.

they would start heading down toward shore here. They did that here, too, here at its point.

They used to have me go first here. I always went first, and I would leave running when I was young. I'd wait for the others in my group when I no longer saw them in view. When they'd appear, I'd go on.

The very first person would leave from here, and then the next people to leave gradually moved farther down toward shore, and the next ones to go would move farther down toward shore as they left.

They also brought [people] from out there, with kayaks along the edge of the water. And other people would be running along the shore, over there, and then they would meet.

Paul John: Our ancestors were knowledgeable about everything having to do with making an effort at living.

John Alirkar: Mainly emperor geese [were driven]. Since these lesser Canada geese tend to try to get out, when there weren't too many, they would remove them and let them get out [of the fence] since they were a waste of time and energy.

But these emperor geese were easy to drive and easy to pursue as they turned when you encountered them. But these lesser Canada geese, although we tried to catch them, they'd constantly try to get out. We'd let them go out.

Alice Rearden: I wonder why those lesser Canada geese are like that.

Paul John: Probably because they don't have the same mind [as emperor geese]. [*laughs*]

Alice Rearden: Probably because they didn't make them into parkas, also.

Paul John: Yes, lesser Canada geese aren't made into parkas, but just emperor geese.

Alice Rearden: What about when they tried to obtain tomcod?

John Alirkar: They would use dip nets to catch them, the kind you have to wade in the water to set, those large dip nets.

Paul John: If you participate in that [way of fishing], if you are about to set the dip net, you'd go down and wade in the water, and you'd wade in the water up to a certain depth and insert their stakes. Women would wade in the water and dipnet.

Alice Rearden: Did they [dipnet] here at Arayakcaaq?

Paul John: Yes, they did.

John Alirkar: They also [dipnetted for tomcod] along the tributaries of the Qalvinraaq River, here in the marshy area. At Isquq [Point of land], Kassigluaralek [Place with a small *kassigluq* (confluence of rivers)]; any of the lower tributaries [of the Qalvinraaq River] were places where they dipnetted.

☙

Nanurrulalek: Wiinga, wiinga tamaa-i ellangelqa yaaqsigpek'naku nasaurlullraulua nallunrilkenka, Aanaq-llu ika-i aipaqtullruamku ullagturatullruamku nallunritaqa.

Augkut tua-i maurluqa aataka-llu wangkutnek ilaluni; ukaqlikacagauluta uitallrulriakut. Yaatemteni-wa kinkut Kangrilnguunkut, maurlullra-w' uatiini, uatiini-w' Nasaalleraam Arnaan, yaatiini-wa uani Akurtuyugaankut, anaanakiiyaurlugka-ll' tayim' nani call' tamaani. Taukut tua-i wii nallunritanka, tuaten yuullemteni.

Tua-i ilumun caitunrilnganateng, uitavkenateng. Wiinga-ll' cumikekacarrluk' cumiksuitellrukenka tamaani.

Allirkaq-llu ikna, Allirkaraam ik'um yaaruiteka tuluq augna pitekluku yaaruicuglua taisquuraqanga ullatullrukek'a. Qulirilgulua.

Tua-ll'-am quliringuaqiinga anqercamiarluni, yaaruitemnek aturluni tulumek. Waten tua-i pillrani ukvekenriqertellruaqa. Kiugna-wa-gguq kiani Tarr'aq. Atemnek acirluku. Tarr'aq-gguq kiani aqumgaluni tua-i piyugcalik'acagarluni iqmigturluni qeciraqluni.

Tuaten-llu tua-i atemnek acirngaku Tarr'amek ukvenriqerrlua, quli'ir' Tarr'amek atengqerrngaicukluku. [*ngel'artuq*]

Tamaani tamaa-i miktellemni ellangeqtaallemni un'gaani ikegkut ika'antellruut Cangarraam angayuqaak, ua-i ugna. Keluani-w yaani qungut. Cangarraam angayuqaak, Cangarraankut.

Tamaani makut pingvailgata nugtarrnemteggun taukut pillruut. Tamaa-i-ll' Iralunkuk Taneksiim-llu Atii aipangeksaunatek. Aipangvailgagnek tamaani maani pillruunga.

Aanaka-ll' tua-i un'gaani cali, caluteng, neqsurluteng pilalliut. Aanaka tayim' ikani qunguni uitauq; qungicimauq.

Tuamtell' augna uyu'urqa tan'gurraq angliriqerterpaagarluni; cali ikani cali qungicimaluni.

Ii-i. Ugkut ua-i Cangarraankunek yungqetullruuq. Tamaa-i Cangarraam aatallni ucikluku ikamrarluni ayautaqluku. Apertuulluku-gguq tua-i cassurviminun pitullrullilria.

Wiinga-w' tamaan una pivailgan ciungani pillrullilrianga. Tuaten tua-i ellangellruunga. Aangaq wii ullalgullruaqa. Arnauyukluku piqarraallemni

Rita Angaiak: Not long after I became aware of life, when I was a little girl, the people who I knew, and since I used to play with Aanaq and always went to see her, I know her.

Those people, my grandmother and my father along with us; we were located the farthest on this side. Beyond us were Kangrilnguq [Paul John] and his family, and his deceased grandmother was downstream, and downstream was Nasaalleraam Arnaan, and beyond them were Akurtuyugaq and his family, and my *anaanakiiyaurluuk* [aunts] were there somewhere. I know of those families back when we lived like that.

Indeed, it seems they didn't lack things and weren't always idle. I didn't really pay close attention to them at the time.

And Allirkaq over there, Allirkaq over there would always want to play story knife with me and would ask me to come because of my ivory story knife, I'd go see him. He always told me tales.

Once using my story knife he started telling me a story with it. When he said this I didn't believe his tale anymore. He talked about the person back there, he called that person Tarr'aq, my name. He said that Tarr'aq was sitting back there, contently chewing tobacco, and would periodically spit.

When he called that person in the tale my name, Tarr'aq, I didn't believe the tale he told, thinking that the person in the tale wouldn't have the name Tarr'aq. [*laughs*]

When I was small and just becoming aware of life downriver, the people across there were Cangarraaq's parents, down there. Then behind their place were graves. There were Cangarraq's parents, Cangarraq and his family.

Before these [others were around], when we first moved there, those people were there. And at the time, Iraluq and Taneksiim Atii weren't married. I was here before they were married.

And down along the coast, my mother, they were doing something along the coast, probably fishing. My mother is across there in those graves; she's buried there.

And again, my younger sibling, a boy [died] when he had gotten big; he's also buried across there.

Yes. The place downstream was occupied by Cangarraq and his family. Cangarraq would bring his father in his sled and take him to places. He was probably showing him his customary hunting and fishing places.

I was probably here before this person was here. That's how I became aware of life. I always went to see Aangaq. I thought that he was a girl at first,

pillruaqa, cunaw' angutnguyaaqellinilria.

Tua-i yaaruiteka, yaaruiteka tegumiaqenrilkumku-ll' aqvavkarluku. Iqluqulua tang pitullruyugnarqell'. Wiinga ukevqeryukaarngama anqercamiarluni, Tarr'amek iliit aterluni. Wii-ll' ukveryuumiirrlua atemnek atengqellinian quliraq. Tuaten tua-i nallunritanka ukut.

Qalulriamek call' iillayullruunga, tua-i iillayuk'acagarlua. Akluni mayurrluki imarniterluni. Ala-i maaten tang im' tekilluni piuq, tua-i uateurluuk qiulutek, ugaan kumlasnguaqtaryaaqem.

Wiinga qanerteksunaitua. [*ngel'artuq*] Irr'itarlua tua-i kaputaqlutek iigka, kaputkacagarlutek. [*ngel'artuq*]

Unangik: Yaa, yaani Atamtaamek atuqangramta amelqapiartuq. Iciw' makut tụqumalriit, nalluyagucimalria amllertuq yuk. Amlleqapiartuq. Agayucestaunani agayucesqumangermi, agayutestekain-llu nalluyagulluku.

Man'a maa-i umyuaqerkaugaput nani, waten kelistanek tangerqumta yuilqumi. Tamaa-i nalluyagucimalriit amllertut. Uani-llu uitavillemteni Umkumiuni yull'erugaat maani acilqami nalluyagucimalriit amllertut.

Taumek waten tua-i tekiteqarraarqama inarteqatarqama agayuaqama nalluyagucimalriit tua-i umyuamnun kangatuut kesianek, waten tekiteqarraarqamegneki waten up'nerkami neqliyarlunuk.

Tamana tamaa-i umyuaqerkaqerput yugni; umyuarkaqsaaqerput. Taugaam nalluyagutaput ilaput ilaitni. Angayuqaput, caput, alqaput, aanaput, ataput; tang tamaa-i nalluyaguskengaput.

Nanurrualek: Niigartelallrulrianga qanelrianek; ava-i iciw' Umkumiunek taillrulriakut Arayakcaamun. Ikaken tailuta Arayakcaamun.

Tamaa-i ellangeqtaarlua mik'nii aanaka nangteqellrullinill' qamiquminek *three days.* Augna tua-i ava-i elliinguyukluku umyuarteqellruunga elliinguyukluku qairrarmun iciw' ellillruatgu.

Ak'a-w' avani qairrarmun ellilallrukait. Augna ava-i qamiquq tangllemku elliingunguarcetellruaqa Arayakcaami.

Ellangeqtaakacagallruuga, aanakellra taugaam nallullruaqa. Maurluugkallu aanama aanii uitaluni, aatii-llu; taukuullinlutek. Aatama-ll' cali aanii aatiillu *sister*-aari-llu uitaluteng; tamakuullrullililuteng. Angliriama, tua-i tuaten pillrulliniluteng.

Uyurangqerrlua-ll' cali piipicuarmek; uyuraqa piipicuayagauluni tamaani, aanairulluni-w' tua-i. Aanairullunuk tua-i, piipiuluni tauna uyu'urqa.

but I learned later that he was actually a boy.

If I wasn't holding my story knife, he'd have me go and get it. I think he used to lie to me. Since I was gullible, when he told a story and one of the people was called Tarr'aq. I didn't want to believe him any longer since that character in the tale had my name. That's what I know of this place.

I was also in awe of someone who was dipnetting, and I was extremely amazed. She lifted up her clothing, wearing a seal-gut rain garment. When she arrived her poor lower body was blue because it was so cold.

I'm not a very good speaker. [*laughs*] I had a tendency to stare, and my eyes would get really stuck on things I was observing. [*laughs*]

Simeon Agnus: Yes, it would be adequate if we sang "Our Father" over there. As you know, many deceased people are forgotten. There are many of them. There is no one to pray for them even though they urge people to pray for them, and people who have a duty to pray for that person have forgotten him.

We have to remember this when we see crosses out in the wilderness. There are many people who have been forgotten. There are also many deceased people at Umkumiut where we just stayed along the land.

That's why when I first arrive there and I am about to go to sleep, when I pray, the people who have been forgotten always come to my mind, when we first arrive there during spring to cut and dry fish.

We people must remember them; they are people we must remember. But some of us have forgotten our families. Our parents, our relatives, our older sisters, our mothers, our fathers; those are the people who we have forgotten.

Rita Angaiak: I briefly heard others speaking in the past; you know how we came to Arayakcaaq River from Umkumiut. We came to Arayakcaaq from over there.

When I was small and going in and out of awareness, my mother was evidently suffering from headaches for three days. I thought that maybe [the grave I saw] was her since they placed her above ground [to bury her].

They used to place people above the ground [when they buried them] long ago. When I saw that skull at Arayakcaaq, I imagined it to be her.

I frequently came in and out of awareness at the time, but I didn't know that she was my mother. And my grandparents, my mother's mother and father were there; that's evidently who they were. And my father's mother and father and his sisters were there; that's who was evidently there. When I grew older, I later found that's evidently what happened.

And I had a younger sibling who was just a baby; my younger sibling was just an infant at the time and lost its mother. We lost our mother, and my

Unugmi-ll' tua-i qiallinillrani tupaglua. Maaten tupagtua aatama tegumiaqluku.

Tua-i-ll' aanaklinikiin qam'um waten piluku, "Taiteqerru kitek. Uryura'arvikqernauqa."

Iciw' piipicuayagaat avani niitelallruanka, camek piluteng mer'urrluki, tua-i-ll' qanemeggnek iciw' qanritgun cukavkenateng iciw' im'urluku, nerqelluku. Aamarkaaiteurlurluteng, canek taugaam neqa mer'urrluku, mer'urrluku. Kiimi-ll' pivkenani tauna, pilallrulriit.

Taugaam waniw' ukunek quyaunga, *seventy-five*-aarlua aanama tuqullra ullagngamku.

Tuani imat'anem tuavet tekicama waten ak'a tamaani, waten ak'a tamaani niitelallruama, nunamek malrurqugnek amllerpek'naku nerlua igluku.

Ii-i, nunallermeggnun-gguq uitavillmeggnun tekitaqameng ak'a tuaten pitullruut. Ii-i tekicaqliraqameng nunarrarmek; tuani pillruunga tuaten. Ii-i, kitek.

Allirkar: Uani-am Arayakcaarmiuni uitayaaqellruukut tua-i-ll' qaillun ulqatallra uksumi nallunrilamegteggu tuani-am nel'iluteng uksuarmi uitaluteng. Tua-i-ll' ulerpagluni.

Uksumi ataucimi. Wangkuta Arayakcaarmiuni pillruukut.

Nurataaq: Uksurpailgan nel'illruut tuani tua-i uitaviteng unilluku nunakegtaraungraan. Taukut taugaam tegganrit ukut tegganrita nalluvkenaku tuavet nel'iluteng.

Tua-i-ll' ulngan tauna patuluku. Ellait-llu ulniurpek'nateng qertulriami uitiimeng.

Allirkar: Man'a ketvut nuna man'a patuyaaqluki taugaam taukut enet cayugnaunateng pikaanlameng. Cakmani taugken uitavilput kangrit taugaam kiimeng pinritqallrulliniluki.

Qaillun tua-i [nallunritatgu]? Allrakumi ataucimi tuantellruukut. Allrakuan-llu uniluki tuavet.

Avegyaq: Qantullrulriit-wa ak'a waten ataucimek anuqlirturluni, atauciq anuqekluku. Tua-i wall'u-qaa negeqvarturluni anuqlirturluni allamun piva-

younger sibling was just a baby at the time.

When the baby evidently cried at night, I woke up. When I got up, I saw that my father was holding the baby.

The baby's mother said to him from in there, "Give it over to me. Let me trickle some food [into the baby's mouth]."

I used to hear that in the past, they'd liquefy something, and then with their mouths, they'd slowly let the food trickle inside the baby's mouth and feed it. When the poor things didn't have milk to drink, they'd liquefy some food. And she wasn't the only one to do that, but others did, too.

But I am grateful to these people here, since at age seventy-five I've come to the place where my mother died.

I forgot to mention that when I arrived [at Arayakcaaq], since I heard of this custom long ago, I took a little bit of soil from the ground twice and placed it in my mouth and swallowed it.

Yes, it is said when they arrived in their hometown where they once stayed, that's what they did long ago. When they arrived after a long absence, they'd take a little bit of soil [and swallow it]; that's what I did there. Yes, okay then.

John Alirkar: We had lived down at Arayakcaarmiut, but knowing that it was going to flood, they made a house there [on high ground] and lived there. And then there was a flood.

It happened one winter. Those of us who were living at Arayakcaarmiut experienced [the flood].

Phillip Moses: They built houses before winter came, leaving the place where they were staying although it was a really nice place. But their elders knew about [the coming flood] and thus made houses at that spot.

And when it flooded, it inundated that land [at Arayakcaaq]. And the flood did not get to them because they were on high ground.

John Alirkar: [The flood] actually covered the land down below us, but the [new] houses that they built were untouched by the flood because they were up there [on high ground]. But those houses downriver where we had stayed before, only the tops of the houses were untouched by the flood.

Now how did they [know]? We stayed at [high ground] for just one year. And then the next year, we moved back.

Sophie Agimuk: They used to say that sometimes it blew from one direction only. Like it would just blow from the north mostly and not from other

karpek'nani. Tua-i qacaqallerkaa tauna aaqellruat.

Ataucimek anuqlirtura'arqan tua-i-gguq qacaqerqami ulenricuituq.

Taumek wani ak'a ulesqiitullruuq augna maraq. Ulerpagluni tua-i piaqluni.
Tua-i ikiugurayuitellruan ella ataucimek tua-i anuqengqerpallurluni piaqan makut wani niicugnillret qantullruut waten. Kegg'um-gguq anuqiin qacaqallerkaa aarnarquq. Qacaqaquni-gguq ulenrilngaituq. Tuaten tua-i qantullruut.

Allirkar: Arayakcaami-llu uqtat mikulallruut cikuqerraami. Kuiggaat paingitni uqtarqami aanaka imna piliqaqluni-ll' tua-i.

Neng'uryar: Imumi-w' uksiqallemteni Arayakcaami uqtaryaumallrulrianga un'gavet uatiitnun; uqtaryaumallruunga pitemssaayuileng'erma-llu. Iliini angullugaat tekitaqlua ikamracuaralriit.

Nurataaq: Uqtaryarangqerrluteng-am tua-i pivimeggni kuigaaraat paingitni; tamaani-am pingnaquraraqluteng.

Allirkar: Taugaam uatairciryalallruut amelkilngurni.

Una tua-i picuciquq. Uatiikun-llu tua-i anleliluni kalveskan picuirulluni! [*ngel'artuq*]

Kuigpagcetun ayuqevknani, Qalvinraacetun, Urrsukvaacetun-llu. Maani kuigpaagni caniqliqngermeng caniqlia picutulria; tuaten pivkenateng. Nakellriit-am tua-i avatiikun-llu pingraaceteng cakaniyuunateng pissuraqameng picutuluteng.

directions that much. They were apprehensive about the wind suddenly shifting to the south in those times.

When the wind continually blows from one direction, when it then switches to the south wind, flooding is inevitable.

Long ago, that marshland used to flood. It used to flood.

Because the weather was not bad all the time, when it started to blow mainly from one direction, these people who listened closely used to say the following. They said that the weather out there will be dangerous if it starts to blow from the south. They said if it blows from the south, flooding will be inevitable. They used to say that.

John Alirkar: And also at Arayakcaaq, smelts used to be abundant at freeze-up. And when my mother fished with hookless lures for smelts at the creek mouths, she used to catch lots.

Lizzie Chimiugak: At that time when we spent the winter at Arayakcaaq, I went to fish with hookless lures for smelt quite frequently downriver; I used to fish with lures quite frequently, even though I didn't catch a lot sometimes. Sometimes some old men who were pushing sleds would come upon me.

Phillip Moses: They had their own spots where they fished with hookless lures for smelt, at the mouths of creeks; they frequently tried to [fish with lures] in those specific spots.

John Alirkar: In narrow creeks, it was easy to take away fish from someone by fishing downriver from him.

So this person who is fishing would be catching a lot. Then someone would poke a fishing hole just downriver from him, and when he let down his fishing apparatus, that person would not catch as much anymore! [*laughter*]

It wasn't like in large rivers, like the Qalvinraaq or Urrsukvaaq. In these large rivers as one fishes, the person next to him is good at catching; it is not like that. When one is lucky, even though people are fishing around him, they are still lucky catching fish.

Ingriaraak

Kangrilnguq: [Ingriaraak] keluaramteni uitatullruuk. Wani-ll' caniani elanellerpallraat augkut.

Ataucirqumek call' tuani uksumi uitavikellruaput. Ulerpakatallinian-am nel'iluteng tuavet, qaill' nallunritatgu.

Ulerpakatallinian tuavet itrarluta ulesqiirluni-ll' tua-i nuna. Uitavikelallerput mer'em tekilluku, nep'ut-llu mer'em itliniluki, tua-i kangrit pagkut pinritqerluki.

Uksuarmi ulerpallrani. Uksuarmi-w' ulel'alria.

Angalgaq: Taukut-mi elanellret camiunguat?

Allirkar: Anguyiurvillret.

Kangrilnguq: Nunallerpagnek aterluteng.

Allirkar: Pikani-am kangratni nel'ilriit, elaturrarput-wa atauciq; pingayuuluteng enet.

Kangrilnguq: Ingricuaraat, malruk Ingriaraak, kiakariigni-w', Ingriayaaqgguq.

Taukut Ingriayaarmi call' elanellertarluteng, ukut-gguq uaqliita uitavikeqallrit; inglukluteng anguyakluteng. Tamaa-i taukut nunallret malruin anguyakelriit-gguq-am tua-i nunallrit.

Tamaa-i-llu-gguq cikuliurutmek-llu navrarqata aipateng tunpiarluki tunyuunaki, kayimqerluki taugaam tun'aqluki.

Neqsurviit pitekluki anguyiit tamakut qanruteksuitellruit, taugaam imumek nauwa taringenrullerkarpeciuggun, waniwa tungayakekuvcia elpeci, ingluvci tuqullua, wall'u tua-i ingluklua pikatnga, elpeci yuryugluci taukut anguyagyugngaaci.

Yurtaagulluteng waten tamaa-i ilateng-llu yurtaagulluteng anguyatullrulliniut, neqa pitkevkenaku, nuna-llu pitkevkenaku, taugaam tua-i ilulnguyulteng pitekluku.

Unangik: Tua-i ukut ingkut yaa-i Ingriarmiut uaqliit-llu, canimeluteng'ermeng inglukulluteng taukut pillrat tamana wii taringesciigataqa. Qanrutkeqatuit tuaten tua-i inglukellruniluki. Qaill'-wa piat nallukeput aka'artaugut ingkut ak'allaugut nunallret.

Ingriaraak Hills[31]

Paul John: [Ingriaraak, Two small *ingrik* (mountains)] were located right behind our place [Arayakcaaq]. And next to them were large, old house pits.

We lived there one winter also. Since there was going to be a large flood, they built a home there, and I wonder how they knew [that it would flood].

Since there evidently was going to be a large flood, we moved up there, and then that land flooded a little. The water reached the place where we had stayed before, and water evidently entered our home and didn't quite reach the top [of the home].

During fall when there was a large flood. It usually floods during fall.

Ruth Jimmie: What was the name of the village where those *elanellret* [old house pits] were?

John Alirkar: It was a site from the bow-and-arrow war period.

Paul John: They were called Nunallerpiit [Large *nunallret* (old villages)].

John Alirkar: They built a home up on top of [the house pits], and we had one adjoining porch; there were three homes.

Paul John: The small mountains, there are two Ingriaraak, and right up above them is what they call Ingriayaaq [Small *ingriq* (mountain)].

There were also old house pits there at Ingriayaaq, and they mentioned that it was a place where the ones downriver had lived for a while; they were enemies. They say those two old village sites were once occupied by two groups that were enemies.

And they say when their enemies would borrow an ice pick, they didn't just hand it over, but they just pushed the ice pick over when they gave it to them.

They never mentioned that they went to war because of fishing sites, but so that you would understand it more clearly, if I was your relative and your enemy warriors killed me, or if I was their enemy, you will want to come to my defense and go to war with those people.

They evidently went to war with one another because people sought revenge for their relatives because they felt defensive, and not because of food or land, but because of feeling defensive.

Simeon Agnus: Those Ingriarmiut [People of the *ingriq* (mountain)] and the people downriver from them, although their villages were situated close to one another, I cannot understand why they were enemies. They mention once in a while that those two villages were enemies. I'm not sure why, and we don't know why since those village sites are ancient.

Makut maa-i anguyiit nunallrit qerturrlainartut. Ingkut kia-i canimun tangerquvciki taum Ingriaraam kellian amatiini tangerquvciki atam nunallerpakayallraat qertukayagtut tua-i.

Taugken taukut Ingricuarmiut keluqliit, tua-i ingrim iggagnerani uitanillrularyaaqekait tua-i tang kit'elliameng alaitenritlalriit. Caneggluut taugaam paugkut tua-i, taukutun uaqlimegcetun ayuqevkenateng. Alaiterpagpek'nateng.

Ingkut yaa-i menglairluki iliini tua-i tangtullrukenka tua-i, menglairluki tua-i. Waten iliini umyuarteqnaurtua, "Anguyiit makut nunallrit waten qerturrlainalarpagtat. Qaill' caliaqelallruitki? Wall'u-q tua-i camkut aciit-llu qerratalartut?" Menglairluki *Ski-doo*-rlua menglairluki qimugtetgun, caniatgun kiturluki.

Paniliar: Qanrutkelarait elanellret. Tamakut maa-i wangkuta mat'um nallini waten tangrraqamteki mik'nateng pilalriit. Tua-i-ll' niitaqluta tamaanigguq ak'a naklekutepiarluteng pillermeggni, tamakut ilateng nuqlitellriit nelgutkaqluki pitullruit.

Tamakut tamaa-i tayima pikangqerquneng ilait, allakarmeng-llu waten uitavingqerrsallilriit. Yugni ayuqenrilata nutaan avani ciuliaput nuqlipallaarluteng ilait pitullruut-gguq. Taumek-gguq tuaten tua-i nuqlitellriateng-llu caka'arpek'naki nelgutekluki pitullrukait.

Nevurtuli

Unangik: Waniw' nunallernun waten ayagluta ak'allanun iillanarqelrianek tangerrngaitut. Taugaam waten ak'allaungameng makut nunallret iillanarqelriartaitut. Waten tua-i can'gurneruut ullagarkaput.

Ukut waniw' nunallret ukut ak'allaugut nunallret, wangkuta-ll' atullruvkenaki augkut taugaam aanamta ciuliarita-llu atulqait. Augkut cali atamta tayima ilait atutullrullikait.

Tua-i waten ukut wani canimelutait pingkut Negtemiut. Ukut waniw' qanrutketullruit. Yungqerrlainatullruut uksurneq tamalkuan, kiagmi-ll' pilallilriit tayima. Waten tua-i can'giirnek neqengqerrameng iqalluanek, naternanek; canek tayim' ilaluk' pitullrullikait tamakut yullret.

Tamaani tamaa-i qungullret atam amllellruyaaqut taugaam tua-i catairulluteng tua-i tayim', nunamun iquluteng caquit augkut muriit. Tuskanek

The places once occupied by warriors during the bow-and-arrow war period are always steep. If you look closely at that place over there, the ones located beyond the area down below one of the [two] Ingriaraak, the very large old village site is very steep.

But Ingricuarmiut [Residents of Ingricuar (Small *ingriq* (mountain)] behind them, they mentioned that it was located along the edge of a mountain, but since it probably sunk, it isn't visible any longer. There is just a grassy area up there, and that place isn't like the one downriver from them. It isn't clearly visible.

I used to see that place over there when traveling alongside it. This is what I would think sometimes, "These old sites once occupied by warriors are all so steep. I wonder how they built them, or is the ground underneath them raised up?" I travel alongside that place with a Ski-doo and dog teams, traveling next to that place.

Theresa Abraham: They mention old house pits. When we see them today, they are small. And we hear that back in those days when they had great compassion for one another, they lived in the same house with their relatives who lacked things.

If those people had homes to stay in, they'd probably live in separate homes. Since people aren't all the same, it is said some of our ancestors lacked things in the past. That's why they didn't ignore people who were poor and lived in the same home with them.

Nevurtuli[32]

Simeon Agnus: When we travel to old village sites, they won't see things that are astonishing. There is nothing extraordinary about these old village sites since they are old. The places that we will go to are grassy areas like this.

These village sites are old, and we didn't use these places, but our mothers and their ancestors used them. And our fathers probably used some of them.

This place [Nevurtuli, Place with an abundance of *nevuq* (dirt, mud)] is close to Nightmute. They used to talk about this place. It was always occupied every winter and probably during summer, too. Since blackfish are available to eat, tomcod, flounder; the past people probably added other things to their diet besides those foods.

There were once many old graves there, but they have disappeared, their wooden casings have fallen to the ground. They didn't bury [their dead]

caquyuitellruit tuskartaitellrani, *plywood*-artaitellrani, taugaam muragaq qupluku tamaa-i tamakunek muraganek caqutullruit. Pikailkuneng-llu nemernginaraqerluki tua-i camek tua-i nunamun patutetullruit.

Augkut ciuliaput waten teguqerrartenrilameng camek, taugaam anrutameng taugaam imarkaaraitnek tua-i taugaam tua-i cumigqurluteng pitullruut. Neqkangengnaqu'urluteng. Calilriartaunani, kipusvigtaunani cataunani, cataitqapiarluni. Camek tamakut tayima yuurqalallrulartat. Cuyaturluteng tuaten, kuingirkaq-llu nurnarluni. Tayim' qaillun tamakut yuullrurlulartat tamakut ciuliaput.

Ukut tua-i waniw', una waniw' qasgillrat qukaatni. Nunaullruut tua-i avaken ayagluteng ukut nunaulliniut, ikegkutun Kanerrlulegmiutun ullagarkamcetun.

Allanek-llu nunacuartaunani. Qaugkut taugaam qava-i ingriim acianelnguut tua-i nunaullruut cali waten ak'allauluteng. Ukut waniw' ak'allaugut, ikegkut-llu Kanerrlulegmiut Cakcaaq-llu. Manrirmiut-llu ikegkut ika-i ak'allanek keluqlingqertut nunallernek malruinek, ak'allaqapiarnek cali.

Ukut wani alailutellrit, alailutait-llu piani pia-i alaitetullruyaaqut taugaam catairutut ak'alqapiaraungameng. Tayim' tua-i yuurpailegma-llu ukut nunaunrillruyugnarqut. Augkut angayuqamta angayuqrita ciuqliita nunaketullrulliniit ukut waniwa.

Kanerrlulegmiut

Unangik: Ava-i tua-i tangvalriakut tamamta tangvakput. Wangkuta waten waniw' Yup'igni pituukut, imarpigmi-llu unani. Makut maa-i makliit, irniaqaa kan'a makliim, angelriim taqukam. Amirkamek pituluki makut maa-i.

Tayima allrakuni pingayuni angtacirkamegcetun. Kan'a kana-i tuqutenrilkumteni aanamitun angtariyartuq waten allrakut pingayun aturluki wall' cetaman.

Ava-i tangvagtuci. Yupiit waten waniw' makunek maa-i taqukanek pissutulriit augkunek tegussuucirluteng. Nutgaarluku tua-i teguteqerluku-ll'.

Unani tua-i imarpigmi waten ikayurnarqelriit waten angyalriit tangrrinayuitait; ikayuraqluki. Cali maa-i qanercuuteryaurcameng ciku man'a umkataqan qayagaurluki call' tamakut angyat unani tumairutqatarniluki qayagaurluki.

Qalvinraaq River shoreline on a July evening, 2007. AFR. (Pages 180–183)

Boat traveling on the Qalvinraaq River. AFR.

Qalvinraaq River from the air. AFR.

Arayakcaaq. AFR. (Pages 182–197)

Group gathered at Arayakcaaq, July 2007. AFR.

Boat grave at Arayakcaaq. AFR.

Riding upriver toward Nevurtuli. AFR. (Pages 200–203)

Nevurtuli. AFR.

John Roy John butchers a seal at Kanerrlulegmiut. AFR. (Pages 202–207)

Group gathered at Kanerrlulegmiut. AFR.

House pits at Kanerrlulegmiut. AFR.

Simeon Agnus speaking at Manriq. AFR.

Manriq. AFR.

Ruth Jimmie and Theresa Abraham cleaning birds at Manriq. AFR.

Manriq River. AFR.

Talarutmiut. AFR. (Pages 208–211)

Joe Felix describing his experiences at Talarutmiut. AFR.

Qavaliriyaq. AFR. (Pages 214–217)

Grave at Qavaliriyaq. AFR.

Woman's sewing machine left on her grave at Qavaliriyaq. AFR.

Anna Agnus speaking at Qavaliriyaq. AFR.

Upper Urumangnaq River. AFR. (Pages 220–227)

Beaver dam on the Urumangnaq River. AFR.

Linda Joe, Ryan Abraham, Ben Angaiak, and Anna Agnus eat raw pike at Urumangnaq camp. AFR.

House pits at the mouth of Urumangnaq River. AFR.

Eroding bank at Urumangnaq River mouth. AFR.

Old village site at the mouth of the Urumangnaq River. AFR.

Kellarvik, on the north shore of the Qalvinraaq River. AFR. (Pages 228–233)

Anna Agnus recounting the story of Kellarvik. AFR.

Nacecararmiut on the upper Cakcaaq River. AFR.

Rita Angaiak, Anna Agnus, Martina John, and Joe Felix at Nacecararmiut on the upper Cakcaaq. AFR. (Pages 232–243)

Camp on the upper Cakcaq River, July 2007. AFR.

inside plywood caskets back when there was no plywood, but they split a log and used those pieces for caskets. And when they had no [wood], they'd just wrap them in something and cover them with land.

Since our ancestors didn't have an abundance of things, they only continually worked hard at obtaining things to fill their stomachs. They continually made efforts at obtaining food. There was no one with a job, there were no stores, there was nothing modern around at all. I wonder what those people drank for a hot beverage. They also had chewing tobacco, and cigarettes were scarce. I wonder how our poor ancestors lived.

At this place here, their *qasgi* was in the center. This was a village site that has existed since long ago, like Kanerrlulegmiut which we will go to.

And there are no other small villages around. But the ones up there down below the mountain were also at an old village site. This village site is old, and Kanerrlulegmiut and Cakcaaq across there. Manrirmiut across there, there is another old village site behind them, two old village sites, also very old village sites.

The grave markers of this place used to be visible up there, but they have disappeared since they are very old. I think this village site existed even before I was born. This place was once occupied by our parents' parents, by those who came before them.

Kanerrlulegmiut[33]

Simeon Agnus: We all just watched [a bearded seal being caught]. This is what we Yup'ik people do, and also down on the ocean. That down there is an offspring of an adult bearded seal, a large seal. They call these *amirkat* [young bearded seals].

They grow to their adult size for three years. If we had not killed that one down there, it would have grown as large as its mother in three or four years.

You just watched [a bearded seal being caught]. The Yup'ik people hunt for seals using those retrieving tools. After shooting it, they harpoon it with a retrieving harpoon.

Boaters don't ignore those who need help down on the ocean; they help them. And now that they've started using VHF radios, when the ice obstructs the area, they also call the boats down on the ocean and tell them that their trail down on the ocean is about to be obstructed.

Tua-llu ukut waniw' Kanerrlulegmiut, angayuqaput ilait wantetullruut. Angayuqaput augkut ciuliartaat, ciuliat atullrit waniw' wani angayuqamta atutullruit ukuni nunallerni.

Ukut wan' ak'allaugut nunallret. Tua-i nunauluteng, uksurpak unicuunaki, kiaguskateng taugaam un'gavet pitullrullilriit neqet malkanirluki, maavet uatmeggnun.

Wiinga waniw' nutaan wii tekipaaluganka waniw', taugaam yaatiitnek tangtuanka nunallret ukut. Yuut ayuqenrilnguut ukut, ingkut-llu Cevv'arnermiut ciuliarit ilait wantetullrungatut.

Ukut nunarraunritut waten amllertang'ermeng.

Ukut kelgitullruut ilameggnek augkunek avaqlimeggnek kelegluki tua-i pitullrullikait tuaten. Wangkuta taugaam aturyugnaitaput ukut tamaani cataitellruukut wangkuta.

Cali tua-i aanama qanrutkeqallrukai; ulerpallermeggni-gguq ukut enet itellrui mer'em, ukut ulerpallrani un'a. Aanaka-ll' wantellrullinilutceng, wiinga-ll' nalluluku yuurpailegma. Makut maa-i ilait, makut Tuqsugmiut ilait angayuqrit wani waniw' uitatullrungatut Kanerrlulegmiuni ukuni.

Angussaagkat amllerrluteng tamaani can'giiret, taugaam manignataunani qaurtutaunani cuukvagtaunani-llu man'a. Taugaam un'gani ava-i nertukemtenek naptanek pitarluni iqalluanek naternanek-llu. Tamakunek tamaa-i neqengqellruut ukut neqsuraqameng. Qavavet kuimtenun qaugkunun qaill' ilait upatullrullilriit tayim' qavavet manignanun tamakunun.

Uani up'nerkituluteng Umkumiuni, up'nerkitullruut. Allgim Atii imna tuaten tua-i uani pitullruuq. Waten nenglairutaqan, uavet ikamrat maaken atam upagatullruut.

Kiaguskateng-llu tua-i maavet nunameggun tailuteng. Cali maani maa-i nunani neqsurturluteng iqalluanek naternanek, tamaa-i. Waten neqkateng yaaveskanirturluki, makunek-llu maa-i nerlaqngamtenek akwaugarpak, naptayagarnek augkunek.

Aanavut-qaa pisciigatuq?

Avegyaq: Wiinga tua-i nalluanka, nunaullrit-llu nalluluki. Taugaam qanrut'lallruatnga wani-gguq yuurtellruunga. Tauna tua-i yuurtelqa kiingan nallunritaqa. Ellangumalua-ll' maani ellangumallrunritua.

Tua-i-w' ava-i qanemcit'lallrukiinga waten, ellait tua-i uitaqallruyaaqniluteng. Elkek wani uitaqallruyaaqnilutek maani tua-i, taugaam tua-i yuurrlua-ll' maani, tua-i yuurteqatallemni-gguq ulerpagluni.

Enet-llu-gguq iteryarpiaraluki tua-i. Uani-llu Negtemi Nupigaankut eniit

Now this Kanerrlulegmiut [Residents of Kanerrlulek (Place with a little bit of *kaneq* or hoarfrost)], some of our parents stayed here in the past. Our parents followed the ways of our ancestors here at these old village sites.

This old village site is old. They were a village, and they didn't leave this place all winter, but they probably went down to the ocean during summer to get closer to the fish, heading downriver.

This is the first time that I have arrived here, but I've seen this old village from a distance. All different people, including the ancestors of the people of Chefornak, stayed here in the past.

This isn't a small village although there are a number of houses here.

The people from this village used to invite people from the surrounding villages, they probably invited them. But we haven't used this village site since we weren't around back in those days.

My mother also mentioned this place briefly; she said when there was a flood, water entered the homes here, when there was a large flood down there. And my mother and father evidently were here, and I didn't know about it, before I was born. I think some of the parents of the people of Toksook Bay lived here at Kanerrlulegmiut.

There were a lot of blackfish to catch in the past, but there were no burbot, broad whitefish, and pike here. But along the coast there are whitefish that we eat, tomcod, and flounder. Those types of fish were available when the people of this place fished. I think some of the people moved up north to our [Toksook] river where burbot are available.

[People from here] used to go spring camping down at Umkumiut. Allgim Atii used to [go spring camping] down there. When it got warm out, sleds moved down there from around here.

And when summer came, they moved here to their home village. They fished around here again for tomcod and flounder. They continually made their supply of food last longer, and they'd also obtain fish that we've been eating since yesterday, the small whitefish.

Does our mother [Anna Agnes] want to add anything?

Anna Agnus: I don't know this place, and I wasn't aware when it was a village. But they used to tell me that I was born here. I only know that I was born here. I wasn't aware when I was here also.

They told me that they lived here once. They said that they lived at this place, and I was born here, and they said that there was a flood when I was about to be born.

And they said water almost entered the homes. And downriver in

iterluku Negtemi, amiigakun. Apac'angaaq-gguq imna Cuk'ayaq yuurrnerrarluni-ll'; tamaa-i tuani amiiga itraku qamigautegnun ek'arrluku Nupigaq aaniin anutellruluku.

Wiinga-ll' angayuqaagka maantellinilutek. Tuani tua-i ulerpakatallranigguq yuurellruunga. Ulerpiimi-llu-gguq cikuq navgurluku nunamun tagerqelluku. Tuaten qanemcitellruanga aanama.

Tua-i-gguq tuaten uksuarmi cikurraarluni ulellruuq, cikuq-llu-gguq navgurluku makut kuiget cikuit navgurluki tagerqelluki elatmun.

Arremaarmiut

Unangik: Pingkut pia-i Arremaarmiut ullakaqsailngatai, pamani tayima ipingaut. Cali tua-i nellret qavciugut cali. Tumyarauluteng yaaken pikuneng tumekluki Negtemek pikuneng tumekluki. Yungqerturatullruut.

Imna tayim' kituullrua-ll' Kass'atun tauna nayurtellra, Allgim Atii tua-i Yugtun. Tuaten piuratullruat. Pia-i kalikami nunanguami uitaut Arremaarmiut tua-i pamkut pama-i.

Aling neq'lirpagtat. Uksurpak qaluyarturalriit arulairvikluki, nerluteng. Neqkameggnek-llu kanavircuunateng, ena atauciq. Tayima yuurqertelluki; caayuutait tayim' cukanralaryaaqellilriit.

Tuamtell' avaken taikuneng qimugteseng neqkarcurraarluki cali tua-i arulairvikluki cali. Qaillun-llu allanernek mernuyuunatek imkuk angayuqaagket. Yugyakallermeggni qavciuluteng nunat pillruyaaqut, yugyakallermeggni tua-i enet.

Ingna-ll' yaa-i Panruk, aug'um ava-i kitulriim atii, ikayurtemta atii.

Ukuk wani caperrnarqellruuk yullregket augkut. Allaneq tamalkuan nerevkaraat uksurpak yaavet up'nerkallranun.

Aling aren mernuqayuunatek, neqkaitniluki-ll' qanyuunatek. Atiit neqnek amllernek kumlanernek unangetullruyugnarquq; uqtaqnganek, can'giirnek, manignanek-llu-w' pilallrullilria.

Wii tua-i caperqellruagka taukuk yuuk piani. Tununermek tuaten Niugtarmek tuaten tamaa-i allanruvikellruak pingkuk pianelnguuk. Yuk tamalkuan

Nightmute, water entered the home of Nupigaq and his family through the doorway. It is said Apac'angaaq, Cuk'ayaq had just been born at the time; when water entered the doorway, they just placed him inside a kayak sled and his mother took Nupigaq out of the home.

My parents were evidently here at the time. They said I was born right before the flood. And they said when it flooded, it broke the ice to pieces and brought it up to the land. That's what my mother told me.

They say that it flooded after it froze during fall, and it broke the river ice to pieces and brought them up to shore.

Arremaarmiut[34]

Simeon Agnus: I don't think he has gone to Arremaarmiut up there, out of view. There are also a number of old houses there. When traveling from over there, they were along the trail when they were traveling from Nightmute. It was always occupied.

I don't know the English name of the person who lived here, whose Yup'ik name was Allgim Atii. That's what they always called him. Arremaarmiut up there is written on the map up there.

My, what an abundance of fish they had. All winter long, people who went to dipnet would stop there and eat. And the one home that was there never worried about lacking food. They'd have them drink tea; their supply of tea probably went fast.

And again, when they came from out there after they had gone to obtain food for their dogs, they'd stop at that place again. And their parents weren't tired of receiving guests in their home. At one point when many people were living there, originally a number of residents were there, when many homes were there.

And Panruk over there, the father of the person who passed us, the father of the one who helped us [lived up there].

The people who occupied that place were unrivaled. They fed all guests all winter long up until spring.

My goodness, they never got tired, and they never said they didn't have food for people who arrived. I think their father obtained many frozen fish to eat; fish caught with lures by jigging, blackfish, and probably burbot.

I found the people who lived up there to be unrivaled. The two who lived up there received guests from Tununak and from Newtok. They helped all

ikayurluku anrutaakun. Ilait nenglliurluteng pirtugmi tekitaqamegteki urugcirvikluki.

Amartuq: Arremaarmiut tumketullruanka pamaken Manrimek. Aug'utun tua-i qanemcillratun tua-i nerviugut, nerviupigtut. Arulairluteng tua-i-ł' nererraarluteng ayagluteng.

Cali-ll' amaken Cevv'arnermek qaluvigmek taikuneng tuani call' arulairluteng ner'aqluteng. Tuaten tua-i ayuqellruut.

Nanurrualek: Quyana. Tua-i wii qanerkaipallaarlua, Arremaarmiut taugaam nallunritanka. Iciw' tamaani Arremaarmiunun aataka imna piaqami, ilu'uqngamiu, maaten tua-i tekiciiqukut ak'a tua-i neqkaput elagyaatni upingaurluteng. Aatama tua-i ilu'uqngamiu neqkainek upluku, tua-i teguqainauluteng.

Kenircuun-llu augkuciq *pump*-arluku caanililuteng. Nerurarraarluta tag'aqluta. Tua-i upingacimalaaku neqkanek ner'aqluta. Tua-i.

Talarun

Amartuq: Tua-i painga ingna Talarutem etgatuq. Tua-i nallunrilamku imkutllu tengalrarluteng itraqameng tuani etgalqiterrlainatullruut paingani.

Taugaam qanemcikcuaqeryugngaanka. Paingani tuani neqlitullruukut cali, neqliqerluta tua-i makunek qaurtunek. Tuani tua-i imkuk Anthony-nkuk neqlitullruuk, neqliuraqatullruuk.

Cali-llu naunranek piaqata naunranek call' pitullrulutek. Tua-i-ll' pinarikatek itrarlutek tua-i kiavet nunallernun.

Aug'utun *three*-aarungatellruut enet. Aataka tuquan taukugni uitalangartellruunga tamaa-i, aulukluta wangkuta im'um maurlullemta tua-i. Tuavet tua-i uitaqalallruukut. Tua-i uksuq-llu tua-i qaill' piqerluku nugtarrluta call' tua-i neqaireskan. Neqairutenqegtuq atam kiugna Talarun nanilami.

Yaa, taum tua-i aulukellruakut Anthony-mek aiparluni tamaa-i. Call' up'nerkami nayutullruaput tua-i. Up'nerkami tevyulinek pissurvikluku. Pissurvikaqluku akikangengnaqutekluku tamaa-i pitullruukut; tamakut tevyulit akikangengnaqutekluki pilallrukait.

Tuani tua-i tuani uitallemteni ca nurnarillruuq tua-i. Cakaunateng caayuutaunateng, iqmigkaunateng-llu tua-i.

Wiinga tamaa-i iqmigyunqellruama cali iruluarnek-llu cikirnanrirlua iruluaraat qelek'ngellermegteki tuani tua-i.

people by feeding them. When some people arrived cold in a blizzard, they'd warm up at that place.

Joe Felix: I used to travel through Arremaarmiut when traveling from Manriq up there. Like he said, it was a place to eat, it really was a place to eat. They'd stop, and they'd leave after eating.

They'd also stop and eat when coming back from dipnetting at Cevv'arneq. That's how the place was.

Rita Angaiak: Thank you. I don't have much to say, but I know Arremaarmiut. When my father would go to Arremaarmiut in the past, since [the person who lived there] was his *iluraq,* we'd arrive to see that our food was ready in their partially underground storage cache. Since he was my father's *iluraq,* he would prepare food for him, and they were ready to eat.

And they'd pump that type of cooking stove and make tea. After eating, we'd go up. Since he had food prepared for him to eat, we'd eat. That's it.

Talarun[35]

Joe Felix: The mouth of Talarun River is shallow. And since I know that it is, when people went inside that river using sails, they always beached and got stuck along shallow water along its mouth.

But I can briefly talk about that place. We also cut and harvested fish along its mouth, cutting some humpback whitefish for a short while. Anthony and his wife used to cut fish there for a while.

And when they picked salmonberries, they also picked salmonberries there. And when it was time, they'd go upriver to that old village site.

Like [Simeon] said, there seemed to be three houses. When my father died, I started to live with them, our late grandmother taking care of us. We stayed there briefly. During a certain part of winter, we'd move again when fish were no longer there. Fish get scarce easily up at Talarun since it's a short river.

Yes, that person took care of us, and Anthony was her spouse at the time. We also used to stay there in spring. During spring, we would hunt for muskrat at that place. We hunted there, trying to obtain an income; they tried to obtain an income from muskrat skins.

Things became scarce while we were staying at that place. They didn't have things, they didn't have a supply of tea, they didn't have chewing tobacco.

Since I liked to chew tobacco, they stopped giving me tobacco leaf stems at that time, when they started keeping the tobacco leaf stems at that time.

Taugaam tua-i tamakut caayut cali nuuqiyutekngamiki maurlumta im'um caayullret egcuunaki kinercirluki. Kinercirraarluki-llu atuumaksailngurnek cali *mix*-arluki. Yaa avuluki tua-i atuumaksailngurnek tuaten caanilitullruluni.

Taugaam wii yuurqayuitellruunga, ellait yuurqatullruut augkut. Caanik aug' angrrarngalengraan nangenqegcaarluku yuurqernauraat tua-i, yuurqaumaluteng. Qaill' augkut pilartat! [*ngel'artuq*] Tua-i nangenqegcaarluku. [*ngel'artuq*] Ii-i aka'arcetun tua-i.

Tuani tua-i neqlitullruukut. Tua-i-ll' man'a qaill' pitariqerluku call' wavet anelraulluta taukunun tua-i nunallemtenun tuavet. Tuani tua-i nutaan uksiluta cali; uitatullruukut tuaten tua-i.

Unangik: Tua-i ava-i iqluvkenani qanelria, maurluugmini uitaqalallruami tuani tua-i Talarutmi.

Cali ikamrat tumku'urpek'naki, ketiikun tamaaggun tua-i maaggun, piavet qam'umun qama-i itratullruut qimugtetgun pitullermeggni. Tumyarauvkenateng kiaqsiameng. Taukut tuan cuukvaguat iquatni; cuukvaguarirtellrani taukut tua-i nunalleruaraat uitaut.

Tua-i wiinga ukut arulairutengramceteng taukut nunallret tekicesciigaciiqaput. Keluqsigtut tuaken, mat'um Qalvinraakun asgullerkamta ceniini.

Callulleq

Unangik: Una waniw' Callullermek pituat, kiugna ingna yaa-i cuukvaguangqelriim nallii. Pingna pia-i alangruviktullrulliniat augkut angayuqamta. Wangkuta, wangkuta mat'um maa-i nalliini alangruniluku ilavut niiteksaitua. Taugaam angayuqaput ilait alangrutullrullniut tuani.

Tuani tua-i qamaken Cakcaamek neqnek aqvaillermini unugluku, qimugtet cukaitellruameng; uqamaitaqagnek ikamrak cukaitetullruut.

Tamaavet elliqerluteng qimugtai ukut ciutait elivluteng, cali cukariluni cukarilliniluni. Tamaa-i ikamragmi aciagnek qalrillagaqan ikamrani-gguq tua-i pegtuqanrilkurrlukek tegumiaqetullruak. Tua-i alangrullra tamana niitellruamku waniw' qanrutkaqa.

Arcariinarluni taugaam tua-i pillra. Tua-i-gguq ikamragken iluani pin-

But since she would run out of tea, our grandmother never discarded the old tea leaves but dried them. And after drying them, she'd add some unused tea leaves and mix them together. Yes, she'd add unused tea leaves to the used tea leaves and make tea like that.

But I didn't drink tea at the time, but they used to drink tea. Although that kettle looked pretty large, they'd finish drinking the whole pot, drinking tea for a long time. What did those people do! [*laughs*] They'd finish the entire pot. [*laughs*] Yes, like the old days.

We cut fish there, and then during a certain time of year, they'd move us down to this place, to that old village site where we stayed. We'd spend the winter there also; that's where we used to stay.

Simeon Agnus: He spoke truthfully just now, since he lived with his grandparents there at Talarun.

And sleds didn't pass through that place, traveling down below them when they went upriver to that place when they traveled with dog teams in the past. [Talarun] wasn't along the trail since they were pretty far inland. It's along the end of those alders; that small old village site is in the area where alder no longer grows.

Although I stop there to show you the place, we will not be able to reach that old village site. It's pretty far inland from the shores of the Qalvinraaq that we are going to go up.

Callulleq[36]

Simeon Agnus: They call this Callulleq [One who fought, from *callug-*, "to fight or challenge"], the place up there where there are alder bushes. Our parents evidently were haunted by ghosts up there. Recently, I've never heard of any of us being haunted by a ghost. But some of our parents evidently encountered ghosts at that place.

At that place there, when [Puyangutem Atii] went to go and get fish from Cakcaaq upriver, in the dark, since dogs were slow; when the sled was heavy, they were slow.

Just when they reached that place, his dogs' ears lowered, and he suddenly went faster. When a sudden noise came from underneath his sled, he held onto his sled and tried not to let go. I'm talking about the haunting he encountered since I heard about it.

The noise only got louder. He said that a sudden noise didn't come from

rilngermi camaken taugaam ikamragken acianek qalrillagaqluni. Tua-i-ll' mat'um, tamaani atam ikavet arvillermini, kuigmun tekican, tua-i tekicami uunguciirutliniluni.

Waten tua-i avani alangruaqameng arulairluteng waten cetruarqait-gguq tua-i ceterluk waten. Cetruarluk' tua-i waten. Qarilkituut.

Ciuqliq tauna cetellra tekitaqamegteggu, ellmeggni tua-i kuiguluku tua-i tang tamana cetellra tangvatungataat. Waten pilangraata cukariinarluteng taugaam, nunat canimelliinallrat maliggluku.

Tauna-am angutet iliit alangrullrani tua-i tuaten tua-i piurluku. Qimugtiin tua-i ataucirraam ikayurturyaaqluku, waten nunallernek pillrani.

Taugaam tua-i tamana cetellrani yaaqsigiyaaqelliniluni, taugaam cukariinarluni-gguq.

Nunat-gguq alairtut kevegluteng tua-i piaqluteng ellami tut'aqluteng.

Tua-i tekitniaraamegteki tekitniaraamiu tua-i tamana cuqluku nunamun pillerkani, mic'an tua-i egmian tamaavet ug'artelliniluni, tua-i aciirutevkenani nunanun.

Augna tua-i qanemcika Puyangutem Atii tamaani taugaam tua-i qimugtai qacigtengellrulliniut.

Tua-i tamatumun kuigmun capenricami tauna tua-i arulaillrungatuq. Waniw' tua-i alangrunek qanemciqertua. Ilait taugaam tua-i nalluanka alangrurpallret.

Cali augna aipaa call' qanruteknaurqa cali. Cali-am una kiirrarmi nunallernun, uksillermun aqvaillinilria.

Piinanrani tua-i atakuqerluku-am tua-i tan'geriqerluku qakemna-am enem kangiraanek migpallartelliniluni. Cali uani cali amiigem taqurraani cali migpallartelleq elliin nalluvkenaku, amigmun itqatarluku. [*ngel'artuq*]

Qerrulliigni yuuqerlukek kangiraq tua-i ikigutlinia. [*ngel'artuq*] Migpallarcan elep'alliniuq. [*ngel'artuq*]

Maaten-gguq ercan anngami pilliniuq enem tua-i tuaken kangiraanek akallrullinilria. [*ngel'artuq*]

Carayiit makut eleq alikaat, alikeqapiararaat. Qaill'-kiq pilriameng pilartatgu. [*ngel'artuq*]

Cungauyaq: Cakcaaq pingna nell'eq tayim' tangtuksi pia-i. *Ski-doo*-gka wani ayagciigalillragni, ukut waniwa umyuaqngamki alangruviktullrit pavagguillruunga *shortcut*-arlua alangruyuumiilama, tua-i-wa wani ukut

inside his sled but from underneath. Then here, when he went across there, when he arrived at the river, he became disoriented.

When they experienced hauntings in the past, they'd stop and pretend to cut [across their trail] like this. They'd make a pretend mark. They stall them.

When [ghosts] came upon that first mark he made, I think they view it as a river. Although they [made a mark], [the ghosts] only got faster, the closer they got to the village.

When one of the men was haunted, he continually did that. One of his dogs continually helped him, when he was returning from an old village site.

But when he made that mark, he evidently got farther behind, but he said that [the ghost] got faster.

He said when the village came into view, it would lift into the air and then touch the ground.

When he was about to reach [the village], he estimated when he would go on top of the village and onto land, when the village touched ground, he immediately got on top of the village and not underneath it.

The story that I told you about Puyangutem Atii, his dogs evidently started to run with ease at that time.

Since he couldn't cross that river, that person seemed to stop there. I'm telling about ghosts now. But I don't know about people who experienced serious hauntings.

Let me tell you another story. There was another person who went to an old village site, to get things at a winter site.

While he was there, when it got dark, a large banging noise came from out along the corner of the house. When another banging noise came from along the side of the door, he knew that it was about to enter through the doorway. [*laughs*]

He took off his pants and bent over and stuck his buttocks out toward the corner of the home. [*laughs*] When a large banging noise sounded, he suddenly farted a large fart. [*laughs*]

When the sun came up and he went outdoors, [the ghost] had evidently rolled from along the corner of that home. [*laughs*]

Ghosts are afraid of gas; they are extremely afraid of it. I wonder why they are. [*laughs*]

John Walter: You see that old home up there at Cakcaaq. When my Ski-doo couldn't run, when I remembered that they encounter ghosts here at this place, I went through the route up there, using a shortcut since I didn't want

niiteqallruamki tuaten alangrunek.

Avaggun. Man'a cataituq. Yaaken Cakcaamek yaa-i pekcimallruunga yaavet Negtemun. Nutka taugaam tua-i teguluku iqalluarpiit, unugpak kangaumallruunga, *thirteen hours*-llu tua-i yaavet tekillua cukailama. Tauna taugaam kiingan piaqa.

Qavaliriyaq

Amartuq: Nallunritqallemnek-wa tua-i wiinga-ll' mat'um uum mat'um Qavaliriyam pillranek.

Wiinga tua-i, qamaantellruukut tuani avani ava-i Manrimi. Tua-i-llu kiagmi waten anelrarluta maavet maa-i; tamaani tamaa-i pelatekarluteng qavcin.

Cunaw' tua-i taukugnun tua-i yugkiuteksarturyaaqlua. Wii tua-i ellangqellruama wii tamaani iciw' tua-i ellangvikellrunrilamkek wiinga ciuniurciiganaku tua-i. Iciw' tua-i piaqaceci qessatulriaci, qessaluci tua-i pitullruuci.

Tuartang ut'ruskiitnga egmian unuaquani. Tamaani anelrautellermeggnia taukugnun tua-i itrucatnga yugkiuteksaaqellemnun, uumek tan'gurrarpaagarmek tangellruunga; cunaw' tauna tua-i Nanugaullinilria. Tauna tua-i anngaqsallrulliniaqa; ellangqerpeknii pillrukatnga aipaagni anngaqsallruaqa, maani maa-i tekiutellratnia.

Tuavet tua-i itrutlermeggnia aturaqsugnailkengamnek aturaqegcilua at'esksiitnga. Augkut-wa qangananek pitukait atkuut cali, atkukegtaaraat tua-i assirluteng. Atkukegciyaaqlua tamakunek tamaa-i. Tauna tua-i tuaten nallunritaqa. Uksumi nalluaqa, nalluaqa man'a uksumi. Kiagmi taugaam ataucirrarmi tekiarrngatellruaput.

Wiinga ellangeqtaarturlua call' tamaa-i pillruunga, taugaam nalluvkenaku tua-i tunyaaqellrak taukugnun, ukuullrullilriik-wa waniwa. Tuani ellangqellruunga.

Avegyaq: Elpet tua-i tegussaagyaaqellruagten. Ping'umun pivkenak, pingna aipaqenrillrani, Navgamek taugaam aipangellrani.

Tua-i nallunritaqa tauna. Tua-i tass'uqsaaqaqagten-llu wiinga tua-i tass'uqesqumanritkacagarnaamken. [*ngel'artuq*] Tua-i uyuracungaqevkangnaqsaaqellruatgen wangnun. Un'gani tuartang Qalvinraam cenakeciqekii.

to encounter a ghost, since I had often heard that this place had ghosts.

I traveled through that route out there. There is nothing here. I walked for a long time from Cakcaaq over there to Nightmute. I only took my gun and some herring and walked all night, and I arrived over there in thirteen hours since I was slow. That's all I'm mentioning.

Qavaliriyaq[37]

Joe Felix: I, too, am going to talk about something that I know concerning Qavaliriyaq here.

We lived up at Manriq. Then during the summer like this, we moved down to this place; a number of people had tents over there.

They evidently went there to give me to a particular couple to adopt me and raise me as their child. Since I had awareness, since I didn't become aware having them as my parents, I couldn't accept the arrangement. You know when they ask something of you, you are reluctant, you were unwilling to do what they ask.

It seems they brought me home right away the next day. When they brought me down at the time, when they brought me inside that couple's home, to the couple who wanted to adopt me, I saw a pretty big boy; that person was evidently Nanugaq. That person would have been my older brother; if they had given me to that family while I wasn't aware, when they brought me here, he probably would have been my older brother.

When they brought me inside that home, they had me put on clothing that wasn't mine that looked very nice. They also had me put on what they call a squirrel parka, a wonderful-looking parka. I had a nice parka at the time. That's what I know. I don't know this place during winter. It seems we only arrived here once during summer.

I was in and out of awareness at the time, but I was aware that they were giving me to that couple to adopt, and it was probably this couple here. I was aware at the time.

Anna Agnus: They tried to take you [to be their child]. Not that person up there; when she was no longer married to that person up there, but when she married Navgaq.

I know about that. And even though they held your hand, I didn't want them to hold your hand at all. [*laughs*] They tried to make you my younger sibling. I think it was down on the coast along the shores of the Qalvinraaq

Navgamek aipangenrakun tuani pillruyaaqaatgen.

Iciw' Navgan aatavet ataatakekii, ataataklinikii. Tamaa-i wiinga-ll' qanruquraraqlua taum Navgan anngallramnek tuqlurcequ'urluku tangssuilkekawa. Ellangeqtaallruunga tamatum-wa nalliini. Tua-i.

Qukailnguq: Ingkut yaa-i mingqessuutellret avani acitullruit tutmaryaranek. Tua-i tutmaryaranek acirturluki pitullruit.

Cali avani murilkellemni qagaani-llu amlleq makungqellrunrituq. Tamaa-i tua-i nukalpianek nulialget melqulegculinek nulialget augkunek ava-i mingqessuutnek tutmaryaranek pingqerrniluki niitelallruunga. Aug'umek tua-i nalluyagutellemnek qanqautekaqa. Tua-i.

Pengurtalek

Unangik: Tua-i-ll' ugkut uaqliit ua-i Pengurtalegmiut, ugkut ua-i nunallequinraat ugkut cali ingrim ug'um ukatiitni, ugkut cuukvaguat iquata nalliitni ketiitni uitaut cakma. Kuigat taugaam iterciigatnarquq maa-i mat'um nalliini; anenra et'galiuq.

Ugna Pengurtalek kipusvigtangqellruuq. Angyakun aklussaagaqluni Bethel-aamek qamaken angyakun. Iiliamek aterluni tua-i.

Tua-i ugna ua-i allanertullruuq ellii. Avaken tuaten ungalamtenek ullagluku kass'arviktullruat. Naken Kayalivigmek-llu ikaken pilallrullikiit. Augkut tua-i unkut ungalaqlimta tua-i ullagluku pitullrukiit-llu, maaken, Tununermek tuaten. Cat ilait kepqutmeng angutet elliin qemangqatullrui. Allanertukayagluni, taugken Yupiuluni wangkucicetun; tua-i Yuuguq.

Camiunguvkenani-ll', aanii-ll' maani maa-i uitallruluni, nunamteni maani. Taugaam Bethel-aami tuqullruuq aanii tauna. Ellii-ll' tua-i uani uitainanermini tua-i assiirucan ayautellruat qamavet Mamterillernun. Mamterillerni tuqullruyugnarquq.

Tauna tua-i laavkaallra tayim' umyuaqaqamku qaill' pillrulartatgu, wall'u-q imtellruat. Nalluaqa qaill' pillra. Taugaam kia yuum aqvaqatarnilukull' niitellrunrilkek'a tauna. Iqua kipusvikluku iqua-ll' nekluku. Angellruuq atam tauna enii.

Isaac, Elia Isaac. Taungullruuq tua-i. Tua-i tamarmeng ilarrai tua-i

River. Right after she married Navgan, they tried to adopt you at that time.

As you know, Navgan is your father's maternal uncle. And Navgan continually told me and had me call him my *anngaller* [bad older brother], but here I had never seen him before. I was in and out of awareness during that time. That's it.

Michael John: Those types of [treadle] sewing machines over there, in those days they called them *tutmaryarat* [lit., "ones you step on"]. They always called them *tutmaryarat*.

And when I observed things in those days, there weren't many people who had these, even in the north. Those who had *nukalpiat* for spouses, those who had spouses who were good at catching fur animals, I heard that they had those types of sewing machines called *tutmaryarat*. I'm just briefly mentioning what I had forgotten to mention. That's it.

Pengurtalek[38]

Simeon Agnus: And Pengurtalegmiut downriver, the small old village that is on this side of that mountain down there, it is located somewhere along the end of those alder trees down there, on the shore below them. But its river isn't navigable today; its outlet has gotten shallow.

There was a store down at Pengurtalek [Place with a *penguq* (hill)] . He'd go and get merchandise from Bethel with a boat. His name was Iiliaq [Elia].

That person who lived down there received a lot of guests. People even came from east of us to purchase goods. They probably went there from Kayalivik over there also. And the people to the east would go to that place also, and people from here, and people from Tununak. He had some necessities that men needed. He received many guests, but he was a Yup'ik person like us; he was Yup'ik.

He wasn't from some other place, and his mother lived here also, in our region here. But his mother died in Bethel. And while he was living downriver, when his health deteriorated, they brought him up to Bethel. I think he died in Bethel.

His frame building, when I think about what happened to it, I wonder what they did with it, or did they tear it down. I'm not sure what happened to it. I didn't hear that someone went to get it. One end was his store, and one end was his home. His home was large.

Isaac, Elia Isaac. That's who he was. All his few relatives died; they all

nangluteng tuquluteng; tamarmeng tua-i nangluteng perrirluteng tua-i, tangrruunrirluteng tayim'. Aaa, Buddy imat'anem, alqaa-ll' pillilria. Irniara-w' tauna tua-i Buddy-q. Cali-am assiirusmiluni-am cali, assinringluni.

Iiliaq tua-i una wani, qaill' nalluaqa tua-i augna piurallra, taugaam tua-i nunat ukut wani tua-i ullaketaallruat amlleret, avaken tuaten ullagluku.

Akinek piyugnaunateng, imarmiutartameggnek, kaviartameggnek, imkunek-llu qatellrianek; uliirnek wangkuta pituaput qatellriit. Tua-i tang mingqaanek pivkarluku, mingqaanek piiyuitellruyugnarquq.

Yaa, kiirrarmi tua-i *Native Store*-aq. Aren cat tamarmeng ikani *Native Store*-ami akiitellrullinilriit. *Drum*-aq-llu *thirty dollars* akiluni. *Five gallon*-aaq-llu uqulkuk *five dollars.* Mukaaq-llu tayima *five*-aaq naavkenaku, *five dollars. Milk*-at-llu *four*-aaruluteng *dollar.* Maa-i-ll' *milk*-aq atauciq *dollar* cipluku maani akingluni.

Avegyaq: Wani waniw' uitallrulliniukut. Tamaa-i illayuyuunii-ll' canek pilallruunga.

Tua-i-ll' upagnariakut upiimta uani ua-i Pengurtalegmi uitallruukut uksurpak. Cali tua-i kiaqlingqerrluta.

Tuartang Aamecaankuk kiimelnganatek uani Talarutmi. Kia-i-ll' eniik alaitaqluni. Tamaa-i tua-i kangangengama kia-i eniik tangrraqluku tua-i.

Tua-i-ll' caqerlunuk caangssiurallmegni pakissaallruukuk tauna-ll' kinguqliirutka-llu maavet uakariitnun, maram mat'um qainganun kuigem ceniini. Taugaam tua-i pakikengarkat atam tuani tua-i amllellruut. Utngungssararugaat negaasget-llu; tamakunek tamaa-i cumertaqlunuk tauna-ll' kinguqliirutka-llu.

Tua-i-am pivakarlunuk taperrnatlemegni cali aanapuk tauna quyak'acagallruuq. Taperrnaqegtaarai-wa maa-i umyuaqaqamki, taperrnaqegcillrullinilriit ugkut ua-i, caugat, Pengurtalegmiut.

Tua-i taukut-llu tua-i Iiliankut uitaluteng. Kipusviuluteng. Iquat tua-i kipusvikluku, iqua-ll' nekluku. Tamaa-i irniari-llu taukut qaqimaluteng. Taugaam atam tua-i uksurpak tua-i nemteni qavarpallurturnaurtut; yugeckacagarluta tua-i tuani uitalallruukut unugmi. Qavarviksugpagluta tua-i taukut irniakenka.

Tuaten tua-i maavaqarrallemni uantellruuk angayuqaagka. Nel'utek tua-i kiimta-ll' tua-i yuuluta; wangkuta, Yuguayiinkuk-llu, ellait-wa. Tua-i kiimta

died and are no longer around. Oh, there's Buddy, and probably his older sister. His child was Buddy. He isn't in good health any longer either.

Elia, I'm not sure how he lived, but many people from the surrounding villages went to him and even came from out there to see him.

They didn't use money at all, but they used the mink they caught, the foxes they caught, and the ones with white fur; we called the white foxes *uliiret*. I don't remember him taking coiled grass baskets; I don't think he took coiled grass baskets [as payment].

Yes, only the Native Store [took baskets]. All merchandise at the Native Store over there [at Tununak] was evidently inexpensive. And a drum [of gas] was thirty dollars. And a five-gallon container of motor oil was five dollars. And flour was under five dollars. And four milk cans were a dollar. These days, one can of milk costs over a dollar.

Anna Agnus: We evidently lived here at this place. I also wasn't in awe of things at the time.

And when it was time for us to move, when we moved, we stayed downriver at Pengurtalek all winter. And there were people living upriver from us.

It seems that Aamecaaq [and her husband] were alone downriver, at Talarun. And their home was visible up there. When I began to walk, I'd see their home up the river.

Then one day, when we were gathering food, my late younger sibling and I were searching for mouse food from underground mouse caches, right downriver from their place, along this marshy area, along the shores of the river. There was a lot of mouse food underground at the time. There were many *utngungssaraat* [mare's-tail tubers] and *negaasget* [edible plants]; my late younger sibling and I would gather those at the time.

One day, when we got some *taperrnat* [coarse seashore grass], our mother was extremely grateful. When I think about the wonderful *taperrnat* at that place, the place downriver, Pengurtalegmiut, had wonderful *taperrnat*.

And Elia and his family were living there. They had a store. One end of their home was their store, and the other end was their home. And all their children were alive at the time. But all winter long, they'd mainly sleep in our home; there were many people who stayed there at night. Their children always wanted to sleep at our place.

When I first came here, my parents lived downriver. They had a home, and we were the only ones living there; there was our family, Yuguayak and

yuullruukut, Panrumek aiparluni irniarunatek taugaam.

Tua-i waten tua-i pitalua qanemciunga taumek maavaqarrallemnek.

Urumangnaq

Neng'uryar: Urumangnami cali alingelqa umyuaqetuaqa-llu. Ayumian tang Qaariitaatullratni, tamaa-i Pangalek, Ap'ankut, Nasgaunkut, tuartang-llu Yuguayiinkut-llu uitaqallrulriit. Ilait cumikellrunritanka. Uyangliinkut-wa. Kangrilnguunkuullratni, Kangrilnguunkut, Uyangliinkut, Nasgaunkut. Nasgauq tuar yuurpailgan pillrulriit. Atsalleq-llu tamaa-i panini-ll' ilakluku Curyak-llu. Yugyagngatlallruut ellait. Uyangliinkut. Elanelput tayim' tangerrsularyaaqanka. Tangellrunritanka.

Qaariitaam-llu tua-i nalliini atakumi tauna cali irr'iktukek'a. Ingelret qaingatni ingelret akiqliqngata, ingkuk-wa Noni-nkuk Qilangaq-llu. Elliraat nayu'urlutullrullinikaitkut.

Acimi uitainanemni atakumi, kankut tang caranglluut cumikua cageskait, qayam ikaraliitai, waten imkut akultutaurluteng tupigat, kelugkaqegtaaraat, tamakut qanemcikellrenka nalacirat. Uavet cageskait, amik-llu ikingqaluni, avatek makuk amiiguluni nem'un.

Cingukan: Apqiitnek amiguyuq.

Neng'uryar: Elaturraq-wa cakemna. Tuani tang amiguyumi angutek waten *white*-amek qasperlutek atkugturlutek. *White*-kacagauvkenani-ll' iqangtageurlullrullilria.

Nacartuumalutek tua-i waten, ilutuluni-ll' nacaak, kegginakek-llu wii tangellrunritanka, uani aqumgalriik amiguyumi. Amik-wa. Kankut-wa tupigat cagingalriit.

Tua-i-ll' tang qantagnek qantarpallraagnek muragagnek, neqnek imarlutek, tamaa-i keviraullrullilrianek cegg'arpallernek qallirluteng, akutartarluni.

his wife, and [Elia's] family. We lived there alone, and [Yuguayak's] wife was Panruk at the time, but they had no children.

I'm telling about when I first came to this place to that extent.

Urumangnaq[39]

Lizzie Chimiugak: Once in a while I recall the time that I was afraid at Urumangnaq [from *uruma-,* "to be warm"]. Back when they used to have [the fall festival] Qaariitaaq, there was Pangalek, Ap'aq and family, Nasgauq and family, and it seems that Yuguayak and family stayed there briefly. I didn't pay attention to some. And there was also Uyangliq and family. When they were Kangrilnguq and family, there was Kangrilnguq and family, Uyangliiq and family, Nasgauq and family. It seems it was before Nasgauq was born. There was the late Atsaq and also her daughter and Curyak. They seemed to have many people in their family. There was Uyangliiq and family. I really desire to see our old house pits. I didn't see them.

Then during Qaariitaaq, in the evening, that was something that I was in awe of. I was seated on top of the bed, since the beds were situated across from one another, and over there were Noni and Qilangaq. Orphans evidently always stayed with us.

While I was sitting on the mattress in the evening, I saw them spread a grass mat, the grass kayak mat, those twined grass mats that had [grass pieces] spaced about this far apart, those wonderful *kelugkat* [coarse grasses], those [grasses] that I talked about that were wilted and cured. They spread them out along the front of the home, and the door was open, since the exitway was like this, and it was a doorway into the home.

Albertina Dull: What they call *amiguyuq* [entranceway].

Lizzie Chimiugak: The porch was down there. Inside the entranceway were two men wearing white hooded garments. It probably wasn't completely white, but dirty.

They were wearing hoods like this, and their hoods were deep, and I didn't see their faces, they were seated out there in the entranceway. Then there was the door. Then down there was a twined grass mat that was spread out.

Then [they brought out] two bowls, two large wooden bowls, filled with food, and there were fish that had been stored inside sealskin containers, very large *cegg'at* [whitefish split in half with small, horizontal splits along the

Cingyukan: Aling ellang[yaraallrulliniuten].

Neng'uryar: Anelrauskekek tang taukuk-llu teguluki. Taukugnun tunluk', kegginakek-llu tangerpek'nakek.

Tua-i-ll' anulluki, cakma neplirlutek, neplirlutek qakma.

Cunaw' tang Qaariitaat qimugtengunguarluteng neqkegnek tegutessaalallinilriit. Marurpagallragni cunaw' taungucingellrunritaqa, kinguakun taugaam nallunrillruaqa qanemcillratni.

Ayaglutek tayima. Tua-i-ll' ayiignek Naulalria tang kanavet tupigat iquatnun ina'arcami uatmun akagartellria ikaraliitet nemerluku iqukliarrluku. Cunaw' tuaten pitullrullinilriit. Piyarait tamakut.

Akagarrluni ngelliarrluni. Natetmun-im' pillrulria.

Angalgaq: Putting away the mat. Inarrluni uivluni.

Neng'uryar: An'aqagnek cunaw' taukuk. Aataullrulriik-qaa imat'anem? Caneg'-im' taukuk arivtelallrukegket.

Akagarrluni. Irr'ikluku cali. Qaill' qavaqerraarlua tang tupallruyugnarqellrianga. Irr'ikluku tuaten akagartellrani, wall'u-qaa uatmun wall'u-qaa kiatmun. Iquklicami qaillun pillrua. Nemrirluni.

Tuamtell' qavarraarlua cam iliini tamaani call' tupakartua Naulalria itellria. Tamaani Qaariitaami piyugnarquq. Waten tang kangiplugmek minguumaluni, maaggun qengaan qaingakun ayagluni maavet. [*ngel'artut*]

Angalgaq: Indian-atun? [*ngel'artuq*]

Neng'uryar: Yaa. Tua-i-ll' angliriama, Naulalria apluku, "Imumi-ggem tangellruamken tupakallemni itellriaten waten pimaluten, kangiplugpall'er mitkacagarluni maani. Qaill' erullruan-qaa?"

"Nuu." Eruyuitellruit-gguq. Inartaqata-gguq qava'arqameng tupalallruut catangssagaunateng. Tamaa-i-gguq Qaariitaat yuita pailallruit, *clean*-arluki.

Angalgaq: Kangipluut-qaa imat'anem aug'arciigatqalalriit?

Cingyukan: Kegginait urasqamek minguggaarluki. Urasqaq urrluku minguggaarluk' tua-ll' kinercirluku. Nutaan-llu kinqaqani qaralilirluku kangiplugmek.

flesh] on top. And there was *akutaq* [a mixture of seal oil, boned fish, berries, and sugar].

Albertina Dull: My, you became aware [early].

Lizzie Chimiugak: He brought them down, and those two took them. He gave them to those two, and I didn't see their faces.

Then they brought them outside, and they were making noise out there.

Evidently the Qaariitaat were pretending to be dogs and were trying to grab their food. I didn't realize that's what they were doing when they were howling loudly, but I learned that afterward when they told stories about it.

They left. And when they left, when Naulalria lay down along the edge of the twined grass mat, she suddenly rolled down toward the front of the house and folded the *ikaraliitet* [grass kayak mats] to the end. That's evidently what they used to do. Those were their customs.

She suddenly rolled, reaching the end. I forgot which direction she [rolled].

Ruth Jimmie: Putting away the mat. She lay down and rolled.

Lizzie Chimigak: That's evidently what they would do when those two would leave. Were [those two] *aatak* [fathers]? I forgot what they used to call those two.

She suddenly rolled. I also watched her in awe. It seems that I woke up after sleeping for a short while. I watched in awe when she suddenly rolled like that, either rolling toward the front or back of the house. I don't know what she did when she finished. She removed the [twined grass] wrapped around her.

After sleeping one time, I suddenly woke and saw Naulalria come inside. I think it was during Qaarriitaaq. I saw that this part [of her face] was painted with charcoal, the paint covering the top of her nose up to this area. [*laughter*]

Ruth Jimmie: Like an Indian? [*laughs*]

Lizzie Chimigak: Yes. Then when I grew older, I asked Naulalria, "In the past, when I suddenly woke, I saw you come inside, and you had a large charcoal painting that was dark here. Did you wash it?"

She said, "No." She said that they didn't wash them off. She said that when they went to sleep they'd wake to find nothing at all [on their faces]. She said that *Qaariitaat yuit* [the persons of Qaariitaaq] used to lick [their faces] clean.

Ruth Jimmie: Isn't it hard for charcoal to come off?

Albertina Dull: After painting their faces with *urasqaq* [white clay]. They dissolved the *urasqaq,* and after painting them, they dried it. Then when it dried, they made designs with charcoal.

Temcinarqaqluteng ilait tua-i temcinaqkacagarluteng. [*ngel'artut*]

Neng'uryar: Tua-i-ll' tang, tamaani-w' pillrullilrianga, Uliggaq anqatalria anuteqatarlua Qaariitaaqatarlunuk. Ala-i. Tamaani cali.

Qantanek tang, muraganek-am tua-i tegumiarluni alqairutka wiinga-ll' call' qantarlua. Minguitellilriakuk-wa.

Ellamun tang an'ukuk atakumi, amkut neplilriit; alingallagyaaqlua tua-i utercullagyaaqlua. Amkut neplilriit, waten-wa tang nepii ellam, "Aaaa, uuuu." Waten piurluteng.

Cingukan: Tua-i-wa Qaariitaat an'aqameng qasgimek tuaten minguggaarluteng tuaten tua-i quyurrluteng qalriatulriit tua-i.

Neng'uryar: Wangni Qulic'ankuk Kangrilnguum-llu Atra. Amllerrnganateng, "Aaaa, uuu." Waten tua-i. Alingyaaqlua ayaullua. Elaturrarpall'ermun tang itruskiinga, wangni mat'utun angtaluni. Angkayagnganani.

Tamaa-i tang mik'nani tangellrat avaurnailnguq. Egkuani elaturrarpallraam kumlanquq cikumalria nevuq uitalria. Cunaw' tang elagyam amiiga, kumlanquq. Nevumek maaken kumlanaku kiiqaarluku maniggluku tayim' tuavet ellilallikiit; elagyam amiikluku.

Ukalirnermi-wa tang amik, enem amiiga, ukalirnermi-w' cali amiik. Tua-i mik'nan tangelqa cumiklua. Ayumian tang iqsulirnermun wavet itruskiinga, qantaqa-ll' tegumiiyulluku.

Itertukuk tang nerpall'er man'a akilvallraak naparyai, ingkuk uqurrarnek kenurraarlutek imkunek piirrayagarnek—Ala-i cumikelallemni!—Piirrayagarnek pilutek akiqliqlutek, Nasgaum Arnaankuk tuartang Atsalleq-llu. Kangrilnguum Arnaan-wa tallirpilirnermi uitallrullilria.

Tua-i-ll' tang itramegnuk aipaan akutamek tuaten qantapuk imirluki, tamakucimek-llu cegg'aqegtaarpall'ermek. Waten tua-i qantaq, navguumavkenani qallilirluku, tamamegnuk, akiqlian tuaten.

Tua-i-ll' tang anngamegnuk natmun-llu itruciirullua.

Cali tayima Kangrilnguunkunun iteryaryaaqellilria. Wall'u-q' elaturrallgutkellruyugnarqut. Tua-i-ll' augna ava-i uunguciirulluku. Itqetaallruyaaqellilriakuk-wa.

Some were funny, they were extremely hilarious. [*laughter*]

Lizzie Chimiugak: Then I think it was during that time, Uliggaq was about to leave, and she was going to take me outside with her, and she told me that we were going to go and attend Qaariitaaq. Oh my. It was at that place also.

My deceased older sister was holding a bowl, a wooden one, and I also had a bowl. We probably didn't have paint [on our faces].

We went outside in the evening, and people over there were making noise; I was suddenly frightened and wanted to return home. The ones over there were making noise, and this is what it sounded like outdoors, "*Aaaaa, uuuu.*" They constantly made that noise.

Albertina Dull: When Qaariitaat leave the *qasgi* after painting [their faces] like that, they gather together like that and make noise.

Lizzie Chimiugak: To me it sounded like Qulic'aq and Kangrilnguum Atra. There seemed to be many people going, "*Aaaa, uuu.*" This is the noise they were making. I was actually afraid, but she brought me along. She brought me inside a very large porch, and to me it was the size of this place. It seemed very large.

One doesn't forget things they see when they are small. Along the corner or back wall of the large porch was a frozen piece of sod. It was evidently the doorway of the *elagyaq* [partially underground storage cache], a piece of frozen sod. After prying it from the ground while it's frozen, they probably smooth it and place it there; it was the door of the *elagyaq*.

On this side was a door, the door of the home, and on this side was another door. I paid close attention to something I saw when I was small. She immediately brought me inside the left [doorway], and she held my bowl.

When we went inside, I saw a very large home and there were two large *akitek* [log headrests], its log posts, and those two over there had a seal-oil lamp, and they had those small, braided ropes [to hang the lamps]. My, when I used to observe things! They had small, braided grass ropes situated across from one another. I think it was Nasgaum Arnaan and the late Atsaq. Kangrilnguum Arnaan was probably along the right side.

Then when we went inside, the other one filled our bowl with *akutaq* among other things, and one of those very large and appetizing *cegg'aq*. A bowl like this, they placed a whole piece on top for both of us, even the one across.

Then when we went out, I don't remember what other house we entered.

She probably would have gone inside Kangrilnguq's family home, or I think they had an adjoining porch. Then I don't have a memory of what we did afterward. We probably went in and out of houses.

Angalgaq: Iciw' Qaariitaalriit.

Neng'uryar: Quyurmeng ayallret ak'a, mikelngurugaat nevum nallumeggni aciakun. Angalkum-kiq pillrullii.

Angalgaq: Under the ground ayagluteng, tua-i-ll' nauggun tayim' anluteng. Tangtullrua-gguq ayagaqami.

Cingyukan: Aipaagni-wa imkut angalkum pivkalallruyugnarqai.

Neng'uryar: Yaa, angalkut pivkalallruit. Nevum aciirulluteng tua-i, qagg'un-llu anlliniluteng yaaqvaggun.

Cingyukan: Ing'errlugarni-am tuar Qaariitaat anellrat. Tua-i-w' tamaa-i Qaariitaat, Ing'errlugarteggun anellrunilarait Qaariitaat.

Augna tang qanemcin aanilrianun ayuqekuskeka. Iciw' piciryauktullruameng yuut imkut, wagg'uq aanirluteng. Aaniquneng tua-i yuuk iterciqelriik.

Neng'uryar: Aanillratni pillrulliniunga; Qaariitaami piyukelqa.

Cingyukan: Nuu Qaariitaaq camek nagutaituq.

Neng'uryar: Aanaullruuk taukuk!

Cingyukan: Ava-i elitaqsaaqekek'a. Yuuk iterlutek, tuaten tua-i aqumlliciumanganatek. Tua-i-ll' uavet elliqagnek akutagnek; akutak tang qaralirlutek waten. Qukaagni-wa naunraquinraak.

Qantaa qaralirluku waten. Tekermek waten piluku. Tua-i-ll' qukaagnun naunraquineq elliluku.

Tua-i-ll' tunkagnek ugkuk uitauraqerlutek. Yuk cakemna qanerturalria, "Aanirtua cikiqercia. Aanirtua cikiqercia." Qaillun cali iqulirluku. Tua-i-ll' tang tuaten pirraartelluku tuaken akutaarmek tegulluteng pamatmun eg'arciiqaa. Qaillun-wa tua-i tuaten taq'lallruyugnarqut.

Neng'uryar: Aanillratni-w' pillrulliunga tuani.

Cingyukan: Piciryauktarluteng waten uksuarmi.

Ruth Jimmie: You know those who participated in Qaariitaaq [the distant past].

Lizzie Chimiugak: Those who went as a group long ago, many children who unknowingly went underground. I wonder if a shaman was responsible for causing them to do that.

Ruth Jimmie: They traveled under the ground, and then they exited somewhere. [Elsie Tommy] said that she used to see [the place where they exited] when she traveled.

Albertina Dull: A shaman was probably responsible for allowing them to do that.

Lizzie Chimiugak: Yes, shamans were responsible for causing them to do that. They went underground, and they evidently exited a great distance away up north.

Albertina Dull: I think the place where the Qaariitaat exited was Ing'errlugaat [Mud Volcanoes north of Nelson Island]. They mention that the Qaariitaat exited through Ing'errlugaat.

That story you told [earlier], I associate it with *aanilriit* [those practicing Aaniq, a ceremony in which *aanak* (two men dressed as "mothers") led children from house to house receiving food]. Since those people had many customs, they would practice what they call Aanirluteng. When they had Aaniq, two people would enter.

Lizzie Chimiugak: I evidently [gained awareness] when they had Aaniq; I thought it was during Qaariitaaq.

Albertina Dull: No, Qaariitaaq has no restrictions.

Lizzie Chimiugak: Those two were *aanak!*

Albertina Dull: I just recognized what you were saying. Two people enter, and they seem to have a [mat] prepared for them to sit on like that. Then when they reached the area out there, [they gave them] two *akutak;* the *akutak* had designs like this. In the center were single salmonberries.

They made a design like this on the [contents of the] bowl. They did this [to the *akutaq*] with a pinky finger. Then they placed a single salmonberry in the center of [each bowl of *akutaq*].

Then when they gave it to them, the two out there would just sit. There would be a person back there continually saying, "*Aanirtua,* give me some, *aanirtua,* give me some." He also said something at the end. Then after he did that, they took a little pinch of *akutaq* from there and threw it behind them. I think they would finish with that.

Lizzie Chimiugak: I must have [gained awareness] when they had Aaniq.

Albertina Dull: They carried out many customs during fall.

Kellarvik

Avegyaq: Uumek niiteqarrallrulrianga Kellarvigmek, kia taum qanrutkellrani, atra nalluyagutaqa. Tua-ll'-am kangiiturtua wiinga, "Ca-gguq pitekluku tauna Kellarvigmek atengqerta?"

Qanemciuguq-gguq. Qanemcim-gguq ilakaa. Ak'a-gguq tamaani yuut ukurmiut tua-i Up'nerkillermiungqellriit ua-i ak'a, cami-ll' tayim' ayagnillrua, ugna Up'nerkillermiuq nunaurtellra.

Tua-i tamatum ciungani ukut-gguq Qaluyaat inerquutangqelalriit makunun irniameggnun, panimeggnun, panimeggnun-wa tua-i inerquutangqelallruut naken aipangesqevkenaki.

Paniteng ilulnguk'lallruit. Arcaqerluku-gguq una nunamiumek tua-i cucukliqaasqevkenaku tukuungraan.

Una-gguq qaraliqniluku, waten tua-i uksurpak yuunginanermeggni neqnun kanarnatkameggni, qaraliqaat-gguq yuum amllerem kainiqurallni.

Uksuq iquklipailgan ak'a-gguq kainiquratullruut tua-i tuaten. Kaigpalriartangqerraqluni-gguq allrakut iliitni.

Tua-i-gguq-am ua-i ugna Kellarviuruyutekellrukii arnam taum, ukurritallrem nunamiunun.

Caurrluni-ll' pia tayima temirnerurrluni-llu-w' pillilria; tua-i taukut ukurrisngaviin tua-i cakairucameng-am tua-i neqkaarairucameng tauna ukurrarteng pilliniat tua-i piyugngaurallrani kingunranun ayaagaasqumaniluku.

Tua-i taukuk cakiigken tua-i qanrutenqegcaarluku, "Tumevni yuukaunring'erpet peknanriquvet tuqungerpet maanicetun pillerkarpetun piciquten."

Tua-i-am tuaten piatni ayalliniluni irniangutminek, irniarraminek aamartetuamiu tunumiayaarluni.

Tuaten tua-i unugcuutengluni wall'u-gguq-qaa ataucimek wall'u-gguqqaa malrugnek. Tuartang wii tangrruallemni atauciuciqelria, aipaa taugaam tekitniararnganaku, tangrruaqallemni tauna mikelnguyagaq.

Ayaagaurlulliniaqelria tua-i canun tekitaqami, iciw' paugna napangqellria; napanun tekitaqami qeltairiluni qeltairiqerluni qemagarciluni-ll' mangirruraqaqluni tamaa-i ayaagallinilria.

Kellarvik[40]

Anna Agnus: I first heard about Kellarvik when someone told a story about it, but I have forgotten the person's name. Then I asked, "Why is that place called Kellarvik?"

S/he said it's a story. S/he said the source [of the name] comes from a story. S/he said long ago, the people of this area, there is a place called Up'nerkillermiut that is down the coast, and I'm not sure when Up'nerkillermiut was founded.

Before that time, they say the people of Nelson Island cautioned their children, their daughters, not to marry someone from another region.

They were protective of their daughters. They especially told a person not to desire to marry someone from the inland region, even though he was wealthy.

It is said that part of their way of life, as they were living, during winter before food was available, many people constantly experienced famine.

Before winter ended, long ago, it is said they constantly experienced starvation. They said people experienced severe famine during some years.

It is said the source of the name Kellarvik originates from a woman [from Nelson Island] who had married someone from the inland region and moved there as a daughter-in-law.

I'm not sure how old she was at the time, she had probably become an adult at the time; they say the people in the village where she came to live as a daughter-in-law, when they ran out of food, they told their daughter-in-law that while she was able, she should return to her hometown.

Her in-laws thoroughly told her, "During your journey, although you are near death and unable to walk and die, your fate will be the same as it is here."

When they told her that, she evidently left, carrying on her back her only child, who she was breastfeeding.

That's how many months old that child was, either one or two months. When I imagined how many months old that child was, it seems that child was a month old, near two months.

She evidently traveled on, and when she'd come upon certain things, you know how there are trees in the inland region; when she'd come upon trees, she'd strip the bark, and she'd store some away and periodically chew on them as she traveled on.

Tua-i camek-llu taquarutkailami taquarraunani ayallrullinilria.

(Ilii katangramku waniw' nallunrilutacirramtun qanemcikqata'arqa.)

Ayaagalliniaqelria tua-i, tua-i-ll' ingrinek tangerkengangengami tua-i cenarmiunguluki ingrit niitetuamiki call' nallunrilamiki tungiitnun ayaagalliniluni.

Tua-i pivakarluni Nanvarugmun-wa tua-i kanallilria, ceniikun-qaa tamaa-i ayagtuq wall'u-qaa ingrit qaingatgun ayagtuq.

Tua-i pivakarluni kangarpakarluni tua-i nanevpall'er pellugngamiu, kuigungalngurmek kanarngami nanvauyuk'ngermiu, agna akia qaillun arvillerkaminek piami, naspaaqerluku pillinia, tuar-gguq arvirciqkii, tamaa-i uksuunrilan pillikii.

Tua-i tuaten tua-i mangirruraqalallminek aamaksuaraagni kanevnengaqagnek tauna irniarraurluni aamarteqaqullmikun anertequraurluan.

Tua-i pivakarluni akulkitaralriamek tekicami tuani tua-i aqumgaurarraarluni, naspaanaluni tua-i tuaggun, uaggun ua-i Kellarvigmek atngelriamun, aqumluni tuavet tua-i naspaanaluni.

Tauna irniani aamarqurarraarluku elliluku, tauna-ll' kellarvini caniqliliulluku.

Tua-i ayarurluni aqvaarkauluku et'utacia nasperturluku tua-i. Aqvanrilngaunaku-w' tua-i unicaaqellikii.

Arvilliniluku, arvirturalliniluku qukani pellugturluku.

Tua-i tekicami qaill' una-qaa nenglengellrunrakun piuq, wall'u-qaa tua-i atu'urkailami tua-i taq'illruuq?

Ikavet akianun tekicami taukut akluni ciurturarraarluki, peluracinraat umyuaqluki uitaluni. Tua-i-am teguqautellruami mangirrurararkami ilarriinek tuavet aqumluni urugciarluni, mangirrurarraarluku, atam-gguq ellii naspaanaluni piiyaaqelriim, tua-i-gguq tang ivenqigtellerkaminek arenqialnguq caperrsullrulria.

Tua-i tayima tamaa-i elpengyugallermini, niitelallruami-llu-gguq unani cenami tua-i-w' upallernek tayima cenami unani uqurcuraralrianek, unani nunaulrianek imarpiim ceniini umyuarteqluni tamatum tungiinun ayagnaluni. Tua-i piiyaaqerraarluni tauna tua-i irniani unitelliniluku, tauna-ll' kellarvini.

Since there was no food to take along during her trip, she evidently left without any provisions.

(Yes, although I've forgotten part of the story, I'm going to tell it now to the best of my knowledge.)

She continued on, and when she started to see mountains, since she had heard that there were mountains in the coastal area and knew about them, she continued walking toward them.

Then after a while, she probably reached Nanvaruk [Baird Inlet, Large *nanvaq* (lake)], and did she travel along the banks of [Baird Inlet], or did she travel along the mountains.

Then after continually walking, when she left the large lake, when she reached a body of water that looked like a river, although she thought it was a lake, since she was pondering how to cross it, when she attempted to cross it, she felt as though she could get across, probably since it wasn't during winter.

Because she breastfed the child from time to time as her small breasts filled with a little bit of breast milk from continually chewing [on bark] like that, her poor child stayed alive.

When she came upon a narrow crossing [in the river], after sitting there a while, she planned to attempt [to cross] along that place, down in the place that is now called Kellarvik [Storage bag]. She sat there planning to try to cross.

After breastfeeding her child, she put him down and set her *kellarvik* beside [the child].

Using a walking stick, she measured the depth of the river, planning to return [for the child]. She probably left [the child] certainly planning to go back and get the child.

She slowly crossed the river, [the water] reaching above her waist.

When she arrived [on the other side]—was it because it had started to get cold, or did she decide not to go back since she didn't have any clothing to use?

When she arrived on the other side after wringing out her clothing, she thought of the bark and stayed. Since she had taken a little [bark] to chew on, she sat down there to warm up, and after chewing on [the bark], after planning to attempt [to return], she felt very hesitant and afraid to wade in the water again.

Back when she became aware of life, since she had heard about people along the coast who had moved in their efforts to obtain seal blubber, thinking about settlements along the ocean, she planned to head in their direction. After contemplating, she left her child, and also her *kellarvik*.

Tua-i pivakarluni natmun una tekita, taukunun nunarrarnun tua-i. Tua-i nalqigutekluni ellminek, tekicami taukut qanrulluki. Ak'a-llu tayima-gguq angayuqairutellrullilria-llu.

Taukuk-am ciuniulliniluku irniangeqayuilnguunkuk; tua-i-w' irniakek unguvasciigalnguurilriagnun taukugnun ciunillinilunі.

Tauna tua-i irniani qanrutekngaku, taum tua-i angutiin egmiakacagaq aqvallruyaaqellinia tauna irniara. Tua-i-wa yugg'ailamek elkek quyalutek tauna tua-i aqvallruyaaqellinikii.

Maaten tua-i tekitaa tekicungami, ayakpanritlilria-ll'-am tayim' cukamek. Tekitaa tauna nunapiim tua-i qainganun elliqallrullinikii waniwa kellarvia-gguq-wa caniani, imarluni-gguq napat qeltaitnek.

Tua-i-gguq tauna imna tukarturayaalliniluni-ll' waniwa tukallrek-llu taukuk iluturillinilutek. Ukuk-llu-gguq ukiutellinilutek tua-i, kakangcaa-llu pikna piurallra call' qeltairutliniluni. Tuqullrulliniluni-gguq.

Tauna tua-i kellarvia taugaam ut'rutliniluku-qaa? Tauna tua-i tayima-gguq tayim' taum yugg'aqlikii ug'um Kellarviim. Tua-i-gguq-am tauna ua-i ugna Kellarvigmek at'lek, taum tua-i Kellarviuruyutekellrua.

Tamaa-i-gguq ak'a kaitullratni yuut inerquumatullruit ukut wan' Qaluyaat yuggaita paugkumiumek kina imna arnaq uingesqevkenaku. Tuaten-gguq amllerqunek tuaten ukurritat ayatullruut kaigem nalliini kingunengyarluteng. Tua-i.

Cakcaaq

Unangik: Waniw' tua-i nangnermun wavet waniw' tekitukut, wavet Cakcaamun waniw'. Tua-i uniciiqluku tua-i.

Wangkuta taugaam ullaketaatuaput man'a. Una wani, man'a maa-i kuik asguqvut, yugnek tua-i avaken ayagluni ciuliamtenek nerqilriaruuq man'a kuik, neqtuluni-llu.

Avaken tailuteng nunat waten tua-i una waniw' tua-i uksuarmi caumatuat man'a kuik. Uksullranun neqairucuituq man'a, yaavet up'nerkallranun, kiallranun.

Makut maa-i kuiget augkut uaqlimta agkut-llu, ing'um taugaam yaa-i Qanrangam aipirturaa, aipirturyaaqekii.

Man'a maa-i neqtuqapiartuq; augkut ciuliamta tayim' ciuqliita-llu man'a maa-i nayutullruat. Taluyarpagpall'ernek augkucinek napalrianek taluyiryugtait taluyituluku, capluku tua-i waten.

As she was traveling, I'm not sure which place she reached, a small settlement. She told her story to the people there when she arrived. And she had probably lost her parents by then.

A couple who had no children received her; she was received by a couple whose children couldn't live.

When she mentioned her child, the husband immediately went back to get her child. They were probably grateful and went to get that child since they didn't have any children.

He finally reached [the baby], and he probably didn't travel very fast at the time. When he reached it, he saw that she had placed the baby on the tundra, and her *kellarvik* was right beside him, filled with tree bark.

They say that small [baby] had been kicking, and the place where his legs had been kicking had made a deep depression. And these two [heels] had formed holes, and the top of his head where [he had been moving] also had no skin. [The baby] had evidently died.

Did he only bring home her *kellarvik?* That person is probably the only person [buried there] at Kellarvik. That place down there called Kellarvik, it is said that story is the reason why it was given the name Kellarvik.

It is said back when people experienced famine, the people of Nelson Island cautioned women not to marry someone from the inland region. It is said many times that women who married people from the inland region and moved there would leave for their hometown during starvation times. That's it.

Cakcaaq[41]

Simeon Agnus: We have arrived at the last village site, to Cakcaaq here. We'll leave this place. But we come to this place often.

The river that we have gone up, this river has fed people from the time of our ancestors, and there are many fish here.

People from villages out there come to this place and spend a lot of time on this river during fall. This river has fish available up until winter, until spring, until summer.

Among these rivers downriver from where we are and the ones across there, Qanrangaq across there is another river that is comparable.

This river has a lot of fish; our ancestors and those before them stayed here [along this river]. Those who wanted to set wooden fish traps in the river would set those very large wooden fish traps by making a weir on the river.

Tua-i man'a kuik man'a avaken ayagluni ciuliamtenek ciuqliitnek-llu nerqiuq man'a kuik.

Uksuqan tuamtell' tua-i kuvyat atam un'gani uaqliqu'urluteng tua-i; maa-i piiyaurtellriit makut tan'gurraat, caman' cikum aciani.

Waniw' uum wani makut maan' avatmini, makut nunarugaat pavavet kelumtenun neqai neqeksaaqekni, kiingan taugaam akakiiget imkut angkayalriit qaurturpallraat, maani tua-i iliini pitauyuitut, mat'umi kuigmi, akakiiget.

Ilumun tua-i man'a kuik man'a nerqiuq, nerqipiartuq yum'inek man'a. Uksumi, kiagungraan neqa tua-i pelluyuunani.

Maa-i atam naunraam nalliini augkut tua-i kenilci qaurtut itetuut. Cikukan-llu, cikuqaqan manignat iterluteng, cuukviit-llu kinguqliuluteng.

Tuaten maa-i murilkelluku pilangamku, maaten piaqa tuaten itetullinilriit. Manignat ciuqliuluteng, taugken qaurtut ak'a asgutuluteng; maa-i atam asgurtut tayima pagaavet. Cikuqaqan-llu cetuluteng.

Qavani-llu kiaqvani qaluluteng capluku, qalurpall'ernek. Anagutsiyaagaqata neqet, qassayagaat mikcuaraat qaill' angtalriit amllessiyaagaqata, tauna tua-i ikirrluku kiturtelluki tuaten.

Tua-i ilumun man'a ukuni kuigni tamalkuitni neqtunqurrauguq. Neqa tamalkuan waniw' qemangqaa mat'um maa-i kuigem.

Takngami amavet, ing'um yaa-i, tevanquulria ingna, kangia tekisngaa qam'um, ingrim qam'um kia-i waten ayuqelriim nangellra.

Amna-llu kuigput, Nightmute-armiuni kuigput kassuusnganritqerlutek waten qemimek avaqlingqeqerlutek ingrimek. Tuaten tua-i ayuquq man'a.

Tua-i man'a maa-i, makut maa-i tan'gurraat elpengameng elpeksagucamegteggu augkut-llu yaaqlimta, uksumi manarluki-ll' manignat mayurqetuit atam, iliini picuaqluteng, manarluki manignat.

Avani kapurluki taugaam pitullruaput tamaani.

Ing'um yaa-i tayim' tekiciiqerput avayaa ukatmun, camaggun taugaam anen'erluni; tamaani tamaa-i kapurluta pitullruukut wangkuta.

Kuik tua-i kepelmun tugerluku qaill' neqututaluku, manignanek. Ki-

This river here, since the time of our ancestors and those before them, has fed people.

When winter comes, fishnets will be downriver situated up and down the river these days; that's what young men are starting to do today, [setting mesh fishnets] under the ice.

This river has all species of fish that are available in all the villages, reaching the area behind our village, but only the large *akakiiget* [broad whitefish] that are large whitefish aren't caught in this river.

Indeed, this river has provided food to people, it has truly fed its people. During winter and even during summer, fish is always available.

During this time of year when salmonberries are ripe for picking, the type of fish you cooked, *qaurtut* [humpback whitefish], enter the river. And when it freezes, right after freeze-up burbot enter, and pike come in next.

When I started paying attention to this place, I learned that they enter the river in that order. The burbot enter first, but the *qaurtut* go up the river first; they are going upriver to the headwaters at this time. And at freeze-up they will go downriver.

And a good distance upriver, they block the river with a weir and dipnet, using very large dip nets. When there are too many fish, when there are a great number of *qassayagaat* [round whitefish] that are small, about this size, they open [the weir] and have the fish pass.

It is indeed true that this river, among all the rivers around, has the most fish. This river has every kind of fish in it.

Since it is a long river, you see how that is a valley over there, the river reaches the upper part of that place up there, the place where the mountain up there tapers.

And our [Tuqsuk] river, the river of those of us who live in Nightmute, [the rivers] almost meet and have a hill, a mountain separating them. That's how this river is.

And this river here, when young men started to learn what this place was like, including people in villages [like Chefornak and Kipnuk] outside our area, in winter they fish for burbot with hooks and bring them up, and sometimes they catch a lot when they jig for burbot.

In the past, we only caught them by spearing them.

We will reach the tributary of that place over there that goes in this direction, but it has an exit down there; we would spear fish there.

We'd chop a hole in the ice crosswise along the river and make it a certain

turturluteng erenrungraan. Kapluki mayurtaqluki.

Ilumun tua-i man'a kuig' man'a neqtuqapiartuq tua-i. Iqluvkenii waniw' qanertua. Neqtuuq. Makuni kuigni am'umi-ll' amalirnemini am'umi, mat'um amatiinelnguq neqtunquqapiarauguq man'a maa-i kuik.

Ukuk-ll' avaqliik paluqtaat pivailgata ping'ermek mat'um taugaam anangqalukek.

Man'a maa-i, man'a kuik qagalvallrii tangrrarci tua-i pian' ankumta. Pavani-ll' akiani qeminun pulamaluteng cali mat'umun maa-i ellngalriit qagatiinun.

Avavet Kassiglurmiut keluat nuuqerluku nanevpallraat kuigluteng, ukatmun taugaam carvanirluteng.

Una tua-i waniw' tua-i makut maa-i kuiget imutun tua-i qagatekelriatun tua-i ayuqluku. Neqet iluvarluteng, taugaam kiimeng akakiiget augkut qanrutkellrenka, caqa'arqameng taugaam pitetuut tamakunek.

Waten-llu kiani, qamani kia-i kiaqvaarni caqutaarluki, caqulluki; kuvyaq atercelluku angyak akiqliqlutek, kuvya-w' call' uatiigni.

Amllessiyaagaqameng neqet qairuluteng ayagaqluteng; tuaten tua-i pituut maani amllessiyaagaqameng neqet.

Cali waten cikuqata'arqan qaurtussuurqameng qamani Qangllurpagmek pitukiitni kiatmun takluni, nakirneruluni; tamaani cali tamaa-i Tuqsugmiut augkut yaaqliput Cevv'arneq, Qipneq, aqvatetuut, maaken maa-i.

Wangkuta-llu nunakestaini maani qaill' yugmek inerqurisciigatukut, wangkuta Yup'igni neq'legmek, taugaam apertualuku pituat; avaken ayagluteng tuaten tua-i ayuqut.

Aperturluku neqnek, can'giiret-llu pugkata nani kuigmi aperturluki, cali apertutuluki. Waten iirumavkenaki. Yuum ataucim nallunritevkenaki, yugnun tua-i angutnun aperturluki.

Taugaam pingraan man'a, neq'lingraan, qessamkani wangkuta uksumi neqput nurutetuut ilaitni. Waten taugken angun pingnatugturalria nurusngaitqapiarluni uksurpak kiagluki-ll' neqai. Tuaten tua-i ayuquq.

Yup'igni wangkuta tuaten tua-i, neqkeurluamteki wangkuta Yup'igni makut neqet, qaillun tua-i waten ilaluta makunek nerengramta tua-i maa-i,

width, and [spear] burbot. They'd continually pass although it was during the day. We'd spear them and bring them up.

Indeed, this river has a large amount of fish. I'm not lying to you now. There are many fish in this river. Among all the rivers around, and compared to the one that is beyond it, this river has the most fish.

And the [Urumangnaq and Talarun rivers] that are situated beside it, before there were beavers around, although they had an availability of fish, this river had more fish than they did.

You will see this [Qalvinraaq] River's very large lake source [Baird Inlet] when we go out up there. And inland on the other side, the tributaries that drain out to this river's lake source go into the hills.

Almost reaching the area behind the village of Kasigluk, there are very large lakes that have rivers, but their currents flow in this direction.

This [Qalvinraaq River] is like a lake source to the rivers around. The fish come around, but they only catch the *akakiiget* that I mentioned once in a great while [in this river].

And upriver, in the upper part of the river, they do the kind of fishing they call *caqutaarluki, caqulluk;* two boats situated across from one another drift a mesh net, with another net downriver from them.

When there are too many fish, they travel in groups like a wave; that's what fish do around here when there are too many.

And right before freeze-up when they fish for *qaurtut* in the place up there they call Qangllurpak [Big *qanglluq* (deep hole in a riverbed)], an area [along the river] that is a long straight stretch heading upriver; people also go there from Toksook Bay and the villages beyond ours, including Chefornak and Kipnuk, to get fish from this river here.

And those of us who live in the area, we Yup'ik people cannot caution other people not to go to a place that has fish, but they reveal a place [where fish are available]; that's how they've been since long ago.

We tell them where the fish are, and when blackfish become available in a particular river, we also reveal that place. We don't hide those places from others. That place isn't known by just one person, but we reveal those places to men everywhere.

Although this river has a lot of fish, those of us who are lazy, some of us run out of fish during winter. But a man who continually makes an effort at subsisting won't run out of fish to eat all winter, and his fish will last until summer. That's what it's like.

Since it's our customary food as Yup'ik people, although we supplement our diet with other foods these days, even the [non-Native] people who are

cangakevkenaki-ll'-am waniw' ilamta nerlaqait taquaput. Cangaksugnaunaki elpecei, assikluki tuaten ilait.

Tua-i Kass'allamek mat'umek nerenritut avaken ayagluteng. Makut maa-i irniaput-llu kass'aturpallungeng'ermeng taugaam neqput nerait makut mikelngumta.

Cakcaaq-llu kiugna kia-i amllerem yuum tua-i uitavikellruluku waten neqa tua-i tamayuilan.

Tua-i kiimi makuni kuigni tamalkuitni neqtanggenqurrauguq kiugna tua-i Cakcaaq kiugna, neqairucuinani kiallminun.

Neqa tua-i tamalkuan kiugem kiugum qemangqaa—qassayagaat, qaurtut, cuukviit, naptat ayuqluki. Avaken neq'lirturta angeng'ami.

Una-ll' Cakcaaq neqairucuilnguq maa-i nallunrilkeci tua-i yaavet kiallranun. Kiagaqan nutaan neqet amllenrit itraqluteng.

Cakcaaq una qagateliami amllernek tua-i maavet taklillranun.

Yaa-i-ll' qagatii ingna Nunapicuarmiut keluqliat, qullik'acagaat qagatnguluni. Paugkut tua-i nanevpallraat paugkut Aruq-llu angkayaglun cali nanvaq angtuaq Niugtarmiut keluatni. Tamaa-i wavet wani ellngaumaluteng tua-i.

Neqet anluteng, asgullret anluteng.

Neng'uryar: Cakcaaq-llu kiugna inerquuterluni neq'lek call' kiugna inerquutetangqellruluni.

Nell'eq, nell'eq muralleq Cakcaakun-gguq asguusngaunaku. Tauna taugaam qanemcikellratni niitellruaqa.

Nell'eq asguusngaunaku, nutaraq taugaam muragaq. Asguuciyuitellrulliniuq qanallernek, nell'ernek Cakcaakun kiaggun. Cali-am tua-i kencikluku.

Nutaranek taugaam-gguq nek'ameggnek asguutaqluteng. Muragamek paivngaliurayuiteurlullrung'ermeng, tamaa-i tuaten-am tua-i inerquutengqellrulliniluni.

Kit'ellria-gguq cali, talligmi avategmikun, Cakcaaq tallingqerrnitullruat, kit'ellria cali qaill' pinrilkatni, pitsaqa'artevkenani kit'ellria unguvangaunani.

Inerquutai kiugum Cakcaam amllellruyaaquq neqelguami-w' tua-i Cakcaaq ukanirpak.

traveling with us have been eating our provisions without minding them at all. You don't find them repulsive to eat, and you even like some of the foods.

Since long ago, the people haven't eaten Western foods. And although our children are starting to eat mainly store-bought food, our children are eating our customary foods [on this trip].

And lots of people lived up around that Cakcaaq area since fish were never scarce.

Of all the rivers, Cakcaaq up there has the most fish, never running out of fish [all winter] until summer comes.

All the fish are kept "in the pockets" of that river—round whitefish, humpback whitefish, pike, and Bering cisco alike. It has had the most fish since long ago because it is large.

And this Cakcaaq, you all know that it never runs out of fish all the way until the coming of summer. And when summer comes, then lots of fish go into it.

This is because this Cakcaaq, being long, has lots of lakes connected to it.

And its connecting lake source is that [lake] behind the village of Nunapitchuk, [that lake] is the upper-most lake that is connected to it. And all those large inland lakes [are connected to it], and Aruq is also a huge lake behind the village of Newtok. So they all flow into [Cakcaaq].

Fish come out of them, those that had gone up come out.

Lizzie Chimigak: There were specific admonishments for the Cakcaaq River up there that has fish in it.

They said they couldn't take an old log frame from a home up the Cakcaaq River. That's the only one that I heard them mention.

They wouldn't take an old log that had been used in a home upriver but only a new log. They never brought old log frames from homes up the Cakcaaq River up there. They also treated [the river] with care and respect.

They said they'd only take new logs to build homes up the river. Although there weren't many logs around for those poor people to use, that was one of their admonishments.

And they mentioned a person who fell into the water, they used to say that the Cakcaaq River had arms along the sides, a person who fell in the water by accident that they didn't rescue wouldn't live.

The admonishments for Cakcaaq River used to be many because Cakcaaq has always had an abundance of fish.

Qukailnguq: Augna ava-i tauna Nakrailnguum Atiin, Ussugan imum Cakcaarmiungurraarluni, Cakcaami uitarrarluni, uitallruuq. Imna apa'urluteng una maurluteng-llu anerteqellratni, allrakuni tayim' qavcini, pingayuni-ll' pilliuq.

Cevtarmun-llu tua-i nugtarcameng unayaqaanga maligtesqelluni. Taluyarpani aqvayugluku maani egumlluku can'giircuuciyugluku.

Tua-i-llu tailunuk akmaken quunillrani. Cakcaamun tekillunuk kiavet.

Maaten tekitukuk pelatekaq inga. Tua-i-ll' ketiinun arulairlunuk. Maaten tauna tua-i atrarluni pian—inialirlutek tua-i qaurtunek—Mancuam Atii. Tua-i tut'garaminek-llu aterpagglua, tauna-ll' tua-i aiggarluku.

Nerlunuk. Tua-i tagluta nerluta. Tua-i ukaqvaggun tuani tua-i tuavet tekitellruunga. Qanengssaarluni, Mancuam Atiin apluku cassuqerluku taillranek. Tua-i-ll' kiugaa taluyarpani manignarcuutni egumlluku can'giircuutekluku neqsuuteknaluku aqvaniluku. Tua-i tauna angerluni Mancuam Atii.

Tua-i nerlunuk tua-i yuurqerlunuk-llu taqlunuk piqanemegnegun navercugluku tamana taluyarpii.

Tuani-gguq uksuivigkamini aqumeqarraalriatun ayuquq.

Augkut avani ciuliaput camek neqsuuteteng tamakut neqsuutaitaqameng tuaten tua-i aqumeqarriirniluteng tuavet uitavigkameggnun, uksivigkameggnun qantullruut.

Tua-i pia, pia navercugluku unarciamek.

Augkut-llu waten uksuarmi tamarmeng unarciat makut neqsurcuutet, neqsurcuutekateng can'giirnun tua-i piitenrilkurrluki pitullruit. Tamaa-i aataka-ll' pilallruuq. Allat-llu cali tangvak'nganka tuaten pilallruut.

Kiaguluku tua-i imarpiim ceniinek tamakunek muragtelallruut; muragtelallruut unarcianek.

Makut tua-i muriit, tamakut aruvikumalriit tua-i cakneq tamakut qelkelallruit. Makut-gguq aruvikumalriit elngulartut.

Tua-i-ll' pia Mancuam Atiin camek qanqerluni, qassayaaryugniluni pian qavartarciqnilunuk. Pia, tuani tua-i unarciamek navrutkaminek aqvaciiqniluni.

Michael John: That person named Nakrailnguum Atii, Ussugan, after living at Cakcaaq, he lived there. When their grandfather and grandmother were alive, they stayed there for a number of years, probably three years.

And when they moved to Cevtaq, he asked me to accompany him. He wanted to go and get his large wooden fish trap here, take it apart, and make a blackfish trap out of it.

Then we came from across there when the weather was calm and windless. We arrived up at Cakcaaq.

There was a tent over there when we arrived. Then we stopped below it. When that person came down—they had a lot of humpback whitefish hanging to dry—it was Mancuam Atii. He called me his grandchild, and we shook that person's hand.

We ate. We went up and ate. I arrived there in more recent times. He told stories, and Mancuam Atii asked him why he came. Then he replied that he had come to get his large wooden fish trap for catching burbot so that he could take it apart and use it as a blackfish trap. Mancuam Atii agreed.

We ate and drank tea, and just as we were done [Mancuam Atii] told him that he wanted to trade for his large wooden fish trap.

He said that in his winter camp, it was as though he was going to sit [and not fish] for the first time.

Our ancestors, when they didn't have implements to fish with, they would say that they were going to sit and not harvest in the place where they were going to stay, *aqumeqarriirluteng,* in their winter camps.

He wanted to trade a straight-grained log for [the wooden fish trap].

And in the past, during fall, they always tried to have all the straight-grained logs for making fishing tools, implements for catching blackfish. That's what my father did also. Others I observed were also like that.

During summer, they would go and get logs from the ocean shore; they'd go and get straight-grained wood.

They really valued those types of wood, those *aruvikumalriit.* They said the type of wood called *aruvikumalriit* is pliable.

Then Mancuam Atiin said something to him, and when he said he wanted to get some round whitefish, he said we were going to spend a night. He said that he would go and get a straight-grained log to trade with.

Tua-i qavartarraarlunuk kiani nunallret kiatiitni qassayaarnek pillunuk. Caqutauglunuk, taugaam piliqevkenanuk.

Tua-i anelrartukuk augna qaill' tayim' taktallruuq, qaillun taugaam tayima ellegtaluni; tauna tua-i unarciam taluyaqsunarqelriim avekluku.

Tua-i tekicamegnuk yuurqerlunuk. Tua-i atraamegnuk cenametlinian, maa-i-gguq man'a qiperrlung'ermi-gguq assirtuq, elngurtuq. Tamana tua-i taluyarpak taumek naverrluku.

Tuaten tua-i pillruuq tuaken tua-i aqvalluni arviutellrulliniamiki. Taum-llu tua-i Nakrailnguum Atiin, Ussugan, ikgelkevkenaku-ll' tua-i cangakevkenak' taugaam quyakluku. Tuaten tua-i pillruuq.

Tuani tua-i qanqertuq, nutaan aqumeqirriiqatallerminek.

Augkut imkut Naulalriinkut tua-i cangakluki tamakut neqsuutellni cikutellritnun tua-i uniteng'ermiu-ll' ikna atulallra, tamakut tamaa-i neqsuutni navgulallritnek.

Tuamtell' qanerluni cali, tuani-gguq tua-i uksuarmi taluyarpituuq ketminun.

Tua-i-gguq unuungraan-llu qacaqautaqaki, unuungraan-llu tua-i makluni atrarluni yuugaqluki pitullrui. Yuunritaqateng-gguq (qalviryagmek) imangyuata. Tua-i augna ava-i uumun ikayuqautua.

Kinguqermiut

Unangik: Tua-ll' waniw' ilu'urqa una qanemcikuni quyanaqsaryaaquq. Qanemcikak waniw' apertuqataragka. Tumaralriinkuk kitek qanemcikqerkek.

Kangrilnguq: Taukuk-am nulirqelriik irniangyuitellinilriik tamaa-i tamatum nalliini. Tua-i-llu angalkuq tauna uingan taum irniangyuilamek pillinia aipani mikelngurmek naugivkaryuumakaku tuunraikun, mikelngurmek-wa tua-i qingallerkaanek piqaasqelluku.

Qamkut ingrit, makut maa-i Qaluyaat Nanvarugmun ngelengqellriit, Nanvaruurtellranun; taukut-gguq tua-i Kinguqermiut paqcullinii.

Tua-i Kinguqermiunun ayiimi, ircenrraunilaqait-wa. Pilliniuq taukugnek anngaquralriignek elliraagnek, apa'urluagnek taugaam tua-i avaliqlukek pitangqellinilria.

After spending a night upriver from the old village site, we caught some round whitefish. We seined for fish, but we didn't catch many.

When we went downriver, that [log] was a certain length, and it was a certain width; that straight-grained log was half of a log that is good for making a wooden fish trap.

When we arrived, we drank tea. When we went down, since [the log] was along the shore, he said although it was a little twisted, it was good and pliable. He traded that large wooden fish trap for that.

That's what he did since he had gone and gotten those [logs] and taken them across. And that person Nakrailnguum Atii, Ussugan, didn't think it was too little and didn't mind it and was happy for it. That's what he did.

He said at the time that he was going to just sit and not do anything for the winter because he didn't have any fishing implements.

He was critical of Naulalria [and others], and how he would just leave his fishing tools, even though they froze [in the river], and how he would ruin his fishing implements like that.

And again, he said that he usually set a large wooden fish trap right down below his place.

He said even at night, when the wind was blowing directly against them, he woke up and went down and took them out of the water. He said when you don't take them out they fill [with quicksand]. I just wanted to add to what he said.

Kinguqermiut[42]

Simeon Agnus: Now, it would be good if my *iluraq* told a story now. I'm going to name the story that he will tell now. Tell the story of Tumaralria and [his brother].

Paul John: There was once a married couple who could not bear children in the past. And so the husband asked an *angalkuq* [shaman], since they couldn't conceive a child, if he could use his powers to help his wife become pregnant, he asked if he could help her conceive a child.

These mountains back here, the Qaluyaat end at Nanvaruk [Baird Inlet], [they end] where Baird Inlet is situated. [The shaman] wanted to go to Kinguqermiut [People from the back, from *kingu-*, "rear, behind, back part"].

When he went to Kinguqermiut, they say [those at Kinguqermiut] are *ircenrraat*. He saw two orphan brothers there whose grandfather was taking care of them.

Tua-i-am taukuk apa'urluagnek elliraak aulukaarraak qarutliniak tauna apaurluak elluarrlukek aulukestekakegnun ayaucuglukek, maligtaqukani taum apaurluagnek.

Tua-i egmian-gguq angenricaaquq. Tua-i qarulluku tauna apaurlua, angutngurrniluku-llu cirlaurrniluku, aulukestekegcillerkaagnun taukuk tut'garak ayaucuglukek.

Tua-i unakiutekliniak. Tua-i ut'rullukek. Taukuk-am tua-i ut'rutellregni taumun arnamun irniaqliutarkaurrlukek piamikek, tua-i Tumaralriamek anngaa aterkiulliniluku, uyuraa-ima kituuyaaquq, avaurqa.

Taugaam tua-i inerqullinilukek nunuyakqaqsaunakek yuk'uraasqellukek. Ukut ingrit amalirneratni angliurngatellrulliniuk taukuk.

Tua-i ikani ika-i Engelullugarmiuni-gguq pivakarlutek, taukuk-gguq tua-i aipaqu'urlutek ellami aquiguratuuk. Ilangqeng'ermek avvupakayuunatek.

Tua-i-am pivakarluni aaniignek taum tungliqu'urlukek tua-i irniaqliutellrulliniamikek, aturatek, mecungtellragni nunuyakliniak mecungpakalallratnek. Tua-i-gguq taukuk irniak angniinatek, angniirrlutek.

Atam tua-i angutet iliit Ceturcuryaramun-gguq wavet. Ceturcuryaramek-gguq tauna pilaraat penaqacuggauluni Engelullugarmiut kanani iquatni. Taugaam-gguq entaqami man'a kelua tua-i nunaurtaqluni taum Ceturcuryaram acia.

Piinanermini tamaatmurtellermini nepelkialriignek mikelnguugnek niigarcami paqnayuami uyangtelliniak, Tumaralriinkuk kankuk uyurani-llu. Elpekevkenaku taugaam uyangtestesek tauna.

Tua-i uyangqaqanrakun anngaan uyurani pillinia, "Aling aanamegnuk tang ing'um nunuryungqataryugnarqekiikuk. Kingunemegnun taugaam ut'reskumegnuk."

Tauna tua-i nunuyaklertek pitekluku kingunemegnun utercugyaaqelliniluni anngaa. Waten imat'am pikii, "Qaillun utercarcenuk kingunerpuk nalluluku?"

Aren anngaan pillinia, "Nallunritaqa. Utercugngaukuk utercukumegnuk. Atam tumkapuk maniqernaurqa."

Mer'em-gguq engeliinun iqelqugni waten inglugtun, iqelqugni, talligni mayureskiik meq kevkili, acia un'a ellaurrluni. Maaten-gguq tang uyangtaa uyuraan tumet makut atauciin.

He gently pleaded with the orphans' grandfather that he wanted to take them to parents who would take good care of them, if their grandfather complied.

They say he didn't immediately agree. He kindly pleaded with their grandfather and told him that he was getting older, that his body was becoming weak, that he wanted to bring his grandchildren to a couple who would take good care of them.

So then, he obtained them [for the couple]. Then he brought them home. The two who he brought home, since he had decided that that woman would bear those children, he gave the elder one the name Tumaralria, and I have forgotten the name of his younger brother.

But he had warned [the couple] never to scold them as they raised them. I think those two grew up along the other side of these mountains.

One day while they were over at Engelullugarmiut, it is said those two would always play outside together. Although they played with others, they hardly played separately.

Then one day, since their mother had them one right after the other, when their clothes got wet, she chided them about repeatedly getting their clothing wet. They say her children were sad, they suddenly became disheartened.

One of the men went to a place called Ceturcuryaraq. It is said that the small cliff along the end of Engelullugarmiut was called Ceturcuryaraq. But it is said when the tide went out, land appeared along the shore, the area below Ceturcuryaraq.

While [the man] was heading that way one day, when he heard some children making noises, he became curious and looked down over at them, and he saw that it was Tumaralria and his younger brother down there. But they didn't sense the person looking down on them.

Just as he looked down, the older brother said to his younger brother, "My, I think that our mother over there is going to develop a habit of scolding us. We should return to our home."

His older brother evidently wanted to return home because they had been scolded. This is what [his younger brother] said to him, "How are we to return home not knowing where our home is located?"

His older brother said to him, "I know where it's located. We can return home if we want. Let me show you the path we can take."

When he placed both his pinky fingers like this [palms upward] along the edge of the water and lifted his arms, the water lifted, and the area underneath turned into air. When his younger brother looked inside, he saw one set of tracks.

"Tua-i maa-i makut aqvastellmegnuk tumellri. Aturluki ayagciqukuk tua-i kingunemegnun-llu tekillunuk."

Tua-i meq ellimariaku uyuraan pillinia, "Aling wanirpak tang pinrilengramegnuk, nunuyakenqigeskakuk taugaam pikumegnuk." Anngaangguq ilumunqaallagaa.

Aren tana tua-i niicugnistiik angun tua-i elpekvailgagni kingupiarluni, aaniik ullalliniluku. Tekicamiu itrami eniinun pillinia, "Irniagken-qaa nunuyakellruagken?"

"Tua-i-wam," kiullinia aaniin. "Tua-i-wam mecungpakaryuagnek, mecungellragnek-am pilua aturakegnek nunuyakellrukegka aturakek piteklukek."

Arenqiapaallinia taum, "Arenqiapaa! Nunuyakenqigcaqunakek. Uumiku nunuyakekuvtek utercugngalliniuk kingunermegnun. Uyuraan uumikutellrunrilkaku tamariyaragput ava-i. Uyuraan taugaam uumikulluku tua-i tamarivkarpek'nata tua-i waniw' piqatartukut, tamarivkenata."

Tua-i aaniignek nunuyakenqigtevkenakek.

Tua-i taqnerurcamek, tauna tua-i Tumaralria angarvauluni, wani waniwa Qaluyaani tuknilriaruluni angalkuullrulliniuq.

Aassaqvigmiut

Neng'uryar: Kiani atam ellangeqtaalallruunga carvani kiani Urumangnamek atlegmi. Cakcaaq, Talarutmiut, Urumangnarmiut-wa. Tamaani tamaa-i ellangeqtaalallruunga. Tamaaken-llu avaurpek'naku, Aassaqvigmiunek-llu qanlallrat.

Tamaa-i angyarualrianun maligucugaqama qessakenglua. Cunaw' qialallrullinilrianga.

Alqairutma-ll' pillrania, Qemirrluilngulleq Kuimaralriim Atii alikerrlulallemni tamaa-i Urumangnami, alqama tang uum maligucugyaaqellemni qanruskiinga Uliggaam Atran Aassaqvigmiut-gguq yugturayulirtangqertut, qanerpaukacagarluni-gguq ciutegni ngeleklukek. Umyuarteqa'artua, "Kuimaralriim Atiitun-wa ayuqellilria." Maligucuumiirrlua.

"These are the tracks of the person who went to get us. We will leave using them and return to where we came from."

When he placed the water back down, his younger brother said to him, "My, we shouldn't go now, but we should go only if she happens to scold us again." His older brother suddenly agreed with him.

Before they sensed the man listening to them, he walked back and went to their mother. When he arrived and entered her home he said to her, "Have you scolded your two children?"

"Well," their mother replied to him. "Because they repeatedly get drenched, I scolded them because their clothing was wet."

That person expressed his concern, "My goodness! Don't scold them again. If you scold them again, they can return to where they came from. We would have lost them just now if his younger brother hadn't suggested they leave the next time. But his younger brother suggested they leave the next time and has prevented us from losing them, and so we didn't lose them this time."

Their mother never scolded them again.

When they became adults, Tumaralria was a powerful shaman, and he was evidently a powerful shaman here on Nelson Island.

Aassaqvigmiut[43]

Lizzie Chimiugak: I used to go in and out of awareness up along the mountain stream called Urumangnaq. There was Cakcaaq, Talarutmiut (Residents of Talarun), and Urumangnarmiut (Residents of Urumangnaq). I went in and out of awareness there. And I never forgot things from that time on, even when the people used to mention Aassaqvigmiut [Residents of Aassaqviq (Place that one kept secret)].

When I wanted to accompany people riding in boats, they didn't want to take me any longer. I evidently used to cry.

And when my deceased older sister told me, back when I was a little afraid of the late Qemirrluilnguq, the father of Kuimaralria, at Urumangnaq, when I wanted to accompany them, my older sister, Uliggam Atra [the one Uliggaq is named after] told me that Aassaqvigmiut was occupied by someone who likes to eat people, that it had a very large mouth that reached its ears. I was thinking, "It probably looks like the father of Kuimaralria." I didn't want to accompany them any longer.

Qavani-gguq-wa egkumi, qecignek neq'liurcuutengqelallratni, *plastic*-aamek piyugnaunani. Aminrarnek piaqluki tua-i inguqerruluteng. Maa-i tungunqut mat'um-llu nalliini atunriqait.

Taum-gguq qainga aulikacaarluni. Taum-gguq tangerqunia tegulua tua-vet pilaglua nerciqaanga. Ayagyunermek taqlua alingkacagarlua.

Angalgaq: Qaillun-tam tauna atngellrua Aassaqvigmiunek?

Cingyukan: Akaar-wa tua-i caqallret at'liutelaqait; aciqautaqluki.

Angalgaq: Kina-qaa tayima aassaqluni tuani piqallrukan Aassaqvigmiunek acirluku?

Neng'uryar: Pillrullian-wa.

Cingyukan: Tuaten ayuqut.

Neng'uryar: Uyangliinkut angyaat angyamteni mikellrullruan tamaaggun ayagluteng kangitmurrnganateng. Wiinga tua-i ayagyuumiirrlua tua-i. Ayagyunqigtevkenii-llu yugturayulimun, ayakataksugtengraata, yugturayulimun nernayuklua.

Tamaani tamaa-i Cakcaami-ll' kiani ellangeqtaallruunga; ellangeqtaalallruunga tua-i cumikepiggluki-ll' cumikevkenaki.

Cali-llu ellat waten ayuqsuksaaqellruanka. Usviinii. Nangertaqama ellavut umyuaqeqa'arqamku qukak'acgaani waten akalriim uitanaurtua.

Tua-ll' umyuarteqlua, "Waniwa ayakumta Talarutmiunun tekiskumta waten call' ellarluteng. Ayakumta-ll' Negtemi waten cali ellarluteng. Umkumiunun cali ayakumta ellartarluni."

Angalgaq: Oh, she thought they were in different spheres.

Neng'uryar: Ikamragni patulluta ayalallruamta cingyaamek, kiarcuunata-ll' patumaluta, qimugtetgun ayagtura'urlutullemteni.

She said [that it was] along the corner or back wall, back when they used skins as mats to work on fish and didn't use plastic at all. They called them *aminrat,* and they were work mats for things. These days, they no longer use adult bearded seal [skins].

She said the surface of one of those [skin-work mats] had a lot of blood on it. She said when that thing saw me, it would take me and place me there and butcher me and eat me. I didn't want to go anywhere any longer as I was extremely afraid.

Ruth Jimmie: I wonder how that place came to be called Aassaqvigmiut?

Albertina Dull: Long ago, they gave names to places based on things that occurred; they gave them names.

Ruth Jimmie: So if someone kept a secret there, they would call it Aassaqvigmiut [from *aassaqe-,* "to have a secret"]?

Lizzie Chimigak: [They probably called it that] because that's probably what happened.

Albertina Dull: That's what [place names] are like.

Lizzie Chimiugak: Since Uyangliiq and her family's boat was smaller than ours, they left with that, seeming to head toward the upper part of the river. I didn't want to leave any longer. And I never wanted to leave again, although they were planning to leave to where *yugturayuli* [one who eats humans] was, thinking that *yugturayuli* would eat me.

I also came in and out of awareness up at Cakcaaq; I used to come in and out of awareness, and I didn't closely observe that place.

I also thought worlds were like this. I had no sense at all. When I'd stand, when our world would come to mind, it seemed that I was standing in the very center of something rolling.

Then I thought, "When we leave and we arrive at Talarutmiut, they have their own world. And when we leave, they also have their own world at Nightmute. And when we travel to Umkumiut, there is also another world."

Ruth Jimmie: Oh, she thought they were in different spheres.

Lizzie Chimiugak: Since they used to cover us with a tarp inside a sled when we traveled, and we never looked around as we were covered, back when we poor people only traveled by dogteam.

Igyararmiut

Neng'uryar: Kiugkuni cali nunallerni Igyararmiullret-gguq.

Pim wani Cakcaam avayaa uatmun, maaggun Amatekun. Cimiugam-am tua-i nalluvkenaki.

Amatekun ayagluta naunrarcurqamta, ayainanemteni-ll' iqua qagatngurrluni, qagalvall'er ingrim mengliini qemirtarluni.

Qaugna-ll' ilii uss'aryugluni, man'a-ll' ukatmurtellra ukalirneq ingriq-wa paugna. Qemilirluni. Angluni tauna nanvaq.

Tuavet ankumta, naken maaken iqvaq'erluta qemit iggagneratnek avatiitnek.

Tua-ll' yaavet Igyararmiullernun ayiimta nunallret qertukayagluteng. Avatiit mayurnaqluni. Nunallret.

Igyararmiullret. Natecaraq un'gantuq. Waten-wa tang neqututalria tamana kuiggaq, angyaq tua-i qacalkurluni.

Qagatem tauna, Qagatem kiatiintuq, ingrim mengliini.

Angalgaq: Tua-i-w' nanvarpaagaat iciw' augkut.

Neng'uryar: Qagatnguuq tauna. Tuavet pikumta, kuicuariitgun asguq'erluta, nequtuvkenani.

Ik'ikik mayurluta elanellret, elivellret ak'allakacagaat ilait neviulluki.

Ala-i caaniigmek atam Noah-q tegutellruuq mingulek tungulria. Ak'allak'acagaq kicarraq-llu cali, tegutellruuq.

Tua-ll' tang tamaani ak'a Cimiugaq-gguq maaten yuurtuq ellanguq Igyararmiunek ukut qanernaurtut, Igyararmiullernek.

Cali-gguq tuavet tekitellria ak'a Agayun nallullemteni alangrunrilngaunani. Alangruviullruut-gguq taukut tekiartestemek ak'allaussiyaagameng.

Unangik qanemcillrani tamana qanrutkellrua. Ellii-gguq Cakcaami yuurrluni ellangellruyaaquq, taukut-gguq nutaraunritut. Igyararmiullernek-gguq ukut qanernaurtut.

Ak'aqucuk tamaani yungqetullrulliniuq. Elivrit-llu alaunateng, ilait ne-

Igyararmiut[44]

Lizzie Chimiugak: And at that old village site up there, the place they call Igyararmiullret [the old village of Igyararmiut (People of the *igyaraq* (lake outlet)].

Along a tributary of the Cakcaaq River that heads down, we traveled along Aman River. Cimiugaq [George Chimiugak, Lizzie's husband] knew where it was located.

We traveled along Aman when we'd go and pick salmonberries, and as we traveled, the end became a lake source, a very large lake source along the edge of a mountain, and hills are there.

And some areas up there were eroding, and this area where it heads this way on this side, and there is a mountain up there. There are many hills there. That lake is large.

When we went out to that [lake], we'd pick berries somewhere briefly, from the area along where the hills slope.

And when we traveled to Igyararmiullret over there, the old village site was very steep. You had to climb up along the side. An old village site.

Igyararmiullret. Nacecaraq [High place to scan one's surroundings] is downriver. That slough was about this wide, enough room for a boat to fit through.

That is above Qagan [Lake source], along the edge of a mountain.

Ruth Jimmie: Those pretty large lakes.

Lizzie Chimiugak: That is called Qagan. When we went there, we'd go up its small slough for a little ways, and it wasn't wide.

We went up high, and there were many old house pits, their old graves that are ancient that the ground had covered.

My goodness, Noah took a kettle that had paint on it and was black. It was very old, and he also took a small anchor.

Then Cimiugaq mentioned that when he was born and became aware, the people around would talk about Igyararmiut, Igyararmiullret.

And he said that a person who arrived there, back when we didn't know about God, would have ghost encounters. He said that people encountered ghosts in that place when they arrived there since that village was extremely old.

When Unangik was telling stories, he mentioned that. He said that he was actually born at Cakcaaq and became aware there, but he said that place wasn't recently founded. He said the people around would talk about Igyararmiullret.

viulluki.

Aka'araungraan caanillregnek tuaken, callruaraat uitaluteng, piuqerraallret makut mingulget, ciuliamta piqarraallrit minguirtetullret.

Caanicuarmek taitellruyaaqut, wiinga tua-i maantesqumavkenaku alinglua ak'allaussiyaagan. Nallumni maani agallrulliniuq.

Egcetellrulliaqa-ll'-am. Wiinga alikluku alangruuyutunilallruitki, piunga, "Caaniik-mi ingna agalria." Akaurrluni maavet tekitellra.

Tua-ll' aiparma pianga, ak'a-gguq agamaaquq. Piaqa, "Aling ciin alangruyutullrungraata."

Tua-ll' pianga canrituq-gguq ak'allauguq nelguteknaurput. Nalluatni-ll' anlluku.

Tamaani tang qaingatni ucuryullrulrianga, man'a qemi qaill' pitaa. Una wani nulkaumaluni nevuq. Maaten tang piunga yull'eq kiugna qamiqukuyua uitaluni. Keggutai ayuqucimegcetun uitaluteng, nulkaumangssaarpek'nateng.

Cingyukan: Kegguteklaki-tuq tayima.

Neng'uryar: Kegguteksugyaaqluki. Tua-i qercurpak imkut.

Assik'acagarluteng, naliat-llu augaumavkenani. Una-w' cali qamiqukuyuk cali uitalria waten.

Angalgaq: Ayagyuarulliami-w' keggutekegcillilria.

Neng'uryar: Ala-i keggutai-w' naamaluteng assik'acagarluteng. Cimiugaam qanlallra neq'aqerluku. Yuurtuq-gguq maaten Igyararmiunek qanraqluteng. Ala-i tauna tang.

Clean-arluteng keggutai. Ucuryuglua. Ak'a-w' man'a mamtulria nevuq cali.

Ak'a yaassiignun ektullratni, ektullrulliniitki waten piqa'urlurluki, tauna tayim' nevum qaingantellruyaaqelria; aciqsigiluni.

Paugkut-wa call' elivellret alailnguut ilait, ilait nevumun ilapliyusngaluteng. Tamaa-i-w' alailuteksuarallrit-llu.

Ingriq paugna canimenaku. Naunrilartuq taugaam taum qainga. Tuaken iqvalallruukut.

Keluvut-llu paugna paqtengssaarpek'naku ingrim tunglirnera. Aling

It was evidently occupied long ago. And their old grave markers were visible, and some are covered by land.

Although it was old, [he took] an old kettle from there, and there were a few belongings there, those painted ones that were the first to come around, those first ones that our ancestors had that would lose their paint.

They actually brought home a small kettle, but I didn't want it to be here out of fear, because it was too old. It was evidently hanging inside [our home] without my knowledge.

I had them throw it away. I was afraid, since they mention that they can cause people to encounter ghosts, I said, "What about that kettle that is hanging over there." It had arrived [in this village] a while back.

My husband told me that it had been hanging for a long time. I said to him, "My, why [is it there], even though they say those things can cause hauntings."

Then he said to me that it's okay to keep it in our home since it was old. Then I removed it from our home without their knowledge.

I was in awe on top of that [old village site], and I'm not sure how tall the hill was. There was a crack in the ground. I saw a person's skeleton with its skull back there. Its teeth were in their original condition, and they weren't cracked at all.

Albertina Dull: I wish they were my teeth.

Lizzie Chimiugak: I really wanted those teeth. They were very white.

They were very nice, and not one of them had come out. Then there was a skull that was situated like this.

Ruth Jimmie: It probably had nice teeth because it was a young person.

Lizzie Chimiugak: My, it had all its teeth, and they were in very good condition. I recalled what Cimiugaq used to say. He said when he was born, they spoke of Igyararmiut. My, it was that place.

Its teeth were clean. I was in awe. And here the ground in the surrounding area was thick.

Back when they used to place them inside boxes, since they placed them inside [caskets] positioned like this, that [dead body] was probably once on top of the ground; it had gotten low.

Then some other graves that were visible up there had become part of the ground. And their small *alailutet* [grave goods] were visible also.

It was close to the mountain up there. But there are many salmonberries on top of that. We used to pick berries there.

naunrilaryaaqsugnarqelria tang. Pengut, pengut-wa makut, ingrim menglekngaki.

Cakcaam Painga

Neng'uryar: Mikcuayagaulua tamaa-i ellangeqtaarlua uani pelatekaratullerput neq'aqerluku tauna ellangeqalqa pelatekarrlainaat, uksiviullrunrilnganateng taugaam.

Pilu'uggaarlua tang imkugnek piluguugnek—kiagungraan pilu'ugteurlutullruamta—anevkaqiitnga. Anlua pelatekat, tuani cunaw' paingani Cakcaam.

Anlua tang piunga tamaa-i cumiksiyaayuitellemni eliverpall'er pikna ingrim qacarnerani. Cunaw' tang Panruum Atra. Ukut wani imkut Nanugaankut aanallrat. Taunaurluq imna Kumlilriim aanapialqellinikii.

Makut tang atralriit ingrimek, uvertengraan-llu pelatekaralallrullinilriit. Naulalriinkut, Canaar-llu, Canaaraurluq-llu, Uliggaam-llu Atra.

Tamaa-i angerturyutullemni kass'allarnek, angerturluteng. *Blue*-aaruluteng tang angrit. Cucuk'acagarlua tangssuarluki. Tua-i-ll' alqaagka kiturlutek.

Tua-i-ll' Canaaraam-am ullagarrlua, waten piqerluni, wangni kass'allaq angeq *blue*-aaq. Tua-ll' pianga, "Pik'um cikillruakut."

Maaten pikavet piaqa eliveq pikna. Tua-ll' ukverlua kass'allauyukluku ava-i ayagarrluni.

Tamuassaagyaaqekek'a tang, maaten tang yuvrirqa, naterkaq. Naterkat iciw' imkut nat'raqatarqata-ll' neruraurlutullrukait maaten cumikua. Waten uum elirqellra naterkam taungulliniluni. Kass'allauyuksaaqekek'a.

Imumi cali angernek tuvqaktullerci neq'ak'laraqa.

Billy-m-llu imum' qavavirqaarluni aataka yuurqerkiteurlulallra caarralatllu avauyuilkenka yaassiigenqupayagaat. Tauna neq'ak'larqa.

And we didn't go to the area behind us, the area toward the mountain. There probably are a lot of salmonberries there. The hills, there were hills around, as they were situated along the edge of the mountain.

Cakcaaq River Mouth[45]

Lizzie Chimiugak: When I was very small and coming in and out of awareness, the place down where we used to have a tent camping site, I recall the time that I became aware when there were only tents around, but it didn't seem like a winter camp site.

After putting my skin boots on—since we used to wear skin boots although it was summer—they had me go outside. I went outside, and there were tents, evidently there at the mouth of Cakcaaq River.

I went outside and saw, back when I didn't pay close attention to things, that there was a very big grave on the side of the mountain. It was evidently Panruum Atra [the one that Panruk is named after]. It was the deceased mother of Nanugaq and siblings. It was that dear one who was evidently the real mother of Kumlilria.

People came down from the mountain, and although it was slanted, they camped with tents there. There was Naulalria and Canaar, dear Canaar and Uliggaam Atra [the one Uliggaq is named after].

Back when I liked chewing store-bought gum, they were chewing gum. Their chewing gum was blue. I watched them and really desired to have some. Then my two older sisters passed by.

Then Canaar rushed toward me, and when he did this, to me it looked like blue, store-bought bubble gum. Then he said to me, "The one up there gave us some."

When I looked up at it, there was a grave up there. Then I believed him and thought it was store-bought [gum], and he ran off.

I tried chewing it, then looked at it, and saw that it was a piece of seal skin used to make boot soles. You know those seal skins used to make boot soles, even when they were going to sew boot soles, I became aware when they used to eat them. It was a piece of leftover seal skin from cutting patterns for a boot sole. I thought it was store-bought.

I remember the time when you [Albertina] used to give us some chewing gum.

And after Billy had gone up north, he used to give my father some tea,

Angeq carpaungatellrani, angrraq im' *bubble gum*-aaruvkenani-llu, mistukekacagallemni.

Taukugnek-am wiinga, augkut arcaqaksugpagluki qanemcit ellangellrenka.

Umkumiuni taugaam Negtemi-llu uitalallrulriakut. Cali-llu kiagmi iluvayuunata *school*-ayuitellratni neqlitullrulriakut piciatun, wavet upagluta; neqnek neqsurtura'urluraqluteng anguarturluteng aataput.

Cat quyurrluki, ininarqelriit iniluki, iniluki. Kiani-ll' cali manignalegmi uitaaqamta, manignanek cali iniangaqluta.

Tua-i-ll' imumek taugaam yuut ayuqluteng neqsutullruut. Caquigaqluteng-llu augkunun tupigarnun naternanek-llu tutmarturluk' imirluki.

Neqtengnaquraurlutullruut augkut cumikellemni. Nutaan-llu cailkaq qakurnaqungekan uksillerkamtenun ayagluta, Negtemun.

Uatmuqrun

Neng'uryar: Augna kinguneqa umyuaqaqamku, tuamtell' tua-i uksillerkamtenun tuavet uksilallruamta kiani Cakcaam ukatiini, pimi wani, Cakcaam im' tungkekii, pi wani. Urumangnaq River. Tamaa-i etgacugnaitkacagallrullinilria Uatmuqrun-llu.

Tua-i-ll' tuavet-am tekitellerput call' tauna nallunritellruaqa. Tekilluta, iterluta, ingelret, amik-wa ua-i, ingelret-wa ukut; nepiamtenun iterluta.

Ayumian tang makut tag'uraqilit inglernun waten ilanka, alqanka. Waten iruteng piluki tagtenqegcarluki waten tua-i, aqumurluteng, iruit-wa nengingauralriit. Wiinga-ll' iquatnun mayurrlua uaqlikacagaulua. [*ngel'artuq*]

Mayurrlua cali ellaicetun, qantaq-llu wavet elliluku, qantanek. Ingelret tua-i imirluki, angayuqaagput ukuk. Qantanek tang cikiqiikut makaullilriit-wa akutat-llu. Tuaten imarluteng.

Tamakut-am tamaa-i kevirateng anerqelluki keviralteng. Tamakunek cali

and I never forget the sugar, those large, square-shaped ones. I remember that.

Back when *angeq* [chewing gum] seemed to be a significant thing, back when just chewing gum and not bubble gum was very noticeable to me.

I'm telling those stories as I consider the things that I have to tell about the time when I became aware of life as important.

We used to stay only in Umkumiut and Nightmute. And we didn't go [to Nightmute] during the summer back when they didn't attend school and just harvested fish all over, moving to this particular place; our fathers would constantly fish by paddling [kayaks].

They gathered things and hung things that needed to be hung. And when we stayed up there where there were burbot, we'd also obtain burbot that were hung to dry.

All the people used to fish similarly in the past. And they stored them inside those twined containers, and they'd fill them with flounder, constantly stepping on them [to pack them down] as they filled them.

Those dear people continually made efforts at obtaining fish when I observed them. And when the ground started to form frost, we'd finally go to our winter village, to Nightmute.

Uatmuqrun River[46]

Lizzie Chimiugak: When I think about my past, [when we'd go] to our winter camping site, since we used to go winter camping up there on this side of Cakcaaq at that [river], the one that is before Cakcaaq, that [river]. Urumangnaq River. It was evidently not shallow at all during that time, as well as Uatmuqrun River [One that suddenly goes down, from *ua-*, "area below"].

I was also aware of the time that we arrived there. We arrived, we went inside, there was a bed, the doorway was out there, and a bed was here; we went inside our sod home.

Then my siblings all went up to the bed, my older sisters. They brought their legs up all the way, they all sat, and their legs stayed extended. They lifted me up along the end of where they were, and I was situated farthest down from them. [*laughs*]

They lifted me up like them, and they placed a bowl here, bowls. We filled the bed, and our parents were here. They gave us bowls, and they seemed to be *mak'at* [mixtures of salmon eggs and berries] and *akutat*. That's what [the bowls] were filled with.

cegg'anek qallilirluk' kepengssaarpek'naki tua-i waten. Canek, akutamek-llu-w' tangellrulrianga.

Wavet tang qantamek elliilriit, ukut-llu call' maaten pianka, qantanek cali piluteng, ayuqurluta, cegg'arpallraat-wa imait.

Cunaw' tang tamaa-i neqliskengtullermeggni-gguq, nunamtenun te-kiteqarrallemteni, maurluirutvut-llu-w' tuantellinian, neqlilluta cunaw'. Tuar-llu tang miiskiikut-llu.

Cingyukan: Mernek tapituit neqlitaqamegteki tua-i, mernek tapirluki. Aviukarteqerraarcelluki, aviukarqelluki cali.

Neng'uryar: Aviukarqura'urlutullermeggni-w' tamaa-i, maurluirutvut atam tuani tuqullrulliniuq, ciuqliirutka Uyangliin Atra piipiullrani.

Tayima tua-i neqemtenek aviukarqerraarluteng nevumun nayukaulluku.

Kiimta tua-i yuungamta, tuaten tua-i aqumevkarluta. Qantat-wam tua-i muragat.

Ilamnek tua-i tuaten aqumgalrianek irr'iqerlua iquatnun-llu aqumllua. Qantanek cikirluta. Kia-kiq wii neqenka nangniartaki.

Qantanek tamamta piluta. Qaill' pisia nerellruunga-qaa, melqa taugaam nalluvkenaku.

Angalgaq: Qantavcenek-qaa tamalkuita aug'aqaulluteng aviukarluteng?

Cingyukan: Yaa, ilangarcecuayaarturluki. Cakuinrayagarmek tua-i.

Neng'uryar: Cakuinrayagaq tuqumalriami amelkacagarnituat, cakuinra-yagaq.

Cingyukan: Tua-i kina tuqullrukan, tua-i-ll' atqeqertai tamakut tuaten, tua-i apqiitnek akiqerluki.

Qanrangarmiut

They took out the dry fish that they had stored in sealskin storage containers. They topped [the bowls' contents] with those *cegg'at* [fish split in half] and didn't cut them to small pieces at all. I also saw some *akutaq*.

They placed a bowl here, and when I looked at the others, they also had bowls, we all had the same thing, and they were filled with very large *cegg'at*.

Evidently, back when they gave food offerings to people on behalf of the deceased, what they call *neqliskengluteng*, when we first arrived in our village, since our grandmother was also evidently buried there, they evidently gave us a food offering on behalf of the deceased, *neqlilluta*. And it seems that they also gave us water to drink.

Albertina Dull: They also included water when they gave them food offerings on behalf of the deceased; they included water. They first had them give a food offering to the deceased, they also gave a food offering to the deceased, *aviukarqelluki*.

Lizzie Chimiugak: Back when they constantly gave food offerings to the deceased, our grandmother evidently died there when my deceased older sibling Uyangliin Atra was a baby.

They first gave an offering from our food to the deceased, just digging the ground and burying it there.

Since we were the only ones, that's how they had us sit. The bowls were wooden.

I watched my siblings who were sitting in awe, and they sat me down along the end of where they were sitting. They gave us bowls. I wonder who finished my food.

They gave us all bowls. I wonder what I did, did I eat, but I only remember drinking water.

Ruth Jimmie: So from your bowl, did they take a small piece of each [food] and give an offering to the deceased?

Albertina Dull: Yes, they took a small piece from each. A very small piece.

Lizzie Chimiugak: They mention that a very small piece is a large amount to a deceased person, a very small piece.

Albertina Dull: If someone died, those named after [the deceased] would do that, what they call *akiqerluki* [giving them something in return].

Quyangun: Qanrangarmiut nunallret akiatnun agaavet nanvallermi ikani, nunallemta akiani tuani tua-i tevyulircutullrulriakuk. Tua-i tevyulit, tevyulit amllerrluteng, amllerraqluteng.

Arcunan: Up'nerkami up'nerkiyalallruut. Tua-i upagluteng, upacuarluteng imkut angutet pilallruut. Pavavet tua-i qayalgirluteng. Qaillun-llu tayim' *month*-artek'lalalliut-llu.

Month-am tua-i nuniini yuilqumtaqluteng pavani. Ellmeggnek amiirluki nillarluki; neqekluki tuaten.

Iniiluteng tuaten, pikartuyiqaqameng yaqulegnek iniiluteng ut'rutarkameggnek, ut'rulluki makunek *geese*-anek, *geese*-at tua-i-w' cipneteng iniluki tamaani *camp*-ameggni. Nutartungnaqu'urlurturluteng taugaam piaqluteng neqkat-ll' amllelaata. Makut aturyunrilkengateng iniluki ut'rutaqluki.

Tua-i upagluteng upacuarluteng.

Cali elitellrat-am tamakut tevyulit tua-i imumi imarpigmi pitarkani cangallruvkenateng pitangyunarqelliniluteng tungunqucetun ayuqluteng.

Uniurterrlugngalngermeng-llu pitaqsukaarluteng.

Tua-i tuaten paivngaliluteng piaqameng tua-i imarpigturqellrata cangallruvkenaki pissurniaqluteng tua-i. Imarpigmi iciw' tua-i pissurturatullrulriit up'nerkami.

Pavani-llu-gguq cangallrunrituq tevyulim pitangyugnarqellra tungunqum pitangyugnarqellrani cangallrunrituq-gguq. Akikaungami neqkauluni tuaten.

Cali imkucirlaameng ilu'urqelriit anagtasiiguterrluarturluteng pilallruameng, piliqeng'ermi tua-i kiiki tua-i pitenruurangnaqluni ilu'urmini. Ut'reskunek *count*-arciqakek nalikek piliqenruarallinilia tuaten. [*ngel'artuq*]

Anagtassiigullutek.

Taumek cakneq pissulallrulriit unisngaurpek'nateng tua-i, tua-i ilu'urmeggnun caunrilkessiyaallerkarteng pitekluku. [*ngel'artuq*]

Unangik: Unuakumi kuimyutuluteng atakumi-ll' call' kuimyutuluteng. Erenrani piqatung'ermeng nurnarqetuluteng, atakumi taugaam tua-i kuimyutuluteng.

Makugtautekellruat atam tua-i. *Fifty cent*-auluni-llu tevyuli atauciq.

Qanrangarmiut[47]

Carl Mark: Across from the old village of Qanrangarmiut, in that old lake across from our old village, we two used to go and hunt muskrats. So there were a lot of muskrats.

Peter Dull: In spring, they went to spring camps. Men used to move for a short while. They went up there with their kayaks. And they seemed to stay about a month.

They stayed in the wilderness for about a month up there. They skinned them by themselves and stretched them to dry; and they also used [muskrats] as food.

They even dried geese when they had more than enough to eat so they could take them home there at their camps. They tried to get fresh food since there was also lots of food. They hung those that they weren't going to eat to dry and took them home.

So they moved for a short while.

And when one learns how to hunt those muskrats, it isn't any different from hunting in the ocean where you want to catch them as much as you want to catch a bearded seal.

And even if one seems to miss them, they are easy to catch.

When they are available like that, they would say it is no different than hunting in the ocean. You know that they always hunted in the ocean in spring.

And likewise, up there in that land, the urgency that one feels to catch a muskrat is not any different from wanting to catch a bearded seal. Because it is a source of money and also something to eat.

And because those who were teasing cousins tried to outdo one another, even though he had caught lots of them, he tried to catch more than his *iluraq*. When they returned home, they would count, and one of them would have a little more than the other. [*laughter*]

They tried to outdo one another.

So they really went all out in hunting [muskrats], and they were not to be found staying behind fearing that they would be belittled by their *ilurat*. [*laughter*]

Simeon Agnus: [Muskrats] like to swim in the mornings and in the evenings. Though they do swim during the day, there weren't as many, but they like to swim at night.

Akiinani.

Makugtautekluku. Qemitgun tuaten qayateng qamurluki tua-i nevum qaingakun tevulluki una pingqelliniaqan ullagaqluku qayateng qamurluki. Qamigaucirluki taugaam.

Tamaani makugtatullruut augkut yuut. Wangkuta maa-i atunritaput.

Wiinga-ll' malrurqugnek tevyulircuqallruyaaqelrianga taugaam piliq-kacagallrunritua.

Tamaa-i akitungataqluteng. Taugaam neqkaq akiitellruuq akiitkacagarluni. *Native Store*-aq ikna ika-i kiimi kipusviullruuq maani tua-i ellange-qarraallemni, kiiqapiarmi Tununermi.

Tuaken-am atam Yuguayak-llu taglunuk pillruukuk miiqaqataan. Tamaani tua-i uruan anguarturlunuk ayaglunuk qavavet Cakcaam uatiinun pillruukuk.

Ilait-llu nani qavani; Piirraq tua-i pingna aptullruat tevyulilitullra. Augkut yaaqlimta ullagatullrukait up'nerkivirvikluku.

Caarrlulilget makut tevyuliyagaat nayutungatelallruit, caarrluliriit tua-i nanvat, caarrlugnek tua-i imalget.

Amelkacagalrianek tang tangerqallrunrilngua; ilait piliqetuyaaqut tua-i ilait tamaani pavani-w' tua-i agaani akimteni pilriit qemini.

Pissurnanriameng-llu tua-i nangluteng tua-i tayima. Nangelriatun ayuqut maa-i mat'um nalliini pinanriitki.

They really suffered in hunting them. One muskrat pelt brought in fifty cents. It was cheap.

They went through hardship [hunting muskrats]. They even portaged over hills by dragging their kayaks on top of the ground when [muskrats] were in a certain place, they dragged their kayaks. But they dragged them with kayak sleds.

Those people went through hardship in the past. We do not experience that nowadays.

I, too, went muskrat hunting twice, but I didn't catch an enormous amount.

At that time, they seemed to to be worth a lot. But store-bought food was really cheap, it was dirt cheap.

The Native Store across there was the only store around this area when I first came to be aware, [located] all by itself at Tununak.

From there Yuguayak [Mickey Abraham] and I went up there when the snow and ice were about to melt and create pools of water. When it melted that time, we went up there by rowing just on this side of Cakcaaq.

And some people were up there; they used to mention [the river] Piirraq [Braided string of fish] as having a lot of muskrats. Those villagers to the east of us used to go there to spend spring.

Small muskrats seem to frequent these with a lot of grass [in the water], lakes where there is a lot of grass, those choked with grass.

I've never seen a lot of [muskrats] though some people catch a lot, those who hunt in the hills across from us.

And since we don't hunt them anymore, they have become scarce. It's as though there are no more of them at the present time since they do not hunt for them anymore.

Cevv'arnermiut

Chefornak

Cevv'arneq

Avegyaq: Kuigat iciw' augna, kuiget maa-i piciunrilriit, tamana piciunrillerkaa kuigteng pitekluku nugtartellruut kiavet.

Ava-i-ll' tua-i maaten qangvaq imumi asgutullruamku asguryaaqaqa wani kiakaraatni nuyaruat amelkacagarluteng.

Aling nangurallinilunі-ll' nunallrat imna ilarugii tayima elanellret-llu kanani kiugkut elanellrit.

Nurataaq: Tua-i-ll' agngami ak'anivkenaku cali nugtartelluki tuavet Cevv'arnermiungurrluku malikluku atra Cevv'arnermiunguluteng yaa-i. Caputnguarmun nugtarrluteng. Cevv'arneq malikluku.

Avegyaq: Cevv'arnermiunguameng-wa tua-i itrarluteng-llu Caputnguanun Cevv'arnermiunguameng tua-i ellaita aprutekluku Cevv'arneq.

Nurataaq: Tamarmeng pivkenateng ilait un'garrluteng. Tua-llu allrakuan quyurrluteng. Yaa-i Caputnguarmun Cevv'arneq malikluku.

Tamarmeng nugtarrluteng. Yuirulluni tauna. Cevv'arnermiungurrluteng.

Avegyaq: Tang avani nasekcugglugaulua wiinga qaillun tayim' angtaurallrusia.

Qavciuluta tuani Caputnguarmi uksillruukut uksumi taitullruukut. Ataucirquqapiarmek tua-i uitaqallruukut imkut Panill'am Arnaan imna atii anerteqellrani aanaminek ilaluni. Ellait wangkuta-wa. Imkut-wa Maggienkut; Uksuarpiinkut-wa augkut atrit qaqimallratni. Ussugankut. Taukut tua-i. Tallimaullruyugnarqukut nen'i tuani.

Uksurpak tua-i uksiluta tuani tua-i tuantenqigtevkenata.

Nurataaq: Nangluteng tua-i itrararkat tamarmeng tua-i piluteng.

Avegyaq: Uksurpak ataucirqurrarmek akaurtellria uitaqallruukut uksuiluta ataucirqumek. Itrarvikluku yaa-i nunalleruartangqerrngan-am tauna.

Nurataaq: Nuniit-llu cakaniqsaunani maa-i man'a tekilluku. Ketiitni taugaam teggalqut amlleriluteng. Tagenricaaqeng'ermeng-am pugluteng teggarvallraat.

Avegyaq: Teggalqut augkut nunaullruuq qaingat takumni tamaantellem-

Chefornak[48]

Sophie Agimuk: Their river there, you know that some rivers can no longer be used, since their river would no longer be navigable, they moved up there.

Since I used to go up that river, just recently when I went upriver, there were a lot of weeds.

My, their former place had eroded quite a bit and also the former house pits [were gone].

Phillip Moses: So when he moved over there, he let them move and kept the name Cevv'arnermiut like it is now. They moved to Caputnguaq [Pretend *capun* (weir, fish fence)]. They took [the name] Cevv'arneq [Cut through place] with them.

Sophie Agimuk: Because they were from Cevv'arneq when they moved up to Caputnguaq, since they were from Cevv'arneq, they named it that.

Phillip Moses: All of them did not move at once, but some stayed. And then the following year they got together. So they stay over there at Caputnguaq with the name of Cevv'arneq that they have assumed.

They all moved. [That old village of Cevv'arneq] does not have people living in it anymore. They became the village of Cevv'arnermiut.

Sophie Agimuk: I was just a small girl [in the early 1930s], and I don't know how tall I was then.

A number of us spent the winter there at Caputnguaq since we always came there in wintertime. We only spent one winter there when Panillaq's [Theresa Abraham's] mother's father was alive along with her mother. So they and our family were there. And there was Maggie [Julius] and family; and when the namesakes of Uksuarpak were all there. There was Ussugan and family. So those families. There must have been five houses there.

So we spent the entire winter there and never stayed there again after that.

Phillip Moses: So everyone who was to move up there all moved [there].

Sophie Agimuk: We stayed there only one time, a long time ago, all winter. We moved up there since there had been a small village here.

Phillip Moses: So their village never changed up to the present time. But down below [their village], there have come to be many rocks. Though they have not come on shore, big rocks have surfaced.

teni; nunami augkut teggalqut pugumalriit ketiini, nunami uitallruyaaqut.

Taugaam call tagluni keluqvanun, tamakut teggalqut nunam aciantellret nunapillemta aciani uitallret alaitelartut ava-i. Nang'uq cal' ingna.

Ingna-ll' mengliitni nanvarpall'er unaken tagluta tumyarartarluni unaken tagluta mertarvikaqluku. Nunaullruut unkut teggalqurpallraat alailnguut, qaingani nunatangqellruuq.

ᴓ

Paniliar: Wiinga-llu ellangellruunga, tua-i waten mat'utun tangvak'ngamcetun ayuqellrunritukut. Uani Cevv'arnermi ellangeqarraallruunga. Qavavet tayima ayaumallemteni pingatuq ellangeqarraalqa nani maani kuigem ceniini, augna-llu maurluqa malikluku.

Tamaani maaten piqertua aanaka, kina-llu tayima malikellruak, qavani pinganii. Tua-i-ll' iqvaryarluta, pilliniluteng iqvaryarluteng.

Tua-ll' tauna maurluqa kuigem ceniini uitaluni, wiinga-ll' cali uitalua, aanaka tangerrluku tua-i, pekluni tayim' natetmurteqatallrua, malingqellrullilria-wa.

Tua-i-ll' tuani taum maurluma maaken cailkamek tegulluni qaltaruarullinilriignek waten tegulluni. Angeng'anatek-llu taukuk malruulukek teguakek tangvakarluku-am teguamikek uuggun canek kep'arrluku pikavet waten piqerluku, tuamtell' akianun kanavet-llu call' piqarraarluku kep'artaqluku.

Maaken call' tegulluni nemerluku kan'a teguyararkaqa. Nemerluku waten tayim' ayuqellria qaltaruaq. Uuggun waniwa ciumek pillruluku, kanaggun-llu kinguakun, uuggun-llu nemerluku, tua-ll' pikna waten pillra elatmun nengqaarluku imumek iki'irtaa tua-i aturyugngaluni avuquma maaken naunranek.

Qaltaruat-gguq, naucetaat augkut. Tamakut-am tamaa-i qaltaruat cali waten nalaaqata ilaita pitaqluki pelurkiutuit. Qaltaruanek pelurkartaqluteng waten up'nerkami-llu nunapigmek pavaken eleggluki pelurkiuraqluteng.

Green-aaruluteng naumaluteng qalcilua tua-i, tua-i-ll' iqvarlua tua-i. Taugaam tua-i iqvainanemni tuani maniluki, tua-i-ll' teguluku, tua-i-ll' tayima

Sophie Agimuk: There was land on top of those rocks in my presence when we lived there; those rocks that are visible down below the land were once underground.

But the land has eroded far back, and those rocks that used to be underground, under our tundra, are now visible [in front of the village]. That land has also eroded.

And that big lake beside it, we used to come up to it using the path and get water from it. Those big rocks that are visible now were once covered by land, there was land on top of them in the past.

Theresa Abraham: I also became aware, and we didn't live the kind of life that we observe nowadays. I first became aware of life down at Cevv'arneq. I think I first became aware of life when we traveled up north, along the shores of a particular river, and we brought my grandmother along.

When I gained awareness, I saw that my mother, and I'm not sure who she was with, but it seemed that I was up north. Then we went to pick berries, they had gone to pick berries.

Then my grandmother was along the shores of the river, and I was there, too, and I saw my mother, and she was walking somewhere, and there was probably someone accompanying her.

Then my grandmother picked what were evidently *qaltaruak* [two lamb's-quarter leaves, lit., "pretend buckets"] from the ground. And those two looked large, and when she took two of them, I watched her, and when she took them, she cut a piece of grass here and placed it up there like this, and then she brought it across and down to the bottom, and then she cut it.

Then she took some again and bound the handle that I held down there. She bound the *qaltaruaq* [pretend bucket] that looked like this. She had first [bound it] here, and then along the bottom next, and bound it here, and when after stretching the top toward the outside, when she opened it, I saw that it could be used if I picked some salmonberries from the surrounding area.

[She was making it out of] what they call *qaltaruat,* those plants. Those *qaltaruat,* when they wilted, some people gathered them and made ash to mix with tobacco. They'd obtain *qaltaruat* to make ash to mix with tobacco from the area up there, even in spring, and they burned them to make ash to mix with tobacco.

They were green and had grown, and she made me a bucket, and then I

kinguakun tua-i ellaka nalluluku.

Cali tamaani tamaa-i ellangellruunga upallemteni cali angyapiakun. Uaken Aqumgallermek kingunerluta kiatmurtellilriakut-wa.

Tua-ll' piunga, angyam-wa tua-i ilua cataunani, aklullruaraput taugaam, massiinartaunani-ll' palayam ilua.

Ingna-wa kingumteni angyallugaq qimugtenek taugaam imarluni, massiinaunani-llu. Ilavkullruarmek nangcauterluni, aataka-w' una alulaaralria, wani uitaluni, wiinga, aanaka-w' kanani. Kiimelnganata-ll' tua-i.

Tua-i-ll' piunga, kiugna-gguq cayartuqerliu, cayartuusqelluku aanaka ellimerluku. Tua-ll'-am cumikarrluku. Itraami angyam iluanun teggliq waten augna teggliq waten ayuqluni, teggliuluni taugaam inangqaluni.

Tua-ll' tauna teguamiu teggliq makluku acitmun kalevvluku. Kalevqaarluku-ll' tua-i uitaluni. Tua-i allamek pinrilan tangvaggaarluku tua-i ulurluku. Tua-i-ll' maaten piunga cali pikani ellami tengalrautaq, tengalrautaullinilria tua-i nengingaluni uitalria.

Ayumian-am umyuarteqkilii angyam ciungakun cali kiarcarturnalua. Iterlua angyaq augna palayaq lumarrall'ermek enetarluni qilii.

Itrarlua-am tua-i kiugna ciungani pakikarluku piunga apqeka una ataatacungaqa Angayiim Atra. Aatama tua-i-w' iqugteklallikii, iqugteklikii. Angyam ciungani qaspell'erturluni qaterlill'ermek iqaitenritliami.

Kinguakun maa-i umyuarteq'lartua tangrruarluku iqangtagluni qaspellrii paltuugnek piiteurlullermeggni. Tua-i irugni imkuk, ciisqugni ukuk uitauralria waten angyam ciungani aqumgaurluni, kiarqurnganani. Tuamtell' tua-i pirraarlua iterlua tua-i.

Egmian-llu tekitelaayuilngatnaurtukut ciunemtenun. Neqliyarluta ayagaqamta uaken tua-i, ciunit'laagngacuunata natmun arulairluta piaqluta.

Tua-i-w' ula aturluku pilallilriit anuqlinritaqan. Arulairaqluteng tua-i, ayagaqluteng. Cayaqlirluta ciunisngataqluta tuavet.

Tua-i-ll' ciuniskumta qimugteteng tua-i yuurraarluki, nutaan tamakut pelatekarkaput aklullruaraput-wa tamakut nutaan tua-i pirraarluki. Qimugteteng tua-i ciumek nekegga'arrnaurait uitaurayuilata.

Pelatekiurraarluteng nutaan unuaquani kuvyarkateng tamakut cauma-

picked berries. But while I was picking berries, I showed them to her, and she took it, and then I lost awareness after that.

And at that time, I also became aware when we moved with a real boat. From down at Aqumgalleq, I think we were heading upriver.

Then I saw that there was nothing inside the boat but our few belongings, and there was no outboard motor inside the *palayaq* [large open boat].

Behind our boat was a wooden boat filled only with dogs, and it didn't have a motor. It had just a tow rope, and my father was steering the boat, seated here, and I was here, and my mother was down there. It seemed we were alone.

Then he said, he told my mother to go and do something to the back [of the boat]. Then I watched her. When she went inside the boat, that metal device that looked like this, a metal device that was laying there.

Then when she took that metal device, she lifted it up and then lowered it. After lowering it, she just stayed there. When she didn't do anything else, after watching her, I looked away. Then I saw a sail outside up there, what was evidently a boat's sail that was stretched out.

Then I immediately thought that I would go and look around along the front of the boat. I went inside, and that boat, that *palayaq* had a cloth canopy on it.

I headed in, and when I opened up the [flap] up front, there was a person who I called my *ataatacungaq* [little father's brother], the person who Angayiq is named after. He was probably my father's fishing helper. He was along the front of the boat wearing a dirty hooded garment.

When I think about it these days, I imagine how dirty his hooded garment looked, back when the poor things didn't have coats. He was on his legs, his knees, and he was just sitting along the front of the boat, as though he was looking around. Then after looking, I went inside.

And it seemed that we didn't arrive at our destination right away. When we'd go and cut and harvest salmon at summer fish camps from down there, it seemed that we didn't arrive at our destination right away and would stop along the way.

They probably traveled following the tide, when it wasn't windy. They'd stop and then they'd leave. It seemed that we'd finally arrive at our destination after traveling for a long time.

And when we'd arrive, after unloading their dogs, they would set up our tents after unloading our few belongings. They first put their dogs in a good spot since they didn't sit still.

rraarluki, cali tua-i cavluteng angyallugarkun tuaggun kuvyiryarturaqluteng.

Tua-i neqliuraraqluteng, neqliurarraarluteng-llu tuamtellu tua-i kinrata puyuqurluki.

Agayuyarnariaqateng ukut Mamterillermun itrarluteng agayuyaraqluteng, Maqinruaqan-wa pilallrullilriit.

Tua-i tamaa-i pinarillikateng cali, neqteng tamakut caquluki tua-i *plastic*-aanun canun caquyugnaunaki taqukat-wa augkut caquit.

Aanaka-w' tua-i cumikelallrukek'a taqukanek neqautai imkut qeciit caqungqerrnaurtut nunutagnek augkunek taqukagnek. Ii-i patgutagnek. Tua-i ekluki, enrirturluki qemagqurnaurait enrit allakaita, cat tua-i makut enqataitllu cali allakaita caqu'urluki.

Tua-i pinarillikateng tayima cam nalliini utertelallruat. Iliini ukaqvaggun massiinangnermegteggun pingatelallruut, *August*-aaq tuan qukarngaqaarluku apqeteng *fifteen*-aaqerraarluku kingutmun uterrnaurtut. Agayunerpauninauraat tauna *fifteen*-aaq. Tamaa-i kinguakun taum utertaqluteng.

Tua-i utertaqamta tayima tua-i cayaqlirluta call' ciunisngatnaurtukut uavet nunamtenun Cevv'arnermun. Taugken tua-i nunalleqengramteggu tekiskumta nunaniryugluta tua-i enemtenun tekiskumta caiteurlungramta.

Nunanikluku tua-i nunaput tua-i. Kingunerput tua-i Ingriik-llu kankuk tangerkengaurtaqamek nunaniqnaurtuk. Tuamtell' nuna alaiqan nunaniryugluta tua-i cakneq tuavet nunamtenun tekiteqatarqamta.

Tua-i imkut angutet-llu uitavkenateng, cali uksuaqegciaqluni. Tuar-im' anuqliyuilnguq. Akercirturngatnaurtuq-llu ellallirturayuunani-llu.

Yuut-llu iniarluteng, neqnek iniarluteng. Tua-i cat imkut angutet-llu kuvyayarturngatnaurtut, iniurluki-llu imarpinrartait-llu iniurluki uitavkenateng.

Makut-llu call' nulirrit naunraat assirilaata tamaa-i *babysit*-arkameggnekllu kepeqsugnaunateng.

Aanaka-w' cumikellrukek'a kan'a uyu'urqa Tarr'aq malikluku, qaspellraminek pamavet amarcuucirluku, issratni wavet elliluku, tamaa-i ayallra murilkellrukek'a tamaani qaillun tayim' nasaurlucualleraulua pillrullilria. Kinguakun tua-i ayalallruunga kingunragengun.

Ivrucirturlunuk tua-i ayagaqlunuk qagaavet neglirnemtenun, paug'umgguq Nemrukaraam kangianun pillilria, pavavet Ilanernun augkunun ayagaqlunuk. Tamakut-llu kavirpaungatnaurtut naunranek; naunrirnga-

After setting up their tents, the next day after fixing their fishnets, they would row with wooden boats and set their fishnets.

They'd cut fish all the time, and after cutting fish, when they dried, they'd smoke them.

When it was time for them to go to church, they'd go up to Bethel to attend church services, probably when it was Sunday.

And probably when it was time, they'd put their fish away in containers, and they didn't put them away in plastic containers at all, but inside sealskin containers.

I watched my mother use seal skins that were connected and sewn together for storing fish. Yes, ones that were put together. She'd put [the fish] inside and remove their backbones and store their backbones separately, and they'd also store their fins separately.

And probably when it was time, I'm not sure when they returned home. It seems in more recent times after they got outboard motors, after the middle of August, they'd return home after the fifteenth. They'd call the fifteenth [of August] Agayunerpak. They'd return home after that day.

When we'd return home, it seemed that we'd reach our village of Cevv'arneq after traveling for a long time. But since it was our village, when we'd return, we'd be so joyous when we got to our homes although we didn't have many belongings.

We found our village to be a joyous place. Our home area, and even when the Ingriik [Mountains] down there became visible, we'd be so overjoyed to see them. And when the village became visible, we'd be overcome with joy when we were about to arrive in our village.

And the men didn't sit around, and the weather would be good during fall. It seemed that it didn't get windy. And it seemed to be sunny and not rainy all the time.

And people had fish hanging to dry. And the men seemed to go fishing all the time, and they'd constantly hang [fish to dry], and they constantly hung the whitefish they caught and didn't sit idle.

And since salmonberries were ready for picking at that time, their wives didn't say they needed babysitters for their children.

I used to watch my mother, who brought along my younger sibling Tarr'aq, using her old hooded garment to carry him on her back, and placed her *issran* [twined-grass carrying bag] here, and observed her when she went, probably when I was a little girl. I would walk behind them.

We'd leave wearing waterproof sealskin boots walking to the north of our village, probably to the upper part of [the river] Nemrukaar [from *nemer-*, "to

tnaurtut tua-i ayagvipuk, keluat neglirneq man'a.

Taugken tua-i tuavet tekiskumegnuk taquani anlluki neqraat nerucuglua nerlunuk, irniani-ll' tauna neqpiarrarmek tamualiartaqluku. Tua-i tamualiqaarluku tua-i nererraarluni taqkuniu aamaraareskuniu qavaqerluni. Taumek-llu amarcuutellranek qaspellraminek, iluanun ek'arrluku una tua-i waten qamiqurran nallii pikalgilalliani qerrataurluni waten pilallrulria, epsalnguyailkutkellrullikii.

Tua-ll' taqkan, qavaqaan piciqaanga, kitak-gguq iqvarnaurtukuk. Aren iqvacuaqerlua qavarnim tua-i tucaaqnauraanga cayuumiitkacagarlua, qavarnim tua-i tucaaqnauraanga, cayuumiitkacagarlua. Kiiki-gguq assigtarpuk una imangekan uterciiqukuk, cumigqurlua iqvarlii.

Issratem-am imaa paqnakluku piaqa aug'umek anrutamek amrayaangqelliniluni, kinguakun egmian elitaqsuitellrukek'a. Cauga-wa cetuam pikenrilkani. Miktevkenani issratem iluani augna anrutaq, amrayaaqluku tua-i.

Qamulria: Kaugpiim piklikii.

Paniliar: Ii-i, wall'u-q' kaugpiim pikaa. Tua-i piyaaqaqama iqvaryuumiirullua qavarninilua, kiiki-gguq una-gguq assigtarpuk imangekan uterciiqukuk. Tua-i qessayaaqerraarlua qavarnilua tuaten tua-i nangertaqlua. Ivrucirturlunuk-llu tamaa-i ivrucirturluta ayatullruamta.

Tua-i-ll' uterrnarikakut quyak'acagarlua uterteqataqumegnuk. Issratni tauna, imangaqan-wa tua-i tauna anrutaq pilallikii, ingna tua-i imircuutellni qillerrluku, tangvauralaqeka-am qillerrluku tua-i-ll' taqkuniu, taqkan una-w' call' qaltacuarii augna teggliq imarluni call' naunranek, wiinga-w' cali tauna assigtarraqa tua-i imarluni cali. Atmakuniu tauna mikelnguq pama'antelleq wavet wani manulirneminun.

Iqsulirnermek waten tuar aciiqerluku pilaqii, tauna-ll' qaltacuarani tegumiaqluku. Kingutmurtenga'arciiqukuk, nunat-wa kankut yaaqvani. Yaavanelnganani tua-i. Wiinga-w' tua-i kingunrakun qaltacualler qaltaq tegumiaqluku, kingunrakun ayagaqlua tua-i.

Tua-i imkut arnat uitaurpek'nateng, aipateng tuaten icaqisteksugnaunaki caluteng tua-i, aulukluki-ll' tamakut pitait, ellaita-w' call' makut cumer-

bind or wrap"] up there, to the Ilanret [from *ila,* "part of, one of"] up there. And those areas seemed to look red from being covered with salmonberries; the places where we went seemed to have an abundance of salmonberries, the area behind their village to the north.

But when we arrived at that place, she'd take out her provisions, a small amount of food, and she would want to eat with me and we'd eat, and she'd chew some food for her baby. After chewing food for him to eat, after eating, when she'd nurse him, he'd fall asleep. And using her old hooded garment that she used to carry him on her back, she'd place him inside, and since she probably placed something along his head, it would be sticking up like this, probably to prevent him from feeling suffocated.

And when she was done, when he fell asleep, she'd tell me that we should pick berries. After picking berries for a short while, I'd suddenly feel sleepy, and I'd feel like I didn't want to do anything at all, suddenly feeling sleepy. She'd tell me to hurry, that if our containers were filled, we'd return home, that I should try my best to pick berries.

Curious to see what was inside the bag, I looked inside and saw that it had a stomach lining, and I didn't know what it was at first, but found out later on. I'm not sure what kind it was if it didn't belong to a beluga whale. That stomach [container] wasn't small inside the bag, and that was her *amrayaaq* [stomach container].

Maria Eric: It probably belonged to a walrus.

Theresa Abraham: Yes, or was it from a walrus. When I would say that I didn't want to pick berries, that I was sleepy, she would encourage me and tell me that we would return home when our container was full. I would stand after being reluctant to pick and sleepy, too. And we'd be wearing waterproof skin boots since we used to travel using waterproof skin boots at the time.

Then when it was time for us to return home, I was so happy when we were going home. Her *issran,* probably when that stomach container was filled, she tied the section that she had filled [with berries], and she tied it as I watched, when she was done, and her metal bucket was also filled with salmonberries, and my small bucket was also filled. When she'd put it on her back, she'd place the child who had been on her back along the front of her body.

She seemed to put her left arm underneath [the baby], and then she'd hold her small bucket. We'd start heading back, and the village would be a great distance away down there. It looked far. I would be holding a small bucket, walking behind her.

Those women didn't just sit around, and they didn't use their husbands

kekngateng cali.

Puckamek tua-i atauciunrilngurmek imirinaurtuq. Caqerlua-ll'-am cumikaqa qayikvayagnek tupilria. Tua-i-ll' piaqa cakiullranek. Nanvamun-gguq tan'gerpiit ekciqai taumek assigcirluni.

Tua-i-am paqnakluku tuaten pirraartelluku, piuq pavaken-gguq quagcinek iluperkanek piqatartuq. Maliklunuk tua-i tauna-ll' uyu'urqa ayagluta.

Tua-i nanvam ceniinek pit'esqenganga pillua. Tua-i tauna-am tua-i qayikvayak tupigaq ilua *line*-irluku tamakunek quagcinek. Tamakut tan'gerpagtani tuaten kuvvrraarluki tuavet kic'elluki, kic'elluku nanvam iluanun.

Cali naunrarmek tangvallruaqa kic'ecillrani. Anglanillrunrilameng assigtarkameggnek waten tua-i assigtarrateng tauna ciptaqan tamaavet nanvanun ek'lallrullikait tamakut.

Qikertaar

Qamulria: Kanani up'nerkitullruukut wangkuta Qikertaarmi, uani-llu mat'um kuigem paingani. Taukugni wii uitatullruunga.

Aling ilagalallrukuvkut. [*ngelaq'ertuq*] Aren tua-i-wa ilii uunguciirucaaqaqa wiinga mik'nii tamaani ellangellruama.

Atam qaillun tayim' angtaurlua tamaantauratullruukut up'nerkami. Qikertaarmi kanani up'nerkiluta aanavut im' tuquvailgan.

Wangkuta tua-i pingayuuluta—Ussugan, pingna-w' alqerra'urluqa, wiinga-wa. Una-ll' uyu'urput yuurteksaunani. Tamaani tuaten, tautun-llu angtallrulliunga.

Tua-i murilketullruunga tamaani ellaka tua-i tamaranrian.

Atam kan'a Qikertaar nunakelallemteni, man'a tua-i qertuuq, man'a-ll' ketmun nengluni, un'a taugken tua-i teggalquuluni.

Kanani-w' nemta ukalirnerani teggarvakayallraak. Tua-i yaassiiguaruluni, neng'uciqnganani tua-i pikna qiliquni. Ukuk-llu iquuk kevirlutek, kelulirneq taugaam keviinani.

Taukut tua-i, ukut alqaanka tuani piaqata ilagaqtarnaunka-am wii, ap-

as babysitters and worked, and they'd process and take care of things they caught, and also things they gathered themselves.

She'd fill more than one barrel [with salmonberries]. One time I happened to watch her as she was twining some wheat grass. Then I asked her what she was making it for. She said that she was going to place the blackberries inside the lake using that as a container.

After she said that, I was curious to see what she would do, and she said that she was going to get some sourdock from up there for lining [the container]. We went together along with my younger sibling.

Since she asked me to gather some from along the edge of the lake, I got some. She lined the inside of that wheat-grass twined bag with those sourdock leaves. After spilling the blackberries she had picked inside there, she sunk it inside the lake.

I also watched her when she sunk some salmonberries inside the lake. Since they didn't have many containers for storage, when they didn't have enough containers, they probably placed [berries] inside lakes there.

Qikertaar[49]

Maria Eric: Our family used to go spring camping down at Qikertaar [Small *qikertaq* (island)] down there, and down along the mouth of this river also. I used to stay in those two places.

My, if you had stayed with us there. [*chuckles*] I've forgotten some things that happened since I became aware of life there when I was small.

When I was a certain age, we stayed there during spring. We'd go spring camping down at Qikertaar before our mother died.

There were three of us—Ussugan, my dear older sister up there, and myself. Our younger sibling hadn't been born yet. I was probably about the age [of Theresa Abraham's six-year-old granddaughter, Angilan] when we stayed there.

I used to observe things at that place when I became fully aware of life and stopped going in and out of conciousness.

Back when we lived at Qikertaar down there, this area is steep, and this area stretches down to the shore, but the shore down there is rocky.

On this side of our home down there were two large boulders. It was square-shaped, and it would look like a home if a roof was placed over it. And the ends were filled in, but the one along the back [toward shore] wasn't filled in.

qiitnek ikna-ll' kia, augnaurluq-wa tuqulleq ik'um Qiuqaam alqallra Aryagmek pilallrat. Tamaani ilagautaqlunuk.

Tua-i cumiknaunka. Cumikellruunga, tamaani-ll' cumikelallruanka tua-i cakneq.

Uitainanemteni qayagaurciquq, kan'a-gguq qayaq kan' mayurluni kana-i napautartuq, mer'em engeliini.

Meq atam yaaqsinrituq kanaken Qikertaarmiuni uitatullemteni. Kituuciirluku tua-i. Kana-i-ggur-am tua-i ikamragnek atrauqutesquuriuq.

Aling ikamragnek atrautaqata, picimegcetun tua-i atraucilaameng ikamranek qimugcirluteng, tauna tua-i napautalleq tagucivkarciquq tua-i ikamrak ucilirlukek, wall' waniw' qayartuq, qayakun qamigalartuq.

Imna tua-i Terkuam atallra, una-i-ggur-am un'a uurcayagaq tag'uq. Tuaten qayagpaganaurtut. Tua-i ciukacagarmek tungunqutetullruyugnarquq.

Aren tauna tua-i tekicarturciquq aqvaisqelleq ikamragni, ikamrak-llu ucilirlukek taqukarugarnek, tungunqunek tuaten.

Aren up'nerkarpak tua-i cayuilama-ll' wii tamaani, qaillun calisciigalama, ellami akusrartelngungaqamegnuk iterciiqukuk ellii-ll' tauna Aryagmek pilallrat, kiugna tua-i nepianek nengqerrameng kiugna acilaqiit egkumek, egkumeggnek, cumiknaurqa, nayiit-wa tua-i uryailkutait. Waten tua-i ukut, ukut taugaam qeciuluteng ukalirnermi qalliqluteng, kemegnek imarluni.

Taqukat tang avani amlletullruyugnarqut. Taumek ucuryulallruunga wii tuaten taguquringartaqata, amtall' qayatgun pissurluteng.

Ilait tua-i tagevkenateng atakuaqan aqvaivkaraqluki, taqukiqkacagaata.

Aataurlullerput imna wangni taqukiqkacagarnaurtuq. Aqvaigaqlutek ukuk alqaagka; alqaqa im' Ussugan aqvailallrulria pissuqengaitnek.

Iciw' imna enem ilua, amiiga-wa, nepiaq marayaq, wani tua-i acingqellriakut wangkuta, ikani-w' cali angayuqaagemta aciak; qaugna. Iqua qaugna, tua-i-gguq egkuq, taqukanek imarluni kiugna tua-i.

Tuamtell' caqerlua ciugtua qulqikarangqerran tauna mat'um qulii, naka-

When my older sisters played there, I would join them, along with that dear person who died, the older sister of Qiuqaaq over there who they called Aryak. She and I would join them there.

I would watch them. I was aware of things, and I would observe them closely at the time.

As we were just sitting, someone would yell out that a kayaker was down there who had climbed and erected a post along the water's edge.

The water wasn't far away down there, back when we stayed at Qikertaarmiut. They'd try to figure out who it was. They said that once again that person down there was signaling for them to bring down a sled.

My, when they'd bring a sled down, since anyone went down using a sled and dogs, the person who had erected a post would have them bring up [their catch] by filling up the sled, and here he had been seal hunting with a kayak.

Terkuaq's late father, they would say that the *uurcayagaq* [little person announcing his catch] was coming up to shore. That's what they yelled out. I think he used to be the first to catch an adult bearded seal.

My, that person who had signaled for them to go and retrieve [his catch] would arrive inside the sled, and the sled would be loaded with many seals, including adult bearded seals.

My, all spring long, since I didn't work during that time, since I was unable to work, when we were tired of playing outdoors, the person who they called Aryak and myself would go inside the home, and in the back area, since they had real sod homes, and see that the home's back area underneath the wall they called *egkuq,* their *egkuq,* I would look back there and see ringed seals being used as a barrier to prevent their catches from moving down. But there were skins on this side piled on top of one another, and it would be filled with meat.

I think there were many seals in the past. That's why I would be in awe when they began to bring seals up to shore, but here they were hunting with kayaks.

Some [men] didn't come up to shore, but they'd have them retrieve their catches in the evening, since they caught many seals.

Our late dear father would catch many seals; to me, he would catch many seals. My two older sisters would go and retrieve his catches; my older sister Ussugan would go and retrieve the seals they hunted and caught.

You know inside the home, there was the doorway, in a real sod home, we had a mattress here, and over there was my parent's mattress also; the area back there. The [house] end back there was called *egkuq.* That area in the back was filled with seals.

cuut pagkut. Mikliriinarluteng uani.

Tangssuarqenka-am tuani aanavut taqukiullrani tuani, tangssuaqainanemni tang niugglullakarluteng, wall' kitumek agturtailnguut; arviqtaarturnaurtut, arulaqtaarturluteng. Qaill'-kiq pitullruat?

Taqukat nakacuit. Irr'ilua tangssuumanaurtua.

Tua-i up'nerkarpak, Qikertaarmetetullermeggni kanani taqukiqkacagatullruut, qagkut-llu elaqliput.

Atam cingiuguq kan'a waten tua-i uatmun nunallerput, una tua-i imarpik engelekluku, teggalqut-wa tua-i engelekluki.

Cingiungami-w' ukut waniw' Aryiinkut ellait, wangkuta-w' nep'ut, kia-w' makut nek'aki; ullayuitellruamki nallukenka.

Kanani-wa acilqerrarmi cingian iquani Iquyuilnguunkut. Nallukenka makut ilaput, kinkuuciinateng.

Neng'uluni tua-i nuutmun waten, nepianek marayanek nel'iqulalliniluteng.

Kan'a-w' call' kana-i qikertaar aprutii. Kana-i tua-i tangertura'aqluku.

Elagyartarluni pingayunek, waten tua-i caniqliqluteng, kia pikatki ukuk. Una taugken aatama itqetaarturluku.

Tuavet tua-i pitami ilait, kemgit-wa tua-i kinelriit, kinengyiqutullruameng, atrauqulalliniluki, cat-llu tayim' pilartatki. Tamanek tua-i.

Tamanek tauna tua-i elagyarput imangqerrngatellruuq maligtellemni, maligarrluku-am maligtesqengan atrallemteni. Tua-i neqnek tua-i, canek ilangqertat. Ayuqenrilngurnek, apqemeggnek tamanek. Tuaten ayuqellruut.

Tuamtell'-am unani tua-i maani nemta ketiini acilqerrarmi unani Aryakllu piurarraarlunuk taglunuk neryarturlunuk.

Neryartuucamni-am taglunuk itertukuk tuaggun nemta qukaakun kanaggun naterkun aanallerput imna, puyuqilria aklullraput an'arrluki puyuqiluni elaturraani. Cunaw' tang nayiit pugtautait.

And one day I happened to look up, and since there were small shelves above [the *egkuq*], there were seal bladders up there. They were lined up from large to small.

As I was looking at them while my mother was working on seals there, as I was watching them, they made a rustling noise, and here no one had touched them; they'd moved one-by-one going across. I wonder what they were doing?

They were seal bladders. I watched in awe for a long time.

All spring, back when they stayed at Qikertaar down there, they caught many seals, and even the people to the north of us outside our area [caught many seals].

The place where we used to stay is a point that extends down the coast, reaching the edge of the ocean, reaching the rocks.

Since it is a point, there was Aryak and their family's home, our home, and I'm not sure who the other houses belonged to; I don't know whose they are since I never went to them.

And down along the edge of the tundra, along the end of the point, there was Iquyuilnguq and family. I don't know who the other families were.

There were homes all the way toward the point, and they evidently constructed real sod homes back then.

Then down below was the small island that the place was named after. It was visible down there.

There were three partially underground storage caches, and they were side by side like this, and I'm not sure who the other two belonged to. But my father would constantly enter this one.

He'd evidently bring some of the animals that he caught inside there, the meat that had dried, since they made dried seal meat, down to that [cache], and I'm not sure what else they placed down there. It was filled with every type of food.

It seemed that our partially underground storage cache was filled with all types of food when I went with him there, when I accompanied him and went down when he asked me to accompany him. There was food inside, and I'm not sure what else was inside. All different kinds, what I call *tamanek* [various types]. That's how they were.

And one time after Aryak and I played down below our home along the edge of the tundra, we went up to eat.

When I brought her to eat with me, we went up and went inside and I saw that our mother, along the center of our house on the floor, was smoking

Inilallinikai tuamtell' imumek tegg'iyarpiaqaqata itrulluki puyuqluki. Puyuqilalliniluni tamakunek.

Uqunek-am tuamtell' imiriurarraarluni taukut-am tua-i puyuqellri cali caqutnun ekluki. Askacagall[ruut].

Tuani tua-i murilkeqarraallemni nerrlemni tang tua-i assiliqalrianga. Cangimirteng'erma-ll' qaillun qanerciiganii cangimircaaqeng'erma.

Askacagalliniut kinerciqerluki pugtautait, *lung*-ait. Puyuqluki assipiat tua-i. Ingqiuraqerluki waten uqumun ektullruyugnarqai.

Waten up'nerkami tayima atrallemteni-am aataka neqsaagyugluni tayim' anluni.

Tekiutuq, qaltarraq augna imirluku tekiutellinilria taukunek puyuqaqlallrinek, kinengyagnek ilaluki, canek-llu augkunek ilaluki, tuartang yaqulget kemgit kinengyiit. Tua-i aanama itran ingqiurluki, qantacuarkun avaggun.

Kinerciqaumanrilameng tuartang imkut cat, neqerrluut-llu puyurniarninaqluteng neqnik'acagarluteng. Tamaani tua-i ellangeqarrallemni tuaten ayuqellruyugnarqut.

Uani taugken Aqumgallermi up'nerkilaryaaqelriit kinguakun, akaurrnerakun-wa anglirinemkun up'nerkilaryaaqellrulriit, taukucicetun taqukiqelriatun amllertalrianek tangerqallrunirtua tayima, taqukatqaquurang'ermeng.

Aling aren tua-i imna-ll' iquat qecigglainarnek iquyailkuterlutek. Kemegnek imarluni tauna neqiviat, un'a-ll' nayirnek elluryailkuterluteng. Elluryailkutengqerraqluteng tuan Qikertaarmi.

Elluarrlua tamaani ellangellruunga, taugaam qaillun mikliama-ll' keveglua-ll' ukut tan'gaurluut qimautelallrukiitnga tamatum nalliini. Ellangyararallruyugnarqua tamatum nalliini.

Tua-i pinga'artaqamegteki taqukat, tua-i-w' un'a tuarirtaqan ketvut taqukanek calingartaqameng, imkut-llu nayiit-llu qiluit cipegqurluki erurturluki ininaurait.

Askacagarluteng-am call' aaqassaarturluki nerellrat. Erurturluki-ll' iniinaurtuq imna aanavut.

Tuartang natkuivkenaki taqukat inilallrukait, anrutaita taugaam imait, qiluita-ll' imait cungait-llu-w' pilallikait. Cumikenqegcaarluki wii tamaani

[food] after taking our belongings out into the porch, she was smoking [food]. They were evidently seal lungs.

She evidently hung them, and then right before they hardened, she'd bring them indoors and smoke them. She evidently smoked those.

And after filling [sealskin containers] with seal oil, she placed the ones that she smoked inside sealskin containers. They were very tasty.

When I first watched her do that and ate them, I found them delicious. And although I wanted more, I couldn't say so.

Their lungs evidently taste very good when slightly dried. They are very tasty when you smoke them. I think she'd place them in seal oil after cutting them to pieces.

When we went down [to Qikertaar] during spring, my father said that he wanted to get some food and went outside.

He returned with something, and he had evidently filled a small bucket with those that she had smoked along with some dried seal meat, as well as some other things that looked like dried bird meat. When he came inside, my mother cut them to pieces [and put them] in that small bowl.

Since they weren't just dried, they tasted like something, like dried fish, and they tasted like smoke and were very delicious. Back when I first became aware of life, I think that's how they lived.

But although they'd go spring camping down at Aqumgalleq after that time, they started going spring camping there much later when I had grown, but I never saw them catch as many seals as they did at [Qikertaar], although they did catch seals from time to time.

My goodness, the edge [of the seals piled along the back wall] was lined with skins to prevent things from falling. The place where they stored food was filled with meat, and there were ringed seals in this area to prevent [the meat] from sliding down. They had places to prevent [the meat] from sliding down at Qikertaar

I became fully aware of my surroundings while there, but since I was probably small then, boys would lift me up and run off with me at that time. I think I became aware of my surroundings early at that time.

When they started to work on seals, when the ocean down below us was free of shore ice, when they started to work on processing seals, they'd squeeze their hands down ringed seal intestines and wash them and hang them.

They were very delicious when we chewed on them when they dried and ate them. And my mother would constantly wash them and hang them.

It seems they hung every part of a seal to dry, only discarding the contents

cumikelallruanka taqukiungartaqata; cumikluki cakneq.

Qapiarturluki amiit, makunun angtuanun, angtuanun caqukiurluki.

Tua-i taugken tamakunun uquiqunegteki qerruallermeggnun caquurluki uquit tamakut-llu pugtautait.

Tamarmeng tua-i ukut tangvak'nganka Terkuam Arnaalleq-llu im' pinaurtuq tuaten. Aklullruarateng an'arrluki puyuqiaqluni, natmegteggun, waten call' marayamek tua-i natengqelaameng nep'ut tamakut.

Tamana tamaa-i nalluyagucuitelaqeka; waten taqukallruarnek, taqukanek piqcaartura'arqama, *lung*-ait maa-i qunukengramki egtelalriit, tamana umyuaqluku naspaaqernalua pilaryaaqeng'erma. Waniw' tua-i canrilkuma qavcirrarnek [piciqua].

Inimaqarraarluki tua-i, iciw' kineryarturqateng ensuqertelalriit. Tuaten elli'irtaqata itrulluki puyuqaqluki, puyuqelalliniluki.

Tua-i taugken caqutnun ekekunegteki uqirluki cali caqutulliniluki. Askacagalliniut.

Tua-i-w' tua-i-gguq cuakaayiluni tamakunek, cuakayagnek aperluki. Askacagalliniut ensuqertaqata puyuqaqluki, kinluaqerpailgata. Ungimayugnaunateng-llu. Neqniqkacagalliniut puyurninaqluteng. Naspaq'ernalua-am waniw' tuquvailegma umyuarteqengyaaqellruunga.

Mark-aq-am maliksukluku itquma waten piarkaulluryaaqaqa, "Wangtun qemageskiu qanemcilqa umyuarpenun anqercetenrilkurrluku." [*ngel'artuq*] Tut'gaqnitkeurluryuamku.

Cucuaq: Augkut-qaa taqukat egkumun itrutaqamegteki tamaani merr'it'lallruit? Tangvallruaten-qaa?

Qamulria: Yaa, tuani-ll' tua-i cali ataucirqumek tangvallruunga. Tua-i-ll' aanaka im' apcaaqluku, "Qaill' pisiu?" "Tua-i-w' pikek'a waten pilaamteki." Tua-i-llu mer'itqerluta pillemteni, qanikcarmek atam call'.

Itrulluku tua-i-ll' aitara'arrluku kuvluku. Tua-i-gguq miilluku.

Ellami taugken keggani tangvallemni call' pimek, ikamranek yuulallrit augkut qanikcaarmek qanritgun kaimqaqluki.

Tamakut-llu tang qulqikarait cali qamiqurritnek, uatmun cauqurluki imirturluki. Atam call' kenirauluteng aspialliniut.

of their stomachs and of their intestines and probably their bile. I paid close attention to them when they started to work on seals; I watched them closely.

They always skinned the seals starting from their neck areas to make sealskin pokes for storing the [seal blubber] of larger seals.

But when they removed their blubber, they always stored their blubber inside the seal skins they inflated, along with their lungs also.

All the people I observed, even the late Terkuam Arnaan, did that. She would take out their clothing and belongings [from their home] and smoke [lungs] on their floor, since our homes had mud floors.

I never forgot that; when I am working on processing seals, these days I discard their lungs although I don't want to, although I think of trying to [smoke them] thinking of what they did in the past. If nothing happens to me, I'll try it with a few.

[They smoked them] after hanging them to dry for a while. You know how they shrivel up and shrink when they are in the process of drying. When they became like that, they brought them inside and smoked them, they evidently smoked them.

But when they placed them inside sealskin pokes, they also placed seal oil inside [the pokes] when they stored them in sealskin pokes. They are evidently very tasty.

She was making *cuakayiit* out of those, and she called them *cuakayiit*. Those are very tasty when you smoke them when they shrivel up and shrink before they fully dry. And they aren't mushy at all. They are extremely tasty and taste like smoked food. I was thinking that I wanted to try making those before I die.

I thought maybe Mark [John] had come with you and I was planning on telling him when I came inside, "Try to store what I told you inside your mind like me, not allowing it to suddenly come out." [*laughs*] I tend to tease him since he is my grandchild.

Alice Rearden: When they brought seals to the back wall of their home in the past, did they give them a drink of water? Did you watch them?

Maria Eric: Yes, I watched that once. I asked my mother, "What did you do to it?" "I did that because that's what we do to them." Then when we didn't have any water, she used snow.

They brought it inside, and then she opened its mouth and spilled [water inside]. They call it *miilluku*.

But when I observed that outdoors, the ones they had unloaded from their sleds, they'd sprinkle a little snow in their mouths.

And they also filled their small shelves with their heads, facing them

It'gait-llu egcugnaunaki. It'gait cali taquaqaqluki neqliya'arqamta.

Tamakut-llu tua-i qamiqut meqngareskata aitaruciqerluki.

Caranglluum-am piakuk, maurluiruteurlumta imum piakuk, "Aling qamiqunek-qaa taquarituci?"

Yaavet Centulimun tagqerrluta ukut-llu Ayak'ankut. Ungalamek anuqengyartuan maaken ayalriakut, kiturluki-ll' Kuigilngurmiut. Yaakariintelliniuq Kuiguilngurmiut tauna Centuliq.

Piakuk-am, "Qamiqunek-qaa waniw' taquarraituci?"

Tua-i-ll' Angilan piluku, "Qavcin-wa ugkut ua-i qamiqut malikellrukput it'ganun ilakluki nerelngunayukluta-am neqnek."

"Kitek taglutek ikayuqlutek kenilaakegteki."

Arenqialan-am tua-i kenirlunuk. Pavaken Centulirmiut akiatnek avuqiirlunuk, ciamrunek.

Agna qertukayalriim acia, taperrnai cali makut keggunret mengliini qercurpak tua-i, qaillun sugtutaurluteng.

Avulalriakuk tuani, cunaw' kiagpak mingqaarkamegnek. Itraugartaqluki Mamterillernun.

Taperrnareskina! [*ngel'artuq*] Arnassagangaraqtalliniluni!

Upagaqluta atam tua-i mat'umi [March], nengqerrameng nepianek. Qerrucugnaunata up'nerkiaqluta. Qanikcangqengraan tua-i waten aterqurluta tekitnaaput tuar qanikcangqerrsugnaitetaciitni.

Uani taugaam pelatekarpalluulartut ulem piiyuaku; pelatekarpallulallruut.

Taukut-llu tua-i Iquyuilnguunkut kan'a qaillun pilria uitavikelallrat atam tua-i cama-i taperrnauguq acetuqitagnek, tauna tua-i uitavillrata nevua.

Waten atralria cingiuluni, uitavikelallerput, qulvani askacagalria.

Kan'a atam tua-i cama-i, Angilan-ll'-am atrarlunuk pillmegni tua-i taperrnarpakayallraat acetukayagluteng, teguneqegtaarcurviksunaqsaaqluni.

Ellait-am Iquyuilnguum Atiin avacirluku waten tuskanek, *plywood*-aat

toward the front of the home. The [heads] are also evidently very tasty when cooked.

And they never discarded their feet either. And we also brought along their feet as provisions when we went to our summer fish camps.

And when the fur started to shed from their heads, they put something in their mouths to keep them open [before cooking them].

Carangllluk said to us, our late dear grandmother said to us, "Did you happen to bring any heads with you to eat?"

We had briefly gone up to Centuli along with Ayak'aq and family. When the wind started to blow from the south, we left from here, and we passed Kwigillingok. Centuli is evidently a little past Kwigillingok.

She asked us, "Do you not have a few heads that you took with you to eat?"

Then Angilan said to her, "We brought a number of heads back there along with some feet just in case we are tired of eating fish."

[She said], "Then come up and help each other quickly cook them."

Since she was so insistent, we cooked. We picked some driftwood from across Centulirmiut.

The area across, the area underneath a very steep area, the *taperrnat* that grew there, and even the grasses that had already been bitten off at the root [by mice] along the edge were extremely light in color and a certain height.

We picked from there, and evidently we'd use them to make grass baskets all summer long. We'd bring [the finished grass baskets] up to Bethel [to sell].

You should go and pick some *taperrnaq!* [*laughs, talking to Ann*] She's evidently becoming an elderly woman!

We'd move [to Qikertaar] during this month [March], since they had real sod homes. We didn't get cold at all and would go spring camping. Although there was snow, we'd arrive there by floating down the river just like there was no snow at all.

But they mainly had tents down there [at Aqumgalleq] since floods tend to cover that area; they mainly used tents.

And the place where Iquyuilnguq and his family had a home, for some reason long *taperrnat* grow on it down there now, the land where their home was located.

The land that extends down is a point, the place where we used to stay, and higher up is very good land.

The area down there, when Angilan and I went down, had large *taperrnat* that were extremely tall, and it is a good place to go and get grass for the stitches on a coiled-grass basket.

pivailgata tuskanek ituqurayaarluki.

Waten tua-i qalliqurluki, elanirluku, pikna-ll' pelatekamek qilirluku. Assirpak tua-i, tan'gercecugnaunateng. Assikeqalqa.

Taqukanek, taqukarrlainarnek tuani pissulallruut. Mat'umi maa-i atrarluteng pilaryugnarqut nengqerrameng-llu. Taqukiqkacagarnaurtut.

Qanikcarpayuilan-llu kan'a Qikertaar, unkut-llu tekitnaurtukut teggalqut alaiterpagluteng.

Aling, iqalluarpiit tamaani pilaryaaqellrullinilriit. Ulerpagaqan teggalqut engeliitni tua-i neqngunaurtut. Pissuyuunaki!

Imkut taugaam, elquat taugaam nevngartaqata qecugnaurtut. Elquarullinilriit tamakut.

Qikertaarmiut kankut askacagallruuq atam up'nerkivikellrat. Naseknacualleraulua tua-i murikengellruunga tamaani allani-ll' up'nerkiyuilamta, tuani taugaam.

Tua-i-ll' im' aatavut qaill' pilriim uani piurangluni mat'um paingani, pissuqcaarturangluni. Ulerpiuryulkugtuq taugaam ugna.

Tuani-ll'-am uitalriakut. . . . Tailriakut Arayakcaamek tailriakut maavet up'nerkiyarturluta. Up'nerkiyarluni-am tuavet upaulluta.

Tekicamta-ll' tua-i qimukcualleraak ingkuk malruk qiluallagtuk tua-i qamigautek mengliigni. Anqertut Aniim Atiinkut.

Anigarmek irniarluteng, maurlurlullrat-wa, elkek-wa; qasgimi uitalliniluteng uani Cevv'arnermi.

Tua-i-ll' itresqelluta, arenqianani ilagaasqelluteng pelatekiurpailgan pelatekangqerqumta. Tua-ll'-am aatama kiuluku, "Pelatekaiteksailngukut-wa up'nerkautaqakut."

Tuani call' tua-i tauna-am murilkeqallruaqa, murilkelluku tangvakallruaqa. Aling nakleurluq, tua-ll' kiungani piuq, ellait-gguq-am waniw' pelatekangenrilkuneng kiagiciqelriit maani.

Taukuk tua-i qimugteklinilukek, ikamrak-wa imkuk iciw' qamigarcuutektullrukait qayanun inguqaqluki qamigautet. Qulel'iqerlukek taillrulliniluteng Cicingmek.

Maurlurteng malikluku. Ek'arrlukek-gguq Anigar-llu. Taukuk-wa qimugteket waten akiqliqa'arrlukek ayautaqlukek, qimugteurluuk. Nangteqeurlullruut atam tua-i cakneq.

For their home, Iquyuinguq's father placed boards along the outside before there was plywood around, connecting the boards.

He stacked them on top of one another and made the outside, and then he placed a tent over the top. It was very nice and didn't get dark inside. I liked it.

They only hunted seals [at Qikertaar]. I think they'd go down during this month [March] since they had homes also. They'd catch many seals.

And since Qikertaar doesn't get a lot of snow, we'd arrive and see the rocks completely visible down there.

Gee, there were actually herring there during that time. When the tide was very high, that kind of fish would be along the edge of the rocks. They never fished for them!

But when the herring eggs started to cling [to the rocks], they'd pull some. Those were evidently herring eggs.

Qikertaarmiut down there was a wonderful spring camping site. I started to become aware of things there when I was a little girl since we never went spring camping in other places, but just there.

And our father for some reason started to [go spring camping] down there along the mouth of this river, and he started to hunt there. But that place down there tends to flood.

While we were there one time. . . . We came to this area from Arayakcaaq to go spring camping. He moved us there to go spring camping.

And when we arrived, two small dogs started barking from along the edge of a kayak sled. A person suddenly came out, and it was evidently Aniim Atii and his family.

Anigaq was their child at the time, along with their grandmother and them; they were evidently staying at the *qasgi* down at Cevv'arneq.

Then they told us to go inside and pleaded with us to join them before he set up his tent, if we happened to have a tent. Then my father said to him, "We always have a tent when spring comes."

That's something that I observed intently also. My, how poor, when my father answered him, he said that if they didn't get a tent, they would spend the summer there [at Cevv'arneq].

Those two dogs evidently belonged to them, and their sled, you know how they used kayak sleds to place the kayak on when they went seal hunting. They had evidently placed a backing and handle bar on [the kayak sled] and had come from Cicing.

They brought their grandmother. He said they had just had her and Anigar get inside [the sled]. They placed their two dogs side by side and traveled,

Tua-i-ll' piuq, ellakegciqallrani-am qaneqtartuq, "Atak wii avavet kangaqerlii yaatemtenun, uliiret kangalalliut."

Angerluku-ll' tua-i aatama. Piuq, ellii-gguq waniw' pelatekiurutkiuryartuqatartuq anelrarluni, muriit paivngallratni.

Pelatekaq tua-i qanagkiurluku tuani, qanagkiulliniluku, acikaa-llu waten ellirraarluku itralliniluni.

Tekituq uliirtellrallinilria. "Aling arenqiapaa-ll' tua-i waniw' uqlaryaaqevkenaku amiirqa. Waniw' unuaqu Tununermun qimugtevet ilaitnek ilaqaqikek qimugtegka Tununertelaakarniartua." [*ngel'artuq*]

Tua-i-ll' pelatekaq ac'arturluku. Ilaitnek tua-i ellii aturluni qimugtenek anelrarluni. Tekitell'ertuq atakuan ut'rarrluni, qaterlimek tua-i pillinilria, qaillun-wa angtauralria augna mukaaq.

Uliirem akianek, nillaumavkenaku-ll' ayaulluku.

Tua-i tekiteurluraput caunateng neqaunateng-llu. Naklekellruanka tuani.

Tua-i-ll'-am aatama tuani atakumi qaluyaasqellunuk Cuyuanguyak-llu kanavet Qayairyaramun. Ikamrak tua-i ucilirlukek taglunuk.

Akleng, Aniim Arnaan anqertuq qantacuaq-wa tegumiara. Elakcarluni cukilget imkut tua-i cimelpakayallraat mikleraitnek avurluni.

Naklekellruanka tuani. Caturaqluteng uitallruat tauni? Tua-i iqmigaqamiki ig'aqluki. Naklekellruanka cakneq.

Uani tua-i up'nerkilangamta taqukamek amllermek tuanicicetun tangerrnanrillruunga. Taqukat-wa amllellruata avani pillrulriit.

Tua-i Mik'ngayam Atii nayirtevlaagaqameng tayim' tuar uyakelli'irtaqan tamarnaurtuq. Piinanermini taugken tua-i tekicarturluni paiminun aqumgaurluni.

Cunaw' Qalvinraamek nayircalallinilria, caqutekassaatullrullinilria. Arenqialami-gguq caqutekailata uqurtaarani.

Taqukiqtullruut atam tua-i. Caqukailata waniwa aqvatellruuq.

Tua-llu-wam nulirran tekican qapiaqai ellami, kemgit tuaten iniluki.

those poor dogs. [Dogs] really suffered in the past.

Then he said, when the weather was good, he said, "Let me go and walk up there beyond our place, as white foxes might be roaming around."

Then my father agreed with him. [My father] said that he was going to go down and set up the tent when there was wood around.

He made roof boards for the tent there, he evidently made roof boards, and after constructung the bottom of the frame, he headed up.

He arrived, and he had evidently caught a white fox. "Oh my, I just skinned this, trying not to make a mess of it. You should let me take some of your dogs to add to my two dogs so that I can run quickly to Tununak tomorrow." [*laughs*]

Then he went to place the tent over the frame. Using some of the dogs he headed down [to Tununak]. He arrived that evening having returned the same day, and he had evidently bought white cloth and a bag of flour that was a certain size.

[He bought it] for the price of the white fox, and it wasn't even stretched to dry when he brought it.

When we arrived upon those poor people, they had nothing and had no food. I felt sorry for them at the time.

Then my father asked Cuyanguyak and I to go and dipnet in the evening down at Qayairyaraq. We loaded the sled and went up.

Poor, Aniim Arnaan ran out holding a small bowl. She dug [inside the fish] and she picked the smaller needlefish, the smaller of the smelt.

I felt sorry for them at the time. What did they eat when they were there? When she'd put them in her mouth, she'd swallow them. I felt really sorry for them at the time.

When we started to go spring camping down there [at Aqumgalleq], I no longer saw many seals being caught like in the past [at Qikertaar]. It was because there were many seals in the past.

When they didn't catch many ringed seals, Mikngayam Atii would disappear when the shore ice got closer to shore. Then after a while he would arrive, sitting along the opening of his kayak.

He'd evidently go and hunt seals for sealskin pokes at Qalvinraaq River. He would say that he went since there weren't sealskin containers for his seal oil.

They caught many seals in the past. He said that he went to go get some since there weren't any storage containers [for seal oil].

When he arrived, his wife skinned them starting at the neck area and

Ellami tua-i urugartaqan urugngikacaaraami-ll' kan'a nunakellrat, qapiaqunaurtut anuquriluteng.

Tua-i-gguq tungunqutellriit uurcarluteng, ayarurluteng.

Tegumiaqurluku nakacuk, aug'umun negcikcuarmun aga'arrluku. Negcikcuarluteng cali ayarukluku tagnaurtut, kangrani-w' tauna tua-i.

Terkuam Atii-w' tua-i ciukacagarmek atam tagtullruuq, upallerput yaaqsigpek'naku atrarqami. Ciumek tua-i tungunquterrlainarluni.

Tua-i amllermek qanemcikaitua aug'umek ciuqvallarmek, ciuqvallaat augkut nalluanka. Kan'a tua-i Qikertaar kana-i ellangvikellruamku maaten ellangua tua-i Qikertaarmun upatullrullinilriakut.

Atam una-i kayangirtuq una uatii. Nangnermek-am Qikertaarmetlemteni Yugissaam Arnaan-llu makiralriakuk. Tua-i-ll' ingna pekvallakan aqvaqurluni curugluku.

Pilaqeka-am, "Aling ciknatalarpagcit!" Ciunemnek-llu pekvallagngan curukarluku eknaurai issratminun.

Paniliar: Aataka-ll' im' qanemcitullruuq avani ak'a Qikertaarmek wall'u-q' naken tayima naliatnek kankut kingunirluni [?] Arnaan maligtaqamiu makiraluni un'gaavet Aqumgallermiut kiatiitnun.

Waten-gguq cikut aterqaqngartaqaki cikut-gguq tamaaggun arviutaqluku taum malian. Atertengraata tua-i canimelkiinun ek'artaqluni, ek'artaqlutek; arviutaqluku atertellriatgun cikutgun.

Tuamtellu-gguq tua-i uterrnarikatek ut'reskunek, iliini-gguq uaqsigitengaqlutek-llu.

Qamulria: Ayaruminek anguaqcaarturluni. Ayarungqetullruut atam waten kapuukartessuutnek.

Paniliar: Kuik un'a iqkitaranrituq. Waten ul'aqami cikut aterqaq'larait navguraqata. Tua-lli-wa-gguq tua-i aturluki tamakut arviutelaqii un'um Urrsukvaam akianun.

Tua-i kiaqsigiterrlugaqlukek, iliini-llu-gguq tuamtell' eneskan uaqsigitengaqlukek ikavet akianun tekipailegmek. Qungvagnaqvaa!

pulling the carcass out, leaving the skin intact outdoors, and she hung their meat.

When the snow melted, since snow melted fast in the place where they stayed [at Qikertaar], people would skin seals starting at the neck to make sealskin pokes, bringing [seals] outdoors.

They say those who caught adult bearded seals would announce their catch, using walking sticks.

They would hang onto the bladder and hang it on the *negcikcuaq* [small gaff]. They'd also use the small gaff as a walking stick when they went up to shore, and that [bladder] would be up at the top [of the small gaff].

Terkuam Atii was always the first to go up to shore, when he went down to the ocean not long after we moved [to spring camp]. He was always the first to catch an adult bearded seal.

I don't have a lot to say about the old days, since I don't know much about the old days. Since I became aware of life down at Qikertaar, when I became aware of life, I saw that we used to move to Qikertaar.

There are many eggs in the area down the coast from that place. When we were at Qikertaar for the last time, Yugissaam Arnaan and I went egg hunting. When a bird flew off, she'd run and get it.

I would say to her, "How jealous you are!" And when it would fly off from the area ahead of me, she would run over to it and place the eggs inside her grass carrying bag.

Theresa Abraham: My father would also tell stories about back when he'd accompany someone's mother from Qikertaar or one of the places down coast to go egg hunting down along the area above Aqumgallermiut.

He said when ice sheets started to float in the water, the person he accompanied would take him across [the river] along those pieces of ice. Although [pieces of ice] were floating, they'd jump onto one that was close and get on it; she'd take him across [the river] through floating sheets of ice.

And he said when it was time for them to return home, on their way home, sometimes they'd float a little too far down along the lower part [of the river].

Maria Eric: She'd use her walking stick to paddle. They had walking sticks they used for obtaining buttercup plants that were shaped like this.

Theresa Abraham: The river down there isn't narrow. When the tide comes up, sheets of ice float when they break into pieces. Stepping on those [ice sheets] she'd take him across to the other side of the Urrsukvaaq River.

Sometimes they'd drift a little too far upriver, and sometimes when the

Qamulria: Imna carvanra tuani eneskan tuknirivailgan, ulkan-llu cali tuknirivailgan arviqcaarluteng ullakengarteng nall'artevkenaku yuugaqluteng.

Paniliar: Arnat tua-i tamakut caperrnaqluteng pilallrulliniut.

Aqumgalleq

Cuyanguyak: Waniwa wangnek call' waniw' qanrutkeqatartua. Cameg' yugmek nallulua ayatullruunga kiagmi issratka atmagluku, ivrucigka-llu wavet tevvlukek, ayaglua yuilqumun.

Umyuartequ'urlua-ll' yuilqumi waten kangarlua, unavet ketemtenun unavet. "Tua-i-qaa waniwa kayangurrarmek unangengaitua."

Tua-i taugken ernerpak piiyualua. Uqsuqaq aipaagni pekvallagaqan ullagluku tekitaqamku quyalua, "Quyanaqva-ll'! Tua-i-ll' kayangullua! Tangrriu! Cikiuteka waniwa."

Issratka cillarrluku ciicailkutkaanek-llu pirraarluki, kayangutanka ek'uraqerraarluki tuavet issratka atmagluku ayaglua.

Yuilqumi piiyualqa cali waniwa piiyualalqa call' waniw' tuaten ayuqellruuq. Tua-i-ll' ernerpak tua-i caqiageurlua kayanguqu'urlua. Neqkaq taugaam umyuaqurluku caqiageurlua, kayangutaqama tua-i caquurarraarluki ayagaqlua.

Tua-i-ll' nutaan taquangqerrama, aglua ing'um nanvam ceniinun.

Tekiskumku neru'urlua, unkut unani yalqulget tengaurturalriit tangvaurluki. Tangvaurluki naruyat tuaten, nacallngaraat, teqiyaaraat, ukut unani. Tua-i tangvaurluki, neru'urlua, nerurarraarlua nerkuanka nanvamun ek'artaqluki.

Tua-i tuaten nerurarraarlua nangertaqama, unkut imkut kiarqurallrenka umyuaqluki nangerrlua issratka atmagluku atraraqlua.

Cali qaltacuarangqerraqlua kayanguyagarcuutekamnek. Tua-i taugken tamakut imkut unani yaquleyagaat, nacallngaraat, teqiyaaraat, naruyacuat; cali tua-i tamakunek qaltacuarqa kayanguyagarnek imiraqluku.

Taugaam makut cali kinerneruaraat, caneggluaraat, qikertarnat-llu ullag-

tide went out, it would drift them a little too far downriver before they got to the other side. How scary!

Maria Eric: They'd cross [the river] when the tide went out before the current became strong, and when the tide came in before the current became strong, and they would not get off in the spot that they had directly aimed for.

Theresa Abraham: Those women were unrivaled in the past.

Aqumgalleq[50]

Martina Wasili: I'm going to tell you about what I was like in the past. Without anyone else to accompany me during summer, I used to travel out to the wilderness with my *issran* on my back, and I'd drape my waterproof boots here and take off to the wilderness.

This is what was constantly on my mind when I was walking around out in the wilderness, when walking down below [Aqumgalleq, One who sat there], "I wonder if I will obtain just one egg."

I'd walk all day long. Sometimes if a pintail suddenly flew off, I'd approach it, and when I came upon it, I'd be grateful, "I'm so grateful! I've found some eggs! See! Here is my gift."

I'd open up my twined grass bag and after placing padding in there to prevent the eggs from getting smashed, after carefully placing the eggs I found inside, I'd put my grass bag on my back and leave.

That's how I used to roam on foot in the wilderness in the past. I'd go back and forth all day long, finding eggs. Thinking only of food to harvest, I'd go back and forth, and when I'd find eggs, I'd put them inside my bag and leave.

And since I had taken some provisions to eat along the way, I'd walk to the edge of that lake over there.

And when I arrived, I'd eat, watching the birds that were flying down below. I'd watch gulls, Sabine's gulls, Arctic terns down there. I'd watch them and eat, and after eating, I'd put my leftovers inside the lake.

When I'd stand after eating, I'd think of the places I'd searched, and stand and go down with my *issran* on my back.

I also had a small bucket with me to hold small eggs. With the eggs of those small birds down there, of Sabine's gulls, Arctic terns, of black-legged kittiwakes; I'd also fill my small bucket with those small eggs.

taarturluki piaqama pekvallagaqluteng. Tuaten tua-i. Tekitaqamki kayanguit caquqerraarluki atraraqlua. Uqamairiaqan issratka uterrnalua umyuarteqaqlua.

Unayaqiyuitellruunga-llu yuilqumun ayakata'arqama. Tua-i ayagaqlua waten tua-i wangnek ayaullua. Tua-i taugken taglua nutaan ilamnun tekillua. Tuaten ayuqellruunga.

Taugaam aatama ayautaqamia un'gaavet ayautaqanga qayamun eklua. Iliini qessalaryaaqelrianga, taugaam qaill' qessasciiganii qanrutesciiganaku.

Kuigeurlurmun uavet Qukalirrarmun yuugaqamia, pinauraanga, "Kitakat waniw' kingumni utaqaurqia." Aling aren nanikuayuunii, camek-llu umyuarteqsuunii, alingellerkamnek-llu umyuarteqsuunii.

Taugaam makut maa-i yaqulet kayanguitnek umyuartequ'urlua. Unillua ayagaqan tayima pellaaqluni. Tuaten tua-i kayangussuaguraraqlua. Yukllu igvayuunani. Unani-llu Urrsukvaam paingani qayamek kiarteng'erma tangyuunii.

Taugaam issratka una tua-i imingnaqu'urluku.

Nanvamun-llu ekqataquma, qerrulliigka mayurqaarlukek issratka atmakluku ullagturluku qikertaarnaq una nanvami.

Piinanemni neqleret pekpallagaqluteng. Tekitaqamku, issratka yuuluku cillarqaarluku ek'uraraqluki.

Uqamairiaqan issratka uterrlua qayamegnun atraraqlua. Atrainanemni yaquleyagarnek kayangutaqama, qaltacuaramnun ek'aqluki.

Tua-i-ll' tekiskuma nutaan issratka yuurraarluku un'gavet ayaglua.

Nauwa-w' tayim' avatemni yuut. Ayaglua muragayagarnek avurlua. Avurturarraarlua amlleriaqata, itrarlua nuna elakarluku, nutaan taukut kayanguyagartanka kenirluki.

Aataka kiarcaaqnaurqa cataunani. Nerinitengnaurtua kayangutuqcaarlua tua-i ner'aqluki.

Nerurarraarlua, tuamtell' issratka imairluku cailkamun. Imairraarluku patuqerraarluki tuamtell' ayaglua.

Cali tua-i issratka cali imingnaqu'urluku kayangunek, caqiagurlua tangaagurlua, pivakarluni pekvallagaqluni.

Tuaten tua-i issratka uqamairiaqan atranqigglua nutaan aqumlua uta-

But when I'd go to all the small dry areas, small clumps of grass, and small islands along lakes, birds would fly off. That's what I'd do. When I'd reach them, I'd put their eggs in my container and go down. I'd plan on returning home when my *issran* got heavy.

And I didn't ask people to accompany me when I was about to travel out on the land. I would just leave on my own. But I'd go back up and reach my family when I returned. That's how I was.

But when my father would take me down along the coast, I'd get inside the kayak. Sometimes I was reluctant to go, but I couldn't tell him that I didn't want to go.

When he'd drop me off down at Kuigeurluq and that slough called Qukaqlirraq, he'd tell me, "Now, wait for me after I leave." Oh my, I never felt distressed and never thought anything would happen, and fear never crossed my mind.

Bird eggs were the only things constantly on my mind. When he'd take off and leave me, he'd dissapear from view. I'd constantly look for eggs like that. And I never saw a person. And although I'd look around for kayakers down along the mouth of Urrsukvaaq River, I never saw them.

The only thing that was on my mind was trying to fill my *issran*.

And when I was about to get in and wade in a lake, I'd pull my pants up first, put my *issran* on my back, and approach a small island inside a lake.

After a while, black brants would fly off. When I'd get to [the nest], I'd take my *issran* off my back, and after opening it, I'd carefully place [the eggs] inside.

When my *issran* got heavy, I'd return, I'd head down to our kayak. As I was heading down, when I'd find eggs from little birds, I'd put them inside my small bucket.

And when I arrived, after removing my *issran*, I'd head down toward the coast.

There were no people around. I'd walk along, picking up sticks. After collecting wood and gathering enough, I'd go back up, dig a small pit in the ground, and cook the small eggs that I found.

I'd search for my father, but he'd be gone. I'd get impatient for his arrival as I ate the eggs, and I'd continue to eat.

After eating, I'd empty the contents of my *issran* onto the ground. After emptying its contents and covering them, I'd leave again.

I'd try to fill my *issran* again with eggs and go back and forth along the land, and upon searching for a while, a bird would fly off from its nest.

qauraraqluku.

Piinanemni ak'aki amaken yugpall'er alairciquq, cugtukayagluni. Utaqaluku tua-i. Aataka tekiciiquq yaquliqkacagarluni uyampagluni yaqulegnek. Piaqa kayangunek kenillrunilua.

Tua-i-ll' taukut kayangut nernginanrani un'gavet tuamtell' ayaglua kuigem painganun. Kuigem painga tekitaqamku muragat tangellrenka avurturluki, muraganek avurlua, equp'aglua itraraqlua.

Tua-i taugken qayam keluanun elliluki muragat. Aataka-ll' qamigautengqerturatullrulria. Cali qayaan qaingani qamigautek taukuk uitalallrulutek. Nererraarluni taq'aqami, taukut imkut muragayagaat atrauqurturarraarluki, naqyulluki, naqyuqaarluki atraraqlua naqyuqaartelluki. Tua-i taugken ek'arrlua qayamun, arvirlunuk itrarlunuk Aqumgallermun. Tekitaqamegnuk tua-i itraqlunuk pelatekamun.

Tuaten tua-i wiinga yuuguralqa ayuqellruuq. Imutun ellaka qinuitqapiaralriatun. Uitaurayuunii waten tua-i-w' yugni. Taugaam uitayuitellruama, yuilquq taugaam kesianek umyuaqluku. Tuaten tua-i pilallruunga.

Aataka-llu kuvyayarraarluni. . . . Qavarcecuitellruanga kiagaqan. Tua-i-llu qavarcecuilanga Arnaucuamek aipirlua unugpak pegg'araqlunuk.

Aatama pinauraakuk, "Ulqaarqan, paq'ertaqluku kuik, ulqaarqan tupageskia tagliarturciqua." Qalurqisqenauraakuk-llu.

Tua-i taugken uitaurlunuk Arnaucuaq-llu piaqlunuk unugmi. Qavarniyuunii. Tua-i taugken kuik paqpakarluku piciqaqa ulqaarallinilria, kiatmurnengaarallinilria.

Tua-i taugken taglua pelatekamun aataka tupaggluku ulqaarniluku.

Yuurqerkiulaagluku. Yuurqalaaggaarluni upluni tayima qayamun atraraqluni ayagaqluni. Wiinga inartaqlua qavaraqlua.

Tua-i tuaten wiinga yuuguralqa maa-i man'a, nalluyagucuunaku-llu. Ellangellemnek ayaglua nalluyagucuunaku.

Ingricuaraak

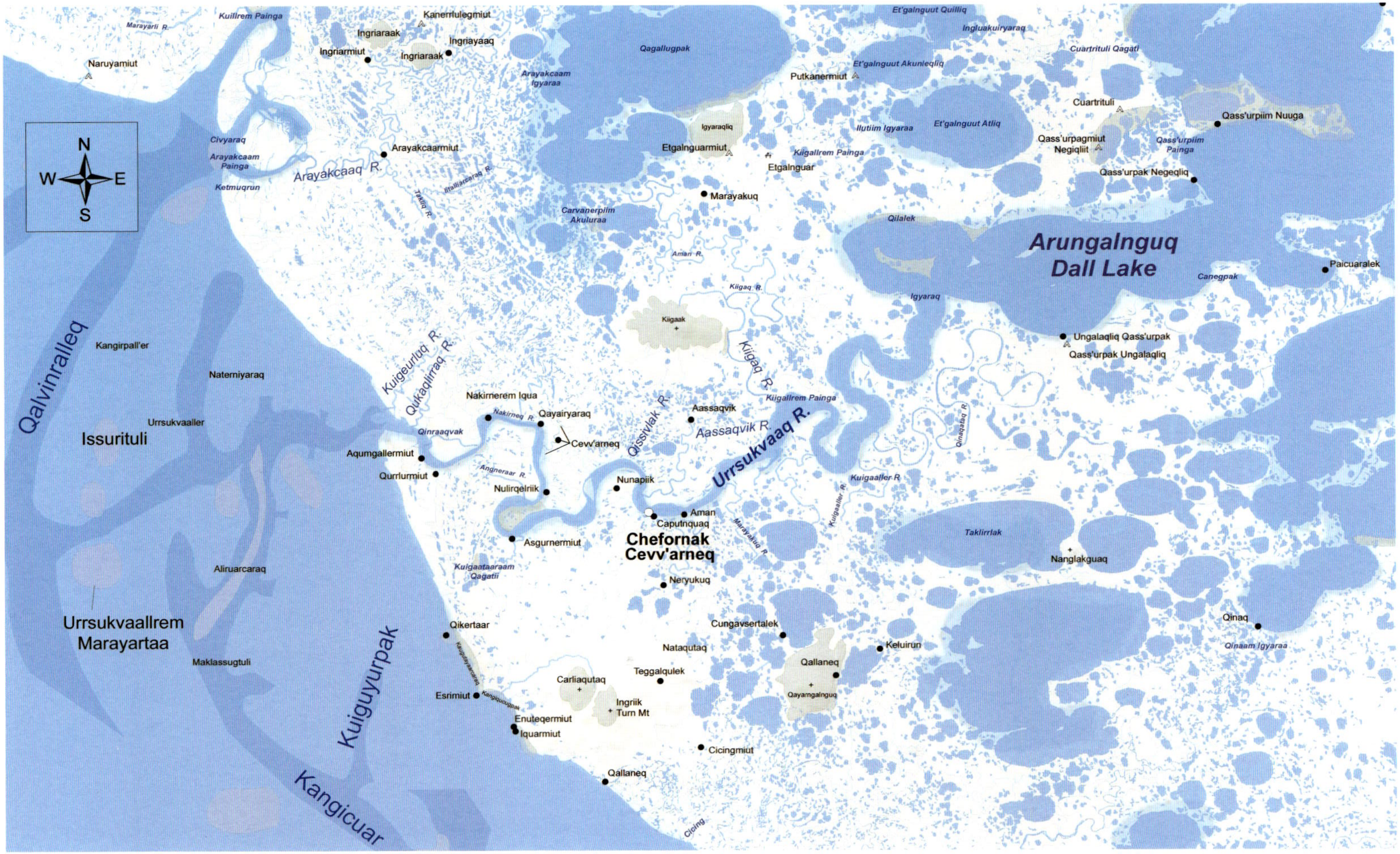

Chefornak area. Michelle Pearson and Alice Rearden.

Wire fish trap on the upper Cakcaaq River. AFR.

Setting a whitefish net below camp on the upper Cakcaaq River. AFR.

Ben Angaiak with beaver on the upper Cakcaaq River. AFR.

Mouth of the Cakcaaq River. AFR. (Pages 254–257)

Village of Chefornak, early 1960s. University of Delaware, University Museums: Mabel and Harley McKeague Alaskan Inuit Collection © Mabel McKeague. (Pages 266–277)

Woman and child pick berries on the tundra near Chefornak, early 1960s. University of Delaware, University Museums: Mabel and Harley McKeague Alaskan Inuit Collection © Mabel McKeague.

Man working on a wooden fish trap, Chefornak, early 1960s. University of Delaware, University Museums: Mabel and Harley McKeague Alaskan Inuit Collection © Mabel McKeague.

View of Urrsukvaaq (Chefornak River), early 1960s. University of Delaware, University Museums: Mabel and Harley McKeague Alaskan Inuit Collection © Mabel McKeague. (Pages 304–309)

Ingriik (Turn Mountain) with Chefornak in the foreground, early 1960s. University of Delaware, University Museums: Mabel and Harley McKeague Alaskan Inuit Collection © Mabel McKeague. (Pages 314–321)

Newtok, 1962. University of Delaware, University Museums: Mabel and Harley McKeague Alaskan Inuit Collection © Mabel McKeague. (Pages 344–349)

John Kassayulie and family at Newtok, 1962. University of Delaware, University Museums: Mabel and Harley McKeague Alaskan Inuit Collection © Mabel McKeague.

Newtok elder Michael John. AFR.

Newtok area. Michelle Pearson and Alice Rearden.

Just as before, when my *issran* would get heavy, I'd go down again and sit and wait for him.

While I waited, a very large person would appear way over there, a very tall person. I'd wait for him. My father would arrive having caught many, many birds, holding many birds over his shoulders and around his neck. I'd tell him that I had cooked some eggs.

Then as he was eating those eggs, I'd take off down there toward the river mouth. When I'd arrive at the mouth of the river, I'd pick up the sticks that I saw as I went, picking up wood, and I'd go back up with a large amount of wood on my back.

But then I'd place the wood up behind the kayak. Back then my father always had a kayak sled. And his kayak sled was situated on top of his kayak.

When he was done eating, after bringing those sticks down [to the kayak], he'd strap them down, and after he strapped them down, I'd go down. I'd get inside the kayak and we'd go across and go upriver to Aqumgalleq. When we'd arrive, we'd go inside the tent.

That's how my life was. It was as though my world was completely calm. I never stayed around people. Since I was never idle, the wilderness and land was constantly on my mind. That's how I was.

And after my father went fishing. . . . He never allowed me to sleep during summer. Since he never allowed me to sleep, Arnaucuaq and I would stay up all night.

My father would tell us, "Go and check on the river once in a while, and when the tide is just coming up, wake me up, so that I will fish for fish when they come up to shore." He'd even tell us to dip [the fish from the beach seine].

So Arnaucuaq and I would just stay at night. I never got sleepy. But after checking the river a number of times, I'd see that the tide was just starting to come up, I'd see that the current was starting to flow upriver.

I'd go up to the tent and wake my father and tell him that the tide was just starting to come in.

I'd quickly prepare some tea for him to drink. He'd quickly drink tea and prepare to leave and go down to the kayak and leave. Then I'd go up and go to sleep.

That's how I lived, and I've never forgotten it. I've never forgotten it from the time that I became aware of life.

Cuyanguyak: Cali ataucirqumek kiani Cevv'arnermun itranemteggun taugaam uitaluta kiaqliqluta, ayallemegni tunturugarnek pavaken, ikaken ika-i Ingricuaraagnek pangalegluteng tungemnun.

Aataka-w' pavani tayim' keluqvani. Alingkacag[arlua]; ircaquqa nutengvagluni. Qimaglua, wiinga-ll'-am tagellrulua tamaavet. Nanvat-wa makut, tua-i tumkarcualuki caqialua ayaglua. Makut-wa tuntut tungemun pangalelriit. Alingkacagarlua.

Tua-i-ll' unkut nanvat ketiitnun elli'irrlua, uka-i tua-i tekitniarallratni, aqvaqurlua ayaglua qayam tungiinun.

Piinanemni kingyalqa nall'arrluku tunturpall'er nanvamun angllurluni. Ala-i tukarluni, maktesciiganani. Cunaw' kana-i cirunrek nanvam terr'anun kaputellinilriik.

Uterrlua atrarlua. Maaten piunga aataka man'a. Tua-i-ll' ullagluku narugluku, tuntut-llu uatmun tayima ayagaluteng. Kan'aruk-wa tua-i pektaunani. Tekitarpuk tuqullinilria tuani.

Tua-i-w' wiinga qimallemni pitaqluku.

Maktengnaqluku aataka-ll' mermun ekluni, qamiqua cirunragnegun teguluku. Tua-i-ll' tagqaarluku pilagluku.

Tallik aug'arlukek, iruk-llu cali aug'arlukek tamarkenka taukut-llu uitaluteng. Nutaan tauna uivai nutaan tuavet nanvamun ekluki. Tamakunek taugaam talliignek irugkenek-llu atraullunuk. Atraulluk' qayamun ekluk' uterrlunuk.

Tua-i-ll'-am aataka qayagaurluni taukunun, "Tuntuyulria kenirkaminek aqvas[kili]." Tailuteng kemginek cikirturluki, kemgitnek. Quyaluteng augkut, tuntutaqngamku-w' wiinga qimallemni.

Uitayuitkacagallruunga wiinga! Qavaqallemni taugaam tua-i uitaaqlua. Ayagallerkartulua nunam qaingani. Arnaullgutemnek-llu maliglua ayayuunii. Kiirrarma.

Nunaniryulaama kiimelngerma camek-llu umyuarteqevkenii, alingellerkamnek-llu umyuarteqevkenii. Camun-llu pinayuklua umyuarteqsuunii. Atam Jesus-aam kangaumallra umyuaqetullruaqa, imumi Jesus-aaq kangaumallrulria yuilqumi natmun-llu ayayuunani. Tamana umyuaqetullruaqa.

Qinaruuq

Ingricuaraak[51]

Martina Wasili: One time right after we moved up to Cevv'arneq and were living there with homes situated upriver from one another, when we went [to hunt and gather food], there were many reindeer running toward me from Ingricuaraak [Small *ingriq* (mountain)] over there.

My father was far inland. I was so afraid; my heart was pounding. I ran off, having gone up to that place. There were lakes around, and I constantly turned as I ran, trying to find a suitable trail. Reindeer were running toward me. I was extremely frightened.

Then when I reached the area down below those lakes, when they were about to reach me, I ran off toward the kayak.

Just as I turned around, a very large reindeer submerged in the water. It kicked its feet down there and couldn't get up. Evidently, its antlers had gotten stuck along the lake bottom.

I returned and went down. I saw that my father was there. I went to him and met him, and the reindeer were heading down toward the coast. That one down there wasn't moving. When we got to it, we saw that it had died there.

I had caught it when I fled.

We tried to get it upright, and my father got in the water and took its head by its antlers. And after we brought it up, he butchered it.

He removed its fore legs and removed both its hind legs, and those other parts were in place. Then he placed its ribs inside the lake. We only brought its legs down [to the kayak]. We brought them down to the kayak and loaded them and returned home.

Then my father called the people there, "Anyone who wants reindeer should come and get some." They came, and he distributed its meat to them. Those people were happy because I had caught that reindeer when I fled.

I never sat still! The only time I was idle was when I fell asleep. I traveled all over the land. And I never traveled with girls my age. I always went alone.

Since I really enjoyed it, I went alone, and I never was worried about anything, and I never thought about being afraid. And I never thought that anything would do something to me. I always thought about how Jesus walked for a long time; Jesus walked a long time out in the wilderness, and he never went anywhere. That's what I used to think about.

Paniliar: Uumi-llu tua-i uyu'urqa-llu imna-llu . . . Nanurrualguuq Tarr'auluni tuaten John Avegyagaaq. *Camp*-allruukuk Qinaruumun. Tua-i-am pianga, quagcinek qanrraarluni maligcugaqa-gguq-qaa allgiarnek uuvlekarkangyuartukuk. Angqerluku.

Ayaglunuk Qinaruumi qikertamun tua-i piiyaaqelriakuk yaqulegtevkenani. Tamaa-i kep'alinrarnek kayangulluni ellii pingayunek. Wiinga kicetaaqerluki kayangut augkut mermek caaniik imirluku. Tua-i pugtarpanrilata, pugtang'ermeng teguluki.

Wiinga-ll' up'nerkaq tayima yuilqumun ayakallrunritua it'ganka puvellratni. Ayakanrilama tuani kayangutaqa, wiinga-am *lucky*-qerlua kayangutanka augkut kep'algem kayangui kitkacagarluteng tua-i tamarmeng.

Tua-ll' taukut tua-i uyu'urma kayangutai, kayanguliurama, ak'a pilallracetun yuurtaqata waten qallarvaagaqaulluki kayangiurlua tua-i. Tua-i yuurrluteng.

Tuamtell' utercama cali taukut kenirallrenka tuamtell' tua-i nerqataamta, aug'umek cali Nellie-m calillgutiinek Hooper Bay-rmiumek nasaurlurmek ilaluta tua-i nerluta. Piaqa, "Kayangutallemegnek waniwa ak'a piciryaraacetun keniumalrianek paivciciqua kayanguturkamtenek."

Tua-i-ll' ikirrluki. Tua-i tangerrluki imumek tua-i melqurluteng augkut yaqulecuaraat. Kiingan *yellow*-aarit alaunateng, augkut-wa tua-i qatellriaquinrayagacuayaar, tegkacagarluni-llu tua-i ellirluni taun qatellriara.

Piaqa, "Makut-gguq maa-i waten avani ciuliamta puguusviitnun tua-i nerumatullruit, taugaam tua-i waten yaqulgurtessiyaagqata qallauquraqerluki tua-i, melquyagait-llu tamakut eritaqerluki nerluki." Tua-i camek piyugnaunani neqnililuni nerluni tauna.

Anguyaluk: Augkut tang ava-i kayanguut nallunailnguut. Yung'elriit pugtaluteng. Yung'aqameng pugtaaqluteng. Taugken tua-i makut yung'eksailnguut kit'aqluteng.

Urrsukvaaq

Qinaruuq[52]

Theresa Abraham: Recently, my younger sibling and I . . . John Avegyaq's names are Nanurrualek and Tarr'aq. [John and I] went camping at Qinaruuq. After mentioning sourdock, he asked if I wanted to go with him, that we might get some long-tailed ducks to eat rare. I agreed to go with him.

We left, and at Qinaruuq we went to the island and he didn't catch a bird. He found three greater scaup eggs. I checked to see if the eggs would sink by filling the kettle with water. Since they weren't really floating, although they did float, I took them.

I didn't travel out to the wilderness this spring when my feet were swollen. Since I didn't go [searching for eggs during spring], I was lucky that the greater scaup eggs that I found all sunk to the bottom.

Then when I cooked the eggs that my younger sibling found, like they used to do when eggs formed into birds, I boiled them hard for a long time to prepare them. They had formed into birds.

Then when I went home, when we were about to eat the ones I had cooked, we ate with Nellie's coworker, a girl from Hooper Bay. I told her, "I'm going to serve some eggs that we found that are cooked in a traditional way that we can eat."

Then I opened them. I looked and saw that the small birds had feathers. Only their yellow parts [yolks] were visible, and that very small white piece had become very solid.

I told her, "They say our ancestors ate these up until they hatched, but when they formed into birds like this, they would boil them for a while, and they just plucked off their small feathers and ate them." She didn't mind at all and found them delicious as she ate.

Martina John: It's easy to tell what stage eggs are in. The ones that have formed into birds float. When they form into birds, they float. But those that haven't formed into birds sink.

Cungauyar: Angullugaat taukut pingayun wii tanglallrenka tayima tua-i catairutellruut. Kaillrullinilriit man'a tua-i una ilakluku Akulmiut-llu man'a-ll' Canineq.

Augna-ll' Angutevialuk tayima nalluketek. Qanemcillruuq kan'a-gguq Arungalnguq cenii ilua-llu nurutellrianek yull'ernek imangqertuq.

Makut akulmiut ayagyaaqluteng, nurulluteng-llu-gguq. Kanavet unavet Urrsukvaamun [ayagyaaqluteng] niicamegteggu cukilegnek.

Tamaani tamaa-i ellii-llu ellangeqtaarluni tauna ayautesteni angun tauna caklikii tayima; kanani Esrimiuni Ingriik ketiigni ellangartuq-gguq amkut yuut.

Ava-i tua-i tangerrnariluteng. Tauna-llu-gguq waten ayauqurtii qavaqernganani tua-i wani ikamrak kinguagni, ellii ikamrak iluagni ekumaluni tua-i mikcami tayima.

Maaten-gguq tauna qavaqeryukellra pillinia tuqullinilria, tua-i-w' kemgilami, piniarulluni. Tua-i tuquluni tuani.

Imkut taugaam taukut Esrimiut neqengqerrameng tamakunek piciatun, tayima-llu mallunek wall'u-qaa mallullernek imarpiim ceniini, cukilegnek-llu tuaken aqvat'lalliniameng Urrsukvaam neqainek.

Aug'um-llu Apacuaraam qanrutkellrukii, aug'um-llu qetunraan Kayiraiyuam cali ukut kankut yun'i qanrutellrullinii kan' Urrsukvaaq unitesqevkenaku, tua-i-gguq-wa cat kuiget allat neqairutengraata taum nalliini neqengqellruuq-gguq cukilegnek, *needlefish*-anek.

Anluat-llu-gguq yuicuunateng *twenty-four hours.* Waten imna qantayagaq mikcuar imangurainaraqluni; uivvaarturluteng.

Cukilget-llu etuami kan'a imna Qayairyaraq, qanglluungami; *seventy-five feet* et'utauq *depth finder*-aakun cuqtaqamni.

Tuani tua-i tauna cing'urteni Mr. Beaver-aam tuqulliniluni-gguq tua-i nurulluni. Taukut tua-i Esrimiut aqvaluku. Cunawa-gguq neqengqelliniameng cukilegnek yaaken Urrsukvaamek.

Urrsukvaaq River[53]

John Eric: Those three elderly men who I used to see have all died. They evidently went through starvation, including the people of this area and the tundra area and the lower Kuskokwim coastal area.

And you two don't know Angutevialuk [Albert Beaver]. He said that the shores and inside of Arungalnguq [Dall lake] down there are filled with people who didn't reach their destination and starved to death.

The people of the tundra region actually traveled [to find food], but they ran out of food and died before they reached their destination. They were traveling down to Urrsukvaaq since they heard that there were needlefish there.

During that time, when he was coming in and out of awareness, and the person had brought him along on his travels, probably one of his family members; he said that he suddenly became aware down at Esrimiut, down below Ingriik, and saw people over there.

They had become visible. He said the person who was taking him seemed to have fallen asleep behind the sled, and he was inside the sled because he was small.

When he checked on the person who he thought had fallen asleep, he saw that he had died, since he was thin and weak. He died there.

But since the people of Esrimiut had all sorts of food, including dead, beached animals or old, dead animals that were beached along the ocean shores, and since they would also go and get needlefish, fish available in the Urrsukvaaq River [they survived].

And Apacuar also mentioned, and his son Kayiraiyuaq also evidently told his children not to leave Urrsukvaaq down there, that although other rivers around no longer had fish in them, that during that [starvation] time, the river had needlefish.

And they mentioned that their [dipnetting] hole in the ice was always occupied by a person for twenty-four hours. A small bowl would slowly be filled [with needlefish]; [the fish] constantly circled.

And there are needlefish since Qayairyaraq down there is deep, since it is a deep hole in the river; it is seventy-five feet deep when I calculate its depth with the depth finder.

During that time, the person who was pushing Mr. Beaver in the sled evidently died, as he didn't make it to his destination and died of starvation. The people of Esrimiut went to get him. [They had evidently survived]

Ukuk waniwa Negtemek qimugterugait ing'um-llu atii cali tangtullruaqa; qimugterugaat qaluyarluteng qimugteteng neqkassaagluki.

Wangkuta-llu watqapiar avirakesciiganaki, neqa amllerrami *needlefish*-aq.

Avani wiinga qimugterlua, cali-llu kiima qimugtenka ukut aulukengnaqevkenaki yullret augkut qaluyaryunqeggamta, augkut-llu Kangrilnguq ilakluku kan'a, unayaqulluta waten, "Ingna qaluyautnaupuk. Wii ingna qaluyauciiqaqa."

Qimugtaitnek aturlua tua-i qaluyautaqluki. Kiituan tang imna Aniim Atii qannguq ellii-gguq nunani cenirtaartengurtuq; wii tua-i aqumlluku uksumi.

Waten wani man'a yuk-wa tua-i tan'gaurluq piyugngaurallermini-w' tua-i augkut qanellruciatun, "Piyugngallerpeni uitanrilkurrluten; atam-gguq pisciigalikuvet pisciigaliniartuten, tua-i-w' cangnaqesciigalikuvet."

Tamana tua-i neq'akluku iliini-w' tua-i uitanrilkurtelaryaaqua. Taugaam angyangqerraqama ayalleralartua massiinaq cayugarrluku.

Cali ukuk qanelkek piciuguq augna. Ap'ama aug'um cali qanrutkellra ava-i qanrutkaa. Allamek-gguq *friend*-aliryaqunii ukut *brother*-aama wall'uqaa uyurama wall' anngama yatiitgun. Una-gguq taugaam anelguka'ar kiimi tua-i takuyarvigkauguq nanikuam nalliini.

Tuaten tua-i aug'um apa'urluma qanrutellruanga. Arnaaraungermi-gguq anelguka'ar takuyarvigkautuuq ukanirpak.

Paniliar: Qayat-llu tua-i tamakut, wiinga-llu qayami, makiraaqamta taugaam uani up'nerkivimteni uitallemteni, agaavet kuigem akianun makiraaqamta arviutaqakuk aanaka-llu aatama, wiinga tua-i qayam iluani. Aling kitnaurtukut pekeskuma!

Kiavet itertellua kinguanun qayam. Uitaurlua tua-i pek'arcaaqevkenii qamani iluani qayam uitaurnaurtua, aanaka alrapaqluku aataka-w' angualria.

Agaavet Urrsukvaam akianun cakmani paingan kiatiinun arviutaqlunuk makirallerkamegnun.

Tuamtell' tua-i pinarikan aqvakunikuk yaani kinguani qamigautek uitalalriik qayam mayurcuutek; tuavet tua-i issratpuk elliqerluki wiinga-

because they had needlefish to eat from the Urrsukvaaq River over there.

These two people from Nightmute and I used to see that person's father also; they'd go and dipnet to get food for their dogs.

And we [from Chefornak] couldn't say that we didn't want them around whatsoever, since there were many needlefish.

I had dogs in the past, and I didn't try to take care of just my own dogs, but since we liked to go dipnetting, those people along with Kangrilnguq down there, we used to tell one another, "Let's go and dipnet for that person over there. I will go and dipnet for that person over there."

Using their dogs, I'd go and dipnet for them. Eventually, Aniim Atii started saying that all he does is visit from home to home in the village; I sat him down [allowing him not to work hard] during winter.

When a person, a young man, was capable of doing things, like those people used to say, "While you are capable, try not to sit around; they say when you become incapable of physical work, you will become helpless, when you are unable to try and carry out labor."

With that in mind sometimes, I avoid sitting around. But when I have a boat, I go places after pull-starting the outboard motor.

Also, what these two said is true. And he also talked about what my grandfather mentioned just now. He said that I shouldn't make friends with a person, disregarding my brother, younger brother or older brother. They said only a relative is someone who one can look to and depend on during desperate times.

That's what my grandfather told me. He said that a relative, even a female, is someone who one can depend on since time immemorial.

Theresa Abraham: And those kayaks, only when we would go and search for eggs and greens when we stayed down at our spring camp, when we would go and gather eggs and greens across the river, when my father would bring me and my mother across, I would be inside the kayak. Gee, we could have drowned if I moved!

He would let me get into the back of the kayak. I would stay and try not to move and stay inside the kayak, and my mother would sit back-to-back with my father who was paddling.

He would bring us across the Urrsukvaaq River, right above the mouth to the place where we would gather eggs and greens.

And when it was time, when he went to get us, the kayak sled is usually

wam tua-i iluani qaman' uitauralrianga.

Taugaam pek'arcaaqevkenii uitaaqlua, meq man'a tangvagluku ikaraliitet maani aciatni. Tangvaglua tua-i pek'arcaaqevkenii uitaaqlua.

Tuaten tua-i qayam iluantelallruunga makiraaqama, aatama kuigkun agaavet arviutaqakuk.

Anguyaluk: Tua-i-gguq pulastenguluten.

Paniliar: Ii-i, pulastengulua.

Anguyaluk: Wiinga-llu.

Paniliar: Tuamtellu cali aataka cali up'nerkami tamaa-i cikuirnatkaani qayarluni cali qavavet tevyulircuutekaqluku qayani. Tamaani ayagluni, qamigani ciumek aturluku tevyulircurluni.

Tamaavet-llu tamaa-i makiraaqamegnuk agaavet arviutaqlunuk. Tuamtell' tua-i anguarturluni nunallernun itrarluni angyarcuquni tayim' ayagluni. Cali tua-i utertaqamta qayani taman' aturluku kuvyaqcaaraliyaraqluni un'gaavet neqnek, tamakut qayat aturluki.

Angalgaq: So, arnat-qaa qayayuunateng?

Paniliar: Naspaq'alallruunga nanvami.

Anguyaluk: Wiinga-w' pilallulrianga. Anglanarquq.

Paniliar: Assirluni, nanvami, ii-i. Taugaam kuigmun pillerkaq alikellruaqa.

Anguyaluk: Ellmikun, kuik-llu arvirluku uterrluta. Taugaam yuilqurruteksuunaki. Tua-i teguqainarluta qayanek anguaruaqaqluta.

Paniliar: Ava-i qanemciunga aataka wan' anguararkaq *front*-ami uitaluni, aanaka-ll' tunuarrluku augna cauluku aqumqerluni. Qaill' waten piqerluni aqumqaumangatelartuq. Wiinga-ll' iterrlua qamavet kinguani uitaurlua camani qayam iluani.

Anguyaluk: Maktesciiganata. Meq-llu maavet tangvaurluku iliini waten elliuirturluni.

Paniliar: Tangvaurluku. Pek'artesciiganii tua-i niicugniurluku. Nunaniqluni.

Anguyaluk: Aling, qiperrluitellruvagceta. Ak'aki uaken Umkumiunekllu apa'urluqa imna maligtelallrukek'a qamavet Nunallernun. Nerinisngacuunani-ll'. Pulastengulua.

Paniliar: Pulastengulleq tuaten nunaniqluni, tangssuarluku man'a luqurquralria.

Qass'urpak

situated on the back of the kayak; we'd place our grass carrying bags on top of that [sled], and I would stay inside.

But I tried not to move and stayed there, watching the water [along the side], and the wooden planked seating was underneath. I would watch, trying not to suddenly move.

Just like that, I would stay inside the kayak when I went and gathered greens and eggs, when my father brought us across the river.

Martina John: You were what they call *pulasta* [one lying inside the kayak].

Theresa Abraham: Yes, I was the *pulasta*.

Martina John: Me, too.

Theresa Abraham: And again, in spring before the river was free of ice, my father would also use his kayak to go north to hunt for muskrats. He'd leave, using his kayak sled at first, hunting for muskrats.

And when we'd go and gather greens and eggs he would bring us across to that place. And then again, he would paddle and go up to the old village when he went to get a boat. And when we would return home, he would use his kayak to go fishing with mesh nets for fish, using those kayaks.

Ruth Jimmie: So, women didn't use kayaks?

Theresa Abraham: I used to try in a lake.

Martina John: I used to [use kayaks]. It's fun.

Theresa Abraham: It's good in lakes, yes. But I was afraid of [using a kayak] on the river.

Martina John: Just for fun, and we would cross the river and return. But we didn't use them to travel out to the wilderness. We would just use kayaks for fun.

Theresa Abraham: I told you just now that my father who would paddle would stay up front, and my mother would sit with her back to him, facing [the other direction]. She seemed to sit like this somehow. And he'd place me inside the kayak, and I'd stay in the back inside the kayak.

Martina John: We couldn't get up. And we'd watch the water sometimes, and it would constantly move like this.

Theresa Abraham: We'd watch it. I couldn't suddenly move, and would just listen to the noise. It was enjoyable.

Martina John: Gee, how we weren't squirmy. I used to accompany my grandfather from all the way down at Umkumiut up to Nunalleq. And I didn't seem to be impatient. I was the *pulasta*.

Theresa Abraham: It was enjoyable lying inside the kayak like that, watching [the water] that was making slapping noises.

Cungauyar: Una umyuartequtelqa, man'a tevyulim akikengnaqutekellra avani ellangellma kinguani.

Maani maa-i *1950*-mi, *51* mat'umi *March, April,* tua-i-ll' *May*-q una qaill' piqerluku, cunaw' pavavet tevyulit ullakatarluki up'nerkiyaqatalliniluta qimugtetgun. Augna-llu Qilangaq cali malikluku piavet Qass'urpagmun. Augkut-llu imna Tutmalria, John Walter-aam atii.

Tua-i tamaani uitallemteni, kiituan tua-i miiqanguq. Cunaw' pelatekamek waten nel'uta uitanaluta man'a qanikcaq, nangluni-llu. Augna-ll' makunek taugaam uqviarnek kaminiarput tua-i muriraqluku avaken yaatemtenek.

Wiinga-ll' piyugngariama tamaa-i augna al'aka ikayurluku iliini kepuriaqlunuk uqviarnek. Nutaan tamaa-i pelatekarput tauna imkurluku tua-i-w' kiirnilengnaqaqluku unuakumi. Cali keniutekaqluki tamakut uqviaraat neqkamtenun. Ernerpak tua-i kumaqaqluni tauna kaminiaq. Augna yaassiiggauluni, imkut augkut *five gallon*-aat tamakuciuluni, amllermek-llu muriyuunani.

Tua-i tuanlluta, tua-i-ll' meq amlleriqerluku al'ama pianga una-gguq ataka Tutmalria-llu tevyulircuqatartuq Qaleqcuugtulimun, wiinga-llu nalluluku tauna. Cunaw' amani Qemilleraam *north*-alirnerani tauna Qaleqcuugtuli uitalliniluni.

Ayaglutek-llu tayima qayatek qamurturluki qamigautegnun ekluki taugaam. Erenret qavcin tayim' aturluku tuanllutek. Tamaani tamaa-i makut tevyulit akingqellratni atauciq *twenty-five cents.*

Tua-i tamatum nalliini ataka qanemciluni miiqaqerluku-gguq tua-i nanvallrem qukaanun atrarlutek yaaqliqlutek qayamun eklutek qanikcangqengraan.

Tevyulit-gguq makut camaken waten pug'aqluteng. Qaillun tamaa-i elliin-wa tua-i nutgaqluki, kiituan-gguq tua-i tayim' naaquciirutut uivetmun. Taugaam-gguq taum malimi tungiinun nuteksaunani.

Tua-i qaill' tayim' pitariata, augkuk-llu nanglutek, imkut *ten*-aanek imalget imkut imayagaat, *fifty*-nek atauciq imangqetullruami, *ten*-aanek caquyaarnek imangqetuameng nangluteng; nangluni tauna.

Tua-i nangeng'ata avurturarraarluki nutaan, qaill' tayim' ella pitarian erneq-wa, amiirluki yaaqliqlutek. Tayim' qavcinek cass'at amiirluki. Nutaan

Qass'urpak[54]

John Eric: Something that I thought about, how they would try to obtain an income from hunting muskrats after I became aware of life.

During this time of year, in 1950, in 1951 during this month of March, April, then during a certain part of May, we evidently were going inland for spring camping with dogs to where muskrats were located. And along with Qilangaq, we went up to Qass'urpak [Place with a big echo] up there. And Tutmalria, John Walter's father.

While we were there, pools of water started to form from melting. We brought the tent along at the time. We evidently would stay inside a tent, and the snow eventually melted away. But we'd get some willows from beyond our place to burn for firewood in our stove.

When I was able, sometimes I would help my older sister and we'd cut willows. We'd try to keep our tent warm in the mornings. And we used those willows to cook our food. That stove would stay on periodically all day. That stove was just a box, a five-gallon [gas] container, and it didn't take a lot of firewood.

We lived there, and when there was a lot of water around, my older sister told me that my father and Tutmalria were going muskrat hunting at Qaleqcuugtuli [Place of many *qaleqcuuget* (grebes)], and I didn't know where that was. Apparently, Qaleqcuugtuli was located to the north of Qemiller [Bad *qemiq* (hill, bluff)].

They left, towing their kayaks, but they placed them on top of a kayak sled. They were there for a number of days. This was back when one muskrat pelt was worth twenty-five cents.

During that time, my father said that just water started to form after melting, they'd go down to the middle of an old dried-up lake and get inside their kayaks, situated a distance away from one another, although there was snow.

He said muskrats would appear like this from down there. He would shoot them, and eventually he said they couldn't count the amount all around them. But he said that he wouldn't shoot toward his hunting partner.

After they caught a certain number, and the carton of shells containing ten boxes of fifty shells each, since they are filled with ten boxes, they were all used up; that was all used up.

When [all the bullets] were used up, after collecting the [muskrats] during

tua-i erenret qavcin kinguatni agiirrlutek.

Atam tauna qaill' tayim' yaaqsigtauq kiaken Qass'urpagmek Qaleqcuugtuliq, pellamiimi augna Qemiller; *ten mile*-aq cipluku yaaqsigtauq.

Cunaw' tua-i wiinga-llu, al'aka augna nillariaqan cali ilakuani meq'errnayukluki kumlamun natmun elliluki uitavkaraqluki.

Nillautait-wa qavcin augkut. Tamakut tamaa-i kaassautellret imkut caquit waten mamtutalriit, qavciuluteng tua-i. Mumigtaqluki waten akertemun kinerciraarluki. Tua-i tayima tamakut qavciullruat pitakek taukuk Tutmalriinkuk John Walter-aam atii ataka-llu.

Tua-i taum kinguani tauna ullanqigtevkenaku taugaam atakualiyaraqlutek maavet yaatemtenun waten anguarlutek.

Wiinga-ll' caqerlua maliklua. Tamaani atakualiyallermini waten alrapaulua. Nutkaqluni, cunaw' tevyulinek.

Tua-i tamaani kinrilliateng cikuq-llu nangluni, nangqertelluku al'ama pianga angyarcuqatartuk-gguq maavet, wavet, tayima-ll' ayaglutek. Tayim' qaill' amatiini-ll' tekitelliuk angyamek maliglutek.

Tua-i-ll' tamakut tamaa-i akluput pelatekat-llu angyamun ekluki, wangni ayagluta nanvaq una, nanvami tuan ernerpak. Al'aka piaqa, "Man'a-q' nanvaulartuq?" Kuiguuq-gguq. Tua-i tayima ellaka nalluqerluku.

Tua-i-llu kiagan, cunaw' qamani Mamterillermiuni cali waten ellangarrlua. Taukunek akilirluni atama pianga angyamek-gguq kiputeqatartuq.

Wii angyaq taman' paqnakluku caucia. Imna aterpaggluku Kassaurlurmekgguq kipukengqatartuq *two hundred fifty dollars* angyaq augna massiinaunani. Taukut tua-i pitami ilaitnek akilirluku. Augna tua-i qanqautaa.

One hundred-aanek qillertarnek tauna qanrutellrua. Aug'umek tua-i waten amllertalriamek, atauciq *twenty-five cents*, tayima *twenty-five cents times twenty*-iuluteng, *five dollar*-auciquq-qaa taum akia?

Tua-i tuaten tamakut-llu tevyulirculallret tamatum nalliini qavciugat tayima, taugaam tauna nallunritellruaqa. Cunaw' Oscar Samuelson, augna

a certain time of day, they skinned them situated a ways from each other. They skinned them for a number of hours. Then after a number of days, they arrived.

Qaleqcuugtuli is a certain distance away from Qass'urpak upriver, since Qemiller is not visible; it's about ten miles away.

When my sister was stretching skins to dry, when there were some left over, fearing that their fur might come off, she'd put them somewhere cold and leave them there.

They had a number of skin-stretching devices. They were old gas container covers that were about this thick, and there were a number of them. They'd constantly turn them over toward the sun when they dried them. I'm not sure how many Tutmaralria, John Walter's father, and my father caught at that time.

They never went to that place after that, but they'd go hunting during the night beyond our place by paddling.

And they brought me with them one time. When he went to hunt for the night, I was sitting back-to-back with him [in the kayak]. He'd shoot once in a while, evidently at muskrats.

Probably when the skins dried and the ice had completely melted, a short while after it was all gone, my older sister told me that they were going to get a boat from this village, then they left. Then after a number of days, probably after a couple of days, they arrived with a boat.

Then we put our belongings and the tents inside that boat, and it seemed to me that we were traveling along a lake, as though we were on a lake all day. I asked my older sister, "Is this a lake?" She said it was a river. Then I lost awareness.

Then when summer came, I suddenly became aware, apparently up at Bethel. My father told me that he was going to purchase a boat using those [muskrat furs] as payment.

I was wondering what that boat was. He mentioned the person's name, that from Kassaurluq he was going to buy a boat for two hundred fifty dollars, a boat without a motor. He paid for it with some of the furs that he obtained. That's what he told someone.

But he told that person about a bundle of one hundred [muskrat pelts]. The price that I mentioned earlier, that one pelt was worth twenty-five cents, and if they were worth twenty-five cents and there were twenty [pelts], will it be worth about five dollars?

I'm not sure how many people hunted for muskrats in the past, but that's

kalikiurta, uani Kuiggayagarmi tamakunek cali kiputetulliniluni.

Tamakunek tua-i maaniunrilnguq, tevyulinek tamatum nalliini akingqelallruut up'nerkami. Up'nerkami taugaam ayuqluteng tuarpiaq tamatum kinguani wii taringellemni tamakut ayuqellrulriit.

Canek-llu augkunek apeqmeggnek elliqeryaranek *nine horse*-anek, tua-i wangni cukaq'apiarluteng waten elevaarnaurtut.

Cunaw' tua-i tamakunek melqulegnek akilirluki pilallrullinikait tamatum nalliini. Augna ava-i wii nallunritelqa up'nerkami tevyulit nallunritellruanka tuaten.

Ingriik

Qamulria: Tua-i-gguq kankuk Ingriik tangnerratakacaarlutek. Tuamtellu-gguq yuut makumiungunrilnguq mayuqan taitungulluku, tua-i tairvangulluku cakneq.

Tua-i-llu-gguq angyam kituqani, kanani tua-i ketiigni tua-i uitaqapiggluni ayagyung'ermi.

Amiiga-gguq Ingriik ketmun caumallrani tuaten pitullruut. Tuunrangayiit tua-i uivtellrulliniagket.

Akak'aq: Taum mumigtellruak Ingriik kankuk, tangnerrayuirucellukek.

Paniliar: Waniwa qanemcitqataramci taum uivitellragnek. Maacungamta qanemcitellruanga Ap'akegtaaraankuk-gguq Luk'aq-llu—Canaarayagaamqaa Atii?—kitumek ilaluteng ayalriit palayakun kiatmurrluteng.

Tua-i-llu-gguq kankuk Ingriik ketaiqerlukek, atuqengaat man'a ayanrirluni, ayagluteng-gguq taugken tua-i.

Pingkuk-gguq Ingriik cakaniirullutek, qaku-gguq kituqatartanki, taugken-gguq tua-i ayaktaryaaqluteng.

Tua-i-llu-gguq taum tua-i iliita pillinia, "Arenqia wangkuta tang caciitenrilngukut." Tauna tua-i Luk'aq tauna pillilria, ilaseng angalkungqellinian caulliniluku qaillukuaqaasqellukek pingkuk Ingriik.

Tuani-gguq tua-i, taulleraam tua-i caqirrlukek. Tua-i angalkumikun caqirrlukek pikiitek aren nutaan ayangartelliniut.

Kelutmun caullukek. Tuamtellu aanaka ingna tua-i cauciak, aanama

what I know. Apparently Oscar Samuelson, the mailman, used to purchase those [pelts] down at Oscarville.

Unlike nowadays, their source of income was muskrat pelts during spring. But it seems to me that they engaged in the same harvesting activities during spring after that.

And they would use those nine-horse outboard motors they called *elliqeryarat* [lit., "ones that you just placed there"], and they seemed very fast to me when they traveled with those outboards.

Evidently, they paid for those [outboard motors] with fur animals during that time. That's what I know about how they obtained muskrats in spring.

Turn Mountain[55]

Maria Eric: They say those Ingriik down there are inclined to react when seeing people for the first time. And they said if someone who is not of this village ascended the mountain, a fog would suddenly form around them, a heavy fog would form when they went up.

And they said if a boat passed by [the mountain], it would just sit there right down below them although it wanted to continue.

They said when the doorway of Ingriik was facing the [ocean], that used to happen to people. Shamans evidently turned it around in the other direction.

David Jimmie Sr.: That person turned Ingriik down there in the other direction so that they wouldn't react when seeing people for the first time.

Theresa Abraham: I'm going to tell you about how that person turned them around. Our grandmother told me that Ap'akegtaar and Luk'aq—was [Luk'aq] Canaarayagaq's father?—along with someone else, traveled with a wooden boat upriver.

Then just as they went down below Ingriik down there, the boat they were using suddenly stopped, but here they continued to move.

He said the Ingriik up there were situated in the same place, and they waited anxiously to pass them, but here they were actually moving.

Then one of them said to him, "Oh my, there's something happening to us." It was probably Luk'aq who turned to one of the people among them who had shaman powers and told him to use his powers on the Ingriik up there.

They mentioned that that clever shaman turned them at that time. When he used his shaman powers to turn them, they finally began to move forward.

call' qanemcik'laraa. Tuani aanani tuqullrani, maurluirutlermini pavani Nanvarnarrlagmi uitallinilriit. Tua-i-llu apa'urluuk taukuk cangerliim nalliini tuquluni apa'urlua, maurlua-llu aanami kinguani uitavikek'ngak.

Tua-i-ll' tuquagnek, tuani kinguqliirutiini, amaumni Anguteurluum Atallrani, Naparyarrarmi uitalliniluni, aug'umek nayagarminek cali nunalguterluni. Tua-i taukuk taum amauriutegma kingunragnek pitaarlutek aulukluku.

Tua-i pivakarluku pilliniluk' amauma taum Anguteurluum Atiin, aatiinun uumun tangerrsularyaaqniluku irniaqngaku. Erenrem iliini aqvakaku naigarteqaasqelluku. Tua-i ellangvikenrilamiki qessayaaqluni.

Tua-i-llu-gguq kiagmi ap'aka, uum waniw' Kangrilnguum Atii tekitelliniuq ilu'urminek Caingilnguum Atranek maligluni cali iqugterluni. Tua-i-ll' pilliniluku waniwa aqvaniluku.

Tua-i amauma taum pilliniluku naigarteqaasqelluku irniaqngaku tangerrsulaaku aqvaniluku, taugaam erenrem cali iliini ut'ruciiqniluku. Tua-i-ll' qessangermi tua-i maligtelliniluku.

Tua-i-ll' taumek tua-i ilu'urminek Caingilnguum Atranek qarutestekalgirluku. Ayiimeng tua-i Kass'atun *boat ride*-aulluku Kuinerramun ayautelliniluku, tua-i nallunrilamiu umyugaa nunairyunrilan, utercuumiinani.

Tua-i tuani arnaurteqarralliniluni Kuinerrami, ak'a piciryaraicetun aqumgalliniluni tua-i ernerni qavcini.

Tua-i-ll' tua-i pinariateng tailuteng. Tuantetullratni pingatut Yugissaam Atii. Aanamnek qanemciunga.

Tua-i-llu unaggun imarpigkun tailliniluteng tua-i uavet uksuaryartuqerluku. Tua-i-llu-gguq inglua man'a cam tua-i pupingtiim nauluku.

Tua-i-llu-gguq piluteng, kankuk-gguq kana-i Ingriik, ircenrraat, caungamek tamaa-i tunglirnellrak tuacetun piuq tangnerrarluku.

Tua-i-llu-gguq arrlugnek tamakut tamaa-i piaqluki. Piqerlutek qagken qayakun angutek malruk cakmavet pilutek mat'umun ukvemtenun tuigculriit anglluryulriit piluki. Tua-i ap'ama-gguq taum tuqunayukluku tua-i angllurcetliniluku. Tauna tua-i kankuk cakuyuullrak call' tamaaggun.

He turned them around toward land. Then again, my mother also talks about what they are like. At the time her mother died, when she lost her grandmother, they evidently lived up in Nanvarnarrlak. Then during an epidemic, her grandfather and grandmother died, those who she was living with after her mother's death.

Then when they died, she evidently stayed at my great-grandfather's, Anguteurluum Atii, in Napakiak, and her younger sister was also staying with her. My deceased great-grandparents who she stayed with took care of her.

Then after a while, my great-grandfather, Anguteurluum Atii, told her that her father longed to see her because she was his child. He told her to oblige him when he came to get her one day. Since she didn't become aware among those people, she was reluctant to go.

Then during summer, my grandfather, Kangrilnguum Atii, arrived along with his *iluraq,* Caingilngum Atra [the one Caingilnguq is named after], as a helper. Then he told her that he had come to get her.

Then my great-grandfather told her to oblige him since he had come to get her because she was his child and he had longed to see her, but he told her that someday he'd bring her back [to Napakiak]. Although she was reluctant, she evidently went with him.

So he had brought his *iluraq,* Caingilnguum Atra, to urge her to come with them. When they left, as they say in English, they brought her on a boat ride to Quinhagak, since he knew that she wasn't too happy about going home.

She evidently had her first menstrual period over at Quinhagak, and observing the custom they followed long ago, she sat and abstained from activity for a number of days.

Then when it was time, they came here [to Chefornak]. I think it was when Yugissaam Atii was there. I'm telling a story about my mother.

Then they evidently came through the ocean route to the place downriver in early fall. Then she said that sores grew on one side of her body.

Then they said that because those Ingriik down there, the *ircenrraat,* since the area [of the mountain] that faced them has some sort of supernatural ability, that's what happened to her because they had reacted to seeing her for the first time.

So they called those things that grew on people *arrluut.* Then after a while, two men with kayaks went down [to Chefornak] to attend to people who wanted to convert and get baptized into our [Catholic] religion. Fearing that she might die, my grandfather had her baptized. The fact is that those two

Ii-i, miluqullrak-gguq. Augna-ll' Ap'akegtaaraankuk cali ava-i atullrat Maacungaam qanemcillra. Kankuk caukuyaggluulliniuk Ingriik. Tua-i.

Qamulria: Aatavut-llu tuatnallruuq. Pavavet-am ayaggaarluni tekicami qanertuq, aren Ingriqtak-gguq kankuk miluquyugnarqaak. Cat-gguq tutmaraat. Tutmarluku, tua-i-ll' tamakut naugarrluku. Arrluluku-am call' unrakun, waten unra piluku. Tamakullinilriit tamaa-i miluqutai.

Unruagucirluku tua-i unran acia uivetmun. Kankuk qaillukuarayullruuk.

Qerrataralria: Tuamtellu cali Ingriik kankuk qanemciullrak amllerrsugnarquq. Ircenrrarnek tuaten yungqerrniaqlukek watua waniwa. Maa-i cali tuaten ayuquk.

Tuamtell' yaani wangkuta Cicingmi uitauralallruukut. Tua-i aug'umekllu, nallunritliken Qayuq'amek piaqluku ilangqerraqluta tamaani. Tua-i uitaaqluta tua-i tuani. Tua-i Ingriik kankuk ircenrrarnek yungqerrnilaragket watua waniwa.

Tua-i tauna tua-i Qayuq'aq waten ayagatullruuq, tua-i ernerpak tayima cataicimaaqluni-llu. Tekitaqan-gguq aaniin piyaaqnauraa neresqelluku ernerpak cataicimarraartelluku. Kiunauraa-gguq nerellruuq-gguq.

Tua-i-ll' pilallinia nani nerellrucianek. Kass'ani-gguq nerlartuq, Kass'at ilagarluki. Tua-i tuaten piaqluki.

Cali tua-i augkut ava-i augkuk qanemcikellrukiik augna tukaratunilukek piaqluteng. Maa-i call' pilaryugnarquk tuaten. Tua-i-gguq tukaralutek, tem'iqtara'arturlutek.

Tua-i-ll' tuaten piameng cali augkut, tuaten ak'a-gguq tamaani qavci *years,* qavci *thousand years ago* qagellruuq. Cali tua-i tamana-gguq tua-i qagrarkaq imumek piaqan tukaralutek-gguq pilallruuk. Cali tua-i cam' iliini-gguq cali tua-i tuaten piciquk pika-i, nut'guciiquk.

Cali-w' keluatni-w' cali, Nenguanek pilaqengait, pingkut enet. Tua-i enet'un ayuqelartut kelulirneragni wani teggalqut quyungqaluteng. Cali caullrak atam amllertuq Ingriik pikegkuk.

Tuamtell'-am tua-i-am wani atmaglutek qagaaken tua-i, qanemciulutek, quliraulutek, taitellinilukek.

Atmautaak tua-i, tauna atmautaa taum wani taisnginanrani kevkartelliniluni.

Kevkarcagnek tua-i pikavet unitellinilukek tua-i wavet tua-i, wangku-

[mountains] down there are also extraordinary in that way.

Yes, it was the things they threw [that caused her to grow sores]. And the story about what Apakegtaar and another person experienced is a story that grandmother told also. Those Ingriik down there are extraordinary. That's it.

Maria Eric: That's what happened to our father, also. After traveling inland, when he arrived he said that those darn Ingriik must have thrown things at him. He said that things landed on him. They landed on him, then [those sores] suddenly grew on his body. Sores grew along his armpit also, *arrluluku* growing like this along his armpit. Those were the things that were thrown at him.

Something grew under his armpit all the way around. Those two down there tended to mess with people.

Paul Tunuchuk: And again, I think there are many stories told about Ingriik down there. And they mention that there are *ircenrraat* living there at this time. They are still like that today.

And again, we used to stay at Cicing all the time. Then that person they called Qayuq'aq, you probably know who he is, was living there with us at the time. We lived there. They mention that those Ingriik down there are occupied by *ircenrraat* at this time now.

Qayuq'aq used to go hunting, and he'd be gone all day long sometimes. When he'd arrive, his mother would tell him to eat after he'd been gone all day. He'd tell her that he had eaten.

And she'd ask him where he had eaten. He would say that he eats with [*ircenrraat* appearing as] white people. That's what he would tell her.

And what they mentioned in their story earlier that [the Ingriik] make rumbling noises like when one is kicking with both feet. I think they still do that these days. They call it *tukaralutek* when they make rumbling noises.

And when those people mentioned that, they said that a few thousand years ago, it erupted. They said when there's activity from an impending eruption, they make rumbling noises, *tukaralutek*. And they mentioned that one day they will erupt again.

And behind them, the features on land they call Nenguat [Pretend houses], the houses up there. The boulders grouped on the backside look like houses. There are many things said about Ingriik up there.

And again, there is a tale about two [huge] people carrying something on their backs who came from the north and brought something here.

The thing he was carrying on his back, while he was bringing that thing on his back, the strap on his backpack broke.

ta-ll' waniw' uverneratni qanemciluta. Tua-i-ll' kinguani-am pilliniut quliraurtuq. Tuar' ilumun.

Uugnaraam elavngavikellinilukek ukuk; pikani kangrani uugnaq elavelliniuq. Qukaani-wa-gguq kanani ilutuluni qallacian-gguq uitavillra.

Tuamtellu uyaqurri tevingalliniluteng amalirnermi. Tuamtell' tua-i pamyuan nel'illiniluku pamyua ukalirnermi tua-i, caqingqaluni-ll' ukatmun pamyuan uitavillra.

Tuamtell' kinguakun tua-i tulukarugtanglliniluni mit'elliniluni kangragnun kelulirnermun. Analliniluni tua-i tungulriamek. Teggalqut kelulirneragni.

Tua-i yaatmegnek tua-i tuaten ayuqaqlutek. Tulukaruum-gguq anallrek. Tua-i quliraullerkaa taum anglanarquq.

Cali-ll' ava-i waten tangnerratarlutek-llu. Piciuguq cali tauna.

Caqerluta-am augna-ll' nengaugput nallunritan Linda-m uinga; up'nerkaryartumi waten tekitellragni cikuciluta.

Qaltaq imirraarluku cikunek piaqa, "Mayuryugtuten-qaa pikavet?" Angerluni. Angran tua-i ayagluta tua-i. Kiarnarqellruluni tua-i.

Atam tua-i mayuinanemteni ayallerput man'a kiarnairutellria. Kangllitniarangluku qanugpangkili tua-i. Kiarnairutkacagarluni, anuqengluni tuaten. Tua-i kiarnaitkacagarluni kangranun tekicaaqukut anuqlirluni.

Atrarluta tua-i. Atrainanemteni-am assirikili tua-i kiarnarqengluni-llu, alaiterpaglutek-llu. Tuaten tua-i pitulliniuq.

Cali tangnerratulutek yugnek. Tua-i-ll' elpet tua-i tangnerralliamegteggen ellavut keggna unuamek assiirutellria. [*ngel'artut*] Tua-i qaingagni uitalriakut waniwa.

Ugirciyaraq

When they broke, he left it at [Ingriik] up there, here in this place, and we are along its slope, telling stories. Then later they found that it had become a tale. It seems to be true.

And evidently [Ingriik] here was where a mouse was crouched down; a mouse evidently crouched down along its top up there. And they mention that the center down there where there's a deep depression is where its bellybutton was situated.

And the place where its neck was situated is hanging over the other side. And its tail was situated on this side, and the place where its tail was situated turns in this direction.

Then afterward, Raven came around and evidently landed up at the top along the back side. It apparently defecated a dark feces. They are rocks on the back side [of Ingriik].

From the surrounding areas, that's how they look. They mention that it's the feces of Raven. That legend is fun to listen to.

And they are inclined to react when seeing people for the first time. That's also true.

One day, when we were with our son-in-law, you know who Linda's husband is; toward springtime like this when they arrived, we went to get some ice [to melt for drinking water].

After filling the bucket with ice, I asked him, "Do you want to go up there?" He agreed. When he agreed, we went. There was good visibility at the time.

While we were ascending, visibility became low in the surrounding area. Before we reached the top, it started to snow heavily. There was no visibility at all, and the wind started to blow. There was no visibility at all when we reached the top, and it was windy.

Then we went down. While descending, the weather started to improve, and once again, the weather cleared, and [Ingriik] were very clear and visible. That's apparently what [the Ingriik] do.

They also react when seeing people for the first time. Since they are probably reacting from seeing you [Ann and Alice] for the first time, our weather has gotten bad today. [*laughter*] We are on top of [Ingriik] now.

Cungauyar: Tauna-w' nunamteni ingna yaa-i Ugirciyaraq; tua-i niitelallruken ing' Ugirciyaraq. Tuavet-gguq ugirtelluki [cetuat] kapurluki tuqutetullruit qayat.

Niitaqluku tua-i Ugirciyaraq, uani nunangellran uakaraani ingna. Itrarluni alqunaq qip'artellra una tua-i Ugirciyaramek acirluku cetuanek tuqucivillerteng augkut, ataatavet tayima augkut angagpet-llu ciuqliita.

Caqerluta taugaam ingna Tuguyak cayugnaunaku un'gaani angyaruallemteni Kayiraiyuaq-llu call' man'a Yang'aq-wa; pingayuuluta angyat. Unguyaaqekput tang tua-i aug' cetuaq kiatmun.

Meq-llu tua-i man' nutgaqluku, cat tua-i kaugtuarluki angyam iluani Kayiraiyuam alerquangakut. Akiqliqluta.

Qavaggun tua-i yaaggun pilaryaaquq. Piqerluni maaggun uatemteggun qakcimaarnaurtuq itrarciiganani, caulliami-w' tua-i pilria.

Piirraq

Akak'aq: Piirraq uitauq waniw'. Kuiguuq.

Yang'aq-llu anngaqa-llu *camp*-aqerpuk tauna. Necuartangqertuq, pama-i uitauq, napauq cali.

Man'a maa-i Piirraq, uksuarmi-am ellimerraanga Yang'am mertaasqellua tekicamegnuk unugmi. Tua-i-ll' anlulilua, caaniik qaluqaarluku atrarlua.

Unuaquan paqnakngamku paqluku. Tekitaqa can'giirnek waten. Anliuralqa im' pakmaarluni can'giirnek imangellinilria.

Tuaken tua-i Yang'am pilua, taluyilartuq-gguq ellii maavet ceniinun naparrluku muiqata-llu-gguq kuvluki. Can'giilinertuuq uksuarmi.

Cungauyar: Augkut ava-i, makucetun, uksuarmi-w' tua-i ullagluki, ayuquq una Piirraq apellra. Up'nerkami-llu maaken uum atiin ullagluku uksuarmi-llu, up'nerkiviketullruluku.

Cali-llu ilaita maani, aug'um-llu makumiullrem Tuqsugmiunun nengaugitam Negtemiunun akagarcailkutekluku ingna ilu'urqa, maantetullrua-

Place Where One Brings Things Up onto Shore[56]

John Eric: Near our village is a place over there called Ugirciyaraq; you heard about Ugirciyaraq over there. They say in the past kayakers drove [beluga whales] into [shallow water] there and stabbed them and killed them.

We used to hear about Ugirciyaraq, that place right along this side where the land begins. When you head up, where it suddenly bends, they called that place Ugirciyaraq where those people, the forebearers of your maternal and paternal uncles, used to kill beluga whales.

But one time when Tuguyak was in good health, when we went boating down along the coast, along with Kayiraiyuaq and Yang'aq; we were in three boats. We actually pursued and drove that beluga whale toward shore.

And we'd shoot at the water and even strike things inside the boat since Kayiraiyuaq told us what to do. [Our boats] were situated across from one another.

The [beluga] would swim out there. After a while, it would resubmerge for a while down below us and couldn't go up, probably because it was some sort of [extraordinary animal].

Piirraq River[57]

David Jimmie Sr.: Piirraq is written down here. It's a river.

That is my older brother Yang's and my camp. There is a small house there, and it's still standing up there.

Here at Piirraq, during fall, Yang told me to get some water when we arrived there at night. Then I made a hole in the ice, and after dipping the kettle in the water and filling it, I went down.

When I was curious about it the next morning, I went to check it. When I came upon it, there was this much blackfish there. The hole that I had made in the ice had filled with a pile of blackfish.

Yang told me that he sets a blackfish trap by setting it upright along the sides of the river, and when it fills, he spills them out. Many blackfish are there during fall.

John Eric: Piirraq that he just mentioned is like these other [rivers around Chefornak], they'd go to them during fall. And this person's father would go to that place during spring and fall and go spring camping there.

And some people here, including [Paul John] who was originally from

mi cali Piirraq paugna tua-i igumaqapiarluku aug'um Paul John-am.

Tauna ilu'uqngamku piciatun acilaqka wiinga. Tua-i tauna tua-i ullagluku akmaken pissutullruuq imarmiutarnek.

Aug'um-llu cali Tuyumiim Anguk'am-llu Ayagalriim-llu cali. Qaugna qava-i augna Urutaq, Piirraq, Penguvagcaraq, tamana tamaa-i, una-llu cali Cuukvagualek qaugkut Akulmiut-llu call' ullagatullruluku avani ciuqvani imarmiutarraq pitekluku wall'u tevyuliq.

Akaurtuq *1951,* augna Tuyumak nalluyagucuilkeka tua-i qimugtai-w' pingayun, maklagmek uciluni miiqanga'arrluni man'a. Aling ak'aki. Wii waten ayagngaitua maaken Naparyarrarmun qimugtenka-w' pingayun.

Tangrriu augkut caperrnarqetaciat maa-i avani-w' tua-i. Tamakut up'nerkami ullalalteng wangkucicetun qaugkunun uum Arungalnguum avatii igaucecugngaluku qanemcikluku.

Makut maa-i Piirraq neq'lian augkunek can'giirnek neqsurviktullruatgguq, imarmiutarnek tapirluki. Up'nerkami-llu tevyulinek avani ciuqvani.

Tevyuliq atauciq nallunritlemni *twenty-five cents* tua-i akiluni. Amtall' kipurqaqluteng angyanek massiinarnek piciatun. Maa-i-llu akiturian wangkuta *twelve dollar*-aam natiini kia pissuyuirulluki tevyulit.

Augkut ava-i, una Piirraq up'nerkami niitelallruaqa uksuarmi-ll' cali. Yullri-ll' tayima nangluteng. Wangkuta taugaam maa-i una-llu kinguvkutaurrluta tua-i tamakunun.

Akak'aq: Caqerluta-am up'nerkiyarluta Piirrarmun pillemteni, ayagassiyaangvailegma-w' tua-i avani; ayagaksaitellrulrianga. Arnapagaankunek ilaluta, tamaa-i wangtun ayanitallrullilria.

Tuyumak tekituq avaken, ikamralugpiak-wa uciarlutek tua-i neqnek, enrualugnek taryaqviit enrualuitnek, qimugtai-w' augkut pingayun. Qayakwa cali malruk nangcak, aipaa egelrutnguluni Anguk'am qayaa.

Tauna tua-i wiinga-ll' tangerrluku caperrsullruunga yaaqsian-llu qamna Naparyarrarmiunek kingunerluni. Tua-i capeqluku wiinga, pingayunek-llu taukunek qimugtenek call' pinikilua. Ikamralugpiak-llu augkuk miktevkenatek; taklutek uciarlutek piciatun tua-i aklukakegnek pelatekanek tuaten.

Up'nerkami waten up'nerkaryartumi tekilluni. Tagumariluta taugaam

this village and moved to Toksook Bay, to Nightmute, when he married, who is the *akagarcailkun* [one who prevents them from rolling], my *iluraq,* since he used to live here, Paul John knows Piirraq up there very well.

Since he is my *iluraq,* I call him all sorts of names. He used to go to that river from [Nightmute and Toksook Bay] and hunt for mink.

Tuyumak, Anguk'aq, and Ayagalria also [went there]. The area inland, including Urutaq [River] [Place with *uruq* (tundra moss)], Piirraq [River], Penguvagcaraq [River] [Route to get to large *penguut* (hills)], and Cuukvagualek [Place with *cuukvaguaq,* "alder"], people from the tundra area also went to that area in the past just to obtain mink or muskrat.

It was a while back in 1951, but I never forgot Tuyumak [Oscar Larson], who had three dogs and was carrying a bearded seal in his sled, and water had started to form from melting ice on lakes and rivers. My, how far [he traveled]. I won't travel from here to Napakiak with three dogs.

You see how amazing they were in the past. The places they traveled to during spring, like we did, they can identify place names and also talk about the area around Arungalnguq.

Since Piirraq [River] has many blackfish, they mentioned that they went to fish there, as well as hunting for mink. And they'd hunt muskrat during spring long ago.

From what I know, one muskrat was worth twenty-five cents. But here they would buy boats, motors, and all sorts of things [with the money they obtained]. Now that it's worth more, around twelve dollars [per pelt], we no longer hunt muskrat.

Those places they mentioned, I used to hear that Piirraq [was used] during spring and fall. And the people who hunted there are all gone now. We are the last ones left after those people.

David Jimmie Sr.: One time when we went to Piirraq for spring camping, before I really started to travel and hunt; I didn't travel and go hunting at the time. Arnapagaq and their family were with us, and he was probably my age at that time.

Tuyumak arrived from out there, and his big freight sled was loaded with fish, with king salmon backbones, and he had three dogs. He was also towing two kayaks, the other a canoe that belonged to Anguk'aq.

I was amazed seeing that [person] also, since he had come from a great distance away, from Napakiak. I was amazed by him, and I was amazed by how strong those three dogs were. And his big freight sled wasn't small; they were long and were loaded with their various gear, including tents.

wangkuta, tauna tua-i ilagaryartulliniluta.

Tua-i-llu angyallugarkun tagellruamta, tainariakut kiani kia-i Qass'urpagmi waniw' tevqatarluta. Tuyumiim qimugteni taukut pingayun uskurarai, angyam-llu taqurraanun petugluki. Ikamralugpiagnek atlilirluku taman' angyaq, aklunek-llu uciarlukek tua-i ikamrak angyaq tamana.

Elisngakellruanka taukut qumugtai. Qatguskiiteng qimugtai augkut uyungluteng angyaq-llu man' ayakataarluni. Uciarluni. Tevulluku tua-i tuavet nanvamun tamaavet.

Uskurairluki tuamtell' angyaq mermun elliamiu ekluki nutaan maavet tailuta.

Taukut tua-i nalluyagucuitanka cali wii uskurallri taukut tevqatallemteni, angyarput-llu augna mikenricaaqluni angyallugpauluni.

Arungalnguq

Cungauyar: Aug'um tamaa-i-gguq kaillratni, ca tayim' engelekluku ungalatmun negetmun kiatmun, niitelallruunga aug'um-wa ap'aurluma qanrutellrukiinga, ellii qanerluni, man'a-gguq kuigput kiimi neqengqellruuq cukilegnek. Unugpak-gguq tua-i qancunguar-gguq imiqaqluku taugaam.

Cali-llu Akulmiunek Arungalnguq-gguq uatmun enertangqertuq yuut enritnek nururqellernek. Tuaten tua-i qanellruuq.

Cali-ll' tamaani nallustai cukilgem tua-i-gguq paluaqluteng ilait cukiitnek. Tua-i *needlefish*-aungameng cukiliameng anrutaat arturluki cukilget.

Taumek maa-i tamaani qanrut'lallrukiikut makunun mikelngurnun cukilget nallunguaresqevkenaki. Neqa-gguq piilkan man'a-gguq kiimi kuigput neqengqellruan, cali neqengqerciqniluku. Cali-llu carvanrunani. Camani aciqvani uitaluteng.

Uani tua-i Qayairyaraq tauna uitavikellruat etuan. *Seventy-five feet* et'utalartuq et'utassiartekun qanglluungami.

Taukut tua-i tamakut Akulmiut, nururqellernek-gguq Arungalnguq, enrit amllertut avani. Anangniyaryaaqelriit-gguq nurutaqluteng.

Uavet-llu Cevv'arnermun. Ukut-gguq nunataitellruut, ugkut-gguq tau-

He arrived during spring, toward spring like this. But we had already gone up to shore [after hunting on the ocean], and he had evidently come to join us.

Since we had gone to shore with a wooden boat, when it was time for us to return here, we were just about to portage overland up at Qass'urpak. Tuyumak put harnesses on his three dogs and tethered them along the edge of the boat. They placed that boat on top of the freight sled and then they piled gear on top of that boat.

I thought his dogs were intelligent. When he shouted at them, his dogs squatted down, and then the boat started moving. It was filled with gear. They portaged it overland and onto that lake.

And after he removed their harnesses and placed the boat on the water, he placed the dogs inside and we came here.

I never forgot those dogs that he harnessed when we were about to portage over land; and our boat wasn't a small boat, it was a large wooden boat.

Dall Lake[58]

John Eric: Someone mentioned that when they were starving, I'm not sure up to which area, to the south, north, and upriver, I used to hear, my grandfather told me that only our river had needlefish at the time. They would only fill one small bowl over night.

And he said that Arungalnguq is filled with the bones of people from the tundra area, of people who ran out of food [and starved to death]. That's what he said.

And it is said that some people who didn't know how to eat needlefish would starve to death because of their spikes. Since they are needlefish and have many spikes on them, their stomachs couldn't handle the needlefish.

That's why they told us that we should not fail to introduce children to eating needlefish. They said that when food is scarce, that in the past only our river had fish, that it would have fish once again. And it didn't have a current. They were very deep inside the river.

They were at Qayairyaraq down there since it is deep. It is about seventy-five feet deep with a depth reader, since it is a *qanglluq* [deep hole in a river].

He said that Arungalnguq is filled with many bones of people from the tundra area who ran out of food [and starved to death]. Those who had gone to survive the famine ran out of food and didn't reach their destination.

gaam Cevv'arermiut kiingan uksiviullratni.

Cali augkut avani tamaani ilait-gguq qasgimi paluaqluteng, tuaten tua-i cukilget nalluluki.

Iliit-gguq tauna qantani tangrraarluku uum payugtaqani tangvaurarraarluki qanernaurtuq, "Iilir."

Tua-i-llu-gguq kelutmun cauluni, qantaa-wa-gguq uitalria. Tua-i paluluni, iirugarnek qanrraarluni.

Tamakut tamaa-i watua ilumun cukilget ilumun piilngaitelliut man'a kuigput tamakunek neqengqevkarluku. Ukuk-gguq avaqliik Qukaqliinkuk Qalvinraaq-llu neqai tuaten qaillun piniluki taum nalliini ayuqellruut. Uum-gguq taugaam mat'um neqai, tua-i-gguq qancunguar-wa imiqatuluku.

Cali-llu-gguq tamakut arnait qelketaameng piciatun avurraqa'aqluki wall' makunek tayarunek wall' tangviarrlugnek pikangqelalliniameng tamaani. Augkut ava-i uum wan' Arungalnguum mat'um-llu kuimta, tuaten tua-i qanrutkelallratni niitelallruanka.

Qaugna-gguq Kusquqvagmiut qagkut, natmun tayima tailaryaaqellilriit-gguq ilait, ellaita nalluluki, taugaam-gguq kingauakun niitaqluki Arungalnguq qaugna tuaten ayuqniluku watua. Qukaa tayima tamana wall'u-qaa avatii man'a, man'a-llu wall' ungalalirnera tua-i-gguq yuut enritnek pingqertuq, tautun tua-i Albert Beaver-aam ayautestiitun.

Ilumun-gguq tua-i man'a Urrsukvaaq elliin tua-i tuaten niitellrua. Cali aug'um apaurlullma Amaqigcim cali qanrutkellruluku tuaten. Tua-i kaigem cami tayim' allrakut iliitni *19*-aam cami tayim' neqaitullrullinii taum nalliini, imarpik-llu cataunani mermek, cikumek muirumaluni.

Augna ava-i tuaten uum Arungalnguum, una-ll' un'a kuigput tuaten pitalriamek niitelallemni ayuquq.

Akak'aq: Yaqulegcurviktuat maa-i mat'um nalliini-llu man'a Arungalnguum [avatii].

Taugaam ellalliyuitaqami etgalituuq man'a. Ellalliyuitaqami etgalituami umyuani aturluku ayaganaituq mat'um iluani.

Cali anuqlirqan mer'a ingluartetuluni, ingluqvani uitatuluni.

Qangvaq-am uumi iqvaryallemteni waken qacaqnermek anurvallrani utercaaqukut. Tua-i-ll' Qass'urpagmek anqatartukut marayaq man'a ciunemteni tua-i uitaluni. Qaillun tua-i ayagngaitelliniamta uterrluta pelatekiurluta qavartatngurrluta tuani.

And they went down to Cevv'arneq. They said there was no village here, but they said it was back when Cevv'arnermiut downriver was the only winter village around.

And it is said some people would starve to death inside the *qasgi* during that time, since they didn't know how to eat needlefish.

It is said one person would look at his bowl when they'd give him some [needlefish], and after looking at it, he would say, "So many eyes."

Then he would turn his back on it, and his bowl would just sit there. He died after saying that there were too many eyes.

There will probably be needlefish for sure in our river. It is said the rivers located on either side, Qukaqliq [One in the center] and Qalvinraaq, their fish was affected at the time. But it is said that they would catch enough fish in this river to fill a small bowl.

And they say since their women tended to keep things stored away, they'd add various foods to the [needlefish], including *tayarut* [mare's-tail plants] or *tangviarrluut* [seal blubber from which oil had rendered] since they had that type of food available. That's what I heard them say about Arungalnguq and our river.

It is said some people from the Kuskokwim River would attempt to come here, but [the people of Cevv'arneq] weren't aware of them, but heard afterward that Arungalnguq [was filled with bones of the dead]. The center [of the lake] or the sides, or its south side, they say it has bones in it, like the person who brought Albert Beaver [and died of starvation].

He said that that's what he indeed heard about Urrsukvaaq. And my grandfather, Amaqigciq, also mentioned that it was like that. They evidently experienced famine sometime in the 1900s, and there was no open water on the ocean as it was filled with ice.

That's what I heard about Arungalnguq, and that's what I've heard about our river, also.

David Jimmie Sr.: Even these days they hunt for birds there, in the area around Arungalnguq.

But when it doesn't rain, this area gets shallow. Since it gets shallow when it doesn't rain, a person can't travel anywhere inside [the lake].

And when it's windy, the water moves to one side [of the lake] and accumulates along one side.

Recently, when we went to pick berries when the wind was blowing strong from the side of a hill, we returned home. When we were about to exit from Qass'urpak River, there was mud ahead of us. Since there was no way we could travel through it, we returned and set up tents and decided to spend

Angutekayak: Qayatgun pilallermeggni yaqulegcutullruut qayatgun, ii-i maavet Arungalngurmun. Augkut wani allgiarnek pilaqengameggnek ungulallruut ingtaqata, ingtellrata nalliini. Augkut-llu call' kep'alget avukluki. Tuaten tua-i ungulallruut qayatgun.

Kuvyirluteng pilallruut. Augkunek piqarralallermeggni, niigartelallruunga piliamegteggun yualunek kuvyarkiurluteng.

Qayatgun tua-ll' akiqliqluteng waten ungulalliniluteng, tuavet kuvyillermeggnun caqulluki.

Cenamun. Tuaten tua-i pilallrulliniut. Taum iluani, avatiini, wall'u allami kia imum' nallunrilkiini.

a night there.

Peter Matthew: Back when they used kayaks for transportation, they used to go bird hunting with kayaks here at Arungalnguq. They would drive what they called long-tailed ducks when they molted, during the time they molted. They also [drove] greater scaups. They would drive birds with kayaks like that.

They used fishnets [when they drove birds]. When they did it the original way, I heard they would make their own nets out of sinew.

Then they'd go with kayaks, situated across from one another and drive the birds, and then they'd drive them into the nets they set.

[They set nets] along the shore. That's evidently what they did in the past. Inside [that lake] or alongside it, or in another place that a person knew of.

Nuigtarmiut Tununermiut-llu

Newtok and Tununak

Kayalivik

Nanugaq: Wiinga cali una angalkunek angulqa iigemkun-llu tangvalqa. Una-llu Tut'garaurluum angalkuunrilngermi imarpigtellra. [*ngel'artuq*]

Tauna cali tua-i aka'artaungan, tuunriluteng waten iqukvaraqan imarpigteng taqukanek paqcet'lallrat; tauna cali tua-i umyuamnek, neq'akngamku tua-i, tamana-llu-w' cali qanrutkekuni tayim' cangaitellilria.

Angalkut waten qasgimi tuunriluteng, taqukangqetassiarluku waten kevgarluteng tan'gurrarnek.

Tua-i-ll' kevgaa tauna taum angalkum piciqaa, "Tua-i carrangqelliniuten. Kevgaukuvet assirciquten."

Angalkut-gguq ilait iqlulartut. Tut'garaurluum qanellra. Angalkut-gguq ilait angalkuunikait iqlulartut-gguq. Agayutem-gguq ikayularngatai; angalkuunrilengraan angalkumek tuqlurluku. [*ngel'artuq*]

Ellii-gguq tua-i imarpigtestelqaat Kayalivigmiuni.

Angalkugglugaam taum angalkuuniluku carrangqerrniluku pissuukarangqerrniluku imarpigtesqelluku qanrutliniluku.

Tuunriluni tauna angalkuq. Kevgaqluku imarpigmun ayaasqelluku waten, pilu'ugluku.

Pipiaryaaqluku. Pipiarluteng-gguq ayatullruut.

Tua-i nayiignek piluguugnek cikiatni tua-i-ll' taum anaaniin-gguq piluguugnek ac'elluku kevgauqatallinian. Naquggluni-llu-gguq tapengyagmek.

Tua-i-ll' taqngami tua-i anaaniin taum pillinia, "Kitek tua-i qasgimun agi." Nayirraagnek-llu-gguq kaumacirluku, agangqerrlutek-gguq taukuk nayirraak.

Tua-i iterngan tua-i piut-gguq tua-i uptelliniluteng. Kitakiilliniluku,

Kayalivik[59]

Elsie Tommy: The following also concerns the time that I happened to catch when shamans were around and something that I witnessed with my own eyes. And also about how Tut'garaurluq [Elsie's husband's father] went to the ocean although he wasn't a shaman. [*laughs*]

Since that concerns something that happened long ago, how [shamans] used their powers and had people go and check seals in their ocean toward the end of winter; since I recalled that story, it probably will be okay if I tell that story.

Shamans used their powers in the *qasgi* to check and see if there were seals, having boys help them carry out the task.

Then the shaman would tell the person he chose to carry out the task, "You have some sort of ability. You will be good as the person to carry out the task."

He said that some shamans lie. This is what Tut'garaurluq said. He said that some shamans, those who people say are shamans, lie. He said that he thinks that God helps them; although he isn't a shaman, they refer to him as a shaman. [*laughs*]

[Tut'garaurluq] said he was the one who would go to the ocean at Kayalivigmiut.

That shaman said that [Tut'garaurluq] was a shaman, that he had some ability, and he told him that he should go down to the ocean.

That shaman used his powers. He let him carry out the task, telling him to go down to the ocean, wearing skin boots.

He actually told him to go down for real. They say they really used to go.

When they gave him a pair of ringed-sealskin boots, he said that his maternal aunt had him put on the skin boots since he was to be the one to carry out the task on behalf [of the shaman]. And he said that he put on a braided grass belt.

Then when he was done, his maternal aunt told him, "Now go over to the *qasgi*." And he said she gave him some ringed-sealskin mittens, and those ringed-sealskin [mittens] hung from a harness.

Then when he went inside, they were getting ready. He told him well

"Kitaki, tumlliquangaituten imarpigmun atraqaquvet. Taqukat paqeskuvki tumlliquangaituten."

Tua-i tuunrissuutni imarnitek piakek, "Kitaki kalevvluten." Tua-i-ll' amigmun tua-i kalevvluni.

Upqaarluni tua-i, amik, amiinga ikingqaluni, kanaggun pitaunani. Tua-i kalevtesqengani kalevvluni, aqumesqengani-ll' waten tua-i aqumluni, uatmun cauluni.

Tua-i-ll' erinani aneskaku aqvaqurluku anesqelluku.

Tua-i erinani ancaku nang'errluni aqvaqurluni anqertelliniluni. Amik-llu-gguq kiugna patuluku kia-i. Patuatgu-llu-gguq cup'urillrakun iterluni. [*ngel'artuq*]

Ukinengqetullruut atam imkut kanaggun amiigem aciakun. Cup'urilleqniluki tamakut ukinret. Tuaggun tua-i kenret alaitaqluteng kia-i amiikwa pikani ukineq. Aciani tua-i kiaken, wangkuta-am tangssunglallrulriakut kenermek kiugumek kumaaqan. Tuaggun-gguq tua-i iterluni. [*ngel'artuq*]

Tuaggun tua-i iterngami kan'a-gguq kana-i aralleq. Tua-i-gguq una piyunarqellinian, pagkut-gguq-wa ukinret, qulinret.

Itlermini-gguq tuani, tua-i-gguq iterciigaterrlugngami nagcarpiarami, tua-i-gguq itenritnayukluni nangteqa'arcaaqellruuq. Tua-i caqirrluni tua-i qamiquni ancamiu. [*ngel'artuq*]

Anqercami tua-i anlliniluni tua-i nutaan. Tua-i-ll' amiinga, taqurraani elaturram amiingan taqurraani nangerrluni tuani, imarpigmun kiartelliniluni, "Qaillun-kiq ayallrusia? [*ngel'artuq*] Qaillun-kiq ayallruyarcia?" Tua-i-llu erinataircan iterturalliniluni tua-i.

Tua-i camek pivkenani iterturalliniluni tua-i. Tua-i-ll' amiinga tekicamiu ikirrluku nugluni. Nugngami-ll' nang'ercami taumun ayaasquurteminun waten piqerluni maniitelliniluku.

Tua-i-ll' taum taukuk imarnitegni waten pim'aurluni evcuggaarlukek nangerrluni tegulliniluku, "Qayumi taqukat up'nerkaqu amlleqatartut." [*ngel'artuq*] Qayumiirluni-gguq tua-i quyak'acagarluni tua-i.

Aren tua-i ellii qaillun-llu-gguq qilagkun pekciiqnillra, qaillun. [*ngel'artuq*] Imarpiim-gguq tungiinun nunamun tutmarpek'naku atrarciqlilria, qaillun-gguq ellii tuavet ayagciqa.

Aqvaquusqelluku tua-i egmianun ayagluni. Elaturrakun anelraqaami

then, "Well then, you won't have a difficult time walking on the trail when you travel down to the ocean. When you go and check the seals, you won't have a bad trail."

When he put on the seal-gut rain garment that he usually wore when he exercised his powers, [he said], "Well then, go down [into the tunnel entrance]." Then he went down into the entryway.

After getting ready, its door was open, and there was nothing down there. When he told him to go down, he went down, and when he told him to sit like this, he sat facing the exit.

And [the shaman] told him that when he let out his voice he should run outside.

When [the shaman] let out his voice, [Tut'garaurluq] stood and ran out. And he said that they closed the door back there. And when they closed it, he went inside through the draft hole. [*laughs*]

They used to have holes down below the door. They called those holes *cup'urillret* [draft holes]. The flames were visible back through there, and the doorway was up there, the hole. And underneath it, we used to watch the flame back there when it was lit. He said that he went inside through there. [*laughs*]

When he went in through there, he said there was some ash down there. Since he was able to [enter through there], he said up there were holes, cracks.

He said that when he entered, since it was a little difficult for him to enter, since he almost got stuck, he suddenly struggled, thinking that he might not enter. He turned and then he took his head out. [*laughs*]

When he got out [of the draft hole], he went outside. He stood alongside the doorway of the porch and scanned the ocean, "I wonder how I went? I wonder how I could have gone?" [*laughs*] Then when there were no longer any voices, he slowly went inside.

He slowly went inside. Then when he got to its doorway, he opened it and went up. When he went up and stood, he showed [the seal model] to the person who had asked him to go.

Then positioned like this, after shaking off his seal-gut rain garment, he stood and took it and said, "Just as could be expected, there will be many seals this spring." [*laughs*] He said it was just as could be expected, and he was extremely happy.

My, though he had said that he would be walking through the sky, he wondered how. [*laughs*] Though he had said he would head down toward the ocean without walking along the ground, he was wondering how he would travel there like that.

[The shaman] told him to run down and leave immediately. When he

akerteggun mayurluni, nutaan igvarcami-gguq tua-i uitaluni.

Tuani tua-i nangerngaurarraarluni yuarutmek-gguq tuunrissuutminek atullermini alaiteqallruuq. Tua-i-gguq nepairucan itqataarluni tua-i piyaaqevkenani

Cup'urillerkun anngami tua-i tuani yuarun iquklitnercirluku.

Ayalleq wani aiparma atallra, Tut'garaurluq. [*ngel'artuq*]

Tua-i-qaa tauna maniaku qayumiirluni, "Qayumi up'nerkaqu taqukat amlleqatartut." [*ngel'artut*]

Tua-i-llu-gguq-am tauna qemanqegcaarluku taum angalkum.

Taqukaruacuayagaq elliin taum angalkum pikluku. Tua-i-llu ayagcetqataamiu tauna tunluku elliinun.

Tua-i-gguq taqukat nurnarqeqatarqata ayagcecillri unangyuitelartut. Taqukat-llu-gguq piarkaukata unangluni. Tua-i-gguq tauna piarkartuyartellra. Up'nerkaan-gguq taqukat amelkacagallruut.

Piciuluni-gguq tua-i. Ikayurtengqellruuq-gguq tangvaumanrilngurmek. [*ngel'artuq*] Kayalivigmiuni.

Uitaqalallruunga yuratullratni, yuratullratni kevgitullratni uitatullruukut Kayalivigmi.

Ikaken Kaviarmiunek Tununermun upagluta. Tununermiut-llu kiatiitnek uksirraarluta up'nerkaan Merr'armun upagluta. Tua-i-ll' Kayalivigmiunun ayagpek'nata uitaluta. Uksuaraqan asguraqluta.

Tua-i-ll' aataka una piniarucami piavet Kuingartellermun uksuiyaurrluta, kanani ket'aramteni taluyat, taluyituami. Wangkuk tua-i ciuqliirutka-ll' alerquaguraarqakuk can'giirrsuutekayagaa civtaqluku. Alerquagurlunuk.

Up'nerkiyaraqluta Kayalivigmun Merr'armun pinritaqamta; pavavet ayagluta up'nerkiyaraqluta.

Uksumi uitatullruyaaqukut Kayalivigmi, allrakuni-ll' tayima qavcini, yuratullratni tuani. Tua-i-ll' piavet elkarrluta allrakuk tua-i ukuk malruk wall' pingayun aturlukek. Yurayuirulluteng. Deschout-am taqevkarluki.

went down through the porch, he went up through the steps, and when he appeared, he stayed there.

After standing there for a while, he said that when [the shaman] sang his incantation song, he could hear him clearly. He said when he got quiet, he slowly went in, trying not to [make noise].

When he went out through the draft hole, he waited for the song to end.

The one who went was the deceased father of my husband, Tut'garaurluq. [*laughs*]

So when he showed him that, he said *qayumi* [just as could be expected], "Just as could be expected, this spring there will be many seals." [*laughter*]

Then that shaman put that [model seal] away carefully.

The small model seal belonged to that shaman. So when [the shaman] was about to let him go, he gave that to [Tut'garaurluq]

They say when seals are going to be scarce, the ones that he sent out didn't obtain anything. And if seals are going to be [plentiful], he obtains something. [Tut'garaurluq] said that was a time when he was clever. He said that spring, seals were abundant.

He said it turned out to be true. He said that the unseen one helped him. [*laughs*] At Kayalivigmiut.

I used to stay there from time to time back when they used to dance; back when they used to dance, back when they had Messenger Feasts, we stayed at Kayalivik.

From Kaviarmiut over there, we moved to Tununak. Then after spending winter up the coast from Tununak, when spring came we moved to Merr'aq [possibly "Small amount of *meq* (water)"]. Then we didn't go to Kayalivik and stayed there. When fall would come, we'd go upriver.

And when my father became weak, we started to go and spend winters up at Kuingartelleq [One that formed a *kuik* (river)], since he used to set a blackfish trap right down below our place. When he would instruct my deceased older sister and I about what to do, we would set his small blackfish trap. He would continually tell us what to do.

We would go spring camping at Kayalivik when we didn't go to Merr'aq; we'd head up to go spring camping inland.

We used to stay at Kayalivik during winter, and we stayed there for a number of years, back when they used to dance. Then we moved up there for either two or three years. They stopped dancing. [Father] Deschout had them stop.

Unangik: Man'a maani curukaryaraat imuuguq tua-i waten, elliraat, atailnguut, angussaagtailnguut tuaggun tua-i angutullruut; ikayurluki. Kass'allauyugnailngurnek neqnek, uqunek tamaa-i. Tamakut tamaa-i pistaiteurlulriit tua-i angurvatullrullinikait.

Tua-i kelellinikait malruirulluki. Kayalivigmiut kelegluki, ingkut-llu keluqliita pingkut, Nunapicuarmiut Kassigluarmiut-llu-w' pillilriit.

Tua-i nalirruggluteng natmunllikiarluteng tua-i, "Natmun atak piqaalta." Naliitnun tua-i ellmeng nunameggni, wall'u Kayalivigmun yaavet.

Kayalivigmiut-gguq tuani cat tua-i uquq amlleq tua-i unakellruat tuani.

Tua-i-am waten maqinerrarallratni angutet iliit itliniuq, nalirrugtaarluteng tamaan natmun pillerkameggnek. Angutet iliit itrami uskurani agartellinii urugcirluki. Ilani ukut pillinii, "Wiinga tua-i uqurturkaaranglerkamnun wii piyugtua; wii piqatartua uqurturkaaranglerkamnun Kayalivigmun."

Aren taukut-gguq tua-i ilain maligartaat tua-i, Kayalivigmun piqatarluteng, yaavet, ikavet Kayalivigmiunun.

Tua-i ayagluteng. Tuani tua-i Kayalivigmiunun pilliniluteng. Nunat malruin pillrungatut tuani.

Tamaa-i tua-i utertellermeggni aruqut'liqsiyaagameng tuan Kayalivigmi neqnek, uqurugarnek tuaten, iliita-am uquq kapqerluku waten ucimeng iliit maq'urtelluku tua-i, tua-i-gguq-wa qimugtemeggnek artuqliteurluata tamaa-i ucimeggnek neqnek.

Neqnek ayuqenrilngurnek tayim' ucingqellrullilriit, kass'allauyugnailngurnek neqerrlainarnek taugaam.

Ii-i, maq'urtelluku tua-i ayagluteng. Iliita tua-i kapqerluku, tua-i ucini ilangaqanirluki, uqeglicarluki.

Tayima-w' tua-i nuqlipallaalria pillrullilria, qimugtelliqenqurriit pillrullilria. [*ngel'artuq*]

Augkut ava-i curukatullret ak'a tamakut, tua-i ilumun yugnek makunek yum'eggnek angussaagtailngurnek tua-i imutun ikayuriq'apiarallruut.

Simeon Agnus: The Messenger Feast was a way in which orphans, those without fathers, those who had no providers survived; they helped them. They gave them foods that weren't store-bought at all, including fish and seal oil. They evidently really helped provide for those poor people who didn't have providers.

Two separate villages evidently invited them [to a Messenger Feast]. The people of Kayalivik invited them, and the people inland from them, probably the people of Nunapitchuk and Kasigluk.

They were undecided about which place they would go to, "I wonder which place we should go to." They couldn't decide if they should go to a village near their village or to Kayalivik over there.

It is said the people of Kayalivik obtained a lot of seal oil at the time.

Right after they took a firebath, one of the men came in while they were undecided about where they should go. One of the men went in and hung up his harnesses to thaw them. He said to his fellow villagers, "I want to go to a place where I will obtain some seal oil; I'm going to Kayalivik where I will obtain some seal oil."

The people there suddenly followed his decision, and they planned to go over to Kayalivik, to Kayalivik over there.

They went. They evidently went to Kayalivigmiut at that time. I think there were two villages there at the time.

When they returned, since they had obtained many gifts of food there at Kayalivik, including a lot of seal oil, one of the people evidently poked a seal poke that they were carrying and had it leak out, since they had a difficult time with their dogs that were carrying the load of food.

They were probably carrying lots of different types of food, not store-bought food at all, but all Native foods.

Yes, they traveled by having [the seal oil] leak out. One of the people there poked it and removed some of the load he was carrying, lightening his load.

It was probably someone who didn't have many dogs, the one with the least dogs. [*laughs*]

Those who had Messenger Feasts in the past, indeed they really helped their own people who didn't have any providers.

Nuyarralek: Agaani yuurtellrusia nani, ingkut Cevv'arnermiut ukatiitni pingatuq. Camiunek apertuqatullruyaaqai aanama.

Tua-i-ll' agken ukatmurulluta. Elevaakun piyugnaunateng taugaam cavluteng, angyaput-wa qeciit. Tamaaken *move*-allruukut.

Kayalivigmun-llu asguulluta. Ingkut Kayalivigmiut yugyaggallruut, Kayalivigmiut. Qaugkut-llu avanelnguut avatiini yugluteng tamarmeng. Taugaam Kayalivigmiut yugtuqaullruut tamatum nalliini.

Tauna taugaam qasgingqellrat malrugnek kingu'urtellruaqa wii. Qasgik-llu malruk elaqliq'ngermek waten canimeluteng'ermek allakarmek aterlutek. Aipaa Qukutvallruluni, aipaa-llu camek aciqalallruatgu.

Cali tamaani qasgimi uitallemteni, Nasgauq kenkeksaicaaqaqa, maa-i qanemcikangqerrsartua. Carayak itqataryaaqelliniluni. Qasgiq yungqellruuq tua-i uivetmun kassugluni. Wangkuta-llu aatamta ketaini aqumgaluta.

Ugna amiigem aciakun im' aurneqegtaar, imna puyuqegtaar, murruggluni-llu. Pinqigcami itraqanirluni, murruggluni-llu.

Nasgauq naken qavaken nangerrluni alingyugnaunani, an'uq. Tua-i-ll' tauna tua-i taqluni.

Taqngan Culungalgem Atii uitauraqerluni qanertuq, "Carayiim aug'um itqataryaaqekiikut." Nallunrilami. "Aug'um anelriim navgaa." Tangerrsarqa carayak.

Tamakut-llu amiigiq'ngelriit kiturciigatnilaqait.

Cali arnaukan naugg'un cavvluku, wall' angutngukan nauggun cavvluku, kiituan pikaggun cavqaarluku aug'um tua-i tallim uqamarraanek atrarturcelluku. Negleraqan qulmuqaniraqluni. Tamakucimek wii tangeqsaitua. [*ngel'artuq*]

Mark Tom: I was born across there somewhere, I think on this side of the village of Cevv'arneq. My mother used to mention the name of the place.

Then they moved us in this direction [north] from across there. They didn't travel with outboard motors at all, but just by rowing, and our boats were skin boats. We moved from there.

They brought us upriver to Kayalivigmiut. Kayalivigmiut had a good many residents at one time. And all the villages to the north out there were occupied. But at the time, Kayalivigmiut had the most residents.

But I wasn't around and happened to miss the time they had *qasgik* [two men's houses]. And although the *qasgik* were situated right next to one another, they had their own distinct names. One was called Qukutvalleq, and I'm not sure what they called the other.

When we were staying at the *qasgi,* I wasn't too happy with Nasgauq, as I would have had a story to tell today. A ghost was evidently about to enter. The *qasgi* was occupied with people all the way around. And we were seated down below our fathers.

From underneath the doorway, a nice mist appeared and then it faded. When it appeared again, it came farther in and faded.

Nasgauq stood from somewhere inside, not afraid at all, and went out. Then that [mist] stopped.

When it stopped, Culungalgem Atii said after a while, "A ghost was about to enter our place." He knew what was about to happen. "The person who went out ruined the process." I would have seen a ghost.

And they mention that people couldn't pass by ghosts who blocked doorways, *amiigiq'ngelriit.*

Also, if it was a female [ghost], they'd touch them along a certain part of their body, or if it was a male, they'd touch them along a certain part, and after touching it, from the [head] they'd use the weight of their hand to bring [the ghost] down [toward the ground]. When pushing down with too much pressure, it would move up. I've never seen one of those. [*laughs*]

Niugtaq

Qukailnguq: Cali tuaken, Qiingssarmi, Qiingssarmi uitanrirluta Cevtarmun nugtarrluta. Tuani-llu tua-i allrakuni qavcini wall'u-qaa pingayuni uitaluta *uncle*-aaqa augna Angayiq tuquluni.

Tauna tua-i tuani tuquan uksuumainanrani aataka tuquvailgan alularlua qamani-llu qavarlua, qavartarlua. Avegyam Atiin tangrramia pianga aataka qanrutesqelluku kiakan nugtartesqelluta, *school*-aliqatarniluku.

Man'a-ll' maa-i Niugtaq Culungalgenkuk Arnapagaq-llu yuvrillrulliniak, paac-am ullagciigatenrilkiinun. Man'a tamaa-i Niugtaq ngellekluku, tua-i mat'umun maa-i Niugarmun taumek tua-i cucuklirlutek, paac-am ullagciigatenrilkiinun.

Kiagngan-llu tua-i qamavet ayagluta up'nerkaan. Taingamta-llu maavet maa-i tua-i-w' ciuneqluku tailuta maavet Niugtarmun arulairluta. Upaggaarluta maanqaarluta enep'ut cali Qiingssarmi aqvaluku.

Tua-i tamaa-i elkek Arnapagaankuk-llu Culungalek-llu kiartellrulliniuk nunakameggnek. Yaaqsillruyaaquq un'a una nunaksagutellemteggu. Tua-i cangalkevkenaku nunakluku. Assirluni.

Paug'umi nunallemteni man'a Niugtaq uksumi qacignarqenruuq, tua-i qacignarqenruuq. Paugna nunallerput uksuurrluku nengllitullruuq tamatum nalliini. Neqmek cali paivngalinrunaqluni. Tua-i cangalkevkenaku assikluku tua-i. Taugaam tua-i nunalillemteni qacignarqellrunrituq.

Nanurniralria: Tua-i-llu *1950*-mi tua-i imkut ilanka aataka-ll' tamaa-i unguvaluni, upengluteng. Maaten tua-i ayagtut tuavet tua-i Niugtaurtarkaullinilriamun ayallinilriakut.

Tua-i-ll' tamaani *1950*-mi kuigmun tua-i kuigkaanun kiagmi piameng pelatekiurluteng nunakamek kiartelliniluteng. Ukut tua-i tegganret qavcin kiarrluteng.

Tua-i nalkucameng, uksuarpailgan tuavet nunakamtenun Niugtaugarkaullinilriamun itraqaniameng, ukut tua-i anngaagka muragaarnek tua-i naken tayima aqvauqurlutek angyangqerramta.

Tua-i-ll' nevumek neliut. Tua-i tamakut tuantarkat yuut, naken-llu tayim' pillruat, nevunek nek'ameggnek piluteng tua-i.

Newtok[60]

Michael John: And at that time, we stopped staying at Qiingssaq, but we moved to Cevtaq [Man-made channel]. Then we stayed there for a number of years, or even three years, and then my uncle Angayiq died.

When he died there that winter, before my father died, I traveled with an outboard motor and spent the night up there. When Avegyaq's father saw me, he told me to tell my father that we should move that summer, that they were going to build a school.

Culungalek and Arnapagaq evidently surveyed Newtok, and they picked a place that barges could reach. They chose this site of Newtok, a place that barges could reach.

And when summer came, when spring came, we traveled up there [to the Kuskokwim River]. And when we returned, we came straight to Newtok and stopped here. After moving, after staying here, we went to get our home at Qiingssaq.

Arnapagaq and Culungalek evidently searched for a spot for our village. The coast was far away when we first moved to this village. We didn't mind the village. It was good.

Newtok is much easier to live in compared to the place where we used to live during winter. It's much easier to live here. Our old village used to get cold during winter. And there is more food available. We didn't mind it and liked it. But it wasn't easy when we formed this village.

Mary George: Then in 1950, my family, and even my father was alive at the time, they began to prepare. When we left, we were evidently traveling to what would become the village of Newtok.

Then in 1950, when they evidently went to the river where [the village] would be located, they set tents along there and searched for a place where [Newtok] would be located. A number of elders searched.

When they found a place, when they headed up to the place that would eventually become our village, the village of Newtok before fall time, my two older brothers [Michael and Peter John] went to get some logs from somewhere since we had a boat.

Then they built a sod home. The people who eventually settled there, and I'm not sure where they all came from, went to obtain sod for homes and built them.

Tua-i-w' tamaani wiinga ellangellemni taukut can'giiret cuukviit-wa makut-llu tengmiat nervallullrukput tamaaken avakaramtenek tamatum nalliini. Watua taugaam maa-i, *'90s*-am-wa tua-i nalliinek ayagluni avakaramtenek neqsurviput-llu, wangkuta arnani cumercaralput tua-i nang'ut.

Cali-llu naullrat tua-i tamatum naumrruyuum, avakaramtenek pisciigaliluta maa-i. Tua-i tamana unangnaqsararput ilii yaani nunamteni tamarluni, kill'uni, nunavut ingna qerkelliami, avatvut.

Cali-llu ustem tamaa-i navgurluku. Cali-llu uksuarmi waten uugnaraat neqaitnek pilalput assinrirluni, piirusngiinarluni taugaam, mer'em-wa tua-i capsugluki.

Wiinga tua-i taumek tuaten pitalua qanemciunga.

Unangik: Augna avani ikayuqernaluku piaqa una wani Qukailnguq.

Ika-i ikegkut Niugtarmiut tanglaqput. Arnaucuam Atiin qanellra waniw' aturluku, ikegkut ika-i yuugut Niugtarmiut, tangvallmegni una-ll' aipaqallu. Waniw' aiparma qanrutketukai.

Ikegkut ika-i Niugtarmiut naken angutnek iluvaupakanritut ikegkut Niugtarmiut. Ilameggnek aipangu'urluteng, nunalgutmeggnek aipangu'urluteng. Tuaten ayuqut.

Arnaucuam Atiin unipailegminiki tuaten tua-i qanrutellrullinikai. Allanek nunanek, arnanek-llu allanek tekiurqessuunateng, arnat-llu nasaurluut agkut angutnek iluvaulluteng tangnerranarqellrianek tekiucuunateng, taugaam ellmeggnek, nunalgutmeggnek, nasaurluut-llu. Ikani Niugtarmiut tuaten ayuqut tangvallmegni wangkuk. Allanek tekiupakarpek'nateng.

Niugtarmiut ikegkut tamanek yungqenritut. Atauciq-wa nauviat. Ataucimek nauvingqertut-gguq ikegkut ika-i Niugtarmiut.

Waten yuraliya'arqamta-ll' tanglaqput. Tangnerranarqellrianek-llu ilangqerpakarpek'nateng. Niugtarmiut agkut, ava-i tan'gurrayaallret agkut irnialiriluteng, wangkutni-ll' kiani yugyanruluteng.

When I became aware, we mainly ate blackfish, pike, and birds, obtaining them from the area immediately surrounding our village during that time.

But at this time, starting sometime in the 1990s, the places where we used to fish in the area surrounding our village and the places where we women used to gather food are all gone now.

And the growth of those plants, we are no longer able to gather things from the area immediately surrounding our village. Some places where we used to make efforts at obtaining things have disappeared over at our village, they have sunk, since our village over there has gradually lowered, the area around our village.

And erosion has also destroyed it. And during fall like this, the places where we once obtained mouse food from underground caches are no longer in good condition, but they are only getting scarce, as water is starting to cover those places.

I'm just talking about that to that extent.

☙

Simeon Agnus: I just wanted to help Qukailnguq [Michael John] by adding a little to what he said.

We see people from Newtok over there. As my wife and I have observed them, the people of Newtok across there are now living by following the instructions of Arnaucuam Atii, by following his instructions. My wife mentions what they are like.

The people across there at Newtok hardly ever bring men from other places into their village. They continually marry their fellow people, they continually marry people from their village. That's what they are like.

Before leaving them, Arnaucuam Atii evidently instructed them to do that. They don't bring people from other villages or women from other places into their village, and the girls across there don't bring men who people haven't seen before into the village, but they [marry] people from their village, including the girls. That's what we have observed the people of Newtok to be like. They hardly bring other people into their village.

The village of Newtok over there doesn't have people from all over. They have one ancestor. They say the people of Newtok come from one ancestor.

We see them when we go and attend dance festivals there. And they hardly have people in their village who we haven't seen before. The people of Newtok across there, the young men across there have many children now, and they have more people in their village than in our village [of Nightmute].

Wangkuta waniw' ukuni qikertam yuini yuilqurraugut wangkuta, ikgelqurraugukut. Niugtarmiut tungliqsaaqekemceteng, amllenruluteng taugaam waten mikelngumegteggun.

Kiani kia-i nunamteni *two hundred*-aaq tayima kitungyaaqngataat aipaagni. Niugtarmiut taugken ukut amllenruluteng.

Arnaucuam Atiin atanrata im' nallunrilkeci; taum tua-i qanaateqallrullinikai ukut Niugtarmiut. Aiparma uum wani qanrutketuaki-ll' ukut Niugtarmiut ukut ilakutaqngamiki, anngaa-ll' imna Qilangaq taukumiungullrulria uum. Ikayuqa'arqa.

Qiingssaq

Qukailnguq: Tamaa-i murilkellruunga ellangellruunga Qiingssarmi. Enet qavciullruut; *four*-aarullruut. Ilakluta.

Tua-ll' un'gavet iliini-llu Engelullugarmiunun Tununermun-llu tua-i iqalluarpagssurluteng. Pirrlainarpegnateng, cam iliini tua-i tuavet upagaqluteng. Iqalluarpagnek tua-i neqsurluteng.

Neqsurraarluta-llu tua-i taqkuneng kinqata neqet Nerevkartulimun itrarluteng, tua-i uterrluteng pikuneng. Tamaa-i-llu tengmiarcurluteng ingtarnek.

Ingtaat cali tua-i ingtanek qavcirqunek kiagpak unguaqluteng; qavcirqunek pingayurqunek aipaagni wall' cetamarqunek pilaryugnarqut. Tamakunek tua-i tamaa-i kemgit iniluki piaqluki. Nacaullget-llu amiit eritarpegnaki amiirluki kinercirluki. Tuaten tua-i piaqluteng.

Tamakut-llu nacaullget amiit atkukluki. Atkuliluki tua-i taqkunegteki aanamta, aatamtenun. Tua-i aataput nacaullekegciaqluteng, wangkuta-ll' tamakunek atkuliyuunata. Taugaam tunutellegnek alkainaunrilngurnek atkuliaqluta. [*ngel'artuq*]

Tua-ll' tuani nacaullget tengmiat tengkata itrarluta tuavet, iliini-ll' wani ataucirqumek pelatekarallruukut. Itraqumta-ll' tua-i Cevtarmun iliini arulairluta. Tua-i cali uitaluteng, uksuangareksan-llu tua-i Qiingssarmun tuavet tua-i upagluta. Tauna tua-i nunakluku tua-i natmun-llu allamun nunamun pivkenata, tuani tua-i uksurpak. Aatallma uksuarmi waten neqsurvikluku pilallrua, neqsurvikluku.

Tua-i kiaguluku waten pivailgan taluyirluni tua-i tamaa-i can'giirnek neqsuraqluni.

We people who reside on this island have the lowest population. Although Newtok was founded later than we were, they have more people due to their children.

I think the population of our village upriver [at Nightmute] is over two hundred people now. But there are more people at Newtok.

Arnaucuam Atii, their leader who you know; that person evidently spoke to the people of Newtok and gave them direction. My wife talks about the people of Newtok since they are her relatives, and her older brother Qilangaq was from that village. I just wanted to help him and add to what he said.

Qiingssaq[61]

Michael John: I started becoming aware of my surroundings at Qiingssaq. There were a number of houses; there were four. We were all related.

Then they'd go to the coast and fish for herring, sometimes to Engelullugarmiut and Tununeq. They didn't always go, but they'd move there sometimes. They'd fish for herring.

And after fishing, when they were done, when the fish dried, they'd head up to Nerevkartuli when they returned home. They'd hunt for molting birds.

They'd drive molting birds a number of times throughout the summer; they went a number of times, either three or four times. They'd hang their meat to dry. And they wouldn't pluck the emperor-geese skins, but they removed their skins and dried them. That's what they did.

And they'd make the emperor-geese skins into parkas. Our mothers would make them into parkas for our fathers when they finished processing them. Our fathers had nice emperor-geese parkas, and they never made us those types of parkas. But they'd make us loonskin parkas that didn't easily tear. [*laughs*]

And when the emperor geese, the birds flew, we'd go up to that place, and we went tent camping at this place once. And when we'd go up, sometimes we'd stop at Cevtaq. They'd stay there, and when it turned into fall, we'd move to Qiingssaq. That was our village, and we never went anywhere else, but we'd stay there all winter. My deceased father used it as a fishing site during fall.

During summer before conditions were like this, he'd set his wooden fish traps to fish for blackfish.

Maani cuukviit mikullrunritut. Tua-i kuvyait augkut piliarraungermeng picunritellrata tamatum ilalqallruyugnarqai. Tamakunek tua-i malrugnek kuvyangqerrluni tua-i piaqluni.

Tua-i tamakut tamaa-i nenglengvailgan taluyai civtellri ukut piculallruut. Tenguitnek qassalallruukut can'giiret. Tamakut tenguirluki initaq tua-i iliini-ll' tua-i takrangraan initaq imiraqluku.

Tua-i tauna uksurpak nunakluku tua-i, pissurvikluku tuaten uksuarmi-llu imarmiutarnek pissurvikluku piaqluta, piaqluni-w' tua-i aatalqa.

Tamaa-i nuna akluklermeggni, neqekluku, akikluku-llu, tua-i tamakut *lucky*-rvimeggnun maa-i makut cagqaqellrat *school*-arviitellermeggni nunaullruut.

Ilait-llu enet ataucirrauluteng; tua-i wani Naruyami uitavalluraqluteng tamaa-i qaciggluteng neqnek cali-ll' akikarcullermeggnek unangenrulallermeggni.

Cali tua-i kaviarnek tua-i cali pissullermeggni tamaa-i paivngalinrulallermegteggun piaqluteng.

Tua-i-ll' iliini up'nerkaureskan, up'nerkangkan, aniullingyaureskan, tuavet tua-i Qiingssam painganun, painganun.

Ayagngamegnuk tua-i tuavet tua-i, wavet ayaglunuk. Kanaqlagcurvikliniluku tauna. Tuani tua-i ernerni qavcini uitalunuk, unugmi makut kanaqliit pissurnaqngameng. Tua-i cassaunanuk-llu.

Aatalma tua-i tuavet tekicamegnuk tunutellget aqesgit-llu tua-i cass'aqluki. Tunutellget tua-i makut unuk qaill' pitariqertaqan tua-i tan'geriqertaqan nepairtelallruut. Tua-i tuani yaqulget tua-i imkut tua-i neplillret nepaiteqerluteng, nepaunateng tua-i.

Tua-i-ll' qaill' pikan tayima tunutellek qalriuqan, aqesgit-llu aqumkallaganga'arrluteng, tengmiat tua-i ayuqenrilnguut nep'ngeciqut, neplirluteng. Tua-i-ll' ak'anun pivkenateng nepaiteqerluteng.

Tuamtell' aqesgiq aqumkallagciquq kelumegni, tunutellek-llu qalrialuni. Tua-i-ll' tauna ayagneqluku nep'ngekuneng tua-i nutaan nepengluteng.

Tua-i tuani pissurraarluta taqkumta *June*-ami, *June*-aullinilriami tamaani kanaqliit nulirtenga'artaqameng allguutetulliniut, tua-i taqluki.

Tua-i-ll' taqkumta tua-i tuani uitarraarluta, imkut-llu Uyuraurluunkut Cakataaraankut-llu Cevtarmun tuavet angyakun anelrarluta; angyangqerrluta augkunek tuskanek.

Tuani-ll' tua-i nutaan tuaten palayamun, palayaakun Angayiim atraqumta,

Pike weren't abundant around here. Although their mesh nets were handmade, I think it was difficult for them because they didn't catch a lot. He had two of those mesh fishnets.

Before it got cold, the wooden fish traps that he set caught a lot. We used to eat blackfish livers raw. She'd remove their livers and sometimes fill a fish rack full [of blackfish] although it was long.

We lived at that place all winter, and we'd hunt there, and we'd hunt for mink there during fall, or rather, my father did.

When the land provided people with tools, food, and income, people were scattered in places where they had the most success and were lucky in obtaining food and other things when they had no schools.

And sometimes there was one home in one place; they mostly lived at Naruyaq, back when they obtained more food and fur animals for income.

And when they hunted for red fox, they'd stay in places where they were readily available.

And sometimes when spring came, in the beginning of spring when the snow began to soften, they'd go to the mouth of Qiingssaq.

When we traveled to that place there, we traveled here. That was evidently his muskrat hunting place. We stayed there for a number of days, since these muskrats have to be hunted at night. We had no watch to tell time.

When we arrived there, my late father used loons and ptarmigan to tell time. During a certain time in the evening, when it got dark, these common loons used to get quiet. Then at that time, the birds that had been making noise were quiet.

Then during a certain time, when a common loon made its call, and ptarmigan started falling on their bottoms, different kinds of birds would start making noise. Then not long after, they'd get quiet.

Then the ptarmigan would fall on its bottom behind us somewhere, and a common loon would make its call. Then from that time on, when they started to make noise, they started to get noisy.

After hunting at that time, during the month of June, during what was evidently the month of June, when muskrats start to mate, they start to tear each other's skin, and [men] stop hunting them.

And when we were done, after staying there along with Uyuraurluq [Andy Charlie] and family and Cakataar and his family, we'd go down to Cevtaq with a boat; we had a plywood boat.

And when we went down with Angayak's *palayaq*, sometimes we would

iliini Tununermun ayagluta. Ayakuneng-llu tua-i caginek manignaleryagnek-llu pissurraarluteng, taqkuneng Nerevkartulimun tuavet tua-i itrarluteng. Tua-i tuaten piciryaraqluku.

Cali-ll' uaken ua-i imumek tunuirutmek, anelrarqamta arulairluteng, tua-i tengmianek tua-i pissurluteng, kayangunek tuaten piaqluteng. Tua-i-ll' tuaken anelraquneng yaavet Nerevkartulimun anelrarluteng.

Tauna tua-i maaken nunat katurrvik'lallruat. Neqsurvikluku tua-i pissurvikluku tuaten taqukanek amirkanek. Tauna-ll' tua-i una waniwa kiagpak yuicuunani. Anssiirvikluku tua-i piaqluku.

Tuaten tamaa-i. Tua-i-llu qaill' pitariqerluku angamta *uncle*-amta, allrakut tayim' qavciatni tuani tua-i kanaqlagcurraarluta taqngamta massiinangluni. Cakayiim kiputestekellrua.

Tuaken ayagluta Kusquqvagmun ayaulluta nangcaqluta. Aren tuani-im' ciuqliullrulria nangcaqluta maaggun asguulluta, piavet Akuluramun. Cimerlituliullinilriamun-llu unilluta. Tuani tua-i uitaluta.

Nutaan *1945*-aami tuavet ayaucamegtekut Kusquqvagmun qavavet ayaulluta nangcaqluta. Naparyarrarmiut-llu uatiitni uitaluta. Tuavet arulairulluta, *red*-anek makunek neqsurluta; neqsuulluta.

Tua-i neqsurluta tua-i kiagpak tua-i. *August*-ami-llu tamaa-i tamaani ut'reskumta natmun ayagpek'nata tuavet tua-i wavet Cevtarmun tagluta. Ut'rulluta, maavet wavet. Tuani tua-i uitaluta Cevtarmi.

Nenglengareskan-llu tua-i wavet cali, tuavet, wavet uterrlua, Qiingssarmun. Tauna uksumi uitavikelallruarput; uksuarmek ayagluta yaavet uksurpak uitavik'lallruarput.

Tua-i makut maani nunarraat tamarmeng *lucky*-rvimeggnun nunaliqulallrulliniut tamatum nalliini, *school*-arviitellermeggni. Tua-i cangakevkenaku tua-i.

Taqikcaq

Qukailnguq: Tua-i allrakum iliini tuntulget waten tuaten maani neqmeggnek nuqlit'ngaqata avavet nunamun nugtarrluteng pitullruut.

Tuani akmavet Qiingssarmun, tamaa-i yuilqumun ayagyaurpailegma, qaill' tayim' angtarilua taugaam, tekitellruut. Waska-mek taukut tuntulget atanengqellruut.

Qulvarkankut iliitnek. Atanruaqluni tamaani tuntulegni. Tangellruaqa.

travel to Tununak. And when they left, after fishing for halibut and Pacific cod, when they finished, they would head up to Nerevkartuli. That was their custom.

And from down along the shortcut, when we went down, they'd stop there and hunt for birds and also obtain bird eggs. And when they went down from there, they'd go down to Nerevkartuli.

The people from the villages around this area would gather there. It was their fishing site and hunting site for seals and young bearded seals. And this site here was occupied all summer. It was a place where they hunted seals in open water.

That's what they did. Then during a certain time of year, our *angak* [older brother], our uncle, during one year, after we went muskrat hunting and were done, he bought an outboard motor. He was a store-keeper for Cakayak.

After that time, he brought us to the Kukskokwim River, towing us. Oh, I forgot to mention that he first towed us and brought us up this river, up to Akuluraq. And he left us at what was evidently Cimerlituli. We stayed there.

Finally in 1945, he brought us to the Kuskokwim River, towing us there. And we stayed downriver from Napakiak. He stopped and left us there and we fished for red salmon; he fished for us.

We fished all summer long. And when we returned home in August, we didn't travel anywhere but we went up to Cevtaq. He brought us home to this place. We stayed there at Cevtaq.

And when it started to get cold, we returned to this place again, to Qiingssaq. That was where we stayed during winter; starting in the fall, we stayed there all winter.

All these small villages, people evidently formed villages in places where they were lucky [obtaining food] back when they didn't have schools. We didn't mind it.

Taqikcaq[62]

Michael John: Some years, when [reindeer] started to lack food in the surrounding area, reindeer herders would move to other places.

At that time, before I started traveling out to the wilderness, and I was a certain age, they arrived across there at Qiingssaq. Waska was the head of the reindeer herders.

He was one of Qulvarkaq and his family. He was the head of the reindeer herders. I saw him.

Tua-i-ll' tamakut, aataka qanemcitaa tekicami tuntut apqucirniluki. Cali-ll' tamaa-i kasmiinanermeggni iquaqata tua-i unilluki ilangcivkenaki piaqluki. Kemgiulluteng-llu.

Tamaa-i tamakut kemgit ilumun assiirutellruut, patrit-llu assiirulluteng.

Tua-i-ll' tuaken ayagngameng tua-i maavet maa-i tailuteng, tua-i kiagpak uitallerkameggnun tamaani up'nerkami unitellerkameggnun tuntut tamakut.

Tua-i-w' makut yuit. Cakcaaq-llu yungqerrluni. Tununeq; natmun tayima tua-i ellaita pillerkameggnun tamaa-i ayautellruit.

Tua-i *company*-rtarnek ilagallermeggni apqucillrulliniut. Qaugkumiutaat *company*-rtarnek acilallruit.

Tuaken tua-i tangenrillruanka. Taugaam ikani Qiingssarmi up'nerkitullemteni, up'nerkaan tamaa-i assiring'ermeng amllellruut tamakut pinritellriit.

Aataka-llu qetraryaurcan ayagaqan maligtaqamni, tuaten tua-i waniw' tekitaqamegnuk tuntut amllerrarluteng katungqaluteng. Tamakunek nut'galuni ikamragni ucilirlukek utertaqluni.

Akmani nunamteni kelumteni qemini tamaani pilallruuq, Qiingssam kelulirnerani.

Tua-i aataka-wa tamaa-i maliggluku piaqamni imkut-gguq cirunrit naugaaralriit, naugaaralriit cakneq pitangyuutek'lallrui. Maaten-gguq pilagciqai, iluit-llu uquriluteng. Tamakut-gguq tamaa-i nerlallruaput. Tamakut taugken tamaa-i neryuunaki, qimugtenun neqkautekevkaraqluki apqucillret.

Amiit taugaam tua-i kinercirluki piaqluki. Tamakut-llu curuqluki inarrvikluki tuaten piaqluki.

Unangik: Ikani Waska-q atanrat canimelan, wangkuta maani nalarqiyuitellruut tuaten. Waska-q taugaam qanrulluku, wall' ataucimek wall' malrugnek nalaciqatarniluteng. Tuaten tua-i piuratullruut wani.

Ikani ika-i ingrirpall'er ikna akemna akma tangerqeci. Amatiini tuntulget uitatullruut. Cali ualirnerani, cali Yuukarmiut kiatiitni tuani-llu uitatuluteng. Tauna kiaqlia una wani Qayairyaramek pitullruat, tauna tua-i tuntulget uitaviketullrat.

Waten kiagmi piciatun ayagangtuut. Anaryugciqaqameng qimagallrata tamaa-i pangalgavkatullruit atam. Un'a-ll' un'a Qalvinraaq nalugluku maavet ukalirnermun piaqluteng.

Then when [Waska] arrived, he told my father that the reindeer had a sickness. And while they were herding them, when they'd topple over, they'd leave them. And they got thin, too.

Indeed, their meat became bad, and their marrow got bad.

And when they left that place, they came here to settle for the summer, during spring, when they left those reindeer.

The people originally from this area [were here then]. And people were living at Cakcaaq also. Tununak; they brought them to the place where they would [herd them].

When the [reindeer] from the company joined them, they evidently got a sickness. They called the [reindeer] to the north "ones from the company."

From that time, I no longer saw [reindeer] around. But when we used to go spring camping in Qiingssaq across there, when spring came and they recovered, many weren't affected by sickness.

And when my father traveled when hard snow crust started to form at night during spring after a warm day, when I'd travel with him, when we'd come upon reindeer, there would be many in a group. He'd shoot at those and load his sled and return home.

He would do that across there in our area behind our village, behind Qiingssaq.

When I'd accompany my father at the time, he'd want to pursue and catch the ones with antlers just growing. When he'd butcher them, we'd see that they were fat inside. We used to eat those. But we never ate those other [reindeer], and we had the dogs eat the ones that were sick.

But we'd dry their hides. And we'd also use those as mattresses and bedding.

Simeon Agnus: Since Waska, the head of the reindeer herds, was close by across there [at Tununak], we didn't kill them around here at random like that. They'd only inform Waska that they were going to kill one or two. That's what they always did here.

You see that large mountain across there. The reindeer herders stayed on the other side. And down below it, and they also stayed above Yuukarmiut. The place up the coast from it, they used to call it Qayairyaraq (Kayak docking place], a place where reindeer herders once stayed.

[Reindeer] start to roam all over during summer. When the flies entered their nostrils and ears and laid their eggs, and they were fleeing, that made them run around. And also the Qalvinraaq River down there, they'd swim across it and come to this side.

Taugaam tua-i amllerrata wii nangenritnayukluki pillrenka, uani ua-i Tununermiut nuniitni amllellruyaaqut, taugaam paluturnilliniut. Nuna man' cikursallrani up'nerkaryartumi tuani tua-i amlleq tuqullruuq, tua-i amelqapiar.

Taugaam tamakut wangkuta neryuunaki, taugaam qimugtemtenun nalamalriit avurluki malrugnek uciluteng utertaqluteng. Qimugciurutekluki.

Qukailnguq: Kiani, ikani, maa-i nugtarrvigkaata uatiini, Taqikcaq; tuani tua-i Waska-q uitatullruuq, Taqikcarmi.

Tauna-llu kiani Qayairyaraq uum apqii ava-i, tamaavet maavet tevyarauluni ikamrakun-llu. Tevyarauluni.

Tuani tua-i laavkaacuarmi, taum kinguakun Taqikcarmi uitallran kinguakun laavkaacuarmek nel'illruut tuntulget, necuarmek-llu tauna acirluku.

Aataka-llu tuavet Taqikcarmun nalaciyarturaqluni, tuntumek ataucirrarmek.

Uani-ll' cali Tununermi iguugiriaqluteng, cali-llu tuntuyagarnek atkugkiuraqluteng. Tuani casgiryarturaqluteng caliyarturaqluteng.

Aataka uksumi caliaqluni. Tua-i calirraarluni taqkuni tuntumek ataucimek-llu iliini-ll' akingluni, iliini-ll' qanerluni aipaa avguluku akingniluni. Tuaten tua-i pillruut.

Unangik: Tuntulget tamakut waten kiagmi pagaani ingrit qaingatni kangatullruut tua-i yuaraluki tamakut tuntuteng tamariaqamegteki.

Qukailnguq: Tuntunek acirpeg'naki tua-i ucuqluki qanemcik'lallruit, curunelegnek.

Cevtaq

Nanurniralria: Uksuiyaraqamek ukuk angayuqaagka tamaa-i cumigyagutellemni, tauna uksuarvigput Qiingssauluni. En'ar tua-i angevkenani uksuarvimteni.

Una tua-i iteryarami iqsulirnermi kaminiarput tauna *tank*-allruar uitaarqelria, tua-ll' kiakariini ca augna muragaaraat murilkellemni, tuani tua-i caaskaarait, caaskaaraput uitaluteng.

Kiugna-ll' tua-i arvitmun, arvitmun aciuluni wavet elliqerluni. Yaani

But since there were many, the ones that I had initially thought wouldn't die off, there were many around the village of Tununak in the past, but evidently they easily starve. When the land froze over in the winter toward spring, many died at that time, a great many died at the time.

But we didn't eat [ones that starved], but we would pick the dead ones and load two and return home to feed our dogs. They used them as dog food.

Michael John: Upriver, over there, down the coast from the place where [the people of Newtok] will eventually relocate, the place called Taqikcaq [from *taqig-,* "to have sexual intercourse"]; Waska used to stay there, at Taqikcaq.

And that place up the coast called Qayairyaraq that [Simeon] mentioned, it is a traveling route, a portage route to [Newtok] and this area. It is a portage route.

Inside that small frame house, after the time that he lived at Taqikcaq, the reindeer herders built a small frame house there, and they called it *necuar* [lit., "small house"].

And my father would go to Taqikcaq to kill just one reindeer.

And down in Tununak they would castrate reindeer and prepare young reindeer skins into parkas. And they'd go and herd them inside fences there, they'd go and work there.

My father would work during winter. When he was done working, he was sometimes paid one reindeer, and sometimes he would say that he was paid one-and-a-half reindeer. That's what they did.

Simeon Agnus: The reindeer herders would roam on foot during summer up in the mountains, searching for their reindeer when they lost them.

Michael John: They didn't call them *tuntut* [reindeer] when they spoke of them out of reverence, but called them *curunelget* [lit., "ones with antlers"].

Cevtaq[63]

Mary George: When my parents would go fall camping when I started to observe things, our fall camp was Qiingssaq. At our fall camp, there was a home that wasn't large.

Along the entranceway, along the left was our stove made of an old tank, and right behind it were some small shelves when I observed, and their few cups, our few cups were located there.

Then going across the back area of the home was a mattress reaching this

tua-i qukaa cali aklullraaranek pimaluni, una-ll' tua-i yaatiini ukuk anngagka qavatulutek.

Wiinga taugken taukuk angayuqaagka unisngangaitelliamkek tuani qavatulua ilagarlukek. Uatiigni-ll' tua-i cat tua-i muragaaraat-llu uitaaqluteng.

Tuani taugken Cevtarmi uksurpak tua-i yaavet angyarnarillranun uitaviketulput inglengqellruluni, inglengqellruluta.

Kassauluta-w' tamaani yuurtellrullilriakut, taugaam ellangeqarraallemni tamaani canek tua-i makunek-llu apqiitnek *junk food*-anek piyuitellruunga. Tua-i caqapigtaqami uum aanama angerpallurmek taugaam cikitullruanga.

Tamaa-i tuantaurallemteni Cevtarmi, canek-llu neqangrussagnek-llu tekiucuunateng ukut kipusviinateng-llu tua-i.

Taugaam tua-i ukut angayuqaagka-w' tua-i, ilangqerrluni tayim' aatalqa pilallrullilria, naken-llu tayima pillrit nalluanka, tua-i mukaaq una, caarralaq, caayut, caqaquneng-llu caalanek tua-i tekiutaqluteng. Tamakunek tamaa-i ellangellrulrianga.

Ellangellemni angeq taugaam una kantiq-llu tua-i ciumek wiinga ellangutkellruagka.

Nanugaq: Kumaurayuitetullruut. Kumayarangqerrluteng waten pingayurqunek--unuakumi, erneq qukaqan, atakumi.

Anguyaluk: Irniayaarluteng-llu tua-i nipumaluku tua-i tan'germi. Taugaam tua-i kumassuukarangqerrluteng tamaa-i irniayaarluteng pilriit.

Nanurniralria: Atam tamakut enet makucetun ayuqenritqapiartut. Kumaqallruaqameng tua-i ak'arpak cass'at amlleret aturluki maqarcecimaaqluteng. Una taugaam wiinga cuqtellemni waniwa kingutmun tayim' kinguneqa umyuaqertellemni, atakuq yaavet tua-i ukuk angayuqaagka kumavkarciqaak tua-i atakumi tua-ll' inarrniaraqumta tua-i murinqigtevkenaku.

Tua-i-ll' unugpak qavallemteni; nengervagaqan-wa taugaam kumlangyararalallilria.

Iliini tua-i tupagciqukut nengllirluni, wiinga-w' tupagciqua nengllirluni tua-i. Cat-llu mer'et cikuluteng.

Anguyaluk: Cikumaluki maktaqluta. Piluguput-wa cali nat'rait tegkacagarluteng.

Nanurniralria: Taugken tua-i ella maqarillikan-wa tayim' pilallilriit, yaavet ertellranun tua-i maqarcecimaluni.

Anguyaluk: Tamaa-i tamakut kaminiaput kenirrsuutekluki. Caani-

area. Then over there, the center was filled with some clothes, and this area beyond it was where my older brothers slept.

But since I probably didn't want to sleep separately from my parents, I would sleep next to them. And down below them would be some things, including wood.

But Cevtaq, the place where we used to stay all winter until conditions became good for boating, had beds, we had beds there.

We were probably Westernized when we were born, but when I first became aware of life, I didn't eat these foods that they call junk food either. Once in a great while, my mother would give me chewing gum.

While we were living at Cevtaq, the people there didn't arrive with snacks either, and they didn't have a store there.

But my parents, and my father probably traveled with someone, and I'm not sure where they purchased goods, but he would arrive with flour, sugar, and once in a while lard. Those things were around when I became aware of life.

When I became aware of life, chewing gum and candy were the first [type of junk food] that I became aware of.

Elsie Tommy: The [stoves] weren't always on [in the past]. They were on three times a day—in the morning, at noon, in the evening.

Martina John: And they'd take care of infants while it was turned off in the dark. But those who were taking care of infants had small lamps that they turned on.

Mary George: Those homes aren't like these homes at all. If the [stoves] had been on for a while, they would stay warm for many hours. But when I think about my past, my parents would have it on in the evening, and then when we were about to go to bed, they wouldn't add wood to [the stove] again.

Then [it stayed warm] while we slept all night; it probably only gets cold right away when it's extremely cold.

Sometimes we woke up, or I woke up sometimes and it was very cold. And things with water in them froze.

Martina John: We'd wake to find them frozen. And the skin soles of our skin boots would be extremely stiff.

Mary George: But probably when the land became insulated [with snow], it stayed warm for a long time up until the sun came up.

Martina John: Our stoves were used to cook things. They used them to

lissuutekluki kenircuutekluki tua-i.

Nanurniralria: Kaminiam-llu tuaggun qaingakun *bread*-aliyugngaluteng. Manianrilkuneng, aanaka-w' augna pilallrulria, manianrilkuni quuleciraminek iciw' *bread*-arkiurluni.

Tua-i-ll' maniarcuun wall' tua-i ca qantaq imiqerluku qainganun elliluku tua-i uitaciquq kumallran nalliini. Tua-i-ll' acia *brown*-aarrlureskan mumiggluku tuamtell'-am tua-i.

Taukuk-llu tua-i apeqminek kelipacuggluliluni. Ernerni tayim' qavcinikiq neqautenglallruat.

Wani, piciatun-llu wiinga nerevkayuunii, wani taugaam tua-i ner'aqameng cikiraqlua.

Anguyaluk: Ayuqluki-w' yuut tuaten pitullrukait. Tua-i ataucikun taugaam, maani-ll' akuliini nercunguayuunateng.

Nanurniralria: Kiakan tuamtell'-am tua-i pikangqelliaqami-w' tayim' pilallrullilria, ellami keneq kumarrluku apqiitnek, wangkuta-wa ellangellemteni, uqulegaliluteng-gguq; uqupiamek uqirluku maniarluteng.

Anguyaluk: Tamaani ayagaqamta, arulaingqaqa'arqamta nevuq, nevuq nayugluku waten tua-i nevur nayugluku kenillerkiuraqluteng. Pagaaggun arvirulluku caaniliaqluteng agarrluku. Kenirluteng cali egan epungqellria cali agarrluku.

Uugikuneng-llu tua-i nutaan nem'un itrulluku nerluteng.

Waten tua-i pelatekat qavciugaqameng avaqliteng kelektuurluki quyurrarmeng ner'aqluteng.

Ciin-llu imkut yuut nerem akuliini-ll' yuurqanrilkaunritetullruat? Caanilivkarnauraitkut ellakun, imna-w' tua-i canigpaagaq, caanik-wa tua-i angtaciqellria, tamalkuan caayirluki avaqliput yuurqeryartuusqengnaurait. Yuurqanertuluteng tuaten. [*ngel'artuq*]

Nanugaq: Qantullruluteng-llu, "Aipirillruunga-qaa?" [*ngel'artut*]

Anguyaluk: Tua-i cuqerluteng, cuqerluteng augkut yuurqatulit piaqluteng.

Cucuaq: Caskameggnek-qaa maligluteng?

Anguyaluk: Yaa, ii-i.

Nanugaq: Ilait-wa, "Pingayiriksaitua-qaa? Pingayiriqeryugyaaqvagcia." [*ngel'artuq*]

Anguyaluk: Naagituluteng yuurqameggnek.

Nanugaq: Naagiyaramek cali qaneryararluteng yuurqaquneng.

make kettles of boiling water and for cooking food.

Mary George: And they could also make bread on top of that stove. If they didn't make fry bread, my mother, when she didn't make fry bread, she made bread out of sourdough she'd prepared.

Then she'd fill a frying pan or a bowl and place it on top of [the stove], and it would stay while the stove was on. And when the bottom turned brownish, she would turn it over.

And when she did that, she referred to it as making *kelipacuggluk* [sourdough bread]. I wonder how many days that lasted.

And they didn't let me eat randomly, but she only gave me food when they ate.

Martina John: That's what they had all people do. They all ate at once, and they didn't eat between meals.

Mary George: And when summer came, probably when she had some ingredients available, she would light a fire outdoors, when we became aware, they'd make what they call *uqulegat;* they'd make fry bread using seal oil for oil.

Martina John: When we'd travel back in those days, when we stopped somewhere briefly, they'd dig a hole in the ground, they'd dig a hole in the ground to make a firepit. They'd put [a stick] across it and hang a kettle there to make boiling water. They'd also cook, hanging a pot with a handle.

And when their food was cooked, they brought it inside the home and ate.

When a number of tents were around, they invited the people around them and ate together.

I wonder why those people always had tea between meals? They'd have us make a kettle of boiling water outdoors, and a kettle that was pretty large, or one that was regular sized, they'd put tea in it, and they'd start to tell the people around us to come and have some tea. And they would also drink large amounts of tea. [*laughs*]

Elsie Tommy: And they used to say, "Did I have a second cup?" [*laughter*]

Martina John: They had limits, those who drank tea would have personal limits.

Alice Rearden: Did they bring their cups with them?

Martina John: Yes.

Elsie Tommy: And some would say, "Did I not have a third cup? I'd really like to have a third cup." [*laughs*]

Martina John: They would drink their limit of tea.

Elsie Tommy: They also used the term *naagiyaraq* [to reach their limit] when they drank tea.

Anguyaluk: Waten caskam imaa nangkuniu, tua-i-llu allamek imiritesqelluni. Tua-i-ll' yuk malrugnek caskak imaagnek yuurqatukuni, tua-i malruurcagnek naagiluni.

Tua-i-llu ilii pingayunek, pingyurqunek una imitukuniu, pingayirikuni tua-i naagiluni.

Tua-i cuqerluteng. Ellaita piciryaraqluku caaskam uum imaa qavcirqunek pituli, tua-i taukut pingayun naangnaqluki wall' malruk naangnaqlukek yuurqatuluni.

Nanurniralria: Iciw' qanemciuraulluteng waten pilliaqameng tayim' qavcirilteng nalluyaguarrluku pitullermeggni, apqauritullrungatut qavciricimeggnek. [*ngel'artuq*]

Anglilqa-wa una kass'aurrneratgun ellangellrulrianga.

Ingna Cevtaq wani nunalput yugyanrituq; qulnguluteng enet, en'araat tua-i. Cali-ll' tuani ilakerpallulriaruluta. Aanamkun, aanama ukut uyurai taukunek tua-i yungqerpallullrulria.

Tua-i uitalput tauna, qasgimek nalluunga, yurayuitellruut-llu tuani. Yuramek nalluluta tuani Cevtarmi.

Nanugaq: Iciw' nunarraat uksuilleruarnek arivatullrukait.

Nanurniralria: Uksuilleruarangqerrluta-llu Qiingssarmek aterluni. Tua-i wangkuta taugaam Apauyulqa-llu tayima kiimta tuantaqluta. Una-wa ilavut, Atuq'aciamek pitullrat.

Iluraanka tua-i ukut uicungaanka ellangutkellrukenka cali tan'gurraat. Nasaurlurmun ellangellrunritua; anngaagka ukuk ellangutkellruagka malruk. Ukuk-llu alqaagka nunamni uitavkenatek; Kayalivigmi uingelriarullinilutek.

Wangkuta taugken tua-i pingayuuluta ukugnek anngaagemnek ciuqligemnek ilalua tua-i ellangutenka. Ukut-wa aanama uyurain qetunrai alqainllu irniari tan'gurrarrlainaullruut. Tua-i taukut tan'gurraat ellangutkellrenka. Aiparnikluki tua-i tuani uitauratullrulrianga.

Tua-i-llu uksuaqan yaavet Qiingssarmun-gguq uksuiyarluta. Tuani tua-i uitaluta, nevurrarnek tua-i nengqerrluta.

Caniaramteni quarruugssuraqlutek uksuaraqan. Keluaramteni-ll' can'giirrsuraqluteng. Yaaqsiyuunani tauna.

Apauyullma tua-i, iliini tua-i tupaumaaqama upciiqaanga, pilu'ugciqaanga can'giirrssuutai-gguq takuyarturnaupuk.

Martina John: When he finished the contents of his cup, then he'd tell them to fill it again. Then if a person usually drank two cups, after he drank two cups, that would be his limit.

And if a particular person usually filled his cup three times, after the third time, that was his limit.

They had limits. A person who regularly filled his cup a number of times had the habit of trying to finish those three cups or two cups that they usually had when drinking tea.

Mary George: When they were probably telling one another stories, when they forgot how many cups they had drunk, I think they asked how many cups they had. [*laughs*]

The way that I grew up, I became aware of life just as people started adopting Western ways.

Cevtaq over there where we lived didn't have a lot of residents; there were ten homes, few homes. And at that place we were mainly related. Relatives on my mother's side, it was mainly occupied by my mother's younger siblings.

That place where we lived, I knew nothing about a *qasgi,* and they didn't dance there. We didn't know about dance there at Cevtaq.

Elsie Tommy: You know how they used to call the small settlements *uksuilleruaraat* [small winter settlements or villages].

Mary George: And we had a winter settlement called Qiingssaq. The only people who resided there were our family and my Apauyuk. Then the other person staying there with us, the one they used to call Atuq'aciaq.

I became aware among my *ilurat* [cross-cousins], my *uicungat* [male cross-cousins], boys. I didn't become aware of life around girls; I became aware of life around my two older brothers. And my two older sisters weren't living in my village; they had evidently obtained husbands and were living at Kayalivik.

But the three of us, I became aware around my two older brothers. Then there were the sons of my mother's younger siblings and also the children of her older sisters, who were all boys. I became aware of life around those boys. I lived there and enjoyed playing with them.

Then when fall came, we went to Qiingssaq over there to spend the winter. We would stay there, and we had small sod homes where we stayed.

They went and fished for needlefish near where we stayed when fall came. And they'd fish for blackfish right behind our place. That place wasn't far.

My late Apauyuk [from *apa,* "grandfather"], sometimes when I was awake, he would get me ready, put my boots on, and say that we should go and check his blackfish trap.

Pilu'ugciqaanga, pilukataqunia evget it'gamnun tapluki, nemerluki-ll', nemrrarluki-ll' piluguugemnun all'ukek piluguugka maatekiirlutek.

Kaamaterlua-ll' tua-i qamigautegnun, camek aug'umek kass'artallruarmek curiqerlua qamigautegnun ekciqaanga. Qimugtepuk-wa una ataucirraq *side*-ami. Tua-i tauna qimugtekluku.

Tua-i-ll' qamigautek waten pissuuterlutek.

Tuaggun tua-i agciqukuk, qanerturluni, una tekitaqamegen'gu wavet tekitniaqlunuk. Wiinga tua-i anglanik'acagarlua. Qamigautek cukak'ayagnganani piaqluni. [*ngel'artut*]

Wavet-llu una kanaqatarniluku. Una tua-i tekitaqamiu tua-i piuraqerluni, "Kitaki waniw' tekitukuk. Kitek can'giirrsuutepuk takunaupuk."

Tuaten tua-i Apauyukniluku tauna angulluaq pilallruat.

Tua-i-ll' augna naparcilluullinilria tua-i cillarciiqaa. Painga waten pimauraasqaqaku, nayumiqaurnaurqa tua-i nangengqalua.

Tua-i-ll' kan'a kana-i qaill' pirraaluku makciiqaa taluyaq una. Tua-i-w' cat unkut pilriit.

Augkunek cali imairiterluni. Tua-i-tang qaluterraarluni uitaurarraarluni tuavet kuv'aqluku.

Tua-i-ll' augna issrallugpak, kingumek tua-i imirraarluku paigna qillercuunaku; waniw' ut'rutarkapuk tauna egaarkat. Qanerturluni, qanerturallrillu taringyuunaki.

Tua-i-ll' tauna ekluku wiinga-ll' eklua qimugtepuk-wa una, iciw' yaani pivkenani, wani taugaam.

Ayaglunuk tua-i. Ayakaamegnuk-llu wangni qavarnaurtua tua-i tayim'. Ellangyungaqama tua-i ellangaqlua.

Canek-llu nunanun-llu ayagayuunateng ukut angayuqaagka-wa. Kayalivigtangqerrsaaqellinilria-ll' tuavet ayayuinateng, yuraliyayuunateng-llu.

Tua-i angyakun maavet neqliyaryaurtelliniluteng. Neqliyalangluteng tua-i cumiksagullua. Maani tua-i *May*-rmi taigaqluteng *September*-aami-ll' uterrluteng tuavet Cevtarmun.

Un'gaan, ingkut wani *gas tank*-at, *gas tank*-at man'a-w' ayalria. Taum

He would put my boots on, and when he was about to put my boots on, he would fold the grass over my feet and bind them. And after binding them, he would put my feet inside my boots, and my boots would be about this high.

Then he'd put my mittens on and put me inside the kayak sled with some sort of padding under me that was Western-made. We had just one dog situated on the side. That was our only dog.

Then the kayak sled had [a raised back and handle bar] to [push it with].

We would leave with that, and he would constantly talk, and when we reached a certain place, he would say that we reached this particular place. I would have so much fun. The kayak sled seemed to go very fast. [*laughs*]

And he would say that we were about to reach this particular place. And when he reached the place, he would say after a while, "Okay then, we've arrived now. Let's check our blackfish trap and remove the catch."

They used to say that elderly man was my Apauyuk.

Then he would open what was evidently a *naparcilluk* [twined grass container]. When he told me to hold the opening, I stood and held it.

Then after doing something to the one down there, he would lift it upright and it was a blackfish trap. Then there were things down there [that were moving].

He had one of those tools to empty [the blackfish trap]. After dipping it inside [the blackfish trap], after a brief pause, he spilled it inside [the grass container].

Then after filling that very large *issran* [grass bag], he wouldn't tie the opening; we were going to take that container home; they were to be cooked. He would constantly talk, and I didn't understand his constant jabbering.

Then he would load that and place me inside [the sled], and our dog wasn't situated over there, but here.

We would leave. When we took off, it felt to me as though I was sleeping. When I would gain awareness, I gained awareness.

And my parents never traveled to other villages. And there was evidently a place called Kayalivik, but they never traveled there, and they never went to attend dances there.

Then they evidently started to come here [to the Kuskokwim River area] to cut and dry salmon. They started to go and cut and dry salmon when I started to become aware of life. They came in May and returned to Cevtaq in September.

[We stayed] downriver [from Bethel], where those gas tanks are located

tamatum amatiini uatmurtellriami uitatullruukut *camp*-arluta, amaqliput-wa Cevv'arnermiut. Caninermiut.

Angalgaq: Elepci-w' tamaaggun akulekun taigaqluci?

Nanurniralria: Imkut, Kassiglurmiut tumekluki pilarngatellrullinilriit. Tua-i-llu *1957*-aami aataka, yaani, *hospital*-aarulriit augkut, tuavet ayaulluku tuani-ll' tua-i yuunrirluni.

Tua-i-ll' neqput kinerngata tua-i Qukailnguum anngaagma aulukeqcarluta tua-i ut'rulluta.

Tuaken-llu tua-i ayagnanrirluta. *1950*-mi-llu tuaken Cevtarmek yaavet Niugtarmun upagluta.

Manuuqinraaq

Nanugaq: Agaaken upallemta kinguani, aanagka pinirrlugarlutek yuullragni, Manuuqinraam paingani ikani tamakussuqcaaratullruukut, qavlunanek, taryaqvagnek pivkenata.

Tua-i-am cali tuani nangnermi cunaw' agaavet ayayuirutlerkamtenek, pinauraitkut angayuqamta, "Pingkeurluugnun tagqeryaqunatek."

Piani kelumteni pelatekaq pingna waten tua-i kaputaarauluni, waten. Ullaasqevkenakek taukuk alerquanauraitkut nasaurlurni. Nasaurlurpaullrulriakut-llu-w' tamaani. Cauciitaqlukek wiinga taukuk.

Tua-i-ll' caqerlunuk Panigkaq-llu pillrungatukuk, ii-i, Panigkaq-llu imum' Arnaqulluum uyuraurlullra, ukut Makliinkut ilaurlullrat. Taunallu inuguaryarturlunuk pavani nunapiim amatiini; inuguaryartuucuanga tamaani inuguaryartullmegni, amiingak amicuaraak ikingqaluni. Aanii qetunraa-wa.

Aling takuyarluki tangrrapuk, aanaurlua aqumgaurluni tua-i waten, qetunraa-wa wani caniani aanani caumaluku.

Takuyallrani tangerrluku. Tua-i nuyaurlui tua-i qulmun tua-i napak'acagarluteng. Tuar' imna kegginaa kalikaq, tua-i kalikatun ayuqluni. Cai tamarmeng migpaulluteng, qavlui migpaullutek, iik-llu migpaullutek.

Nangerngaurlunuk-ll'-am tuani. Ayagarteqataryaaqelrianga, Panigkam

over there, then [the land] extends beyond it. We stayed on the other side of it, camping along the river that heads down, and across from us were people from Chefornak. They were people from the Lower Kuskokwim coastal area.

Ruth Jimmie: So you would come here [to the Kuskokwim River area] through the inland route?

Mary George: They seemed to travel along a route that went through Kasigluk. Then in 1957, my father, over there where the hospital buildings were once located, they brought him there, and then he died there.

Then when our fish dried, my older brother Qukailnguq [Michael John] took care of us and brought us home.

Then from that time, we stopped going [to cut and dry salmon]. Then in 1950, we moved from Cevtaq to Newtok.

Manuuqinraaq River[64]

Elsie Tommy: After we moved from across there, when my mother and father were still pretty strong and in good health, we used to make efforts at catching those silver salmon and not king salmon along the mouth of Manuuqinraaq [possibly from *manu-*, "area at the front"].

And at that time, evidently during the last time we went before we stopped going across there, our parents would tell us, "Don't ever go to those two dear ones up there."

There was a tent inland behind our place that was erected simply, with stakes in the ground like this. They would instruct us girls not to go to those two. We were big girls at the time, too. I didn't know who those two were.

Then one time, I think it was Panigkaq and I, yes, Panigkaq, who was the dear deceased sibling of Arnaqulluk, the dear deceased sibling of Maklak and his siblings. That person and I went to play with dolls inland on the other side of the tundra; since she wanted to go and play dolls with me there, when we went to play dolls there, and their entryway, their small entryway was open. There was his mother and her son.

My, when we turned our heads and saw them, his poor mother was just sitting like this, and her son was sitting next to her facing his mother.

When he turned his head, we saw him. His poor hair was sticking straight up. His face looked [white] like paper; it looked like paper. Everything on him was very clearly visible, his eyebrows stuck out, and his eyes stuck out.

We just stood there. When I was about to take off, when Panigkaq suddenly

nuqleranga tua-i irr'ilunuk tangvaglukek tua-i tangerrlukek.

Tua-i-ll' tangvaagarraarlukek tua-i yaatmun ayaglunuk. Cunaw' tua-i tauna qumaqitleq-gguq tauna tan'gurraq.

Tua-i-tang tangvayunaunani. Nuyai-ll' tua-i napak'ackacagarluteng.

Pekcuunani. Tua-i-ll' tuquniluku niilluku. Aanamta qanrulluta.

Tua-i-ll' un' piuraqerluni aanama piakut maligglarput-gguq. Negaryamllu cali tua-i tangvallruluku, Nuyarralgem taugaam tangvallrunritaa.

Nakleng! Angyak qeciik akivingqalriik, pagna qelpaluni, taugaam ikaraliitnek patumaluni. Aciani-llu kanani tauna tua-i taklalria ikaraliitet qaingatni.

Aanii-wa qamiqurran taqurraani nangerngalria naquguterturluni kaumatek-wa kumluunatek, kaumaksuaraak kumluunatek. Cumikelqa cali cakneq.

Tua-i-llu qaqitelliamta tan'gurrait ataita ciuqerratnun aqumlluki, wangkuta-llu caggluta cali aanamta ciuqerritnun aqumluta. Tua-i aanaput tunuqliqluki, alqairutka, wiinga-ll' caniani.

Taum tua-i aaniin qetunrani tauna unitekanirluku nangerrluni, nasaurlurni tua-i waten nirturturluta, tauna-llu qetunrani niiraqluku. "Tan'gurrarmek ungacariciqelriaci quuyuaraulluku. Quuyuaraucukuvceni kana-i, kat'um tan'gurraam unguvakuni, quuyurniarauskuvni tua-i ung'aqerrvikciqaaci tua-i ataucirquungraan quuyuarautelaquvgu." Tuaten aaniin qanrulluta.

Tua-i-llu apqapigtevkenaku waten piciqaakut, "Ukaniqutassaagteskuvgu tua-i waten kana-i qumaqilluni tuquciquq." Tua-i tuaten. Wagg'uq-gguq aulukevkaquma ukaniqutarluni.

Tuamtell' tua-i taqngamikut tan'gurraat cauluki. "Arnaq takuyaquvgu quuyuarauciiqeken. Arnam-llu tua-i kat'utun kana-i cikirluten. Elpet ukaniqutassaakuvgu nasaurluq tauna, tua-i tuaten kat'utun ayuqliriluten tua-i-ll' tuquluten." Tuaten tua-i qanrutaqluta.

Tua-i ikani ika-i Manuuqinraam paingani qungitelqaat. Ussuteurlullrullikii-w'.

Kangia tekilluku qanruyutnguluni tauna, wagg'uq qumaqitellria. Tamana-ll' tang niitnauyuirulluni.

pulled me, we watched them in awe. Then after watching them, we headed out to the area beyond.

That boy was evidently one whose health deteriorated as a result of being preoccupied with sex because of having sex, what they call *qumaqitleq.*

He wasn't good to look at. And his hair was sticking extremely straight up.

He didn't walk. Then we heard that he died. Our mother told us.

Then after a while my mother told us that we should follow her. And Negaryaq witnessed it, but Nuyarralek didn't witness it.

How pitiful! Two skin boats were placed on their sides, and the top [in between the boats] was open, but it was covered with a grass kayak mat. And down below it was that [boy] who was lying on top of a grass kayak mat.

His mother stood along the side of his head, wearing a belt, and her mittens were thumbless, her small mittens were without thumbs. That's something that I observed very intently.

Then when we were probably done, they seated the boys in front of their fathers, and we also scattered and sat in front of our mothers. With our mothers behind us, my deceased older sister was there, and I sat next to her.

His mother moved a little farther away from her son and stood, and she went around continually pointing at us girls, and she also pointed at her son. [She said], "You will try to attract a boy by smiling at him. If you tend to smile at him, if that boy down there is alive and you smile at him, he will suddenly be attracted to you, even if you smile at him just one time." That's what his mother told us.

And without saying it explicitly, she told us, "If you try to get him to have sex with you, his health will deteriorate as a result of becoming preoccupied with sex and he will die like the one down there." That's what she told us. She meant that if I allowed him to have sex with me, *ukaniqutarluni.*

And again, when she finished talking to us, she turned to the boys, "If you turn your head to look at a girl, you will smile at her. And a girl will give you [an ailment] like that one down there. If you try to have sex with that girl, you will become like that one down there and die." That's what they told us.

They buried him over there along the mouth of Manuuqinraaq. The poor [grave] probably eroded away.

That instruction was given down to its source, what they call *qumaqitellria* [one whose health deteriorates from being preoccupied with sex]. And that [condition] is no longer heard of.

Merr'armiut

Cucuaq: Iciw' agnilaqiit ella. Ella-wa tamaani ag'aqan-llu pissurciigat'ngaqameng iciw' imarpiitaqameng-llu kainiqlallrullilriit ella agluni piaqan.

Nanugaq: Ee-m. Kainiqeurlutullrulriit-wa.

Wiinga angullruaqa ataucirqumek, Merr'armiunun kanavet upagniararluta, anngarma aqvaniarallranikut.

Tua-i pugssuutevut-llu picuirulluni, can'giirssukarput picuirulluni. Ciuqliirutka-llu takuurlurqamegnegu qavcirrarnek picaurrluni.

Aanama-am qunavutminek kapurturluki aunrarcequrarraarluki, tauna tua-i aunrarviinani egatmun kuvluku keniraqluku.

Neqkaicungluta. Kiagnaciarluni.

Cucuaq: Ciin-gguq tuaten tamakut can'giiret pillruaki?

Nanugaq: Tua-i-wa auggait wani imarkuaranun tamaavet.

Neqkengnaqluki, qayuqengnaqluki. Qayurrluqengnaqluki imarrluarait.

Egaat iciw' erup'aumanrilnguut imarkuarat *soup*-angelriatun ayuqliriqertetulria; qayurrlirluteng. Tua-i-gguq qayurrlungqengnaqluki auganek tamatum.

Tua-i taluyarput tauna tua-i pitesciigaliurluan yuuluku.

Anngarma-ll' tua-i tekilluni nayicuaraam kemganek tekiulluta, amiinani taugaam uqurrartarluni. Aqvaluta Merr'armiunun kanavet [agulluta].

Cali tua-i ellait Merr'armiut taqukanek tuavevkenateng qamigaryararteng kessissiiyaagngan.

Tua-i neqkuinraat tua-i neqakuinraat tua-i nerengnaqaqluki. Tayarunek cali makunek avuluki cali tua-i nerengnaqurutkaqluki.

Cali Merr'armiuni kanani angalkumek tangvallruunga.

Tayima Kangrilnguum Atii, anqerrivikluni tulimag akuliignun puuliaramek.

Imum Angassaaraam Qissunamium taklarrluku tupigat qaingatnun

Merr'armiut[65]

Alice Rearden: You know how they say the weather stays cold beyond its usual time, *ella agluni.* When the weather extended beyond its normal time and stayed cold, when they could no longer hunt, and when their ocean conditions prevented them from hunting, they probably experienced starvation when the weather stayed cold beyond its usual time.

Elsie Tommy: Yes. The poor people also used to go through famine.

I experienced it during my lifetime just once, right before we moved down to Merr'armiut [Place with a small amount of *meq* (water)], close to the time when my older brother was to get us.

And our *puggsuun* [wooden fish trap that was set upright] no longer caught [fish], our small blackfish trap no longer caught fish. Although my older sister and I checked the trap, it started to only catch a few.

My mother constantly poked [the blackfish] with a sharp sinew-splitting tool and let them bleed, and when that [fish] could no longer bleed, she spilled it inside a pot and cooked it.

We started lacking food. The summer season was delayed.

Alice Rearden: Why did she do that to the blackfish?

Elsie Tommy: To have their small amount of blood seep out to its broth.

They tried to make it into food, trying to make it into broth. They tried to make their small amount of contents into broth.

You know how cooked food that isn't completely washed and cleaned, their broth forms soup; they have some broth in them. They tried to make the blood of that [fish] into broth.

Since our poor blackfish trap couldn't catch fish any longer, we removed it.

Then my older brother arrived and brought us the meat of a small ringed seal, but it didn't have a skin attached to it and had a little bit of blubber on it. He came to get us to bring us down to Merr'armiut.

And the people of Merr'armiut didn't catch a lot of seals since the place where they usually hunted seals was too far down [in the ocean].

We tried to eat the small amount of food that was available. And we also added these mare's-tail plants for food.

I also watched a shaman down at Merr'armiut.

Kangrilnguum Atii accidentally shot himself and lodged a bullet between his ribs.

That Angassaar from Qissunaq had him lay on his back on top of a woven

taklarrluku, kalikat alaillrata tamaa-i, qainganun kalikaarmek qatellriamek elliivkarluku.

Tengmiam-llu nuqaruaranek cuplungqelriamek qengamegteggun iqmigssuutektullritnek tamakucimek, qanen'i-ll' agtuumavkenaku, kan'a-ll' ekia cali agtuumavkenaku, waten pimallrani, waten tua-i arviagurluku camek-llu tua-i nepmek-llu cangssagaunani.

Tua-i-ll' nallaiquniu agtuumangssaarpeg'naku, piaqan, tauna tua-i, agtuumangssaarpek'naku.

Tua-i-llu tauna melugcuutni aug'aqerluku kalikam qainganun uryuqauciiqaa auguluni.

Tua-i-ll' tamana qecirturatni ikeglian, iciw' carrarmek-llu tua-i avuqetaangluni tua-ll' piirucan qanerluni elliin-gguq waniwa puuliq kan'a artucuararaa.

Piuguranran-gguq angalkuunerraan, piuguranran-gguq aug'aryugngayaaqaa, taugaam-gguq ikiurrngaituq aug'anrilngermi.

Tuaten carririllrani Merr'armiuni tangellruaqa, tangvallruaqa.

Engelulluut

Nanugaq: Cali-llu Engelullugnun cali ayallrulunuk ikamrarlunuk, ak'a anguyiit nalliitni nunaliallritnun.

Nanvaq-llu-gguq tauna pugluni up'nerkaan, up'nerkaryartuan tua-i taukut kainiqluteng. Tua-i qungumeggnek nerengluteng.

Tua-i nangteqluteng taugaam pillernek piyuunateng, taugaam tua-i tuquqallernek piaqluteng.

Nunarraat-gguq tua-i taukut taumek yugmek qunguk narulkarlukek tua-ll' ikirrlukek kemga tauna anlluku tua-i ? vvluku, taukut tuani tamatum iluantellriit en'arraat enet, nekuinraat aruqeqcaartura'aqluki-gguq tua-i, taqukaliulriatun.

Tuqunerramek tua-i allragnitamek-llu tuqullermek. Ner'aqluki tua-i kenirluki.

Yualuit-gguq nulirrita qelekluki. Yualiluki qip'iluteng kuvyaliluki.

Tua-i tuani neqet amlletuata kuvyarluteng kiagucateng tua-i kuvyarluteng neq'liqluteng.

Tua-i-llu-gguq allamikuan tauna tua-i nanvep'akayall'er pugluni.

grass mat, and back when paper first came around, he had someone place a small white piece of paper on top of his body.

And using a bird's wing bone, one that was hollow in the middle, the ones they used to sniff snuff through their noses, and not touching his mouth and his skin down there, while he was [laying] like this, he brought it across [his body], not making noise at all.

Then when he reached [the wound], not touching [his body] at all, he wasn't touching [his body] at all.

Then he removed the device that he used to suck with and let it leak out on top of the paper, and it was blood.

When the [blood] that he spit out became less with other substance in it, when there was no longer [any blood in it], he said that it was a little difficult for him to [extract] the bullet down there.

He said that a shaman who was more powerful than he could remove it, but he said that his condition wouldn't worsen although it wasn't extracted.

When he cleaned [a wound] at Merr'armiut like that, I watched him.

Engelulluut[66]

Elsie Tommy: We also traveled to Engelulluut [from *engelu,* "muskrat's covered exit hole"] by snowmobile, to the village that they made long ago during the bow-and-arrow warfare period.

They say that lake surfaced when spring came; toward spring, those people experienced famine. They started eating [people] buried in their graves.

They didn't [eat] people who had been ill, but only people who died suddenly.

They said that the few people of that village would come to a grave and open it, take the body out, and the few homes that were there, they said they'd pass out [human flesh] to the few people in the homes, like they do with seals.

A newly dead person and one who died the year before. They'd eat them by cooking them.

They say their wives kept their sinew. They'd make them into thread by twisting the strands together and make them into fishnets.

Since there are many fish at that place, they set nets to catch fish when summer came, and they fished with nets and caught many fish.

Then they say the next year, that very large lake surfaced [dried up].

Pugngan-llu-gguq tamana cali kuiga waten quuyarturluni cali quuluni. Quungami-llu-gguq tua-i cali tua-i etgaliaku angyakun piyunairulluni.

Nanevpall'er tauna neqet asgurviat, qassayagaat, akakiiget, cuukviit, imairulluni tua-i pugluni tua-i.

Tengutellret

Nanugaq: Ugkut ingrini, ak'a-gguq tamaani Tengutellernek pilarait, taugaam teggalqurruut. Atam avani nasektallraullemteni yugngatqapiaratullruut. Ilait tev'ayagangqerraqluteng.

Tevaangqerrngataqluteng. Naqugutait-llu teggalqut, naqugutekniluki pitukait, ukut teggalquk qalliqumaaqlutek.

Iciw' Iqallugtulirmiut kiatiitni uitalriit pikani. Aciatni iciw' taperrnarrlugtelallrulriaci up'nerkami.

Ekvicuarauluni uqvigalirluni. Tuani cali elegcitullruut.

Atam mayurluni nanvacuartarluni pakemna; taukut tua-i teggalqut yaaqliqluteng pikani-llu maani-llu. Ilait atam tua-i yugngatqapiarluteng, tuarpiaqllu tevaangqelalriit, taugaam tua-i teggalqurruluteng.

Canek tua-i waten qaterturngalngurnek teggalqunek qaralingqerrnaurtutllu, taugaam kegginait ikiurrneratgun tanglallrulliketek.

Piliaruvkenateng.

Wagg'uq atrit Tengutellret, nerestet-gguq tengutellrit. Ilait tevaangqerrngataqluteng.

Makut-llu teggalqut keneknaqluteng qevlaanek qaraliarluteng qaralingqerrngat'lartut. Teggalquk-llu ukuk manigpaulutek qalliqlutek. Aqumgallrungataqluteng manuitni piaqluteng.

Tua-llu tauna tevaartulria tuamtellu tangelriani makut tuar kuiguayagaulalriit teggalqut; tamaa-i-gguq nuyait. Pamna-wa nacaan iluani iluanek pugumalria qamiqcuayagarngalnguq nuyangqerruciilnguq-wa.

And when [the lake] surfaced, its river started closing in and disappeared. They say when it closed in when it became shallow, a boat couldn't travel through it any longer.

That very large lake that fish headed upriver to reach, including round whitefish, broad whitefish, and pike, became empty and surfaced.

Ones That They Flew Off With[67]

Elsie Tommy: Those down the coast in the mountains, they said long ago they called them Tengutellret, but they are rocks. Back when we were girls, they looked like real people. And some were carrying small babies on their backs.

They look like they are carrying children on their backs. And their belts were rocks, those that they said were their belts, were two rocks piled on top of one another.

You know, they are up the coast from Iqallugtulirmiut up there. You used to gather some *taperrnarrluut* [wilted beach grass] during spring from down below them.

It's a small bluff with a lot of willows on it. They used to burn [willows] there also [to make ash for their tobacco].

When climbing, a small lake is up there; those rocks are situated right beyond one another and up there and here. Some closely resemble people, and they look as though they are carrying children on their backs, but they are rocks.

They even had light-colored rock designs on them, but you two probably saw them after their faces started to become unrecognizable.

They aren't man-made.

They are called Tengutellret [Ones that they flew off with], the ones that the lice flew off with as they say. Some look as though they are carrying babies on their backs.

And the rocks situated here that look like shimmering designs are beautiful. And these two rocks are very smooth and situated on top of one another. They look as though they had been sitting, and they are situated along their laps.

And when looking at the one carrying a baby on her back, the rocks here resemble small rivers; they say those are their hair. And the one on her back inside her hood, the thing visible from inside her hood looks like a small head, appearing as though it has no hair.

Tauna-llu nacaa engelkarrluku pamaken engelkarrluku qaterturalriamek man'a teggalqumek assirpak tua-i qaralingqerrluni. Tua-i-gguq tevaartulria tauna; tevaarturngatuq. Ua-i tua-i piciunrirtuq.

Tekilluki avani ciuqliirutka-llu tangvallruaput Negaryaq-llu malikluta. Iqallugtulimek ullagluki, Iqallugtulimun tuavet arulaingqallemteni.

Paqtelput taukut Tengutellret, tengutellret-gguq ak'a tamaani avani.

Ullagnaqluteng kiatemteni. Unaggun cenakun ayagluta tua-i-ll' tuaggun mayurluta, mayuamta-llu elakacuarmek nanvacuarmek tekilluta, ukalirnerakun-llu mayurluta tamakut yugngalnguut tangvagluki.

Quyigtut. Unaken angyarluni pitulriani tua-i alaitelaryaaqut, taugaam yugngairutut.

Imumi Iqallugtulimi uitatullemteni Pete-aq-am piluni kiavet-gguq angyarluta itraqaalta elegcissuutmek nalkutqeryuartukut.

Tua-ll'am angyarluta itrarluta tuavet tua-i ketiitnun arulairluta tuaggun tua-i mayurluta.

Tua-i tamakut tangllemtun avani ayuqenritut; yugngairutliniluteng. Yugtun-gguq avani ayuqeqapiaratullruyaaqut yugcetun yugnganateng.

Pingairutsiyaagpailgata tangvallruanka.

Qanemcikngamteki aatama tua-i waten pilqaakut, yugngairutut-gguq. Avani-gguq tangvalallrani yugngatqapiaratullruut-gguq, tuar-gguq yuulalriit.

Waten-llu ilait qamiqurrita qaingit imkunek qevlercelngurnek, qevlercelngalngurnek tua-i qaraliayagangqerrnaurtut tamakut tev'artulriit ilait tev'artunrilnguut-llu ilait. Tamaa-i-gguq ingqit.

Tua-i atengqerrluteng tamarmeng.

Anguyaluk: Ala-i tua-i pingariluteng-am pilaqait. Nerestait-llu-w' call' alaitellrullilriit. [*ngel'artuq*]

And up to its hood from back there, this area has white rock on it, and it looks very nice and has designs on it. They say that one is carrying a baby on its back; it looks like it's carrying a baby on its back. It no longer looks like that now.

My deceased older sister, Negaryaq, and I reached them and looked at them together. We went to them from Iqallugtuli, when we were stopped at Iqallugtuli.

Those that we went to see are called Tengutellret, those that [lice] flew off with long ago.

We had to approach them as they were situated up the coast from us [at Iqallugtuli]. We traveled along the shore down there, and then we ascended there, and when we climbed, we came upon a small water hole, a small lake, and then we climbed along this side of it and looked at the ones resembling people.

They are high. When traveling by boat down there, they are actually visible, but they no longer resemble people.

Back when we used to stay at Iqallugtuli, Pete said that we should head up the coast by boat, that we might find a place to burn [willows].

Then we headed up by boat, and we stopped down below them and climbed up along there.

Those [rocks] didn't look like they did the first time I saw them; they evidently no longer looked like people. They say long ago they looked exactly like people, they resembled people.

I saw them before they stopped resembling [people] completely.

When we told about them, my father told us that they no longer resembled people. He said when they saw them long ago, they closely resembled people, that they looked like live people.

And he said that some had designs on them that looked like sparkly [rocks] on their heads, some that were carrying children on their backs and some that weren't. He said those were nits.

All those things [on the rocks] had names.

Martina John: My, they cleverly stated things. Their lice were probably visible too. [*laughs*]

Iqallugtuli

Cucuaq: Tauna qanellruuq Iqallugtulimun-gguq ayallermini qaillun pinillrulria mikliriluni tauna-llu kuigpaurrluni.

Angalgaq: Nanvaq iciw' imarpiurrluni nanvacuar elegciyartullratni.

Nanugaq: Tua-i-gguq ircenrraat, ircenrraat pivkarlukek.

Imna-llu kuigaacuayagaq kuigpakayall'er ameltukayagluni. Qaillun-gguq amlliyunaunani.

Kan'a-llu-gguq nanvaq uitayaraata keluani nanvarra'ar akia-llu-gguq cataunani.

Camna-gguq-wa qetunraan puyua, keneq cali cam qevleqtaalria, kaviqetaarluni; yaaqsigluni-gguq.

Tamarmek-gguq tangvallruakek. Nakrialngurluum qanemcikuraqalqaa cali tauna.

Ircenrraat-gguq umyuaqellrunritai. Nutaan-gguq pellugngamek ircenrrat umyuaqluki.

Anguyaluk: Aling aturakek-kiq anglirivagtat. [*ngel'artuq*]

Angalgaq: Aturatek-wa malikluki pillilriik.

Anguyaluk: Aling, igcukluki aturakek. [*ngel'artuq*]

Angalgaq: Igeskata-w' cangalliuryallilriik iciw'.

Anguyaluk: Kiituan anglinrillik. [*ngel'artuq*]

Engelullugarmiut

Nanugaq: Engelullugarmiuni uitatullruukut. Up'nerkiluta.

Cucuaq: Teggalqurtangqellruuq-qaa igalegmek tamaani?

Nanugaq: Yaa. Tulukaruum panian yaaruillri. Cali-wa pikani imna qantaq. Qantatun ayuqluni teggalquq.

Nanurniralria: Taukut taugaam qamigautiin pillri, yaaruillri-llu tanglallruanka. Maa-i cali uitaut. Teggalqum qaingani.

Qaillun atam waten ellegtauq taukuk qamigautek ilukek qaterrluarlutek, cakneq taugaam qaterpek'natek, teggarvallraam tua-i qaingani.

Elausngalutek. Taukut-wa teggalqut qaingatni yaaruillri. Ceteqcaumalriit

Iqallugtuli[68]

Alice Rearden: [Pauline Pitka] said that something happened to her when she traveled to Iqallugtuli, that she got smaller and that river became a large river.

Ruth Jimmie: When they went to burn [willows] that lake became an ocean, that small lake.

Elsie Tommy: They say *ircenrraat* caused them to do that.

And that small river became a very large river that was very wide. They said there was no way to step over it.

And she said the lake situated down behind their place, the area across from it wasn't visible.

And the smoke from her son's [bonfire], she said the fire was twinkling, glaring red and then waning; she said it was far away.

She said they both saw that. Nakrialnguq also told that story.

He said while it was occurring, *ircenrraat* didn't come to mind. After they got through that experience, *ircenrraat* came to mind.

Martina John: My, I bet their clothing got large. [*laughs*]

Ruth Jimmie: Their clothing probably also got small with them.

Martina John: My, I thought their clothing fell off. [*laughs*]

Ruth Jimmie: If they fell, they probably would have known that something was wrong, you know.

Martina John: My, they could have gotten large. [*laughs*]

Engelullugarmiut[69]

Elsie Tommy: We used to stay at Engelullugarmiut. We went spring camping there.

Alice Rearden: Was there a rock with etchings on it there?

Elsie Tommy: Yes, they are etchings that Raven's daughter made when she was playing with her story knife. And there is also a bowl up there. It was a rock that resembled a bowl.

Mary George: I only saw the tracks made by [Raven's] kayak sled and the story knife etchings he made. They are still there today. On top of a rock.

The kayak sled tracks are about this wide and a little light colored inside, but not very light, on top of a very large boulder.

They are burrowed. Then on top of those rocks are the story-knife etchings

cali nallunaunateng. Maa-i cali uitaluteng.

Nanugaq: Tauna taugaam qantaq Irniiliingaam qantaqaa.

Pikani quliitni *baseball*-araqata kellirneran tungiini teggalquq imna tua-i teggalqurruluni. Tua-i-llu wani qukak'acagaani-w' pivkenani nayuumaluni, ilua manigpauluni.

Tua-i-gguq Irniiliingaam qantaa. Taukut-llu Tulukaruum panian yaaruilqelluki.

Anguyaluk: Ateqluku-qaa tauna Irniiliingaaq; yuuluni?

Nanugaq: Yuullrullilria-wa.

Anaanairutma-wa quliriluni tua-lli-wa-gguurluni tamakut pitullrukai, qulirauniluki Tulukaruunkut Irniiliingaaq-llu.

Engelullugarmiuni, taugaam ikiurtuq Engelullugaam pagna qulii. Ikiurtekacagartuq.

Imkut elegciviketulput pagaaken uryuum patuluk. Pikna-llu yaatmun imna Iqallugtulim tungiintellria iggluni cali.

Nanurniralria: Taukut-llu Kelliruat teggalqut ulem patutullri, tua-i-ll' eneskan alairluteng; taukut-llu yaa-i qaill' tayim' qertutaria, qerturiut, ulemllu tekitesciigaliluki, Kelliruat.

Pagna atam nallunaituq ava-i Engelullugarmiut kepellra ingriq atralleq, pagaa-i nallunaunani tamakut-llu Kelliruat mayulliniluteng.

Nanugaq: Qallaneq-llu nanvacuaraam, uum ingricuaraungalnguum qaingani cali qungurtalilria, ak'allallernek qungullernek; imna qallaneq, taum wani ellurvikluku patullruluku.

Tauna-llu nanvacuar imaiyuilnguq kuigaarangqerrluni, aciani-ll' kuigaacuar carvarraq mermek imairulluni, taum tua-i nanerngaku qallaneq.

Nanurniralria: Tauna qallaneq qaill' tauna qertutaluni uitallruyaaquq. Tua-ll' kiak wani tekitellemni tauna piaqa atrallinilria maavet, nikuyamek cali taman' patungluni.

Tamaaken qallanelleq nikuyam nevurrluum mat'um pianek, imuunani-ll' an'urluni taugaam. Ilungqellruyaaquq tuantellermini ellurpailegmi.

Taugken maa-i watua mat'um-wa nikuyam qainganek maaken-llu nunam qainganek meq an'urluni.

she made. The etchings are obvious. They are still there today.

Elsie Tommy: Just that bowl is Irniiliingaaq's bowl.

Up above [the village], in front of the place where they played baseball is a rock. And not along the very center of it, there is a hollowed-out place, and the inside is very smooth.

They say that is Irniiliingaaq's bowl. And those ones are etchings made by Raven's daughter when she played with a story knife.

Martina John: Was Irniiliingaaq his name; was he a person?

Elsie Tommy: He was probably a person.

My late maternal aunt, telling tales, would say "*Tua-lli-wa-gguq* [Then, they say]" and would tell stories about them and say that stories about Raven and Irniiliingaaq were *qulirat* [legends].

[They are] at Engelullugarmiut, but the area above Engelullugaq has become unattractive, it has become completely unsightly.

The places where we used to burn [willows], the things falling down from up there have covered them. And the area toward Iqallugtuli has also collapsed.

Mary George: And those Kelliruat, those rocks that used to be covered by the high tide, then they used to appear when the tide went out; those [rocks] have also become steep, and the high tide no longer reaches them, the Kelliruat.

The area up there at Engelullugarmiut where part of the mountain broke off and slid down is obvious up there, and those Kelliruat evidently rose.

Elsie Tommy: And the spring [beside] the small lake on top of what looks like a small mountain has a lot of graves on it, old graves; that slid down on that spring and covered it.

And that small lake that doesn't empty that has a small stream attached to it, and underneath it is a small mountain stream that has no more water because that [land] has covered that spring.

Mary George: That spring of a certain height was once located there. Then when I arrived there this past summer, I saw that it had moved down to this area, and that area is now covered with *nikuyaq* [sticky, gray kaolin clay].

That old spring [was cascading down from] the *nikuyaq,* from the land, and it didn't have [a hollowed-out place] but it just continually came out. When it was located there it used to have a hollowed-out place before the land slid down.

But today the water constantly comes out of the surface of the *nikuyaq* and on top of the surrounding land.

Angalgaq: Tuaten ayuqlirivailgan tekitellruunga. Nunaniqluteng tang taukut. Tua-ll' kinguakun tekitellrianga tang kelliat qaillun ayuqluni; imkurluni, ellullrullinilria nuna.

Nanurniralria: Maa-i qerturiut.

Narukacuk

Nanugaq: Ap'allulleq-llu tauna imumek pavani Narukacuum kangrani asguulluku qayarugaat narulkatgun tuqutellrat tauna; yuraarqameng alerquciararaqluteng tauna iquklitaqan, arvermek.

Alerquciaraluteng-llu erintukayaglutek-llu ukuk alerquciarastekek Tomas-ankuk Ap'alluk-llu; erintukayaglutek alerquciaralallrulriik.

Tuani-wa tua-i unuakumi pilu'ukcaaralrianga maa-i kevgak aqvaiqatarlutek Cuukvagtulimun, Ap'alluk iterluni aataka cauluku qanerluni, "Angacungaqa, arvertaqa-qaa anernemteggun qaraliqkumteggu cangaciiqa?"

Tua-i-ll' tangcuararraarluku pia, "Yurami-wa tua-i aneskuvceni kinguvarciqelria."

Ap'alluk. Angalkuunricaaquq, ikiungan, carayagtun ayuqngan aliketulqaat. [*ngel'artuq*]

Atam tauna Ap'allulleq ikiuk'acagartuq tua-i; kegginvakayallrii, qamirvakayallrii.

Yugpaullruuq. Angulluangellrani tamaa-i. Qengalleraak-wa maksugtekacagarlutek. [*ngel'artut*] Cuplukek-llu alaunatek qengalleraagkeni. Erinvaukacagarluni!

Ikiuqtangraan ungavikluku. Tua-i pinqegcaarauluni, amtall' tang tua-i alikesteminek alingcetaariqtarluni, taugaam wangkuta alingcetaayuitelqaakut.

Aling! [*ngel'artuq*] Qanerpallrii-wa, qengagni ikiuniteklukek qanerpallrii, erinvaukacagarluni!

Maacungarmek nuliangqellruuq. Irniyuunatek. Angurvagmek taugaam angulluangluni yul'illruuq, Atrilnguum-llu atiinek. Taukugnek tua-i yul'illruuk. Taukuk tua-i anglicaraqellruak taugaam.

Ruth Jimmie: I arrived there before it started looking like that. That place was beautiful. Then when I arrived later, the area down below looked strange; the land had evidently slid down.

Mary George: These days, they have gotten steeper.

Narukacuk River[70]

Elsie Tommy: Also, the late Ap'alluk, the [bowhead whale] they drove up to the upper Narukacuk River [possibly from *narug-,* "to intercept, to encounter"] that many kayakers killed with spears; when they'd dance, they would loudly proclaim their accomplishment when that song was over, about a bowhead whale.

And they would loudly proclaim their feat, and the two who were loudly proclaiming their feat, Tomas and Ap'alluk, had very loud voices; they who loudly proclaimed their accomplishment had very loud voices.

I was putting my boots on in the morning, and the messengers were about to go and get people from Cuukvagtuli, Ap'alluk came inside and turned to my father and said, "My *angacungaq* [little *angak* (maternal uncle)], what do you think if the bowhead whale that I caught became our insignia through our breath?"

After looking at him for a short while he said to him, "If you let it out during the dance, it will be passed down from generation to generation."

Ap'alluk. He wasn't actually a shaman, but since he was ugly, since he looked like a monster they were afraid of him. [*laughter*]

The late Ap'alluk was extremely ugly; his very large face, his very large head.

He was a big person. I used to see him when he started to become elderly. His terrible nose was extremely upturned. [*laughter*] And his nostrils were visible on his terrible nose. He had an extremely loud voice!

Although he was ugly, we were fond of him and were affectionate toward him. He did things with thought and care, but that darn one tended to scare those who were afraid of him, but he never tried to frighten us.

My! [*laughs*] And then there was his large mouth, as if his nose wasn't ugly enough, he had a very large mouth, and he had such a loud voice!

His wife was *maacungaq* [grandmother]. They couldn't have children of their own. But when he became elderly, he adopted Angurvak, and also Atrilnguq's father. They adopted those two. That person raised only those two.

Anguyaluk: Anerquciarautekluku?

Nanugaq: Arvertaa, arvertallra tauna Narukacugmi narulkaquurluteng.

Nanurniralria: Alerquciarluni-mi qaillun?

Nanugaq: Alerquciarautellra-qaa? "Aa-rraa, Aa-rraa, nuyurqevkenaku-ata piurallraqiciu-uu-uu!"

Anguyaluk: Angutait anerquciaraluteng. Qanruciqluku tua-i piku'urluku, piciryaraqurluku yuram qaingani.

Nanugaq: Yuram qaingani, yuraqatarluteng maa-i kevgak ayaglutek Cuukvagtulirmiunun.

Tua-i-llu yuraqatallermeggni kevgak ayagngagnek Ap'alluk tauna iterluni unuakumi, tua-i-w' unuakuqvani, aataka cauluku apluku tauna pitallni maniyugyaaqluku qanerkun.

Tua-i-ll' aatama tua-i tangssuararraarluku tua-i tuaten qanrulluku kinguvararkauluni augkunun kinguliarkanun tamarngaunani; alerquciarallra tamarngaunani augkunun kinguliarinun.

Anguyaluk: Kinguvrin pikurararkauluku, ayagcequrararkauluku. Yurat tamalkuitni. Yuram nalliini taugaam tamakut pituut.

Nanugaq: Atam yuralriit uitaqa'arqata, taqniararqameng tang pitulallruyugnarqelriit.

Tua-i taun alerquciararkaq itqertaqelria. Tua-i taugken yaggluni, "Talligkaa! Talligkaa! Arverssurrsuutegka-aa! Aa-rraa, aa-rraa!" Tuaten. [*ngelaq'ertuq*]

Aaraluni. Tauna-llu tua-i narulkakun pitallni aperturluku.

Piarkauluni pitaqestii. Tua-i-llu tuqullmi kinguani tauna tua-i ilakutain tungelqurrin anqurararkaullruyaaqluku. Tua-i kep'eurlurluni.

Anguyaluk: Yuraq taqenrilkan kinguvrin aturtuarararkauyaaqluku tua-i aug'utun piurluteng ilai, kinguvri, ilakutai. Taugaam yuramun taqrutmun taqrutngullrullilria.

Nanugaq: Allrakugni tua-i malrurraagni aturngatellrua.

Martina John: So he verbally proclaimed [that bowhead whale they caught] as an accomplishment during the dance festival?

Elsie Tommy: The bowhead whale that he caught at Narukacuk River by spearing it.

Mary George: How did he proclaim his accomplishment and ability?

Elsie Tommy: Are you asking about what he said when he proclaimed his accomplishment? "*A-rraa, A-rraa,* now [pursue it] without being afraid of it!"

Martina John: Their men boastfully proclaimed their accomplishments. That became his customary pronouncement during the dance festival.

Elsie Tommy: During the dance festival, when they were about to have a dance festival, the messengers went to Cuukvagtulirmiut.

Then when they were going to have the dance festival, after the messengers left, Ap'alluk came inside in the morning, sometime in the early morning, and turned to my father and told him that he would like to verbally reveal the animal he caught and asked for permission.

Then after looking at him for a short while, my father told him that it would be passed down to future generations and not be lost; his verbal pronouncement about his accomplishment would not be lost and would be passed down to his descendants.

Martina John: His descendants would always keep it, constantly passing it down through the generations. During every dance festival. Those are only revealed during dance festivals.

Elsie Tommy: When the dancers were idle for a short time, I think they did that before they were done [dancing].

The one who would verbally proclaim their accomplishment would suddenly enter. He would raise and extend his arms [and say], "My arms! My arms! The ones that I use to hunt bowhead whales! *Aa-rraa, aa-rraa!*" That's what he would do. [*chuckles*]

He would yell. Then he would reveal [the animal] that he had caught with a spear.

The one who caught it would do that. Then after his death, his relatives, his family members were responsible for constantly revealing [that pronouncement]. Nowadays, it has sadly ended.

Martina John: If dancing hadn't ended, his descendants would be responsible for constantly revealing it, and would constantly do what she just mentioned, his family, his descendants, his relatives. But that probably was the last time they performed it before dancing ended.

Elsie Tommy: He seemed to perform it for only two years.

Aling tua-i augkut cayarateng tua-i piciruimun elliluki piciruinguniluki Tuunrangayagmun pikniluki tua-i waten kepellruit.

Nanurniralria: Agayulirtet-wa makut, agayulirtenun taqevkarnillrukait.

Tua-i-ll' maa-i *2004*-aami qanrutaatnga augkut wani agayuvigmun-wa calilriit ilakeqataryaaqellratnia, piut maa-i-gguq taum *2004*-aam ciunganek ayagluteng agayulirtet *Pope*-amek ayagarrluteng maa-i augna wani taqevkallrat ca imna pugtengnaqu'uryaaqaat, iciw' cayarallrat ataam ukut nunat cayarallrat ayagniisqelluku, taqevkalteng. Ayuqenritut-gguq nunani cayarallrit.

Tamana tamaa-i pinilriarullinian-gguq piciulriarullinian-llu qessanayugtut agayulirtet taqevkallermeggnek. Yugmun-gguq ikayuutngullruyaaqelliniuq *instead of doctors or* augkut iciw' cat ayuqucinek-llu ikayuristet; tamakunigguq pininrullruyaaqelliniut.

Anguyaluk: Kangingumavkenateng tamaa-i ellait angalkut makutgun taugaam angalkutgun yuunguartelluki, cayarait tamakut eyagyarait man'a-ll' yuraq ilakluku, iciw' tamakut angalkut cauyarturluteng piniaqekait; tamatumun elliluki tamakut, yuraq-llu man'a aug'artelluku.

Maaten tua-i ellangukut wangkuta yuralrianek tangerqayuunata, makut taugaam maa-i ciuliaput yuratullruyaaqluteng avani, taugaam waten nunani allanek elaqlimeggnek kelegluteng, nunami ataucimi pivkenateng.

Maa-i pingualallrulriakut imumi ak'a pitullracetun, taugaam nunalgutkengramta.

Ukut angutet allanrunguartelluki arnat-llu nunamiungunguartelluki. Tuamtell' tua-i kinguqlilirikuneng mumigarrluteng cali, ukut nunamiungunguarluteng ukut-llu allanrunguartelluki.

Iciw' nulirqetaarturaruarluki pitullrukait, ak'acetun waten nunanek allanek kelegluteng piciryarallmeggnek, ukut allanrunguartelluki.

Tua-ll' irniangqerkuneng, irniangqerkata taukuk yuralriik irniangqerruartellukek cali apqunegtekek uivtaartiignek, uivaartiitnek aperluku.

Ava-i tua-i yuraryaurteqarrallermeggni tamana atuqeryaaqellruat.

Tamaa-i agayulirta nalqigulluku ak'a tamaani tang man'a yuraq ilaitnun ellirarnun ikayuutngupiallranek tamaa-i iciw' yurautetgun cangaqluteng,

My goodness, the people of the past stopped practicing their customs, stating that they were taboos that belonged to the Devil.

Mary George: These priests, they said that priests had them stop practicing them.

Then recently they told me in 2004, when they were going to have me become one of the church workers, that starting before 2004, the priests with orders from the Pope were trying to get people to start practicing customs that they had them stop practicing, asking people in villages to start practicing the traditions that they had them stop practicing. They stated that the traditional customs they practiced vary from village to village.

They said the priests were regretting that they had people stop practicing them since [those traditions] were powerful. They mentioned that it actually helped people instead of doctors or those mental health workers; they mentioned that [traditional ways] were more effective than those.

Martina John: They didn't understand and mistakenly believed that people were living lives that were dictated by shamans, and their traditions and their abstinence practices including dance, you know how they used to mention that shamans were constantly drumming; they considered [those customs] to be related to [shamanism], and they even had them stop practicing dance.

When we became aware of life, we never saw people dancing, but our elders had danced in the past, but they would only invite people from other villages outside their own and didn't hold dancing in just one village.

We used to have an imitation [dance festival] like they used to have long ago, even if we were from the same village.

They would pretend to have the men be the guests and the women the host village. And when they held [the imitation dance festival a second time], they would switch roles, and the [men] would pretend to be people from the host village, and they would have the [women] pretend to be guests.

You know how they used to pair them into pretend married couples, and they would carry out the custom of inviting villages [to a dance festival] like they did long ago, and they pretended to have a group of people be guests.

And if they had children, they had the dancers pretend to have a child, and when they referred to [the children] by name, they called them *uivtaartiik* [lit., "ones circling them"].

When they started dancing again for the first time [in the 1950s], that's the custom they carried out for a short time.

They explained to the priest how dance was a great help to some people, to orphans, and those orphans obtained things through dance. They continually

tamakut-wa elliraat. Waten tua-i akluteng navqetaagulluki. Tamana ikayuutngullra nalqigulluku tua-i yuram ayuqucillranek.

Taugaam-am tua-i taum Deschout-am taugaam-gguq tua-i tuunrangayiim, angalkum-wa tua-i piciryarallra peggluku. Nutaan tamaani kangingellermini tuaten tuunrangayiim-gguq piciryarallra peggluku tamakutgun imkutgun assillrakun taugaam ayasqelluku.

Nerevkartuli

Nuyarralek: Kayalivigmiut tua-i tamarmeng Merr'armun pitullrulriit, tuavet. Up'nerkarpak-llu tuanlluteng, uqurrsullermeng qaingani.

Cali nutaan up'nerkaq taqkan tuamtell' upanqiggluteng tengmianun pingnatullerkameggnun. Tengmialilria upagvikluku. Ikna-w' ika-i Kuilleq upagvik'lallrukiit tengmiarcuryarturluteng, Nerevkartuliq-llu.

Nerevkartuliq tauna tua-i, pelatekat amlletullruut uaqliqluteng. Kiaqliit, qukaqliit, uaqliit-llu.

Unguqata'arqameng qanruyulluteng pilallrungatut. Elevaarluteng curukaryugnaunaki, taugaam anguarluteng.

Tauna-ll' unguvigkarteng ullakunegteggu quyurrluteng qanaalluteng. Quyurtelalriit caqatarqameng. Tuaten tamana tamaa-i atuqerluku piaqluteng.

Tua-i-ll' ayagceciqataquneng uqilanqurraq taugaam ayagtelluku, uqilauralria. Aarrarraarluni aqumleryugnaunani.

Augna imna Culungalek ciuqliuvallutullruuq, ciuqliqvallutullruat. Akultutaciqeggluki ayagcequ'urluki.

Cali natmun piqataquneng akirtekaa call' ayagtelluku. Tauna akirtii yugyuarrlainarpek'naku cali qanrulluku, cali yugyuaqaqluku piuraasqelluku.

Tengmiat makut takvillruyugnarqut; takvigngalnguut-wa.

Piyullrat-am tua-i aturluku piaqluteng. Iliini taugaam picurlagaqluteng. Picurlagaqameng unangyuitellruut.

traded their belongings. They explained how dance helped people and what it was like.

But [Father] Deschout told them to abandon the ways of the shamans and not include them [when they started dancing again]. When he finally understood [the purpose of dance], he told them to abandon the ways of the shamans but to only practice dance customs following the good ways.

Nerevkartuli[71]

Mark Tom: All the people of Kayalivik used to move to Merr'aq, to that place. They stayed there all spring during the time they made efforts at obtaining seal oil.

And when spring was over, they'd move again to a place where they would make efforts at subsisting for birds. They'd move to a place where birds were abundant. They would move to Kuilleq over there to make efforts at hunting birds, and also to Nerevkartuli.

At Nerevkartuli there were tents situated up and down the river from one another. There were [tents] that were upriver, in the middle, and downriver.

When they were about to drive birds, I think they would discuss what to do with each other and make plans. They wouldn't pursue them with outboard motors but by paddling.

And when they went to the place where they would drive the birds, they would gather and discuss what they would do. You know how they have meetings when they are about to plan something. That's what they would do briefly.

And when they were about to send someone, they sent the fastest runner, someone who was a fast runner. He wouldn't say "*Arrarrarraa*" [an expression used when tired] and give up easily and sit down.

Culungalek mainly went first. They'd send people out a good distance from one another.

And when they were about to go somewhere they'd send out the one who would meet him from the other end. And they'd tell the person who would meet him from the other end not to be too visible, to be visible once in a while.

I think those birds had good eyesight; they seemed to have good eyesight.

They'd do as they wanted them to. But sometimes they didn't accomplish what they set out to do. When their plan didn't work, they didn't obtain [any birds].

Nacaullget amllepiatullruut ikani ika-i akimteni. Anglanaqluteng qalriuqaqu'urturluteng piaqluteng. Amllelallruut. [*ngel'artuq*]

Inerciigatut tuutangayiit; ciumurngaqtartut. [*ngel'artuq*] Anssaakata'arqameng yuum tungiinun, ilaita-ll' kinguatgun maligarrluki. Tuatnatullruutam cali. Tayima-w' qanaatullilriit tengmiat makut wangkucicetun anerteqsugluteng, ellmeggnek taringulluteng.

Piliqelallruut. Qayat ucilirluki. Qimaguyut-llu ak'aki tua-i, amlleriluki quyurrluki. Tengmiarugarnek tamaa-i irniaritnek.

Tuutangayagnek pinritut, nacaullget taugaam tua-i kiingita pitangyuutekluki atkulitullruamegteki qeciit. Angutait taugaam atukuliluki, arnait evacukarpalget pivkenaki.

Iniarit-llu amlleraqluteng ilaita tengmiat. Taukut tua-i tengmiaraat taukut kinercirateng neqkurluki, neqmeggnun makunun usguku'urluki.

Cali tauna kuvyacuaq piitenrilkurrluku ellaita; angussaagcuukaraqluku. Unugmi naptaat naptayagaat.

Camek egciyugnaunateng naternaq-llu egcugnaunaku, kayurrlugaq-llu egcugnaunaku. [*ngel'artuq*]

Anrutamtenek anglanillrunritukut avani ayagassuutvut assiitellratni. Tamalkumta ayuqluta ayagassuutelliqluta pillemteni.

Ikna ika-i nacaullelinqurraungat'lallruuq, ikna akivut. Waten ayuqevkenani.

Tuani ungutullruukut; yug-amlleq quyurtetullruuq Kuillermun. Tuani tua-i ungulngukuneng tua-i tengeng'ekata call' tua-i neqaralegmun, naunrarcurluteng tuaten tamaani upagaqluteng.

Taukut-llu tua-i pitateng, naunraat-llu pinriqata cali asgullerkameggnun, cali iqallualegnun.

Nerevkartulirmiut yugyatullruut. Makut maa-i atrarluteng unguyartut tuani uitaqutullruut, quyurrvikluki tua-i nerangnaqurallerkameggnun, ca neqa amlleq teguluku piyuitellermeggni kass'allaq-llu nurnaqluni.

Egciyuitellruut. Kinercirluki, kinerciqcaarturluki.

Cali umyugiurcecuunata neqmek camek. Neryaraq tua-i una nall'arrluku pilallrungatut. Anglanivkallrunritaitkut angayuqamta.

Many emperor geese were across from our village. They were fun to listen to when they made their calls. There were lots. [*laughs*]

Canada geese are rebellious; they aren't easily herded. [*laughs*] When they are trying to escape, they run toward a person, and the others follow. That's what they did. These birds probably talk as they like to live like we do, and they understand one another.

They used to catch a lot. They would load the kayaks. And they'd gather the many goslings together. They got many birds, their offspring.

They didn't prefer Canada geese, but they only wanted to catch emperor geese since they made their skins into parkas. They only made parkas out of the males and not the females that had worn spots on their skin from sitting on eggs.

And some people had a lot of bird meat hanging to dry. They always ate their dried bird meat, always eating them along with other things they ate.

And they tried to have a small mesh fishnet; they used it to try to catch fish. They'd fish for small whitefish at night.

They didn't discard anything at all, and they didn't discard flounder, and they wouldn't discard devil fish. [*laughs*]

Back when we didn't have good transportation, we didn't have a lot of food to fill our stomachs. We were all in the same situation, back when we didn't have good transportation.

The area across from our village seemed to have the most emperor geese. It wasn't like it is now.

We used to drive birds there; many people gathered at Kuilleq. When they were tired of driving birds, when the birds started to fly, they'd move to places where there was fish and would also pick salmonberries when they moved all over.

When they were finished processing the things they caught, and when salmonberries were no longer there to pick, they moved to places where they would go upriver to stay, including places where there was tomcod.

There used to be lots of people at Nerevkartuli. The people here who went down to drive birds would stay there and gather in places where they could subsist, back when they didn't catch large amounts of fish and store-bought goods were scarce.

They didn't discard things. They hung them to dry; they'd continually hang things to dry.

And they didn't let us eat as much food as we wanted. They seemed to eat only at mealtimes. Our parents didn't let us do as we please.

Pistailnguut naklegnarqetullruut cakneq, aturallraput tuaten.

Tua-i wangkuk Tuqulleq-llu urussiyaagpailgan kamilartetullruukuk pilugungqesciigalilunuk. Qanikcaq-llu una-w' tua-i qanikcaq qaillun pitalria aqvaqurlunuk arviraqlunuk. Tuskumegnegu-llu it'gapuk urugcirluki. Wii tua-i kamilangqiimegnuk akekatak. [*ngel'artuq*]

Anglanarqellrunrituq augna atullerput. Atunqiggnarqenricaaqluni, tamaa-i uterrvikluku.

Tua-i kiagpak kamilangqalunuk, tua-i-w' tamamta pikailamta. Nenglengkan nutaan nenglengluni pikan pilugull'erkaput angayuqamta paivvluki. Cap'akirkaitellruukut.

Kuimliruaq

Arcunan: Man'a-ll' maa-i man'a, tuavet tua-i Nanvarugmun anumallrunircaaquq, kuigtaitellruyaaquq ak'a avani tayima. Man'a kuigtaicaaqellra wavet. Qanemciullrulria tauna arnassagaq.

Quyangun: Kiugna Kuimliruamek pitukiit. Tauna-w' tuani angalkuullrullilria agiyautacuaraagnek atulleq.

Ussugcitet imkut nallunritaten, nunaliurcuutet Yup'igtaat. Tamakut tamaa-i agiyautarnek pilallrungatait.

Kiugna im' Kuimliruaq cevumallrunrituq. Tua-i tevyaraullrungatuq cali.

Tayima arnallruaraam taum tuquqataami agiyautacuaraagnek avaqliliisqelluni.

Tuqullran tuan kinguani kiugna Kuimliruamek pitukiit kuigurrluni, kia-i cayunairutellria, ameltukayagluni.

Arcunan: Qanemciullermini tauna tutgarani qavavet ayangnaqkan-gguq cakviurnayukluku, tutgarani tayim' tua-i kiimaungan, kingumini tua-i tuaggun pikan tuaten tua-i tuquqataami taukugnek pisqelluni.

Ak'anivkenani tua-i tauna cev'artelliniuq. Maaten-gguq tua-i piat tuarpiaq-gguq tamakut tamaa-i kapullret.

Muriit-am augkut ussugcitnek maani pitullruaput wangkuta. Aatama

Those without providers were so pitiful, and even our poor clothing.

Tuqulleq and I would start going without skin boots before the snow fully melted, we couldn't wear boots any longer. And we'd run across a patch of snow that was a certain size. And when we stepped on it, we would warm our feet. Since we were barefoot, how painful. [*laughs*]

What we experienced was no fun at all. It isn't something to long to return to and experience again.

We'd go barefoot all summer, we all did, since we didn't have boots. When it started to get cold out, our parents would take out the boots that we would use. We didn't have shoes to wear at the time.

Kuimliruaq[72]

Peter Dull: And this here, they say that [this river] didn't flow out to Baird Inlet at one point, that there was no river there long ago. The fact was that no river was here at one time. A story is told about that elderly woman.

Carl Mark: The river up there they call Kuimliruaq [from *kuime-*, "to swim"]. That person who had an *agiyautacuar* [small, land-prying tool] was probably an *angalkuq*.

You know about those *ussugcitet* [land-prying tools with sharp ends], a traditional Yup'ik tool used to work on land and soil. I think they called those *agiyautat*.

Kuimliruaq up there didn't have a channel. I think it was a portage trail at one point also.

When that small woman was about to die, she told them to give her an *agiyautacuar*.

After she died, that river they call Kuimliruaq up there became a river, and now it is a very wide river.

Peter Dull: When that story was told, it is said that she was worried that her grandchild might have difficulty when he started traveling north, when he traveled through there alone after she passed on, since her grandchild was an only child, that's what they told them to give her when she was about to die.

Not long after [she died] that river cut through the land and formed a channel into another source. When they looked at that place, [the sides of the river] looked as though they had been pierced with a sharp object.

Those wooden tools, we called them *ussugcitet* around here. My father

tegg'eraraat muriit, iquit cingikeggluteng, ukut tua-i cingiumaluteng, nunaliurcuutekluki. Capuciuqata'arqami tamatumek nuna kapurraarluku ekiterraarluku capuciaqluni. Tuaten.

Elisngastiin niitetullran qanemcikekani atam anglanaqsartuq niicugniurallra. Ayagneranek-llu qanemciksaraa.

Ningliq

Miisaq: Una-llu-w' cali, manignitullruyaaquq, una, ak'a avani.

Tua-i-am taum naken tayima naunranek aqvatellria tamaaken nunallernek, up'nerkaryartumi. Tua-i tauna qimugkarmek-gguq ikamracuaraak tua-i maani kasmurraukaraagni petuumaurluku ikayungqetullruuq.

Tua-i qanikciurluku tua-i taukut naunraat. Anqaarluku tua-i pilliniuq, anguyain makut ak'a avataillinikiit.

Tua-i elpeka'arcamiki-am tua-i pileryagpek'nani.

Tuavet tua-i elallerminun ekngami, tanglugni-llu maliklukek tuavet ekluni. Cingigni tua-i cagnitlinilukek, tua-i aqvaqurturquni ang'iqerrngairullukek. Tanglugni-ll' all'ukek tua-i.

Anngami tua-i qamuutani aqaarluku Ningliim tungiinun ayagartelliniluni. Tua-i caqtalriamek, qimugglugii una, ingna qamurluni. Petuilaakarraarluku nutaan.

Ningliq qerarluku, naugg'un tayim' qerallruagu.

Akianun tus'arcami kingyallinii ikegkut-gguq nutaan Ninglim akiakun taukut malirqertai, nutaan ika-i nangengqaqerluteng.

Tauna-am tua-i ciuneni pivkenaku ayallinilria tua-i taukunun-llu waten caqirrluni.

Taukunun tua-i tekicami, aniguyaralrianun taukunun manignanek, iliita-am tua-i neqliullinia, egalliniameng neqliulliniluku qamiqumek.

Aqumngami tuavet-am tua-i tangssukarluku. Qanerpegnani taukunek qanrutevkenaku anguyagnek.

Qantani tua-i teguamiu calligtelliniluku, calligqaarluku-llu egmian anngami naugg'un tua-i ciunerminun ayagpegnani, naugg'un taugaam uterrluni, qanrutevkenaki.

Tua-lli-wa-gguq-am taukut tua-i ciunrin taringekiit anguyaminek qimallra. Tua-i ellait upluteng call' tua-i taukut qimagluteng ellait.

used those hardwood tools with sharp ends, with this end made sharp, to work on land. When he was going to build a fence, after piercing the ground with that tool, after prying it, he'd put a fence there.

If a person who knew it well told the story, it would be fun to listen to. And they would have told the story from the beginning, too.

Ningliq River[73]

Peter John: And they say this place had a lot of burbot, this place, long ago.

A person had gone to retrieve some salmonberries from an old village site somewhere toward spring. It is said that he would keep a dog tied to his small sled to help him haul things.

He shoveled the place where the salmonberries were. After taking it out, he saw that his enemy warriors had already surrounded him.

When he realized they were there, he didn't react right away.

When he went inside that pit that he had shoveled, he took his snowshoes with him and went inside there. He tied his boot straps tightly, so that they wouldn't come loose when he ran. And he put on his snowshoes.

When he came out [of the pit he had made], after putting on his tow rope, he fled toward the Ningliq River. When he felt something, he saw that he was dragging his dog. After quickly untying [the dog], he [ran].

He crossed the Ningliq River, and I'm not sure where he crossed it.

When he landed on the other side, he looked back at them and saw that those pursuing him had finally appeared and were standing along the other side of the Ningliq River.

He didn't head toward his destination and turned, and turned toward those people.

When he arrived among those people who had built snow shelters and were fishing for burbot, someone there dished him food since they had cooked, dished him a fish head.

When he sat down he looked at it. He didn't say a word, he didn't tell them about the warriors [pursuing him].

When he took his bowl, he set it aside, and after moving it aside when he went out, he didn't head directly toward his village but took a different route home, not telling those people what had happened.

The people that had taken him in understood that he was running away from enemy warriors. They also prepared and fled.

Taringketallruut-gguq augkut ciuqliit. Yuk-gguq tua-i qanenrilengraan tuaten tua-i taringetullruat.

Tauna qanemciutullrulria, taukut-llu tua-i ukut qanrutekluki tuavet manignarnek nerengnaquralriit qanikcamek aniguyirluteng tuantellrat. Qanemcingssaarai call' mat'um amllermiyaaqut Ningliim.

Tununeq

Maklak: Up'nerkami nallunritlemteni agaaken Cakcaamek-llu wall' allanek iqalluarpagnek piyulriit wavet taitullruut Tununermun.

Tua-i-ll' imumek tuariqan ayagluteng kiavet imum' Uyaqurruamun. Kuvyiviutuluni, iciw' cingiggaar. Qalirneranun ayauquriurluteng.

Augkut-llu iciw' ikani Qanrangarmiut-llu tuaten Cakcaarmiungulallruriit. Iqalluarpagcutuluteng kiagmi tailaraluteng. Piyulriit tailaraluteng, wall' Negtemek tailuteng piyulriit. *Everybody was brothers and sisters, big family.* Tuaten tua-i pitullruut taringkumallemteni wangkuta waniwa.

Neqsulallruut angyartaunani iqalluarpagnek, qayatgun tua-i qayarluteng taugaam.

Cali avaken Cakcaamek-llu tailuteng, agken-llu Merr'armek-llu iqalluarpagcutullruut. Kiaguluku tailuteng, tua-i-w' up'nerkami. Qayarturluteng taugaam qayanek maavet kanavet taiqurituluteng.

Qayailnguut-llu upagluteng kiavet Uyaqurruamun. Kuvyait-llu naninateng tua-i nanitkacagarluteng, ilait tua-i *twenty feet*-aq nuringaluku, *twelve feet long.*

Ul'aqan pissuraqluteng. Ul'aqan muiraqluteng. Eneskan-llu tua-i taguquriluteng.

Enet-wa pagaani, enetaunani. Teggalqut ikayuqluteng anerqelluki waten ilutulriamun uitavilingnaqluki. Qalirnera-llu canek cingyaalleruarnek-wa pikat, nurnarqellruameng. Tuaten tua-i piuratullruut, Cakcaami-llu.

Ungalangqata'arqan nalluvkenaku pikaken pingaqan uptaqluteng. Makut maani petuktuurluki qimugteteng, cat tua-i aturluki. Tuaten tua-i piuratullruut.

Neqliluteng-llu unani cenami; piviggangqerrluteng. Tangtullruanka.

They say those first ones were very perceptive. Although a person didn't say anything, they understood his circumstances.

That was a story that was told in the past, and they also mentioned these people who went there to fish for burbot and were staying there in snow shelters. There are actually many stories about the Ningliq River.

Tununak[74]

Edward Hooper: During spring, from what we know, from across there, including Cakcaaq or other places, those who wanted to fish for herring would come here to Tununak.

And when the shore ice was gone, they'd head up the coast to Uyaqurruaq. It was a fishing place, that small point. They'd bring supplies to the top of that place.

You know how people from Qanrangaq were also from Cakcaaq. They'd come here [to Tununak] in summer to fish for herring. Those who wanted would come here, or those who wanted came from Nightmute, too. Everybody was brothers and sisters, big family. That's what they used to do from what I know.

They used to fish for herring when there were no boats around, with kayaks, only with kayaks.

And they'd also come here from out there, and from Cakcaaq, and from across there, and from Merr'aq to fish for herring. They would come during summer, or rather in spring. They only used kayaks to haul equipment down there.

And those without kayaks would move up the coast to Uyaqurruaq. And their fishnets were short, very short, and some were shorter than twenty feet, about twelve feet long.

They'd fish when the tide came in. When the tide came in, [their fishnets] would be full. And when the tide went out, they'd haul [their fish] to shore.

There were no homes up there. They helped one another to remove the rocks and tried to make a place for [the fish] in a deep area like this. And they placed some old tarps up on top since they didn't have many items back in those days. That's what they always did, even at Cakcaaq.

When the east wind was about to start blowing, they knew, and when it started to blow from up there, they'd prepare. They would tether their dogs, using something. That's what they always did.

And they cut fish along the shore down there; they had places [to cut and

Augkunek-am kenurqutat pillrit augkut *glass*-allrit anumaluteng, tamakunek-ll'-am *matches*-aalirluteng kenilleq kumartaqluku, akerta pikna. Puyungaqluni tua-i, tua-i-ll' ekuangluni. Waten pinrilngermi tua-i, *glass*-arrarmek piluteng akerta pikna kumarrluku kenillerteng. Tuaten tua-i piuratullruut.

Elquarugaat-wa unkut unani cali. Kinercirluki tuaten ilait tageskengameng. *No freezer, no* tengssuun, *no* elevaaq, *nothing.* Niicuunata elevaamek, taugaam waten angyacuar tua-i kiimi angyauluni.

Nunivaarmiut tag'aqluteng tua-i cali piyarturluteng. Tuaten tua-i neqtengnaquralallruut. Atmaagarluteng unaggun itraraqluteng qayailameng. Ikayulallruit qayarluteng taicilluki neqnek, neqautaitnek.

Uugarcimarpallurturluteng taugaam, taugaam nerellrit assirluteng. Tuaten tua-i, kuvyiqcaarluteng-llu *red fish.* Atam amllellrunritut *red fish*-at. Pitaqluteng.

Up'nerkillermiuni-llu qilagluteng *king-salmon net*-aliluteng, pitaqluni ataucirrarmek *king salmon*-aamek iliini. Cunaw' una-i ketiikun unaggun neqrugaat ayagluteng. Pikartuyiqenrilameng.

Taqukaq imna, issurim-llu amia wall' nayiim-llu amia meqcirraarluku akurqaurraarluku taryumi ekumavkarluku *string*-aliaqluteng.

Qukaanek ayagarrluki *string*-arluku *skin*-aq. Taqkan-llu ekluku; *string*-alirluteng kuvyakiurluteng tamaa-i taqukarcuutekiurluteng.

Kaugpiit-llu cali ekiarrluki unkut uqum tunglirnellri; wagg'uq qavyat.

Cali tamakut augauskuneng *rope*-arkalirluteng, *rope*-alirluteng *from walrus hide.* Cali tuaten. Taryumi ekumavkarraarluki naparyaq imna, nuqluku kinercirluku *rope*-aq. Tua-i *rope*-arkaqluki *like manila rope, nylon rope.* Tamakut tamaa-i tuaten.

Augkut-llu cetuamek piskuneng yualuit amllelalriit; yualuit aug'arturluki qip'iluteng yualukiurluteng. Tuaten yualukiurluteng-llu augkunek *twine*-anek pikuneng averqurluki caliluteng yualukiurluteng kuvyamek iqalluarpagcuutmek. Tuaten tua-i.

Kuvyaq civqaarluku, wagg'uq cayukaucirluku *both ends.* Aanat piluteng,

dry fish]. I used to see them.

They used old glass that had been removed from old flashlights as matches to light the fire pit, using the sun. It would start smoking, and then it would start burning. Although they didn't do this, they used just a piece of glass, and using the sun up there, they'd light their fire pit. That's what they always did.

And there were also many herring eggs down there. And they also dried some of the ones they brought to shore. They didn't have freezers, no airplanes, no outboard motors, nothing. We never heard the noise of outboard motors, but a small boat was the only boat.

People from Nunivak Island would also come up [to fish for herring]. That's how they always tried to obtain fish. They'd carry loads on their back and walk up along the shore since they didn't have kayaks. They helped them using kayaks, bringing the fish they caught here for them.

But [herring] were mainly overexposed to the sun and cooked, but they were good eating. That's what they did, and they'd also set nets to catch red salmon. There weren't many red salmon around in the past. They'd catch them.

And at Up'nerkillermiut, they'd tie a king-salmon net together, and sometimes they'd catch just one king salmon. Evidently, there were many fish that passed down below [that they didn't know about]. Because they didn't have a lot of equipment [they didn't catch them].

A seal, either a spotted-seal or a ringed-seal pelt, after letting the hair fall off, after keeping it in salt water for a while, they'd make string.

Starting along the center [of the pelt], they'd make string out of skin. And when it was done, they'd put it in; they'd make string to make mesh nets for catching seals.

They also removed a layer of the walrus skin that had been along the blubber; they called them *qavyat* [walrus-skin ropes].

When they removed those also, they prepared rope from the walrus hide. They also did that. After keeping them in salt water for a while, they'd pull [the skin line] along a post and dry the rope. They used those as rope, like manila rope, nylon rope. That's how they used those.

And when they caught a beluga whale, you know how they have a lot of sinew on them; they'd remove their sinew and twist the strands to prepare thread. And when they prepared twine, they'd split them and prepare thread for making a herring net. That's what they did.

After setting the net, they placed what they call *cayukautet* [grass mats to

piirriluteng iqalluarpiit uitavigkaitnek.

Tua-i-ll' iqalluarpak pirraarluku waten kingumun egqurluku.

Tua-i-ll' pingqataqan tuamtellu yaatmun tuamtellu neqtairingluni.

Nasperturluku tua-i uciangekuni-llu tua-i taqluni uterrluni. *One load per tide,* unugtuumaan tuaten tua-i.

Aatavut qantullrulria *fifteen* qayam imai *that will be enough for winter, for the whole family.* Tuaten tua-i.

Wangkuk-llu taguciqcaararaqlunuk, issratyaarlunuk. Imiqerluku akiqliqu'urlunuk, kuvqaqluku. Qavciulartat-llu tayima.

Uliggaq: Cangalliuryugnaunanuk akiqliqa'arrlunuk. Iliini-llu tuaten pirraarlunuk iqalluarpiit maavet.

Unani-llu-w' ketemteni enucetaarluteng pitullruyaaqellriit. Kuvyaq imna enuskani qertuluni tua-i unavet kuvya; iqalluarpiit qalliqluteng enutaqateng. Neq'liqaqluteng tamaa-i enucetaarluteng.

Maklak: Tuaten tua-i *salmon*-at-llu pitullrulliniut; napluteng qertuluteng. Caperrnaqluteng tua-i tangvallrat; taguqurimamaluteng.

Tuaten tua-i iqalluarpiit-llu naptetullruut amllerqameng. Iliini-ll' malrurqugnek tull'uteng amllerameng.

Quunengluni; anuqlingraan quunirluni ugaani *spawn*-arqameng, *fertilize*-arluteng malaku'urluni tua-i qagna.

Maa-i pinritut. *Two years* maa-i. *Three*-aarurciiqlilria maa-i. *No spawning area.*

Uliggaq: Iqalluarpiit imumi amlletullrulriit.

Un'a tang cenaq un'a uatvut tamaa-i qurrelriit iqalluarpiit tua-i qurrayirnaritullrulriit. Una-i-ll'-am piyuirusnganateng.

hold herring, from *cayug-*, "to pull toward oneself"] inside both ends [of the kayak]. The mothers would twine [grass] for the area where herring would be placed [inside kayaks].

Then after removing the herring [from the net] like this, they'd throw it in the back [of the kayak].

And when the [kayak bow was about to rise out of the water from the weight in back], they'd remove the fish and place some in front.

Determining how much he could carry, when he obtained a load, he'd finish and return home. They'd get one load per tide, even at night.

Our father used to say that fifteen kayak loads [of herring] would be enough for the winter, for the whole family. That's how it was.

And we two would slowly haul [fish] to shore, using small grass carrying bags. We'd fill it up, and situated side-by-side [we'd haul it up] and spill it out. I'm not sure how many [loads we carried].

Susie Angaiak: We didn't mind at all and would be situated side by side. And sometimes after we did that, we'd put the herring here.

And down below our village, they also set nets until the net was exposed when the tide went out. When the fishnet was exposed at low tide, the net would be in a steep pile down there; herring would be piled on top of one another when the fishnet was exposed at low tide. They would catch a lot of fish when they set nets along the shore that were exposed at low tide.

Edward Hooper: That's what salmon evidently did, too; they'd get caught on the net in a steep pile. It looked like hard work to bring them up to shore; they'd haul [fish] to shore for a long time.

That's how herring used to get caught on nets, too, when they were abundant. And sometimes there would be two herring runs because they were abundant.

The weather would get calm; although it was windy, it would be calm when they spawned, and when they fertilized [their eggs], that area to the north turned white like the color of milk.

They didn't [spawn] this past year. It's been two years now. It will probably be three years. No spawning area.

Susie Angaiak: In the past there were many herring.

Along the shore down the coast from our village, the herring that spawned used to cause it to become slippery. And they don't seem to do that any longer down there.

Maklak: NC Company-q ciumek piullrulria. *NC Company from* St. Michael-aamek aklunek piaqluni. Angyaq-wa augna *Aglade*-amek atengqerrluni.

Aglade-amek atengqerrluni. Tauna tua-i taigaqluni, massiinaa-wa *Widdy*-q *one cylinder*-aq. Egilraurluni tua-i. *Not fast, but it's moving. Spark*-arluni *igniters,* ellakun, tua-i amatiikun. Tauna tua-i taitetullruuq aklunek. Aatavut *he's the captain and the cook,* tuani. St. Michael-aami.

Two times kiagpak. Tauna-ll' *Aglade*-aq kanani kelumteni mayurrluku. Tuq-tukayagmek akaggluku tua-i ayagcetaqluku tua-i, kiituani tuk-tunguq. *Igniter*-aara-wa ellami, qamaggun kenerpallagaluni. Tauna tua-i taitetullruuq neqkanek.

Augkut-llu Kayalivigmiut avaken-llu aqvaqerpagangraan nangyuunani. Taringnaqluni ilatii pakmaken pimalria.

Mukaat saayut-llu taum qemangqaluki. Nutget, *sewing machines by hand operating,* puyurkat-llu, *those black powder.* Augkut-llu *primers, what they call primers,* kenret, puulirkat-wa, *lead*. Uruggluki puulikat piaqluki.

Makut-wa *twenty rounds ammunition* uitalriit. Tangerrluku *dollar seventy-five a twenty-round box.*

A big rifle, shiny, new, never been used, forty-five dollars. Sewing machine, the whole works, forty-five dollars. A big scoop of sugar, fifty cents. A big scoop tea, seventy-five cents. Those, boy, it's really something.

Nangucuunani-ll' tauna kipusvik.

Cugg'alit-llu, *I don't know,* qaill' pilallrat. Tegularluki *palm*-arluki pilallruuq. Ilaita-llu kalmanamnun qemagarciluteng, kalmaanamnun; kipucartut avaken wall' agken, nakleklua. Tamakut tayima umyuaqanka, naklekesteklallrenka. Tuaten tua-i ayuqellruuq.

Augkut-wa kalkiissat tengmiarcuutet imarkait, cat, *sack*-ayagaat mamtuluteng caquit, *shotgun*-aanun aturarkat *hundred pounds;* teguqang'ermi pekcuunateng. *It's hundred pounds.*

Sears Roebuck-aartaunani-ll'. *Nothing. After so many years, Sears Roebuck*-aam *catalog*-ai waten mikcuaraat qaill' mamtutaluteng tekilluteng, nakenllu pillruat; aklut qaill'-kiq taiyartat? Akiitqapiarluteng, cat tamarmeng akiitqapiarluteng.

Edward Hooper: NC Company was the first [store] around. NC Company would obtain merchandise from St. Michael. That boat that was called *Aglade.*

It was called *Aglade.* That [boat] would come here. Its motor was a Widdy, a one cylinder. It was always moving. Not fast, but it's moving. It had igniter sparks, located on the outside, on the other side. That [boat] used to bring merchandise here [to Tununak]. Our father was the captain and the cook there. At St. Michael.

[It would come] two times each summer. And we'd haul up the *Aglade* down below behind our village. It had a large inboard motor, and they'd start it by turning it, and eventually the inboard motor would start running. Its igniters were located outside, and inside a flame would burn. That [boat] used to bring food.

And although people from Kayalivik and out there would go and get a large amount of goods, [the store at Tununak] never ran out. It was obvious that they were given help [by God] from above.

There was flour and tea. There were guns, sewing machines that were hand operated, and powder, those black powder. And there were primers, what they call primers, *kenret,* and their *puulirkat* [metal for bullets] were lead. They would melt them to make *puulit* [bullets].

Then there were twenty rounds ammunition. It was a dollar seventy-five for a twenty-round box.

A big rifle, shiny, new, never been used, forty-five dollars. Sewing machine, the whole works, forty-five dollars. A big scoop of sugar, fifty cents. A big scoop tea, seventy-five cents. Those, boy, it's really something.

And that store never ran out of merchandise.

And Pilot Bread crackers, I don't know how much they cost. They used to take a handful. And some people would just place some in my pockets; people who came to purchase goods from out there or across there, they felt compassion for me. I think of those people who felt compassion for me. That's how it was.

And those lead pellets, the lead pellets for bird guns, those in small, thick sacks, the ones that would be used in shotguns, were a hundred pounds; although you took [the sack], they didn't move. It was a hundred pounds.

And there was no Sears Roebuck [catalog] in the past. Nothing. After so many years, Sears Roebuck catalog that was small and was about this thick arrived, and I'm not sure where they came from; I wonder how the items would get here? They were very cheap, all things were cheap.

Assilriit, *different colors,* yaggluni, *no yards. Yard for fifty cents.* Maa-i *nine dollars or ten dollars a yard.*

Fox-aamek assilriamek tun'iluni. *Storekeeper book*-arluni. Kaviaq ellirraarluku, *forty-five dollars.* Akitullruuq atam kaviaq, ataucirraungermi.

Kalikamun elliluki kipussaakuni; kipukengkan, avga-llu *draw*-qerluni pilria, augaq'erluku tauna. *That's a mathematic.*

Waten piluteng, tuaten tua-i akiuteksagulluku waniwa, waniw' akiurtuq. Atra-llu ellillerkaa pivkenaku. *This is ten cents, twenty-five and fifty cents.*

Kan'a igaq *fifty-cents* pikan avegluku, yuum-llu piksagulluku. *Fifty-cents*-aryulriamek pikan x-arluku igalriim. *That's a mathematics.* Tuaten piurturluni.

Wall'u, *what they call* punerneq. *Those are like coins. Fifty cents and dollar.* Punerneq, punerneret. Tamaa-i akit.

Kaviaq tauna, *aluminum coins,* elliivikluku tua-i *forty-five dollars.* Camek kipukengkan ukut aug'arluku wavet, aug'aqtaarturluku. Iliini waten piaqluku. Yugualiqerluni nallunailkucirluku. *Like Japanese* igarluni.

Wall' aqvaqurtelluku pikan taringluku taum, tua-i-w' igaqngamiki elliin. Call' uunguciilkuniu pilinguaqerluku natii assinritniluku.

Iqmigmek pikuni, *that's the* kipukengarkaata quyilriit iliit cuyaq. Imkut tua-i angkayalriit muraganek caquterluteng. *Ten*-aanek imangqelarngatut.

Tang-ata murilkuratullruanka. *One, two, three, four, dollar seventy-five.* Augkut taugaam amllerrluteng tua-i.

I just like joking right now, but it's there. Cigarettes-aanek tangerpakayuitellruunga *and matches,* taugaam atulallruit. Iliini *ignite*-arcuutnek pingqelallruut, kenerpallagaluteng.

Nasgauq: Kuvya civvluku, iciw' qaluq civvluku, wangkuta-ll' tangssuarluku.

Tua-i-w' anluarluteng. Tangssuarluki. Tuaten piaqata wiinga manalall-

The good [kinds of cloth], different colors, they'd extend their arms [to measure them], not using yards. One yard cost fifty cents. These days it's nine or ten dollars a yard.

They'd sell a good fox pelt. The storekeeper had a book. After recording a fox [in his book], it was forty-five dollars. A fox pelt was valuable, although it was just one.

They'd write them down in a book when they purchased things; when they purchased items, when they'd draw a mark, they'd remove the other half. That's the math they used.

They'd [make this mark], and that was their money, it became credit. And they didn't write down its name. This is ten cents, twenty-five and fifty cents.

When they wrote down fifty cents, they'd put a half mark on the drawing they put down, and it belonged to a person. If he purchased something that cost fifty cents, then the person who did the writing would place an x mark on it. That was the math they used. That's what they continually did.

Or, what they call *punerneq*. Those are like coins. Fifty cents and a dollar. *Punerneq, punerneret.* Those were money.

That fox pelt, aluminum coins, they'd put down forty-five dollars. If they purchase something, they'd remove it from [the book], constantly removing it. Sometimes they'd [make this mark]. They'd draw a person. They'd write like Japanese.

Or if they drew that person running, the person would understand what that meant, since that was his writing. And if he didn't understand something, he'd make a drawing on it indicating that some part wasn't good.

If they bought tobacco; one of the most expensive items was tobacco. Those large ones that had wooden containers. I think they were filled with ten.

You see, I used to pay attention to them. One, two, three, four dollar seventy-five. But there were many of those.

It's just like I'm joking right now, but it's there [true]. I hardly saw cigarettes and matches, but they used them. Sometimes they had igniters; they would spark.

Helen Walter: [When I was young at Tununak] they'd set a net, they'd set a dip net, and we'd watch.

They had holes in the ice. We'd watch them. When they would do that, I

ruunga. Tua-ll' paqnakekumki paqluki, kuimalriit. Amllerikata-ll' nucugluku tamakulriit.

Kanani iciw' kill'uni qaluq, avatii taugaam uitaluni.

Tua-ll' pikestiin tangssuarluku, wiinga paqnayuglua. Paqtellemni kuimaralriit unkut neqet iqalluat, amlleriqerreskata-ll' nucugluku.

Cingyukan: Epuluteng, pikaggun nucugyararluni. Uivenqeggluteng.

Anguyaluk: Nucukcuarluteng-gguq.

Nasgauq: Alingitlallrullinilriakut. Imarpigmi. Entaqan-llu ala-i, iciw' entaqami cikuq pagaani, wangkuta-ll' ukinerkun atrarluta camavet. Ilaput angutet augkut yaaqvanun ayagaqluteng.

Anguyaluk: Ala-i, imuteksailkiici! Qerratarrluni.

Nasgauq: Iciw' marayauluni, marayaurtaqluni. Anluakun pug'aqluta. Ila-i alingitellrullinivagceta.

Iciw' *echo*-rtangqerraqluni-llu. Aaqetqalriani *echo*-t ayakpagaluteng. Cikum aciani kanaraqluta ulnerciraqamteggu.

Anguyaluk: Aling ulqauskaci-mi qaill' piyarceci? Qungvagnaqluni.

Nasgauq: Yaaqvanun wangkuta arnani [piiyuitellruukut]. Ukinerteggun, anluatgun.

Iliini nangpagciigataqluta. Ala-i cikuq-wa pagaani. Nengelvalaami-wa, mamtulaami-ll'.

Anguyaluk: Imuskiinek-llu niicuunata. Kiingan-wa wiinga nucukcualrianek niitetullrulrianga tangerqallruvkenii-llu.

Nasgauq: Manaraqama tuaten pelatekaassualriit paqtelallruanka, manalnguqertaqama.

Anguyaluk: Pelatekaassuarluteng-gguq tua-i anluaq neqet quyurrvikaqatgu tamakut nucugaqluki. Pitaqluki tamakut kuimalriit anluam paingani.

would fish with hooks through the ice. And when I was curious to watch, I'd go over and see fish swimming. And when there were lots, those people who fished like that would pull up [the dipnet].

The dipnet would be submerged, but its frame was visible.

The one who owned it would keep an eye on it, and I watched with curiosity. When I went to check it, tomcod were swimming down there, and when there were a large number, they'd pull [the dipnet] up.

Albertina Dull: They had handles, and there was a place up there where they pulled it up. They were round.

Martina John: They called [that way of fishing] *nucukcuarluteng* [fishing for tomcod using dipnets under the ice, from *nucuk-*, "to pull out"].

Helen Walter: We weren't afraid back then. On the ocean. And my goodness, when the tide went out, the ice was [hovering] above, and we'd go down through the [fishing] hole [in the ice] and go down there [under the ice]. Our companions, the boys, would venture far.

Martina John: My, how [the ice] didn't collapse on you! [The ice] hovered above the ground.

Helen Walter: There was mud, it became mud [when the tide went out]. We'd appear through the [fishing] holes. My, how unafraid we were.

There was an echo also. When saying "*Aaa*" the echo would travel. We'd walk underneath the ice when we'd wait for the tide to come up.

Martina John: My, what would you have done if the tide came in [while you were under the ice]? How creepy it was.

Helen Walter: We girls [didn't] venture far. [We climbed up] through holes, through the [fishing and dipnetting] holes.

Sometimes we couldn't stand straight. My, the ice was up there. Since it used to get extremely cold, since the ice used to be thick.

Martina John: And we never heard of [ice] collapsing on someone. I only heard about *nucukcualriit* [those pulling out fish], but I never saw them.

Helen Walter: When I'd fish with hooks through the ice, I would go and check on people who were fishing in small tents, when I got tired of fishing with hooks.

Martina John: They'd use tents, and when fish gathered along a fishing hole, they'd pull those [fish] out. They'd catch those [fish] that were swimming along the opening of the fishing hole.

Tununermun Tumyaraq

Anguyaluk: Piuralallruut. *Saturday*-mi piurluteng. Tua-i irniangqeng'ermeng amarluku, aqumluteng arulairluteng elaqvanun aanat irniateng aamarrluki.

Wangkuta taugaam tamaani mernuyuitellruukut. Aqvaquagaqluta maani piciatun. Mernuyuunata *young*-arluta.

Wangkutni *first time* yaaqsigluni. Tua-i-llu kinguqlilirikumta canimenani. Yaaqsingraan canimenani. Maaken cali, ugg'un ayagluteng amavet.

Yuukaq

Ayaprun: Uksiluta-ll' uksurpak, up'nerkaqan-llu *school*-alriit iliini taqluteng, iliini-ll' taqvailgata tekilluta.

Neqsura'arlutek neqkamtenek uksurpak.

Cuk'ayaq: Iqalluanek. Yaa, kinercirluki atam pitullruit. Ataucirqumek iqallualiqellrulliniuq-am tua-i.

Tua-i tuavet cali tua-i kuvyitullruut, kuvyitullrulria-wa tua-i tauna, tauna tua-i uksurpak tua-i. Neqngunriyuunateng taugaam. Neqnguluteng. Ilait-llu qimugcitekluki pilallrukai.

Ayaprun: Ivrallaurrluteng aipait-wa nutaqat. Nutaqat, ivrallat ak'a-llaurrluteng. Nerairluki-llu, nerairraarluki-llu ak'alliciriaqluteng cali, kami-nialleramta uatiini. Tua-i-ll' tep'ngareskata kenirluki.

Tua-i-ll' cairuteurlurluta, *no* caarralaq, *no* caayuq, tua-i caunata. Aanaka tengucualillruluni, iqalluat meluitnek kenirluni. Melugglainarmek, kingua-kun-llu tengugglainarmek. Caturyungeqcaarlua tua-i. Mukaarrartangqell-rulria imat'am, maniallruluni aanaka.

Tua-i-ll' tuaken melugnek uungaki, qantall'erqa augna, ciurluki makut qaingit aug'aqa'aqluki. Cali-ll' caarralaqaquinrat. Umyuanglua tua-i wiinga. Augkut-ggem Apassugam atrautallri *school*-amek *cornmeal*-amek aterluteng. Ciamlluki meluit, *eggs*-at, tua-i makut aug'aqcarluki. Angayuqaagma nalluagni, catailan.

Trail to Tununak[75]

Martina John: They always [traveled from Umkumiut to Tununak for church]. They always went on Saturday. Although they had children, they'd carry their child on their back, and then the mothers would move a distance from the trail and nurse their children.

But we never got tired back then. We'd run around everywhere. We never got tired when we were young.

To us, when we went for the first time, it was far. Then when we went again, it seemed close. Although it was far, it seemed close to us. And from this village, they'd travel through this route over there [to Tununak].

Yuukaq[76]

Pauline Pitka: And we spent the entire winter camping [at Yuukaq], and sometimes when spring came and school ended, sometimes before it ended, we'd arrive [at Tununak].

They'd fish for fish that we ate all winter.

Tommy Hooper: Tomcod. Yes, they used to dry them in the past. At one time, he caught many tomcod.

They also set mesh nets there, that person used to set a mesh net there, all winter. [Tomcod] were eaten all winter. And he used some for dog food.

Pauline Pitka: They were made into *ivrallaat* [old, frozen tomcod that were thawed] and the others were *nutaqat* [fresh ones]. There were *nutaqat* and *ivrallaat* that were aged. After removing their innards, they'd age them for a little while down below our small stove. And when they started to smell, they cooked them.

And we ran out of goods, no sugar, no tea, and we didn't have anything. My mother had made *tengucuat,* or rather, had cooked some tomcod roe. [She cooked] only roe, and afterward, only liver. I wanted to eat something. I forgot that there was some bread, as my mother had made fry bread.

And from there, when the roe was cooked, I got my bowl, and I squeezed the water out of them and removed their casings. And there was a little bit of sugar. I got an idea. I thought of the ones called cornmeal that Apassugaq had brought down from the school. So I crushed their eggs and removed the casings.

Apassugaq-ll'-am aanaka-ll' camek piluni, iirtuqcaarlua caarralamek tegutelaaglua, caarrilirluku, *cornmeal*-aq umyuaqluku. Neqniatkacagarluni.

Aren carraugurluku-am piurqilaku, kiituan neqniringuq, kiituan nang'aqa.

Amatiikuan-llu tengucuat ua-i ilait waten ceterluki uquit kanangcilaqait.

Maniamek cikianga aanama, tengucuat tua-i ikegkut tenguit ulurciiganaki wii. Tua-llu-w' umyuangekilii, augkut imkut *peanut butter.* [*ngel'artuq*] Tamakuunguartelluki.

Tuamtell' aanamnun nalluvkarluku tegullua assaliaq tamana tua-i umyuaqluku. Keggucaaqlua neqniapalkackacagarluni. [*ngel'artuq*] Tua-lliwam tua-i neru'urqilii, kiituan nang'uq. Tuatnallruunga cali.

Tuani Yuukami arnat qalutullruut. Aañanka Nalugalria.

Tangvatullruanka. Apassugaq-llu ungumrarluni qayarluni, kaugtuarluni.

Uksuarmi-llu cikuqami-llu Amatmi uatemteni ipukaquluteng angutet. Kuvyaq camavet iterrluku, Apassugaq muragamek or qanikciurutmek qamaken naken ungumraarluni, kalegturluku cikuq. Nucugluki-llu. Uksuarmi. Miknaurtut tayim'.

Apassugaq-am cumikaqa. Elli-gguq kumlanertuqatartuq. Can'giircetun ilait angtaaqluteng. Nerelria tamak'acagaita qamiqurritnek nerkuiluni kiirraan. Can'giircetun kumlanerturaqluni, mikcuayagaat tamakut. Naspaalua. Enernek asqialliqkacagarlua, nerkuiqaqlua. Tua-ll'-am neryaurrluki.

Qinaruuq

Kangrilnguq: Tua-i tamaa-i ayagavakarlutek [Tumaralriankuk uyurani-llu] tuntussulliniuk-am Qinaruum pavavet qagatii tekilluku, asgurluku Qinaruuq. Qagatiini tua-i tamaa-i tuntunek ucianglutek piamek utertellinilutek.

Waniw' tua-i itqatarlukek narungraicetek, anngaa Qinaruumun, igyaraanun itqertelliniluni.

Uyuraa-ll' tua-i umkaucatni, caq'iqerrluni nunam tungiinun ayiimi

Without my parents knowing, since Apassugaq was gone and my mother was doing something, I hid and quickly took some sugar and put sugar on it, thinking of the cornmeal. It tasted very bad.

I ate small amounts at a time, and eventually it started tasting good, and eventually I finished it.

And the day after the next, you know how they try to get the oil to render from tomcod liver after cutting a slit in them.

Since my mother gave me a piece of fry bread, I couldn't look away from the livers. Then I had an idea, that peanut butter. [*laughs*] I pretended it was that.

Then without my mother knowing, I took the fry bread, thinking about that [peanut butter]. I took a bite and it tasted terrible. [*laughs*] Then I ate a little at a time, and eventually it finished. I also did that.

The women dipnetted there at Yuukaq. My mother, Nalugalria.

I used to watch them. And Apassugaq would strike the water with a stick to drive the fish using a kayak.

And during fall at freeze-up down below our place at Aman, the men would fish with dip nets with wooden frames and handles. They'd push the net down, Apassugaq would use a piece of wood or a shovel and start to drive the fish from somewhere upriver, continually scraping the ice. And then they'd pull them up. During falltime. [The tomcod] would be small.

One time, I was watching Apassugaq. He said that he was going to have frozen fish. Some were the size of blackfish. He ate and ate the entire thing, and the only things that he didn't eat were their heads. He would eat frozen fish like blackfish, eating those small ones. I tried one. I didn't like the bones at all, and I would remove [bones] once in a while. Then I started eating them.

Qinaruuq River[77]

Paul John: Once, during their many travels, [Tumaralria and his brother] went caribou hunting reaching the lake source of Qinaruuq River, traveling up the Qinaruuq River. After they obtained a load of caribou meat up along its lake source, they returned home.

Just as they were about to go into [the outlet of the Qinaruuq River], and they happened upon [enemy warriors] there, his older brother suddenly went into the lake outlet of the Qinaruuq River.

And when [the warriors] blocked his younger brother's path, he suddenly

nunamun-gguq tua-i tekitessiyaagpailegmi, ceturyamikun aqvaqurluni nunamun qecengluni ayakalliniluni. Pitgaquyaaqekseng tua-i uqiliin pitaqevkenaku, yaaqsigiqerrluni.

Tua-i anngani tua-i imna tayima malirqerluku. Tuqucukluku ping'ermi uatmun aqvaqulliniuq. Uaqsigiqerluni, waten Qinaruuq man'a qipneret iliit uyanglluk' pillinia anngaa-ll' ugna uaggun qip'arrluni tayima.

"Arenqiapaa anngaqa tua-i anerteqliniuq." Aren tua-i ciunringnaqluku, cingik tevluku. Uyangcaaqelliniuq-am augna-ll' qayaa qip'arrluni.

Paillipailgan tua-i ciunringnaqsaaqekii, tua-i tuaten qipneq nalkuaqerluni uyangnauraa-gguq ugna-ll' qip'arrluni. Aqvaquryaaqluni.

Nutaan tua-i cakmani Qinaruum paillitellrani uyangtellinia, kan'a-llu-gguq qayami paingan tunulirneranun qetqataarluni, tua-i mernuirciqallerkani umyuaqluku pillikii.

Qusemliqalria niigarcamiu tangerqerluku, anngaan pillinia, "Aling tua-lli-w' anguyagpenun tuqucukluten atanqevkenak cetulrianga."

Tua-i-gguq-am anngaan alrapaqluku. Anguyamek tua-i pingraiceteng anaglutek, piturnilliniamek.

Anngaa-am anqaraucilliniluni yuarutmek aturluni:

Angaa-raa-ii-aa-a, agii-aa-yii-iya-raa.
Angaa-raa-ii-ya-iya-aaa.
Angaa-raa-ii-yaa, agi-yaa-rra-nga-ii-aa-a.

Mat'umek maa-i anngaa anqaraucilliniluni yuaruciluni, tuani tua-i anguyamek piyarpiangraicetek anallermegnek.

Tua-i piinanermegni taukuk imarpigtaalaamek-am, pivakarlukek wagg'uq ukunun uqitelliniuk Kavialegnun.

Taum-llu-gguq Tumaralriim apqiitnek maaggun imarnitek allgarrlutek; alleglutek waten qairem imiqallrani man'a imarnitegken qacunrak, allgarrlutek, meq tua-i qayaanun ellngallagluni.

turned, and when he escaped toward the land, before reaching the land, he stretched out his legs as he ran and jumped onto the land and ran off. Although they shot arrows at him, they didn't catch him since he was a fast runner. He quickly got pretty far ahead of them.

He ran after his older brother. Although he thought he had been killed, he ran downriver. Just as he got pretty far downriver, when he peered around at one of the bends on the Qinaruuq River, he saw his brother suddenly turn and disappear around the bend down below.

"Oh my, my brother is actually alive." He tried to cut across to reach the area ahead of [his brother], and he cut across the point along the river bend. When he peeked around the bend again, he saw his [brother's] kayak disappear [around the bend].

Before he reached the mouth, he tried to cut in front of him, but when he'd reach the end of one bend and peek around it, the one downriver would disappear around the bend. Here he was actually running.

Finally down along the mouth of the Qinaruuq River, when he peeked at him, he saw that the one down there was lying along the back of his kayak cockpit, probably just resting.

When he coughed a little and he heard him, his older brother saw him and said to him, "My, here I thought your enemies had already killed you, and so I just went downriver without waiting for you."

Then they say his older brother sat back-to-back with him in his kayak [and they left]. Although their enemies pursued them, they escaped since they were adept.

His older brother composed an *anqaraun* [warrior song], singing a song:

Angaa-raa-ii-aa-a, agi-aa-yii-iya-raa.
Angaa-raa-ii-ya-iya-aa-a.
Angaa-raa-ii-aa-a, agi-yaa-rra-nga-ii-aa-a.

His older brother composed this *anqaraun*, about a time when they escaped although their enemies almost captured them.

One day, those two, since they would travel out to the ocean, one day they went to seek shelter from the wind at [piled ice] called Kavialget.

Then they say Tumaralria's seal-gut rain garment tore from the waves hitting it; they tore when the wave that splashed on him collected along the area here, and the loose section of his seal-gut rain garment tore, and the water suddenly poured inside his kayak.

Tuani-gguq tua-i tauna Tumaralria angarvaungami tua-i tuunrituuq yuut tangvallratni, tua-i tuunriskengai-llu assiriaqluteng. Cat-llu umyuaqluki yuut ikayuutekaitnek tuunramikun call' tua-i piaqami tua-i yugnun tangvagcetaqluni.

Tuaten tua-i Kavialegnun uqicamek, uyurani pillina, "Aling wangkuk tang waken waniwa Kavialegteggun iterlunuk kingunemegnun taugaam ayagturqumegnuk canricaaqelria."

Tua-ll'-am tua-i uyuraan pillinia, "Aling yugnun tangvagtelluten tuunertaarpakalalriaten, ngelaicuklunuk yuut waten qanlarciqelriit, 'Tumaralriankuk-wa imkuk picurlalriik Tumaralria angarvaungraan.' Yuut tuaten pilarciqut. Yuarciqaatgen. Angarvaullren pitekluku ciin ananritlem'egnek, iterlunuk ayagyaaqekumegnuk ukutgun."

Tua-i-am uyuraan ellaliqallinia. Tua-lli-wa-gguq-am tua-i Tumaralriim, ellangarcecani uyu'urmi, imarnitegni tamakuk iquugkengun allgarnerak teguluku nalugluku. Iquakun tua-i iqmiamiu ageskii, iqukliarrluku-gguq pegtaa, imarnitek allganengssagaunatek. Mamtellinikek-am tua-i iqmiglukek allganrak tauna.

Uyurani pillinia, "Kitek qerruinan piluku kingunemegnuk tungiinun piqrutqerru mermun."

Uyuraan tua-i qerruinani tauna kingunermek tungiinun piqrutliniluku. Tua-lli-wa-gguq tua-i piqrucaku meq tevalria qupnertun, imarpiim mer'a. Tua-i anurvangraan kingunemek tungiignun tua-i iluturiluni.

Ayakatangarcamek tamaaggun uyurani pillinia, "Qayaqa taugaam puukaryaaqevkenaku piurqina."

Aren maaten-gguq ayagtuk tevagnerkun anuqliuryugnaunatek, ayuquciak-wa-gguq cersertell', mer'em qairi. Tua-i quuniulriatun tevagnerem iluakun qailiuryugnaunatek ayaglutek.

Tua-ll' tua-i ingrit makut canimelliluki, uyurani kingyarluku pillinia, "Arenqialnguq tang anuqlirpakaami Tununermun kautellerkarpuk pilria."

Qinaruumek augna Tununermiut kiatiitni acitmun ellngalria pilaraat. "Qinaruukun iterlunuk Mertaryarakun cetuyarturluk." Uyurani piani,

They say that at that time, since Tumaralria was a powerful shaman, he would use his powers while people watched, and the people who he healed with his powers would recover. And he allowed people to watch him when he used his powers to do things that helped people.

When they sought shelter from the wind in Kavialget, he told his younger brother, "My, it would be good if we just entered Kavialget and headed toward the place where we came from."

Then his younger brother said to him, "Gee, because you have constantly practiced your powers in the presence of people, this is what people will say when they think we've gone missing, 'Tumaralria and his brother died accidentally although Tumaralria is a powerful shaman.' That's what people will say. They will look for you. If we happened to enter and leave through here they will wonder why we didn't survive because they know you are a powerful shaman."

His younger brother put some sense in him. Then, they say, when his younger brother caused Tumaralria to suddenly come to his senses, he took his seal-gut rain garment along the ends of the torn section and lifted it up. When he placed his mouth over one end, moved across, and reached the [other] end, he let go and there was no hole at all in his seal-gut rain garment. He had closed the tear by placing it in his mouth.

He told his younger brother, "Now take your sealskin float and strike it down in the water in the direction of our village."

His younger brother struck his sealskin float on the water in the direction of their village. Then, they say, when he struck it down, a gap formed in the water like a crevice in the ocean water. Although it was extremely windy, the gap became deep and led toward their village.

When they were about to leave through that route, he told his younger brother, "Try not to bump my kayak as you're going."

My, when they left they went through the gap [in the ice] in calm and windless weather, and the area surrounding them was making splashing and crashing noises from the water's waves. Like they were traveling in calm weather, they traveled through the gap without going through large waves at all.

And when they got close to these mountains here, he looked back at his younger brother and said, "My, since it's so windy, it's going to be difficult to reach Tununak."

They call the river that trickles down behind the village of Tununak Qinaruuq. "We will go in through Qinaruuq to head down Mertaryaraq."

"Tua-i-w' piyugngakumegnuk."

"Aren piyugngaukuk." Aren tua-i kuigmun kaucartulliniuk. Qinaruukun; imna ellngatuli tua-i ellngaryugnaunani kuiguluni kauyartullragni.

Kuigkun asgullinilutek, tua-i qagatiinun anqertelliniuk. Ikna call' ika-i kuigem igyaraa nallunaunani.

Arvirlutek, kautuk-gguq kuig-man' ciunragnek tungiinun carvanirluni.

Qayaq-wa-gguq una igyaraani kuvyaminek neqtairiuralria, qayaa-gguq tua-i napangyagcet'ngelliniluni.

Tekicamegnegu anngaan neqkamegnek cikiisqessaaqelria, taum tua-i kuvyaminek neqtairiuralriim qunutelliniluku. Qunucagni tua-i kiturluku.

Uyuraan taum kingyarluni tangllinia naruya, imna qayauluku neqtairiuralria tekiteltek. Naruyaq-gguq imna qamiquni angllurrluku cenakun maaggun ayagnaurtuq, ciuggluni-llu.

Taumek tang tuatnaaqata imkut naruyat kuvyauqcuarnilallrukait. Taukuk tua-i tuaten naruyaq tauna yuuluku tekiqaarluku kitunermegnegu tangllinilukü.

Tua-i kuigkun cetulutek, ikaggun-llu-gguq tua-i Tununermiut mertaryaraatgun kuicuarkun Tununermun anlutek. Tua-i qairitkacagarkun tekitellinilutek.

Tua-i tauna amllerqunek tua-i caperqek'ngait yuut tuunramikun pilalliniamiki Tumaralriim, ellatelalliniuq tua-i ellatesqaqatni, pakmavet ellamun ayagluni. Tua-i utertaqluni.

Unguvayugmiut

Maklak: Tua-i-gguq taukut atengqertut Unguvayugmiunek, taukut nunallret ingrim qacarnerani. Unguvayugmiut.

Iciw' ulerpiurluteng kanani nanikualuteng, tua-i-ll' tagluteng unguvaluteng pikani. Tua-i taunguuq. Mermek alingluteng.

When he told his younger brother, [he replied], "Well, if we are able to."

"My, we can do that." They approached and were about to enter a river. They traveled through Qinaruuq River; that river that usually trickles wasn't streaming down at all but it was a river when they reached it and were about to enter.

They headed upriver and suddenly went out to its lake source. The outlet of another river into the lake was visible over there.

They crossed and reached it, and the current of the river they reached was flowing toward the place they were heading to.

They say there was a kayaker along its outlet who was removing the catch from his gillnet, and they saw that his kayak had started to tip up [from the load in the stern].

When they reached him, his older brother asked him to give them some food to eat, but the one who was removing fish from his gillnet didn't want to give them any. They passed him since he didn't want to give them any.

When his younger brother looked back, he saw that the one who they had come across as a kayaker removing fish from his gill net was a gull. That gull would dip his head underwater and swim along the shore, and then it would lift its head up.

That's why, when gulls do that, they refer to it as *kuvyauqcuarluteng* [lit., "using a small net to acquire small amounts of fish"]. After reached that gull in human form, they saw it [as a gull] after passing it.

They went downriver, and then they went out into Tununak through the small stream where Tununak people go and haul water. They arrived through a route that had no waves at all.

Since Tumaralria would use his powers to do things that other people found impossible, he would travel up to the sky when they would ask him to travel through the sky using his powers, traveling up to the sky. He'd return.

Unguvayugmiut[78]

Edward Hooper: They say that place is called Unguvayugmiut [Those who want to stay alive], that old village site along the side of the mountain. Unguvayugmiut.

There was a large flood down there and they were in a desperate situation, and so they moved up there and stayed alive up there. That's what the origin [of the name] comes from. They were afraid of the water.

Caputnguat

Uliggaq: Imkut teggalqut naumalriit Caputnguat, tuani-gguq tua-i akaar tamaa-i taukut yuungnaquralriit, tamaani wani nulirqelriik taukuk irniarlutek. Tuani tua-i uitatullruuk kiagmi waten. Tua-i taukurmiut ellukaulluki tua-i tuqutellrullinikait.

Tamakut-am ilaita, tua-i-w' ullallermeggnitki, atiit-gguq tekitnerra-ralliniluni, qayaa unani cenami waten ugingqaluni uitalria.

Atiit, qanlallruut taumun-gguq tua-i atiitnun nallunricaaqsukluku tauna tuaten piqatalria pillruut. Tauna tua-i qayaa unani cenami ugircimaluni tekitnerra'arluni.

Tua-i-gguq imumek elagluki pillratni irniarin-gguq iliit tauna nang-tequralriarullruuq; tua-i-gguq taum tua-i nangtequralriim qaingani waten patumallrua palurcimaluni. Tua-i qanerluteng-llu nallunricaaqellruyukluku taumun atiitnun.

Tua-i-gguq taukurluut tua-i pelatekarallratni kanani cenami pikaken quliitnek nuna tua-i imna aug'aqerluni ellu'urrluni tua-i patullrullinikai. Taukut tua-i Caputnguarmiunek-am acirluki pitullruit.

Nanugaq: Engelullugarmiut uatiitni uani. Tuani tua-i ellukautelqait taukut nulirqelriik irniakek-llu, tua-i tamanqegcaaraita.

Tauna-gguq panian iliit Tununermi nunasngayaaqluni, atiin-llu-gguq aqvaluku. Tua-i-ll' aqvallra unukuan pikaken qeciirnerutullruuq; ellukaulluki patulluki.

Imum-llu al'ama Panuuyaam aanalleurluan qanemciktulqai. Caqerluni-gguq waten tan'gerpiit amllerillratni pagaaggun maligulluni tan'gerpaggluni tuaken amllerniiceteng tang'erpiit.

Issratmek tua-i atmagluni ayagluni. Pikaggun-llu-gguq caknerluni ellu-qaqluni tua-i irugni akitmiarcetaqlukek nunarrluni maavet tan'gerpaqutarnek.

Tua-i-ll' kanavet tekilluni. Tekicami pingayurqunek-gguq amlliqerluni aqumluni teggalqum qainganun kiarqurallinilunii tua-i.

Caputnguat[79]

Susie Angaiak: Those rocks that are there, the Caputnguat, they say there was a family living at that place long ago, a married couple with a child. They lived there during summer. The people of that village there, a landslide evidently killed them.

When others went to those people, they saw that their father had just arrived, and his kayak was docked along the shore.

They suspected that their father knew that [the landslide] was about to occur. His kayak was docked along the shore, and he had just arrived there.

They say when they dug the people out, they say one of his children was suffering from illness; it is said that [the father] was on top of that one who was constantly suffering from illness, on his belly. And they suspected that the father knew [that the landslide was about to occur].

They say those poor people, while they were living in tents down along the shore, a piece of land suddenly broke off above them, and it slid and covered them. They used to call that place Caputnguarmiut [from *caputnguaq,* "imitation weir"].

Elsie Tommy: Down the coast from Engelullugarmiut. The land slid on top of a married couple and their children there, their entire family.

They say one of his daughters was actually at Tununak visiting, but her father went to get her. Then the evening after he went to get her, that area above, that area had no ground covering on it; the land slid down on them and covered them.

And my older sister, the dear deceased mother of Panuuyaaq, told the story about what happened to them. She said one day when there were many blackberries around, she accompanied others along the mountain up there and went to pick some blackberries from there since they said there were lots.

Carrying a twined grass bag on her back, she left. Then she said she had a difficult time traveling up there and would slide down once in a while and brace herself with her legs to stop herself from sliding, and she went overland to that area to pick large blackberries there.

Then she reached the area down there. When she reached that place, after taking three wide steps, she sat down on top of a rock and scanned her surroundings.

Kiarqurarraarluni iigni cayuamikek piqalliniuq-gguq tegglirugaat-gguq ayuqenrilnguut, aqlitet. Cakneq-gguq augkut cungavserit tuar-gguq tanqillagauralalriit cungavseret imkut, ak'a avani cigviktullrit.

Tua-i-gguq taukut tua-i ellukautellri umyuaqelqai maniicukluni tamakunek, tamakunek aklullritnek arnat taukut.

Tua-i-am yuvriararraarluki umyuarteqliniluni ak'a-ggem avani inerquutaq tamana atutullratni-gguq yuum tuqumalriim akluanek cailkami uitalriamek teguqautesqevkenaki inerquaratullruniluteng. Tegucaaqekanllu-gguq tua-i putukua aqvaluku. [*ngel'artut*]

Anguyaluk: Tauna-qaa tua-i ellimalriim pikliniluki taukut tegglit?

Nanugaq: Taukut tua-i alqaqelriit anngaqelriit angayuqaak-wa. Qayaat-gguq tang taugken tua-i tuani mayungqaurlulria tua-i ellukam tekisngavkenaku. Taukut-llu tua-i enemi uitaurlulriit tamanqegcaaraita tua-i ellukaulluki. Tua-i elagluki, elagluki-gguq tua-i, *line*-aumaluteng-gguq waten enem tamatum iluani qavaatni ellukaulluki.

Tua-i qaill' picirkailamegteki-gguq tua-i waten ayuquciicetun tuaten patutelqait.

Anguyaluk: Tua-llu-qaa taukut tegglit tua-i uitalluki teguvkenaki?

Nanugaq: Tegglit tua-i taukut teguvkenaki tua-i uitalluki.

Tua-i-llu taukut tua-i tuaten umyuartequqaarluki tua-i nallunairtuqerluki cali tua-i unitelliniluki. Maaggun nunapigglugmek taperrnaqutarrlugnek mengliitnun elliqervikluki, mengliit tauna taumek tamaaken nunamek elliqervikluk nallunairturluku atrarluni ikavet-llu arvirluni. Unataarallruuq-gguq ilai-llu-gguq tua-i tekilluki.

Tua-llu-gguq tua-i augna yugnikek'ngani aqumngamek qanruqurallininiluku taukunek. Tua-i yugnikek'ngaan taum paqcullagluki. Paqculliiki-gguq tua-i paqyulluku.

Tua-i-gguq tekitaak maaten taukut tua-i uitallrit tua-i nallunaunani. Makut taperrnaqutat pellukutayagarrluut uyungumaluteng, tauna-ll' nallunailkutaa uitaluni mengliitni, cataunateng.

After scanning her surroundings, when she turned her eyes, she saw many different kinds of beaded jewelry that included earrings. She said their beads looked like they would shimmer, those beads, those that they used as nose adornments long ago.

She said she recalled those people who had been covered by a landslide, thinking that she was shown the old belongings of the women there.

After looking at them, she recalled the admonishment they followed long ago, and how they were told never to take a dead person's belonging that was along the ground. And if they took something, [the dead] would go and get that person's toe. [*laughter*]

Martina John: So that beaded jewelry belonged to the people who were buried there?

Elsie Tommy: Those sisters and brothers and their parents. But their kayak was brought up to shore there, and the landslide hadn't reached it. Those poor people who were inside the home, they all died when the land slid over them. They dug them out, they say they dug them out, and they were lined like this as the land slid over them while they slept inside that home.

Since they didn't know what to do with them, they say they just covered and buried them as they were.

Martina John: So she didn't take the beads and left them?

Elsie Tommy: She didn't take those beads and left them there.

Then after thinking those thoughts about them, she left them there, placing a marker on them also. She placed some tundra and some wilted coarse grass along the edge of where they were, placing some land along their edge to mark their location, and she went down and went across to that place. She said she picked berries and reached the others in her group.

Then she said she told her friend about that [beaded jewelry] when they sat down. Her friend suddenly wanted to go and see them. When she wanted to see them, she brought her there to see them.

When they arrived at their location, she said the place where they had been situated was obvious. The beach grass and small leaves were pressed down, and her marker was located along the edge of where they had been, and they were gone.

Akruat

Uliggaq: Cali-ll' imna aanavut qantullruuq imumi naunraam nalliini ayagaluteng maani arnat pitullruameng, avavet-gguq-am Akruat aciatnun ayalria, naunrarcurluni.

Tua-i-llu-gguq avani Akruat aciatni, nani-ll' evegpiit augkut avataitnek piurluni pillermini, camek-gguq imumek niitelangengluni.

Maaten-gguq tang imna qasturiinaan taringcaurturluku pia imumek waten, qa-qa-qaarturluni pilallinilria. Avaken-gguq tua-i tailuni, ukaqsigiinarluni.

Tuaten-gguq qalrianqigtaqami ukaqvaqanirluni piaqluni. Ellii-ll' tua-i pagaani Akruat aciatni piluni.

Tua-i-ll' neq'aqalliniuq tamakucim pikani tua-i avatii mer'urtarkauluni, mer'urtetuluni, amikuum. Tauna tua-i amikuuluni qa-qaa-qaarluni qalrialria. Qalrianqigtaqami-gguq ukaqvaqanirluni piaqluni.

Tua-i-llu-gguq qalriullra tamana unavet ketminun elillrani agayullerkani neq'aqerluku. Tua-llu-gguq ciisqumiggluni, imumek-gguq tua-i atamta aturluku. Agayuqcaarluni. Maaten-gguq tang imna agayuqcaarallrani tuani qalriurtuq kinguqvaqanirluni. Tua-i tamana iquklilluku.

Imna-gguq tang ukaqsigiinallmitun yaaqsigiinarturluni qalriurturalria.

Tuaten tua-i qanemcitellruanga caqerluni. Tauna tua-i tuaten qalriulria amikumek atengqerrluni. Tua-i-llu-gguq tayima taillermitun nepa tamana ayagluni tayim' tamarluni.

Cuk'ayaq: Tua-i ullagyaaqluku. Tamakut-gguq tua-i avatairqaceteng tua-i avatii tua-i taum tua-i yuum mer'urtelartuq tua-i. Mer'urrluni qaillun tuani piviirulluni, tuquarkaurrluni.

Tamakut tamaani tuaten tua-i qanemcingqelartut. Augkut ciuqliput, angayuqaput-wa augkut ciuqliput tua-i-wa iliini canek pilallruut. Ilait nanikuanarqelrianek-llu piaqluteng.

Akruat[80]

Susie Angaiak: And our mother used to say, since women used to travel all over the place during the salmonberry-picking season, she said she traveled down below Akruat to go and pick salmonberries.

Then underneath Akruat, when she was picking berries around those long grasses, she started hearing something.

When the sound started to get louder, she tried to figure out what it was, and it would make *qa-qa-qaa* sounds. She said it came from out there and got closer.

When it would make that noise again, the noise would get closer. And she was up there underneath Akruat.

Then she suddenly recalled that if that *amikuk* [legendary creature] got to her, the area surrounding her would turn into water. That thing that was making a *qa-qa-qaa* sound was an *amikuk.* When it would make another sound, it would get closer.

When the sound it was making reached the area down below her, she remembered to pray. Then she said she got on her knees, and she sang the Our Father song. She continued to pray. While she was praying there, it made its noise from farther back. She ended [the Lord's Prayer].

In the same way that [the creature] had gotten closer, it got farther and farther away as it made noise.

She told me that story one time. That thing that was making noise like that was called an *amikuk.* And just like it approached, that sound disappeared.

Tommy Hooper: It was approaching her. They say when those [*amikut*] surround them, the area surrounding that person turns into water. It turns to water, and they cannot do anything, but they end up dying.

That's the story that is told about those. Those first people, our parents, those before us, encountered strange things in the past sometimes. Some encountered terrifying situations.

Paluallermiut

Cuk'ayaq: Cali-ll' kan'a cali imna, Paluallermiut kana-i.

Uliggaq: Kumegturviim kiatiini unegna penaq, mat'utun kat'utun kiugutun penacuggauluni.

Cuk'ayaq: Ingkut call' yaani Ilutagmi uitalriit taukut tua-i Paluallermiut, tua-i-gguq amaken avatiinek neqkairucameng tuavet tua-i.

Enet'arluni tauna; tua-i-gguq neqkairucameng tuavet tua-i quyurtellruut. Ukut-gguq tua-i cenat pitekluki waten ullatullruat neqkairutaqameng. Imkut tua-i cenat qapilaat-llu alairqata tua-i tamaavet piluteng nerangnaqtullruut tamaani.

Tua-i imkut ilait-gguq taugaam paluallermeggni tuani yugviqluteng-gguq tuaten tamakut, terr'et-wa tua-i yugvissiyaalaameng; tua-i tamakut tamaa-i yugvertuumaita-ll' tua-i ner'aqluki. Tamatum-gguq tamaa-i tuqurqai-llu yuvgerem qamani anrutaatni.

Tua-i-gguq tauna tua-i up'nerkaan tua-i nuyait imkut meqngameng tua-i-gguq tauna tua-i *area*-q tauna nuyanek tua-i nuyallernek pimallruuq taun.

Tuani-gguq tua-i maaken-wa tua-i iluvaqcaaraurlullret anangniarluteng, tuani-gguq tua-i paluluteng tua-i tuani tuquallruut. Tua-i tauna, augna ava-i pitekluku, tauna tua-i pitekluku Paluallermiunek imkut angayuqamta qanruteklallruat.

Unguqutaq

Uliggaq: Pik'um pika-i Unguqutam uum quleqlimta. Imna iciw' ciuliarput Tumaralria. Tuantuq. Tauna-gguq uyurani qanrucartullrua uitaviminek paqyucugluku.

Nani tayim' maani-w' uitallrani, kanani-wa Tununermi uitallratni, tauna-gguq-am uyuraa nem'ini tuani uitallermini enem qaugna kiatii qat'rikili, imutun-llu qerratarrnganani.

Maaten-gguq kiarrluni piuq yuk ukna agiirtellria. Anngaa tauna ak'a tuqullruluni, Tumaralria.

Tauna tua-i uyuraa Qaltayauguq. Tua-ll' maaten-gguq tang tekituq, tauna anngaa Tumaralria. Tuqullruan tauna tua-i uyuraa alangaarluni tuaten agiirrluni tekitellranek yuuluni.

Tua-llu-gguq taum anngaan pia, nani-gguq uitallni nalluyukluku aper-

Paluallermiut[81]

Tommy Hooper: And that one down there, Paluallermiut down there.

Susie Angaiak: The cliff up the coast from Kumegturvik is a small cliff like the one down there, like the one up the coast.

Tommy Hooper: And those located at Ilutak, Paluallermiut, they say when they ran out of food, people from the surrounding area went there.

There was a home at that place; they say when they ran out of food, they gathered there. They say they'd go there for seafood located along the coast when they'd run out of food. When that coastal seafood including mussels became available, they'd move there and try to subsist.

But they say when some people were starving, they consumed too much slime because those sea anemones have too much slime; they'd eat those along with the slime. They say that slime inside their stomachs killed those people.

They say when spring came, when their hair fell out, that area had a lot of hair, hair that had fallen out.

They say at that place, the poor people who came from this area to obtain food in order to survive starved and died at that place. For that reason, our parents mentioned that that place is called Paluallermiut [Place where people died of starvation].

Unguqutaq[82]

Susie Angaiak: Unguqutaq [Cliff] above [Tununak] up there. You know our ancestor Tumaralria. He is there. It is said that he went to his younger brother, wanting to show him where he lived.

When he was living somewhere here, when they were living down there at Tununak, they say when his younger brother was staying at his home, the area above that home up there started to turn white, and it looked like it was up in the air.

When he searched his surroundings, he saw a person coming his way. His older brother Tumaralria had died at the time.

His younger brother was named Qaltayak. Then when he arrived, he saw that it was his older brother, Tumaralria. Since he had died, his younger brother was surprised that he arrived there as a living person.

Then his older brother said to him that he had come to get him to show

tuutnaluku aqvaa. Tayima aqvaniani maliggluku ayalliniluni, ayallinilutek quletmun.

Tua-llu-gguq pikna Unguqutaq tekilluku piqanragen'gun-am, tamana tamaa-i im'um Unguqutam man'a acia qat'rilliniluni-am kevegluni-llu.

Maaten-gguq tang kevegluni pillrani taum Qaltayiim un'a tangerrluku imumek *TV*-tun qatraarluni alairluni, alairtuq nunat-gguq kankut.

Tua-llu-gguq taum anngaan pia, "Kana-i-tang nunanka. Kanani uitaunga. Nani uitalqa nalluyukluku maniicarturamken." Tuaten tua-i tauna pik'um aciani uitallini-ll'.

Ugna cali ua-i waten ayuqelria unguqutauguq.

Ak'a-gguq tamaa-i tuntut maani pitullratni *caribou*-t, cali-w' maa-i pitangqeqatuyaaqellria. Iciw' unguqutaq ugna carrartangqerrngataaqelria yaatiinek atam tangrraqavgu. Tua-i-gguq tauna imkut teggalqut qalliqurluki iirvigkaq.

Iciw' iirvikluku tauna. Un'a-gguq tua-i ketseng tamakunek tuntunek kiarqurluteng tuani uitatullruut, pitullruut tuani, uani ug'um kangrani.

Tua-llu-gguq tua-i kiarqurainanrani, cataiterraarluteng una-i ketiini tuntuq-gguq nangerciiquq. Tua-i aqumgarraarluni nangreskan alairaqluteng; tuaten tua-i un'gaani taum unguqutam aciani.

Tuaten-gguq tua-i ugna ua-i unguqutam carraq pikna kangrani, tua-i-w' kiarrviullruluni; tauna tua-i caskukluku.

Maklak: Tamakut atam amllertut wani Nelson Island-aami.

Qavani-llu tamakucit qaingatni, teggalqut atam ilululeng kiarrviit. *Fawn*-anek, irniaqata, curukarluku aqvaaqluku tuntuyagaq.

Amllertut pektetullemni avani tuntut nalliitni. Tamakucit amllellruut iirviit.

Cuk'ayaq: Makut-am tuntut qaillun-wa tua-i ayuqnilarait. Tua-i ayagyukuneng ayagluteng natmun, tum'uruqurluteng, ellakun-llu piyukuneng ayagluteng cali tum'uruqurluteng.

Tauna tua-i qanruteklallruat augkut angayuqa'urlumta, waten upagluteng natmun. Tamaryukuneng tuanelnguut tamararkauluteng. Tuaten tua-i qanrutketullruit.

Cali tua-i tuntut amlleriyaaqellriit, amlleriyaaqelliniut, amlleriniluki-w' tua-i qanlalriit pavani Mamterillermiut akmani akiatni, iciw' imkut ingrit,

him the place where he was living, thinking that he didn't know where he was staying. Since he said that he went to get him, he left with him, and they ascended together.

And just when they reached Unguqutaq up there, the area underneath Unguqutaq turned bright and then lifted.

When it lifted, Qaltayak looked down there, and after turning bright like a television, when it became visible, a village appeared down there.

Then his older brother evidently said to him, "My village is down there. I am living down there. I came to show you, thinking that you didn't know where I was living." That person was evidently living underneath that place up there.

And there is another cliff down the coast.

They say long ago there were caribou in this area. These days, there are still some around sometimes. You know the cliff down coast, when you look at it from a distance, it appears as though there is something there. They say those piled rocks were a hiding place.

That was their hiding place. They say they stayed there looking out for caribou in the area down below them, down the coast along the top of that place.

They say while one was searching, although none were there before, a caribou would stand down below him. After sitting, when it would stand, they'd become visible; that's what they would do down coast below the cliff.

They say that small thing on top of the cliff down the coast was a lookout place; it was used as an aid to pursue animals.

Edward Hooper: There are many of those here on Nelson Island.

And up north, on top of those, there are rocks that are steep that are lookout places. When they gave birth to fawns, they would attack it and go and get the small caribou.

There were many [lookout places] back when I used to travel all over during the time of reindeer. There are many of those hiding structures.

Tommy Hooper: They mention that these caribou are somewhat extraordinary. When they want to go somewhere, they leave one after the other, and if they want to travel through the air, they can leave one after the other.

Our dear parents used to mention that [caribou] move elsewhere. If ones located in a particular area want to disappear, they disappear. That's what they used to say about them.

And also, caribou populations are evidently increasing, they mention that caribou are becoming abundant up in the area across from Bethel along those

tamaa-i amelkacagangniluki. Tua-i ak'acicetun ilangciyuilkuneng tuatnangyaryaaqsugnarqut. Maaggun ayagluteng negetmurrluteng-llu avaggun-llu tua-i cali pituluteng.

Ircaqurrnaq

Cuk'ayaq: Tua-i wii tua-i tungaunii tua-i ircenrraullinilriignek Niugtarmiungulukek taugaam tangssuglukek, wii tua-i tangellrulrianga.

Tua-i ernerpak tua-i Al Frances-aq-llu tua-i cenarcaaqlunuk, tua-i taugaam enutenrilakuk, augna avani kialirnerpuk aug'um ava-i Evelgem kat'um kana-i kiaqlikacagaam, kanani tua-i kicaqerlunuk, ennerciryaaqlunuk.

Tamaaken agiirtellria angyaq, *Lund*-aq. Tamaani maaggun-llu tua-i canimegnegun kiturluni uatmun, augkut ava-i Engelullugarmiut tungiitnun. Cangaksugnaunaku.

Tua-ll'-am tauna Al Frances-aaq piaqa, "Ava-i-w' tua-i Niugtarmiut cenartellriit tua-i uavet tua-i Engelullugarmiut ukalirneratnun." Ayaglutek-llu ava-i.

Tua-llu uum pianga, "Iluq atam augkuk tangerqerkek." Tangrragka uatmurtellriik augkuk, ciuqliqu'urlutek.

Aipaa alularluni pillruyaaqelriim, augkuk avani aipaa waten piluni, cukanrarlutek tua-i ayalriik tua-i.

Aipaa tauna ciuqlia una, ciuqaqlia alulanrilnguq tungurrlainalrianek qaspellugmek aturluni, nacarturluni ilutuluni-llu una nacaa. [*ngel'artuq*]

Tua-i tangellruukuk tua-i taumek tua-i. Ernerpak-llu tuanllunuk. Tuavet tua-i qapilaanek pissurlunuk. Taglunuk imaitkacagaan. Qaugna-ll' tua-i kiatii marayauluni tua-i, *all the way*.

Tua-i tuani tua-i pit'elnguqercama, amllerriata augkut pitanka taqlua, maani tua-i *four* 'klaam natiini.

Tua-ll' tua-i aipaqa piaqa, yurvirraarluku man'a cenaq, piaqa, "Ulqatarngatliniuq man'a. Tua-i yuurqernaurtukuk." *Thermos bottle*-aalgillruama *two quart*-amek, piaqa, "Yuurqernaurtukuk. Saanigpuk una nangeksaituq." Tuani angqerluni. Imirillunuk tua-i yuurqerlunuk tua-i.

Tua-ll' tua-i una-i ciuqaqliqa piuq, "Iluq, atam augna, tangerqerru atam." Apertuyuunaki-ll' angyanek, taugaam augnaaraqluni.

mountains. I think if they left them alone like they did long ago, they would [come to this area]. They used to travel through here and head up north and out there also.

Ircaqurrnaq[83]

Tommy Hooper: I saw with my very own eyes two people who were evidently *ircenrraak,* but I saw them as people from Newtok.

Al Frances and I were out all day having gone to get seafood, but since the tide didn't go out while we were there, the area up the coast from us, the area up above Evelek, the [point] farthest up the coast, we anchored down there, and we waited for the tide to go out.

A boat approached from that area, a Lund boat. It passed close to us heading down the coast, toward Engelullugarmiut. We didn't find it strange at all.

Then I told Al Frances, "People from Newtok are going to get seafood down the coast along this side of Engelullugarmiut." The two continued on.

Then this person said to me, "*Iluq,* look at those two." I looked at them, and they were heading down the coast, seated in the boat, one in front of the other.

Although the other had previously been driving the boat, those two, the other was like this, and they were traveling fast.

The one up front, the one seated in front of the one driving the boat was wearing all dark clothing, wearing a *qaspelluk* [old, dirty hooded garment], wearing a hood, and his hood was pretty deep. [*laughs*]

We saw that. And we stayed there all day. We gathered mussels there. We went up since the water was very low. And the area up the coast was all mud, all the way.

When I got tired of gathering [mussels] since I had obtained lots, I quit around four o'clock.

Then I told my partner, after checking the shore, I told him, "I think the tide is going to come up here. Let's have some tea." Since I brought a two-quart thermos bottle with me, I told him, "Let's have some tea. Our tea hasn't finished." He agreed. We filled our cups and had tea.

Then the one ahead of me said, "*Iluq,* look at that over there." And he never called them boats, but he'd refer to it as *augna* [that one].

Piunga, Engelullugarmiut tungiitnek angyaq man' agiirtellria *Lund*-aq kavirliuluni kingua, kavirliullruluni. Tua-i piunga, "Aren tua-i-w' maa-i Niugtarmiuk piliqngamek utertellriik cenanek." Aa-gguq.

Tamana-ll' tamaani ciunerkaak imailnguq *sandbar*-aurtellria tamana ciunerkaak umyuaqsugnaunaku. Tuatnanarqelliniuq tamakucimek tanglleq, cangayuyuunani pinarqelliniluni.

Tua-i maa-i tekicartuagnek tua-i taqlunuk up'arrlunuk taugaam tua-i. Maa-i-ll' tua-i canikun tua-i elitaqnaiqurlutek taugaam kiturlutek maa-i. Tauna-ll' tua-i kiartaayuunani caniqlia tauna qaspellugmek tungulriamek atulria, nacarpauluni ilutulriamek. Carayauyugnarquq tauna. [*ngel'artuq*]

Tauna taugken tua-i alulartii tua-i waten tua-i atkucuarrararluni waten tua-i atkucuarrararluni, waten tua-i *light, green*-arrluarauluni. Nacaunani-ll', nuyai-w' tua-i naparrlugluteng, kavirrlugcenani kegginaa.

Aling tua-i tang makut maani ircenrraat cangatenricaaqelliniut qaingit makut, taugaam ilangciitelliniut yuut tamakut. Arulacillukek tua-i maavet. Tua-i ilangciqayuunanuk tua-i ayaglutek taugaam tua-i. Taugaam tua-i cak'ngengaicugnarqut.

Tua-i-ll' maa-i kiturlutek, yaavet tua-i taum tua-i nuugem tungiinun. Tamana-w' marayaulria tua-i *sandbar,* kinerluku. Cangayugyugnaunanuk.

Tua-i-ll' cama-i ipteqertellukek tayim' arulairlutek massiinakek. Piaqa, "Iluq, ama-i-w' tua-i nallunrilamek cenanun arulailriik." Ullakerlapuk-gguq. Angqerluku.

Tumellragnegun ayaglunuk. Igvaryaaqerpuk tang kangiqutaq cataunani; teggarvallraam uum kelua cataunani. Piaqa, ing'um Pilagviaraam amatiini, ug'um ava-i apertullvet, Pilagviar.

Nutaan wii ellangartua. Tangrraqa, "Iluq, tangrriu ircenrraagnek tangvalliniaqelriakuk ernerpak. Tayima tamartuk. Yaavet Ircaqurrnamun taglutek nunamun." Temciyukarlunuk-wam tua-i.

Uliggaq: Ircaqurrnarmiungullrullilriik-wa.

Cuk'ayaq: Ircaqurrnarmiuk taukuk cenarrlutek.

Uliggaq: Tauna-llu-ggem yungqerrnilaraat.

Cuk'ayaq: Ircaqurrnaq-gguq yugyagtuq tua-i. Tua-i augna ava-i tangrrualqa, tangvagluku pilqa qanemcikaqa; qanemcik'larqa.

I looked and saw a Lund boat heading our way from the direction of Engelullugarmiut, with its aft section a red color. Then I said, "Since those two from Newtok have obtained a lot of seafood, they are returning home." He agreed.

I didn't even think that the area where they were heading had no water, the area that had turned into a sandbar that they were heading toward. That's what one tends to do when seeing those [*ircenrraat*]; one tends not to be suspicious.

When they were arriving, we stopped [having tea], and we quickly got ready. They passed close by, but they were hard to recognize as they passed. And the one next to him didn't look around, the one that was wearing a dark *qaspelluk,* one who had on a large, deep hood. I think that one was a monster. [*laughs*]

But the driver of the boat was wearing a small parka, wearing a small parka like this, a light one that was greenish. And he didn't have a hood, and his hair was sticking up, and his face was a little reddish.

My, the bodies of these *ircenrraat* aren't actually any different [from ours], but those types of people tend to ignore others. We waved at them. They ignored us completely and continued on. But I don't think they'd do anything to anyone.

Then they passed, toward that point. Here that area was all sandbar and was dry. We didn't suspect anything at all.

Then just as they went out of view, their motor stopped. I told him, "*Iluq,* since those two know that there are some, they've stopped by some seafood." He said that we should go to them. I agreed.

We traveled along the path they took. When the bay came into view, there was nothing there; there was nothing behind that large boulder. Beyond Pilagviar, the place that you mentioned, Pilagviar.

I finally came to my senses. I looked at him, "*Iluq,* all day we've been watching *ircenrraak.* They have disappeared. They have gone up Ircaqurrnaq over there, onto land." We laughed.

Susie Angaiak: They were probably residents of Ircaqurrnaq.

Tommy Hooper: Those two from Ircaqurrnaq were gathering seafood.

Susie Angaiak: I thought they mentioned that that place is occupied.

Tommy Hooper: They say Ircaqurrnaq has many residents. I am telling you about something that I imagined, that I saw; I tell about it from time to time.

Notes

1. Paul John and Michael John (July 2007:270, 282–285); Paul John and Simeon Agnus (December 2007:367, 377).
2. Michael John, Simeon Agnus, and Paul John (July 2007:258–261).
3. Billy Lincoln and Marie Brite (July 1985:5–9). Ann Fienup-Riordan recorded Billy Lincoln's account in Toksook Bay in 1985 while working on an earlier Nelson Island Oral History Project. Billy Lincoln was born in Kayalivik in 1906. We include his words here in recognition of the detailed knowledge of place names Nelson Island elders possess.
4. Susie Angaiak (March 2007:1410).
5. Ruth Jimmie, Elsie Tommy, Martina John, and Alice Rearden (March 2009:350); Albertina Dull (June 2009:1).
6. Albertina Dull (June 2009:10); Susie Angaiak (March 2007:1246, 1347).
7. Simeon Agnus (July 2007:176–178).
8. Paul John and Simeon Agnus (July 2007:213–214, 262–263).
9. Paul John (July 2007:113–118).
10. Simeon Agnus and Paul John (July 2007:1–11).
11. Simeon Agnus and Paul John (July 2007:12–15).
12. Martina John (July 2007).
13. Martina John and Simeon Agnus (July 2007).
14. Rita Angaiak and Martina John (July 2007).
15. Martina John and Simeon Agnus (July 2007).
16. Simeon Agnus and Paul John (July 2007:143–159); Albertina Dull (November 2007:138); Lizzie Chimigak and Phillip Moses (January 2007:229).
17. Simeon Agnus, Paul John, and Martina John (July 2007:84–99); Albertina Dull (November 2007:67, 133).
18. Simeon Agnus and Paul John (July 2007:194–195, 203–206).
19. Martina John (March 2009:36–41); Simeon Agnus and Paul John (July 2007:222, 206–210).
20. Paul John (July 2007:210); Phillip Moses (January 2007:223, 469).
21. Martina John, Theresa Abraham, and Paul John (July 2007:210–212).
22. Simeon Agnus and Paul John (July 2007:217–221); Peter Dull (March 2007:504); Simeon Agnus, Paul John, and Stanley Anthony (December

2007:273).

23. Simeon Agnus and Paul John (July 2007:197–200, 549).
24. Phillip Moses and John Alirkar (January 2007:495); Simeon Agnus and Paul John (December 2007:56).
25. Simeon Agnus and Stanley Anthony (January 2007:93).
26. Simeon Agnus and Camilius Tulik (March 2007:613).
27. Simeon Agnus (January 2007:129).
28. Maria Eric (March 2007:295).
29. Simeon Agnus (July 2007:351–354).
30. Paul John, John Alirkar, and Alice Rearden (March 2008:415–425); Rita Angaiak and Simeon Agnus (July 2007:331–340, 598); John Alirkar, Phillip Moses, Sophie Agimuk, and Lizzie Chimiugak (January 2007:527, 583).
31. Paul John, Ruth Jimmie, John Alirkar, Simeon Agnus, and Theresa Abraham (July 2007:502–503).
32. Simeon Agnus (July 2007:395–398).
33. Simeon and Anna Agnus (July 2007:449).
34. Simeon Agnus, Joe Felix, and Rita Angaiak (July 2007).
35. Joe Felix and Simeon Agnus (July 2007:465–471, 550).
36. Simeon Agnus and John Walter (July 2007:491–495).
37. Joe Felix, Anna Agnus, and Michael John (July 2007:497–499)
38. Simeon and Anna Agnus (July 2007:535–544).
39. Lizzie Chimiugak, Albertina Dull, and Ruth Jimmie (June 2009:49).
40. Anna Agnus (July 2007:648–652).
41. Simeon Agnus (March 2007:472), Lizzie Chimiugak (January 2007:436), Michael John (July 2007:575).
42. Simeon Agnus and Paul John (July 2007:178–191).
43. Lizzie Chimiugak, Ruth Jimmie, and Albertina Dull (June 2009:29).
44. Lizzie Chimiugak, Ruth Jimmie, and Albertina Dull (June 2009:40).
45. Lizzie Chimiugak (June 2009:45).
46. Lizzie Chimiugak, Albertina Dull, and Ruth Jimmie (June 2009:63).
47. Carl Mark, Peter Dull, and Simeon Agnus (March 2007:518).
48. Sophie Agimuk and Phillip Moses (January 2007:532); Theresa Abraham and Maria Eric (March 2008:226).
49. Maria Eric, Alice Rearden, and Theresa Abraham (March 2007).
50. Martina Wasili (March 2007).
51. Martina Wasili (March 2007).
52. Theresa Abraham and Martina John (July 2007:308–310).
53. John Eric (December 2007:349); Theresa Abraham and Martina John (November 2007:100).

54. John Eric (March 2007:81).
55. Maria Eric, David Jimmie Sr., Theresa Abraham, and Paul Tunuchuk (March 2007:166).
56. John Eric (December 2007:318).
57. David Jimmie Sr. and John Eric (March 2008:78).
58. John Eric, David Jimmie Sr., and Peter Matthew (March 2008:84, 91).
59. Elsie Tommy (March 2009:198); Simeon Agnus (July 2007:316); Mark Tom (March 2007:1007).
60. Michael John (March 2007:1109); Mary George (March 2009:4); Simeon Agnus (July 2007:166–167).
61. Michael John (March 2007:1013).
62. Michael John and Simeon Agnus (July 2007:525).
63. Mary George, Elsie Tommy, Martina John, and Alice Rearden (March 2009:49–54, 290).
64. Elsie Tommy (March 2009:266).
65. Elsie Tommy and Alice Rearden (March 2009:318, 373).
66. Elsie Tommy (March 2009:328).
67. Elsie Tommy and Martina John (March 2009:333–340).
68. Alice Rearden, Ruth Jimmie, Elsie Tommy, and Martina John (March 2009:333).
69. Elsie Tommy, Alice Rearden, Mary George, Martina John, and Ruth Jimmie (March 2009:356–365).
70. Elsie Tommy, Martina John, and Mary George (March 2009:386).
71. Mark Tom (March 2007:1110).
72. Peter Dull and Carl Mark (March 2007:1209).
73. Peter John (March 2007).
74. Edward Hooper and Susie Angaiak (March 2007:1313, 1449); Edward Hooper (March 2007:1455); Helen Walter, Albertina Dull, and Martina John (June 2008).
75. Martina John (January 2007:415).
76. Pauline Pitka and Tommy Hooper (June 2008).
77. Paul John (July 2007:184–190).
78. Edward Hooper (March 2007:1252).
79. Susie Angaiak (March 2007:1257); Elsie Tommy and Martina John (March 2009).
80. Susie Angaiak and Tommy Hooper (March 2007:1329).
81. Tommy Hooper and Susie Angaiak (March 2007:1411).
82. Susie Angaiak, Edward Hooper, and Tommy Hooper (March 2007).
83. Tommy Hooper and Susie Angaiak (March 2007:1347).

References

Andrew, Frank, Sr. 2008. *Paitarkiutenka/My Legacy to You.* Seattle: University of Washington Press.

Balluta, Andrew. 2008. *Shtutda'ina Da'a Shel Qudel/My Forefathers Are Still Walking with Me: Verbal Essays on Qizhjeh and Tsaynen Dena'ina Traditions.* Anchorage: Lake Clark National Park and Preserve, National Park Service, U.S. Department of the Interior.

Basso, Keith. 1996. *Wisdom Sits in Places: Landscape and Language among the Western Apache.* Albuquerque: University of New Mexico Press.

Becker, A. L. 2000. *Beyond Translation: Essays toward a Modern Philology.* Ann Arbor: University of Michigan Press.

Bolanz, Mark. 1976. "Alaskan Missionary." *Great Land Outdoors* 8(11):5.

Boyscout, Andrew. 2005. Chevak Place Name Mapping and Documentation Project. Chevak Traditional Council, Chevak, Alaska.

Braund, Stephen R., and Associates. 2005. "Nelson Island Roads Project Revised Section 106 Report." Prepared for KAE, Inc. and Alaska Department of Transportation and Public Facilities, Anchorage, Alaska. 38 pp.

Burch, Ernest, Jr. 1984, ed. *The Central Yup'ik Eskimos. Special supplement, Études/Inuit/Studies,* Vol. 8.

Collins, Henry B. 1927. Typed manuscript of Henry B. Collin's travel diaries from Alaska between April 23 and September 25. Henry B. Collins Papers, National Museum of Natural History, Washington, DC.

Cruikshank, Julie. 1990. "Getting the Words Right: Perspectives on Naming and Places in Athapaskan Oral History." *Arctic Anthropology* 27(1):52-65.

1998. *The Social Life of Stories: Narrative and Knowledge in the Yukon Territory.* Lincoln: University of Nebraska Press.

2004. "Uses and Abuses of 'Traditional Knowledge': Perspectives from the Yukon Territory." In: *Cultivating Arctic Landscapes: Knowing and Managing Animals in the Circumpolar North.* David G. Anderson and Mark Nuttall. New York: Berghahn Books.

2005. *Do Glaciers Listen? Local Knowledge, Colonial Encounters, and Social Imagination.* Vancouver: University of British Columbia Press.

Deschout, Paul, S. J. 1937. Letter to Father John Fox. Oregon Province Archives, Spokane, Washington.

1949. "Varia." Woodstock Letters, p. 181. Oregon Province Archives, Spokane, Washington.

Drebert, Ferdinand. 1959. *Alaska Missionary.* Bethlehem, Pa.: Moravian Book Shop.

Drozda, Robert M. 1998. *Qikertamteni Nunat Atrit Nuniwarmiuni, The Names of Places on Our Island, Nunivak.* Manuscript in possession of author and NPT, Inc. Mekoryuk.

Evanoff, Karen. 2010. *Dena'ina Elnena/Voices of the Dena'ina: A Celebration.* Research/Resource Management Report NPS/AR/CCR/2010-75. Anchorage: Lake Clark National Park and Preserve, National Park Service, U.S. Department of the Interior.

Fair, Susan W. 2004. "Names of Places, Other Times: Remembering and Documenting Lands and Landscapes Near Shishmaref, Alaska." In: *Northern Ethnographic Landscapes: Perspectives from Circumpolar Nations.* Krupnik, Igor, Rachel Mason, and Tonia Horton, eds. Smithsonian Institution, Washington, DC: Arctic Studies Center.

Fienup-Riordan, Ann. 1983. *The Nelson Island Eskimo: Social Structure and Ritual Distribution.* Anchorage: Alaska Pacific University Press.

1984. "Regional Groups on the Yukon-Kuskokwim Delta." In: *The Central Yup'ik Eskimos.* Ernest Burch, Jr., ed. Special supplement, *Études/Inuit/Studies* 8:63-93.

1988 (ed.). *The Yup'ik Eskimos as Described in the Travel Journals and Ethnographic Accounts of John and Edith Kilbuck, 1885–1900.* Kingston, Ontario: Limestone Press.

1991. *The Real People and the Children of Thunder: The Yup'ik Eskimo Encounter with Moravian Missionaries John and Edith Kilbuck.* Norman: University of Oklahoma Press.

2000. *Hunting Tradition in a Changing World: Yup'ik Lives in Alaska Today.* New Jersey: Rutgers University Press.

2005a. *Wise Words of the Yup'ik People: We Talk to You because We Love You.* Lincoln: University of Nebraska Press.

2005b. *Yup'ik Elders at the Ethnologisches Museum Berlin: Fieldwork Turned on Its Head.* Seattle: University of Washington Press.

2007. *Yuungnaqpiallerput/The Way We Genuinely Live: Masterworks of Yup'ik Science and Survival.* Seattle: University of Washington Press.

Fienup-Riordan, Ann, and Alice Rearden. in press. *Ellavut/Our Yup'ik World and Weather: Continuity and Change on the Bering Sea Coast.* Seattle: University of Washington Press.

Goulet, Jean-Guy A. 1998. *Ways of Knowing: Experience, Knowledge, and Power among the Dene Tha.* Lincoln: University of Nebraska Press.

Hunn, Eugene, with J. Selam and Family. 1990. *Nch'i-Wana/The Big River: Mid-Columbia Indians and Their Land.* Seattle: University of Washington Press.

Ingold, Tim. 2000. *The Perception of the Environment: Essays in Livelihood, Dwelling and Skill.* New York: Routledge.

Iutzi-Mitchell, Roy D. 1994. "Definers of a Pan-Yupik Ethnicity: Yup'ik Cultural Authorities across Regional Groups." *Études/Inuit/Studies* 18(1–2):137–153.

Jacobson, Steven A. 1984. *Yup'ik Eskimo Dictionary.* Fairbanks: Alaska Native Language Center, University of Alaska.

1995. *A Practical Grammar of the Central Alaskan Yup'ik Eskimo Language.* Fairbanks: Alaska Native Language Center, University of Alaska.

Judge, W. H., S. J. 1890. Letter from Father Cataldo from St. Michael, July 20. Woodstock Letters 19(3):356–357. Oregon Province Archives, Spokane, Washington.

Kari, James, and James A. Fall. 2003. *Shem Pete's Alaska: The Territory of the Upper Cook Inlet Dena'ina.* Fairbanks: University of Alaska Press.

King Island Native Community, in collaboration with Deanna Kingston. 2010. http://kingislandplacename.com.

Kingston, Deanna. 2010. "'Almost Every Place, Every Rock, Had a Name': A Consideration of Placename Density on King Island, Alaska." *AlterNative* 5(1).

Koutsky, Katherine. 1981. "Early Days on Norton Sound and Bering Strait: An Overview of Historic Sites in the BSNC Region, Vol. I, The Shismaref Area." *Occasional Paper No. 29.* Fairbanks: Alaska Native Language Center, University of Alaska.

Krupnik, Igor, Rachel Mason, and Tonia Horton, eds. 2004. *Northern Ethnographic Landscapes: Perspectives from Circumpolar Nations.* Washington, DC: Arctic Studies Center.

Marino, Elizabeth. 2005. *Negotiating the Languages of Landscape: Place Naming and Language Shift in an Iñupiaq Community.* M.A. Thesis, University of Alaska Fairbanks.

Mather, Elsie P. 1995. "With a Vision Beyond Our Immediate Needs: Oral Traditions in an Age of Literacy." In: *When Our Words Return: Writing, Hearing, and Remembering Oral Traditions of Alaska and the Yukon.* Phyllis Morrow and William Schneider, eds. pp. 13–26. Logan, Utah: Utah State University Press.

Meade, Marie, and Ann Fienup-Riordan. 2005. *Ciuliamta Akluit: Things of Our Ancestors.* Seattle: University of Washington Press.

Menager, Francis, S. J. 1962. *The Kingdom of the Seal.* Chicago: Loyola University Press.

Menzies, Charles. 2008. "Negotiating Indigenous Agendas: Perspectives on Collaboration with/in American Indian Communities." *American Anthropological Association Abstracts for 107th Annual Meeting.* Arlington, Va.: American Anthropological Association.

Miyaoka, Osahito, and Elsie Mather. 1979. *Yup'ik Eskimo Orthography.* Bethel, Alaska: Kuskokwim Community College.

Okada, H., A. Okada, K. Yajima, O. Mikaoka, and C. Oka. 1982. "The Qaluyaarmiut: An Anthropological Survey of the Southwestern Alaska Eskimos." Department of Behavioral Science, Faculty of Letters, Hokkaido University. Sapporo, Japan.

Orth, Donald J. 1967. *Dictionary of Alaska Place Names.* Geological Survey Professional Paper 567. Washington, DC: U.S. Government Printing Office.

Oswalt, Wendell. 1990. *Bashful No Longer: An Alaskan Eskimo Ethnohistory, 1778–1988.* Norman: University of Oklahoma Press.

Pratt, Kenneth L., ed. 2009. *Chasing the Dark: Perspectives on Place, History, and Alaska Native Land Claims.* Shadowlands, Vol. 1. Anchorage: U.S. Department of the Interior, BIA Alaska Region, Division of Environmental and Cultural Resources Management, ANCSA Office.

Ray, Dorothy Jean. 1971. "Eskimo Place-Names in Bering Strait and Vicinity." *Journal of the West* 6(3):371–394.

Rearden, Alice, Marie Meade, and Ann Fienup-Riordan. 2005. *Yupiit Qanruyutait/Yup'ik Words of Wisdom.* Lincoln: University of Nebraska Press.

Reed, Irene, Osahito Miyaoka, Steven Jacobson, Pascal Afcan, and Michael Krauss. 1977. *Yup'ik Eskimo Grammar.* Fairbanks: Alaska Native Language Center, University of Alaska.

Samuels, David. 2001. "Indeterminacy and History in Britton Goode's Western Apache Placenames: Ambiguous Identity on the San Carlos Apache Reservation." *American Ethnologist* 28(2):277–302.

Society for Propagating the Gospel. 1884–1931. *Proceedings of the Society for Propagating the Gospel among the Heathen.* Moravian Archives, Bethlehem, Pa.

Swann, Brian, ed. 1994. *Coming to Light: Contemporary Translations of the Native Literatures of North America.* New York: Random House.

Thornton, Thomas F. 2008. *Being and Place among the Tlingit.* Seattle: University of Washington Press.

Woodbury, Anthony C. 1984. "Eskimo and Aleut Languages." *Arctic, Vol. 5, Handbook of North American Indians.* David Damas, ed. pp. 49–63. Washington, DC: Smithsonian Institution Press.